ROMAN IMPERIAL THEMES

ROMAN IMPERIAL THEMES

P. A. BRUNT

CLARENDON PRESS · OXFORD

This book has been printed digitally and produced in a standard specification
in order to ensure its continuing availability

OXFORD
UNIVERSITY PRESS

Great Clarendon Street, Oxford OX2 6DP

Oxford University Press is a department of the University of Oxford.
It furthers the University's objective of excellence in research, scholarship,
and education by publishing worldwide in

Oxford New York

Auckland Cape Town Dar es Salaam Hong Kong Karachi
Kuala Lumpur Madrid Melbourne Mexico City Nairobi
New Delhi Shanghai Taipei Toronto
With offices in
Argentina Austria Brazil Chile Czech Republic France Greece
Guatemala Hungary Italy Japan South Korea Poland Portugal
Singapore Switzerland Thailand Turkey Ukraine Vietnam

Oxford is a registered trade mark of Oxford University Press
in the UK and in certain other countries

Published in the United States
by Oxford University Press Inc., New York

© P. A. Brunt 1990

The moral rights of the author have been asserted

Database right Oxford University Press (maker)

Reprinted 2006

ISBN 0-19-814476-8

Preface

This volume comprises essays that bear on the imperial aims and ideals of the Romans, the character of their administration of the empire, and the attitudes to Roman rule of peoples they conquered. Chapters 17 and 18 are new, the rest have appeared before and are presented in order of publication. In these I have made a few verbal alterations, and some corrections and additions of more substance, the latter normally enclosed in square brackets. In some cases where I have changed my mind, or new considerations have occurred to me, I have found it more convenient to append addenda rather than to rewrite the original text. There has, however, been no systematic revision (nor updating of bibliographies). Throughout each chapter the footnotes are numbered serially, and for this and other reasons footnotes frequently have different numbers from those in the original publications, but otherwise the varying format of those publications has been preserved, with diverse modes of reference and abbreviation, all of which I expect to be intelligible to the readers for whom they were designed. The original pagination is noted at the top of each page.

I wish to thank the holders of copyright in the essays previously published for authorizing their inclusion in this volume. Acknowledgements are due to *Latomus* for chapters 1, 2, 3, and 8, to the Franz Steiner Verlag, Wiesbaden, for chapter 4, to the Society for the Promotion of Roman Studies for chapters 5, 7, 10, and 15, to the Cambridge University Press for chapters 6 and 14, to *Scripta Classica Israelica* for chapter 9, to *Phoenix* for chapter 11, to Les Belles Lettres, Paris, for chapter 12, and to the Akademie der Wissenschaften der DDR for chapter 13.

P.A.B.

Contents

Sulla and the Asian Publicans[1]

In his recent work on the *equites* (*The Roman Middle Class*, Oxford 1952)
H. Hill has re-asserted a view, which goes back to Mommsen, that
probably 'Sulla, whose hostility to the publicani and the whole Middle
Class is well-known, kept them out of Asia as long as he could by
continuing the collection of the revenues on the system he had
established in 84 BC', i.e. that of direct assessment of the cities (p. 69).
This view has never found universal acceptance. Rice Holmes, for
instance, held that there was no evidence that Sulla abolished the tax-
farming system in Asia, and T. R. S. Broughton has maintained that
the operations of the *publicani* were never suspended there.[2] In my
opinion a controversy that has long divided scholars admits of a simple
solution. In 84 Sulla resorted to direct assessment of the cities because
he had no choice; he had no intention of abolishing the publican system
for ever, and in fact it was restored as soon as he had re-established
order in Italy and the unity of the empire.

After the Peace of Dardanus in 84 Sulla's most urgent need was for
money, principally to finance the impending civil war. He accordingly
laid Asia under heavy financial contributions. Appian (*Bell. Mith.* 62)
makes him tell the provincials that he will impose on them the taxes of
five years, to be paid at once, together with the cost of the war and of
the re-organization of the province; a time limit was fixed for payment.
Appian speaks of this imposition as a fine, and Plutarch (*Sulla* 25, 2;
Luc. 4, 1; 20, 4), who uses the same term, gives the sum as 20,000
Talents. Scholars are not agreed whether the fine of 20,000 Talents
includes or excludes|the payment of five years' taxes down; for my own
part I agree with the arguments of Broughton that the former must be
correct and that the average annual taxes of Asia in this period
amounted to 2400 Talents; on this view the indemnity alone amounted

[1] I am indebted to Professor R. Syme and Mr E. W. Gray for criticizing an earlier draft of this
paper.
[2] For these and other modern discussions see D. MAGIE, *Roman Rule in Asia Minor* (Princeton
1950) II p. 1116 n. 17 with notes 15–16 on p. 1115 and n. 27 on p. 1121. [See my *Fall of the Roman
Republic* (1988), ch. 3 for general rejection of Hill's thesis on the *equites*, and esp. pp. 154–6, 159*sq*.,
514 on Sulla's relationship with them.]

Latomus, 19 (1956), 17–25.

to 8000 Talents, which seems ample.[3] However this question be decided, it does not affect my thesis.

Appian says that the total fine was apportioned among the cities. Soldiers were sent to see that the money came in. From Plutarch we learn that the quaestor, Lucullus, superintended the collection of the money. The division of the province into 44 *regiones* (Cassiodorus, *Chron.* 670) need not concern us here; what is to the point is the fact that apparently the cities were left to find the sums required for themselves and that Roman publicans were not used.

This need not surprise us. During Mithridates' invasion of Asia most of the local agents of the Roman companies must have been killed or fled. They can hardly have returned in strength by 84, or indeed for a few years thereafter; conditions both in Italy and the East were too disturbed. The companies themselves had lost heavily, so much so that credit was destroyed at Rome (Cic. *de imp. Cn. Pomp.* 19).[4] In any case— and this is the fundamental fact—the head offices and [part of] the capital were at Rome, under the hand of Sulla's enemies. The Roman publicans in 84 had neither the men nor the money available to assist Sulla in collecting the funds he required (as, for instance, according to Caesar *BC* III 31 the publicans of Syria assisted Metellus Scipio in 49). Vindictive as he was, Sulla confined his threats to his personal enemies at this time (Appian *BC* III 78), and he was not so imprudent as to alienate the publicans by a calculated attack on their financial interests. Necessity, not policy, excluded them from any part in collecting the fine of 84.

For the same reasons it must have remained impracticable to employ publicans from Rome in collecting any monies from Asia until (say) 80. It is not quite clear what demands were made of the Asian cities during the years from 84–80. Justin XXXVIII 3, 9 says that Mithridates in 88 had granted the Asiatics 'vacationem quinquennii', and it is clear that between 88 and 84 the Romans had|been unable to collect any taxes in the province. It may then be thought that the five years' taxes which Sulla demanded were *arrears*, and in that case that normal taxes were levied year by year after the collection of the enormous fine of 84. On this view the references to an Asian *vectigal* in this period cited below from Cicero may be interpreted as alluding to the annual taxation. On the other hand, Cassius in 43 and Antony in 41 demanded ten or nine years' taxes *in advance* (App. *BC* IV 74; v 5–6); and it may be thought that Sulla had proceeded in the same way. It might then be urged that the whole of the fine could not be levied at once but that

[3] *Economic Survey of Ancient Rome* IV (Baltimore 1938) pp. 562*sqq.*
[4] [Cf. my *Fall of Rom. Rep.* pp. 158*sq.*]

part continued to come in later, and that Cicero was justified in calling it 'vectigal', since the fine did include the equivalent of five years' *vectigalia*.

We may now turn to the well-known references made by Cicero to the Sullan system. In *pro Flacco* 32 he says that Flaccus, proconsul in 62, apportioned the burden of ship-money on the Asian cities 'ad Pompei rationem, quae fuit accommodata L. Sullae discriptioni. Qui cum in omnis Asiae civitates pro portione pecuniam discripsisset, illam rationem in imperando sumptu et Pompeius et Flaccus secutus est.' This does no more than confirm that Sulla apportioned a levy of some kind directly on the cities: Pompey and Flaccus used his *discriptio* as a basis for their own imposition of ship-money. Again in *Verr*. II 1, 89 he says that on the order of Murena, whom Sulla had left in charge of Asia, Miletus built ten ships for operations against the pirates 'ex pecunia vectigali' and that other cities did the same 'pro sua quaeque parte'. Evidently the costs of ship-building were deducted either from what was still due from the levy of 84 or from an annual *vectigal* collected thereafter. The date cannot be precisely determined; Murena remained in Asia till 81 and may well have given orders for ship-building even after the outbreak of the second Mithridatic war; he does not seem to have taken any effective action against the pirates. These orders must be subsequent to Sulla's departure (Sulla needed every penny he could get); whether the 'pecunia vectigalis' be taken to refer to payments in arrears of the Sullan fine, or to an annual *vectigal*, the text of Cicero shows that the Sullan *discriptio* (as we should expect) outlasted his own stay in Asia.

Writing to his brother in 59 (*ad Q.f.* 1 1, 33) Cicero says of the Asiatics:—'Nomen autem publicani aspernari non possunt, qui|pendere ipsi vectigal sine publicano non potuerint quod iis aequaliter Sulla discripserat'. Here again the term *vectigal* may denote either the Sullan fine or an annual tax; but even in the latter case the passage does not imply that the Sullan *discriptio* was in force beyond (say) 80 BC. What of the words 'sine publicano'? Some have translated 'without borrowing from publicans' and assumed that Roman publicans are meant. It is known that to meet Sulla's demands the cities had to borrow at high rates of interest and that as a result by Lucullus' time they were heavily in debt to Roman creditors, some of whom were no doubt publicans (App. *Bell. Mith.* 63; Plut. *Luc.* 20).

However the translation is forced and the context is surely against it. Cicero is arguing that the provincials cannot justly complain of Roman taxes (since they had to pay taxes before subjection to Rome) or of the publican system; they themselves had resorted to publicans to meet Sulla's demands. This ought to mean that they employed publicans as publicans, not as money-lenders. The next sentence surely implies that these publicans were not Romans but Greeks:—'Non esse autem leniores in exigendis vectigalibus Graecos quam nostros publicanos hinc intellegi potest quod Caunii nuper omnesque ex insulis quae erant a Sulla attributae confugerunt ad senatum, nobis ut potius vectigal quam Rhodiis penderent'. This I take to be a sophistical argument: 'we can infer how oppressive Greek publicans in general must have been in their home towns from what we know of the Rhodian publicans at Caunus'. There is certainly no difficulty in taking the passage to refer to Greek publicans. The tax-farming system was endemic in the Greek world. Broughton[5] has shown that we have references to such local tax-farming in the immediate post-Sullan epoch from Tralles in Asia (*pro Flacco* 91) and from Cilicia (*ad Att.* v 16, 2; *Fam* III 8, 5; xv 4, 2). In these cases the cities had presumably resorted to tax-farmers to collect from the individual tax-payers the sums required under *pactiones* with the Roman publicans. It is probable enough that they employed their own tax-farmers to raise the sums at which they were assessed under the Sullan *discriptio*.[6] It is true that at Tralles the Roman Fal|cidius bought the contract. That shows that Romans might be employed as publicans within an Asian city. But it does not of course show that local men could not also get the contracts. In 84–80, if there were not Roman publicans on the spot, this must have been the practice. At any rate the passage cited from Cicero affords no proof that *Roman* publicans were at work in Asia under the Sullan régime.

In 84 then and the succeeding years Sulla dispensed with Roman publicans for the collection of all the taxes; Appian's term φόρους need not, and must not, be restricted to the *decuma* alone, in distinction from the *portoria* and *scriptura*.[7] But he acted thus, from administrative necessity, not political spite. In much the same way Vitellius 'ministeria principatus per libertos agi solita in equites Romanos disponit' (Tac. *Hist.* I 58), probably just because he had no freedmen to fill the posts. Until Sulla recovered control of Rome, there could be no effective *locatio* of taxes for provinces under his power; and we should be obliged to assume that the tax-farming system of Asia was in abeyance even if this were not explicitly stated. Hence Broughton has gone too far in rejecting Mommsen's view when he claims that the operations of the publicans in Asia were never suspended.[8]

---

[5] *Am. Journ. of Phil.* 58 (1936) pp. 173–6.

[6] This is not to say that there was nowhere direct collection by officials, as by *eclogeis* at Messene (*IG* v 1, 1432), before or in this period, cf. Rostovtzeff, *Soc. and Econ. Hist. of the Hellenistic World* III p. 1507 n. 20.

[7] Cf. Mommsen, *St R*[3] III 227 n. 4.

[8] *Ec. Survey* IV p. 519 n. 96.

But it is quite another matter to hold that when Sulla as dictator reviewed the taxation system of the empire (App. *BC* I 102), he retained the emergency method of direct assessment of the cities. For this there is no positive evidence at all. On the contrary it can be decisively refuted. In the *SC de Asclepiade* of 78 we hear of [magistrat] us nostri queiquomque *Asiam* Euboeam locabunt vectigalve *Asiae* [Euboeae imponent].[9] Hardy took this to refer to the leasing of public lands,[10] but this interpretation is refuted by the parallels he himself gives,[11] and by the context: Asclepiades and his co-beneficiaries are to be immune from Roman taxes on their own property in the territory of Asian cities. There is no sound|reason for believing that there were *agri publici* in Euboea.[12] The same holds good for Boeotia, where we find publicans in 73 active in collecting dues from land which can hardly be anything else but tribute; taxation of Boeotian land goes back at least to Sulla, and probably the use of publicans too.[13] But if Sulla retained or introduced publicans for collecting taxes in Boeotia, why not also in Asia? In Cilicia P. Servilius Vatia, proconsul 78–5, approved the rates of interest set out in existing *pactiones* between the publicans and the cities.[14] In Bithynia Roman publicans at once entered city territories in 74 (Memnon, *FGH* no. 434, 27, 5*sq.*). True, they might have been merely contractors for the *portoria* [or for the royal lands which had now passed into the domain of the *populus Romanus* (Cic., *de leg. agr.* II 50).][15] But as early as 74 Asia was again gravely afflicted by Roman publicans; the situation that Plutarch describes could hardly have arisen except over a period of years, and it is barely credible that it is to be ascribed entirely to the activities of farmers of *portoria*, *scriptura* and other rents on public lands.[16] It is quite certain, of course, that the tithe of Asia was again subject to *censoria locatio* at Rome in 70.[17] Mommsen and others have thought that it was revived along with the censorship in that year. Tenney Frank took this to be a concession to business

[9] Riccobono, *FIRA* I[2] p. 257.

[10] *Six Roman Laws* (Oxford 1911) p. 87.

[11] *Verr.* II 3, 12; *Att.* I 17, 9; Fronto p. 125 N (II 140 Haines).

[12] S. Accame, *Dominio Romano in Grecia* (Rome 1946) pp. 189–92.

[13] *FIRA* I[2] p. 260, cf. Accame p. 201.

[14] *Att.* VI 1, 16.

[15] The same might be said of the publicans mentioned in the *lex Antonia de Termessibus* (Riccobono p. 137); but I date this to 68, following Broughton, *Magistrates of the Roman Republic* II p. 141; as the rights of the publicans had on any view been restored by then, this document is irrelevant for my thesis.

[16] [*Luc.* 7 and 20. He lays most stress on the rapacity of usurers. The cities had had to borrow heavily since Sulla (*supra*), but by 70 the Roman publicans were surely among their chief creditors, cf. my *Fall of Rom. Rep.* p. 169 n. 90.]

[17] *Verr.* II 3, 12 (with no hint that there had been any intermission); *de imp. Cn. Pomp.* 15; *Att.* I 17, 9 and other texts cited by Marquardt, *Röm. Staatsverw.* I[2] 338.

interests by Pompey.[18] There is not a tittle of evidence for either view. It need hardly be said that censors were not needed to let out public contracts; in their absence, consuls could act in their stead,[19] and so, presumably, could Sulla himself as dictator. As it is known that some publicans, even if not *decumani*, were active in Asian provinces between 80 and 70, it is evident that contracts were made|in this way; why not for the *decuma*? Finally the law which governed Asian tax-contracts after 70 was still the *lex Sempronia*;[20] therefore Sulla had not repealed it, nor, we may reasonably add, terminated its operation.[21]

Thus the evidence shows that the Gracchan system of tax-collection was revived long before 70 and presumably by Sulla himself. This need occasion no surprise. Much has been written of his hostility to the *equites*. Certainly they suffered heavily in the proscriptions, but so did his enemies in the senate. Sulla deprived the *equites* of those judicial functions by which Gracchus had made the state *bicipitem*. But at the same time he strengthened the senate by enrolling 300 new senators 'ex equestri ordine' (Livy *Per.* 89; Ap. *BC* I 100). No doubt as senators these new recruits may have ceased to represent specifically equestrian interests; none the less their enrolment shows that Sulla had his friends in the order. It would be rash to treat the *populares* of the 80s simply as the friends of 'business interests' and Sulla simply as their foe; how many capitalists must have been alienated from the 'popular' cause by the 'turpissima lex' of 85 BC remitting debts (Vell. II 23; Sall. *Cat.* 33)?

Sulla, we may think, sought to restore the traditional order and the ascendancy of the senate. This did not lead him to undo all Gracchan measures as such. *Leges Semproniae* remained on the statute book, where they did not conflict with his principles (e.g. the *lex de provinciis consularibus*, and the *lex ne de capite civium Romanorum iniussu populi iudicaretur*). Tax-farming was part of the traditional order; Gaius Gracchus had only given it a new extension in Asia. In doing so, he might be held to have had the interests of the state at heart. He had claimed to be 'patronus aerarii' (*Tusc. Disp.* III 48, [cf. Gell. XI 10, 1]), a fine Optimate role, perhaps on the ground that he had made better provision for the collection of the revenues. Whether the Asian cities had been *vectigales* before 123 is a question that perhaps should be left

---

[18] *Class. Phil.* IX 192–3.

[19] *Verr.* II 1, 130 (upkeep of temples at Rome in 80 and 75); 3, 18 (letting of certain Sicilian tithes in 75). There is of course no ground for thinking that Sulla intended the censorship to lapse (cf. H. M. LAST, *CAH* IX p. 300), any more than he intended the courts to be corrupt, another example of senatorial laxity.

[20] *Verr.* II 3, 12; *Schol. Bob.* 133.

[21] It might be added that in the resumé of the history of Roman taxation in Asia in App. *BC* V 4 there is no mention of a change made by Sulla, but the argument *e silentio* is here very weak.

open,[22] but even|if they had, much was apparently to be gained by the introduction of tax-farming. Ancient states had not the statistical skill or information available to modern Ministries of Finance for assessing the future yield of taxes. It was because the publicans contracted to pay fixed sums at fixed times and gave security for payment that the government could calculate in advance the revenue on which it could count. As Rostovtzeff says,[23] they acted as underwriters and guarantors of the revenue. True, their profits, legal and illegitimate, made the system costly both in money and goodwill; and the Sullan direct assessment in 84 and indeed the resort to *pactiones*, first attested under Servilius in Cilicia (*supra*) but not necessarily new then, foreshadowed the abandonment of tax-farming in the East by Caesar; it is none the less easy to understand that Sulla should not have chosen to break with all the previous experience of Roman administration in Asia.

Another consideration may be suggested. If Sulla was a traditionalist in intention, we may ask what conception he had of the traditional order. The Scipionic circle had liked to see in Rome an example of the mixed constitution. Many of Sulla's measures were clearly designed to strengthen the hands of the senate, but that need not deter us from conjecturing that he too had some regard for this doctrine; he may have conceived himself not as the champion of oligarchy, but of that true balance of powers which within the last 50 years had been upset by an undue weighting of the democratic element. It was such a deviation from the mixed constitution, according to Polybius (VI 51), that had partly led to Carthage's decline; and Polybius (II 21) had also hinted at a fatal tendency to democracy at Rome since the Flaminian law as early as 232. Now in applying to Rome the doctrine of the mixed constitution, Polybius (VI 17) had urged *inter alia* that the power of the senate over the people was fortified by its right to vary the terms of public contracts. When speaking of the people he is clearly thinking of the *equites*, who alone had money to invest in such contracts and who constituted (as C. Gracchus saw) a potentially independent|political force. It is clear that the greater the financial interests involved in such contracts, the stronger the contol of the senate over the *equites* must have been. If Sulla wished (as he surely did) to make the capitalists dependent on the senate and to prevent them from lending their support to future opposition to his régime, he could have found no better method than to restore them their opportunity for profit in Asia,

---

[22] Rostovtzeff *op. cit.* pp. 812–3 (Gracchus reforms the collection of taxes); *contra* Magie *op. cit.* pp. 1054–5.

[23] *Op. cit.* p. 966. [Cf. pp. 378–80.]

while of course depriving them of the rights of jurisdiction which made the senators dependent on them. The ascription of motives to Sulla is necessarily problematic; but it may at least be said that this conjecture fits the known facts; the motive of revenge and blind enmity to business interests does not.[24]

[24] [The suggestion that Sulla wished to maintain a balance in the constitution now strikes me as fanciful.]

2

The Revolt of Vindex and the Fall of Nero

The revolt of Vindex has often been seen as a national movement for Gallic independence, or at least in Professor Syme's words, as 'a native insurrection against the Roman power'. Schiller, who held the more extreme of these views, depicted Nero's fall as an almost fortuitous aftermath, brought on by his own timidity and indecisiveness. In his, and other modern accounts,[1] the conduct of Verginius Rufus is (I believe) misrepresented and the true order of events distorted: while his interpretation of the Gallic revolt is altogether mistaken. In this paper I propose first to reconstruct the sequence of events from the time of the revolt to Nero's death, when he was already abandoned by every one, and secondly to show that Vindex rose to end oppression, not only of the senatorial class to which he belonged but of all Rome's subjects. Like the Gordians in 238, he perished, but his cause triumphed, for he had not risen against Rome, but against Nero.|

---

[1] *Gesch. d. röm. Kaiserzeit unter d. Regierung d. Nero* (Berlin, 1872), cf. *Bursians Jahresb.*, 1876-1878, 509; *Hermes*, XV (1880), 620; he is basically followed by e.g. B. W. HENDERSON, *Life and Principate of the Emperor Nero* (London, 1903) and E. G. HARDY, *Studies in Roman History*, 2nd Series (London, 1909), 130ff. Cf. also A. MOMIGLIANO, *CAH*, X, 739. The account given by MOMMSEN, *Ges. Schr.*, I, 333-53 is in many points nearer the truth, but vitiated by his curious assumption that for Vindex *libertas* meant the restoration of the Republic; for its meaning under the Principate see Ch. WIRSZUBSKI, *Libertas as a Political Idea at Rome* (Cambridge, 1950), chs. 4-5, and for the character of the propaganda of Vindex and Galba the excellent article of C. KRAAY, *Num. Chron.*, 1949, 129ff, cf. also G. E. F. CHILVER, *JRS*, XLVII, 29ff. For Syme's views see his *Tacitus* (Oxford, 1958), I 462-3. C. JULLIAN, *Hist. de la Gaule* (Paris, 1920 IV, 179ff. is rather ambiguous on the nature of Vindex' revolt. H. DESSAU, *Gesch. d. röm. Kaiserzeit* (Berlin, 1926) II, 277ff. is (as always) usually sound and judicious. But I differ on various points even from those modern accounts which seem to me the best; hence it is convenient to retell the story. References to Plutarch are, throughout, to his *Galba*. [In *Epigraphica*, 1961, 37-151, M RAOSS published an account of the revolts of Vindex and Galba, independent of this and the following essay, but (as he says, n. 1) generally in agreement with them.]

Latomus, 18 (1959), 531-59.

I

In March 68,[2] C. Julius Vindex, the legate of Lugdunensis,[3] a man of royal 'Aquitanian' stock, called together a Gallic assembly and raised the standard of revolt (Dio, LXIII, 22). In view of the aristocratic character of Gallic society, it is clear, as Josephus says (*BJ*, IV, 440), that he must have acted in concert with the Gallic magnates, men whose rank or adoption of Roman culture had earned them the Roman citizenship (cf. *Hist.*, II, 94, 2). No doubt he had sounded them much earlier; for the revolt spread rapidly, and beyond the confines of his own province. The Arverni in Aquitania and the Sequani in Belgica[4] and the titular colony of Vienna in Narbonensis are named among his adherents;[5] Tacitus speaks as if the Gallic provinces supported him almost unanimously, though the Treveri and Lingones, closely connected with the Rhine legions, and the colony of Lyons, out of enmity to Vienna and perhaps gratitude for Nero's recent munificence (*Ann.*, XVI, 13), remained firm against the rebels.[6] At the outset Vindex claimed to have 100,000 men under arms, besides others whom he might raise (Plut., 4, 5). This was doubtless an exaggeration; at Vesontio, according to Tacitus (I, 51), his army was annihilated, yet Plutarch (6, 4) set his losses at only 20,000. Moreover, however widely the revolt may have spread in Gaul, and however martial the spirit of the Gauls, his levies were inevitably ill-armed and ill-trained, no match for the Rhine legions. As an ex-praetor, Vindex could not have been ignorant of the strength of the Roman state, nor could he have failed to see that his chance of success depended on the extension of the revolt to the armed forces of Rome.

It was, therefore, natural that he had already sought to win the support of other governors (Plut., 4, 4). The prospects of suc|cess would not have seemed poor. Nero's crimes and follies had disgusted the classes from whom the higher officials were drawn, and not them alone. Tacitus tells of the repugnance felt at his conduct in Rome by visitors from distant provinces and the remote towns of Italy (*Ann.*, XVI, 5).

It was from such places that centurions and higher officers generally came. Of sixteen tribunes in the praetorian guard three were implicated in Piso's plot (*ibid.*, XV, 49, 2; 50, 3) and four more were discharged as unreliable after its discovery (*ibid.*, 71, 2). Centurions

---

[2] Nero received the news at Naples, on the anniversary of his mother's death (SUET., *Nero*, 40, 4), i.e. during the *Quinquatria* (*Ann.*, XIV, 4, 1) held 19–23 March.

[3] Not Aquitania [whose legate is clearly distinguished from Vindex by SUET., *Galba*, 9, 2, and is generally taken to be hostile (Betuus Cilo?—cf. *Hist.*, I, 37, 3), *contra* RAOSS, 81 n. 9] and the course of the war excludes Belgica.

[4] PLIN., *NH*, IV, 106, 109.   [5] *Hist.*, I, 51, 4: 65; IV, 17, 3.

[6] *Hist.*, I, 8; 51; 65; II, 94; IV, 17; 57; 69.

must often have passed through Rome when transferred from legion to legion; it must have seemed likely, and events confirmed, that discontent had spread from the capital to the camps. Nero had recently placed most of the armies under the command of *novi homines*, but they too could share the senatorial ideal of *libertas*, and the more widespread disapproval of Nero's breaches of decorum and morality; and just because this disapproval was widespread, they could have better hope than ever before that, if they were disposed to rebel, their soldiers would follow them. It cannot have endeared Nero to the armies that he had fallen into arrears with their pay and had been forced to defer the discharge of veterans and the expenditure on *praemia* (Suet., *Nero*, 32). In 67 the situation was in fact so dangerous to Nero that his freedman, Helios, had urgently recalled him from Greece (Dio, LXIII, 19).

Yet timidity reigned. Plutarch says that, with the exception of Galba in Tarraconensis, the governors whom Vindex approached sent word of his treason to Nero.[7] Presumably his emissaries did not return. From this alone he must have inferred that he had been delated. Despite his lack of promised support, revolt was forced on him. But his prospect of successful revolt still turned on his ability to mobilize Roman discontent against Nero.

Dio (LXIII, 22) makes him inveigh in the Gallic assembly against Nero's despoliation of the Roman world, his destruction of the flower of the senate, his murder of his mother, his outrages and theatrical performances. The speech, like others that Dio composed, is probably free invention. Syme calls it 'miserable and un|real'.[8] This is too harsh. Vindex may not have addressed Gauls in this way, though in Spain Galba too is said to have harangued his audience on Nero's executions of distinguished men (Suet., *Galba*, 10, 1; Plut., 5, 2). But Dio has chosen to illustrate in this form the propaganda by which Vindex sought to subvert the loyalty of Romans to Nero. To the historian this was the more important matter, since it was Roman, not Gallic discontent that brought Nero down. We know from Suetonius that such propaganda was employed by Vindex; his edicts taunted Nero as an incompetent lyre player and actor, and also as an Ahenobarbus, no true scion of the Julio-Claudian line (Suet., *Nero*, 41; cf. 45, 2). Such abuse was well chosen; the praetorian tribune, Subrius Flavus, had avowed to Nero that he had begun to hate him *postquam parricida matris et uxoris, auriga et histrio et incendiarius extitisti* (*Ann.*, XV, 67), and Nero was much disturbed by Vindex' insults. In Dio's speech Vindex appeals to the Gauls to help not only themselves but the

---

[7] It was perhaps somewhat later that Fonteius Capito on the lower Rhine executed one Batavian chief and sent another, Civilis, in chains to Rome, where he survived to be acquitted by Galba (*Hist.*, IV, 13); evidently Vindex was intriguing with the Batavians. [RAoss 83 n. 1 is sceptical. On Fonteius see n. 35 with text.]   [8] *O.c.*, 463, n. 1.

Romans and to free the whole world from one who was no worthy emperor; and in Zonaras' version of Dio's narrative Vindex swore to act entirely in the interest of the senate and people of Rome. His coinage, as Kraay has shown, offers confirmation. Not one of the legends has a Gallic ring; on the contrary, they allude to Rome (e.g. Roma Restituta), and Roman deities, notably Rome's tutelary god, Jupiter Optimus Maximus; to the senate and people; to Salus Generis Humani, Pax, Libertas. The re-appearance of the oak wreath symbolizing *clementia*, and on one issue, of the inscription *ob c(ives) s(ervatos)*, or the allusion to Mars Ultor, whose temple Augustus had built, suggest a programme for the replacement of tyranny by the constitutional Principate of Augustus, and the legends *Signa P. R.* or *Fides Exercituum* seem to constitute an implicit appeal to the armies to fulfil their proper role as guardians of the Roman people, whom Nero oppressed.[9]|

It is unlikely that so late as 68 any one thought it practicable to restore the Republic, least of all a Gallic noble. But though all might concede that the empire needed a *rector* (*Hist.*, I, 16), a Gaul could not hope to usurp that dignity. The revolt required a leader of more prestige and power than Vindex himself possessed. For this part Vindex selected Galba, not indeed, as Dio seems to have thought (LXIII, 23), because he had no small military strength; his army consisted of only one legion. The choice was perhaps forced on him, since alone of the governers whom he had solicited for aid, Galba had temporized, and not reported his overtures to Nero. However, it had many merits. Galba's reputation stood high: *omnium consensu capax imperii*. It was not yet known that torpor had advanced on him with years. The Rhine legions might recall that he had once commanded them with distinction.[10] His *claritas natalium* might win over the soldiers as well as respectable public opinion.[11] Dio (*l. c.*), like Plutarch (*Galba*, 22, 2), seems to have held that Vindex actually proclaimed Galba emperor. Suetonius, however, tells that he wrote urging him *ut humano generi assertorem ducemque se accommodaret* (*Galba*, 9, 2). Vindex' letter must have reached him before the end of March.[12] He did not hesitate for long. As Vinius observed, *qui deliberant, desciverunt*.[13] Suetonius says

---

[9] CHILVER, *o.c.*, 29 says: 'This numismatic argument must not be overstated. We know something of the message being issued in Gaul to Romans but nothing of what Vindex was saying to the Gauls he enrolled under his colours'. Were not the coins minted to pay these Gauls? Could only a few read the legends or interpret the images? The coinage of the so-called *imperium Galliarum* (*RIC*, I, pp. 191–2) is rather different. (KRAAY, n. 57 associates an altar near Le Puy dedicated *Saluti generis humani* (*ILS*, 3827) with the revolt; that is conjectural.)

[10] In Upper Germany 39–41 (SUET., 6, 2; PLUT., 3; *Hist.* I, 49, 4; DIO, LX, 8, 7), when he won triumphal ornaments (SUET., 8, 1).

[11] Cf. *Hist.*, I, 49, 3; II, 76, 2; ZONARAS, XI, 13. Note the choice of Vitellius, too (*Hist.*, I, 9, 1; 52, 4; III, 86), and later of Nerva; and Vespasian's hesitations (II, 76).

[12] Cf. p. 532, n. 1. Galba should surely have heard the news at least as soon as Nero.

[13] PLUT., 4, 6; transposed to another context in *Hist.*, II, 77.

that Galba had intercepted despatches in which Nero had ordered the
procurators to put him to death; probably Nero suspected him of
receiving earlier overtures from Vindex and treasonably failing to
report them. This failure, as Vindex may well have surmised, left
Galba with no option but to revolt. [Early in] April he threw off his
allegiance. But, though later his reign was counted from that moment
(Dio, LXIV, 6), he did not yet assume the style of an emperor.[14] He
professed to be only legate of the senate and people of Rome (Plut., 5,
2), and | both in Spain and Gaul the coins do not bear his image and
superscription. This numismatic evidence makes it likely that Vindex
too, while marking Galba out as his candidate for the succession, had
not gone so far as to proclaim him emperor.

Such caution was prudent. To the rebels Nero presented the most
urgent danger, and they needed aid in resisting his forces even from
those who might not be prepared at once to endorse Galba's candida-
ture, for which they had as yet had no time to organize support. They
could calculate that, if Nero were once removed, Galba's birth and
reputed ability would put rivals out of court, especially as it was likely
that he would prove the most acceptable choice to the senate, whose
prestige still counted for much.[15] Certainly events justified such hopes
or expectations; widespread defections followed the news of Galba's
revolt, and on Nero's death the lead given by the senate induced
universal recognition of his claim. Chilver has indeed suggested that
Galba, faced with a threat to his life, 'reacted by building *partes* on
traditional Roman lines', and that it may be doubted whether he
needed to be prompted by Vindex.[16] But all the evidence makes the
initiative come from Vindex; nor is it in keeping with the inertia (cf.
Suet., *Galba*, 9, 1) that Galba displayed from his insurrection (and
earlier) to his death to conjecture that he had himself taken the lead.
There is no ground for thinking that Galba's attested partisans had
been seduced from loyalty to Nero, before Galba's own hand was
forced; and though [he may well have been in communication with Ti.
Julius Alexander, prefect of Egypt, before he was recognized at
Rome,[17] Alexander, however secretly partial to Galba, did not actually
give him his avowed allegiance before the news of Nero's death
reached him.]

[14] [Scholars have variously fixed the date of his proclamation as 2, 3, or 6 April. *RE* ivA 778.]
[15] Cf. *Hist.*, I, 76; 84 on the importance to Otho of recognition by the senate.
[16] *O.c.*, p. 32.
[17] Alexander issued a complicated edict in Galba's name redressing grievances on 6 July. He
might have heard of Nero's fall on 9 June by about 20 June (cf. FRIEDLÄNDER, *Sittengesch.*, I³, 338);
and as Galba had received official news of the same event on 16 June (PLUT., 7; cf. n. 26), it is just
possible that he then also knew that he had been confirmed in office. But he could hardly have had
time to draft the edict; and indeed Galba's confirmation of his tenure suggests some prior
understanding between them. See WILCKEN, *ZSS*, LXII, 146–8; E. G. TURNER, *JRS*, XLIV, 60
(citing other literature); [see now CHALON (n. 20) pp. 43ff].

Galba occupied himself in raising troops and money (he sold some of Nero's estates) and in the issue of propaganda; thus he sent | edicts to the other provinces, calling on individuals and communities to aid the common cause (Suet., 10; cf. Plut., 5). His coinage, which resembles that issued by Vindex, illustrates the constitutional aims he professed. His propaganda did not lack effect. In Africa Clodius Macer, the legate of III Augusta, also rose in revolt and levied troops; he did not attach himself to Galba but avowed similar aims.[18] The proconsular province, to judge from coins that apparently belong to this time, unambiguously supported Galba.[19] We have seen that the prefect of Egypt was probably [sympathetic to] Galba's cause; his edict in July reflects the claim of Vindex and Galba that they stood for 'the safety of mankind'.[20] But the fate of the empire hung on the armies of Rhine and Danube: their defection was decisive.[21]

The ease with which the Rhine armies had suppressed the revolt of Florus and Sacrovir showed that a Gallic insurrection presented no serious danger. In 68 their commanders showed no lack of zeal for Nero at first. Verginius Rufus in Upper Germany, who had received the ordinary consulship in 63, for a 'new man' a special mark of imperial favour, had not thought fit to rely only on the three legions under his own command, but had summoned *vexillationes* from the legions in the north under Fonteius Capito, together with some *auxilia* normally stationed there, such as the Batavians (*Hist.*, I, 51, 3; 53, 2; IV, 17, 3). With these overwhelming forces he besieged Vesontio. Vindex came to its relief (Dio, LXIII, 24, 1). A battle ensued; the Gallic army was destroyed, and Vindex perished, it was said by his own hand.

At first sight it seems like unreflecting temerity on the part of Vindex to have confronted the superior Roman army and not awaited the forces that Galba might bring up, or the further defections from Nero that their appeals might stimulate. But the sources suggest a very different explanation. According to Dio, Vindex and Verginius exchanged messages and conferred before the battle. This is recorded as a fact, and ought not to be rejected: Dio was careful to state it as a mere conjecture of the time that they | agreed on common action against Nero. Whether or not the conjecture was correct, it was treason for Verginius even to negotiate with a rebel, and from Dio alone we must infer that he himself was now in revolt. Both Dio and Plutarch (6,

[18] *PIR*², II, pp. 276-7.

[19] Mattingly and Sydenham, *Rom. Imp. Coinage*, I, pp. 179-80; 187-90.

[20] Lines 7 and 65 (for a better text than *OGIS*, 669, see Evelyn White and Oliver, *Temple of Hibis in El Khargeh Oasis*, Part II, nos. 3 and 4); [and with admirable commentary, G. Chalon, *L'Édit de Tib. Jul. Alexander* (1964)].

[21] [Raoss collected data on Galba's partisans and found further evidence for support of his cause in the provinces; this involves much speculation; in particular I put no faith in any statements in Philostr., *v. Apoll.*]

3) relate that the battle resulted from a clash between the troops, not intended by their commanders, and Dio adds (ch. 25) that Verginius greatly mourned the death of Vindex. According to his account, it was after the battle that Verginius' soldiers sought to proclaim him emperor and that he refused and persuaded them to submit the question of the succession to senate and people; but Plutarch (6, 1) expressly says that before the battle many were falling away from Nero, that of these all but Clodius Macer and Verginius attached themselves to Galba and that Verginius, though often saluted emperor by his men, had declared that he would recognize only the nominee of senate and people; he records (6, 4) the prevalence of a rumour that *after* the battle the soldiers threatened to *return* to their allegiance, unless Verginius would accept the purple. In my view it is Plutarch's version that deserves the preference. In general his narrative is more detailed than Dio's; and by accepting his testimony here, we can make better sense of the conduct of Vindex and the facts that Dio himself relates. If Verginius had already before the battle thrown off his fealty to Nero, we can understand why Vindex dared to approach the Rhine army and why Verginius consented to confer with a rebel. Nor are the hints supplied by Tacitus (*Hist.*, I, 8) inconsistent. *Germanici exercitus... tarde a Nerone desciverant.* True enough: their generals mobilized them against Vindex, and only later, after Galba's revolt was known, did they cast off their allegiance, [presumably in May, *infra*]. *Nec statim pro Galba Verginius.* It is certainly true that Verginius did not at once declare himself for Galba; he remitted the choice of a new emperor to the senate. But, if Vindex and Verginius were agreed, how did the battle come about? Here there is little difficulty. Dio ascribes it to a misunderstanding, but the passion for killing and looting the legions later evinced, not only in Gaul[22] but in their native Italy,[23] provides an even more plausible reason.

In later years the historian, Cluvius Rufus, sought the pardon of Verginius for an account of these transactions in which he had pre|ferred truth to friendship (Plin., *epp.*, IX, 19, 5). Kraay supposes that Cluvius had asserted that Verginius defeated Vindex in the name of Nero. Under Vespasian that would have been a serious imputation: Nero was a tyrant, and for that loyal Flavian, the elder Pliny, Vindex was *adsertor ille a Nerone libertatis* (*NH*, XX, 160). Kraay's view indeed makes nonsense of Verginius' reply; he said that he had acted as he did in order that men might be free to write as they pleased, but it would have been an absurdity for any one to identify the cause of Nero with

---

[22] *Hist.*, I, 51; 51; 64–8.
[23] *Ibid.*, II, 56; 87–8. Cf. Jos., *BJ*, III, 586–7; Dio, LXV, 15.

that of freedom of speech. Moreover there were too many witnesses for Verginius to have gained credence for a fabricated story. His claim to have been a champion of *libertas* is best understood to refer to his refusal to usurp the Principate himself and thus to deprive senate and people of their freedom of choice.[24] If this be so, what could Cluvius have written at which he might have taken offence? Had Cluvius anticipated the doubts voiced by Tacitus (*an imperare noluisset dubium*, *Hist.*, I, 8)? It would surely have been unpardonable for one senator to have alleged that another, still alive at the time, might have aimed at supreme power; that would have marked him out for the suspicions of the dynasty, and no one could have relied on the clemency of Vespasian's sons. The tradition suggests another explanation. The undesigned attack on Vindex, the persistent and unpunished attempts of the legions to proclaim Verginius emperor, their reluctance to acknowledge Galba even at the end, when commanded to do so by Verginius, would have made it easy, and probably correct, for a historian to put Verginius' character and ability in much the same light as Tacitus sets those of Trebellius Maximus or Hordeonius Flaccus. Verginius, it could be said, had failed to maintain discipline and control. To such a criticism he replied that he had done all in his power to preserve liberty of action to the senate and people at Rome. |

Nero had received news of the Gallic rising with indifference or pleasure; it was thought that he actually welcomed an excuse to pillage wealthy provinces; for eight days he took no action (Suet., *Nero*, 40). Very possibly, the Rhine armies had begun to mobilize against Vindex without instructions from him, in late March. But he was seriously alarmed by the report of Galba's revolt, which must have reached him by mid-April (*ibid.*, 42, cf. Plut., 5, 3). In the new situation he rightly distrusted the fidelity of Verginius. Such distrust accounts for his new measures, for Verginius, if loyal, had ample strength to suppress Galba as well as Vindex. We are told that he now began to recruit soldiers from the urban proletariate, who were alone to mourn his death,[25] even from slaves (Suet., 44), and it must have been now that he sent for the legions of Illyricum, which had reached Italy by the time of his death

---

[24] Cf. Verginius' epitaph (PLIN., *epp.*, IX, 19, 1):

Hic situs est Rufus, pulso qui Vindice quondam
Imperium adseruit non sibi, sed patriae.

MOMMSEN (*o. c.*, 341, n. 6) rightly said that the ablative clause must be taken in a purely temporal sense. The tradition is favourable to Vindex; and Verginius, who mourned his death or gave out that he did so, would not have boasted of defeating him. Moreover, it was not *by* defeating Vindex that he claimed *imperium* for Rome and not for himself.

[25] *Hist.*, I, 4; 78; SUET., *Nero*, 57.

(cf. below) on 9 June,[26] and presumably it was now that he recalled troops in Alexandria or on their way to the East (*Hist.*, I, 6, 2; 31, 3; 70, 1) and began to form a new legion from the Misenum fleet.[27] At some stage he actually despatched forces into Gaul. The presence at Lyons in early 69 of I Italica (*ibid.*, I, 74, 2), a legion raised in Italy for his projected Eastern expedition (Suet., 19), can hardly be explained except on the supposition that it had reached Gaul before his death and had then remained there; there was no later occasion for its transference. Now Dio says that he sent Rubrius Gallus and others against the rebels after he had heard not only of Galba's but also of Verginius' revolt; the advance guard, which doubtless included I Italica, was commanded by Petronius (Turpilianus) (LXIII, 27). On the usual view these forces were sent only after the battle of Vesontio. In itself that is not impossible. Vesontio cannot be precisely dated, but might well be placed as early as the beginning | of May, and Nero could well have heard of it, though the news would have brought him no comfort; the defeat of Vindex was more than balanced by the defection of the Rhine army.[28] However, on my view Verginius' revolt preceded the battle, and Rubrius could have received his orders before Nero was informed of it. In any case this concentration of forces, superfluous to crush Galba, betokens grave apprehensions, if not actual knowledge, of the disloyalty of the Rhine armies themselves.

These measures were in vain. Plutarch (6, 1) speaks as if even before Vesontio there were numerous defections from Nero and as if all the rebels but Clodius Macer and Verginius attached themselves to Galba. That may go too far; but there is truth in his other statement (10, 2) that Verginius' revolt rid Rome of the tyrant. For Nero was now deserted by the Illyrian legions in Italy, who made overtures to Verginius (*Hist.*, I, 9). Chilver dates these overtures after Nero's death, since one legion, the 14th, was 'obstinately loyal to Nero', (*ibid.*, II, 11). But Tacitus' allusion to their *longa erga Neronem fides* does not compel us to assume that by the end, more or less reluctantly, they too had not deserted him. Moreover the claim of the Batavians *coercitos a se quartadecimanos, ablatam Neroni Italiam* (*ibid.*, II, 27), whether true or not, could scarcely have been made, if their resistance to the 14th were to be set at a moment when Nero was already dethroned or dead. Dio

---

[26] Date of Nero's death, *PIR*, III[2], p. 38. [One Pannonian legion had just arrived at Bedriacum on 14 April 69; other Illyrian legions had not come up; all must have received their marching orders in early March (K. WELLESLEY, *JRS* 1971, 471ff.]. In 68 the Illyrian legions can hardly have been summoned later than mid-April.]

[27] *Hist.*, I, 6; PLUT., 15, 5; SUET., *Galba*, 12, 2; it cannot have shown much zeal for Nero, since Galba incorporated it in the army (DIO, LV, 24, 2; cf. RITTERLING, *RE*, XII, 1381–3); he did not do as much for another new legion, that raised by Clodius Macer.

[28] CHILVER, *o. c.*, n. 40 rightly rejects a date in early June as too late for Vesontio.

(Xiphilinus) says that at the last Nero was abandoned by everyone, even (Zonaras) by Petronius Turpilianus,[29] and Suetonius makes his despair follow on the revolt of 'the other armies', i.e. the armies other than Galba's.[30] Even if Nero heard (as I believe) of Vesontio, he now knew that he had, except perhaps in the East, whither he thought of fleeing, no armies left to face the rebels. His praetorian prefect, Nymphidius Sabinus, was no less aware of his helplessness. Sabinus' one hope of expiating his | own crimes was to give Nero the final push and earn the gratitude of Galba, by securing his constitutional election as emperor. Nero's cause was desperate, as Plutarch says,[31] when Sabinus persuaded the praetorians to proclaim Galba by promises of enormous largess. Schiller had indeed not been alone in thinking that Nero was ruined by his own hesitancy.[32] In a speech Tacitus makes Otho deliver to the praetorians we read: *et Nero quoque vos destituit, non vos Neronem* (I, 30, 2); and Tacitus depicts Nero as: *nuntiis magis et rumoribus quam armis depulsus* (I, 89). But Nero had shown no lack of vigour or speed in mobilizing far distant armies to quell what was at first a minor rebellion, and though it was true enough that at the last he did not fight for his throne, it was, if we believe the rest of the evidence, because the messages and rumours of revolt were correct, and he had no troops to fight with, save at most the praetorians and the armies of the East. For Nero the desertion of the praetorians sealed an inevitable fate: to Galba it was of immense value since it enabled the senate to recognize him and thereby precluded all other claims to the succession.

On learning of Vesontio, Galba had all but taken his own life and retired with dismay to Clunia.[33] This does not imply that he thought Verginius was still loyal to Nero; had that been so, he would hardly have written to him, urging his co-operation in securing Roman freedom (Plut., 6, 5). Plainly he feared Verginius as a potential rival,[34] and diplomatically proposed that, in accordance with the pretensions of both alike, they should overthrow Nero and leave the succession to the senate. But the death of Nero, and his own recognition by the senate, smoothed his path. True to his professions, Verginius at last

[29] PLUT., 15, 2, says, however, that he remained loyal to Nero, and Tacitus recording his execution by Galba as *dux Neronis* (I, 6; cf. 37), may have been of this opinion; he and Cingonius *inauditi atque indefensi* tamquam innocentes *perierant*; however, his ruin was deferred till Galba reached Rome.

[30] *Nero*, 47, 1; earlier rumours that he thought of deposing and executing all governors (43, 1) probably ensued on earlier reports of their disloyalty.

[31] 2, 1. The accounts in Suetonius and Dio of Nero's last days differ in some details.

[32] O. c., p. 280.

[33] SUET., *Galba*, 11, 1; PLUT., 6, 6; cf. *RIC*, I, 215, no. 151. At Clunia on 16 June Galba heard of his recognition, PLUT., 7.

[34] Cf. PLUT., 10. The overtures of the Illyrian legions, and the inscription, *ILS*, 982 (cf. MOMMSEN, *o. c.*, 353), illustrate the general uncertainty on Verginius' real intentions.

prevailed on his troops to swear allegiance to Galba, though not before the more forceful legate of the 1st legion in Lower Germany, Fabius Valens, had set the example (Plut., 10). The attitude of the commander of the | Lower Rhine army, Fonteius Capito, was suspect; he was removed, whether by Galba's orders or not was never known.[35] Clodius Macer likewise perished, and others who incurred Galba's suspicions (*Hist.*, I, 37).[36] Galba was not noted for clemency (Suet., *Galba*, 12, 1) and the Rhine soldiers later apprehended decimation for their recalcitrance to his cause (*ibid*, I, 51). But Verginius, though defamed as a traitor by Valens (III, 62), escaped with the loss of his command; and if neither he nor any high officer of the Illyrian legions suffered death, that is further proof that they were prompt to obey after Galba's official recognition, and that intrigues to set Verginius on the throne must be dated before Galba's proclamation at Rome had rendered such activity treasonable.

II

Vindex was dead, but his avowed aims were fulfilled. In the movement he had initiated against Nero armies and unarmed provinces had shared, and the very man he had designated to take Nero's place now held it, though there was little enthusiasm for him. Yet it has been commonly believed that his real aims were very different and indeed incompatible with what he achieved; that he had risen not against Nero, but against Rome, to establish Gallic independence.

This view is founded partly on texts that speak of a war with the Gauls, or use similar expressions.[37] Since, however, the men | who actually fought for Vindex at Vesontio were Gauls, such language is justified, even if they were not fighting for a national cause. Much weight has been laid on four texts in which Tacitus has been thought to

---

[35] Cf. *PIR²*, III, p. 197, no. 468.

[36] Pedanius Costa *adversus Neronem ausus et Verginii exstimulator* (*Hist.*, II, 71, 2) earned Galba's gratitude and the prospect of a consulship; he had presumably urged Verginius to revolt, but favoured Galba.

[37] E.g. *BJ*, I, 5 (where contra SCHILLER, 266: τὸ Κελτικὸν refers to the German revolt under Civilis, cf. *AJ*, XIX, 119); IV, 494; PLUT., 10, 1–2; *Hist.*, 1, 65; 89 (where Tacitus speaks of the war *quod inter legiones Galliasque* velut *externum fuit*); II, 94. All allusions to a 'revolt' are just as uninformative. Schiller 267 adduces the following words of PLUT., 29, 3: Γάλβας δὲ καὶ κληθεὶς καὶ ὑπακούσας αὐτοκράτωρ καὶ τῇ Οὐίνδικος ἐκπαρασχὼν ὄνομα τόλμῃ κίνημα καὶ νεωτερισμὸν αὑτοῦ λεγομένην τὴν ἀπόστασιν ἐποίησε πόλεμον ἐμφύλιον, ἀνδρὸς ἡγεμονικοῦ τυχοῦσαν to show how Plutarch 'clearly unveils the self-seeking aims of Vindex'; certainly the words are as 'clear' as anything else he quotes, and prove nothing of the sort. In *Hist.*, I, 6; 51; 53; 65; 70; IV, 69 Tacitus speaks of the *bellum Vindicis* or the like; this is warranted by the mere fact that such fighting as took place in 68 was with Vindex and his followers, but does not show that in his view Vindex was actuated by personal or national aims.

support the theory that Vindex was the leader of a national revolt. In fact, whatever Tacitus' own opinion may have been, he does not betray it in any of these passages. In the first, he is merely reporting the attitude of the Rhine legions; the others come from speeches of Civilis and Vocula. Doubtless these speeches are inventions of the author, but it is a strange assumption that Tacitus is incapable of writing dramatically, of ascribing to the speakers views appropriate to them in the circumstances, which he himself may be far from endorsing. If indeed we make this assumption, we shall be bound to attribute to Tacitus many self-contradictory opinions, and others refuted by facts he records. Moreover of the following texts only the second suggests that Tacitus even imputed to others the interpretation of Vindex' revolt that Schiller made fashionable.

(a) Tacitus (I, 51) says of the Rhine legions that after their victory over Vindex they spoke of the Gauls no longer as *socios* but as *hostis et victos*. Since they had fought against and beaten the Gallic levies, this manner of speaking was not without reason, but it does not prove that even they felt themselves to have saved Roman dominion; nor would the sentiments of these bloodthirsty, rapacious and ultimately disloyal troops be good evidence that the movement they had temporarily repressed was anti-Roman. Chilver[38] rightly says that the taunt they applied to Vindex' supporters as *Galbiani* bespeaks a quite different view.

(b) Civilis represents the Gauls (IV, 14, 4) as sharing the desire of the Germans for national freedom. It was his cue to say this, to encourage the Batavians; the later course of events showed that the great majority of the Gauls were not prepared to join him.

(c) Again, Civilis appeals for Gallic support (IV, 17, 3): *ne Vindicis aciem cogitarent; Batavo equite protritos Aeduos Arvernosque; fuisse inter Verginii auxilia Belgas, vereque reputantibus|Galliam suismet viribus concidisse.* Civilis is certainly depicted as urging the Gauls to seek 'freedom'; but his argument does not imply that they had been doing this in 68. He is simply meeting the objection that no revolt in Gaul, whatever its object, has any chance of success, because of the great military superiority of Rome.

(d) Conversely, Vocula (IV, 57, 2) maintains that the defeat of the risings led by Florus and Sacrovir and then by Vindex shows that no Gallic revolt can be successful. It does not follow that (even in the view ascribed to him) all these risings had precisely the same object.[39]

---

[38] *O. c.* (n. 1) p. 30.

[39] Vocula also says: *Galbam et infracta tributa hostiles spiritus induisse.* In fact it was the Gauls who had been punished for siding against Vindex, not his sympathizers whom Galba had rewarded (*Hist.*, I, 8; 51), who joined Civilis (cf. G. WALSER, *Rom, das Reich* etc. (Baden-Baden 1951) 113); another oratorical distortion.

We are thus not entitled to ascribe to Tacitus, nor to any other extant writer, an interpretation of the revolt led by Vindex divergent from that clearly expressed by Dio, and implied in the elder Pliny's praise of him as: *adsertor ille a Nerone libertatis.* Nor, as shown above, may we, in contradiction of the evidence, maintain that Verginius saw in the revolt a danger to Roman rule. Galba at least saw none, yet in his slow progress through Gaul (*Hist.*, I, 6) he had ample opportunity to learn the truth. He gave Vindex a public funeral (Plut., 22, 2); he rewarded the Gallic states that had supported him with grants of citizenship and remission of taxation[40] and mulcted the 'loyal' states of land, which probably went to the 'rebels'.[41] By such measures an emperor reputed to be *pecuniae publicae avarus* (*Hist.*, I, 49, 3) diminished the public revenues when the state was all but bankrupt, and fatally alienated the Rhine legions with the object, we are asked by moderns to believe, of recompensing subjects for a revolt against Rome! There could hardly be another instance in history of political gratitude so remarkable or so untimely. The legends on coins issued by Vindex gain in significance from their repetition by the mints the new | emperor controlled. If indeed evidence for Gallic nationalism were to be sought in the coins, we should identify its leader as Galba, not Vindex; for it is only Galba's issues that celebrate the names of Gallia or Tres Galliae.[42]

It has been assumed that since Vindex was a Gaul, his aims must have been purely Gallic. The premise in this argument is not quite certain—it is conceivable, though not likely, that Vindex came from one of the true Aquitanian peoples, which were not Celtic[43]—but in any case the inference is unwarranted. A senator and the son of a senator (Dio, LXIII, 22), Vindex may well have been born and educated in Rome; he could easily have been moulded by senatorial tradition and *esprit de corps*. It is erroneous to think that only the old noble families at Rome shared senatorial ideals; remember the Patavine Thrasea (*Ann.*, XVI, 21), Helvidius Priscus, the son of a *primipilaris* (*Hist.*, IV, 5), the Spaniard, Herennius Senecio (Plin., *epp.*,VII, 33, 5), or Tacitus himself, of equestrian and perhaps Gallic origin.[44] Julius Graecinus of Forum Julii perished for flouting Gaius' unjust orders

[40] *Hist.*, I, 8; 51, 4; cf. Plut., 18, 1. The remission of the *quadragesima*, attested by coins (De Laet, *Portorium*, 171), is distinct from the reduction in tribute. For grants of citizenship cf. Jullian, IV, 185. To Schiller Galba was 'kein politischer Kopf'!

[41] *Hist.*, I, 53,3; Suet., *Galba*, 12; the Lingones probably forfeited land to the Sequani, whom they therefore attacked in 70, IV, 67.

[42] *RIC*, I, p. 210. nᵒˢ 108; 110–12.

[43] For the Aquitanians and their incorporation with true Gauls in the Roman province of Aquitania, Jullian, II, 449ff.; IV, 67ff.; even in the third century they preserved their sense of being distinct from the Gauls, *ILS* 6961. But their *civitates* were small; one might think that a praetor was more likely to come from a Gallic *civitas*, such as the Arverni, in the province.

[44] Syme, *o. c.*, ch. XLV.

(*Agr.*, 4), and an Allobrogan from Vienna, Valerius Asiaticus, justified the killing of that tyrant in a harangue at Rome.[45] There is nothing implausible in what the sources tell us, that Vindex too was zealous for 'liberty'.

A single issue of coinage, if it was due to Vindex and not to Galba,[46] might confirm his familiarity with the ideals of the Roman opposition. The legend on the obverse HERCULES ADSERTOR is unprecedented, and thus no mechanical imitation of earlier propaganda; nor, despite the vogue that Hercules had in Gaul,[47] | can it be interpreted as an appeal to Gallic sentiment; the image of the god seems to be Graeco-Roman, and on the reverse we read FLORENTE FORTUNA P. R. Now it was only a few years earlier that Seneca had contrasted Hercules who *nihil sibi vicit ... malorum hostis, bonorum* vindex, *terrarum marisque pacator* with Alexander, *a pueritia latro gentiumque vastator, tam hostium pernicies quam amicorum, qui summum bonum duceret terrori esse cunctis mortalibus*,[48] and it was precisely Alexander whom Nero professed at this time to be emulating (Suet., *Nero*, 19, 2). It is of course not irrelevant that Hercules reached Italy on his beneficent progress from Spain, as Augustus too had done in 24 B.C.[49] and as, if the hopes of Vindex were realized, Galba would do. If indeed it was Vindex who authorized this issue, prefiguring the propaganda of the ideal monarchy for which Trajan claimed to stand,[50] it shows that he was saturated in the ideas of just those men at Rome who rejected Nero as an immoral tyrant, without rejecting the Principate, in the very manner of the speech that Dio ascribes to him.

King Agrippa is said to have warned the Jews of the futility of resisting the invincible might of Rome (Jos., *B. J.*, II, 345ff.). An oppressed, fanatical and ignorant peasantry would not heed his warning. In Gaul itself a popular rising had been stirred up against

---

[45] *Ann.*, XI, 1; Jos., *AJ*, XIX, 159: Dio, LIX, 30; cf. KRAAY, 137–8.

[46] *RIC*, I, p. 184 no. 1, (for Vindex); STRACK, *Untersuch, zur röm. Reichsprägung* I, p. 96 favours Galba.

[47] JULLIAN, II, 120, n. 6; 142, n. 1; 145; 155, n. 2; VI, 34, n. 11. For the Gallic portrayal of Heracles see LUCIAN, *Heracles*, 1ff. JULLIAN, IV, 575–8; and A. N. SHERWIN-WHITE, *Roman Citizenship*, 277–9, have shown that the frequent issues of Hercules coins by the Gallic emperors of the third century are not evidence for the (mistaken) view that they were nationalists.

[48] *De Benef.*, I. 13. I had already reached this view when I found welcome confirmation in W. DERICHS, *Herakles, Vorbild der Herrschers in der Antike*, Inaugural-Dissertation, Köln (1950), of which there is a typed copy in the Ashmolean Library, Oxford; he cited parallel texts from SENECA, c.g. *de benef.*, IV, 8, 1; *de constant.*, II, 2, 1: *Herc. Fur.*, 882–94; *Herc., Oet.*, 794; 1990, and shows that identifications of Nero with Hercules (e.g. Dio, LXIII, 20, 5) or his liking for the acting role of Hercules do not attest Nero's acceptance of the role of Hercules as the beneficent 'pacator' and model-king.

[49] Cf. HOR., *Odes*, III, 14; cf. HEINZE on line 1; Dio, LVI, 36; this too may have been remembered by Vindex.

[50] Cf. DERICHS, *o. c.*, 49ff.

Rome in A.D. 21, but the magnates seem to have taken little part in it (see below). Educated and well-informed, they would, as in A.D. 70, resist enticements to revolt with reflections on *vim Romanam pacisque bona* (*Hist.*, IV, 69). None could have had a better appreciation of Roman strength than an ex-praetor. Vindex risked rebellion, and the Gallic magnates followed him, because they knew that it was not Rome they had to fight, but a tyrant hated throughout the Roman world. If the programme under | which they fought had masked disloyalty to Rome itself, the very candidate Vindex sponsored for the succession must have turned against him, as soon as he was emperor, and Vindex had thrown off the mask. Thus, if the ultimate aim of Vindex had been national independence, immediate success, no less than immediate failure, must still have led to final disaster. Strong evidence should be required before we tax Vindex with failure to see so patent a truth. He has indeed been represented as an earlier Civilis. If Tacitus is right, as I believe,[51] Civilis did from the first aim at independence for his people, while professing to support Vespasian. But the circumstances were very different. On the very edge of the empire, the Batavians could look for help to their kinsmen in free Germany and hope that Rome would tolerate their independence as for almost twenty years she had tolerated that of the Frisians (*Ann.*, IV,72–4, XI, 19). The Gauls could not expect, nor even desire, German aid; and the riches and location of their country·made it a possession that no Roman emperor would abandon. When Civilis framed his plans, the empire seemed to be in dissolution; no one could be sure that Vitellians and Flavians would not wear each other out in endless war. Even when he threw off the disguise of loyalty to Vespasian, he was encouraged by the weakness and indiscipline of the Rhine legions; and there were rumours of Roman disasters in Britain and on the Danube (*Hist.*, IV, 54–5). But in 68 Roman strength was intact and likely to remain so, if (as the survival of Vindex required) Nero were overthrown by general revolt.

It is thus neither attested nor probable that Vindex personally aimed at Gallic independence. This is not to say that he did not act both as a Gaul and as a Roman senator. He may well have sympathized with the oppression the Gauls suffered (see below) and incurred disfavour at Rome by seeking to protect them against procurators: a Gallic noble lost his authority if he failed to protect|his dependents (Caesar, *B. G.*, VI, 11), and the authority Vindex enjoyed is plain from the way in

---

[51] See *contra* G. WALSER, *Rom, das Reich* etc. (1951), 86ff. By arbitrarily accepting or rejecting statements of Tacitus (our only source), it seems to me that he gives a less coherent and credible picture than that which he criticizes; in particular, he cannot adequately explain why Civilis, if really loyal to Vespasian, should have attacked troops who had sworn allegiance to him, and joined forces with those troops, after they had foresworn this allegiance. [See ch. 3.]

which the Gauls rallied to the standard of their compatriot. Moreover the aims of a rebel leader and of his followers need not coincide. Nero's crimes and follies at Rome could have made little, if any, impact on Gauls, even on the magnates. It might be argued that some of his followers, less aware than he of the hopelessness of the attempt, did aim at Gallic freedom.

The elements of national feeling had certainly once existed in Gaul. United in language, customs and religion, linked by a lively commerce and possessed of lays that reminded them of the heroic deeds of their past,[52] the Gauls of Caesar's day had some consciousness that they were a single people and had a common interest in preserving their freedom from Germans or Romans.[53] But even then internecine quarrels had divided them till it was too late for the common resistance under Vercingetorix to triumph. Did an effective sentiment in favour of national freedom outlast the conquest? It has been thought that the Druids fostered such a sentiment. Yet neither Caesar not later writers represent the Druids as leaders in Gallic resistance to Rome. Their proscription by Rome is not ascribed to such a cause.[54] Once proscribed indeed, they were naturally hostile to the state that persecuted them. It is no surprise that Druids proclaimed that the burning of the Capitol was a sign that the gods were transferring dominion from Rome to Gaul (*Hist.*, IV, 54). But the Druids who for centuries survived Rome's prohibitions cannot have been the great nobles of Caesar's time, 'observed of all observers', but rather humbler prophets and sorcerers, without influence over aristocratic governments.[55] In 69 a lowborn prophet, Mariccus, raised an insurrection of villagers, to secure Gallic freedom,[56] and the local Aeduan government put down the fanatical mob with some Roman help.

After Caesar's conquest only minor operations were needed to | complete or maintain the subjection of Gaul.[57] Foreign help to throw off the yoke was not available, or, from Germany, not desired. The nobility retained its local authority. The persecution of the Druids did not entail intolerance of Gallic religious beliefs.[58] Rome did not impose but offered for acceptance a higher and more attractive culture. At

[52] Cf. *Ann.*, III, 45, 2—perhaps a reminiscence of such lays.
[53] JULLIAN, II, ch. XIII.
[54] H. M. LAST, *JRS*, 39, ff. summarized evidence and rival views. I am not quite happy about his interpretation: JULLIAN, IV, 173, n. 4; VI, 5, n. 5 offers a corrective. [Cf. pp. 483 ff.]
[55] JULLIAN, VI, 80.
[56] *Adsertor Galliarum et deus* (*nam id sibi indiderat*), *Hist.*, II, 61.
[57] JULLIAN, IV, 21; 57–67 (21–8 attempt an explanation of Gallic loyalty during the Roman civil wars).
[58] JULLIAN, VI, 1–8; the religious troubles that have plagued some modern empires were felt by Rome only in Judaea.

least among the upper classes Romanization proceeded apace.[59] By disseminating their own ideas among their subjects, the British and French have sown the seeds of movements for national independence, for everywhere they have taken with them the ideal of free self-government. But from the Romans men learned that a beneficent Providence had ordained eternal rule for Rome and the duty of obedience for her subjects. The Gauls were apt pupils, showing (if we may believe Claudius) *centum annorum immobilem fidem obsequiumque multis trepidis rebus nostris plus quam expertum* (*ILS*, 212). As early as 12 B.C. Augustus thought it safe to let the notables meet yearly in national conclave. Claudius admitted them to the senate—at their own request.

Claudius overlooked a revolt that had occurred so recently as A.D. 21. This Schiller adduced as proof of the persistence of nationalism. The causes are clearly given by Tacitus (*Ann.*, III, 40)—the annual levies of tax, the burden of debt and the cruelty and arrogance of the governors: in brief, the oppressiveness of Roman government.[60] Thus a longing for national freedom was not the | prime motive, though it was the aim: only independence could secure the Gauls from the Roman tax-gatherer, and the rods and axes. The sedition, says Tacitus (III, 41), infected almost every *civitas*, yet its extent may easily be overstated. The two chief leaders were nobles (III, 40), and they had some *primores* as accomplices (III, 41, 2), but the following of Florus among the Treveri was a 'mob of debtors and clients'; few nobles were involved (III, 42). Sacrovir seized Augustodunum, precisely to secure as hostages the children of the Gallic nobility at school there (III, 43). Tacitus can even suggest that the rebels were mere beggars and criminals (III, 40). Local governments were hardly involved. The

---

[59] See the useful sketch by Dessau, *o. c.*, II, 480ff.

[60] For heavy taxation as a grievance under Tiberius. cf. *Ann.*, I, 76, 2; II, 42, 5; IV, 72. A. Grenier, *REL*, XIV, 373ff., plausibly suggested that the curious complaint *de continuatione tributorum* relates to continued levy of taxes on federate or free civitates, previously immune, cf. perhaps *Hist.*, IV, 17, 4; A. H. M. Jones, *Greek City*, 131–2 supplies Eastern parallels. Tax-demands could easily produce indebtedness, as in pre-Roman Gaul, *BG*, VI, 13, and often in the Republic to Roman usurers; note the massacre of Roman *negotiatores Ann.*, III, 42; cf. n. 70. Grenier makes too much of the supposed shortage of money as the main cause of the debt problem, and therefore of the revolt. Though some nobles may have fallen into debt, the *vulgus obaeratorum* were clearly indebted bondsmen, cf. *JRS*, XLVIII, 168, and the revolt was not (as he thinks) essentially aristocratic, any more than Catilina's. Grenier will not hear of injustice by Roman governors under Tiberius, citing *Ann.*, IV, 6, 4. But what evidence could Tacitus have had for that sweeping generalization? The chief value of this text is the proof it gives that Tacitus knew that at some times and places under the early Principate abuses occurred in tax-collection of the kind well known in the late Empire (see texts cited by O. Seeck, *Gesch. d. Untergangs d. Ant. Welt.*, II², 553, n. to 278, 16). For such abuses in the early 1st century in Egypt, cf. *SEG*, VIII, 527 = Ehrenberg-Jones², 320a; Philo, *de spec. leg.*, III, 159 [which gives the direct lie for Tiberius' reign to Tacitus' *corporum verbera aberant*;] H. I. Bell, *JRS*, XXVIII, 1 ff. Cf. also *Ann.*, IV, 19, 4; 72. Perhaps Egypt differs from other provinces chiefly in that there conditions are better documented.

Aedui and others retained their old treaties with Rome years later;[61] it is clear that officially they had not infringed them. Probably the grievances that prompted revolt were real enough, but the majority of the governing class could see that there was no reality in the hopes of success the leaders held out (III, 40, 3). It was reasonable for Tiberius to keep calm, and Claudius to forget the whole affair. It had been no proof of disloyalty to Rome that good government could not dispel.

No better evidence of a persisting nationalism in Gaul is to be found in the attempted establishment in 70 of an *imperium Galliarum*. Though loath to submit to ever new demands for men and money,[62] no Gauls gave ear to Civilis' solicitations that they | should rise for freedom (*Hist.*, IV, 17); they actually fought against him.[63] The situation changed on the news of Vitellius' death, and then only for those who had been from the first committed to his cause (IV, 54ff.); perhaps they feared punishment from Vespasian, as from Galba. The lead was taken in revolt by the Treveri and Lingones. To the former, as to the Nervii who joined them, co-operation with the German Civilis was easy, as they liked to think themselves of German stock, superior to the effete Gauls. The other rebels were German or half-German.[64] Naturally there was an urgent need for wider support. The insurgents sought to seduce the rest of Gaul (IV, 56) and proclaimed an *imperium Galliarum* (IV, 57; cf. 55, 3). That the forms of this new state were Roman,[65] just as its leaders were Roman citizens and officers, does not prove that its conception was not genuinely national; such phenomena have been frequent in the disruption of our own empire. The offer of the purple to Cerealis (IV, 75) is more disturbing; it seems that the

[61] *Ann.*, XI, 23, 1; 25, 1; PLINY, *NH*, 106–7 mentions the Lingones, Remi and Carnutes as other *foederati*. The Treveri, *antea liberi*, had perhaps forfeited freedom for a revolt in 29 BC (DIO, LI, 20, 5).

[62] *Hist.*, IV, 26; cf. 15, 3; 71, 2. Vitellius had previously levied troops for legions (II, 57, 1; cf. perhaps IV, 61, 3) and *auxilia* (II, 69, 1). Abuses in the *dilectus* need not have been confined to the Batavians (IV, 14). Obviously the Gauls had suffered much from Vindex' defeat (I, 51) and later Vitellian depredations (I, 63–9); and Galba's tax-remissions can never have taken effect.

[63] *Hist.*, IV, 18; 20; 25; 28; 33; 37. (I follow Tacitus throughout, not Walser, cf. n. 51.)

[64] For Treveran and Nervian claims see *Germ.*, 28, 4 (cf. *BG*, VIII, 25; II, 4; 15); STRABO, IV, 3, 4 concedes the Nervian claim. There was even a tradition that all Belgae were of German origin, *BG*, II, 4. For my purpose the validity of such claims is immaterial; that they were believed helps to explain the relation of the Treveri etc. to Civilis. Other rebel peoples were the German Ubii (IV, 55; 77; but cf. 63 ff.), Tungri (IV, 55, 66 etc.; cf. *Germ.*, 2, 5), Vangiones and Triboci (IV, 70; cf. *Germ.* 28, 4), and the Sunuci, Baetasii and Caeracates (IV, 66; 70), probably of the same race. The Lingones were the only incontestably pure Gallic people involved. See DIO, LI, 20, 5 for Treveran co-operation with Germans in 29 BC.

[65] Classicus assumed the *fasces*, IV, 59. WALSER, 104, thinks oaths were taken to him as Roman (*sic*) emperor, not to a mere abstraction; but in 68–9 many armies had sworn obedience to SPQR. (Augusta Treverorum was a Latin colony, cf. F. VITTINGHOFF, *ZSS*, LXVIII, 48off.; hence tinctured with Roman ideas).

'nationalists' were readier to fight Vespasian than to secure their own freedom from rule by a Roman. But what is fatal to the view that the revolts of 68 and 70 sprang from a common desire for Gallic freedom is that the second revolt was quasi-German, that its leaders had actually opposed Vindex and now found no support among his old followers. A pan-Gallic congress at Rheims rejected their solicitations (IV, 69). For Tacitus the issue posed was one of liberty or peace (IV, 67). But | in fact the Sequani had already fought hard against the rebels (*ibid.*), and the Gauls could not yet know that Cerealis would dispense with their assistance (IV, 71). The true question at Rheims was whether the Gauls would fight for Rome or against her. It was the former course they chose. There was indeed little positive enthusiasm for Rome, though men of sense are said to have felt 'reverence and loyalty'. Roman strength was stressed, and the blessings of peace; the younger men were restrained from revolt by fear. Still more important, according to Tacitus, were the bitterness still felt at the conduct of the Treveri and Lingones in opposing Vindex, and the rivalries of the *civitates*, precluding unity, as in Caesar's time. There is at least nothing of a passionate longing for Gallic freedom and unity. And after the congress the insurrection soon petered out. The Nervii even took up arms again to fight the Germans on Rome's behalf (IV, 79).

In 70 Gallic nationalism gave but a specious colour to a rising of a few quasi-German peoples, prompted by their individual anxieties or ambitions. As an explanation of the great revolt of Vindex it is not attested and should not be invoked. Rather we should look for a cause that will explain why not only Gallia Comata, but the titular Roman colony of Vienna, which is no more likely to have been anti-Roman than was Cologne (*Hist.*, IV, 64–5), and the largely unarmed Spanish and African provinces at once rose against Nero. Dio supplies it. In his account Gauls (and Britons) were infuriated by the taxes (Zonaras, XI, 13). Vindex is made to say that Nero had despoiled the whole empire and to exhort the Gauls to help not only the Romans but themselves and all the inhabitants of the empire. The new insurrection indeed resembles that in A.D. 21, but not at all points. On this occasion the local governments were engaged, and their aim was to end oppression, not by escaping from Roman rule, but by replacing the ruler. For it was not regular taxes that they so much resented, as the new exactions to which Nero had been led by his extravagance.

Et laudatorum principum usus ex aequo quamvis procul agentibus: saevi proximis ingruunt. This much quoted dictum (*Hist.*, IV, 74) should not be invested with the authority of Tacitus: it is part of an apologia for Roman rule that he puts in Cerealis' mouth. Tacitus knew that the task of an orator was to persuade, not instruct his hearers, and his aim plausibility, not truth, and if he had composed this and other speeches according to this principle with such skill | as to deceive modern scholars, the blame attaches to their gullibility.[66] Our evidence about the 'cruelty' of certain emperors relates chiefly to their victims of the upper class of Rome, and less is known in detail of their conduct as it affected humbler persons or provincials, but it is imprudent to assume that they were not affected. It was not only Domitian who was *inopia rapax, metu saevus*; and though the fears of such emperors were directed mainly against the Roman governing class, their rapacity could have wider scope. Hints of this are not lacking in several reigns,[67] and the exactions of Nero are stated to have been universal.

Even the early part of Nero's reign hardly deserves the praise sometimes bestowed on its provincial administration. Analysis of the eleven or twelve trials for misgovernment will not suggest that the subjects found it easy to obtain redress.[68] After 61 no more trials are recorded. In Judaea Felix was retained for six years to misrule the country.[69] In Britain the confiscations and outrages among the Iceni and the absence of the legate provided the occasion | for revolt; the burden of taxation and conscription, Roman usury, the encroachments of veteran settlers on native land, and the heavy costs of the imperial cult imposed on the notables had accumulated a long resentment. To avoid oppression, the Britons were forced to seek freedom.[70] We may absolve the young emperor from responsibility,

---

[66] In Cerealis' speech observe the half-truth that Rome taxed her subjects only to pay for their defence, ignoring the heavy costs of court, building at Rome, corn-dole etc.; also the falsity of the claim that Gauls often commanded legions and governed provinces. Cf. n. 39.

[67] E.g. those of Tiberius (SUET., *Tib.* 49), Gaius (DIO, LIX, 21–2 [Jos., *AJ* XIX, 1 and 14]) and Domitian (SUET., *Dom.*, 12, 1: *usquequaque*; PHILOSTR., *v. Soph.*, II, 547; cf. *IG*, II–III², 110; v. *Apoll.*, VII, 23–5 [probably fiction based on Philostratus' knowledge of later tyrannies]; *Dig.*, XLVIII, 22, 1, presumably addressed to a provincial governor). Some provincials were, of course, involved in the ruin of senatorial patrons, e.g. Asclepiodotus (*Ann.*, XVI, 33) or (under Domitian) Dio Chrysostom.

[68] Of five persons convicted, one was soon restored to influence (*Ann.*, XIII, 33; cf. XIV, 48; XVI, 17; 28), another secured mitigation of sentence (XIV, 28); other cases XIII, 30; XIV, 18; 46 and perhaps *Hist.*, I, 77 (Scaevinus). Tacitus marks two acquittals as unjust; for one of these Nero was responsible (XIII, 52), and Eprius Marcellus (*ibid.*, 33) later enjoyed his favour; other cases *ibid.*, 30; 52; XIV, 18. Nero prevented the trial of his infamous agent, Celer, XIII, 33. Later in the reign the rapacious Salvius Otho Titianus (*Agr.*, 6) apparently escaped prosecution. So did the procurators of Judaea whose maladministration finally provoked revolt. Lucceius Albinus even received from Nero a new post in Mauretania, where he may have continued to practise collusion with brigands, as he was able to call on their help in large numbers in 69, *Hist.*, II, 58. Cf. *AJ*, XX, 204–15; *BJ*, II, 272–6. [Cf. ch. 4 Part II.]

[69] *Ann.*, XII, 54; *Hist.*, V, 9; Josephus' narrative perhaps suggests little more than incompetence.

[70] *Ann.*, XIV, 31ff; *Agr.*, 15 and DIO, LXII, 1ff. may be combined. Walser's criticisms of Tacitus here (*o. c.*, 128ff.) are mistaken, cf. SYME, *o. c.*, 762ff.: note also (a) the parallel between Catus' conduct and that of a Syrian procurator on Herod's death (*BJ*, II, 16–19; 23–5; 39–79); (b) the unpopularity of a veteran colony is no more surprising than that of Athenian cleruchies;

though *they* are unlikely to have done so. With Corbulo's appointment, *videbatur locus virtutibus patefactus* (*Ann.*, XIII, 8); yet governors at best incompetent were retained at their posts,[71] a legate of Upper Germany, guilty of initiating a useful canal project, was removed in the same year,[72] and favouritism determined several new appointments.[73] All through the reign men of low moral repute were entrusted with positions of high responsibility, and we ought to be wary of accepting statements (that may depend on the dubious testimony of provincial *laudationes*) that some of them displayed unexpected vigour or justice.[74] In Spain Galba saw that inertia was the course of prudence, and kept his post for an exceptionally long period (Suet., *Galba*, 9; cf. Plut., 4). By contrast, the distinquished services of Plautius Silvanus in | Moesia (where, it is true, he had a long tenure) went without reward or praise (*ILS*, 986), and the justice and vigour of Barea Soranus in Asia—he improved the harbour at Ephesus and refused official aid to the depredations of Nero's agent, Acratus, at Pergamum—contributed to his ruin.[75]

By this time Nero's administration had long deteriorated. The days were past when he could dream of abolishing the *portoria* and ending exactions by publicans, which must have been even more oppressive in the provinces than in Italy[76]—it is significant that Galba rewarded Gaul by remitting the customs dues there (n. 40)—and the reforms he had once made in their collection were mostly not effective for long.[77] The lavishness of his court, his shows and buildings, his largesses to favourites (*Hist.*, I, 20), necessitated new financial expedients, though these did not suffice; even the costs of the army were not met, and at his

---

(c) *ILS*, 5163, 16 and 23ff. illustrates the costliness of the imperial cult; *Ann.*, 1, 57, 2, shows that a provincial priest was not always a faithful pro-Roman. Syme is too harsh to Dio. Leaving Seneca aside (but cf. *Ann.*, XIII, 42), Roman usury is probable, as in Gaul in AD 21. Romans massacred may well have included money-lenders (for other such massacres cf. VELL., II, 110; *Ann.*, III, 41). For poll-tax on the dead (DIO, LXII, 3, 4) cf S. L. WALLACE, *Taxation in Egypt* (1938), 124-5. Conscription, *Agr.*, 15, 3; cf. *Ann.*, IV, 46; *Hist.*, IV, 14; [cf. chs. 3 and 9]. *Agr.* 13, 1 suggests there were abuses in tax-collection and conscription.

[71] E.g. Ummidius Quadratus, Felix and Didius Gallus (*Ann.*, XII, 40).

[72] Antistius Vetus, *Ann.*, XIII, 53; cf. 56 for his removal.

[73] Cf. A. N. SHERWIN-WHITE, *PBSR*, XV, 16–17; Otho's appointment is a flagrant example.

[74] See *Ann.*, XIII, 46; SUET., *Otho*, 3, 2 (Otho); *Hist.*, I, 48 (Vinius); *Ann.*, XVI, 18 (Petronius); *Hist.*, II, 97; SUET., *Vit.*, 5 (A. Vitellius). For *laudationes Ann.*, XV, 20ff. and FURNEAUX, *ad. loc.* Tiberius indeed held that responsibility could inspire such men to better conduct (*Ann.*, III, 69) and the zeal for Vitellius shown in Africa confirms one such encomium. There is no such testimony for Fonteius Capito (*Hist.*, I, 7) or Clodius Macer (*ibid.*, 11; cf. PLUT., 6, 2). Trebellius Maximus (*Agr.*, 16; *Hist.*, I, 60) illustrates the premium set on inertia.

[75] *Ann.*, XVI, 23. Pergamum lost its art treasures despite his attitude (DIO CHRYS., XXXI, 148) and probably suffered other penalties (PLUT., 815D).

[76] CIC., *ad. Qu. fr.*, I, 1, 33, cf. also the implication in *Ann.*, XIII, 30: *velut infimam nationum Italiam... adflictavisset.*

[77] *Ann.*, XIII, 50–1; cf. SUET., *Nero*, 10, 1.

death the treasury was bare. As early as 63 he reduced the weight of the gold and silver coinage.[78] In 62–64 Albinus was levying extraordinary taxes in Judaea, perhaps not without authority (*BJ*, II, 273). After the fire at Rome Nero's agents pillaged the empire for works of art. But money too was required. We are told that the contributions demanded devastated Italy and ruined the provinces, including free communities.[79] Dio dates still further exactions to his visit to Greece and his project for an Isthmus canal (LXII, 17). The presence of an emperor and his cortege was always burdensome to a province,[80] and even Greece paid dearly for the freedom and immunity he granted (Dio, LXII, 11). There were useful windfalls in inheritances from freedmen and the confiscation of the estates of his political victims at Rome.[81] Suetonius records how, | presumably at this time, he encouraged delators and claimed the estates of all who were 'ungrateful to the emperor'.[82] It is a delusion to think that delation endangered only the eminent. Even provincials could incur charges of treason, with or without justification.[83] *Fiscales calumniae* (Suet., *Dom.*, 9) could be brought wherever it could be alleged, more or less speciously, that a man had defaulted on his taxes, or appropriated imperial property (widely scattered throughout the provinces), or infringed the marriage laws; these, indeed, applied only to citizens, but the citizenship was enjoyed by numerous rich provincials.[84] An unscrupulous ruler in need of money would not confine his attention to Rome and Italy, ignoring

---

[78] *RIC*, I, p. 31.

[79] *Ann.*, XV, 45; XVI, 23; SUET., *Nero*, 32, 4; DIO, LXIII, 11, 1; DIO CHRYS., XXXI, 148–9 for works of art; *Ann.*, XV, 45; SUET., *Nero*, 38, 3; cf. PLUT., 4: τὰς ἐπαρχείας for money.

[80] ROSTOVTZEFF, *SEH²*, ch. VIII, nn. 4 and 6.

[81] T. FRANK, *Econ. Survey*, V, 43–4, collects the evidence; cf. SUET., *Nero*, 32, 2 for freedmen's estates.

[82] SUET., *Nero*, 32; cf. *Hist.*, II, 10; IV, 42. On imperial claims to inheritances see R. S. ROGERS, *TAPA*, LXXVIII, 78ff. (He is mistaken as to the later part of Domitian's reign, on which SUET., *Dom.*, 12, 2 agrees with *Agr.*, 43, 4; PLIN., *Paneg.*, 43. *Dom.*, 9, 2, evidently refers to his early years.)

[83] Cf. the second Cyrene edict (*SEG*, IX, 8); PLIN., *epp.*, X, 81–2; the Acts of the Alexandrine Martyrs, *passim*; PHILOSTR., *v. Apoll.*, VII, 23; *Dig.*, XLVIII, 4, 6 and 19, 6 *pr.*

[84] The titles *de iure fisci. Dig.*, XLIX, 14 [and *CJ* X, 1, 1] concerning fiscal claims, including those that arose under the marriage laws (cf. *Ann.*, III, 25–8 [PLINY, *Pan.* 42]), constantly alludes to delators and cites numerous rescripts to provincial governors. For delation in regard to tax-payments or census returns cf. also *Dig.*, V, 1, 53; XLVIII, 18, 1, 19–20; in regard to encroachment on imperial land [under Domitian] DIO CHRYS., XLVI, 8. Note *Hist.*, II, 84: *passim delationes* (in the East), *et locupletissimus quisque in praedam correpti;* [the exactions to fill Vespasian's war-chest continued 'etiam in pace' (*ibid.*, cf. Jos., *BJ* VII, 446; SUET., *Tit.* 8, 5; DIO LXVI, 2, 5; 8, 2–4]. In Italy we hear at times of the punishment of delators (e.g. DIO, XVI, 19; LXVIII, 1; SUET., *Dom.*, 9; PLIN., *Paneg.* 35); but the accusers of prominent persons rarely suffered; such delators were clearly little men, and so were their victims (cf. *Ann.*, IV, 36; *Hist.*, II, 10, 1); [see also BRUNT, *Sodalitas, Scritti in Onore di A. Guarino*, 479f.].

the wealth of Gaul[85] and other provinces. Nero would tell his procurators *Scis quid mihi opus sit*, or *Hoc agamus, ne quis quicquam habeat* (Suet., 32, 4), and since Claudius' ill-conceived innovation (*Ann.* XII, 60), they were judges in the *fiscus'* own cause. A prudent governor, like Galba in Spain (Plut., 4), or later, Agricola (*Agr.*, 9, 4), would not dare to interfere with their exactions. Tiberius Julius Alexander declared that in 68 Alexandria had been almost desolated by the number of sycophants and that every household had been thrown into confusion. For two years he had heard complaints of this and many other abuses, but had not ventured on any remedy. His edict cites precedents for many of his reforms in the edicts of earlier prefects, but there is no | allusion to any such edict issued by his immediate predecessor, Caecina Tuscus;[86] doubtless Caecina had known well enough what was expected of him by Nero. It has often been asked how it was that Alexander felt entitled to proclaim such comprehensive reforms, evidently drafted before he had received express authority from Galba. Surely the reliefs he granted corresponded with the general promises that the new 'saviour of mankind' had made in his edicts, when calling on all the provinces to rise against universal oppression. We are well informed of the miseries that Britain, Judaea[87] and Egypt suffered under Nero: it would be strange indeed if all was well in the provinces we know less of. On the contrary, they all suffered from similar wrongs, as our sources unanimously state.

Revolt broke out, because redress could be had no other way; the armies, short of pay and contemptuous of an unworthy prince, were ready to obey commanders hostile to Nero because they were drawn from the senate which Nero had terrorized, and Nero perished, friendless (except among the urban plebs) and alone. Court intrigues had brought him into absolute power, and his personal license and extravagance had then deprived him of all effective support. Tacitus has often been criticized for concentrating his attention on the doings of the emperor and the court to the neglect of the state of the empire at large. But reflection on the great crisis | that began in 68 ought to

---

[85] A. GRENIER, *Ec. Survey*, IV, 518–30 and *passim* on Gallic wealth.

[86] For Alexander's edict cf. nn. 17, 20. Delation, see vv. 35–45. The omission of an edict of Caecina in section 4 is notable; cf. also O. W. REINMUTH, *TAPA*, LXVI, 248ff., whose views in general I do not accept. Caecina was prefect 63–?66, cf. A. STEIN, *Die Präfekten von Aegypten*, 35–7. On Egypt under Nero see H. I. BELL, *JRS*, XXVIII, 1ff. [Chalon, cited in n. 20, and discussions cited by A. BOWMAN, *JRS*, 1976, 169].

[87] The origins of the Jewish revolt were remote and complex; but Josephus' narratives and Tacitus' terse comment (*Hist.*, V, 10) compel us to ascribe it in part to Roman misgovernment, especially from 62 to 66. [cf. ch. 13.]

silence such criticism. Its consequences, but for Vespasian's wisdom, might have been as disastrous to the empire as those of the similar crisis in 193 ultimately proved to be; and its causes are to be found in just those events at Rome which Tacitus describes. The crimes and caprices of an autocrat and his favourites, though at first sight affecting a narrow circle, determined the destinies of millions.[88]

[88] [I doubt if the view (cf. M. P. CHARLESWORTH, *JRS*, 1950, 72ff.) that Nero was popular in the East is warranted. DIO CHRYS. XXI, 9f. says that all now wish Nero were alive, as most believe him to be; the discourse was probably composed in his exile under Domitian (H. VON ARNIM, *Dio von Prusa*, 291ff.) and implies that men were now suffering a worse tyranny, cf. the adverse opinion in XXXI, 150. Greece and Asia were *terrified* by the advent of the first false Nero (who got hardly any local support (*Hist*, II, 8f.); his two successors only found favour with the Parthians (*PIR²* D 129 at p. 39) who were ready to reciprocate Rome's support of pretenders to their throne. For PLUTARCH Nero's liberation of Greece is his one good deed (567 F); for hostile verdicts in his writings (implicit in his *Galba*) see *Ant.* 87, 2; 505 C. PAUSANIAS regards the liberation as evidence of a generous nature which was none the less corrupted (VII, 17, 3f.); he records his robberies of Greek shrines (V, 25, 8; 26, 3; IX, 27, 4; X, 7, 1; 19, 2), and alludes to his crimes (IX, 27, 4). Cf. PHILOSTR., *v. Apoll.* V, 7 and 41. Christian writers in East as well as West confidently adduce Nero to illustrate the rule that it was tyrants who persecuted their faith.]

3

Tacitus on the Batavian Revolt

For the revolt of the Batavians and some other peoples in Gaul and Germany in A.D. 69–70 Tacitus is virtually our only source.[1] This does not mean that we may properly succumb to the temptation of adopting his account without reserve and without subjecting it to critical examination. There is, however, a high initial probability that it deserves respect. In the rest of his work, though his interpretations have often been questioned, too often indeed without sufficient reason,[2] by critics who have neither experience of the kind of conditions he represents nor the imagination to recreate them,[3] his reputation for veracity on particular matters of fact is good, and has been upheld by some of his severest critics. Moreover Tacitus was a contemporary of the events of 69–70, and though he was too young to have had first-hand knowledge of affairs on the Rhine at this time, we should not expect to find that his account is here distorted by preconceptions drawn from the experience of a later age. It is indeed probable that he derived his account chiefly (though not only) from the elder Pliny, who was a contemporary of the revolt and well acquainted with the region where it broke out.[4] Modern scholars have therefore, for the most part, been content to follow Tacitus' account, in which they discern | no incoherence or implausibility. However, G. Walser has recently developed a theory of Münzer (n. 4) in such a way as to impugn the reliability of his interpretation and narrative.[5]

---

[1] Josephus *BJ* I, 5: VII, 75–88; Dio LXVI, 3 (cf. p. 47 below) add almost nothing to our detailed knowledge.
[2] The great work of R. Syme, *Tacitus* (Oxford 1958) (cited as Syme) should silence many such criticisms.
[3] Cf. K. von Fritz, *Cl. Phil.* LII 73 ff.
[4] F. Münzer, *Die Quelle des Tacitus für die Germanenkriege* in *Bonner Jahrb.* CIV (1899), 67 ff. His case depends in part on imputing to Tacitus' account a bias derived from Pliny: this I reject below (pp. 46 ff.). But his argument from the detailed knowledge of geography and customs seems valid, cf. Syme, *o.c.* 173–5. (Syme 675 rejects his identification of the common source of *Hist.* I–II and Plutarch's *Galba* and *Otho* with Pliny). Cf. also n. 5. For use of other sources cf. n. 47.
[5] *Rom, das Reich, und die fremden Völker* etc (Baden-Baden 1951), pp. 86–128 (followed by E. Paratore, *Tacito* (Milan, 1951) n. 245), cited as Walser.

No detailed attempt has yet been made to answer him.[6] It is the purpose of this article to do so.

According to Tacitus' account in the fourth and fifth books of the *Histories*,[7] the Batavian chief, Julius Civilis, was impelled to revolt by private grievances[8] and ambitions, and followed by his people because of the distress caused by the Roman *dilectus*; he was soon joined by eight Batavian cohorts at Mainz, long noted for their mutinous conduct in the civil wars. From the first Civilis aimed at independence, and even at founding a Gallo-German empire for himself; and from the first he strove to incite other German and Gallic subjects of Rome to revolt, and called in the aid of free Germans. But, conscious of Roman power, he did not at once disclose his true objectives. Flavian partisans had encouraged him to take arms in Vespasian's interest; and initially, he claimed to be fighting on Vespasian's behalf, and even made the Batavian cohorts take an oath to Vespasian (IV, 21). With the news of the Flavian victory at Cremona, the situation changed (IV, 31). The Rhine legions reluctantly swore allegiance to Vespasian, yet, though informed of this, Civilis still attacked them (and actually did not desist from attacks, when they temporarily reverted to the Vitellian cause). Thus he was now in open revolt, from Rome and not merely from Vitellius. The news of Vitellius' death, and reports of Roman disasters on every frontier and of the burning of the Capitol, stimulated disloyalty in Gaul (IV, 54); hitherto Civilis' | overtures to the Gauls had had no success.[9] Tacitus' later narrative shows indeed that this independence movement in Gaul was of very limited scope; only a few Belgic states actually revolted. The most prominent among them were the Treveri and Lingones. Under the leadership of Julius Classicus and others, they forced the Rhine legions to swear allegiance to the 'imperium Galliarum' (IV, 59–60). Civilis, though collaborating with the Gallic leaders and assisting to impose this oath (IV, 60, 2), would not take it himself nor allow any of the Batavians to do so; he hoped that in the end he could use the superior strength of his German followers to subject the Gauls to his own dominion (IV, 61). But Roman power proved too strong for the rebels. The disloyal legions

---

[6] Cf. however, F. Altheim's review in *Gnomon* XXIII 432–4 and my brief expression of dissent in ch. 2 n. 51.

[7] All references to chapters and sections only are to the *Histories* (ed. Koestermann, 1957).

[8] His brother (IV 32, 2), Claudius Paulus, had been executed by Fonteius Capito *'falso rebellionis crimine'*; he himself had been sent up in chains to Nero; acquitted by Galba, he was again in danger of death from the Vitellian legions in Jan. 69, and spared by Vitellius, only 'ne supplicio eius ferox gens alienaretur' (IV 13; I 59). For the possibility that Civilis and Paulus were inculpated as partisans of Vindex and Galba cf. Walser pp. 89–90; ch. 2 n. 7.

[9] Walser p. 96 seems to assume that (*contra* IV 17) he can have made no such early overtures, because they did not succeed!

were easily won back for Rome; the revolt in Gaul was crushed; the
war was transferred to the Batavian homeland, and with the desertion
of his allies from free Germany imminent, Civilis himself sued for
peace. Here Tacitus' record breaks off.

Very little of this is accepted by Walser. In his view neither Gallic
nor German subjects of Rome had any desire for independence, nor
could the notion of a Gallic or German empire ever have been
entertained; it is a Roman invention. Civilis took arms as a partisan of
Vespasian, in truth and not merely in appearance; as an adherent of
Galba (see n. 8), he was (it is assumed) adverse to Vitellius. The alleged
grievances of the Batavians at the *dilectus* are not to be taken seriously.
The core of Civilis' support consisted in the eight Batavian cohorts,
which joined him, because they had been denied the rewards they
expected for their services to Vitellius. Even the continuance of the war
after Vitellius' defeat and death became known on the Rhine is not to
be ascribed to a wish for liberty. It was prolonged by Vespasian's
reluctance to reward his Batavian supporters. To extract such rewards,
Civilis now co-operated with Gallic chiefs, who had served Vitellius,
and with the Vitellian legions, who had nothing to hope from
Vespasian. They resorted not to proclaiming a Gallic empire, but to
making Classicus Roman emperor; from his gratitude they could claim
the material benefits they sought. When it appeared that the Roman
general, Cerealis, was too strong for them, they were no less ready to
offer him the imperial title (IV, 75). It was as yet far from | clear that
Vespasian was firmly in control, and they hoped to gain from a new
ruler, who owed everything to them, what they had expected from
Vitellius. Thus, from first to last, the war was a civil war, which Tacitus
has misrepresented as a *bellum externum*. That distortion of the truth was
the work of Pliny, whom he followed,[10] and who aimed at exalting
Vespasian's prestige by crediting him with a great victory over Rome's
foreign enemies. In earlier parts of the *Histories*, however, traces of the
correct view may be found.

Walser denies (pp. 103–9) that either Gauls or Germans could have
aimed at independence or at establishing a powerful Gallic or German
empire. There is force in his view of the revolt in Gaul. I myself have
already sought to prove that at this time there was no widespread
passionate longing in Gaul for freedom and unity.[11] As Walser argues,
the Gallic rebels were peoples who had been too closely attached to
Vitellius and who had some reason to fear the displeasure of Vespa-

[10] Walser holds that Tacitus drew on Pliny's *German Wars*, rather than on his *History*; see *contra* Syme, 174 n. 5.

[11] Ch. 2 Part II.

sian. It is true that in general the Gallic magnates were well satisfied
with the local authority Rome left them, and knew that it was hopeless
to resist Rome's superior power. The course of events makes it plain
that they were not disloyal to Rome throughout Gaul. But these events
are known precisely from the account of Tacitus; he was not misled
himself, and he has not misled us. (He only gives it as a *fama* that the
primores Galliarum earlier in 69 had plotted a general insurrection, IV,
54, 3). Moreover Walser has pressed his case too far. Though nationalism had no sufficient hold over men's minds in Gaul, we need not
claim that it had wholly expired. The alleged Druidic predictions of
Rome's fall (IV, 54, 2) must not be lightly discounted (p. 110) on the
ground that 'the political role of the Druids had long been played out';
doubtless they were humble prophets, but they could have had
influence on the masses, and they were naturally hostile to the state
that persecuted them.[12] Having decided on revolt, Classicus and his
coadjutors had little choice but to try to stir into flame the dying
embers of Gallic nationalism; knowing that a few *civitates* could not
hold out by themselves, they were bound to work for the | creation of a
larger unit of resistance, and to make what play they could with
slogans of Gallic freedom, perhaps blinding themselves to the facts,
'mainly influenced by their not wishing to accept the truth' (Thuc. III
3). (It may also be that they, like Civilis too, entertained vain hopes
that peoples on the very extremity of the empire would be allowed, as
the Frisians had once been allowed, to make good their independence.)
We must not assume with Walser (p. 113) that because they were
Roman citizens, who had served the Roman state and had some
familiarity with Roman ideas and institutions, they were necessarily
loyal to Rome; by parity of reasoning Sir Roger Casement and other
Irish patriots could not have turned traitors to Britain. Doubtless the
new *imperium Galliarum* was modelled on the Roman;[13] it was the only
model they knew. Similarly peoples who have asserted their independence of British rule have readily adopted British practices and
conceptions. The rebels had little conviction[14] or success in their
nationalism; it does not follow that their rebellion had no national
colour at all.

Let us grant that the Gauls in general were not prepared to fight for
their freedom. It does not follow that freedom had no attraction to
those subjects of Rome who were, or accounted themselves to be,
Germanic. They could see that their kinsmen across the frontier were

---

[12] *Ibid.* nn. 54–6 with text.
[13] IV 59, 2 cf. Walser p. 114. (IV 55, 4: *disceptaturas Gallias quem virium suarum terminum velint* also
springs from Roman ideas of world-rule.)
[14] Cf. the offer of the purple to Cerealis, IV 75.

free and pined for the same independence. Walser indeed asserts that primitive peoples, like the Germans of those days, care nothing for high ideals such as liberty (p. 106). This bold generalization, for which he offers no evidence, we may leave to the judgement of the social anthropologist. In his view (p. 104) anti-Roman movements among the Germans were invariably plundering raids or revolts against taxation. Of course it is true that the free Germans usually invaded Roman territory in search of booty, or sometimes of land. According to Tacitus, it was the prospect of plunder that induced them in AD 69–70 to aid Civilis (IV 21, 2; 37, 3; 78, 1). It is also clear that Roman rule subjected Germans to burdens they resented. Walser is quite right in holding (106–7) that Arminius' revolt was provoked by the demands Varus made on the Germans.[15] | But what of this? The value of liberty may be realized, by both primitive and civilized peoples, when its loss is found to involve interference with their customs and the imposition of material hardships; and men may come to desire independence, when they see that only by securing it can they free themselves from these hardships and resume their traditional mode of life. We need not then doubt that Arminius led a freedom movement. The Batavians too had their grievances. They were exempt from taxation (IV 17, 2) but liable to conscription. The rigour and abuses of the *dilectus* caused them to revolt. But they could escape the *dilectus* only by regaining their freedom (IV 14).

At this time the Batavians supplied, besides some rowers for the Rhine flotilla (IV 16, 3), at least one *ala* and nine cohorts to the Roman army,[16] and probably more, perhaps 10,000 men.[17] The *ala* and one cohort were still stationed at home,[18] and it was apparently a recent

[15] Walser makes Varus' avarice alone responsible. Velleius' indictment of his conduct in Syria (II 117) [insinuates the adverse view explicit in Florus (II 30, 31 f.) and Orosius (VI 21, 26) on] his lust, arrogance and cruelty in Germany. But we must not neglect allusions to the imposition of taxes (*Ann.* I 59; Dio LVI 18), [the detailing of troops for policing (Dio 19) and interventions in local administration (18, 3)], the introduction of Roman jurisdiction (Vell. *l. c.*; Florus *l. c.*, cf. *Ann.* I 59: *virgas et secures et togam... supplicia*) and the rumours that colonies were projected (*Ann. l.c.*), which would have involved the appropriation of land (cf. *Ann.* XIV 31) (cf. Dio's reference to the 'synoecism of cities'). It seems clear that Augustus was converting 'Germany' into a province (cf. *Ann.* I 57 for a provincial cult of the Emperor at Cologne with a Cheruscan priest). It was the whole complex of provincial organization the Germans resisted; 'liberty' (*Ann.* I 59; II 10; 15; 44–5; 88) sums up their aims. (Syme, *CAH* X 374, doubts the introduction of 'Roman methods of taxation'. Of course we must not think of a census or of tribute in money. But cf. *Ann.* IV 72; more rudimentary methods could first be adopted. App *Ill.* 30 probably means that Moesia was first subjected to the census under Tiberius, not that Roman forces did not make levies on the population, so soon as they occupied the country.)

[16] The *ala*, IV 18, 1, cf. *domi delectus eques* in 12, 3; one cohort at home under Civilis, IV 16, 1; eight cohorts, previously in Britain, then under Valens, and in summer 69 at Mainz, I 59, 1: II 27–9; IV 15, 1 etc.

[17] Caecina too had Batavians under his command, II 17, 2.

[18] The cohorts were *equitatae*, IV 19, 1; and *after* 70 some at least were *milliariae*, though one was *quingenaria* (Cichorius, *RE* IV 251); Hyginus *de munit. castr.* 26 gives 1000 as the nominal strength

innovation that most of these regiments had | been posted abroad (IV 12, 3). It has been shown by K. Kraft[19] that in the Julio-Claudian period cohorts commonly formed a sort of local militia, serving under their own chiefs; it was only gradually that they were incorporated as regular regiments in the Roman army, and only then were men liable to serve for 25 or 26 years in any part of the empire, in units commanded by Roman *equites* and usually recruited locally, wherever they had first been raised.[20] In 69 we find that the Batavians' status in the army was transitional. They had not long ceased to be a local militia, but they still served under their own chiefs (IV 12, 3). Walser (p. 89) thinks it a *suggestio falsi* on Tacitus' part that this was a special privilege. More probably, the practice had become uncommon when Tacitus wrote, or even as early as 69; it was a relic of a disappearing system. It is likely that the Batavians lost it after their revolt, for it is not mentioned among their privileges in the *Germania* (ch. 29).

Walser has rightly stressed (103 ff.) that many free Germans desired nothing better than to serve as volunteers in Roman armies. Many such adventurous spirits there must have been among the Batavians. Yet not enough to meet Vitellius' needs. He resorted to conscription, 'suapte natura gravem' (IV 14,1). A man enlisted at the age of 17 for 25 years of service abroad had perhaps at best a 60% chance of surviving till discharge, and, if repatriated, of seeing his home and family again.[21] Thus the levy could separate children from parents, brothers from each other, virtually for life (IV 14, 3). It would seem that the unpopularity of long and distant service had led to the suspension in normal times of conscription among the favoured Italians,[22] whose numbers in the legions then | progressively declines.[23] Its introduction

of a *cohors miliaria equitata*, but cf. G. L. Cheesman, *Auxilia of the Roman Imperial Army*, Oxford, 1914, 25–30. The estimate of 10,000 depends on the view that there were more than 9 cohorts: this is not excluded by the fact that after 70 only nine are known to have existed. [Gaius had Batavian bodyguards, Suet., *Gaius* 43.]

[19] *Zur Rekrutierung der Alen u. Kohorten an Rhein u. Donau*, Bern, 1951, 35–42.

[20] Probably only such regular soldiers obtained the privileges attested in *diplomata*. No *diploma* earlier than AD 52 is extant; hence A. N. Sherwin-White (*Roman Citizenship*, Oxford 1939, 191–3) conjectures that Claudius devised the system. But *ILS* 2531; 2567 may illustrate pre-Claudian grants; and *diplomata* only become common in the Flavian period. The system perhaps developed gradually, applying to auxiliary units, possibly with a time-lag, after they had been incorporated in the regular army. The lack of early *diplomata* for *alares*, who (as Kraft shows) were usually regular soldiers from the first, remains notable. [Cf. Brunt, *Italian Manpower*, Oxford 1971, 242 f.]

[21] [Brunt, *Italian Manpower* 332–41. I originally wrote 50%, citing A. R. Burn, *Past and Present* IV (1953), p. 16, but see *Italian Manpower* 132 f.]

[22] Cf. Vell. II 130, 2; Ann. IV 4, 2 (despite lack of suitable Italian volunteers, Tiberius contemplated conscription only in the provinces). Liv. V 11, 5: *quibus dilectus... quibus diutina militia longinquitasque belli sit gravis* probably reflects the dislike of long, distant service in and after the second century BC in Italy.

[23] Cf. G. Forni, *Reclutamento delle Legioni*, Milan, 1953, Appendice B.

in Thrace had provoked a revolt under Tiberius (*Ann.* IV 46, 2). It is not surprising that it was resented by Batavians, and also by Gauls (*Hist.* IV 26, 1).

Confirmation of this resentment may be found in the constant turbulence of the famous eight cohorts which had been serving in Britain.[24] There they were not too far from their home, but it was another matter when they were posted to the east by Nero. Naturally they had no love for that Emperor, and they boasted that it was they who had wrested Italy from him (II 27 cf. 11). On his fall, while the 14th legion with which they were brigaded returned to Illyricum, they made for Britain again (II 27). Or so it was given out. In fact, some seven months later, they were still near Langres (I 59). Plainly, they had been in no haste to cross the Channel, away from their native land. At Langres they were incorporated in Valens' expeditionary force. Their mutinous conduct gave continual trouble;[25] Tacitus offers no explanation, but it seems likely that they were averse to campaigning far from the Rhine. After Bedriacum it was decided first to send them back to Britain, and then to keep them in Germany *ne quid truculentius auderent* (II 66; 69). When in September 69 they were ordered back to Italy, they proved recalcitrant. They demanded fulfilment or confirmation of promises to pay them a donative, to double their pay, and to increase the proportion of the better paid cavalry in their regiments. Walser assumes (p. 89) that these demands represented their real aims. That is directly denied by Tacitus. He says that their demands were pretexts for disloyalty; the more | Hordeonius conceded, the more they pressed claims that they knew he must reject (IV 19). Marching north, they at last disclosed, near Bonn, their true objective: *longa atque inrita militia fessis patriae atque otii cupidinem esse* (IV 20,1) Tacitus' account is consistent and credible, and the conduct of these soldiers harmonizes with the resistance in their homeland to new levies for distant service.[26]

Like the Britons (*Agr.* 13,1), the Batavians might have submitted to the levy but for the wrongs that accompanied it. The recruiting

---

[24] Probably they are not identical with the eight cohorts sent to Britain in AD 60 or 61 (*Ann.* XIV 38); Suetonius Paulinus already had Batavian troops, see Münzer *o.c.* 92–3, arguing from *Ann.* XIV 29, 3; *Agr.* 18, 4 (cf. *Ann.* II 8, 3; *Hist.* IV 12, 3; add *ILS* 2558). [They might have taken part in the invasion of Britain in 43, the year when Civilis entered Rome's service (IV 32, 2); he might have known Vespasian there, but see n. 48.]

[25] I cannot follow Walser's criticism of II 47–8 in n. 393. He admits in the text that Valens proposed to send some of them to Narbonensis, and then says in the note that Tacitus cannot be right in stating that the legions objected to the detachment of such fine troops, and that he has put into their mouths the views of the generals! His view that they were for Galba and therefore hostile to Vitellius disregards 66, 3; IV 17, 3.

[26] Cf. 'Calgacus' complaint (*Agr.* 31, 1): (*liberi et propinqui*) *per dilectus alibi servituri auferuntur.* The desertion of the *cohors Usiporum per Germanias conscripta* (*ib.* 28) comes to mind; they took ship, obviously intending to return home.

officers[27] conscribed the old and infirm, exacting bribes for their release, and handsome boys, to satisfy their lusts (IV 14,1). Walser rejects this as a colourful invention (P. 91). But, though homosexual passion may perhaps have caused a stir only in a few cases, corruption was widespread in an administration where it was accounted a singular virtue to keep one's fingers off the public funds (*abstinentia*).[28] Abuses in the levy had been envisaged and forbidden by the *lex Julia repetundarum,*[29] but practised by Q. Cassius in Spain in 47 BC and under Nero by Pedius Blaesus in Cyrene.[30] Hadrian is said to have prohibited the enrolment of mere boys in the army, but perhaps to no effect; at least inscriptions reveal legionaries aged sixteen or less.[31] It shows an ingenuous faith in the probity of Roman officials and an arbitrary disregard for the evidence to reject Tacitus' account. Its historicity is not to be impugned, as Walser argues, because it is followed by a probably invented speech of Civilis; and even that speech was doubtless composed on the basis of what Tacitus knew of the facts. |

Tacitus places Civilis' decision to revolt after he received a letter from Antonius Primus (IV 13, 2; 32, 1). As Walser remarks (p. 91), this letter cannot have been written before Vespasian was proclaimed on 1 July 69. Walser further infers that the *dilectus* was ordered, and that resistance to it took place, only when a Flavian agitation had begun; this enables him to substitute friendship between Vespasian and the Batavians for the cause clearly attested by Tacitus. In fact there is no reason to date the levy so late. As early as May Vitellius had directed that levies in Gaul, to fill gaps in the legions, should be more speedily carried out (II 57, 1), and similar measures were probably taken to augment the regular *auxilia,* even though untrained Gallic auxiliaries, raised 'prima statim defectione', were demobilized (II 69, 1). By the late summer of 69 ample time can have elapsed for Batavian resentment to have grown to the degree that made them ready to follow Civilis in revolt.[32]

For Tacitus the revolt originated with Civilis' personal indignation and aspirations (IV 13, 1). But a leader needs followers, and he is

---

[27] i.e. the tribunes and centurions of IV 14, 3 cf [ch. 9 n. 68]

[28] For centurions cf. e.g. I 46; 58, 1; *Ann.* IV 72.

[29] *Dig.* XLVIII 11, 6, 2: *lege Iulia repetundarum cavetur ne quis ob militem legendum mittendumve aes accipiat.*

[30] *Bell. Alex.* 56, 4; *Ann.* XIV 18, 1; cf. for abuses in Egypt in 183 *P. Lond.* II pp. 173–4. For similar abuses in Tudor and Stuart England, illustrated by *King Henry IV*, Part II, iii 2, see C. H. Firth, *Cromwell's Army,* London 1902, ch. 1. [See generally ch. 9.]

[31] HA *Hadr.* 10, 8; cf. Forni, (*o.c.* n. 23) p. 27.

[32] Walser p. 97 treats Labeo and Briganticus as partisans of Vitellius, as Civilis was in his view a partisan of Vespasian. When Civilis revolted, loyalty to Rome and loyalty to Vitellius might have seemed coterminous; but in the end we find Labeo and Briganticus fighting for Vespasian and Civilis against him!

unlikely to find them, unless there are more causes for rebellion than his private wrongs, or ambitions. Of royal stock and 'praepotens inter Batavos' (IV 13; I 59), Civilis could not count merely on the influence that flowed from personal rank. He had rivals, who opposed the revolt, the prefect of the *ala*, Claudius Labeo (IV 18; 56; 66; 70), and his own sister's son, Julius Briganticus, who, as commander of the *ala Singularium*, died fighting for Rome (IV 70; V 21). Though he concerted his plans with the *primores* (IV 14), in the end they came to fear his ambition (V 25). [By then the masses too were war-weary, and partly on that account Civilis decided to sue for peace and pardon (V 25 f.). But their earlier readiness to follow him is best explained if] we accept Tacitus' account of their grievances, and admit that, though they may have had no ideal passion for liberty in the abstract, they could and did seek liberty, in order to escape from Roman oppression.

To secure their liberty the Batavians needed help from other peoples. Civilis was intriguing with the Gauls from the outset (cf. | n. 9), and after Vitellius' death he succeeded in obtaining the co-operation of some Gallic *civitates*. But his true purpose, according to Tacitus, was to found a Gallo-German empire in which the German element should preponderate and of which he himself would be ruler (IV 61, 1 cf. 17, 6). Possessed of more cunning than most barbarians (32, 2), he disguised this aim, just as he had at first disguised his disloyalty to Rome by ostensibly espousing the Flavian cause, and was content to postpone conflict with his Gallic allies till the Romans had been repelled; he even seems to have conceded the supreme command to Classicus (76), and only assumed it himself, when the Gallic insurgents had been subdued, and Classicus and the other leaders were refugees; they were then given subordinate commands (V 20), perhaps because of their military experience. But he was careful not to take an oath himself to the *imperium Galliarum*, nor to let any Batavian do so (IV 61). And from the first he had also appealed to the free Germans (IV 14, 1). They soon offered help (17, 1) and in the narrative of the fighting his German allies constantly recur.[33] The rebels themselves were of German stock, or Gauls who mostly claimed affinity with the

---

[33] Bructeri (IV 21, 2; 77; V 18), Chatti (IV 37), Chauci (V 19), Mattiaci (IV 37), Tencteri (IV 21; 64; 77), Usipi (IV 37) and Transrhenani generally (IV 23; 64; V 25); [the Mattiaci, previously Roman vassals, were included in the province of Upper Germany under Domitian (see J. G. C. Anderson on *Germ.* 29), when the Usipi (cf. his note on *Germ.* 32 and *Agr.* 28)] became subjects of Rome. The term *Germani* sometimes includes the Batavians and other rebel subjects (IV 16, 1; 18, 3 etc.), but sometimes distinguishes the free Germans from them (78, 1; V 17, 1); in IV 33, 1 'Germans' are contrasted with the veteran Batavian cohorts. Terminology is loose: in IV 32, 3 Civilis is made to call the Batavians and Canninefates *exigua Galliarum portio*, but in 76, 1 'Germans' even includes rebel Gauls, e.g. the Lingones (77, 1) [cf. C. M. Wells, *German Policy of Augustus*, ch. II.]

Germans.[34] It is not surprising that Josephus treats the revolt as primarily a German revolt[35] and that Frontinus refers to a *bellum Germanicum* (*Strat.* IV 3, 14).

Walser will not accept Tacitus' account of Civilis' aims, because he denies that the Germans had any sense of nationality or hope of uniting. It is true that hitherto the German tribes had achieved no lasting political unity. It does not follow from this that they | had no sense of nationality. In the fifth century BC the Greeks were no less politically divided than the Germans in AD 69, yet they were conscious that they formed one people, with a community of descent, language, religion and customs (Herodotus VIII 144). Ancient testimony credits the Germans with similar sentiments:[36] to reject it is capricious. The fact that Germans were ready to serve in the Roman army no more proves that they did not feel themselves to be Germans than the readiness of Greeks to enlist as Persian mercenaries proves that they did not feel themselves to be Greeks. It is true that Arminius had only organized a minority of tribes in resistance to Rome, and no less true that only a minority of Greeks repelled the invasion of Xerxes. Neither Arminius nor Maroboduus had founded a durable German kingdom; that need not have prevented Civilis from seeking to emulate and surpass them; in Greece too one city after another sought hegemony, undeterred by previous failures. In 69 the time was apparently propitious. The Roman empire was torn by civil war when Civilis conceived his design, and it was not certain that Vespasian would restore stability when he finally threw off his allegiance. It may indeed be thought strange that Civilis, hitherto *consilii ambiguus et vim Romanam reputans* (IV 21, 1, cf. 14, 1) should have abandoned his initial caution, just when the Flavian victory at Cremona had been announced, and when the Rhine legions, however reluctantly, had taken the oath to Vespasian. [In fact, he continued at first to dissimulate in words (IV 32, 3), but his persistence in besieging Vetera revealed that he was in revolt against Rome.] One might have expected that he would have waited to see whether the Flavians could consolidate their success and that in that event he would have put in a claim to the new emperor's gratitude and renounced his grandiose plans. There is a hint in IV 32 that he was spurred on by his early successes and by the hope of a general revolt in Gaul. Perhaps he had already been encouraged by the

---

[34] Cf. ch. 2 n. 64.

[35] *BJ* VII 75–88. Walser n. 535 retains in 80 the impossible MSS reading which makes Classicus and *Vitellius* the local leaders: Vitellius must be a *lapsus calami* by Josephus or a scribe for Civilis.

[36] Cf. IV 64 for common religion; *Germ.* 2 for common descent; and in general Caes. *BG* VI 21–24 and *Germania* passim. It is not of course denied that the Romans looked on the Germans as a nation; and Civilis at least must have become accustomed in the Roman army to this conception.

prophecies of Veleda and believed that her authority and support would provide a religious sanction for his kingdom.[37] He may have gauged the true feeling of the legions and | counted on winning them over. Perhaps his true aims had (despite his own caution) become too widely known for him to trust any Roman ruler (cf. Appendix 8). In the end he failed. The free Germans joined him, not out of solidarity, but for booty (*supra*); it was thus impossible to keep them permanently in the field (IV 37, 3; 76, 1), and defeats made them tire of an unprofitable war (V 24–5). Even during the fighting a divergence of interests appeared between Civilis and the Tencteri over the fate of Cologne (IV 63), and it is possible that he was hampered by rivalries between the free German tribes.[38] In any event, his enterprise was doomed by the termination of Roman civil wars. But all this shows only that he miscalculated, not that he could never have entertained plans which did not turn out well, nor that he did not seem to be a dangerous enemy at Rome. According to Walser (pp. 107–8) the German menace was a fiction of declamatory rhetoric at Rome: the government knew that the Germans could safely be left, as Tiberius had held (*Ann.* II 26), to internal quarrels. Why then did the government retain seven or eight legions, the largest army in the empire, on the Rhine for eighty years? And why were no less than six legions mobilized to crush Civilis (IV 68)?

Walser constantly objects to the presentation of the war in Tacitus as a German war. Thus he takes exception (pp. 88–9) to Tacitus' description of the Batavians, because it assimilates them in character to free Germans. He does not indeed impugn the truth of Tacitus' statements, but seems to suggest that he has presented a one-sided and misleading picture. He complains that Tacitus does not expressly say that the Batavians were subjects of Rome. But that was doubtless well known to his readers (cf. *Germ.* 29) and is implicit on almost every page. Only subjects could be exempt from tribute and liable to conscription (IV 14; 17, 2), or be said to desire 'freedom' from 'servitude'. He alleges that Tacitus overlooks the fact that Civilis and other chiefs were Roman citizens. But *we* only know this from the *gentilicia* Tacitus records, and every *Roman* reader could draw the same inference as we do. It is simply not true to say that the ethnographical excursus (IV 12) is intended to suggest that the Batavians were a *gens externa*. It was, however, necessary to make the course of the revolt intelligible. | The Batavians were the core of the rebels and the last to be subdued. Few

---

[37] IV 61 cf. 65; V 22; 24; *Germ.* 8. In the first text Tacitus represents her as ruler of the Bructeri; this is contradicted, without argument, by Walser *RE* VIII A, 620 in a useful article, which assembles the other evidence on Veleda.

[38] Cf. Walser's article cited in last note.

Romans would have been familiar with their country or customs. It was important that they should be told that the Batavians lived in an 'island', which proved hard to conquer, and that their regiments in the Roman army were under the command of their own chiefs; but for this, their defection would have been more difficult.

Other criticisms are no better founded.[39] For instance, he objects to the contrast Tacitus draws in IV 16, 2 between the German *cunei* and the Roman *acies* and says that the fighting was between Roman *auxilia* (p. 95). But at this time Civilis had in his forces only one Batavian cohort (16,1) and German marauders who would have been organized in *cunei*. When Tacitus says that after taking up arms Civilis let his hair grow and dyed it red in the German fashion (IV 61), Walser remarks that no prefect in the Roman army would have so behaved (p. 115); here and elsewhere, he rejects passages in which Tacitus brings out the Germanic character of the revolt. But, if Civilis did intend to establish a Germanic kingdom, it was natural enough for him to conform to Germanic ways. All such criticisms rest on the assumption that Tacitus' account of his aims is unsound, but they do nothing to confirm it.

According to Walser and Münzer Pliny, whom Tacitus was following in books IV-V, represented the war as *bellum externum*. Now in 70 Rome had to fight at once against revolted provincials, citizens (the Vitellian legions) and foreigners from outside the empire. If the epithet *externus* is limited to the last class, as it sometimes is (e.g. III 33; IV 12), it is still clear that in some degree the war was in fact *bellum externum*. However, *externus* may also connote 'non-Roman' or 'non-Italian' in a sense which includes 'provincial',[40] and in this sense a war with the Batavians and other rebel subjects was *bellum externum* too. If Pliny did hold the view ascribed to him, it was at least no more one-sided than Walser's contention that the war was *bellum civile*. In fact, Tacitus' own opinions in books IV–V do justice to the complexity of the facts; he writes of | *externarum sociarumque gentium motu* (IV 12, 1) and says that the enemy presented the appearance *belli civilis externique* (IV 22, 1). Since an attempt has been made to show that in earlier books Tacitus was using another authority, who treated the war as *bellum civile* (cf. *infra*), it is worth noting that there too he refers to *interno simul externoque bello* (II 69, 1) and says (III 46): *et socordia ducum seditione legionum, externa vi, perfidia sociali prope adflicta Romana res* (III 46). This somewhat exaggerates the gravity of the peril, but otherwise it would be hard to give a

---

[39] Cf. Altheim (cited n. 6) on his criticism of IV 18, 2; and Appendix 2–3 on the rising of the Canninefates; Walser p. 94 suggests that by falsely stating that they acted at Civilis' behest Tacitus builds up the misleading picture of a *bellum externum*.

[40] *Ann*, II 73, 2; III 40, 3; 54, 4; *Hist*. III 48, 3; contrast the more rigorous distinction in III 33 of *cives, socii, externi*.

better summary of the account in book IV, which is supposed to come from a different and incompatible source.

What indeed is the basis for this theory that a contradictory interpretation of the revolt lies behind the earlier allusions? So far as I can see, it is chiefly one text.[41] In II 69 Tacitus comments on the return of the Batavian cohorts to the Rhine with the words: *principium interno simul externoque bello parantibus fatis.* Undoubtedly in their most natural meaning these words suggest that the war originated with the mutiny of the cohorts. Walser appears to accept this as the truth. Yet it stands in flagrant contradiction with the narrative in book IV. There the revolt begins with the grievances of Civilis and his people; the cohorts at Mainz joined it later. If that narrative is rejected, what are we to put in its place? The reconstruction Walser would approve is obscure, since he has not offered any straightforward narrative of his own. Perhaps he would accept Mommsen's.[42] In his account Vespasian's commissioners communicated with the commanders of the Mainz cohorts and Civilis, who, it is implied, was one of them, then resorted to his home and gained the assent of his people to a rising; the revolt began; Civilis 'with his cohort—which he had caused to follow, ostensibly to employ it against the insurgents—threw himself openly into the movement' and summoned the other cohorts to join him. This is sheer fiction, even if Tacitus is wrong and the fiction happens to coincide with the truth. There is no record of commissioners sent by Vespasian (nor indeed could they have arrived so early as September);[43] and Civilis is never stated to have been | at Mainz, but was from the first in the home-land;[44] though he counted on the support of the cohorts (IV 17, 3), he had to seek it, after he had formed his plot (IV 16, 1), and first secured it, when he was already in open revolt (IV 19–20). Münzer refers to this narrative in Mommsen's history as a combination of contradictory data given by Tacitus. But need we assume that there is any contradiction? By winning the support of the cohorts Civilis first became *iusti iam exercitus ductor* (IV 21, 1); till then, the rising was a relatively inconsiderable affair; even the free Germans only joined him later. Hence the despatch of the cohorts to the Rhine could truly be said to have begun what merited the name of a *bellum*, even though the origin of the war lay elsewhere, in the grievances and aspirations of the Batavian people—which the cohorts naturally shared.

But suppose that II 69 does imply a view of the revolt divergent from

---

[41] Some minor alleged inconsistencies are discussed in the Appendix 8–10.

[42] *Provinces of the Roman Empire* I 130 ff. = *RG* V⁴ 119 ff.

[43] The letter Hordeonius read out at Mainz in late October (IV 42, 3) was very probably the first communication received on the Rhine direct from Vespasian; it is at least the first mentioned.

[44] Cf. n. 16; Münzer (n. 4) p. 86 n. 1.

that which underlay books IV–V: which are we to prefer? Mommsen in describing the war as 'more a soldiers' rising than an insurrection of the province, or even a German war' or again as primarily a struggle between legions and auxilia[45] showed that he was most impressed (like Walser) by the references in earlier books to the turbulence of the cohorts. Münzer (p. 92) ascribed this interpretation to some senatorial author of narrow vision who misunderstood the situation in frontier provinces. On his view, which has gained acceptance, Pliny was Tacitus' chief source in books IV–V, a laborious and well-informed historian, thanks to whom Tacitus has recorded at least the military operations with unusual precision (p. 98). Why should we reverse (from our imperfect knowledge) Tacitus' own preference and adopt a hypothetical reconstruction of a rival account given by a writer whose identity and reliability cannot be ascertained? Unfortunately Münzer himself showed the way by arguing that Pliny was over-partial to Vespasian. Yet Tacitus was not incapable of correcting such bias; he was suspicious of adulation by pro-Flavian writers[46] and even in books IV–V recounts incidents not very creditable to Vespasian's kinsman, Cerialis, which can hardly have come from Pliny.[47] We | must not lightly assume that he was credulous of pro-Flavian distortions.

Civilis claimed old ties of friendship with Vespasian;[48] he rose initially in Vespasian's behalf; his rising plainly helped the Flavian cause; and in the end he expected, and probably secured, pardon from Cerialis (V 24). Under the final settlement his people retained their old immunity from tribute (*Germ.* 29), and even though they were not released from liability to distant service,[49] this clemency contrasted with the treatment of the renegade legions. Hence suspicions could be engendered that Vespasian had stirred up a dangerous war. Pliny, it is supposed, met such (unspoken) charges by laying the responsibility on Hordeonius and Antonius Primus.

There was of course a straightforward answer to any imputations on Vespasian; he was too distant to have directly incited the revolt himself (cf. n. 3). But Tacitus, and presumably Pliny, make it plain that both Antonius and Hordeonius initially encouraged Civilis.[50] Surely this was not with the purpose of exculpating Vespasian (it was rather maladroit

---

[45] L.c. in n. 35 cf. p. 142 of Eng. tr. = *RG* V⁴ 129.

[46] I 1: II 101; cf. A. Briessmann, *Tacitus u. das flavische Geschichtsbild* (Wiesbaden 1955).

[47] See Syme 175 (esp. on IV 71; 77; V 22, 3), cf. 675 on Caecina.

[48] V 26, 3, relations perhaps contracted when Vespasian was legionary legate on the Rhine, Suet. 4. [But cf. n. 24.]

[49] *Agr.* 36; *CIL* XVI 174; 178–80; 183; 185; 187; the lists given by Kraft (*o.c.* n. 19) give further evidence of Batavian units or individuals serving abroad after 70.

[50] On Hordeonius see Appendix 8.

to mention his old ties with Civilis) but because the facts were so, and too well known to be denied. Nor is there any sign that Tacitus (or Pliny) *blamed* either of them. Hordeonius is exonerated (as Münzer admits) in the same breath as his complicity is stated; he acted not only out of sympathy with Vespasian—not in itself a discreditable motive (cf. III 86, 2), but also *rei publicae cura*, to spare Italy the horror of prolonged fighting (IV 13, 3). Pliny was certainly hostile to Antonius (III 28), yet the narrative in book IV is not to his discredit; he was too far from the Rhine to have surmised Civilis' real aims, and it is odd to suppose that the historian shared the feelings of the disreputable Vitellian legions, when they heard of his letters to Civilis *tamquam ad socium partium scriptae et de Germanico exercitu hostiliter* (IV 32, 1). Antonius is not implicated in the rising at the stage when it had become overtly anti-Roman. It is not proven to any degree that the account in books IV-V has been distorted by bias of the kind Münzer suggested. |

Walser imputes a very different twist to Pliny's account. In his opinion Pliny turned a civil into a foreign war, to credit Vespasian with a glorious victory; his version, like that of Josephus (and he might have added, Dio's) was official history, not the truth. I would concede (for reasons Walser does not adduce) that to make good the prestige he lacked at his accession (Suet. 7) Vespasian welcomed and inflated military successes. For reducing once more to subjection a rather unimportant people,[51] Vespasian and Titus celebrated a pompous triumph; and the mendacious words later inscribed on the Arch of Titus, ignoring Pompey and Herod (to name no others) claimed that Titus had destroyed Jerusalem, *omnibus ante se ducibus regibus gentibus aut frustra petitam aut omnino intemptatam* (*ILS* 264). Like Claudius who craved for military glory on similar grounds but with still less justification, they extended the *pomerium, auctis p. R. finibus*, a step Augustus had never taken,[52] though he added great provinces to the empire, while Vespasian merely rectified frontiers. Augustus was hailed imperator 21 times for great victories in a long reign, Vespasian 20 times in under ten years (*ILS* 254). It would not have been amiss to his propaganda, if a flatterer had magnified his victory over Civilis.

But the narrative in Tacitus creates no impression of military glory. Most of the rebel *civitates*, and the renegade legions, were brought back to their allegiance with little hard fighting; and the submission of the Batavians themselves was preceded by a battle, which was almost a catastrophic defeat, and accomplished as much by diplomacy as force (V 24-6). It is no wonder that only one of Vespasian's imperatorial

---

[51] The Jews were as little a *gens externa*, in Walser's sense, as the Batavians!
[52] Mommsen, *StR* ii³ 1072, n. 3; Furneaux on *Ann.* XII 23.

salutations can be associated with a success that is depicted as far from brilliant.[53]

A decisive objection to Walser's theory remains. In the autumn of 69 Civilis attacked the legions just after they had taken the oath to Vespasian; this is recorded in a part of Tacitus' narrative (IV 31-7), which Walser himself describes as reliable and accurate (p. 102), though he has not mentioned this attack. The fighting continued on a still more extensive scale after Vespasian's recognition at Rome. How can this be reconciled with the hypotheses that | Civilis had risen in support of Vespasian, and never became an enemy to Roman rule? Walser supposes that for lack of money Vespasian could not meet Civilis' demands for rewards (pp. 108-9). There is not a jot of evidence that before the operations described in IV 57 ff. Civilis preferred any such demands to the far distant emperor and persisted in revolt because they had been refused, and no probability that there was time for such negotiations, or that Civilis thought the best way of enforcing his claim to the gratitude of a Roman emperor was to destroy his troops, and to co-operate with allies who on Tacitus' view were seeking to establish an independent *imperium Galliarum*, and on Walser's to put forward a rival claimant to the *imperium Romanum* itself. And it is quite certain that Civilis had no means whatever of knowing that his rewards would be refused when he launched the autumn attack (IV 33 ff.). From that time forth he must be considered as a rebel against Rome, and whatever it had once been, the war had turned into a true *bellum Germanicum*.[54]

Our gratitude is due to acute and intrepid critics who force us to think again of the veracity of Tacitus or any ancient authority. In this sense Walser has rendered a service to historians. But in the end the judgement Fustel de Coulanges passed on another scholar is applicable: 'il apporte à l'appui de son système beaucoup de raisonnements, mais aucun texte'.[55] Tacitus' account is coherent and credible; that of his critic (I submit) is not.[56]

APPENDIX

1. The stages of Civilis' revolt can be dated only by synchronisms with events elsewhere. Vespasian was proclaimed emperor in Egypt on 1 July and in Syria before 15 July (II 79; 81); his recognition first in Moesia and then in Pannonia (85) may be set in August; hence

---

[53] Weynand, *RE* VI 2649 (not 2653 cited by Walser n. 537).

[54] *Contra* Walser 124-5, the same was probably true of the civil war of AD 89 cf. Weynand, (n. 53) 2569; Syme, *CAH* XI 172-5.

[55] *Recherches sur quelques problèmes d'histoire* p. 73 n. 2.

[56] For some details of chronology and source criticism see the Appendix.

Suetonius' error in dating the rising to the eighth month of Vitellius' reign; he has in mind primarily the revolt of the Danubian legions (*Vit.* 15, 1). Antonius Primus was le|gionary legate in Pannonia and at once, perhaps in [early] August, sent letters to Gaul and elsewhere, urging support for the Flavian cause (86,4). It was after receipt of such a letter and after Hordeonius Flaccus too was informed of the revolt that Civilis planned his insurrection (IV 13). This can hardly be before early September.

2. According to IV 15–16 Civilis' overt insurrection was preceded by a rising of the Canninefates, which he undertook to repress; Tacitus records that they captured and sacked two *castella* held by *cohortes* (IV 15, 2). [This event is mentioned by Tacitus after he has told that Civilis had planned revolt. L. A. W. C. Venmans has shown by an ingenious archaeological argument in *Mnemosyne* 1935/6, 83 ff., that a fort in N. Holland was burned down about 1 May. On the *assumption* that it was one of the very forts whose capture Tacitus relates and that the incident did not belong to unrecorded troubles in another year Tacitus has fallen into a chronological error. If this is so, it may be that he was not informed of the true date of the rising of the Canninefates, and knowing that Civilis promised to suppress them, but that they united in the same cause (IV 16; 32; 56 etc.), he assumed that they rose first at Civilis' instigation (IV 16, 1); K. Wellesley, *JRS* 1974, 230 suggests that the narrative of the rising in 15, 2–3, is 'a typical Tacitean regression in time', and that Tacitus does not imply that it occurred after Civilis began to organize his revolt.]

3. If in fact the Canninefates had already risen independently, this will require explanation. They were associated with Frisians beyond the Rhine (16, 2) and Walser assumes (p. 94) that they too were not subjects of Rome, and that their action was one of the usual plundering raids of tribes beyond the frontier. But the Canninefates had been subdued by Tiberius (Vell, II 105); they resembled the Batavians *origine, lingua, virtute,* and they lived in the same 'island' (16, 1); where was the frontier drawn? Moreover they already (19, 1), as later (*CIL* XVI 178 cf. Münzer p. 95), supplied troops to the Roman army. A Roman reader could not be in doubt that they were subjects of Rome; the Frisians are *distinguished* from them as *Transrhenana gens.* If indeed their revolt is earlier than Tacitus implies, it must be ascribed to causes similar to those which later actuated the Batavians, belief in Roman weakness and resentment at subjection. |

4. The battle of Cremona was fought on 24/5 October (K. Wellesley, *Rh. Mus,* 1957, 244 ff.). The news could well have reached Hordeonius at Neuss (cf. IV 26, 3) very early in November. Its arrival is recorded in IV 31. The events described in IV 13–30 may then be placed

between early September and early November; I assume that *haec in Germania ante Cremonense proelium gesta* is slightly inaccurate, since the events mentioned should be set before the battle was known, but not necessarily before it was fought.

5. In IV 24 Tacitus says that Hordeonius ordered troops at Mainz to proceed by forced marches to the relief of Vetera. We might allow at least 3 days for the march to Bonn, at least a day's pause there (for *legio I* to be set in motion and for the minor mutiny there), and another day for the march to Cologne (IV 25); here there was more trouble with the troops, and the need for foraging must have delayed progress, and two more days might be allowed before the army reached Neuss. Here *legio XVI* joined the army and presumably the advance guard under Vocula and Gallus moved out to Gelduba the next day (IV 26). The drilling of these troops (26, 3) and the incidents described in 27 might occupy a few days. It is likely that Hordeonius left Mainz 15–20 October. The operations recorded in 28–30 were contemporaneous.

6. Hordeonius had moved on learning of the siege of Vetera (IV 24, 1); a courier might have covered the distance in two days. Civilis began his attack on Vetera after he had been joined by the cohorts from Mainz and, so Tacitus relates, after then calling the whole Batavian nation to arms and securing aid from the free Germans (IV 21). However, he had sought and obtained German promises of help earlier (IV 17, 1), and at the same time he must have begun to mobilize his own people. We do not therefore need to think that between the arrival of the Batavian cohorts near Vetera and Civilis' attack on the camp there must have been a long interval, during which an extensive mobilization took place. If the camp was first attacked 13–18 October, when the courier went off to Mainz, the Batavian cohorts need have arrived only a few days before. The cohorts had to fight one engagement on their march north, and to avoid Cologne (IV 20); they may well have taken a fortnight *en route*, and started at the beginning of October or in late September. According to IV 19, 1 their sedition began with the | receipt of a message from Civilis. They then proceeded to demand concessions from Hordeonius, and continually to raise their demands. A few days may be allowed for these negotiations. In IV 18 Tacitus describes Civilis' defeat of the legions based on Vetera, and then states that *isdem diebus* his messenger reached the cohorts. It is not, however, certain that he means to make the defeat and the arrival of the messenger contemporaneous; conceivably *isdem diebus* is intended to convey a synchronism between the operations that culminated in Civilis' victory over Munius Lupercus and the whole account of the cohorts' sedition and march northwards. Hence the operations in IV 18 could extend into mid-October; they should,

however, have begun in late September, and Hordeonius must have
sent his instructions to Munius before that month was out. I incline to
suppose that Civilis needed about two weeks to organize his rising,
that he cleared Roman troops out of the Batavian 'island' in mid-
September, and that Hordeonius gave his orders to Munius towards
the end of the month.

7. Vitellius' first and incomplete news of the Flavian revolt had come
from the legate of Moesia; only later did reports stream in from all
sides (II 96; 99, 1). [Tacitus has previously recorded the celebration of
his birthday (95, 1), which is variously given as 7 or 24 September
(Suet. *Vit.* 3). But here he has carried his narrative beyond the time of
the situation in Rome described in 95, 2, not yet four months after
Bedriacum, i.e. the first half of August; it was then that the Moesian
report came in.] In 97 he states that Vitellius, on receipt of the news
from Moesia, ordered reinforcements from Germany and elsewhere,
but *segniter et necessitatem dissimulans*. These tardy orders need not have
reached Hordeonius till the middle of September. They were also
tardily obeyed; the Batavian cohorts, which Vitellius had sent for (IV
19, 1), were still at Mainz, or not far south, in late September or in
early October, and no other troops are known to have moved.

8. In II 97 Tacitus explains Hordeonius' dilatory conduct with the
words *suspectis iam Batavis anxius proprio bello*, though he adds that his
loyalty was dubious. But in IV 13 (cf. V 26), he represents Hordeonius
as an accomplice of Civilis, who urged him, as Antonius had done by
letter, *avertere accita a Vitellio auxilia et tumultus Germanici specie retentare
legiones*. Münzer (101–2) has ascribed | this apparent discrepancy to a
change of source. Need this be so? It is apparent on the chronology
proposed so far that there is some verbal inaccuracy in IV 13. When
Antonius wrote to Civilis, he could not have known whether Vitellius
had in fact sent for troops on the Rhine, and in fact he had not. But
Antonius and Hordeonius could have anticipated that he would do so,
as he eventually did. Thus Hordeonius was encouraging Civilis early in
September; *primos Civilis conatus per dissimulationem aluit* (IV 18, 1). On
this view his appointment of Civilis to curb the Canninefates, whose
activities he had perhaps ignored since May, acquires a sinister
significance. When Hordeonius first received orders from Vitellius to
send troops to Italy, he now had an excuse for inaction in the Batavian
rising. It is true, however, that in II 97 Tacitus implies that his fears of
the Batavians were genuine. But this is in accord with the implications
of IV 18. Hordeonius abetted Civilis at first; but after the expulsion of
Romans from the island etc., he began to take action as energetic as his
phlegmatic nature permitted, even asking for help from Gaul, Britain
and Spain (25, 2); the suspicions of his own soldiers (24 etc.) were

justified by his early intrigues, not by his later conduct. Germans could not keep a secret for long (16, 1); Civilis' followers were doubtless less discreet than he was himself, and Hordeonius' attitude naturally changed as he became aware that Civilis' aims were not those he stated. In II 97 Tacitus has neglected his early complicity with Civilis, because it was not this but his subsequent alarm at Civilis' designs that ultimately dictated his slowness in obeying Vitellius. No contradiction need be assumed between this text and the narrative in book IV.

9. Münzer (n. 4) p. 88 held that the reference to the Mainz cohorts in IV 15, 1 is an interpolation by Tacitus in a narrative that otherwise depends on Pliny, derived from the source Tacitus had used for their activities in books I–II; similarly the allusion to them in I 59 is intruded by Tacitus from Pliny into a context drawn from another source (p. 86). In both cases, he argues, the relevant sentences interrupt the flow; remove them, and you would not notice the gap. This argument has no force; it is equally true of many other sentences (e.g. I 65, 1 on the feud of Lyons and Vienne; I 46, 1 on Flavius Sabinus' appointment), inserted for explanation or proleptic significance. I do not doubt that Tacitus drew on more than one source; but a change of source is not to be determined in this mechanical fashion. |

10. Münzer also fancied that he could detect incongruities between IV 15 and 19, though he recognized that they could be resolved. Thus in 15 Tacitus says that Civilis sent secret *nuntii* to the cohorts, while 19 mentions the arrival of a *nuntius*. In fact there could have been several; in 19 Tacitus records the decisive message. In 19 we first learn that the cohorts included Canninefates; but this information is only supplementary to what went before, mentioned now, because the Canninefates had been the first to take arms. In 15 Tacitus describes the cohorts as *missas in Germaniam*; but in 19 they are on their way to Italy. But in 15 we are still in early September; the cohorts had not yet been recalled by Vitellius. In 19 some weeks had elapsed, and I believe that the cohorts had left Mainz (cf. IV 24, 1), on their way south, though they had not marched far. Such discrepancies prove illusory. [Nor is it inconsistent with the narrative in 19–20 that in 17 Civilis is made to claim 'esse secum veteranas cohortes'; this means that they were on his side (cf. I 38, 2; IV 69, 2; *Germ.* 29, 2). Of course Civilis could not yet count on their adherence, but Tacitus imputes to him, plausibly enough, allegations which, though not true, were likely to impress his audience. Whether Tacitus or his source was reliably informed of all the propaganda he employed to incite the Batavians to revolt, or supplemented testimony from imagination, we cannot say.] Münzer has shown only that Tacitus did not tell a plain story according to the artistic canons he desiderated, not that he was incapable of combining different sources in such a way that we cannot find the seams.

4

Charges of Provincial Maladministration under the Early Principate

The oppression of the provinces in the late Republic is a familiar story. Cicero observed that it continued in spite of the increasing severity of the laws and the condemnation of many defendants (*de off.* ii 75). Tacitus thought that the provinces were not averse to the institution of the Principate since under the government of senate and people the laws had given them little protection against the greed of the magistrates; violence, influence and money had prevailed in the courts (*Ann.* i. 2). Among modern scholars there is a strong impression that with Augustus a great improvement in the standards of government set in. The correctness of this belief cannot be strictly refuted; yet the extent of the improvement may be exaggerated. The mere maintenance of the *pax Augusta* rendered incalculable benefits to Rome's subjects, and may in itself be enough to account for the material well-being that so many of them patently enjoyed in the two and a half centuries that followed Actium; it is unsafe to argue that because the provinces were more prosperous than they had been in an age of constant civil wars, foreign invasions and endemic piracy and brigandage, they were necessarily governed with far more honesty and justice than in the late Republic. It is my purpose here to show from an analysis of what little is known of the working of the law *repetundae* and from some other scattered evidence that it would be wrong to assume that abuses were infrequent or redress easy to secure. The Principate perhaps often gets more credit than is due for its provincial government, and the Republic perhaps too little.[1]

[1] For brevity I have kept to a minimum references to modern works. Mommsen's *Strafrecht* (1899) remains fundamental; since its publication our knowledge has been extended chiefly by the discovery of the *SC Calvisianum* (*FIRA* i no. 68, V = *SEG* ix 8 = Ehrenberg and Jones, *Documents illustrating the reigns of Augustus and Tiberius*, 311), cf. F. de Visscher, *Les Édits d'Auguste découverts à Cyrène* (1940) with bibliography; A. N. Sherwin-White, *PBSR* xvii (1949), and the *fragmentum Leidense* of [Paul's] *Sentences*, edited with notes and essays by C. G. Archi, M. David, E. Levy, R.

Historia (1961), 189–227.

I

The emperors have often earned praise for their professions of care for the subjects' welfare.[2] But Republican statesmen made similar professions and | castigated the misgovernment of the provinces as sharply as any modern historians.[3] Words count for little; more important, the senate, or 'popular' leaders, recognized the subjects' right to redress by passing ever stricter laws [p. 319 f.]. The last and most severe of these (Cic. *Vat.* 29; *Rab. Post.* 8), the *lex Julia* passed by Caesar as consul in 59 BC, ran to at least 101 chapters (*Fam.* viii 8, 3) and seems to have been a consolidating rather than a controversial measure; Cicero himself thought it excellent (*Sest.* 135; *Pis.* 37). It was this statute, though modified by senatorial decrees or imperial constitutions and subject to fluctuating interpretation in practice, that remained the basis of imperial law right down to the time of Justinian [pp. 492 f.].[4] In most essential principles and in much elaboration in their application the law of *repetundae* was the creation of the Republic and provides the proof that in its intentions the government of senate and people was no less honourable than that of the emperors.

The Republic of course failed to realise these intentions. But we must not assume that the emperors were much more successful. And, to whatever extent they did provide more effectively for just administration, they were building on the foundations laid by Republican law.

The Republican law of *repetundae* penalized only offences [committed by holders of offices which involved or might lead to membership of the senate (p. 499)], and to some extent other senators and their sons when engaged in official business;[5] even the *lex Julia* did not cover

Marichal and L. W. Nelson (Leiden 1956), cf. F. Serrao, *Il frammento Leidense di Paolo* (Milan 1956); in reviewing these works in *ZSS* lxxiv (1957) 461 ff. T. Mayer-Maly cited the chief discussions of *repetundae* that have appeared in recent years.

I am grateful to Mr. J. P. V. D. Balsdon for criticizing this paper in draft; he must not be taken to concur with the views expressed.

[2] E.g. *SEG* ix 8 (= Ehrenberg and Jones 311) vv 73 ff.; iv 516 (cf. F. K. Dörner, *Der Erlaß d. Statthalters v. Asia* etc., 1926); Plin. *ep.* x 18. Tiberius' much praised dictum that he wished the Egyptians to be sheared, not shaved (Dio lvii 10; Suet. *Tib.* 32) does not improve on sentiments Cicero attributes to senate and people (II *Verr.* iii 48), nor go beyond recognition that exploitation must be intelligent.

[3] [See now ch. 14 s. xi.]

[4] *Inst.* iv, 18, 11 cf. *Dig.* xlviii 11; *CJ* ix 27; *CT* ix 27. Mrs Henderson regards all the *leges de repetundis* as merely procedural and suggests that by 4 BC 'such statutes were now archives' (*JRS* xli [1951] 87 n. 110), [*contra* (rightly) A. N. Sherwin-White, xlii (1952) 43 ff.] The *lex Julia* was still cited by *caput* in the early third century (*Dig.* xlviii 11, 7, 1); and so far from being merely procedural, it forbade specific offences (Cic. *Pis.* 50; 90) and prescribed penalties (Cassius Longinus ap. *Dig.* i 9, 2).

[5] Details in Mommsen *o. c.* 710–12 = *Dr. Pén.* iii 7–9. According to [Paul's] *fr. Leid.* 3–4 senators as such were forbidden by the *lex Julia* (a) to own ships (cf. *Dig.* xlix 14, 46, 2; l 5, 3; the old ban on

equestrian officers of the state.[6] This was, however, not a serious defect in days when *equites* could at most hold only subordinate official posts. |

We are apt to render *repetundae* as extortion, and it was of course extortion that the law sought to prevent.[7] But force or menaces could be employed in secret and might be hard to prove. What purported to be gifts or business transactions could be a screen for violence or corruption (cf. II *Verr.* iv 10). The law, therefore, forbade all enrichment by senatorial officials, allowing only certain specific exceptions; thus under Sulla's law a governor might not lend money in his province,[8] nor buy a slave except by way of replacement (II *Verr.* iv 9–11); it was open to question whether he might carry on any business or accept an inheritance in his province.[9] If both the *lex Cornelia* (II *Verr.* ii 142 ff.) and the *lex Julia* (*ad Qu. fr.* i 1, 26) expressly allowed the governor to take money for building temples or monuments, and the *lex Julia* authorized him to accept hay and some other commodities needed on his journeys (*Att.* v 16, 3), we may infer that such practices required explicit sanction just because in general the acceptance of gifts in cash or kind was banned. The Gracchan law had allowed gifts but only up to a certain maximum (*FIRA* i[2] no. 7 v. 2), and an unknown Republican plebiscite sanctioned acceptance of food and drink for immediate consumption (*Dig.* i 18, 18). The rule in the Principate forbidding officials to take presents (Plin. *ep.* iv 9, 7), except in fairly well defined circumstances,[10] accords with a principle stated by Cicero in his ideal system of laws, which was based on Roman models and drafted after the *lex Julia* (*de leg.* iii 11; 46) and which is likely to go back to that law. The very length and complexity of the *lex Julia* suggest that it dealt fully with innumerable types of illegal

this, attested by Liv. xxi 63, 3, had not been revived by Sulla, II *Verr.* v 45); (b) 'vectigalia publica conducere'; (c) to supply horses for the games; (d) to use the slave of another, or a free man, as their own slave. All this may go back to the terms of the law rather than to later interpretation [but cf. pp. 492f.]; for (b) cf. Mommsen, *StR*[3] iii 509; 899 n. 1; since laws often passed into oblivion, it is not surprising that Hadrian had to reaffirm the ban (Dio lxix 16); he need not have made it more rigorous; (c) is confirmed by the exception Augustus allowed (Dio lv 10, 5); (d) may be connected with the abuse of their authority by senators when travelling e.g. on *liberae legationes*.

    [6] Cic. *Rab. Post.* 13 on a vain effort in 55 to extend the law to equestrian officials.

    [7] [But see pp. 493 ff. modifying part of this paragraph.]

    [8] II *Verr,* iii 169; cf. the provisions of later law in *Dig.* xii 1, 33–4, modified in AD 408 (*CJ* iv 2, 16).

    [9] Flaccus' prosecutors urged 'non debuisse, cum praetor esset, suum negotium agere (cf. *Dig.* xii 1, 33) aut mentionem facere hereditatis': Cicero replied that such practice was common, no more than Pliny said (*ep.* iv 9, 17), in exculpating Bassus' flagrant illegalities (*Flacc.* 85). If Republican law forbade a governor to take under an inheritance, the rule had passed into neglect in Pliny's day (*ep.* x 75–6), which is likely enough.

    [10] In the mid-second century, and probably much earlier, urban magistrates might take gifts up to 10,000 HSS (*Dig.* xlviii 11, 6, 2; cf. p. 194, n. 19). Severus permitted acceptance of *xenia* in moderation (*ib.* i 16, 6, 3). Gifts from near relatives were allowed, if not made to distort the course of justice (*ib.* xlviii 11, 1, 1 with 11, 7 *pr.*–1.)

enrichment. Late jurists ascribe to it, for instance, specific prohibitions of the acceptance of bribes for conscribing or discharging soldiers, for speaking in the senate, for wrongful exercise of judicial powers and so forth.[11] We cannot be certain that every such rule comes from its text and not from later developments by *senatus consultum* or imperial rescript. But we can be sure that rules of this kind stood in the *lex Julia* itself. Presumably, they were not designed to be exhaustive, but to call the attention of the subjects to their rights of redress, if the principle of the law were violated in the particular ways that | experience had shown to be most common. The principle of the law had already been defined long ago; it was illegal for the official 'pecuniam auferre capere cogere conciliare avertere' (*FIRA* i² 7 v. 3). At all times the offence is briefly described as 'pecunia capta'.

In the late Republic this principle had been further extended. Thus the *lex Julia* forbade a governor to deprive cities of 'libertas' or individuals of 'praemia' and, like Sulla's law on *maiestas*, to leave his province or wage war without the sanction of senate or people.[12] It would seem that it also banned the levy of unauthorized taxes or requisitions,[13] at least when the governor could not justify them by public interest.[14] In such cases it was apparently not necessary to prove that the governor had derived any personal profit from his illegal acts. *Aurum coronarium*, for instance, was due to the public treasury, whenever levied (*de leg. agr.* ii 59), yet it was an offence under the *lex Julia* for a governor to levy it, unless a triumph had been voted to him (*Pis.* 90). Cicero does not argue that the accusers of Flaccus must prove that he had appropriated ship-money, but only that they must show that its imposition was not authorized by the senate nor warranted by an emergency; this, he says, they cannot do (*Flacc.* 27 ff.). If it had been necessary to prove enrichment in such cases, it would have been too easy for a governor, whatever his original purpose, to meet a threatened prosecution by paying the proceeds of his exactions into the treasury (cf. n. 55). Such acts were forbidden simply because they were oppressive to the subjects and at the same time contrary to, or not required by, the interests of Rome. It is evident, for instance, why

---

[11] *Dig.* xlviii 11, 6–7. Mommsen assembles more fully the various kinds of prohibition that we happen to know, e.g. on buying and selling by officials in their province.

[12] *Pis.* 90; 50. Hadrian had to re-affirm (cf. n. 5) a rule ascribed to the *lex Julia* that a governor might not release his legate before he left the province himself (*Dig.* i 16, 10, 1); but this can hardly have stood in the *lex*, cf. *Att.* v 21, 9; vi 3, 1. [See p. 495 f.]

[13] *Pis.* 90; cf. *Font.* 19 (for *lex Cornelia*); Mommsen *o.c.* 718 = *Dr. Pén.* iii 16–17 (with later evidence).

[14] It was presumably in such cases that the onus was on the prosecution to show that the governor had acted 'adversus leges, adversus rem publicam' (II *Verr.* iii 194); personal enrichment as such always fell in this category.

many laws, including the *lex Julia*, forbade a governor to start an unauthorized war (*Pis.* 50). An unprovoked attack on some as yet unoffending people might entail disasters for Rome.[15] But it was also likely to involve the provincials in many burdens. It was good sense to make them the watchdogs of Rome's interests as well as their own, and to permit them to prosecute a governor for such conduct. And it was convenient that they could include such charges along with others, more proper to the original purpose of the *repetundae* process, in a single indictment before the same court. There is indeed more than one instance of overlapping between the law of *repetundae* and other penal laws. These too could indirectly protect the subjects. After his misgovernment of | Cilicia, Appius Claudius was charged with *maiestas*, and there was provincial testimony against him (*Fam.* iii 11, 3). [Verres' malpractices also exposed him to indictment for *maiestas* (II *Verr.* v 50 and 79).] The *lex Cornelia de sicariis* forbade magistrates or judges to engineer the conviction of an innocent man on a capital charge (*Dig.* xlviii 8,1 *pr.*). Severus punished a prefect of Egypt for forgery under the *lex Cornelia de falsis* (*ib.* xlviii 10, 1, 4). Verres could have been charged with *peculatus* as well as *repetundae*.[16] Kidnapping of *servi alieni* or free men was penal for senators under both the *lex Julia* and the *lex Fabia* of unknown date (Paul, *fr. Leid.* 4). Later, Tiberius made it possible to charge officials with adultery after they had demitted office (*Dig.* xlviii 5, 39, 10). The *lex Julia de vi publica* contained guarantees to the subjects. Thus it forbade the imposition of new taxes (*Dig.* xlviii 6, 12). It also included the old provision that a governor might not execute, flog or torture a Roman citizen 'adversus provocationem'. With the ever increasing extension of the citizenship in the provinces, this afforded protection to many of Rome's subjects though in the second century the right of appeal was restricted to the upper classes.[17] When Marius Priscus put a Roman *eques* in Africa to death for a bribe (Plin. *ep.* ii 11, 8), he offended not only against the *repetundae* law, but others (*ib.* ii 19, 8)—to be precise, against the *lex de sicariis* and the *lex de vi publica*.[18]

[15] Rome's first encounter with the Teutones resulted from such an unprovoked attack, App. *Celt.* 13 [cf. Ascon. 80, 21C.]

[16] II *Verr.* iii 168 cf. 83; iv 88; (cf. Sherwin-White, *JRS* xlii (1952) 54).

[17] *Dig.* xlviii 6. 7; Paul. v 26, 1; Isid. *Orig.* v 26, 6. A. H. M. Jones, *St. in Roman Government and Law* (1960) ch. IV argues that the right of appeal was limited to cases not covered by laws that set up *iudicia publica* at Rome, in which the governor had inappellate jurisdiction; but I doubt if he is right in thinking that Marius Priscus' conduct was criminal only because it was corrupt; nor can we be sure that Flavius Archippus was a citizen already, when condemned to the mines (Plin. *ep.* x 58–9). [Cf. now P. Garnsey, *Social Status and Legal Privilege in the Roman Empire* (1970) ch. 3, for different views; he also discusses petitions for redress to the emperor.]

[18] I think Lucilius Capito (App. I no. 8) was convicted for *vis.* Procurators in senatorial provinces, though not in imperial (Dio liv 21: Strabo 167C), had as yet no public functions (cf.

Cicero indeed, speaking in 70 BC, describes the *repetundae* law as the 'lex socialis', apparently their one protection (*Div. in Caec.* 17–8). The explanation of this cannot be found in the hypothesis that it was only under this law that peregrines could accuse a Roman official. That right had indeed been accorded to them, for the first time, by the Gracchan law and was (I believe) again granted by the Julian; but under the *lex Cornelia*, which was then operative, as before 123 BC, it was apparently only Roman citizens who could prosecute on behalf of the subjects; and citizens were of course free to bring other indictments connected with provincial grievances.[19] (Under the Principate it is | likely that peregrines could themselves initiate prosecutions under laws other than the *lex de repetundis*.[20] And then many provincials were citizens and enjoyed such rights, if any, of criminal prosecution as were reserved to citizens.) The context of Cicero's statement makes its meaning clear. It was only by securing a conviction for *repetundae* that peregrines could hope to obtain compensation for the losses they had

p. 165); but only public officials and their accomplices could be indicted for *repetundae*. Capito used 'vim praetoris' and military force, perhaps to assert claims of the *res familiaris*, which should have gone to the courts (*Ann.* iv 6, 4), perhaps to collect public taxes, a matter for the proconsul (Dio liii 15, 3). Cf. n. 40.

[19] F. Serrao, *St. in onore di P. de Francisci* ii 473 ff. (Milan) 1956. The *SC Calvisianum* (vv. 98–100, 104–5) implies that provincials can bring charges themselves. But if this had been an innovation, explicit language would have been used to confer the right upon them; and I read the preamble as implying that they already possessed it. thus, *contra* Serrao, it had probably been restored to them by the *lex Julia*, which, like the law of 123, was the work of a *popularis*. That they enjoyed the right under the Principate is also clear from the cases in Appendix I, nos. 6, 16, 21, 23–5, 28–31, 33–40. Citizens could also bring charges in this period (nos. 4, 5, 18); hence the fact that they are attested as accusers under the *lex Julia* in the late Republic is no proof that they then had a monopoly of the right. Serrao, like Mrs. Henderson (*o.c.* 74), doubts if claims from *cives* lay under the later *repetundae* procedure. On this view provincials who had secured citizenship could not have brought claims, and the continuing right of citizens to prosecute (for damage to non-citizens only!) would have been an anomaly. But *Ann.* xi 7; Suet. *Dom.* 8, 2; *Dig.* xlviii 11, 6, 2 should dispel such doubts. (*Div. in Caec.* 17–18 naturally does not mean that citizens could not claim under the *repetundae* law, but that they had an alternative remedy.) [On the right to prosecute see also pp. 497 f.]

[20] Mommsen *o. c.* 366–8 = *Dr. Pén.* ii 35–7 held that strictly only a citizen could prosecute under criminal law, since only he could be a substitute for the magistrate and represent the community. Whatever the role of the magistrate had once been, however, this notion was so alien to Roman thinking in the classical period that the right of a magistrate to prosecute could be impugned (*Ann.* iv 19). In late juristic texts (*e.g. Dig.* xlviii 2) peregrines are not denied the right to prosecute; admittedly, when they were written or remodelled, most subjects of Rome were *cives*. Mommsen's explanation of what he regards as the exceptional right of peregrines to prosecute for *repetundae*, viz. that that process originated in civil law, will not stand against Buckland's arguments (*JRS* xxxvii [1937] 37 ff.) that foreigners could not bring civil suits against ex-magistrates for their official acts. The *repetundae* procedure must be regarded as unique, instituted by senate or people in a sovereign capacity. Mommsen (p. 368) seems to admit that peregrines were allowed to prosecute in other cases 'by way of analogy'. If the capital charges they were entitled to bring against ex-magistrates by 4 BC (*SC Calvisianum* v 99) did not fall under the *repetundae* law (as Mommsen's followers hold), it would be certain that by that date they could prosecute under other laws, [but I now reject the premise, see p. 505].

sustained from an official's illegal enrichment; they had no right, as citizens had, to sue for damages under the civil law.

Before 123 BC the rate of compensation had been simple; C. Gracchus made it twofold. Mommsen has found general assent for his doctrine that Sulla reduced it once more to simple compensation, and that the *lex Julia* made no further change. Sherwin-White has restated Zumpt's argument that on the contrary Sulla increased the rate to two and a half times the value of what had been taken; the Julian law was more severe and will hardly have made the financial penalty milder.[21] The possibility exists that it was now fixed as fourfold. That was the penalty fixed by Augustus in 17 BC for breaches of the *lex Cincia* (Dio liv 18), which later at least were treated as offences of *repetundae*,[22] and by | Severus and later rulers for contraventions of the *repetundae* law itself.[23] Whatever be the truth about the rate of compensation after 81 or 59 BC, it is clear that at all times, even when other than pecuniary penalties were also exacted,[24] the victims had the right to claim damages for the losses they had incurred. To this extent an indictment for *repetundae* resembled a civil suit, and the prosecutor is therefore said 'petere' or 'repetere' as well as 'accusare'. The *SC Calvisianum* (vv 89 ff.) views reparation as the main purpose of previous legislation.

Under the Gracchan law conviction was followed by a *litis aestimatio* in which the liability of the defendant was assessed and damages apportioned among the several claimants. The State itself undertook the responsibility of execution. The defendant had to furnish sureties for payment; if neither he nor sureties paid up, the State sold his assets. The State made the appropriate payments to the victims out of the proceeds of the sale, or from what the sureties had to pay up; what was not claimed remained in the *aerarium(FIRA* i[2] no. 7 vv 57-68). [It is not certain that the victims could obtain more than simple compensation and that the treasury did not always retain the surplus arising from the imposition of double damages.] There were similar provisions in the *lex Julia* (*Rab. Post.* 37). They undoubtedly remained valid in the Principate, when the consuls seem to have been responsible (Plin. *ep.* vii 33, 4). Modestinus is quoted as saying that the property of a person

---

[21] *PBSR* xvii 8-10.

[22] *Ann.* xi 7; note that the upper limit for sums advocates may receive is the same as that fixed for gifts that may be taken by urban magistrates under the law of *repetundae* (*Dig.* xlviii 11, 6, 2). [For other fourfold penalties in civil suits under Republican law see J. M. Kelly, *Roman Litigation* (1966) 153 ff., who argues that they were ineffectual.]

[23] *Dig.* xviii 1, 46; texts from late Empire in Mommsen *o. c.* 728 n. 2 = Dr. *Pén* iii 28 n. 3.

[24] Compare the Marius Priscus and Classicus cases (App. I nos. 36, 38), especially Plin. *ep.* ii 11, 19. The theory of Serrao (*o.c.* in n. 1) that once the capital penalty was exacted—first, as he thinks, in the third century—the victims had to seek compensation by a distinct civil action breaks down in view of this evidence; he himself admits that in the late Empire compensation could be secured to the victims at the same time that the defendant was punished by loss of *caput*.

convicted for *repetundae* was claimed by the *fiscus* (*Dig.* xlviii 2, 20). This does not imply that the *fiscus*, like the *aerarium* under the Gracchan law (and still in AD 100), had not to pay out what was due to the plaintiffs.[25]

In a purely criminal process it was naturally not possible to inculpate the innocent heirs of the accused. But under the Gracchan law, once a *repetundae* charge had been brought, it was not terminated if the accused died or forfeited citizenship (*FIRA* i[2] no. 7 v. 29). Thus the victims of extortion could still seek compensation from his sureties, or from his property at the expense of the heirs. Similarly in the penal actions of civil law claims still lay against the heirs if the defendant died after the *litis contestatio*. In Pliny's day the law remained at least as favourable to the victims. Charges against Classicus were tried after his death (*ep.* iii 9, 6; 4, 3–7), and compensation was awarded out of his estate (9, 17). Pliny | says that the laws provided for such a posthumous action, but that the practice had long fallen into desuetude. It therefore seems unlikely that this provision was an innovation of the Principate; more probably, the *lex Julia* at least repeated the comparable provision in the Gracchan law. Texts in the *Digest* even say that the process could actually be begun after the death of a delinquent, with a view to recovery from his heirs (xlviii 2, 20; 13, 16; 16, 15, 3), provided that not more than one year had elapsed (*ib.* 11, 2). This rule is analogous to the right the lawbooks give plaintiffs under penal actions to initiate proceedings, even after the death of the delinquent, with a view to recovering from the heirs to the extent of their enrichment. In both cases, however, interpolation has been suspected. It is unfortunate that we cannot say for certain, on the strength of Pliny's statements, whether Classicus was already dead at the time the charges were brought. If this were so, the juristic texts could be regarded as authentic.[26]

From the late first century BC, under the *lex Servilia Glauciae*, and again under the *lex Julia*, where the property of the defendant did not suffice to meet the claims of the victims, they could recover by the clause 'quo ea pecunia pervenerit' from any third party who could be shown to have benefited from the delinquent's enrichment (*Rab. Post.* 8 ff.; *Fam.* viii 8, 2). [Cicero indicates (*Rab. Post.* 10) that there had been much case law by 54 under this rubric, but that it was hard to

---

[25] Payment to *aerarium*—of precise sum due to victims—in AD 100 (Pl. *ep.* ii 11, 19). Other references to 'confiscation' may be similarly explained. The treasury kept the money when there were no claims (*Ann.* iv 20), and in later law, sometimes shared it when damages were multiple (*e.g. CJ* i 51, 3, 1).

[26] Serrao (*o.c.* in n. 1) n. 71 hesitantly repeats doubts on their authenticity, but cites *HA Pius* 10 in their support. The *Historia Augusta* is reliable only when confirmed; and here, it does not even indicate that actions had been brought in the first place against the heirs.

collect from the beneficiaries.] It must have been under this rule that Classicus' creditors were required to disgorge what he had repaid them from his illegal gains (*ep.* iii 9, 17).

It is clear that Republican law, had it been enforced, held out fairly adequate prospects of reparation to the victims of extortion.

The law also had a deterrent character, and not only in the period when it certainly prescribed multiple damages. Conviction led to *infamia*. Under the *lex Julia* the person condemned cannot act as *iudex* or witness, and in the Principate he forfeits senatorial and priestly dignity.[27] In the orthodox doctrine reparation and *infamia* are all the law demands; the offence was never capital, and if Republican defendants generally took refuge abroad and lost citizenship, they did so of their own volition. By flight they might convey their movable assets out of Roman jurisdiction and retain their riches, as did Verres at Massilia (Plin. *NH.* xxxiv 6). Their powerful connexions at Rome could also assure them honour and influence in their new homes; witness Memmius at Athens (*Att.* v 11, 6). At home, by contrast, they might be financially ruined and would feel most keenly the loss of rights and dignity that *infamia* entailed [cf. p. 503]. Mrs. Henderson has indeed argued (*o.c.* in n. 4) that at all times *repetundae* could legally be capital, and Sherwin-White (*o.c.* in n. 1) that the *lex Julia* | (but no earlier law) appointed a capital penalty for offences where illegal enrichment was aggravated by 'saevitia' or for acts that were already penalized as capital under other laws, in which personal enrichment was not the essence of the offence. His view would accord with the scale of penalties that Cicero thought appropriate for *pecunia capta*: 'noxiae poena par esto, ut in suo vitio quisque plectatur, vis capite, avaritia multa' (*de leg.* iii 46 cf. 11). Further, by 4 BC, provincials could certainly bring some capital charges against officials, and it is the most natural philological interpretation of the *SC Calvisianum* (v. 9 cf. 130) that these were charges under the law of *repetundae*; those who cling to Mommsen's doctrine that in law *repetundae* was still not capital must therefore repudiate his view that peregrines were barred from other criminal accusations (n. 17). (The possibility that the penalties of the *lex Julia* had been stiffened by a subsequent measure, altogether unknown, perhaps need not be taken seriously.) In the early Principate the more heinous offenders undoubtedly suffered punishments more severe than damages coupled with *infamia*; but it is not so clear that a capital penalty was ever inflicted, except when the defendant had faced additional charges under some other law. Not till the third century was death made the punishment for *repetundae* alone in the

---

[27] *Dig.* i 9, 2; xxii 5, 15 (*contra* 13); Pl. *ep.* ii 11, 12.

gravest cases (*Dig.* xlviii 11, 7, 3). On Mommsen's view this was the result of imperial development of the law, on Sherwin-White's it could illustrate the prescriptions of the *lex Julia* itself. If only because Sherwin-White's thesis has not won general acceptance, it must be pronounced uncertain.[28] The question need not be re-argued here, not only because I have little to add (but see p. 69), but because broader ground can be taken to assess the deterrent effect of Republican law. It is clear that, whatever penalties the laws appointed, in practice conviction for *repetundae* under the Republic did involve exile and the loss of citizenship. At the same time it must be added that the retirement of defendants into exile with their assets tended to make the provisions for compensation of the victims, which otherwise were so carefully framed, quite nugatory.

The great demerit of Republican law was indeed simply that it was not enforced; it did not guarantee good government because acquittals were too | easily procured. I need not enlarge on this, nor on one qualification that must be made: a Verres or an Appius was not necessarily typical, and conscience could make governors upright, though the courts were partial or corrupt. It was also an advantage to the subjects that the Romans governed little; much responsibility was left to the cities, and if officials were oppressive, they were at least few.

Under the Principate there were developments in the law itself, apart from further refinements in defining offences, and these must be reviewed, before we turn to the vital issue of enforcement in this period.

1. A third century jurist writes: 'Lex Iulia repetundarum pertinet ad eas pecunias, quas quis in magistratu potestate curatione legatione vel quo alio officio munere ministeriove publico cepit vel cum ex cohorte cuius eorum est' (*Dig.* xlviii 11, 1). Other evidence shows that whether or not this text has been interpolated, it [correctly represents the substance of the law, after its extension in the Principate, cf. pp. 492 f.,] to non-senatorial officials and their agents. This was a natural consequence of the use of *equites* as provincial governors and in procuratorial posts which were recognized, either from the first or in

---

[28] [Paul,] *fr. Leid.* 7 reads: 'Leg(e) Iul(ia) repetundar(um) nemo in p. ..... satur, sed id q(uod) dat(um) e(st) repeti p(otest).' Archi, supplying 'in p[oena ver]satur' or the like, holds that 'Paul' is writing throughout of the terms of the *lex Julia*, and attests that it provided only for pecuniary compensation (see his essay in the Leiden edition, cf. *St. et Doc. Hist. et Iuris* xxiii (1957) 423 ff., where he retracts the supplement but not the substance of his thesis, in criticizing Serrao). Serrao (*o.c.* in n. 1, 43 ff.), adopting the supplement 'in p[ublico iudicio accu]satur, and building on it a theory which Archi has refuted, also comes to the conclusion that it implies that the *lex Julia* did not provide for a capital penalty. I gravely doubt if all the statements in the fragment really go back to the *lex Julia*. In any event valid historical conclusions cannot be based on lacunae, especially where (as in this case) no one has yet proposed a supplement free from objections to the language and substance. [On this text and on the existence of a capital penalty see pp. 505 ff.]

course of time, as official; the extension of the scope of the law no doubt went hand in hand with this development. Naturally the law never applied to *equites* who were merely active in a province as businessmen or even as publicans; it lay with the governor (as under the Republic) to protect subjects from wrongs at their hands. Under Claudius and Nero, if not earlier, equestrian officials were indicted for *repetundae*, and many legal texts attest their liability.[29] Under Trajan even non-official agents of a guilty governor were successfully impleaded as his 'socii ministrique'; apparently this was an innovation.[30] The wife and daughter of the same governor, Classicus, were accused, probably under the same principle.[31] According to the Pauline *Sententiae* it was an offence under the *lex Julia* to make or procure a motion in city council or provincial assembly in honour of a governor or his *comites*. The probable explanation of this rule may best be deferred, but it can hardly have stood in the text of the law, or be earlier than AD 11, if not 62 [cf. p. 81].[32]

2. Under the Republic charges of *repetundae* went before a *quaestio publica*, in which senators had been in a minority since 70 BC. From Tiberius' accession at latest all cases we know of were tried either by the senate (or a judicial committee of the senate) or by the Emperor.

Our earliest evidence of senatorial jurisdiction for *repetundae* is the *SC Calvisianum* of 4 BC, initiated by Augustus himself. To obviate delays, it sets up a new and rapid procedure, with simple compensation as the only penalty, though *infamia* perhaps remained a consequence of condemnation. Under this procedure the court consists of senators, appointed in a way I need not examine, who try the charges and fix the compensation due. It is generally supposed that hitherto the old *quaestio* had continued to operate (no cases are known) and that the senate as a body had not yet assumed jurisdiction. If this be so, the institution of a

---

[29] App. I nos. 19, 22, 23, 30; possible earlier cases (nos. 1, 8—on which cf. n. 18—13, 14, 17) are less clear, but the *comites* in no. 12 were presumably non-senatorial. Procurators, *comites* etc. are treated as liable in e.g. *Dig.* i 16, 6, 3; xii 1, 34; xviii 1, 62 *pr.* xlviii 1, 5; xlix 14, 46, 2. [Paul] *fr. Leid.* 5 makes the law apply to *equestres* by doubtful supplement. [Cf. p. 499.]

[30] Plin. *ep.* iii 9, 12–22; vi 29, 8. In the Republic civil actions lay against such persons, II, *Verr.* i 97 ('coniunctione criminum', i.e. 'associated charges'); iii 152.

[31] Plin. *ep.* iii 9, 6; 12; 14–20. After discussion in AD 21 (*Ann.* iii 33) a SC of AD 24 (iv 20, wrongly dated in *Dig.* i 16, 4, 2) made a governor liable for his wife's offences, but proceedings in the Classicus case went further. Plancina (*Ann.* iii 15; 17), Sosia (iv 20), Paxaea (vi 29) and Cornelia (Dio lix 18) probably all incurred or feared prosecution not for *repetundae* but for *maiestas*.

[32] *Fr. Leid.* 2. The honours voted to Ap. Claudius before he left Cilicia do not seem to have been illegal under the *lex Julia*; the only illegality consisted in the excessive sums voted for embassies of the cities to Rome—in violation of a *lex Cornelia*, presumably on *maiestas* (*Fam.* iii 8, 2–3; 10, 6). Cf. Dio lvi 25, 6 (AD 11); Tac. *Ann.* xv 20–2 (AD 62) for later restrictions on such *laudationes*; Thrasea's speech seems to exclude the view that he (or Tacitus?) knew of such a rule in the *lex Julia*, and the well-known practice of jurists of ascribing to *leges* rules arising out of a later development makes it unwise to prefer 'Paul's' authority.

senatorial court was an innovation. It must then be said that this change bore no relation to the evils the decree professed to remedy. The *longueurs* of the old procedure could have been abridged without altering the composition of the court. Indeed the grounds given for the precise changes made seem altogether specious. The decree laments the hardships of witnesses for the prosecution, compelled to attend from distant provinces at their own cost. We might expect that it would have provided that the prosecution or the state should bear the cost. Instead it limits the number of witnesses the prosecution may subpoena to five, if the charges are laid by private individuals, or ten, if by cities; and all must actually be in Italy, when summoned. The effect of this might easily have been fatally to weaken the weight of the evidence for the prosecution.[33] In any event, the transference of jurisdiction to senators, whenever it occurred, was inspired by the desire rather to please the senate than to protect the subjects. From C. Gracchus to Severus it was the persistent claim of the senate that senators should be judged only by their peers. But senatorial judges usually favoured senatorial defendants.

It seems to me probable that the procedure established by the *SC* was not in force for long. Admittedly the new court can be seen at work in AD 15 when charges of *repetundae* against Granius Marcellus were referred to 'recuperatores' (*Ann.* i 74). Tacitus does not record whether he was condemned or not; probably he did not know. The *SC* does not provide that the court must report to the senate, and the result of a trial need not have been entered in the *acta senatus* from which, directly or indirectly, Tacitus probably drew his information. In all later cases, even when only pecuniary penalties were exacted, | he can tell us the outcome of the trials, and this suggests that they took place before the full senate. For what he is worth, Juvenal (viii 92–4) also speaks of condemnation by the senate in such a case. In Pliny's time the senate heard even the less serious charges agains Marius Priscus who 'omissa defensione iudices petiit';[34] similarly Julius Bassus confessed, while excusing, his crime in the senate, which then passed sentence (*ep.* iv 9). Both indeed had to go before *iudices* thereafter (cf. Suet. *Dom.* 8, 2), and these *iudices* have been identified with the judicial commission of the *SC*. But that commission was responsible for hearing the substance of accusations of 'pecunia capta'; under Trajan this was a matter for the whole senate. 'Iudices dare' is indeed tantamount to 'condemn' (*ep.* iv 9, 19), and the only functions that can have been left to the *iudices* are

[33] Under the Gracchan law (*FIRA* i² no. 7 v. 34) 48 and under the Julian (Val. Max. viii 1, 10) 120 witnesses could be summoned from provinces.

[34] *ep.* ii 11, 2 cf. 4 'cognitionem senatus lege conclusam'.

those of assessing and distributing damages among several claimants and perhaps (as Mr. Balsdon has suggested to me) of deciding which specific claims could be established; these were tasks inappropriate for so large a body as the senate, though on one occasion the senate did assess the compensation due (*ep.* ii 11, 19). De Visscher has sought to reconcile the Trajanic procedure with that envisaged by the *SC*, which, he believes, was still in force, by postulating that from the first the senate was intended to conduct an 'examen du fonds même de l'affaire' (*o.c.* in n. 1, 153). Of this there is no word in the document; the senate simply has to verify that the charges are non-capital, and in that case to set up the court that very day; there is no time for the investigation he assumes. Bassus' trial occupied at least two days (*ep.* iv 9, 9). If the new procedure soon lapsed, the provincials may soon have lost the advantages of rapidity it guaranteed.

The senate also acquired jurisdiction in cases not covered by the *SC*, those in which capital charges were preferred. We do not know whether in 4 BC such charges would have been heard by a *quaestio* or whether the senate already claimed competence. In AD 22 Silanus was tried by the senate for *repetundae* and *maiestas* (App. I no. 6). For the penalties to be imposed Tiberius invoked the precedent of a *SC* on the occasion of the trial about AD 12 of Volesus Messala, who had also been guilty of *saevitia*, and, like Silanus, presumably suffered exile (*ib.* no. 2). De Visscher has suggested that this *SC* was purely prejudicial and that Messala was formally tried by the permanent court.[35] This need not be so. The 'sentence' of the senate presumably took the form of advice to the presiding consul, whose *imperium* justified the proceedings, and is in fact described by Pliny (*ep.* iii 9, 22–3) as a *SC*. It may be added that, when in AD 19 Cn. Piso was tried by the senate on various counts, they in|cluded charges of *repetundae* arising from his government in Spain, which were preferred before the consuls and heard in the senate (*Ann.* iii 10, 1; 13, 1). At latest from AD 22 the more serious charges of *repetundae*, and on my view all charges of *repetundae*, regularly came before the senate, in so far as they were directed against senators. [They were not tried by the emperor.] I know of no clear exception in the period before Trajan's death.[36] Later emperors continued to observe, and even to promise observance of, the rule that senators should be tried only by their peers; doubtless exceptions occurred, but

---

[35] *o.c.* 167. For a prejudicial *SC* cf. Dio liii 23, 7; Suet. *Aug.* 66. De Visscher's view is not proved by Sen. *Controv.* vii 6, 22: 'Saturninus Furius, qui Volesum condemnavit (i.e. as counsel for prosecution), maius nomen in foro (i.e. in forensic work) quam in declamationibus habuit.'

[36] If Nero is said to have acquitted two senatorial defendants (*Ann.* xiii. 52), that need mean only that he promoted their acquittal by the senate; Tacitus naturally cared little for the formalities.

more probably under the law of *maiestas* than that of *repetundae*.[37] The statement by Macer in the third century that 'hodie ex lege repetundarum extra ordinem puniuntur' (*Dig.* xlviii 11, 7, 3) certainly does not prove that senatorial jurisdiction was then at an end and that all cases came before the Emperor;[38] for the senate too claimed that it was not bound by the prescripts of the law,[39] and its proceedings could be described as 'extra ordinem'. The senate still tried a case of misgovernment under Severus (Dio lxxvi 9, 2).

Even *equites* were sometimes tried by the senate under Tiberius and Nero for *repetundae* or other offences of misgovernment (App. 1 nos. 8, 22, 30), but Claudius (nos. 17, 19), Nero (no. 23) and Vespasian (Suet. *Vesp.* 16, 2; Tac. *Dial.* 7, 1) heard such charges in their own court, and Philo (*Flacc.* 106) may have similar cases in mind when he speaks of the impartial justice with which Augustus and Tiberius heard complaints against ex-governors. After AD 60 we have no record of the trial of any *eques* for misgovernment by the senate. It seems probable that in such cases the emperor now reserved jurisdiction to himself and that for that reason they are less apt to figure in our sources. Suetonius mentions, with evident surprise, that Tiberius forced a *praefectus alae* to plead before the senate 'de vi et rapinis'.[40] In his own day this would not have occurred. By the removal of equestrian cases from senatorial jurisdiction the subjects probably gained nothing and lost nothing: senators might have been impartial to *equites* in the dock, and an emperor might be complaisant to the faults of his own agents (App. 1 no. 23).

3. As the senate could exercise the right 'et mitigare leges et intendere' (n. 39), and the emperor obviously possessed it, penalties fluctuated at the discretion of the court, with little regard to the prescripts of the *lex Julia* (even if that statute itself provided for a scale of penalties) or other laws; as early as AD 22, or even AD 12, the sentence to be imposed was a matter for debate in the senate (*Ann.* iii 68). |

(a) *Infamia* normally flowed from conviction, yet men condemned could be restored to a senatorial dignity after an interval, sometimes by senatorial partiality to persons whose guilt was assured (*Hist.* i 77): but Nero pardoned offenders whose merit was to have secured the corrupt intercession of Otho (App. 1 no. 20) or married Tigellinus' daughter (ib. no. 24). Much to Pliny's indignation the senate retained in its ranks Marius Priscus' legate and accomplice in cruelty, and merely debarred

---

[37] Mommsen, *StR* ii³ 960–2; for late instances of senatorial jurisdiction, *ib.* 124 n. 3.
[38] *Contra* Serrao (*o.c.* in n. 1) 49 ff., if I understood him aright.
[39] Plin *ep.* iv 9, 17 cf. ii 11, 4; ii 12; iii 9, 29–34; v 20; vi 29, 7–11.
[40] Suet. *Tib.* 30.

him from a future proconsulship (no. 37); and Pliny himself saved Bassus from loss of dignity (no. 39). Yet we need not believe that Bassus, an elderly and experienced man, was as guileless as Pliny made out, and had done no more than take gifts from friends; there was much evidence against him, lightly dismissed by his counsel as due to the conspiracy of factious subjects he had treated sternly;[41] what he represented as gifts the prosecution regarded as thefts, and the government had so little confidence in his integrity that it annulled all his acts (*ep.* iv 9 cf. x 56, 4).

(b) The *SC Calvisianum* proves that in 4 BC provincials had the right, whether or not under the *lex Julia*, to prefer capital charges against ex-governors, and this right the *SC* did not take from them. In practice, no one to our knowledge was ever executed for oppression of the subjects, and though some were banished after trials resulting from their misgovernment, it is clear that such banishment was not always technically 'capital'. Exile was by now a legal penalty; or rather, the term 'exile' may denote very different legal penalties. A man may be merely banished from Rome and Italy, or perhaps his home province, by simple *relegatio*; he may be 'relegated' to an appointed place of residence, such as an island; or he may be 'deported' to an island; according to the later jurists, only the last punishment, which developed out of *aquae et ignis interdictio*, was necessarily accompanied by confiscation of property and involved the loss of the *caput*, i.e. of all citizen rights, even that of making or taking under a will, though *relegatio* may also be associated with pecuniary penalties. Deportation is lifelong, relegation may be temporary.[42] These distinctions of third-century law were doubtless gradually evolved. As late as AD 12 interdicted persons could still live in luxury and outside the areas appointed for them; only then did Augustus enforce their residence in islands and forbid them to enjoy the attendance of more than twenty slaves and freedmen or the possession of more than 500,000 HSS (Dio lvi 27). It was perhaps only Tiberius' enactment in AD 23, that they might not make wills, which deprived them of citizenship (Dio lvii 22). Still later, Gaius is represented as incensed that | such internees could live in luxury (Philo, *Flacc.* 184). The later distinction between *relegatio in insulam* and deportation may only have been established by Trajan's rule, ending 'the avarice of former times', that relegation should not

---

[41] *ep.* iv 9, 5; cf. perhaps Quint. v 7, 5 for the practice in *repetundae* trials of treating those 'qui se reo numerasse pecunias iurant' as 'litigatores', not as 'testes'; and v 7, 23 for the device of discrediting a large number of hostile witnesses as 'conspirationem'. For the reference to factious persons cf. Cic. *Flacc.* 87; in provincial government 'diligentia plena simultatum est... severitas periculosa'—no doubt a common line of defence (cf. the Thorigny inscription, see n. 88).

[42] The evidence is fully given by Mommsen, *Strafrecht*, book v chapters 5, 7 and 10.

entail confiscation, except in so far as the court directed.[43] Literary sources for the period down to Trajan's death have small taste for legal technicalities; and it is in any event unwise to assume that a term when used in the first century has the same sense as in the third. All this often makes it uncertain how severe a sentence of 'exile' may have been.

Deportation (or what would later have been so described) was certainly imposed for *vis publica* under Tiberius (App. I no. 7). It was also probably incurred by Silanus in AD 22, as by Messala in AD 12, but the former certainly, and perhaps the latter, had also been charged with *maiestas*.[44] Avillius Flaccus too was deported, but the nature of the formal charges preferred against him is unknown (*ib.* no. 14). Some defendants committed suicide before trial or sentence, proof not that they were conscious of guilt, but that even if innocent, they entertained no hope of acquittal; their motive was to avoid confiscation and secure the property for their heirs.[45] Confiscation, however, was not a penalty for *repetundae*; only simple compensation was now payable, even when enrichment was aggravated by atrocities (cf. below). Some of these defendants are recorded to have faced charges of *maiestas* as well as *repetundae* (*ib.* nos. 4, 9, 18); in the other instances the charges are vaguely described in our sources (*ib.* nos. 1, 11, 13), but the mere fact of suicide suggests that *maiestas* was involved. In several such cases it is clear that misgovernment was not the real gravamen of the prosecution, even when there was any guilt at all (nos. 1, 4, 9, 14, 18). Some believed that Classicus took his life, when simply accused of *repetundae*; Pliny can think of no explanation for this but shame, and clearly finds this implausible (*ep.* iii 9, 5). Classicus' offences under the law of *repetundae* were indeed heinous (*ib.* iii 9, 2), yet even so he could not have expected them to attract a 'capital' penalty. After his death, at Marius Priscus' trial, the defence claimed, and the prosecution did not contest, that the penalty under the law of *repetundae* was merely pecuniary, coupled of course with *infamia* (*ep.* ii 11, 3–4 and 20; vi 29, 9). Classicus could not have envisaged that he would have suffered even the relegation imposed on Marius. Very probably, his death was natural, though opportune. There is no instance before Trajan's | death in which a man, charged with *repetundae* alone and not also with

---

[43] *Dig.* xlviii, 22. 1 but cf. 20, 8, 3; 22, 7, 4 cf. 19, 38, 8. Mommsen *o.c.* 1010 n. 3 = *Dr. Pén* iii 364 n. 3 is wrong in assuming that pre-Trajanic cases of exile with total confiscation must be cases of *deportatio* with loss of *caput*.

[44] Of Silanus Tacitus confusingly says that he was 'aqua et igni interdictus' and 'relegatus'; his property was confiscated, in part, and he was interned in an island; probably this amounts to 'deportation' (App. I no. 6). Messala's case was a precedent (*ib.* no. 2).

[45] *Ann.* vi 29, 2; Dio lviii 15–16; their testimony on the law was rightly upheld by C. W. Chilton, *JRS* xlv (1955) 73 ff. and has now been confirmed by *AE* 1957, 250, proving that Macro made a will that remained valid after his suicide.

maiestas, is known to have suffered or apprehended either death or 'deportation'.

Exile in a milder form was indeed sometimes the sentence. Thus in AD 60 a procurator was 'banished from Italy' (App. 1 no. 30). Tacitus suggests that but for his brother's influence a sterner penalty would have been inflicted (and properly), perhaps relegation to an island. No doubt he had been guilty of atrocities as well as illegal enrichment. In AD 70 a proconsul condemned for *repetundae* was banished for his cruelty (*ib*. no. 33); in the light of the other evidence his banishment is best taken as relegation. Marius Priscus was ultimately 'relegated' from Rome and Italy (Plin. *ep*. ii 11, 19; vi 29, 9). *Repetundae* was the only formal charge against him, though he was also amenable on counts of murder and *vis publica* (p. 57 above). Even banishment was held to be an extension of the legal penalty. This does not indeed imply that the *lex Julia* provided for nothing beyond pecuniary compensation; the law to senators of AD 100, as to jurists later, was what current interpretation and practice demanded. The precedents of AD 60 and 70 had perhaps not been repeated (cf. p. 87) and were now forgotten. The senate only rallied to the severer penalty proposed, when it was seen to be favoured by those nearest the consuls' seats—where Trajan himself was presiding (*ep*. ii 11, 22). In accordance with the new decision some of Classicus' accomplices were relegated for two or five years or even for life (*ib*. iii 9, 17–18; 22).

Macer tells us that in his day exile was the punishment for *repetundae*, and that in extreme cases (like taking money to convict an innocent man) death was appropriate. This reflects the stricter practice of a later time[46] and may have been a return to the prescriptions of the *lex Julia*. We have a choice of believing that in heinous cases under the early Principate the senate either mitigated the capital penalty the law required, or that it aggravated a merely pecuniary penalty. Certainly, the first alternative best suits what else we know of the senate's attitude. [cf. p. 503.]

(c) Under the *SC Calvisianum*, if the provincials did not choose to bring capital charges, they could only sue under the new procedure for simple compensation. Thus, if the *lex Cornelia* and *lex Julia* had provided for multiple damages, as Sherwin-White holds, the law was now altered to the advantage of senatorial delinquents. It is clear that down to Trajan's death no more than simple compensation could be exacted. Men who were convicted and later restored to the senate had not been ruined by damages; one of them could even pay a large bribe

---

[46] *Dig.* xlviii 11, 7, 3; cf. Mommsen *o. c.* 731 n. 3 = *Dr. Pén.* iii 32, 1 for later evidence. In AD 205 only clemency saved a defendant from death for misgovernment, Dio lxxvi 9. For later severity cf. also n. 48, and the contrast of *Dig.* xlviii 8, 4, 2 and 8, 16.

for his restoration (App. i no. 20). It may be assumed that when defendants were banished a pecuniary penalty was also imposed. Marius Priscus had to repay the precise sums he had taken for executing an innocent | man (Plin. *ep.* ii 11, 19). Presumably the money was due to his victim's heirs. Even here compensation is only simple. Tacitus implies that the Gauls could have claimed from Silius' assets (*Ann.* iv 20) and no doubt the treasury met claims from provincials out of the confiscated property of Silanus. It may be said that though Republican law may have been nominally more severe, there was now more chance that the victims would get something. This is not certain. Silanus' *materna bona* were reserved for his son (*Ann.* iii 68). [In one case, which Dio (lx 25, 4) perhaps recorded as unusual, Claudius, in banishing a guilty governor,] confiscated only the gains he had made in office. So too only Classicus' illegal acquisitions in Baetica were assigned to meet provincial claims; his daughter was to inherit all he had owned before his proconsulship (Plin. *ep.* iii 9, 17). It is not obvious that in any of these cases care was taken to ensure that all the assets of the delinquent should be available for reparation until all claims had been satisfied. Pius is indeed credited with a rule to that effect, which might have been new, but in an unreliable source (n. 26). After a man's conviction the consuls in Pliny's day were supposed to take custody of his assets, evidently to secure that reparation was made, but it would seem that they were not always zealous in performing this duty. Hence when Baebius Massa was condemned, Herennius Senecio, as counsel for the provincials, went to them to demand that they should not allow the assets to be broken up. One can conceive that a defendant would convey them to some friend in a sort of trust, and that the victims might hardly get a penny. Senecio's action was so unusual that Massa claimed that he was showing 'non advocati fidem sed inimici amaritudinem'.[47] A satirist is not a sober historian, and Juvenal may have taken the name of Marius Priscus, because he figured in a *cause célèbre*, without knowing the facts of the case. But his gibe (i 49–50) would have missed fire, if it bore no relation to the probable effects of condemnation.

> Quid enim salvis infamia nummis?
> Exul ab octava Marius bibit et fruitur dis
> Iratis, at tu victrix, provincia, ploras.

Thus the provincials might fail to get compensation, even when they won their case. Severus' enactment that defendants might not alienate any of their property—if they did so, it was fraudulent and the assets

---

[47] Plin. *ep.* vii 33.

could be recovered after conviction—was perhaps a novelty and is characteristic of the greater severity of the law in his time, when multiple damages were also revived.[48]

On balance the law does not seem to have become stricter in practice than in the Republic. Then almost all who were convicted forfeited citizenship, but enjoyed a comfortable exile. Now exile was a more wretched fate [in the form of relegation (if not deportation) to an island,] but only that minority of offenders who had other counts against them stood in | much danger of these sentences. Compensation for the victims was perhaps as hard to secure as it ever had been. None the less the deterrent effects of the law may have been much greater than in the Republic if the prospects of bringing the guilty to book had substantially improved.

II

We must therefore ask how easy it was for provincials to bring charges and obtain convictions.

While in office a man could not be prosecuted [cf. pp. 501 f.]. The Leiden fragment of Paul's Sentences (section 5) ascribes (with doubtful truth) to the *lex Julia* a rule that no governor or quaestor might hold a new office in the year of his return to Rome. This rule enforced an interval during which charges could be brought before the culprit could be protected by new immunity. It existed before Claudius, but he had to re-enact it, at least in regard to proconsuls.[49] Their tenure was normally annual, and in so far as this rule was observed, trial and punishment need not have limped too far behind the crime. Yet in the Republic governors such as L. Metellus in Sicily [whose own integrity Cicero concedes (II *Verr.* iii 158)] and Cicero in Cilicia, while reversing the acts of their predecessors, Verres and Appius Claudius,[50] had sought to impede their condemnation by threats to deter hostile witnesses and procure laudatory testimony.[51] Were such practices unknown in the Principate, when senators were ready to condone each other's crimes even in the city: 'nulla innocentiae cura, sed vices impunitatis' (*Hist.* i 72)? Plautius Silvanus was at least more disposed to send up a Moesian embassy to Rome, because its purpose was to commend his predecessor,[52] and a Gallic magnate who resisted the

---

[48] *Dig.* xlviii 2, 20; 20, 11, cf. nn. 23, 46.
[49] Dio lx 25, 4–6.
[50] II *Verr.* ii 62–3; iii 123 etc.; *Att.* vi 1, 2 etc.
[51] II *Verr.* ii 64–5; 139; iii 122; iv 141 etc.; *Fam.* iii 10, 1; 11, 3.
[52] *SEG* i 329 (= Abbott and Johnson, *Mun. Admin. in Roman Empire* no. 68), 40 ff.

prosecution of one governor earned the approval of the next (n. 88 below). In most cases of trials it is merely assumed by scholars that a man was tried shortly after his tenure of a province. Two proconsuls of Africa were indicted in 58 (App. I nos. 26–7); it may well be that the later had made it hard to prosecute the earlier of the two, [whose tenure went back to 54.].[53] The question of prosecuting P. Suillius for misgovernment in Asia did not arise till 58 (*Ann.* xiii 43); yet his proconsulship was under Claudius.[54] It is true that it was then broached by his enemies, not by the provincials, and that they eventually took a shorter path to ruin him; but they do not seem to have doubted that evidence against him could have been collected, his past suggests his guilt (cf. iv 31), and his great influence under Claudius will explain his previous immunity.

Governors appointed by the Emperor held office normally perhaps for three years, sometimes for much longer, and imperial officials were freely moved from post to post. | From such officials the provincials might suffer long, if they had no means of making their grievances known to the Emperor, before they had the right to prefer formal charges.

Few Emperors travelled constantly round their dominions to see the condition of the subjects with their own eyes. Augustus did so (before 13 BC); hence the Gauls could bring to his notice the illegal exactions of his procurator, Licinus. To little purpose: Augustus condoned them, when Licinus pleaded that they had been for the profit of the public purse.[55] In his unceasing journeys Hadrian is said to have corrected abuses and punished unjust officials with such rigour that it was thought he incited the accusers (*HA Hadr.* 13, 10; cf. 12, 4) [The source is unreliable (n. 26), but in any case Hadrian's supposed practice] deserved remark precisely because it was so uncommon. And the progress of an Emperor and his entourage was in itself a heavy burden to the provincials.[56] Pius would not follow Hadrian's example. The contemporary panegyrist would have us think that the autocrat had no need to exhaust himself in travel, that though he remained at Rome, provincial officials felt that he knew more of what they were doing than they knew themselves, and stood in more awe of him than a slave in the presence of his master (Aristides xxvi 32–3). Panegyric is not to be taken for truth. Josephus makes king Agrippa tell the Jews that it was not by Rome's command that a governor was oppressive but that what occurred in Palestine could not be seen or easily heard of at Rome (*BJ*

[53] [B. Thomasson. *Die Statthalter des röm Provinzen Nordafrikas* 37 f.]

[54] Waddington, *Fastes des provinces asiatiques* 129.

[55] Dio liv 21.

[56] Rostovtzeff, *SEHRE* ch. viii n. 4; 6; ix n. 46 (with some exaggerations).

ii 353). As in Judaea, wrongs were sometimes left so long without redress that they culminated in revolt.[57] Russian peasants had a proverb: 'Heaven is high and the Tsar far off'. Perhaps the experience of Rome's subjects was not greatly different.

How was the Emperor to hear of his subjects' grievances against a governor or procurator? It is doubtless true (as Mr. Balsdon has pointed out to me) that both under the Republic and under the Principate there were many Romans resident in the provinces and that news of occurrences there could be communicated in their letters; and individual provincials often visited Rome and had friends or patrons in the Roman upper class. Yet in Cicero's time 'ita multa Romae geruntur ut vix ea quae fiunt in provinciis audiantur' (*Planc.* 63). Had conditions so much changed in the Principate? Ideally an Emperor was prompt in giving audience and answering provincial embassies; not so Domitian, if we believe Pliny (*Paneg.* 79), and certainly not all Emperors were industrious and conscientious. Moreover complaints communicated through private channels, or even by embassies acting without their cities' authority (cf. *CT* xii 12, 11), could not have the same weight as official petitions. But the Jews of Alexandria could not petition against an oppressive governor without his own consent (Philo *Flacc.* 97) and under Hadrian the Greeks there seem | to have alleged that the prefect had suppressed their letters to the Emperor.[58] Even to leave Alexandria by sea required an official pass.[59] The same close control could not be exercised in other provinces. However the Jews of Palestine needed the consent of the procurator, or of the legate of Syria who had some supervision over him, to approach the Emperor (Philo *Leg.* 247; Jos *AJ* xx 7; 193–4). Elsewhere governors could certainly, in the interests of economy, prohibit official deputations from cities to Rome[60] and Moesians seek the legate's sanction before sending an embassy to praise his predecessor (n. 52). Even if governors had not the right in general to bar petitions to the Emperor from cities,[61] they may have exercised the power; a city could hardly take action unknown to

[57] *Hist.* v 9–10 cf. Dio lvi 16, 3; *Ann.* iii 40; 3; *Agr.* 19.

[58] *Acta Pauli et Antonini* vi (H. A. Musurillo, *Acts of Pagan Martyrs*, Oxford, 1954, 49 ff.: on p. 102 he refutes a supplement of A. von Premerstein, relevant to this theme; but I am indebted to the latter. *Philol. Supp.* xvi 2 p. 6, for other references).

[59] *Gnomon of Idios Logos* 64, 66, 68, cf. Strabo 101C.

[60] Dio lii 30; cf. Plin. *ep.* x 43–4.

[61] In the fourth century governors are sometimes authorised (*CT* i 16, 2: xii 12, 3), sometimes prohibited (xii 12, 4; 12, 8, 12, 9; 12, 12 *pr.*) to censor municipal or provincial petitions: I am not clear whether i 16, 6 allows provincials to acclaim or complain against governors in office. From these (contradictory) rules we can of course make no inference about earlier practice. [H. W. Pleket, *Mnem.* 1961, 314 accuses me of neglecting the numerous inscriptions which refer to city embassies to the emperor and other measures cities took to preserve their rights. Robert's articles which he cites mention no examples of protests against misconduct by governors; many concern embassies etc. to governors.]

them. Alexander Severus had to legislate against the practice of legates and procurators of violently obstructing appeals to him from their sentences.[62] If cities took the course of stating their grievances without any direct complaint against an official, the Emperor might refer the question back to the officials concerned.[63] Individual petitioners might elude the governor's surveillance, but would they have obtained a ready hearing at Rome? To secure the removal of a minor Claudian official who was exacting 3000 *denarii* a year was not the least achievement of a munificent notable of Cibyra (*IGR* iv 914). To assail a legate, whose very position suggested that he enjoyed imperial favour, must have seemed, all too often, perilous beyond consideration. The young Pliny felt the difficulty of pleading, even in a civil case, 'contra potentissimos civitatis atque etiam Caesaris amicos' (*ep.* i 18, 3). It was obvious that, if the complaint was rejected, the province would be likely to suffer even more. As Agrippa is made to tell the Jews, the governor would then feel free to despoil them openly, instead of doing so in secret (*BJ* ii 351). At this time the Jews did not venture to appeal against the procurator to the neighbouring legate of Syria (*ib.* 280), as they had done against Cumanus (*ib.* 239–40). To appear before the Emperor himself demanded in Plutarch's estimate (805 A) an ardent audacity combined with intelligence; how much audacity the Jews had learned when admitted to Gaius' presence (Philo *Leg.* 349 ff.). Philo commends Augustus and Tiberius, perhaps in exaggerated | terms, for punishing avaricious and cruel governors *after* their retirement; he knew of none before Avillius Flaccus who had actually been removed from office for trial (*Flacc.* 105–7). And Flaccus fell, not for his flagrant misgovernment, but because he had incurred Gaius' personal enmity. We too shall hardly find evidence that high officials in the Principate were deposed and then punished for crimes against the subjects.

Of course legate and procurator might reciprocally control each other's activities. Julius Classicianus secured the recall of the harsh Suetonius Paulinus from Britain, a unique incident in our records (*Ann.* xiv 38–9), and Pliny reported (favourably) on a procuraor and other officials in Bithynia (*ep.* x 85–7). They might also pursue 'vices impunitatis'; or a legate might think it prudent not to interfere with the operations of the imperial financial agents, and earn commendation thereby (*Agr.* 9), or find himself helpless to stop their exactions (Plut. *Galba* 4). In Maecenas' speech Dio (lii 37) advises Emperors to have their spies in every province, but warns them against the lies and malpractices of such people. This system of espionage was highly developed in the late Empire. The governor was to check his *officium*

---

[62] *Dig.* xlix 1, 25 cf. *Pap. Oxy.* 2104.

[63] *CT* i 16, 2; xii 12, 3; for a much earlier instance cf. *ILS* 6092; Dio lii 30.

and the *officium* was to check the governor. But there was no salvation for the subjects in the costly multiplication of rapacious officials, *omnibus pariter corruptis.*[64]

It was undoubtedly of some advantage to the provincials if they were governed by nominees of the Emperor and not by men chosen haphazardly by sortition. The continued use of the lot for proconsulships was an abuse in itself and by Dio's day appointment was vested in the Emperor, because so many proconsuls had governed badly.[65] By contrast, though some Emperors might wish to plunder the provinces for their own ends,[66] none could wish officials to despoil them for their own private profit. But even the ablest were not necessarily good judges of ability or integrity. Offices sometimes went by favour,[67] and even by sale;[68] and an official who had squandered his patrimony in obtaining an appointment (Columella i *pr.* 10) hardly looked only to his salary for reimbursement. If a man holds important posts, that is at most proof that the ruler delighted to honour him, not that he deserved to | be honoured. Such men, as already remarked, might be beyond the attacks of subjects. Under Augustus M. Lollius and Quinctilius Varus were given more than one great command, yet both, if Velleius be trusted, were distinguished for their greed; his charges do not lack plausibility.[69] Not till AD 19, when he was politically ruined, was Cn. Piso indicted for misgovernment of Tarraconensis under Augustus.[70] Dio makes the Dalmatians blame the Romans for their revolt in AD 6: 'you send to your flocks as guardians not dogs or shepherds but wolves' (lvi 16). Tiberius is often credited with special care in provincial administration. Yet in his reign a Gallic revolt was provoked 'saevitia ac superbia praesidentium' (*Ann.* iii 40), none of whom was punished if our records are complete, and illegal exactions led to a Frisian rising

[64] O. Seeck, *Gesch. d. Untergangs der antiken Welt* ii[2] 96 ff.

[65] Dio liii 14, 3. Appointments or prorogations *extra sortem* were earlier made fairly often in special circumstances, but Tiberius refused to exclude manifestly unfit persons from the sortition, to the senate's delight (*Ann.* iii 69); later he did so exclude C. Galba—perhaps for political reasons (vi 40 cf. Suet. *Galba* 3). In Dio's day a man could be denied a province (in AD 217) on the protest of the provincials (lxxviii 22).

[66] E.g. Nero, cf. pp. 28 ff. and with different purposes, Vespasian cf. Suet. *Vesp.* 16, 2 (which can have a basis of truth); *Hist.* ii 84; 95, 3.

[67] See A. N. Sherwin-White, *PBSR* 1939, 16–17; H. G. Pflaum, *Les procurateurs équestres*, 1950, 195–209; cf. Dio lx 18, 2; Quint. vi 3, 68; Suet. *Claud.* 29, 1; *Vesp.* 4 (Claudius); [Epict. iii 7, 31 (Trajan)]; Plut. 814 D; n. 112 below.

[68] Suet. *Claud.* 29, 1; Dio lx 17, 8 (Claudius); Suet. *Vesp.* 16, 2; Dio lxvi 14 (Vespasian).

[69] ii 97, 1; 102, 1 on Lollius, whose fall suggests that Velleius, though biased against Tiberius' enemy, cf. *Ann.* iii 48, may not have been wrong; Horace's panegyric of a powerful court figure (*Odes* iv 9) is also a suspect estimate, and Horace could have been deceived by Lollius' alleged *dissimulatio.* On Varus ii 117 cf. Florus ii 30, 31: *Ann.* ii 15.

[70] Tacitus, *Ann.* iii 13 calls the charges 'vetera et inania': they were *inania* in that Piso's fate did not depend on their outcome, but they were not necessarily false, cf. E. Koestermann, *Historia* vii (1958) 336, and on Piso's later misgovernment in Syria (*Ann.* ii 55, 5; iii 13, 2; 14, 1), 341; 368.

(iv 72–3); the legate, Apronius, was as impotent to repress it as he had been tolerant of the abuses by which it was caused, yet it seems likely that he was still in command six years later.[71] Long tenures, so marked a feature of Tiberius' policy, are no proof of the excellence of the governors concerned; that is a modern theory that finds little support in ancient writers, who better understood conditions in the empire. Josephus reports a remark on the subject by Tiberius: 'it is better to leave the gorged flies on a sore than to drive them off' (*AJ* xviii 174). This may be invention, and it need not be the true explanation:[72] it shows that a provincial did not assume that when a man was kept long in a province, he was necessarily or probably one who dealt well with the subjects. Of long service governors under Tiberius we can name eleven. P. Petronius, proconsul of Asia *extra sortem* for five years, by his later conduct in Syria proved that he had provincial interests at heart, and Tacitus notes the adequacy of Poppaeus Sabinus (*Ann.* vi 39). Of the qualities of four others we can say little.[73] There remain Apronius, of whom I have spoken; C. Silius, legate of Upper Germany from AD 14 to 21, and manifestly guilty of *repetundae*, even in the view of Tacitus, who sees his ruin as the result of Sejanus' machinations (*Ann.* iv 19–20); Pomponius Labeo, who was accused of maladministration in | Moesia after he had been there eight years and who killed himself;[74] Pontius Pilate, who governed Judaea for ten years and who was not merely blackened by perverse Jews—Vitellius as legate of Syria had to take the extraordinary step of removing him on his own responsibility,[75] and C. Galerius, prefect of Egypt from 16 to 31, under whose regime the abuses which Philo praises Flaccus for checking (*Flacc.* 3–5) must, if we believe his account, have flourished.[76] Long tenures may have satiated the avarice of the governors; they also postponed the day of reckoning. It is merely an *a priori* assumption that in themselves they testify to the worth of the men who enjoyed them.

Considerations of space forbid me to examine even briefly the less copious evidence of this kind from other reigns. It has often been noted that there are less prosecutions from imperial than from senatorial

[71] *Ann.* vi 30; the inference is doubted in *PIR²* i 190.

[72] I favour Tacitus' final conjecture (*Ann.* i 80 cf. vi 39); Dio lviii 23 is obviously wrong.

[73] viz. P. Cornelius Dolabella in Dalmatia (AD 14–20)—a man of some talent, who was at least vocal against misgovernment (*Ann.* iii 69; *PIR²* ii 318); Cn. Cornelius Lentulus Gaetulicus, in Upper Germany (AD 30–39); M. Silanus in Africa (AD 32–38); Valerius Gratus in Judaea (AD 15–26). [See pp. 490–2.]

[74] App I no. 11: I do not share the certitude of Tiberius' apologists that his suicide was proof of guilt.

[75] Philo *Leg.* 299 ff; Jos. *AJ* xviii 55–62; 85–9; *BJ* ii 169–77.

[76] Evidence of officials' misconduct in his time in the Germanicus Edict (Ehrenberg and Jones² 320 = *Sammelbuch* 3924) and, by implication in *SEG* viii 527 = Ehrenberg and Jones² 320a; cf. ch. 2 n. 60.

provinces (cf. Appendixes I and III). Of course it is only for certain periods that we have detailed records of trials, and even these may not be complete; we cannot be certain that Tacitus chose to mention every trial for maladministration that was attested in the *acta senatus*;[77] and after Nero the trials of *equites* seem to have been conducted by the Emperor, and might not have figured in his sources. If all these lacunae in our evidence were filled, it might still be found that proconsuls appeared more often than agents of the Princeps as defendants. The inference that they were more often guilty of extortion need not, however, be sound. It probably seemed too hazardous to assail one who appeared high in the Emperor's esteem. A former prefect of Egypt (App. I nos. 1, 14) or a consular legate (nos. 4, 9, 11) was attacked for misgovernment when he was known to have lost favour, and not always then by provincials. Moreover a large proportion of officials the Emperor appointed served in regions which down to Trajan's death were still relatively uncivilized. We should as little expect Britons to litigate as Greeklings to revolt.[78] The former could hardly know their legal rights; the latter had lost the habit of arms. Rebellions in imperial provinces are the counterpart of prosecutions from senatorial. Of fifteen *imperial* agents whose prosecution is attested nine had served in Hellenized areas (Egypt, Syria, Asia, Bithynia, | Cilicia, Lycia and Cyrene); two others in Sardinia and Mauretania, where there were cities of the Italian type. By contrast, it was not the Gauls who accused Silius, though he had oppressed them; they did not claim compensation, and probably did not know how to do so. There is indeed no certain instance of any governor before Hadrian being prosecuted for *repetundae* by Rome's more barbarous subjects.[79] But this was not because no such governor ever gave grounds for an indictment.[80]

Charges could be preferred by individuals, cities and even whole provinces. A Roman court was as apt to decide a case in the light of general testimony on the character of the accused as by what we should think the weight of the evidence. Proof of particular illegalities could be offset by eulogies on the defendant's virtues. It was of clear advantage to the defence if it could produce such testimony from the very province which the accused had plundered,[81] and to the prosecu-

[77] Even political trials are not all recorded by Tacitus, cf. *Ann.* xiv 12, 4 for restoration of two ex-praetors whose banishment he had passed over; for Tiberius' reign E. Koestermann, *Historia* iv 1955, 72 ff. Clearly the loss of parts of his narrative makes our knowledge defective.

[78] Yet even in Greece there was a revolt under Pius (HA *Pius* 5, 5: *AE* 1929, 21: Lucian, *Peregr.* 19), [probably expressing lower class grievances].

[79] Unless the Jews are so described (App. I no. 17). We do not know where Mela served (no. 13) nor whether Moesians prosecuted Labeo (no. 11).

[80] Cf. *e.g. Agric.* 13, 1; 19 (perhaps refers to procurators); *Ann.* iii 40.

[81] Cic. *Flacc.* 100; *Scaur.* 40, cf. nn. 84–5.

tion if that province could unite in pressing the charges. It is often held
that the Emperors facilitated such unity by creating *concilia* or *koina*
which embraced a whole district, province or group of provinces. Such
councils were not indeed unknown in the Republic;[82] and if most of
them originated after Actium, their institution was not always as early
as has sometimes been believed,[83] nor are they attested in all provinces.
Moreover their principal business seems to have been the celebration of
the imperial cult; it was perhaps by an afterthought that they were
allowed to commend or indict officials and receive communications
from the Emperor on other matters. It was not a novelty for the cities
of a province to combine in accusing an ex-governor. Apart from
Messana and some individuals who were, according to Cicero, accomplices in his crimes and who testified in his favour,[84] and at first
Syracuse,[85] Sicily had combined against Verres; and Cicero had to
meet 'a common charge of Asia' against Flaccus.[86] In the Principate we
often read in our sources that men were tried 'accusantibus Bithynis' or
the like (App. I no. 16 cf. 19, 21, 24, 25, 28, 29, 30, 31, 33, 37), and it is
possible that such language generally indicates prosecution by a
concilium, though in one such instance | we know that this was not so
(Plin. *ep.* ii 11, 2 cf. iii 9, 4). In three trials action by the *concilium* is
clearly attested by Tacitus (nos. 6, 8, 23), as in five mentioned by Pliny
(nos. 34, 35, 36, 39, 40). We may readily admit that the existence of a
concilium made it somewhat easier for a whole province to take united
action. It is less certain that agreement could often be obtained. *Concilia*
could probably take decisions by majority votes; unanimity was not
required.[87] Still, in the third century a single Gallic magnate, T.
Sennius Sollemnis, boasted that he had successfully resisted a proposal
to accuse the ex-governor, Claudius Paulinus, 'provocatione scilicet
interposita, quod patria eius cum inter ceteros legatum eum creasset,
nihil de actione mandassent, immo contra laudassent, qua ratione
effectum est, ut omnes ab accusatione desisterent'.[88] It was probably

---

[82] E.g. in Sicily (II *Verr.* ii 114; 145; 154) and Asia (D. Magie, *Roman Rule in Asia Minor*, 1950,
ch. vii nn. 41, 48; ch. xvii n. 9; ch. xviii n. 4), besides several small Greek *koina*. On the whole
subject see Kornemann, *RE* v 801 ff.; and *Supp.* iv 914 ff.; J. A. O. Larsen, *Representative Government
in Greek and Roman History* (1955) chs. VI–VIII (the only good accounts). [But see now J.
Deininger, *Die Provinziallandtäge der röm. Kaiserzeit*, 1965, esp. 161 ff., whose view of their functions
may well be preferred to that suggested above.]

[83] Vespasianic in Narbonensis, Baetica and Africa *proconsularis*.

[84] II *Verr.* ii 13–14; iii 109 f.; v 47–59; 160.

[85] *Ib.* ii 15; iv 136 ff.; under pressure from Verres' successor Syracuse passed a decree in Verres'
favour but later co-operated with the prosecution.

[86] *Flacc.* 34.

[87] Larsen *o. c.* in n. 82 has shown that in Lycia and Thessaly (pp. 101–3), Asia (121) and Gaul
(138) cities were represented in rough proportion to their size (for a change in composition later
cf. 151); this would have been pointless unless majority decisions had been the rule.

[88] *CIL* xiii 3162 (Thorigny); see the edition by H. G. Pflaum, *Le Marbre de Thorigny* (1948).

hardly worth while for a council to proceed if it were strongly divided. In 106 the *koinon* of Bithynia sought to prosecute Varenus; he secured the right to summon witnesses from the province in his defence, and the *koinon* then officially abandoned the charges, though its chief representative at Rome tried to persist, and the true will of the province remained in doubt (App. I no. 40). It is a fair inference that Varenus had his friends in Bithynia, and that though the majority of the *koinon* was adverse, it despaired of success, once it knew that he could count on laudations from provincials.

Now many, if not all, provinces were deeply divided by the mutual rivalries of cities.[89] Πρός τε γὰρ ἀστυγείτονας πᾶσι τὸ ἀντίπαλον καὶ ἐλεύθερον καθίσταται (Thuc. iv 92). Restricted in peace to empty disputes over titles and the like, their animosities could break out into fighting, when civil war in the empire gave the opportunity.[90] Even within the cities *stasis* was often endemic.[91] Rival parties were all too apt to invoke the governor's support | (Plut. 814–15). In the Principate, as in the Republic (nn. 81, 84–5), an unscrupulous governor could curry favour with one city or faction and shield his crimes with the eulogies he thus procured. Dio Chrysostom reminded the people of Nicomedia, as a matter of common knowledge, that their quarrel with Nicaea gave the governors 'tyrannic' power; by pretending to side with one or the other, they were free to wrong all alike (xxxviii 33–7). Similarly he told the Prusans that persistent faction deprived them of strength in dealing with the proconsuls (xlviii 7), and the Nicaeans that rulers were most likely to respect a city where concord reigned (xxxix 4). The withdrawal by the Bithynian *koinon* of charges against Varenus (above) is a mystery; who can say what hidden connexion there may be with his intervention in the *stasis* at Prusa, where he restored the meetings of the assembly (xlviii 1), and perhaps elsewhere? Dio

[89] See generally Plin. *Paneg.* 80, 3; Dio lii 37, 10; *Dig.* i 10, 3; *Agric.* 32, 3; for Asia Dio Chrys. xxxiv 48; *SIG³* 849; Aelius Arist. xxiii Keil *passim*; for Bithynia, Dio Chrys. xxxviii; xl–xli *passim*; for Cilicia, xxxiv 7 ff; for Syria, xxxiv 48 cf. Dio liv 7, 6; for Lycia, Suet. *Claud.* 25; for Sicily, Philostr. *v. Apoll.* v 13, 1; for Egypt, Plut. 380 BC; Juv. xv 33; for Africa, Suet. *Galba* 7; for Italy, *Ann.* xiv 17; *Hist.* ii 21; the.enmity of the Jews and the partly Hellenized peoples in Palestine is well-known. Cf. n. 90.

[90] *Bell. Alex.* 62, 2 (Spain 47 BC); Dio xlvii 31, 2 and App. BC iv 79 (Cilicia and Lycia 43 BC); *Hist.* i 65; iv 67 etc. (Gaul AD 68–70); iv 50 (Africa 69–70); Herodian iii 2–3 and Dio lxxv 14, 3 (Bithynia and Syria, 193); [Philostr. *v. Soph.* 529 (Athens and Megara).]

[91] Plin. *Paneg.* 80, 3; Dio lii 30, 2; [liv 12, 1]; *Dig.* i 10, 3. Plut. *Praec. reip ger. passim* (esp. chs. 19; 32) treats factions as familiar in Greece; cf. Paus. vii 17, 4. See also Dio Chrys. xxxix; xliii; xlv–viii *passim*; Plin. *ep.* x 34; 56; 81; 93; 96, 7 (Bithynia); vi 31, 3 (Ephesus); Philo, *Flacc. passim* (esp. 4) and H. A. Musurillo, *Acts of the Pagan Martyrs*, cf. *Hist.* i 11; Amm. Marc. xxii 16, 15 (Alexandria); Cic. *ad Qu. fr.* i 1, 25; *Ann.* ii 54 (Asia); xii 58 (Rhodes); Dio Chrys. xxxiv 20 (Tarsus); *ILS* 140; *Ann.* xiii 48 and Pompeian *graffiti* (Italy); *ILS* 112 (Narbo). Class struggles and rivalries of great priestly families, as well as religious differences, complicated the problems of Judaea [ch. 13 and Addenda; cf. also Sall., *BJ* 77 (Lepcis Magna); Vell. ii 121, 1 (Vienna).]

Chrysostom himself was accused of complicity with a tyrannic governor, who cannot be identified,[92] and persuading him to torture, banish and execute citizens of Prusa (xliii 11). The possibly corrupt favour Cumanus showed the Samaritans against the Jews did not indeed save him from punishment; at Rome powerful forces worked against him.[93] But some of his successors were more fortunate. The quarrels of Jews and 'Greeks' at Caesarea and the factions among the Jews themselves permitted Felix,[94] Albinus and Florus a harvest of plunder. Florus is said to have finally provoked the Jews to revolt, in order to screen his iniquities (*BJ* ii 282). The history of Judaea happens to be relatively well known; if we had similar evidence from other provinces, we might well find that *mutatis mutandis* like conditions prevailed to some extent. In AD 57 Nero forbade a governor or procurator to give shows in his province; 'nam ante non minus tali largitione quam corripiendis pecuniis subiectos adfligebant, dum quae libidine deli|querant, ambitu propugnant'. What cases occasioned this edict (*Ann.* xiii 31), or how effective it was, we cannot say; it is evidence that officials sought to cover up their offences against the law by ensuring the good-will of a section of their subjects.

It might be enough for them to form connexions of reciprocal advantage with one or two powerful provincials. The patronage of an eminent Roman was useful in municipal politics (Plut. 814C); and Sollemnis was doubtless not the first provincial who earned lucrative employment and high respect at Rome through standing by an ex-governor in danger of prosecution (n. 88). But some provincials, like Plutarch or Dio Chrysostom themselves enjoyed influence with the Roman government, nor were they all men of such estimable character; [it was plausible that] the charlatan prophet, Alexander of Abonuteichos, had such credit with a Roman consular that no governor of Pontus dared attack him, whatever crimes he committed; and such a man could surely have helped a governor to immunity for his own offences.[95] Tacitus speaks of 'praevalidi provincialium et opibus

---

[92] Not necessarily either Bassus or Varenus; we have no right to assume that they were the only oppressive proconsuls in Bithynia during Trajan's early years.

[93] *BJ* ii 232–46; *AJ* xx 118–36 (for Cumanus' corruption 119; 127). Josephus was doubtless better informed than Tacitus, but *Ann.* xii 54 can hardly lack all basis in fact. Conceivably Felix was a domanial procurator under Cumanus, like Herennius Capito (*PIR²* H 103) under Tiberius. He may well have sat on the *consilium*, by whose advice Quadratus sent Cumanus back to Rome for the trial Josephus records. Josephus traces the condemnation of Cumanus to the influence of Agrippa (cf. Musurillo *o.c.* no. IV; *AJ* xx 12) and says that Claudius' friends and freedmen intrigued for his acquittal; but presumably Pallas was against him, and Narcissus, now Pallas' enemy, on his side.

[94] *Hist.* v 9; Josephus, however, records little to his discredit except the murder of the high priest, Jonathan (*AJ* xx 162–4). But note *Acta Apost.* xxiv 26–7.

[95] Lucian, *Alex.* 57 (cf. 30; 48). for Plutarch's Roman friends and *ornamenta consularia* cf. K. Ziegler, *RE* xxi 21–3; 51–8. Dio Chrysostom claimed friendship with Nerva (xlv 2; xliv 12) and

nimiis ad iniurias minorum elati' and instances Claudius Timarchus, who boasted that it rested with him whether proconsuls of Crete should receive thanks from the *koinon*.[96] If this boast was justified, it is plain that by compact with Timarchus a governor could do as he pleased in Crete under Nero. From the first century provincial magnates rose in increasing number to senatorial rank. None was more conspicuous than the Athenian millionaire Herodes Atticus. Violent as he was eloquent, he more than once sustained the accusations of his fellow-citizens. In about 144 he had to answer the charge of defrauding and beating Athenians, even of killing one. Fronto appeared for the prosecution; the young Marcus Aurelius urged him not to press the charges with the vehemence which, however uncongenial to our tastes, was expected of an ancient advocate who acted for his clients with zeal. Herodes was duly acquitted, and Fronto later expressed warm friendship for him. A few years later, Herodes alleged that the brothers Quinctilii as proconsuls of Achaea had once more stirred up the Athenians against him. Yet another charge was preferred against him before Marcus c. 170–174. Consul in 143, he survived all attacks.[97] It seems unlikely that a proconsul who enjoyed his backing had much to fear from other Greeks, whatever he did.

In the Republic provincials often voted honours to a governor while still in office, and a prudent culprit, like Appius Claudius,[98] used his power | to extort them from the people he had despoiled. This abuse persisted under Augustus. In AD 11 he forbade subjects to bestow any honours on a governor in office or for sixty days after his departure; Dio comments that by obtaining such eulogies in advance some governors were securing the opportunity for wrong-doing on a large scale (lvi 25, 6). [We learn from the Pauline *Sententiae* that at the time of their redaction] the provincials themselves who initiated such honours were liable under the *repetundae* law (n. 32). Evidently there could be such collusion between an oppressive governor and oppressive magnates in the province that the latter could be treated as his accomplices. One may doubt if the *SC* was observed.[99] In AD 62 Timarchus' boast led Thrasea Paetus to inveigh against the whole

influence with Trajan (which he perhaps overrated, see Trajan's cold allusion in Plin. *ep.* x 82) and eminent Romans (xlvii 22; xli 7).

[96] *Ann.* xv 20, cf. perhaps *CT* xii 12, 1.

[97] *PIR* ii² C 802 for evidence.

[98] *Fam.* iii 10, 6; cf. n. 32 and the honours voted to Verres when still governor, II *Verr.* ii 114; 144–50; 154. [See also *Flacc.* 36; 100.]

[99] See *Fouilles de Delphes* iii 4, 71 n. 47; *IGR* iv 1410; 1413 for later honorific decrees apparently passed for a man in office; there must be many more, cf. the honours bestowed on men who merited prosecution, *IGR* iii 553 (Eprius Marcellus); *AE* 1934, 90 (Lucilius Capito?); *IGR* i 139 (Cadius Rufus?): 972; 995 (Suillius); *AE* 1939, 294 (Bassus).

practice of *concilia* voting thanks to governors. He argued that it was invidious that senators should have to fawn on provincials. This argument hardly wins our sympathy, but perhaps it was a clever appeal to senatorial pride in the interest of true reform. Thrasea was an upright man, who helped the Cilicians to convict a dishonest legate (*Ann.* xvi 21), and was perhaps provoked more by the injuries Timarchus did to his own people than by his arrogance. He was careful not to limit the subjects' right to claim redress, and the real gravamen of his speech may be found in the attack on 'laus *falsa* et precibus expressa', and on the crimes that might be committed by collusion with the local magnates. As a result of his initiative Nero approved a *SC* which totally prohibited votes of thanks in a *concilium* or embassies to convey them to Rome (*Ann.* xv 20–2). It is not recorded that a like restriction was imposed on individual cities, though that would have been logical. Certainly cities, if not *concilia*, continued to pass honorific decrees for officials, of which countless specimens survive, and Pliny went so far as to say that, if the provinces found that such expressions of gratitude for good service furthered a man's career, there would be no more need for prosecutions.[100] At first sight this observation seems so just that the wisdom of Thrasea's measure might be questioned. Yet it was passed by the senate, to whom, as the Mantineans recognized under Augustus (*SIG*[3] 783), an embassy that brought encomia was more welcome than one that came to accuse. The truth must be that the senate could not deny that encomia too often bore no relation to the facts. Some were merely procured by a league between the governor and some faction.[101] Moreover prosecution, as we shall see, was difficult and dangerous, and provincials who would not risk it might feel that their next best course was to flatter a man who could person|ally oppress them no more, but who as a member of the senate might render them services at Rome.

Thus, despite the institution of *concilia*, there was small likelihood that a province would combine to seek retribution from an unjust official; the marvel is that united action was sometimes achieved.

The prosecutors had to indict a senator before the senate. Dio Chrysostom reminded the Tarsians that they could prosecute their former governors, the legates of Cilicia, only before a court of governors, apt to suspect them of acting simply out of restiveness with Roman rule (xxxiv 9). It was indeed notorious that the senate, with

---

[100] *Paneg.* 70; this does not necessarily refer to *laudationes* by a *concilium*, nor prove the obsolescence of Paetus' *SC*, though I doubt if it remained in force. Cf. n. 88. [See now J. Nicols, *Chiron* 1979, 245 ff., also on rules against cities making a governor patron, which may not have been observed.]

[101] Plut. 794 A; 808 C expresses contradictory opinions on laudatory embassies. Cf. *HA Al. Sev.* 22, 6: 'Praesides provinciarum, quos vere non factionibus laudari comperit . . .'

rare exceptions, was partial to its own members, and not only for the tactful reason Dio gave. Under Trajan the people of Vicetia objected to the request of a man of praetorian rank that he should be allowed to establish *nundinae* on his estate. Their advocate failed to appear, and later confessed that he had been terrified by the warnings of his friends not to enter into a contest with a senator 'quasi de gratia, fama, dignitate ... *praesertim in senatu*' (Plin. *ep.* v 13 cf. 4). In a case of *repetundae* the 'dignitas' of a senatorial defendant was much more clearly at stake. Pliny found it hard to speak against Marius Priscus at his second trial; despite the transparency of his guilt and the atrocity of his crimes, the sympathy of the senate was engaged for its old fellow member, already deprived of his status (ii 11, 12–13). It was easier to plead against Classicus, because he was dead, 'amotumque erat, quod in eius modi causis solet esse tristissimum, periculum senatoris'.[102] The personal quality of the defendant counted for something; the court was swayed by 'vel amor vel odium rei' (v 20, 3). The high birth of Bassus and his sufferings under Domitian (iv 9, 1–4) outweighed the evidence and the law. By contrast, it was a grateful duty to punish the *delator*, Tarquitius Priscus (*Ann.* xiv 46) and probably Baebius Massa. Yet in 97 the senate had the reputation of clemency even to *delatores*, if they were senators (Plin. *ep.* ix 13, 21), and in 69 Vibius Crispus, though hated as a *delator* himself, obtained vengeance on the accuser of his brother, who had been justly, but leniently, sentenced for *repetundae* under Nero (App. I no. 30); indeed only Vibius' unpopularity saved the accuser from being condemned unheard (*Hist.* ii 10).[103]

The provincials could be heard through their own deputies. All the eloquence of Asia was arrayed against Silanus (*Ann.* iii 67); the Bithynians, Theophanes, 'fax accusationis et origo' (Plin. *ep.* iv 9, 3) and Fonteius Magnus (*ib.* v 20, 4; vii 6, 2; 10, 1) showed in prosecuting Bassus and Varenus that such deputies were sure to press charges to the uttermost. But Asian oratory was frigid and displeasing to a Roman ear (*ib.* v 20, 4). Worse still, it was the height of impudence for a Greekling and a subject to answer a Roman and a consular (*ib.* iv 9, 14). Less civilized provincials clearly needed the help of practised advocates. All were entitled to receive them. They were appointed by the | senate,[104]

---

[102] *ep.* iii 4, 7.

[103] [In general it was only delators of relatively low standing, like Norbanus (p. 86), who suffered retribution on the fall of emperors regarded as tyrannical, cf. ch. 2, n. 84.]

[104] Plin. *ep.* ii 11, 2 and 19; iii 4, 5; vii 33, 4; x 3 a. Under the *SC Calvisianum* v. 102 the magistrate initiating the process appoints *patroni* (of the prosecution's choice) for the formal proceedings in the senate. Serrao (*o.c.* in n. 19, p. 193) doubts if they appeared before the *iudices* and then naturally finds it hard to explain why they were needed at all. His doubts are unreasonable. A much more complex document would have been necessary to regulate the procedure, unless it had remained unchanged, except where expressly modified. Hence the prosecutors retained the (indispensable) services of *patroni* in the trial; what is new is the appointment of *patroni* for a session of the senate which is no part of the trial.

but [as under the Gracchan law] the provincials might designate the counsel of their choice,[105] men perhaps bound to them be ties of birth or past connexions,[106] and senators could decline only if they had a legal right to exemption.[107] They took their instructions from the provincial prosecutors (*ib.* iii 9, 35). It was clearly a hard and irksome task. True, Pliny appeared thrice for the prosecution and only twice for the defence, and since he was not unmindful of the fame to be won in such causes (vi 29, 3)—he even recited his speech against Marius Priscus (ii 19)—it might seem that there had been a change since Cicero held that the greatest glory was to be obtained by counsel for the defence.[108] The impression is illusory. Pliny's first brief was against a man the senate hated, Baebius Massa; for undertaking other prosecutions, he could exculpate himself by the bidding of the senate, and various excuses;[109] he gladly graduated to advocacy of defendants. In his day, it must be granted, the senate appointed competent patrons for provincials, though the later pre-eminence in reputation of Tacitus and Pliny (*ep.* ix 23) must not make us think that they were leaders of the bar when they acted against Marius; his counsel, Catius Fronto and Salvius Liberalis, were eloquent orators and men of greater age and standing, who could exert on their client's behalf more of that *auctoritas* which Hortensius and later Cicero himself abused in their forensic speeches.[110] Much depended on the *fides* of the patron (*ep.* ii 11, 2; vii 33, 7); Pliny earned the trust of the Baeticans (iii 4, 4)—as perhaps other orators did not—and Herennius was charged with showing more zeal than his *fides* required (vii 33, 7), more indeed than seems to have been customary (p. 70).

The prosecution had first to demand an *inquisitio*, [without which it might be unable to prove its case. Already under the *lex Cornelia*, this entitled it to impound documents, with sanctions against refusal to produce them (e.g. II *Verr.* ii 182; iv 36, 149). But though this right was conferred by law (Pliny, *ep.* vi 5, 2)], the court might | refuse it (*Ann.* xiii 52), or grant it only after argument (*ep.* vi 29, 8). It was only after debate that the senate authorized inquiry into Marius' more serious crimes (ii 11, 2–7). The law did not allow defendants to compel their witnesses to attend, but the senate gave Varenus this right. That was

---

[105] Plin. *ep.* iii 4, 2; v 20, 1; x 3 a; *SC Calvisianum* (cf. n. 104).

[106] Plin. *ep.* vii 33, 5 (birth); i 7, 2; iii 4, 4–5 on his own 'patrocini foedus' with Baetica.

[107] Plin. *ep.* i 7; iii 4; x 3a; *SC Calvisianum* (in n. 104).

[108] E.g. *de off.* ii 49–51 (cf. the sophistry in *Div. in Caec.* 5); for accusation being honourable for revenge cf. Plin. *ep.* ix 13, 2.

[109] *ep.* iii 4 and nn. 105–7.

[110] E.g. II *Verr.* v 175; *Mur.* 59; 86 etc. On the orators in trials Pliny records see R. Syme, *Tacitus* (Oxford 1958) ii 668–9. In the Bassus trial Pomponius Rufus (for the prosecution) was perhaps the senior counsel. But the only named Roman advocate for the Bithynians against Varenus, Nigrinus, was of tribunician rank and appeared against two consulars.

equitable (as Pliny says), but equity is not usually observable in the senate's proceedings. The true motive was surely partiality to a senator. The *inquisitio* for grave charges could take a year (*Ann.* xiii 43). The slowness of the procedure, which the *SC Calvisianum* was designed to abate, continued. The trial of Caesius Cordus was not decided for a year (App. I no. 5). Marius Priscus and Caecilius Classicus were proconsuls at the same time (*ep.* iii 9, 2), not later than AD 97–8; Pliny undertook the former case in 98, the second somewhat later (iii 4, 8); yet Marius' first trial belongs to 99, the second to January 100, and the Classicus case came on perhaps only in 101.[111]

The senate evinced its partiality also in the lightness of the penalties it sometimes imposed (*supra*), occasionally in unjust acquittals; at least Tacitus castigates the acquittal of Eprius Marcellus,[112] and Pliny, while regarding the guilt of Classicus' widow as unproven, remarks on the inconsistency of pronouncing her not guilty after punishing her provincial and odious accuser for *praevaricatio* (*ep.* iii 9, 19 and 34). Emperors too might distort the course of justice. Nero prevented the condemnation of the infamous Celer (App. I no. 23) and procured the acquittal of two proconsuls (*ib.* nos. 26–7); of these Pompeius Silvanus escaped 'pecuniosa orbitate et senecta, quam ultra vitam eorum produxit, quorum ambitu evaserat'.[113] Thus, despite Tacitus' own earlier testimony (*Ann.* i 2), 'ambitus' and 'pecunia' had not been eliminated from the courts. Claudius, if we may believe a rather absurd story, had turned a deaf ear to complaints against a Bithynian procurator (App. I no. 19); and in his reign, we are told, pardons or punishments went by the profit or caprice of the freedmen, while Vespasian sold acquittals to guilty and innocent alike.[114] Perhaps Herodes escaped because of the influence of the young Marcus (p. 81). If Emperors at other times manifested hostility to defendants, that may have been due less to a rigorous respect for the law than to political or private motives. Tiberius left Silanus little ground for hope (*Ann.* iii 67)—and two at least of his accusers | were creatures of Sejanus.[115] [Silius is held to have been another of his victims.] Few charges of *repetundae* were preferred (it is said) against Statilius Taurus,

---

[111] [See now Sherwin-White, *Letters of Pliny*, 56 ff., with conjectural explanations of the delays.]

[112] *Ann.* xiii 33. Tacitus' dislike of Eprius (which commends him to perverse modern critics) need not discount his testimony; no doubt he had fuller information than he gives (e.g. from the *acta senatus*); and his judgement on Silius (cf. p. 76 above) is impartial. Eprius' promotion by Vespasian is no proof of his good character or ability, any more than those of Caesennius Paetus (*PIR²* c 173) or Pompeius Silvanus (n. 113); and there must be some basis for *Hist.* ii 95, 3. *Hist.* ii 84; *Agr.* 19 should disturb Vespasian's admirers, cf. n. 114. For Tacitus' impartiality note also *Ann.* vi 32, 4.

[113] *Ann.* xiii 52; he lived to be legate of Dalmatia in 69, *cur. aqu.* 71–3; *cos.* II 74; cf. n. 112.

[114] Suet. *Cl.* 29, 1; *Vesp.* 16, 2; *Tit.* 7.

[115] *Ann.* iii 66 (Junius Otho); Juv. x 83 (Bruttedius).

but Agrippina coveted his gardens (App. I no. 18). The course a trial took often depended, whatever the issue, on factors wholly irrelevant to the conduct of the accused in his province.[116]

Thus prosecution often resulted in unjustified acquittals or in penalties unduly light or soon remitted, of little deterrent force;[117] at worst, it was dangerous. Epictetus suggested that a proconsul of Achaea, with powerful friends at Rome, could plunder with impunity; the Greeks would not dare bring charges (iii 7, 10–13). Provincials had to weigh the chance that some friend of the accused might be his successor. Their delegates incurred more immediate risks. Some of Eprius' accusers were banished 'tamquam insonti periculum fecissent' (n. 112). Norbanus suffered the same fate in the Classicus trial, because he had imperilled a consular under Domitian, and his colleagues whom Pliny thought excellent men barely escaped (*ep.* iii 9, 29–33; 36). The majority of the senate would gladly have punished Bassus' accuser, Theophanes (*ep.* iv 9, 20–1). Even senatorial *patroni* were not safe. Thrasea assisted the accusers of Cossutianus Capito, and Capito later encompassed his ruin; Herennius Senecio's zeal against Baebius Massa led to his own downfall (App. 1 nos. 24, 34), and there must have been plausibility at least in Pliny's claims that he too was implicated in Senecio's danger (*ep.* i 7, 2; iii 4, 6). An *eques*, Annius Faustus, was 'destroyed' for proving the guilt of Vibius Secundus (App. I no. 30).

The *koinon* of Asia thought its success in convicting Silanus and Lucilius Capito so remarkable that it voted a temple to Tiberius, Livia and the senate in gratitude (*Ann.* iv 15). If this is proof of a new severity under Tiberius, there can be little truth in Tacitus' estimate of justice in Augustus' reign (i 2). Asia remained 'dives et parata peccantibus', and it is by accident that we learn that under Nero a proconsul 'in omnem avaritiam pronus' escaped the punishment he deserved (*Agric.* 6). Under Trajan the *koinon* voted that in no circumstances would it indict a governor. Dio Chrysostom warned the people of Tarsus by this sad example not to indulge in frequent accusations, even though they had had more than one recent success. They would be taken for 'sycophants' and disloyal subjects. They must not expect their ruler to be a Minos, nor blunt by common use a weapon to be used only in extremity (xxxiv 9: 38–40). In the same spirit Agrippa is made to tell the Jews that their rulers must be appeased by flattery, and that there was nothing like submission to check blows (*BJ* ii 350–2). Subjects who had retained the use of arms and were less conscious than Asians of the hopelessness of revolt sometimes rose in rebellion against prolonged oppression, which would otherwise have been | hidden from us and the

---

[116] Cf. also App. I nn. 1, 4, 9, perhaps 11, 14, 17 (with n. 93), 31, perhaps 34, 39.

[117] Cf. Juv. viii 94 ff: 'sed quid damnatio confert? ... cum Pansa eripiat quidquid tibi Natta reliquit... furor est post omnia perdere naulum'.

ancient sources. Elsewhere men often suffered in silence, and are taken
to have enjoyed the benefits of honest government.

Possibly there were periods in which better standards of administration were maintained. Certainly we cannot generalize from the misgovernment under Nero.[118] Tacitus commends Tiberius in his early
years, and Suetonius Domitian.[119] Since neither author is friendly to
the Emperor praised, we are tempted to accept their judgements, and
to reject the very different picture that Pliny presents of Domitian.[120]
Yet doubts may supervene. The Gallic and Frisian revolts under
Tiberius and what little is known of some of the men he kept so long in
office are dark features we must not overlook. We have to reckon with a
kind of principle of *chiaroscuro* in ancient literary portraiture, expressly
avowed by Philo (*Flacc.* 6–7), and pervading Suetonius' biographies; a
man is first praised, to set his wickedness in higher relief. We must also
ask what evidence lay behind such generalizations. Tacitus and
Suetonius could not go to periodic reports on the condition of the
provinces, compiled after patient inquiry by impartial observers. Nor
could contemporary authorities, whom they might have consulted,
whose testimony could, moreover, have been tainted by adulation.
Provincial eulogies of governors would have been unsure bases for
inference (*supra*). Nor could firm conclusions be drawn from the
relative frequency of convictions for *repetundae*, or the relative infrequency of trials. If within any period trials are rarer, this might be
explained either by the better quality of governors or the reduced
expectation of convictions, and if more trials result in condemnation,
this might be either because the courts or government were more
severe, or because there were more officials whose guilt was so flagrant
that the most partial judges could not acquit them, [or who were
vulnerable for extraneous reasons]. It is no doubt an accident of our
meagre evidence for the reign that we know of only one trial under
Domitian. Yet in fact they may have been few. Suetonius remarks that
since his time many governors had been charged with all manner of
offences. This suggests that he did deduce the excellence of Domitian's
administration from the paucity of recorded prosecutions (cf. p. 489).
The deduction was unsound, whether or not we credit Pliny's insinua-
tion that Domitian neither punished the crimes of his officials nor
rewarded their merits.[121]

[118] See pp. 28 ff.

[119] *Ann.* iv 6; Suet. *Dom.* 8, 2; the flatteries of Vell. ii 126 (critical by implication, but perhaps
not design, of Augustus) and Stat. *Silv.* v 1, 79; Sil. Ital. *Pun.* xiv 685 ff. are not evidence.

[120] *Paneg.* 17; 20 (cf. n. 56); 29, 4 and 41, 1 (cf. *AE* 1956, 90; *Dig.* l 4, 6, 5; *Germ.* 29, 1; *Ann.* iv 6
for extraordinary taxes); cf. n. 121 and see the anecdote in Macrob. vii 3, 15. But Domitian
avowed care for the subjects, cf. *SEG* xvii 755 = McCrum and Woodhead, *Select Documents of . . . the
Flavian Emperors* 466, see nn. 130, 132.

[121] *Paneg.* 14, 5; 44–5; 70; *cp.* v 14, 6; viii 14, 7, cf. *Agric.* 1, 4.

In truth the most conscientious Emperors could hardly maintain generally high standards of administration. Augustus reformed the state: he could not reform society. Public morality remained what it had been under the Republic. | To say nothing of laments by contemporary observers,[122] the prevalence of dishonesty among officials is best proved by the frequency with which individuals are lauded in literature and inscriptions for their 'innocentia' or 'abstinentia' or the like. No one will believe that all these eulogies were deserved; Pallas, for instance, did not make his millions by scrupulous integrity. But the servility of the senatorial decree commending him for virtues he did not possess is not its most significant feature; rather it is the fact that it was thought proper to praise him at all merely for keeping his fingers off the public funds.[123] To-day we would not think this worth mentioning of a Secretary of the Treasury; we take the honesty of an individual public servant for granted, because we believe honesty to be the mark of his class. This was not always so: in 17th-century England, for instance, men were held up to admiration as incorruptible, precisely because corruption was then common in public life. In the Roman Empire, as under the Republic, there were of course many upright men in high posts at all times, yet corruption was rampant. In the cities it led to ever increasing control by the state, which was probably ineffective as the controllers themselves did not come from a milieu in which sounder standards prevailed; indeed the cities were the seminary from which higher officials were drawn. In the imperial service offices were bought and sold (n. 68). A procuratorial career was viewed as a short path to wealth (*Ann.* xvi 17). Not to mention powerful imperial freedmen, the slaves of Caesar acquired riches, which can hardly have been accumulated by savings from their salaries.[124] Even in the army soldiers had to buy 'vacationes' from centurions, and the only remedy the government could find was to pay the bribes out of the treasury.[125] Indeed, corruption sometimes extended to the courts, even with the Emperor as judge.[126]

In such conditions many old abuses persisted, and new ones arose. Flavian officials in Britain adopted with impunity modes of enrichment Verres had practised.[127] Publicans were as extortionate and uncontrol-

---

[122] E.g. Sen. *de benef.* i 9–10; *Ann.* iii 34, 3.

[123] Plin. ep. viii 6, 7: 'abstinentissimi fidelissimique custodis principalium opum'; cf. *ILS* 1403: 'ob innocentiam iustitiamque eius *singularem*'.and many similar testimonies. According to Juvenal i 74 'probitas laudatur et alget'.

[124] *CIL* viii 12314; *ILS* 1514; Plin. *NH* vii 129; xxxiii 145.

[125] *Ann.* i 17, 4; *Hist.* i 46; 58.

[126] Cf. nn. 113–14; Petron. 14 [Cf. J. M. Kelly, *Roman Litigation*, chapters II and V].

[127] *Agric.* 19 cf. ii *Verr.* iii 190–2; Marquardt, *StV* ii² 103, 1 gives later parallels to which add *CT* xi 1, 21–22.

lable as ever,[128] save that their field of activity was reduced. Other methods of collecting direct taxes were now more common, but they might involve brutality that is more amply attested in the fourth century.[129] Officials multiplied, but both Clau|dius and Domitian confessed the impotence of the government to restrain their wickedness.[130] Laws could more readily be passed than enforced,[131] 'quid leges sine moribus vanae proficiunt?'. Of these matters, it is true, we know relatively little. This is an accident of our evidence. In Egypt papyri give us plentiful information of official abuses; it is optimistic to assume that the misery and injustice they attest were mainly confined to that province. For the empire at large we have no equivalent in the first century AD, and still less in the second, to Cicero's speeches or the Theodosian Code. But we must not neglect hints in our meagre material of malpractices that are more clearly revealed in this earlier and later evidence.[132] It is often said that Tacitus and our other authorities for the Principate tell us little of the state of the empire. But they tell more than those can see who look for a historical commentary on Aristides' Panegyric. Tacitus had no illusions about the character of Roman rule. Even the invented rhetoric of Calgacus' speech (*Agr.* 30–2), which naturally does not represent his own final judgement, may have as much truth in it as the effusions an Asian orator produced to flatter his Roman masters. It is certainly unwarranted to ignore or reject plain statements that revolts were provoked by misgovernment.

We may grant that the Principate made some improvements in the standard of administration. And it was of course of great benefit for all that peace was maintained, and for the local ruling classes that they were gradually admitted to parity with the old Romans. But there was also deterioration. Rome tried to govern more and more, and slowly extinguished what remnants of liberty were left to her subjects. Hence the increase of the bureaucracy, sometimes justified in the name of efficiency. There was little efficiency in the late empire, when the process was consummated. The government could not control its own agents. 'Quis custodiet ipsos custodes?' might be a motto for the Theodosian Code. Given the prevalence of corruption at all times, can it ever have been of benefit to the subjects that the central government extended its own responsibilities? |

---

[128] *Ann.* xiii 50–1; *Dig.* xxxix 4 *passim*; *Cl. Phil.* xxxi, 146 ff.

[129] *Ann.* iv 6, 4 [implies that this was familiar except in Tiberius' early years; the exception may be doubted, cf. ch. II n. 62.]

[130] *ILS* 214; *SEG* xvii 755 (n. 120), cf. n. 132.

[131] See nn. 5; 9; 12; 46; *Ann.* xi 7 cf. xiii 5; Plin. *ep.* v 13; Suet. *Dom.* 9, 3; *Hist.* i 22; and much else. [Egypt: see e.g. V. Chalon. *L'Édit de Tib. Julius Alexander.*]

[132] [See e.g. the scattered evidence from the Principate on abuses in the so-called *cursus publicus* collected by S. Mitchell, *JRS* 1976, 106 ff., to be compared with *CTh* viii 5.]

APPENDIXES

I. List of attested cases from Augustus to Trajan.

(Officials appointed by the Princeps in capitals)

Date	Province	Name & Sources	Office	Charge	Result of Trial
1. 26 BC	Egypt	Cornelius Gallus (Dio liii 23–4; Suet. *Aug.* 66; cf. *PIR²* c1369	PREFECT	*Maiestas & Repetundae*(?) [Cf. p. 499.]	Suicide before trial; confiscation proposed.
AD					
2. 12	Asia	Volesus Messala (*Ann.* iii 68; Sen. *de ira* ii 5, 5)	Proconsul	*Repetundae* (saevitia) *? maiestas*	Condemned; punished like no. 6
3. 15	Bithynia	Granius Marcellus (*Ann.* i 74)	Proconsul	*Maiestas Repetundae*	Acquitted. Not known.
4. 19	(a) Tarraco- nensis	Cn. Piso (*Ann.* iii 13; cf. E. Koester- mann, *Historia* vii (1958) 336)	LEGATE	*Repetundae*	Suicide before sentence; the posthumous penalty of confiscation was remitted. (The charges under (a) were not important;
	(b) Syria	Cn. Piso (cf. *Ann.* iii 10 ff)	LEGATE	*Maiestas* etc.	those under (b) included true counts of misgovernment, cf. *Ann.* ii 55, 5; iii 13, 2; 14, 1, Koester- mann, *o.c.* 341, 368, but were not the real grava- men of the case against Piso.

Date	Province	Name & Sources	Office	Charge	Result of Trial
5. 21–2	Crete/Cyrene	Caesius Cordus (*Ann.* iii 38, 70)	Proconsul	*Maiestas* *Repetundae*	Acquitted. Convicted; penalty not known.
6. 22	Asia	C. Silanus (*Ann.* iii 66–9)	Proconsul	*Maiestas* and *Repetundae* (*saevitia*)	Convicted; *aquae et ignis interdictio* = 'relegation' to island with partial confiscation.
7. 23	Baetica	Vibius Serenus (*Ann.* iv 13; 28–30	Proconsul	*Vis Publica*	Condemned. 'Deported' to island. |
8. 23	Asia	Lucilius Capito (*Ann.* iv 15)	PROCURA-TOR	*Vis Publica*(?)	Convicted. Penalty unknown.
9. 24	Upper Germany	C. Silius (*Ann.* iv 19–20; Vell. ii 130)	LEGATE	*Maiestas*	Suicide before sentence; posthumous confiscation.
				Repetundae	? (No claims for compensation; yet guilt manifest.)
10. 25	Asia	Fonteius Capito (*Ann.* iv 36)	Proconsul	?	Acquitted.
11. 34	Moesia	Pomponius Labeo (*Ann.* vi 29; Dio lviii 24)	LEGATE	'Maladministration' & other charges (Tac.); taking bribes (Dio).	Suicide before trial.
12. under Tiberius	Crete/Cyrene	Julius Sabinus and Turdus (Sen. *controv.* ix 4, 19–21)	Comites proconsulis	*Repetundae*(?)	Unknown.

Date	Province	Name & Sources	Office	Charge	Result of Trial
13. under Tiberius		Mela (Plin. *NH* xix 110)	PROCURA-TOR	*Repetundae*(?)	Suicide.
14. 38	Egypt	Avillius Flaccus (Philo, *Flacc.* 125–7; 147–51; 181–5)	PREFECT	Charges preferred by Alexandrines	Convicted; deportation to island and confiscation; executed later by Gaius.
15. 44	Baetica	Umbonius Silo (Dio lx 24)	Proconsul	*Maiestas*(?) (hardly *repetundae*)	Convicted; expelled from senate.
16. 49	Bithynia	Cadius Rufus (*Ann.* xii 22; *Hist.* i 77)	Proconsul	*Repetundae*	Convicted; *infamia*; restored in 69.
17. 52	Judaea	Ventidius Cumanus (Jos. *AJ* xx 134–6)	PROCURA-TOR	Charges brought by Jews.	Convicted; 'exile'.
18. 53	Africa	Statilius Taurus (*Ann.* xii 59)	Proconsul	*Maiestas Repetundae* (the charge was frivolous)	Suicide before sentence.
19. c.52	Bithynia	Junius Cilo (Dio lx 33, 6)	PROCURA-TOR	*Repetundae*	Acquitted.
20. under Claudius	Asia or Africa(?)	Lurius Varus (*Ann.* xiii 32 cf. Suet. *Otho* 2)	Proconsul (?)	*Repetundae*	Convicted; *infamia*; restored under Nero.
21. 56	Crete/Cyrene	Cestius Proculus (*Ann.* xiii 30)	Proconsul	*Repetundae*	Acquitted.	
22. 56	Sardinia	Vipsanius Laenas (*Ann.* xiii 30)	PROCURA-TOR	*Repetundae*	Convicted; penalty unknown.
23. 57	Asia	P. Celer (*Ann.* xiii 33)	PROCURA-TOR	Charges brought by province	Guilty, but Nero protracted trial till death.
24. 57	Cilicia	Cossutianus Capito (*Ann.* xiii 33; xiv 48; xvi 21)	LEGATE	*Repetundae*	Convicted; *infamia*; restored by 62.

Date	Province	Name & Sources	Office	Charge	Result of Trial
25. 57	Lycia	Eprius Marcellus (*Ann.* xiii 33)	LEGATE	*Repetundae*	Acquitted (unjustly).
26. 58	Africa	Sulpicius Camerinus (*Ann.* xiii 52)	Proconsul	*Repetundae*(?) (*saevitia*)	Acquitted.
27. 58	Africa	Pompeius Silvanus (*Ann.* xiii 52)	Proconsul	*Repetundae*	Acquitted (unjustly).
28. 59	Crete/Cyrene	Pedius Blaesus (*Ann.* xiv 18; *Hist.* i 77)	Proconsul	*Repetundae*	Convicted; *infamia*; restored in 69.
29. 59	Cyrene	Acilius Strabo (*Ann.* xiv 18)	LEGATE (given special mission by Claudius)	*Repetundae*(?)	Acquitted.
30. 60	Mauretania	Vibius Secundus (*Ann.* xiv 28; *Hist.* ii 10)	PROCURATOR	*Repetundae*	Convicted; banished from Italy.
31. 61	Bithynia	Tarquitius Priscus (*Ann.* xiv 46)	*Proconsul*	*Repetundae*	Convicted; penalty unknown.
32. ?	?	Paquius Scaevinus (*Hist.* i 77)	?	*Repetundae*	Convicted; *infamia*; restored in 69.
33. 70	Crete/Cyrene	Antonius Flamma (*Hist.* iv 45)	Proconsul	*Repetundae* (*saevitia*)	Convicted; 'exile'.
34. 93	Baetica	Baebius Massa (Plin. *ep.* vii 33, cf. i 7, 2; iii 4, 6; vi 29, 8)	Proconsul	*Repetundae*	Convicted; pecuniary penalty.
35. 100	Baetica	*Ignotus* (Plin. *ep.* i 7)	Proconsul(?)	*Repetundae*	Unknown.

Date	Province	Name & Sources	Office	Charge	Result of Trial
36. 100	Africa	Marius Priscus (Plin. *ep.* ii 11 cf. ii 19; vi 29, 9)	Proconsul	*Repetundae* (*saevitia*)	Two trials; the first led to conviction with *infamia*; the second to payment of (further) compensation and 'relegation' from Rome and Italy.	
37. 100	Africa	Hostilius Firminus (*Ib.* ii 11, 23–4; ii 12)	Legate of proconsul	*Repetundae* (*saevitia*)	Convicted; no *infamia*; barred from future proconsulship.
38. 100	Baetica	Caecilius Classicus and accomplices (Plin. *ep.* iii 9 cf. iii 4; vi 29, 8)	Proconsul	*Repetundae* (violence)	Died before trial (suicide?) but posthumously condemned; compensation granted to provincials; accomplices 'relegated' for periods.
39. 102	Bithynia	Julius Bassus (*Ib.* iv 9; vi 29, 10)	Proconsul	*Repetundae*	Convicted; no *infamia*; pecuniary penalty.
40. 106	Bithynia	Varenus Rufus (*Ib.* v 20; vi 5; 13; 29, 11; vii 6; 10)	Proconsul	*Repetundae*	Unknown.
41. c. 107	Egypt	C. Vibius Maximus	PREFECT	?	Convicted (see ch. 10 n. 13).

II. Analysis of attested cased by reigns.

Figures in brackets relate to persons appointed by the Princeps.

Suicides appear under 'condemnations'.

	Condemnations	Acquittals	Unknown	Total
Augustus	2 (1)	—	—	2 (1)
Tiberius (a)	8 (5)	1 (0)	2 (0)	11 (5)
Gaius	1 (1)	—	—	1 (1)
Claudius (b)	5 (1-2)	1 (1)	—	6 (1-2)
Nero (c)	6 (3-4)	5 (2)	1 (1) (d)	12 (6-7)
Vespasian	1 (0)	—	—	1 (0)
Domitian	1 (0)	—	—	1 (0)
Trajan	7 (1)	—	2 (0)	7 (0)
Totals	28 (12-14)	7 (3)	5 (1)	41 (15-17)

Notes. (a) including Piso. (b) including Lurius Varus.

(c) including Paquius Scaevinus. (d) Celer.

III. Analysis of attested cases by provinces.

There are 7 known cases from Bithynia, 5 from Asia, Baetica, Crete with Cyrene, and Africa, 3 from Egypt; Upper Germany, Moesia, Lycia, Syria, Judaea, Sardinia and Mauretania figure once each. There were of course even in this period cases not known to us by name (cf. Dio Chrys. xxxiv 9; 38–40).

5

Augustan Imperialism

HANS D. MEYER, *DIE AUSSENPOLITIK DES AUGUS-TUS UND DIE AUGUSTEISCHE DICHTUNG* (Kölner Historische Abhandlungen, Bd. 5). Cologne: Böhlau Verlag, 1961. Pp. 108.

In a brief introduction the author maintains that Augustus broke with the tradition of the late Republic and adopted a fundamentally defensive policy, making annexations only when it seemed necessary for security, to round off frontiers. He then systematically reviews the allusions to foreign policy in the poets. He assumes that all were supporters of the regime and representative of public opinion. Yet before 20 B.C. all had envisaged far-flung conquests, especially of Britain and Parthia, and had supposed that Augustus would fulfil Rome's mission to exercise dominion without limit in space or time. The Parthian settlement in that year should have undeceived them. But Propertius (IV 6, 79 ff., cf. p. 79) could not accept it as permanent, and Horace chose to misconceive it as an extension of Roman authority over Parthia (*infra*). Horace's tone does indeed somewhat change. He no longer predicts great conquests, because he regards all the peoples of the world as already subject to Roman *maiestas*, cf. *Odes* IV, 14, 5 and 41 ff.; 15, 21 ff. This view re-appears in Ovid (p. 98, n. 24) and foreshadows the unrealistic later panegyrics of emperors as world-rulers. (Meyer might here have cited the prescript to the *Res Gestae*). Horace is also now more prone to stress the role of Augustus in guaranteeing Rome's security (IV 5; 15, 17 ff.; cf. *ep.* II 1 ff.), while Ovid prefers to celebrate *pax* as *otium*, a condition in which wars have simply ceased (pp. 89 ff.).

A few words first on Meyer's interpretations of Horace's later poems and of Ovid. I cannot follow him in attaching significance to Horace's ostensible refusal to commemorate the victory over the Sygambri in a Pindaric ode (IV 2); as often in the past, he contrives under the guise of a *recusatio* to honour the victor in the most striking way. Again in IV, 4, though there is no express allusion to future conquests, the idea is surely implicit that Rome will go on invincibly from triumph to triumph. The *tutela* theme is not wholly new (cf. *Odes* iii 14, 14 ff.; *Georg.* 1 498 ff.). As for the conception that Roman authority is already world-wide, it is at least closely akin to the proleptic celebrations of Augustus' victories in e.g. *Georg.* iii 25 ff. (on which cf. Meyer 22 ff.), and it was given colour by the interpretation which Augustus himself chose to put on his diplomatic successes, cf. *infra*. It was not at all incompatible with recognizing the need to enforce Roman authority by arms, wherever that authority might be neglected.

Ovid, as Meyer has to admit, predicts great eastern conquests in 2 b.c. quite in the old style (*AA* i, 171 ff.). Moreover (*contra* Meyer 87 ff.) the prophecy of world-rule in *Met.* xv, 829 ff. is reminiscent of that in Jupiter's speech in *Aen.* i, 278 ff. In the *Fasti* Ovid certainly tends to glorify peace rather than the warlike process of pacification (though I do not agree with Meyer that ii, 18 can be cited to illustrate this). Ovid envisages Rome as fighting only defensive wars (i, 715; v, 555 ff.). But in their own estimation the Romans had never fought without a 'iusta causa' (Cic. *de off.* i, 35 ff.), a practice of which Augustus himself boasted (*RG* 26, cf. Suet. *Aug.* 21). Yet, even if Lactantius is too cynical on the use of the fetials (*Div. Inst.* vi, 9, 4: 'legitime iniurias faciendo'), it is naïve to take such claims as invariably sound. When expansion was desired, pretexts were always to hand. And Cicero, in asserting the claim, had recognized glory and empire as reasonable motives for war (*de off.* i, 38, cf. *de imp. Cn. Pomp.* 6; *Phil.* viii, 12). Ovid prays that any land which did not fear Rome may come to love her (*Fasti* i, 718). This seems to exclude universal conquest, but an isolated text cannot be pressed. In any event he revised the *Fasti* in exile, and in these years, when his later poems were also composed, the government had abandoned hopes of further expansion; this may have influenced his attitude, though even now he hopes for and predicts the conquest of Germany (pp. 99 ff.).

Since Meyer does not think that any of the poets were deliberate opponents of Augustus, he seeks, quite rightly, to explain the contradiction between their ideals and the policy that he ascribes to Augustus. He argues, particularly in the last chapter, that Virgil and Horace expected Augustus as *restitutor rei publicae* to fulfil Republican ambitions abroad. They also suggested that by conquering the world he would manifest his divinity in his own lifetime. Augustus could not clear away their misunderstanding of his foreign policy, because it was linked so closely with those ideas of the Principate and of his own charismatic position which he desired men to accept. Ovid, representing a younger generation, no longer believed in the restoration of the Republic—and less politically conscious than his predecessors, he wished only to 'be a member of the country's peace' and to enjoy it. His ideas therefore came closer to the Emperor's, though he too lacked real understanding of his aims.

Meyer's view is then that the earlier poets were the heirs of Republican aspirations and the spokesmen of a public opinion which shared those aspirations. But this view requires support in the evidence which he does not give. Perhaps it might not be so easy to find. In the Republic the Senate had sanctioned annexations slowly and reluctantly, nor had prolonged campaigns overseas been popular | with the masses in the second or even in the first century, when conscription was still often necessary and always hateful (R. E. Smith, *Service in the Post-Marian Roman Army*, 46 f.). The victories of Pompey and Caesar brought them, no doubt, prestige, and helped to make good Roman claims to world-rule which Cicero and others (cf. *SEG* I, 335, 19) advanced. In public Cicero was eloquent on Caesar's achievement in Gaul (e.g. *Prov. Cons.* 32 ff., cf. *Fam.* I, 9, 12–14, a letter meant for publication), but his intimate correspondence at the time displays little enthusiasm or even interest in the war, and his later verdict is condemnatory (*de off.* II, 27 f.). H. Strasburger (*Hist. Zeitschr.* 1953, 236 ff.) has given further evidence of senatorial opposition to the Gallic conquest. Crassus' levies for the Parthian war were resisted, and he left Rome amid tribunician imprecations (Dio xxxix, 39). Dio indeed says that Caesar's projected revenge on Parthia was popular (XLIII, 51). It may be so, yet it had been the military leaders, Pompey, Crassus and now Caesar who had desired to emulate Alexander (cf. A. Heuss, *Ant. u. Abendland* IV, 1954, 79 ff.); a good Republican like Cicero was of another mind. When he exhorted Caesar to re-establish the Republic, he had nothing to say of foreign conquests (*Marcell.* 23 ff.), and he soon despaired of giving advice to the new Alexander: 'de Parthico bello quid spectare debui nisi quod illum velle arbitrabar?' (*Att.* XIII, 21, 1). Clearly he did not share Caesar's passion for the subjugation of an eastern empire. No doubt Augustus must have consolidated his authority by setting to rest the rational fears which men entertained that Rome's very survival would be at stake, if civil wars persisted (Hor. *Epod.* VII and XVI; *Odes* III, 6 etc.), and after 27 his victories and annexations will have gratified public opinion and further enhanced his prestige. But it is another matter to hold that public opinion pressed expansion on a reluctant ruler. 'Pacato orbe terrarum, restituta republica, quieta deinde et felicia tempora contigerunt' (*ILS* 8393, 35); the old Republican senator shows the same attachment to *otium* as Ovid. Augustus 'cunctos dulcedine otii pellexit'. The Italians were war-weary. Perhaps no verse is more characteristic of prevailing attitudes than Propertius' 'nullus de nostro sanguine miles erit'. Horace indeed sought to inculcate martial spirit among his upper-class readers (*Odes* III, 2), just as Augustus did by the institution of the *iuventus*, or by trying to give all senators experience in the army (Suet. 38), probably to little effect. It is hard to imagine that either the heirs to senatorial tradition, or the peasantry who might be called on to serve in the army, still harboured a passionate desire to avenge Carrhae, if it entailed prolonged and arduous fighting—was this why Horace assailed thoughts of a compromise in the Regulus Ode?—or that many Romans were really zealous to visit the ends of the earth under a new Alexander (*Odes* III, 3, 53 ff.). Fewer and fewer Italians were prepared to join the legions, especially when conscription ('res perpetui praecipuique timoris', Vell. II, 130, 2) was at last given up in Italy, and even when Augustus applied it in A.D. 6 and 9, he could not replace three legions—from a people who fifty years before had been contributing 200,000 men to Roman armies. [cf. chapter 9.]

But, if it is implausible that the poets represented Republican tradition or clamorous public opinion, for whom did they speak? For themselves, and some kindred spirits? Judgment can only be subjective.

> Vivite felices, quibus est fortuna peracta
> Iam sua: nos alia ex aliis in fata vocamur.
> Vobis parta quies. (*Aen.* III, 493 ff.)

In such words as these some may discern sentiments more natural to Virgil than the glorification of 'lacrimabile bellum'. Again, would it have been impossibly hard for the poet who commends above all 'desiderantem quod satis est' (*Odes* III, 1, 25) to have entered into the views of a statesman who was content with Rome's existing possessions? Can we really suppose that Tibullus, Propertius and Ovid were ever passionate for wars and conquests? But if the poets were bellicose neither under the influence of tradition nor by their own innate spirit, did they not after all speak for Augustus? This would not necessarily mean that they were mere 'squeaking puppets'. Most readers will feel in the most imperialist verses of Virgil and Horace accents no less sincere than in any parts of their work. In Jupiter's prophecy (*Aen.* I, 278 ff.), as earlier in the Messianic Eclogue, universal conquest heralds the unending rule of world peace. This was an ideal which could inspire Virgil and others, even though it came to them no more naturally than devotion to the task of founding a new city in Italy came to Aeneas. Aeneas had to be prompted; similarly the spring of Virgil's or Horace's conceptions of Rome's mission was surely not in their own hearts.

Nonetheless, the assumption is commonly made that nothing could have been further from Augustus' own intentions than any attempt to realize the grandiose ambitions the poets ascribed to him. It is because Meyer not only makes this assumption but faces the difficulties which then arise in interpreting the poets, as few others have done, that his book merits extended discussion.

In examining this assumption we must naturally (like Meyer) disregard the 'consilium coercendi imperii intra terminos' which Augustus bequeathed to Tiberius at the very end of his reign (*Ann.* I, 11; Dio LVI, 33, 5) and which Tiberius sedulously obeyed (*Ann.* I, 3; II, 26; VI, 32; *Agr.* 13). Unlike Tiberius, Augustus had been no 'princeps proferendi imperi incuriosus' (*Ann.* IV, 32); no | one in past history had added more terrritory to Rome's dominions—Egypt, Pannonia, Moesia, Noricum, Raetia. Even in his last decade he had sought to incorporate Bohemia and Germany, at least west of the Elbe. As Nicolaus of Damascus observed (Jacoby 90 F 125, cf. 126), he had enormously enlarged the empire and subdued peoples whose names were hitherto unknown. The frontiers with which he bade Tiberius be content were not those at which he had recently been aiming. Old, tired, and alarmed by the apparent inadequacy of Roman resources (cf. especially Pliny, *NH* VII, 149), he felt obliged to abandon plans which he had pursued for years.

> Per damna, per caedis, ab ipso
> ducit opes animumque ferro.

After the disaster of the Teutoburg Forest it could no longer be said of Rome [that she had lost many battles but no war (Lucilius 613 f. M.; Livy IX 18, 9).] Augustus' long reign ended in a reverse which was treated as irreparable, but from which the principles of his earlier policy cannot be properly inferred.

The final *consilium* may, however, have influenced the opinions of later writers in antiquity. Writing under Hadrian, whose policy was notoriously defensive, Suetonius claims that Augustus was so far 'a cupiditate quoquo modo imperium vel bellicam gloriam augendi' that he would sometimes bind barbarian chiefs to peace merely by oaths or hostages (*Aug.* 21). Yet in the *Res Gestae* we read of his victories throughout the world (3, 1), of the honours they evoked (4, 1), of his extension of every frontier province (26, 1), of his pacification of western Germany and annexation of Egypt and Pannonia (26, 2; 27, 1; 30, 1); his fleet had sailed on the unknown northern sea (26, 4) and his armies had been the first to reach and cross the Danube (30). Meyer concedes that even late in his life, when drafting or revising this memorial, he 'promoted the conception of world-rule inherited from the Republic' by his imperialistic description of his achievements (p.

61). Again in 16 B.C. a coin proclaims that he had put the Republic 'in ampliore et tranquilliore statu' (Ehrenberg-Jones, *Documents* 35). In 2 B.C. the Forum Augusti and the temple of Mars Ultor were at last complete. Augustus had decided in 20 to place the standards recovered from the Parthians in that temple (Dio LIV, 8), and Meyer argues that he thereby divested the god of his function as a war god, since the standards had been recovered peacefully (p. 6). I shall revert later to his interpretation of the settlement of 20, but what happened in 2 B.C. is hardly reconcilable with his view. The Forum on to which the temple opened was adorned with memorials of Augustus' own conquests (Vell. II, 39) and with statues of old triumphators 'qui imperium p. R. ex minimo maximum reddidissent'; Augustus announced in an edict that he had set them there in order that the citizens might require him and *principes* of later generations to follow their example (Suet. 31, cf. Ovid, *Fasti* v, 563 ff.); Cicero's statement that the monuments of such men bore the inscription 'Finis imperii propagavit' (*de rep.* III, 24) is not borne out by the extant *elogia*; nonetheless they breathe a martial, imperial spirit and must have provided a symbolic and visible commentary on the catalogue of heroes in *Aeneid* VI, whose deeds witnessed to Rome's mission 'parcere subiectis et debellare superbos'. If Augustus' edict implied that much was still left to conquer—and it was in the new temple that future triumphs were to be voted and the triumphators to dedicate their sceptre and crown (Dio LV, 10)—we may be reminded of Propertius' suggestion (IV, 6, 79 ff.) that the settlement of 20 B.C. had only postponed the subjugation of the East until the time of Augustus' children. The author of the *Res Gestae* and the builder of these monuments was not oblivious of military glory, and we cannot exclude this as a motive in considering his programme of expansion.

Dio, however, makes Augustus advise the Senate in 27 to 'guard strictly what you have already, and not to seek what is not yours; ... not to injure or fear your enemies' (LIII, 10), and Tiberius is given words praising him for being content with what Rome had acquired of necessity and for refusing to subdue additional territory, when an attempt to do so might have imperilled Rome's existing possessions (LVI, 41, cf. 33; 57). Dio's fictitious speeches have little authority, and Meyer has not cited these texts. But they are good evidence for Dio's own interpretation of Augustan policy. It is what we might expect; as Mr. Fergus Millar has pointed out to me, Dio was always opposed to expansion (cf. LXVIII 7, 5; LXIX 9, 5–6; LXXV 3, 3; II, 1); he would have been very ready to make Augustus, the exemplar for later emperors, more pacific than he really was. This consideration must be kept in mind in weighing another text of Dio, on which Meyer lays great stress (*infra*).

Modern historians are apt to think that after 27 B.C. Augustus' imperial objective was solely to establish the most defensible frontiers, his aim mere security. Thus Meyer holds that in the East Augustus regarded the settlement of 20 B.C. as permanent, and could do so with the more confidence because across the Euphrates he had another civilized state to deal with (p. 9). In the north this was not so; but Augustus was able 'to fix the limits of required expansion with great exactitude'. What these limits were and how he fixed them he does not say. But no doubt he has in mind Tacitus' summary of Augustus' achievement: 'mari Oceano aut amnibus longinquis saeptum imperium' (*Ann.* I, 9). Sir Ronald Syme once argued that he aimed at the line Hamburg–Leipzig–Prague–Vienna (*CAH* x, 351 ff.). Modern maps make this look plausible enough, but they were not at Augustus' | disposal. There is no ancient testimony. Strabo 291 says that he once forbade his generals to cross the Elbe, so as not to unite in a common resistance peoples on both sides of the river. This is no proof of his ultimate intentions, any more than the facts that Drusus did try to cross the Elbe (Dio LV, 1) and that Domitius Ahenobarbus succeeded (ibid. 10; Tac. *Ann.* IV, 44). Dacia lay beyond the frontier designated by Syme, but Strabo 305 asserts that the Dacians had been almost subdued, and only refused complete submission in reliance on German help. What then if the Germans had been reduced? Of course no permanent and secure frontier could ever have been attained; Rome could not expect to enjoy the certainty of peace (as Virgil saw) so long as any potential enemies remained. A chapter title in a recent book on British imperialism (Robinson and Gallagher, *Africa and the Victorians*, 1961) might serve as a motto for each stage of Roman expansion— 'New Frontiers of Insecurity'.

But was security Augustus' sole aim? Certainly not at all times. Aelius Gallus' Arabian expedition was designed for conquest in the pursuit of revenue (Strabo 780). Difficulties forced Augustus to desist, but the enterprise cannot be reconciled with a purely defensive policy.

Meyer's conception of Augustan policy in fact rests on three bases, which may be considered in turn.

(1) *The symbolic closures of Janus* (pp. 3; 29 ff.), which Meyer contrasts with the glorification in *Aen.* VII, 601 ff. of the opening of the temple. (He does not indeed ignore I, 291 ff., but misinterprets it, arguing that Virgil makes it appear that the closure only symbolized the end of civil wars, and not—as Augustus intended—of external fighting too. On this passage *v. supra*.) Dr. Weinstock has shown that the cult of Pax was designed by Caesar and that no idyllic peace was intended (*JRS* L, 47 ff.). Augustus closed the temple to celebrate 'parta victoriis pax' (*RG*

13). The closures do not support the conception of an emperor pacific in the modern sense.

(2) *Britain.* Meyer has taken no account of the important article by C. E. Stevens in *Aspects of Archaeology, Essays presented to O. G. S. Crawford,* (1951), 332 ff. As Stevens shows, Caesar could be held to have made the peoples of S. E. Britain subject. On some he had imposed tribute, and this was certainly not paid in the time of which Strabo wrote under Augustus; the treaty was also broken in other ways. From the Roman standpoint the Britons were in rebellion. This will, I think (differing from Stevens in many details), explain the fact that Augustus was credited with planning invasion in 34, 27 and 26 (Meyer believes in the first plan but not the rest) and that down to 23 (cf. A. Momigliano, *JRS* XL, 39 ff.) the poets assume that he intended to conquer the island. Whatever be the truth about Augustus' alleged plans in this period, I agree with Meyer, following Mommsen, that Strabo 200 preserves an official justification for Augustus' eventual renunciation of armed invasion. The kings had secured his friendship by sending embassies and paying him court and had made offerings on the Capitol; they had virtually made the island Roman; the cost of occupation would absorb the tribute that might be levied, and the value of customs duties on British trade would decline, if tribute were imposed. (In 115–16, not cited by Meyer, Strabo adds that Britain was inaccessible and unaggressive.) To what date does Strabo refer? Stevens rightly rejects Collingwood's view (*Roman Britain and the English Settlements* 2, 73) that the British embassies can be identified with the appearance of Tincommius and Dubnovellaunus as suppliants at Rome (*RG* 32). But I think that he is wrong in supposing that Strabo has in mind embassies from Tincommius' successors after A.D. 7, Epillus and Verica. The legend REX on their coins indicates only a growing degree of Romanization, not that they were the first or only British princes to enter into a relation with Rome which Augustus could regard as one of vassalage. This relation may have subsisted much earlier, with Tincommius, Dubnovellaunus and perhaps other princes; we must not, of course, infer from the fact that only Tincommius had been issuing coins closely imitated from Roman that he alone had had friendly political connections with Rome. The cessation after 23 B.C. at latest of poetic demands for conquest of Britain is significant, and even more emphasis should be placed on Horace, *Odes* IV, 14, 41 ff. than Stevens has done.

Horace there depicts the Britons among a number of peoples as in some sense subject to Rome; the verbs used 'miratur', 'audit' and 'venerantur' all indicate this. The peoples comprise Cantabrians,

Medes, Indians, Scyths, Egyptians, dwellers by the Danube and Tigris, Britons, Gauls, Spaniards, i.e., some who were under provincial government and some who were not. Now of the latter class the Parthians could after 20 be represented as having recognized Roman supremacy (*infra*), and Augustus records in *RG* 31 embassies from Indians, Scyths, Medes etc., who sought 'nostram amicitiam'. Because he does not mention Britons in this place or in 26, 4, it does not follow that he had received no British embassies; the catalogue is obviously incomplete, and his remark in 32: 'plurimaeque aliae gentes expertae sunt p. R. fidem me principe, quibus antea cum populo Romano nullum extiterat legationum et amicitiae commercium' suggests that he was primarily concerned to record new contacts (although the mention of the Albanians, Hiberi and Medes must be noted as an exception): Britons had been nominal vassals of Rome since 54 B.C. The embassies | mentioned by Strabo can well belong, like those named by Augustus, to a time before Horace wrote *Odes* IV, 14. Horace chose to construe their appearance as a token of dependence. By contrast Meyer seems to think that *amicitia* implies equality (pp. 28; 53; 62). But this is not so; in Roman thinking it merges into clientship (E. Badian, *Foreign Clientelae*, II, 111). As Strabo says, the Britons paid court to Augustus and brought gifts. They could be regarded as clients. Augustus treated client states as 'membra partisque imperii' (Suet. *Aug.* 48). There was thus no call for an invasion, and the poets drop the idea. Of course the notion that the British kings were vassals was unrealistic. But it was enough to justify the 'longa oblivio Britanniae', while more urgent tasks had to be carried out. For Tiberius this 'consilium' became a 'praeceptum' only when expansion in *all* directions had been given up.

(3) *Parthia*. The necessity of settling veterans, of remodelling the constitution and of organizing and pacifying Gaul and Spain, whose resources were valuable for any forward moves, are enough to explain why Augustus took no occasion to resume the Parthian war till 20 B.C. And even then he was satisfied with a compromise which restored the standards to Rome and placed Roman nominees on the Armenian and Median thrones. The character of this settlement is the strongest support that Meyer can find for his interpretation of Augustus' policy (4 ff.). But he has misconceived its nature. Armenia was 'capta' or 'recepta' or 'redacta in potestatem populi Romani' (Vell. II 94); it became a client kingdom and therefore a part of the empire, and when the people overthrew the Roman nominee, Augustus could regard them as rebels (*RG* 27). It is simply not true that by making Armenia a client state (whereas Antony had temporarily annexed it) Augustus was aware of accepting a contraction in the Roman sphere of influence. Lucullus and Pompey had done the same, after conquering

the country (cf. *Ann.* XIII, 34), and Augustus could properly claim to be acting traditionally. As a client state, Armenia could be regarded as a part of the empire, left under native rule only for administrative convenience (cf. Strabo 671 on Cilicia Tracheia). In 20 B.C. Augustus could not foresee the persistent recalcitrance of the Armenians, but when confronted with it, he never failed to reimpose the original settlement—at least, when his hands were free to intervene (cf. Strabo 288).

What of Parthia herself? Had Augustus implicitly recognized Parthia as a fully independent power? So Meyer thinks. Yet according to Horace 'ius imperiumque Phraates Caesaris accepit genibus minor' (*ep.* I, 12, 27–8); henceforth the Parthians fear Roman axes and obey Roman edicts (*CS* 54; *Odes* IV, 15, 23). For Meyer this is mere distortion not only of the realities (on which we should agree) but of Augustus' own views. But coins too depict Phraates as kneeling, like the Armenian king (H. Mattingly and E. A. Sydenham, *Rom. Imp. Coinage* I, p. 70) and other subjects or captives (ibid., nos. 175; 226), and Augustus himself says that he *forced* the Parthians to restore the standards and to *supplicate* for Roman *amicitia*, and later that Phraates sent his sons and grandsons to Rome 'amicitiam nostram per liberorum suorum pignora petens' (*RG* 29; 32). [In this sort of context *amicitia* is certainly a designation for vassalage.] Equals do not kneel or supplicate, nor give pledges. Of course Augustus knew that his writ did not run in Parthia. But he could have thought that with Armenia, a valuable *offensive* base (M. Rostovtzeff, *CAH* XI, 106–7) and potential pretenders in his hands, he had placed the Parthian king on the slope from which so many monarchies had descended into complete subjection.

In fact Augustus never had leisure or resources to extend Roman control beyond the Euphrates. But the ideal persisted. In 2 B.C., when trouble recurred in Armenia, Ovid could again prophesy the conquest of Parthia (*AA* I, 171 ff., esp. 202). On this occasion Augustus' other pre-occupations forced him to go further than in 20 in admitting Parthian parity (Vell. II, 101; Strabo 515; *CAH* x, 275–6), when renewing the old compromise settlement. Ovid duly celebrates this settlement as satisfactory, once it has been renewed (*Fasti* v, 580 ff.). Even after this more extravagent claims were not forgotten. It was probably with reference to the Parthian appeal to Rome in A.D. 6, when they asked Augustus to send them Vonones as king, that Strabo remarks καὶ σχεδόν τι πλησίον εἰσι τοῦ ἐπὶ Ῥωμαίοις ποιῆσαι τὴν σύμπασαν ἐξουσίαν (288). And who knows what might have ensued but for Rome's exhaustion in the northern wars? Later still men could speak of Parthian 'reverentiam in nos' or 'de fastigio Romano Parthorumque obsequiis' (Tac. *Ann.* VI, 37; XII, 11).

Against this interpretation of Augustus' hopes Meyer sets the evidence of Dio. Augustus, we are told (LIV 8, 3), treated the settlement of 20 B.C. as equivalent to a victory in war, all the better as there had been no need for fighting. This was natural enough, and does not prove genuine 'pacifism': the most aggressive rulers seldom desire war for its own sake, when they can take the fruits of victory without it. Augustus accepted a triumphal arch; but to celebrate a diplomatic success as a military triumph was hardly (as Meyer thinks) the best way of allaying warlike ambitions. It is more important for Meyer that Dio says that in a despatch to the Senate, which he assumes to be verbally correct (without warrant), Augustus declared that he did not think it necessary to augment the territory of Rome or the number of her client states; Rome was to be content with her existing | possessions (LIV, 9, 1). Meyer contradicts himself by saying that thereafter his pacific intentions could not have been in doubt (p. 51) but also that he never made his principles of foreign policy plain (p. 104). Even on his own theory the second view must be right, or else the poets, Propertius in particular (cf. p. 1) and Ovid in 2 B.C., must have been in open disagreement with the Emperor. But in that case Augustus' despatch must have been less categorical than Dio supposed. At most he may have advised against further annexations in the East for the present. Dio's bias then made his advice much too absolute. In any event we are all too familiar with imperialists who declare that their last demands have been met, only to present new ones. Within a few years Augustus was engaged in large scale offensive operations in the north which alone could explain why he attempted no expansion beyond the Euphrates.

It was natural that expansion should be directed first of all to the north. Here barbarian raids on Roman territory were chronic [cf. Brunt, *Italian Manpower* 98 f.]; they provided pretexts for intervention and also determined the direction in which any imperialist ruler who cared for his subjects' welfare would wish to move first. The Cimbri and Teutones were not yet forgotten. Augustus' alarm at the Pannonian revolt (Vell. II, 110–11), and the apprehensions expressed about Maroboduus (ibid. 109; Tac. *Ann.* II, 63) show that Italy was not yet regarded as safe. To this extent at least Augustus' policy was prompted by the search for security. Yet Velleius, a contemporary, bears witness that Maroboduus displayed no offensive intentions; he merely indicated that he would resist attack, and at times claimed to deal with Rome as an equal (II, 109). To Romans who divided the rest of mankind into 'subiecti' and 'superbi' and saw it as their mission 'debellare superbos' this was in itself an offence. The projected conquest of Bohemia can only be explained by Rome's need for security, if this word is used in a rather odd sense. And Velleius had no illusions that it was the chief motive. He introduces the story of the attack on Maroboduus with the words that there was nothing left to conquer in Germany (sc. west of Elbe) except Maroboduus' kingdom (108, 1), and he explains the abandonment of the project, when the Pannonians rebelled, with the remark: 'tum necessaria *gloriosis* praeposita.' Maroboduus was no real danger; he lent no aid either to the Pannonians or to Arminius and his power was soon destroyed from within.

Before Augustus could move in the north at all, he had had first to safeguard the eastern frontier by the compromise of 20 B.C., and to make other preparations. North Spain was not pacified till 19, the Alpine valleys not before 14. Velleius rightly saw these operations as a sequel to the ending of civil wars (II, 90). Augustus himself twice had to stay for long periods in Gaul, the land which was to be his western base. Noricum was peacefully incorporated in 16–15. The great campaigns of Tiberius and Drusus in 15 only heralded systematic attempts to reduce all the lands up to the Danube–Elbe line, which occupied the rest of his reign, postponed thoughts of conquest in Britain or Parthia and ultimately ended in partial failure. Who can say what might have followed had Augustus been wholly triumphant here?

At the inception of this vast enterprise the prospects must have seemed favourable. Caesar had conquered the Gauls in less than ten years with an army which never exceeded ten legions. The Germans were regarded as a people similar to the Gauls and akin to them (Strabo 196; 290); they should then have seemed equally easy to subdue. The *commentarii* on which Agrippa based his map seem to have given the dimensions of Gaul from west to east (Pyrenees to Rhine, conceived as roughly parallel!) as 920 miles, from north to south (Channel to Cevennes) as 463. Germany with Raetia and Noricum was probably held to measure 636 or 686 miles from Rhine to Vistula, and 388 or 338 from north to south. Now beyond Germany, according to Agrippa, one came successively to Dacia, Sarmatia with Scythica and Taurica, and finally to Armenia and the peoples round the Caspian sea, which was thought to be an inlet of the encircling Ocean. The eastern border of this last area was the Chinese sea; in other words one reached the Ocean in the East. The measurements from north to south were given for the eastern regions as about 400 miles. The total measurement from the Vistula to the Chinese sea was held to be $1,200 + 880$ or $980 + 480 = 2,560$ or $2,660$ miles; from the Rhine about 3,300 miles, or only about $3\frac{1}{2}$ times the distance from west to east across Gaul. (These figures are taken from the plausible reconstruction made by A. Klotz, *Klio* xxi, 386 ff.; there are some uncertainties.) It was rightly thought that all these lands were sparsely inhabited by nomadic peoples, or in part uninhabitable because of the intense cold. Difficulties of terrain and supply in subduing Germany could easily have been underestimated. Of course there were rival guesses about the *terrae incognitae* of the north, but Posidonius and Strabo also thought that the Caspian was an inlet of the ocean, and it was common practice to measure the *orbis* from Gades to the mouth of the Ganges (cf. O. Thomson, *Hist. of Anc. Geography*, 1948, 159 ff.; 211 ff.; 321-2; Pliny, *NH* II, 242-5). Agrippa himself evidently had no notion of the size of the land-mass east of the Rhine. We are not then justified in saying *a priori* that conquest beyond the Elbe was unthinkable.

Agrippa stood closest to Augustus and we must also ask why he chose to set in his portico a map of the whole world. It served no practical purpose. Surely it embodied an official claim or aspiration | to universal rule. Coins too, some issued as late as A.D. 7, represent the figure of Victory standing or sitting on a globe (Mattingly and Sydenham o.c. pp. 62, 90). Augustus' own decision to record among his memorable successes the arrival of embassies from India, and from the Bastarnae, Scyths and Sarmatians, who sought 'our friendship', points the same way, when we remember the nuance of the term *amicitia*; Horace surely preserves the official interpretation in *CS* 53 ff., and *Odes* IV, 14, 41 ff.; 15, 21 ff., even though the silence of Augustus himself must make us regard the allusion to Seres as poetic hyperbole (despite the unreliable Florus II, 34). Augustus' avowed admiration for Alexander is also significant. He paid homage to the great conqueror's mummy; he at one time put Alexander's image on his seal, and he claimed to have received an omen vouchsafed to no one previously except to Alexander (Suet. 18; [cf. Dio LV 16, 5] 50; 94, 5). It can only have been congenial to him when Virgil in *Aen.* VI, 794 ff. (as Norden showed, *Rh. Mus.* LIV 468 ff., cf. commentary on *Aen.* VI, p. 322-3) and Horace (*Odes* III, 3, 53 ff., cf. Kiessling-Heinze[8] *ad loc.*) bestowed upon him eulogies which derived from traditional encomia on Alexander. His taste for military glory is conspicuous, as already noted, in the *Res Gestae* and in the edict justifying his adornment of the Forum Augusti. How can we dare to be so sure as Meyer is that he did not share the ambitions of the poets and did not aim at achieving the perfect security which only conquest of the world would provide, a world much smaller for him than we know it to be?

The notion of course appears too extravagant for those who see in Augustus only a cool, calculating and prudent statesman. But do they see more than half the truth? Suetonius (*Aug.* 25, 4) says that σπεῦδε βραδέως was one of his favourite maxims. This is easily credible. It explains why he deferred, but did not necessarily discard, the romantic aims of conquering Britain, Parthia and India in favour of more urgent enterprises, which were still not at all incompatible with the most far-reaching ambitions. The maxim illustrates his prudence in choice of methods: it tells us nothing about the designs he pursued. The man who had resolved at the age of nineteen to enter into Caesar's heritage and by steady and subtle procedures made himself autocrat of the Empire at the age of thirty-two was not wanting in audacity or largeness of vision. We cannot read his mind, but there are at least some indications in his own words and acts that the contemporary poets whom he honoured understood him better than Suetonius and Dio did, or than we can hope to do, if we impose upon him conceptions which alone seem rational in a very different age.

I wish to thank Mr. Colin Hardie and Mr. A. R. Birley for help; any errors that remain are my own.

[Note. This chapter has been reprinted with only minor changes, but some of the views expressed are modified in chapters 14 and 18.]

6

Reflections on British and Roman Imperialism*

I

In the heyday of British imperialism some fifty years ago, when Lord Cromer could find that the empire was 'the main title which makes us great', imperialists were apt to compare the British with the Roman empire and to seek 'in the history of imperial Rome for any facts or commentaries gleaned from ancient times which might be of service to the modern empire of which we are so justly proud'.[1] A critic of imperialism, J. A. Hobson, sourly remarked of such enterprises that 'history devises reasons why the lessons of past empires do not apply to our own'.[2] *Prima facie*, however, the comparison was encouraging. Both the Romans and modern imperial powers claimed that it was their purpose to govern in the interests of the subjects; both had undoubtedly established peace and order in a large part of the world; both had extended their own law and their own civilization. The Romans, moreover, had in some measure created a genuine sentiment of unity and loyalty among all the peoples of their empire, and when it disintegrated, it was amid the lamentations of at least the most vocal of its inhabitants. In the provinces Rome first acquired her rule lasted for 600 years. Could not Britain expect a like success? Could she not even avoid the errors that had led to Rome's decline?

To the first question events in our lifetime have now given the

---

* I write as a historian of Rome, and for the British empire draw on scattered reading. I exclude from consideration the 'first British empire' and the white Dominions. [The essay appeared in 1965. I have not altered any remarks on modern imperialism in the light of subsequent events, and have only inserted some new references, or up-dated others.]

[1] *Polit. and Lit. Essays*, 5 and 86 (where he is quoting Sir Alfred Lyall, 1835–1911). This paper had its origin in a revaluation of comparisons between British and Roman Imperialism drawn by Cromer (also in his *Anc. and Mod. Imperialism*), Lord Bryce, *The Roman and the British Empires* (in *Stud. in Hist. Jurispr.*) and Sir Charles Lucas, *Greater Rome and Greater Britain*, which all appeared between 1900 and 1914. They discuss points of defence policy and administration ignored here.

[2] *Imperialism*, revised ed. (1938), 221.

Comparative Studies in Society and History, 7/3 (April 1965), 267–88.

answer. Less than 200 years separate Plassey from the grant of independence to India. Everywhere British rule has now ended or is crumbling away. Compared with the Roman dominion, the British was an ephemeral growth.

Comparisons between the two empires were in fact always rather forced: there were more points of contrast than of likeness. The Roman example | probably had little, if any, influence on the pragmatic evolution of British policy, though it doubtless stimulated the French ideal of assimilation. It was rather the experience of modern imperialism that influenced the interpretation of Roman history with false analogies.[3]

The British acquired their earliest possessions for purposes of trade and settlement. In the late nineteenth century they sought to seize territories that were held to be of strategic value for the security of their existing empire; 'in the main British Africa was a gigantic footnote to the Indian empire'.[4] Similar motives were invoked to explain Rome's annexations.[5] The Romans themselves always claimed that their wars were strictly defensive, and from Augustus' death security was certainly the generally dominant key of their policy. But in that age they made few further conquests, and in the great period of expansion preceding it security was not in fact their only object. Thucydides traced Athenian imperialism to three motives, fear, profit and honour, and this analysis holds good for Roman as well. But the profit they sought was not principally that which came from trade or settlement. The trading class was never influential, and outside Italy lands were not annexed to provide Romans with new homes.[6] Rome practised more direct methods of exploitation. Victories brought in booty and, more important, conquered peoples paid tribute. Honour or glory was no less important a motive. Generals were ambitious for triumphs, and the Romans came to believe that they were destined by providence to rule the world [chapters 5 and 14]. Cecil Rhodes entertained not much dissimilar ambitions for Britain, but sober statesmen like Salisbury hardly gave such dreams a thought. It is, however, a mistake to conceive that Caesar or Augustus had the same mentality as Salisbury. (Perhaps the French attached more value to 'la gloire'.) Roman policy cannot be explained by the analogy of British imperialism.

Again it may be that English scholars have unconsciously pictured

[3] So Lucas (n. 1).

[4] *New Cambridge Modern History*, XI, 616, summarizing the contention which the writers, R. Robinson and J. Gallagher, argue at length in *Africa and the Victorians* (1961), esp. 17 ff.; 462 ff.

[5] T. Frank, *Roman Imperialism* (1914), took this too seriously. [See ch. 14.]

[6] [Brunt, *Fall of Rom. Rep.* ch. 3. Some provincial land was eventually allocated to Italian settlers, especially by Caesar, the triumvirs and Augustus.]

Roman administration after the pattern of their own. Sir George Cornwall Lewis said in Parliament in 1858 that there was never a civilized government 'more corrupt, more perfidious and more capricious' than that of the East India Company from 1758 to 1784,[7] but thereafter there was an immense rise in moral standards, which Professor Stokes has traced to a change wrought in the character of the British at home, 'the product of advancing industrialism, | of the ascendancy of the new middle class, and of the emergence of a new ethic for a new society', an ethic that grew out of the Methodist and Evangelical movements.[8] So too in the Roman Republic the violence and rapacity of Roman officials and tax-farmers made Roman rule, according to Cicero, universally detested,[9] but these abuses were at least limited from the time of Augustus. It was not in the interest of the emperors themselves that the provinces should be impoverished for the benefit of individual officials. But there is no indication that there was any moral reformation comparable to that in British society, and supervision could never be close enough to put down all oppression. In all regions and times where we have abundant evidence we find that bribery and extortion continued. Officials (including a secretary of the treasury) were sometimes extolled for keeping their fingers off public funds. Such encomia on individuals do not speak well for the integrity of the class to which they belonged; honesty was not something that could be assumed.[10] As the bureaucracy grew, the emperors were less and less able to check rapacity.[11] The fact that the subjects did not often revolt is no proof that they were well-governed; they lacked power to rise in arms; moreover, they had no experience of incorruptible administration; they were used to exploitation and expected it; perhaps the standards of Roman rule were somewhat higher than those they had known earlier, and the law provided some occasionally effective means of redress. Above all, Rome brought them the benefits of peace and, to many who had hitherto been barbarous, of civilization.

This was the closest analogy that could be found in the Roman achievement to that of modern empires, and here too the latter had the advantage. The change in moral standards meant that they offered a more humane civilization. Slavery was unchallenged in the ancient world,[12] but modern empires set themselves to stamp it out. Torture

---

[7] Quoted by Cromer, *Essays*, 68.

[8] E. Stokes, *English Utilitarians and India* (1959), xiii and 27.

[9] *De imperio Gnaei Pompeii*, 65.

[10] Ch. 4. Others take a more favourable view.

[11] A. H. M. Jones, *Later Roman Empire* (1964), 1053 ff.

[12] W. L. Westermann, *Slave Systems of Greek and Roman Antiquity* (1955), though often inaccurate, is the fullest general account; the best introductions to the subject are the essays of A. H. M. Jones

was a regular concomitant of Roman criminal procedure in certain cases[13] and was eventually used to extract taxes. In Egypt no peasant enjoyed respect unless he could show on his back numerous marks of the tax collector's courbash.[14] The practice persisted until the British occupation: it was then abolished at once.[15] The Romans too brought with them, even to the Greek world, the barbarity of gladiatorial games. Again, modern progress in science and technology made it possible | for modern empires to spread knowledge to an extent to which there is no parallel in Roman times.[16] As the much smaller benefits Rome had conferred on provincials undoubtedly helped to reconcile them to her rule, it was natural for modern imperialists to entertain the persistent fallacy that good government would have the same effect on their own subjects.

For anti-imperialist writers on the Left, Britain had indeed very little to learn from Rome. According to Hobson the Romans used their power to transplant large numbers of the conquered peoples to Italy as slaves; here their competition ruined the peasantry, deprived Rome of her supply of native soldiers and forced her to rely on provincial mercenaries, whose disloyalty subverted Roman power.[17] Somewhat similar views have been advanced more recently by John Strachey[18] and by Mr Michael Brown who classes the Roman dominion among 'slave empires, designed to keep up the supply of slaves for a dominant exploiting class' which 'collapsed from internal decay before they yielded to external attack',[19] a collapse he thinks inevitable on the ground that there is no possibility of technical improvements in an economy in which slave labour prevails. However strongly such writers held that British imperialism too rested on exploitation, the form that it took was plainly of a wholly different kind. In fact, however, their interpretations of Roman history are mere travesties of the truth.

In order to show this, and at the same time to bring out the features of Roman imperialism that differ most markedly from British and do most to explain the far greater longevity of Roman rule and the greater

and M. I. Finley reprinted in *Slavery in Classical Antiquity*, ed. M. I. Finley (1960). Cf. n. 34. [T. Wiedemann, *Greek and Roman Slavery* (1981), provides a useful introduction and anthology of translated texts.]

[13] Mommsen, *Röm. Strafrecht*, 400 ff.

[14] Ammianus Marcellinus, XXII, 16, 23. [cf. Tac., *Ann.* IV, 6. Roman citizens were long exempt.]

[15] Lord Cromer, *Modern Egypt*, 771 ff.

[16] [See M. I. Finley, *Economy and Society in Ancient Greece* (1981). ch. 11.]

[17] *Imperialism*, 247–8, cf. 136.

[18] *The End of Empire*, 283–9.

[19] *After Imperialism* (1963), 26.

readiness of the subjects to accept it, I shall describe the character of the Roman empire at some length.[20]

II

The Romans first conquered Italy, and then mainly with Italian arms the dominions overseas which ultimately extended from the Solway Firth to the Sahara and from Rhine and Danube, or even beyond, to Euphrates.

The conquest of Italy was certainly not a process of enslavement. It was attacks by their neighbours, or the fear of such attacks, that gave early Rome the pretexts or motives for reducing them to submission; in addition, by confiscating some of their lands, the Romans were able to satisfy the land-hunger of their own peasantry. Despite such confiscations, Roman policy was on the whole conciliatory. The Italian peoples were bound to fight in Rome's wars | at their own charge, but they paid no tribute, and retained self-government in their local affairs. Rome did indeed support the rule of local aristocrats, noble landowners of the same type as ruled at Rome itself, who might be closely linked to the Roman nobility. Some peoples were actually given Roman citizenship, and their chief men secured high office at Rome. The Romans themselves saw in this practice a major factor in their rise to world power and traced it back to the legendary origins of their city. Archaeological and philological evidence in fact confirms that early Rome was the product of a union of Latin and Sabine communes, and there can be no doubt that Rome's readiness to admit new citizens gave her at each successive stage of her history superiority in sheer manpower over her enemies, which was usually decisive in ancient wars. Roman citizens, new and old, were settled all over Italy, and these settlements served to diffuse among peoples of diverse race and speech knowledge of the Latin language and of Roman institutions, which they were increasingly ready to adopt for themselves.[21] Moreover the Roman citizen communities also enjoyed a substantial measure of municipal self-government. It became more and more evident to the other Italians that they would lose little in local autonomy and gain much in prestige, protection from Roman magistrates and even

---

[20] Hugh Last gave a learned but too favourable account in *Cambridge Ancient History*, XI, ch. XI. For a recent balanced survey see Michael Grant, *The World of Rome* (1960). For the extension of the citizenship and Romanization see A. N. Sherwin-White, *Roman Citizenship* (1973). [A Marxist interpretation of the Roman empire will be found, despite its title, in G. E. M. de Ste Croix, *The Class Struggle in the Ancient Greek World* (1981), a work of immense learning and powerful argument; he knows of course that slaves formed only a minority of the exploited lower classes. For criticisms see my review in *Journal of Roman Studies* (1982).]

[21] [Brunt. *Fall of Rom. Rep.*, ch. 2.]

political power, if they too could secure the status of citizens. It was only the rejection of this demand that led them to rise in revolt in 90 B.C., and in the stress of war Rome conceded what they had sought. Thus all the Italians came to be Romans, and by the time of Augustus we might speak with reason of the Italians as the imperial people.

It is indeed tempting to say that at this time the Italians had become a nation. Cicero constantly appealed to the sentiments of all Italy, and Virgil celebrates the prowess of the Italians who had resisted Aeneas, the prototype of the conquering Roman, and looks forward to the circumstances of his own day, when all had been reconciled and had become 'Latins of a single speech'. Augustus mobilized Italian prejudices against Antony, who had been seduced by a barbarian concubine into forgetting the gods and customs of Italy.[22] Still, it was not Rome that was merged in Italy, but Italy that was absorbed into the Roman citizen body; the rulers of the world were the Romans, and the same process that had made Romans out of Italians, many of them derived from an ethnic stock·distinct from the first inhabitants of the city, could be, and was, continued to transform provincials in the same way. I have indeed dwelt on the unification of Italy because in many respects it set the pattern for the wider unity that was to follow.

From the third century B.C. Rome was enlarging her dominions beyond the seas. I shall not seek to determine the question how far aggression or fears of aggression by Carthage or by Hellenistic kingdoms or later by northern or eastern peoples provided Rome with motives, as they often provided | pretexts, for expansion, or how far the real cause of expansion must be sought in the mere desire for power and glory, or in greed for the profits of empire (cf. n. 5). Schumpeter, in his book on imperialism, traces the 'unbounded will to conquest' which the Romans displayed to a 'policy of continual preparation for war, the policy of meddlesome interventionism', and this seems an apt description of much of the process.[23] But a historian of Rome can hardly follow him when he ascribes conquests to the need of the landowning class who governed to divert the minds of the people from agrarian reform to military glory. To say nothing of the fact which he acknowledges that the nobility might themselves be unconscious that their domestic class interests dictated sincerely felt fears for Rome's safety and of the doubt we might feel in making unconscious motivation a determining factor in events, it was often not the governing class, but agrarian reformers or popular leaders who carried out annexations. Nor, to turn to Marxist or quasi-Marxist interpretations, is there

---

[22] R. Syme, *Roman Revolution* (1935), ch. XX.
[23] *Imperialism*, ch. 3. His account contains many historical solecisms.

any evidence that slavery was a decisive factor. Like all ancient peoples, the Romans had always had slaves, and their wars increased the supply. Never were slaves so numerous as in Italy during the first century B.C. But there is hardly a hint in the texts that any war was prompted by the need for slaves. At most some generals may have embarked on unauthorized expeditions in a lust for booty which included slaves. And in the spoils of empire tribute must be accorded a larger place than booty. Once a people had come under Roman rule, it paid taxes to Rome, but it was of course immune from slave-raiding. Free subjects of Rome could not legally be made slaves. It is thus absurd to suggest that the empire was designed to keep up the supply of slaves, especially in the period after Augustus, when the policy was normally to defend the provinces already annexed without enlarging Roman dominions.

The provincials were worse off than the Italians in that they had to pay taxes to Rome. The Romans justified this on the ground that they needed a revenue to pay the army which protected the provincials.[24] It is significant that they thought it necessary to provide any justification at all. In their own estimation their rule rested on right and not on mere force; they were accepting the established doctrine of Greek political philosophy that government exists for the welfare of the governed. The apologia is not quite convincing, since Italy profited as much as the provinces from the Roman peace, and far more from public expenditure, and yet paid little in taxes until c. AD 300 [p.515], long after it had lost other privileges. But at any rate from the time of Augustus Roman arms did secure peace and order. An Asian orator said in the second century A.D. that men had long thought that the peace was a dream and had woken up to find that it was real.[25] It lasted | on the whole for 250 years: nothing like it had been known before, or has been repeated since.

For long it was not the practice of the Romans to govern much.[26] The governor had only a small staff, and he did little more than defend his province, ensure the collection of the taxes and decide the most important criminal and civil cases. The local communities were left in

---

[24] E.g., Tacitus, *Histories*, IV, 74.

[25] Aelius Aristides *To Rome*, 69. This panegyric, translated with commentary by J. H. Oliver, *The Ruling Power* (in *Transactions of the American Philosophical Society*, 1953), is the fullest statement of the admiration for Rome that the upper class in the empire had come to feel. [See ch. 12 n. 1.]

[26] No comprehensive works on Roman administration have superseded J. Marquardt, *Röm. Staatsverwaltung* (1884); cf. W. T. Arnold, *Roman System of Provincial Administration* (1914). On the cities see F. F. Abbott and A. C. Johnson, *Municipal Administration in the Roman Empire* (1926), especially A. H. M. Jones, *The Greek City from Alexander to Justinian* (1940); the last chapter gives a just appreciation of the limitations of the civilizing work achieved by cities in the eastern part of the Roman empire, cf. now his *Later Roman Empire*, ch. XXIV, also dealing with the west. Cf. also the great work of M. Rostovtzeff, *Social and Economic History of the Roman Empire²* (1957).

the main to run their own affairs, though everywhere Rome supported oligarchies and would not countenance disorder or attacks on property rights. By the end of the pre-Christian era, the local communities had become responsible for collecting the imperial direct taxes. Their functions were all the more considerable because their territories were sometimes extensive—about as large as a French department or even larger.

Men of rank and education in the provinces understood that the preponderance of Roman strength doomed resistance or revolt to failure.[27] Time helped to reconcile them to a yoke they could not throw off, the more readily because Rome preserved peace, and guaranteed their local liberties and power, and their economic interests. Gradually they were to gain still more. In the west groups of Italian settlers provided their neighbours with patterns of a higher and more attractive civilization then they had developed for themselves. Without compulsion, though sometimes encouraged by the Roman authorities, the natives began to adopt the Latin language, to build towns of the Italian type, to imitate Graeco-Roman architecture and sculpture, to copy the manners of the Romans. The process was a long one; round Trier Celtic was spoken in the early fifth century.[28] In the Basque country and in Wales the indigenous languages have actually survived, whereas in Gaul Celtic ultimately disappeared with few traces except in place names. But of course the upper classes, who had most dealings with Roman officials and traders, were most susceptible to Romanization. As early as the first century A.D. Gauls and Spaniards were contributing to Latin literature. These *évolués* sought citizenship[29] and preferment, and the government, conscious of their merits and of Rome's traditions, gratified their ambitions. |

Rome also relied more and more on provincials to fill the ranks of the army. They too were partly Romanized by long service in a Latin-speaking force,[30] and were rewarded with the franchise at latest on discharge.

Since the bureaucracy remained small, the government depended for essential administrative tasks on local magnates in every region; they too were enfranchised in increasing numbers even in the East, where Latin did not spread, and where Rome was content to uphold and diffuse Greek culture and the Greek language. Rome had no need,

---

[27] Josephus, *Jewish War*, II, 345–401.

[28] [See ch. 12 App I.]

[29] There is a good instance in Claudius' grant of citizenship to a town in Morocco, half Berber, half Punic, which had rendered the Romans good services in suppressing nomad tribes, and petitioned for the grant [E. M. Smallwood, *Documents ... of Gaius Claudius and Nero*, 407].

[30] Velleius (II, 110) says that Pannonians in the army in AD 6 had learned to speak and even read Latin. Latin papyri of soldiers in Egypt (e.g., private letters) illustrate the process.

said Aelius Aristides (cf. n. 25), of garrisons in the cities; they were held
for her by the best people, who had become Romans. Thus the upper
classes in the East too were Romanized at least in sentiment; here the
empire lasted longest, and the subjects of Byzantium were to call
themselves Rhomaioi.

Early in the third century the citizenship was bestowed on almost all
the inhabitants of the empire by a single edict. This was only the
culmination of a long process. But citizenship no longer carried with it
equal rights under the law; the upper classes were privileged, enjoying
a sort of benefit of clergy.[31] Nor did it involve the intense patriotism of
the old city state. Its chief importance lay in the fact that by luck or
merit citizens could rise to the chief posts in the government.[32] Under
Rome such men as Nehru or Nkrumah would have been eligible for the
highest imperial offices. In the third century most senators were not
Italians. From Trajan onwards most emperors came from the provinces and the eternal city celebrated its millennium in A.D. 247 under
the rule of an Arab sheikh.

The empire had now long ceased to be an alien dominion imposed
on unwilling subjects by force. Its structure was certainly stratified
socially. At the top the landed aristocracy provided the ruling class; at
the bottom were the peasantry and the slaves. Fortune or talent,
however, permitted a few men to rise from the lowest ranks of society
to affluence and power. In the army a peasant might be promoted to
the highest offices; thus Marcus Aurelius' praetorian prefect and chief
minister had started his career in the ranks, and in the late empire,
when the hierarchical social order had become more rigid, cases of such
promotions actually became more common.[33] Roman slavery again
differed markedly from that known in modern western society, for
instance in the United States. In the fields or the mines slaves had little
hope of freedom, but the slaves who were extensively employed in the
household, in trade and industry and even in public administration
and the professions, | were manumitted in thousands; the prospect of
freedom was an incentive to good work, which it was in the interest of
the masters to provide. It is no surprise that the finest manufactured
products, such as Arretine ware, were often made by slaves or
freedmen. If the master was a Roman citizen, his freedman normally
obtained the citizenship with his liberty. Many of them became rich
and influential, especially the emperor's freedmen. Their sons, born in

---

[31] [P. Garnsey, *Social Status and Legal Privilege in the Roman Empire* (1970), with my review in *JRS*
1972.]
[32] R. Syme, *Colonial Élites* (1958), ch 1, illustrates the process.
[33] Jones, *Later Roman Empire*, 1052–3.

freedom, might have still better prospects. Pertinax, the son of a freedman, became emperor in 193.

Though slavery was ubiquitous and never died out in the empire, it is generally held that it was relatively uncommon at all times in some of the most prosperous provinces such as Egypt and Gaul, and that it diminished as the Roman peace reduced the opportunities for making slaves.[34] If this last view is well-founded, slavery was less important just at the time when the empire began to decline. It is not then very plausible to ascribe the decline to the prevalence of slave labour and its supposed inefficiency. Indeed from the ancient evidence it would not be easy to prove that it was inefficient. The technical writers on agriculture assumed that on good land and with good management a farm would bring in higher profits to the owner if it were worked by slaves than if it were let to free tenants.

It is of course true that the empire was technologically backward [n. 16], even in comparison with the early Middle Ages when the stirrup, the heavy plough, improved harnessing which made the use of horse-power possible, water-mills and windmills were either first invented or came for the first time into common operation, with enormous benefits to military tactics or to the economy.[35] If the Romans had been more advanced technologically, the barbarians would have found it harder to disrupt their power. Their backwardness has been attributed to the use of slave labour. Slaves, it is thought, were so cheap as to make the invention of labour-saving devices appear unnecessary, they were incapable of making inventions themselves and their use discredited labour, so that the best minds could have no interest in technology. In fact, many of the slaves were highly skilled and inventions are attributed to them, nor were they particularly cheap. And even when free labour has been used, not many well-educated people except in rather recent times have displayed much concern in the processes of manufacture. There are, moreover, many other factors that help to explain the technological backwardness of the classical world. Fuel was scarce, and social and legal institutions[36] did not favour the accumulation of capital. Transportation was slow and costly, and so long | distance trade was limited in the main to luxury or semi-luxury goods which could stand the charges. The mass of the population, peasants as well as slaves, lived at or near a subsistence level; there was conse-

[34] I have discussed the effects of slavery in [*Storia della Società Italiana*, ed. G. Cherubini and others, vol. 2 (1983) 95 ff. with particular reference to Italy, and more briefly for the empire at large in *The Roman World*, ed. J. S. Wacher (1987), 701 ff.]

[35] Lynn White Jr., *Medieval Technology and Social Change* (1962).

[36] For security and social prestige the rich preferred to invest in land, and spent lavishly on shows, doles and monuments to earn popularity and commemorate their names. Roman law did not permit the formation of joint stock companies or the limitation of liability.

quently no demand for manufacture on a large scale, at any rate unless a 'break-through' had first been achieved in modes of transport. The whole or chief responsibility for the decline of Rome cannot be laid on slavery.

Historians are never likely to agree on the causes of Rome's decline. The most obvious explanation, to which some recent writers have given the most weight, is external attack.[37] From the middle of the third century A.D. onwards the empire was subject to ever more serious barbarian irruptions. In the West it finally disintegrated, and it was in the West that the barbarians attacked in most force. Still, their success is mysterious. They do not seem to have been more numerous than in the past. The Roman army was actually larger numerically though evidently less efficient. Caesar conquered Gaul with no more troops than Rome had to defend it in A.D. 400. It seems probable to me that the empire was irreparably damaged in the third century by constant mutinies and civil wars in which the armies set up one usurper after another and preyed on the civil population.[38] In some 70 years out of 16 emperors, not counting local pretenders, not one died in his bed. The spectacle of Rome's internal weakness encouraged the barbarians to lay waste almost every province. Plagues and famines also depleted the population. Diocletian and his successors only restored the position by laying almost insupportable burdens on the subjects. They had also to rely increasingly for defence on the barbarians themselves, who often asked for nothing more than to be taken into Roman service and to be allotted lands in Roman territory. Thus the barbarians overran the empire as much by infiltration as by open attack.[39] Over-taxed and oppressed, the subjects had little enthusiasm for their own defence.

Discontent of the subjects with foreign rule was not, however, the cause of disruption, if only because the rule was not foreign. Rostovtzeff thought that the armies, who were recruited from the peasantry, vented the resentment of their class on the bourgeoisie of the cities who were exploiting them. The exploitation cannot be denied, but as the armies treated peasants just as badly as the bourgeoisie and were hated by them, his theory will not work.[40] There was no class-consciousness of the modern type, and no Marx to formulate it. In any case, the bourgeoisie in every area tended to be people | of the same ethnical origin as the locally recruited armies; they were not comparable with

---

[37] See the discussions of various theories by Rostovtzeff (n. 26), ch. XII, A. Piganiol, *Hist. Romaine*, IV (1947), 411 ff. and Jones (n. 12), ch. XXV. Both the last writers stress the invasions.

[38] Jones, *Later Roman Empire*, 1033, notes that there were fewer civil wars after c. 300, but perhaps the harm had then been done; and he admits that the record in the West is worse than in the East; this may be a major factor in explaining the greater endurance of the eastern empire.

[39] [Ste Croix (n. 20) 509 ff.]

[40] N. H. Baynes, *Byzantine Studies and other Essays* (1955), 307 ff.

French *colons* or British settlers in Africa. Again we sometimes find that the peasants rose in revolt or assisted foreign invaders.[41] This shows how bitterly they resented the oppression of imperial or more often of local authorities. But these risings were *jacqueries*, not national movements of subject races. The rebellious conduct of soldiers and peasants alike does indeed attest a fearful lack of solidarity among the inhabitants of the empire. In name they were all Romans, but they lacked the active patriotic sense displayed by citizens in ancient republics or in modern national states. The real sentiments of the masses cannot be inferred from the verbose laudations of Rome penned by the literate and wealthy few, who alone understood the values that Rome defended and whose interests were preferred by the Roman government. In the main the masses were probably indifferent; kingdoms might rise and fall, without changing the dreary routine of their lives or the exactions to which each successive government subjected them. The humblest among them benefited from the Roman peace, but they had neither the knowledge of the past nor the foresight to see how they might suffer when it came to an end.

Even the upper classes were more ready to praise Rome than to serve her. The armies were not only composed of peasants and later of barbarians, but they were led by men of the same type, for men of high rank and culture were no longer ready to hold military commissions. Nor did they lead resistance movements when provinces were overrun. In Gaul the Merovingian kings found numerous Gallo-Roman magnates to serve them as administrators and generals and their armies were as much Gallic as Frankish. The Gauls were as loyal to them as they had been to Rome, and took Germanic names, as they had once taken Roman.[42]

Under the Roman autocracy men had come more and more to rely on the providence of the emperor 'vigilant with unceasing care for the interests of mankind' and to believe that his care assured the eternity of the empire.[43] Emperors, moreover, were jealous or thought to be jealous of initiative and enterprise.[44] These qualities then faded away. With only limited political outlets for their energies, many of the best spirits turned to creeds that promised philosophic calm or celestial sabbaths to those who found no satisfaction in the peace of this world. Talent was thus directed into paths that led away from the welfare of the empire. To such men as Augustine the city of Rome mattered little

[41] E. A. Thompson, in *Past and Present*, II; [Ste Croix (n. 20) 474 ff.]
[42] F. Lot, *Les invasions germaniques* (1945), 249 ff.
[43] *Fontes Iuris Romani Anteiustiniani*, I² ed. Riccobono no. 102. See M. P. Charlesworth, in *Harvard Theological Review*, 1936.
[44] See for instance Tacitus, *Annals*, VI, 39; XIII, 53; *Agricola*, 1–3.

in comparison with the city of God. All this may be seen as the result of the progressive loss of liberty. In the name of efficient govern|ment even the liberties of the cities had been whittled away, and the local governments became little more than agents of a fiscal system as oppressive to them as to every one else. Indeed from the late third century the manpower shortage induced the government to regiment every order of society, binding most men to hereditary occupations. There was no refuge beyond the frontiers, and no pattern of a more liberal society; as Mommsen said, in the absence of all material extraneous complications absolutism developed 'more purely and freely' in the Roman empire then elsewhere.[45]

Yet those who were politically conscious were seldom disaffected. In the very century when Roman rule was to vanish in Gaul a Gallic poet celebrated Rome as the city which had unified the world by giving the conquered a share in rights, and a Gallic orator in the city of Vercingetorix, the hero of Gallic resistance during the Roman conquest, chose to honour the memory of Caesar. What a contrast with the jubilation that marks the independence days of British colonies!

III

Modern empires have had more powerful enemies than the Roman, inspired by a more deliberate hostility. Their wars with other well-organized states weakened their power and prestige, and often brought wider horizons within the vision of subjects who had served them abroad. The second world war, above all, drained their strength away, and defeats and temporary losses of possessions encouraged nationalist movements. When peace came, they could count on the enmity of the communist states, but not on the sympathy or support of their ally, the United States, save in so far as its policy was governed by antagonism to communism. Yet only in Indo-China was imperial domination ended even in part by foreign armed intervention. Elsewhere it was the revolts of the subjects or more commonly in British territories their non-violent resistance that gained independence. Thus their empires were dissolved by internal discontent.

This was not because their rule was more oppressive then Rome's, or because it conferred fewer benefits. The contrary was true.[46]

In British territories, for instance, the standard of integrity among

---

[45] *Hist. of Rome*, Everyman ed., IV, 439 f. (Book V, ch. XI). Mommsen clearly had in mind the memorable passage of Gibbon at the end of ch. 3 (Bury's ed. I, 78 ff.).

[46] Many, if not all, of the statements about British rule that follow would also be true of other modern empires.

the administrators was undoubtedly far higher. Like the Romans they maintained peace and order and the reign of law. And the law they enforced was more equal and more humane than the Roman.

Unlike the Romans, Britain did not levy tribute, except for a relatively brief period in India; it was soon abandoned there, partly in the belief that India would then be able to buy more British goods. Of course, Indian revenues were often spent in wars dictated by British interests, but this practice | was subjected to criticism by radicals at home and officials in India. They were also the source of pay for numerous British officials and soldiers; the empire was thus profitable to individuals (especially people of influence) and could be described as 'a vast system of outdoor relief for the upper classes'. But exploitation was much less *direct* (in so far as it existed at all) than in the Roman empire, except in colonies where white settlers were permitted to appropriate the best lands or to turn mineral resources to their own exclusive profit. And in the last epoch of British dominion the colonies were actually subsidized on a growing scale by the British taxpayers.

The Romans had built roads, conserved water and stimulated the cities to construct aqueducts, drainage systems and pompous monuments which served more for display that for augmenting wealth. Their work was more than matched by the railways, mills and irrigation schemes of the British. This is not surprising: Britain gave more because she had more to give. Technologically the ancient Italians were not much, if at all, superior to the provincials, and in so far as the Roman empire became more prosperous, this was due primarily to the simple fact that peace was maintained. (The empire also constituted a great common market, but the benefits of this were limited by the cost of transport.)

The privileges of European settlers in some areas, and more generally the immense power of European capital and technical skill no doubt diminished the material gains of the subjects in modern empires. In India the imposition of free trade in the interest of Lancashire millowners was believed to have ruined the native craft industry and retarded industrial development.[47] Economic analysis may show that there was much *indirect* exploitation of overseas possessions, not necessarily to the ultimate advantage of the ruling power itself. In India again the introduction of British concepts of property and debt seems to have favoured the concentration of landed wealth in the hands of the old tax-gathering class or of moneylenders. Yet despite the poverty of the masses and the recurrence of famines, the huge growth of population shows that the expectation of life actually rose.

[47] Perhaps mistakenly. See M. D. Morris, *Journal of Economic History*, XXIII (1963), 612–13.

This can hardly have been so in the Roman empire where each district had to depend almost entirely on the food it could produce itself.

Economic grievances such as the preference apparently enjoyed by British firms or in government service of British as against native officials naturally played a part in the agitation against British rule, especially when the interpretation of imperialism given by Marx, Hobson and Lenin had become known. But Marx himself, while castigating the bourgeois exploitation of India, emphatically declared that British rule was destined to regenerate the country by promoting political unity, 'private property in land—the great desideratum of Asiatic society' (!), better communications and industrializa|tion.[48] And it does not seem that purely economic discontents gave the chief impetus to independence movements.

The British were also more deliberately active than the Romans in diffusing their own knowledge and ideas. The elder Pliny, expanding Virgil's famous dictum that it was the Roman mission to rule and spread the ways of peace said that Italy had been marked out by providence to unite scattered dominions, to make manners gentle, to draw together in the converse of a common language the discordant and barbarous tongues of innumerable peoples, to civilize mankind and to become a common fatherland of all the races in the world (*Natural History* III, 39). In general, however, the Romans left it to their subjects themselves, encouraging them perhaps chiefly because they had found by experience that civilized subjects were more docile. The British had other motives for spreading western beliefs and practices. The Churches condemned the 'beastly devices of the heathen', and in attempting to propagate the true faith, they also promoted a secular western education. Utilitarians had no use for native institutions which did not make for the greatest happiness. Commercial interests wished to push western manufactures and favoured a legal and social structure with which they were familiar and which would assist trade. The romantic admiration that some early administrators of India felt for Indian culture was submerged by a confident belief in western superiority. Contemptuous of Indian literature, Macaulay by his education policy sought to create a class of persons 'Indian in colour and blood, but English in tastes, in opinions, in morals and in intellect'. The existence of printing made it easier for the British to Anglicize their subjects than it had been for Rome to Romanize hers. Schools and Universities (four founded in 1854) made English the *lingua franca* even for Indian nationalists. All this made western science more accessible in the east. The subjects received the new ideas with alacrity, even in Africa where in some colonies the

[48] Marx and Engels, *First Indian War of Independence* (1939), 32 ff. (from *New York Daily Tribune*) 22 July 1859).

administrators for a time sought to insulate the natives from the modern world and to preserve indigenous culture.[49]

An Indian scholar, K. M. Panikkar, has analysed the British heritage to India.[50] By establishing peace and unity, a stable and uniform currency and easy communications British rule promoted large scale economic organization and an increased demand for goods. The spirit of critical inquiry was revived, and under the influence of Christianity led to a re-examination and purification of Hindu religion. British scholarship renewed interest in India's past. There was an increasingly widespread demand for scientific and technological knowledge. The Indians adopted the British ideals of national independence, of representative government and of law as a guarantor of liberty, | and in local and regional government they acquired some political experience. The English language was the essential medium for the acquisition and extension of a western civilization modified by the older ideas of India. Much of this must be true elsewhere, though in Africa the civilizing and unifying process has been curtailed. In Nigeria the sense of nationality has apparently been stimulated by absorption of the country into the the world economy and the consequent urbanization that has here and elsewhere helped to break down tribal barriers.

It is curious that writers in this century like Bryce and Cromer, in comparing the extension by Rome of Graeco-Roman civilization and by modern imperial powers of the civilization of contemporary Europe, were hardly aware of the profound contrast due to the scientific revolution which made the transformation of life and thought effected by modern imperialism far more total than Rome was able to bring about. Perhaps the reason for their failure in comprehension was that they themselves had been nurtured in the classical tradition. This was also true of most British administrators, and their deficiencies may help to explain why Japan went ahead more rapidly than India did.

The Romans were not given to critical inquiry, one part of the Greek heritage they did not accept. It is significant that the same word 'disciplina' stands for instruction in the schools and the unquestioning obedience drilled into the soldier. They relied heavily on tradition, custom, 'the wisdom of our ancestors'. They valued liberty, but what they mostly had in mind were the private rights of free men under the law—a law that in classical times left great freedom to the individual but gave little protection to the economically weak.[51] Even in the

---

[49] Stokes, *op. cit.*, see index under Anglicization; J. S. Coleman, *Nigeria: Background to Nationalism*, 63 ff.

[50] *Foundations of New India* (1963).

[51] F. Schulz, *Classical Roman Law* (1951), 463; 542 ff. [But in fact different Romans had different and contradictory conceptions of liberty, which included political rights especially in the Republic; see my *Fall of Rom. Rep.*, ch. 6.]

Republic most citizens had not much liberty, if by liberty we mean a share in effective political rights. The Principate was an autocracy. The schools taught that monarchy was the best form of government and democracy one of the worst. If the cities, or rather the upper class in the cities, were for long allowed to manage most of their own concerns, that was a mere matter of convenience: self-government was not an ideal. A Roman could acknowledge the leader of German resistance to Roman conquest, Arminius, as 'liberator haud dubie Germaniae'; he could understand that a people would fight against subjection; but he did not recognize any right in other peoples to be free. On the contrary, Rome was divinely destined to rule all peoples. As the subjects were Romanized, these were the ideas they imbibed, and were the more ready to accept because of the undoubted benefits that Roman rule brought. No Gaul would have had an experience like that of the young Nehru at Harrow, reading Trevelyan and writing a prize essay on Garibaldi. Nehru was to say, criticizing the British, that 'an authoritarian system of government ... must encourage a psychology of subservience, and try to limit the mental outlook and horizon of the people. It must crush ... enterprise, the spirit of adventure, originality .... Such a system does not | bring out the real service mentality, the devotion to public service or to ideals'. (*Autobiography* 19; 439) These remarks seem much more applicable to the Roman empire than to the British.

In the ancient world there was hardly any nationalism in the modern sense. A nation, according to J. S. Mill, is constituted by common and exclusive sympathies, generated by 'identity of race and descent, ... community of language and community of religion, ... geographical limits' and above all by 'identity of political antecedents, the possession of a national history and consequent community of recollections, collective pride and humiliation, pleasure and regret, connected with the same incidents in the past' (*Representative Government*, ch, xvi). Such a nation wishes to be united in a single, national state. This concept of the nation has its origin in modern Europe and was exported to the subjects of modern empires. It has no ancient analogy. Sir Keith Hancock, after quoting Claudian's saying of the subjects of Rome, 'we are all one people', rightly adds: 'Within the British Commonwealth during the past century the movement has been in a contrary direction—from the ideal of a single political nationality to the ideal of a variety of nationalities'.[52]

Most Roman provinces comprised a hotch-potch of tribes and cities,

---

[52] *Survey of British Commonwealth Affairs* (1937), I, 175–6. [See for what follows F. W. Walbank's excellent paper, *Nationality as a Factor in Roman History* (*Harv. St. in Class. Phil.* 76 (1972), 145 ff.) i *inter alia* he points out that the survival of indigenous cultures under Roman rule is no proof of the survival of anti-Roman feeling.]

mutually hostile, and not linked by any of the ties mentioned. Spain, for instance, was no more than a geographical expression. The Greeks indeed were conscious of their identity of race, community of language and religious cults, similarity of customs (Herodotus VIII, 144), and they did look back to a common war against barbarians recorded (as they thought) in the Iliad. But they were far too weak to resist Roman supremacy, and the very traditions that united them in sentiment had always obstructed the development of political unity; their collective pride consisted in memories of the autonomy of separate cities. Caesar depicts the existence of pan-Gallic feelings at the time of his conquest of Gaul, and the Gauls could meet in councils to organize the struggle against Rome. But they were just as deeply divided by reciprocal animosities as the Greeks had ever been, and it could be said that Gaul had been conquered by her own strength (Tacitus, *Histories* IV, 17), for Gauls were an important element in Caesar's army. Forty years after the conquest the Romans were so little apprehensive of Gallic national-ism that they instituted annual councils for the whole of Gaul, to honour the emperor as a god and represent the wishes of the subjects to Rome. Similar councils were set up elsewhere on an ethnical basis. The maxim 'Divide et impera' is not Roman, and in fact the tendency of Roman policy was normally to unite her subjects. It was safe for Rome to do so, in part because few of her subjects had any proud memories of independence that might have enshrined past renown and perpetuated the longing for independence. The Gauls are known to have sung rude lays, but they were not committed to writing and their recollection faded, as the upper classes learned to prefer the more sophisticated pleasures of Latin literature. The Romans themselves had | no curiosity in the past of their subjects and did not seek to preserve or recover its records. By contrast British philologists and archaeologists resurrected the Indian classics and the old glories of Indian civilization, which Nehru was to popularize in his *Discovery of India*, and according to Panikkar 'the growth of a historical sense, giving to Indian life an increased sense of its continuity, a growing appreciation of its political and social roots, a pride in its past achievement, has been an important factor in the development of modern India'. In much the same way more recently European scholarship has been helping to recreate or create the past of Africa and thereby contributing to African nation-alism, indeed to the pan-African movement, which exalts the ancient greatness of Egypt or Ethiopia or Ghana or depicts a golden age of perfect equality, liberty and fraternity before the European slave-trader or settler arrived.[53]

[53] Brunt in *Latomus*, XVIII, 543 ff.; XIX, 497 ff. For the councils J. A. O. Larsen, *Representative Government in Greek and Roman History* (1955), chs VII–VIII. A. H. M. Jones, *The Roman Economy* (1974), ch. XV, convincingly argues against the view that religious differences in the late empire

In modern times religion has often been a divisive force that has helped to distinguish kindred peoples into different nations, for instance the Belgians and the Dutch. In modern empires it separated the rulers from the ruled. 'We are not liked anywhere', wrote a Punjab administrator (Lyall) in the nineteenth century: 'there is no getting over the fact that we are not Mohammedans, that we neither eat, drink nor intermarry with them.' In Algeria few Moslems could take advantage of the offer of French citizenship when it involved surrendering their right to be governed in part under Moslem law. In different ways Hinduism or paganism also constituted barriers to assimilation.[54] In antiquity this was not so. Polytheists were not intolerant of each other's cults, as were Christians of other religions or even of heretical forms of their own. They looked for points of identity, not of difference; they were ready to admit that other peoples knew of other true and powerful gods, or to suppose that the gods of others were the same as their own, though worshipped under different names and in different modes. Roman emperors sought the patronage of Isis or Baal or Mithras without disowning Jupiter. Hence the mystical religions of the East spread under the Roman peace, until Christianity actually became the public religion. By contrast in the modern age Europe's debt to the East has remained small.

There was indeed one subject people whom the Romans failed to assimilate—the Jews. Judaism, like Christianity, was exclusive; it claimed to be the one true religion, and though the Romans were prepared to tolerate it, because it was the traditional religion of the Jews, the intolerance of the Jews | themselves obstructed mutual understanding. In Judaea, as elsewhere, the Romans protected the interests of the upper classes, and the high priests and rulers were always inclined to prudent submissiveness. But in Judaea their acquiescence in foreign domination did not suffice to ensure loyalty. Knowledge of the sacred books was widespread; even the son of a carpenter could expound the Scriptures. And these sacred books kept alive, among humble folk who had little to lose, the memories of past achievements, the conviction that they were God's chosen people and the hope that He would arise and put down the mighty from their seats [pp. 528 ff.]. These circumstances confronted Rome with a problem similar to those of modern imperial powers, and like those powers, Rome too failed to solve them.

can be explained by national (or social) quarrels. Panikkar, *op. cit.*, 68, 131–2, and T. Hodgkin, *Nationalism in Colonial Africa* (1956), 170 ff. on connexion of historical studies and modern nationalism.

[54] Cromer, *Modern Egypt*, 909; E. Behr, *Algerian Problem* (1961), 35 ff.; Nehru, *Autobiography*, 24 (connecting nationalism and Hinduism).

The principles or practice of the imperial peoples of modern Europe also ruled out the chance of assimilation, or of the creation of a single state embracing the colonial possessions with their consent and allegiance. From modern France the subjects learned to know the ideals of liberty, equality and fraternity.[55] These secular concepts of the Revolution actually coloured the teaching of Christian missionaries who tended to discard the Pauline conception that the equality and brotherhood of men was merely spiritual, not affecting nor affected by inequalities in this world. The British brought with them the belief that self-government and representative institutions should ultimately prevail everywhere. After the loss of the American colonies it was widely held that other European settlements overseas must eventually acquire self-government, whatever links they might retain with the ·mother-country. This belief was verified, and the white Dominions provided Asiatics and Africans with a pattern to follow. In Britain this had always been widely envisaged, though it was held that a long period of education was a necessary precondition. 'It may be' said Macaulay in the Commons in 1833 'that the public mind of India may expand under our system till it has outgrown that system; that by good government we may educate our subjects into a capacity for better government; that, having become instructed in European knowledge, they may in some future age demand European institutions. Whether such a day will ever come I know not. But never will I attempt to avert or retard it. Whenever it comes, it will be the proudest day in English history.'[56] This ideal, of educating the subjects for self-government, was never lost sight of at home, even though in practice during the nineteenth century the British administration in India moved towards it with laggard steps, and even though liberals like Gladstone and Bright were convinced that if Britain surrendered her power, the result must be bloodshed and anarchy, | that for the time autocracy was justified in the name of peace.[57] Such caution, prolonged into our own time, irritated nationalists like Nehru; 'even peace can be purchased at too great a price, and we can have the perfect peace of the grave, the absolute safety of a cage or a prison'.[58] This is a comment in notable contrast with the endless panegyrics of provincials on the *pax Romana*.

[55] The decree of 16 Pluviôse 1792 proclaimed that 'all men, without distinction of colour, domiciled in French colonies, are French citizens and enjoy all the rights assured by the Constitution.' Paternalistic in practice, the French could not withhold these ideas from their subjects.

[56] *Complete Works*, XI, 585 f.

[57] For analyses of views of British nineteenth-century statesmen and thinkers on the empire see C. A. Bodelsen, *Studies in Mid-Victorian Imperialism* (1960); Barie, *Idee e dottrine imperialistiche nell'Inghilterra vittoriana* (1953); A. P. Thornton, *The Imperial Idea and its Enemies* (1959).

[58] *Autobiography*, 436.

Some, like Cobden, Dilke and Hobson, actually feared that autocracy abroad might adversely affect the spirit of liberty at home. Dilke did not think India ripe for independence because the Indians were not sufficiently attached to liberty and did not constitute a nation. He also believed that the Anglo-Saxon race ought to dominate the world. Yet he wished the idea of liberty to be disseminated in India. Some held that it was the British role to break down all physical, racial and social barriers in preparation for creating a united Indian nation. Perhaps no one would have denied that if nationalism in India grew and if the demand for liberty strengthened there, concessions would have to be made, as they were, though Cromer and others wished to retard the day of independence, justifying their view by fears that the educated and unrepresentative minority who were already clamouring for it would exploit 'the voiceless millions' whom in their judgement British rule protected. But Cromer quotes a remark of Sir Alfred Lyall, a distinguished Indian civil servant, that 'the universally prevalent belief that education, civilization and increased material prosperity will reconcile the people of our India to our rule' was 'the wildest as well as the shallowest notion'; the Indians 'prefer a bad native government to our best patent institutions'.[59] Cromer added that these opinions 'have become the commonplace of all who deal with questions affecting India'.[60] If 'the universal prevalent belief' was in conflict with these opinions, it was thus not held by the well-informed. It followed that British rule could be perpetuated only by force, in contradiction of the principles the British espoused and at home applied. This was known to be impossible. Self-government was the recognized goal. Even Kipling saw it as the task of the British proconsuls

> to quicken, tend and raise
> Power that must their power displace |

Similarly in Africa Lord Lugard held that unrest and desire for independence among the subjects was a measure of their progress.[61] All that was in doubt was the pace of development. And not even liberals like Hobson who questioned whether 'we are giving (our subjects) those arts of government which we regard as our most valuable

---

[59] *Essays*, 25 ff.; 167 ff.; *Ancient and Modern Imperialism*, 118 ff. Bryce and Cromer thought that centuries would elapse. Robinson and Gallagher (n. 4) 274 ff. criticize Cromer for paternalism in Egypt and not nursing the Egyptians more quickly into independence. Paternalism was natural in those who thought that centuries were needed to educate Asiatics for self-government.

[60] *Essays* 84. Cf. 50–1 for view that repression would be 'false to our acknowledged principles of government and our civilizing mission'.

[61] Perham, *Lugard, Years of Authority*, 645.

possessions'[62] imagined that it would be so fast as it has proved. The French indeed, by contrast, were deluded into thinking that they could emulate the Roman achievement and turn Africans into French citizens; but nationalist concepts have been too strong for them as well.

European principles undermined European imperialism all the more rapidly because the practice of the rulers was so much at variance with their principles. Paradoxically they allowed in some ways less self-government and equality to the ruled than Rome had done, except under pressure when their control began to slacken. Thus in India municipal councils with Indian members were created only gradually in the nineteenth century and with restricted powers; Nehru complains that as a member of one he was constantly obstructed by the administration and that no radical measures were open to them;[63] they seem to have resembled the Roman municipal councils only as they were in their later days, miserable instruments of the bureaucracy. In general British rule was more bureaucratic than the Roman in its heyday; the civil servants governed more, and until after 1919 there was a great preponderance of British in the higher ranks.[64] In the army the high command was entirely British. Bryce remarked that Indians could sit in both Lords and Commons, but there were only two or three instances. Indians had no place in either local or central government analogous to that which provincials could reach under Roman rule. One underlying reason was clearly the British sense of superiority, supported by colour prejudice. Even so intelligent a man as Cromer thought that there was some congenital difference in the mental make-up of westerners and all Orientals from China to Algeria which made the latter incapable of logical, rational thinking; the progress of Japan in his own day was a curious and unexplained exception.[65] It is notorious that the arrogance of this attitude, what Nehru calls the 'overbearing character and insulting manners of the English', bred bitter resentment.[66] As a result the educated élite did not become, as

[62] *Imperialism*, 117.

[63] *Autobiography*, 142.

[64] Indians preponderated in the lower ranks of the administration, but though higher posts had been open to them since 1833, over 80 per cent of these were still in British hands in 1913, and Indians were likewise debarred from all but subaltern army commissions. See R. Coupland, *India, a Restatement* (1945), 46 ff.

[65] *Modern Egypt*, 572 ff.; cf. 882 f. where he professes ignorance of Japan.

[66] *Autobiography*, 6. There is a curious instance in Cromer, *Essays*, 13: 'though we can never create a patriotism akin to that based on affinity of race or community of language, we may perhaps foster some sort of cosmopolitan allegiance grounded on the respect always accorded to superior talents and unselfish conduct, and on the gratitude derived both from favours conferred and from those to come.' This claim to

> The debt immense of endless gratitude,
> So burdensome, still paying, still to owe

could only evoke resentment.

Macaulay had | hoped, 'interpreters between us and the millions whom we govern';[67] they were alienated by the exclusiveness, social no less than political, of the foreign rulers. In practice the ideals of equality, fraternity and liberty were not realized.

Romans too could speak with contempt of peoples born to servitude, or deplore race mixture—Orontes flowing into Tiber. But the ever increasing importance of provincials, even from the east, demonstrates that occasional expressions of racialism were of no great moment. Certainly there was no colour bar, perhaps because the empire contained no negroes and because the physical characteristics of some Italians do not differ much from those of most Syrians. If by culture and sentiment men were Romans, Romans they were. The term 'Wog' cannot be translated into Greek or Latin.

In the end the principles of the modern West prevailed over the practice of those who went out to govern or settle or trade. Those who sat at home did not feel the force of prejudices or dictates of expediency to which they would mostly have succumbed if they had gone out themselves. And the ultimate control lay at home. In Britain there were always politicians and pressure-groups who encouraged nationalist "agitators" with their sympathy, and who indeed represented the most enduring trend in British policy[68] towards the subjects, whatever pauses or setbacks there might be. Even those most prone to talk of vital strategic interests or unrepresentative agitators could hardly reconcile with the liberal and humane principles they too accepted a policy of permanent repression or the savagery to which it almost inevitably leads. In 1919 at Amritsar General Dyer shot down an unarmed crowd of demonstrators. His conduct and the apologies made for it exacerbated Indian opinion and helped on the nationalist cause. But the government at home did not apologize; it disavowed him. Its spokesman in the Commons declared that such 'frightfulness' was 'absolutely foreign to the British way of doing things'. That spokesman was Winston Churchill, and it is not surprising that a generation later he did preside, for all his imperialism, over one stage of the liquidation of the British empire. To the Romans General Dyer's conduct would have seemed very moderate. One of their favourite methods of discouraging rebels was to cut off their right hands. But, as was observed in fifth-century Athens and verified in our own time, a democracy cannot govern an empire. The thing is inherently contradictory. |

[67] Quoted by Stokes (n. 8) 252.
[68] See Perham, *Colonial Reckoning*, 41–3 and 106 ff. For British criticisms of British rule in India, *Historians of India, Pakistan and Ceylon*, ed. C. H. Philips (1961), 332 ff., 382, 391. Administrators and ex–administrators also often stood up for native interests, for instance Lugard, against the Kenya settlers.

The Romans cared too little for liberty and gradually extinguished it. Thus they promoted apathy which destroyed their empire when confronted by foreign attacks. The modern empires were dissolved from within because they disseminated a spirit of liberty which they could not satisfy by any concessions short of independence. But the Romans left behind them not memories of discontent but a continuing aspiration for European unity, and as Christianity took on a Roman colouring, for Christian unity: 'extra ecclesiam nulla salus'. Perhaps the British or French will have bequeathed to their former subjects enduring love of the freedom that destroyed their empires (though, except in India, there is little sign of this). Who can say which ideal is most likely to be realized in a world where disunity prevails and tyrants flourish?

7

The 'Fiscus' and its Development

In a recent article Mr Fergus Millar has propounded the hypothesis that in the first two centuries of the Principate the term 'fiscus' always refers to the emperor's private wealth and is indistinguishable from such terms as 'res familiaris'.[1] In support of this view he has collected a great mass of useful material where the term 'fiscus' is actually used. Some of this evidence undoubtedly accords very well with his contention, and indeed no one can reasonably deny that the term is often employed in the sense stated. But many other texts which he cites only fortify his thesis if what he seeks to prove is already assumed, and can readily be interpreted in accordance with the view that 'fiscus' has more than one meaning. In my judgement he has failed to disprove Professor A. H. M. Jones' theory that 'fiscus' has diverse senses:[2] it may mean

(1) in the Republic the private funds of an individual;

(2) in the Principate the private funds of the emperor;

(3) in both the Republic and the Principate a chest, provincial or departmental, containing public monies;

(4) in Jones' words, 'the whole financial administration controlled by the emperor';

---

[1] F. Millar, *The Fiscus in the First Two Centuries*, *JRS* LIII, 1963, 29 ff., cited as 'M'. Unless otherwise stated Jones = A. H. M. Jones, *St. in Roman Government and Law*, 1960; *KV* = O. Hirschfeld, *Die kaiserlichen Verwaltungsbeamten*[2], 1905 (Rp. 1963); Pflaum = H-G. Pflaum, *Les carrières procuratoriennes équestres sous le haut-empire romain*, 1960. I am indebted for critical comments to Mr. J. P. V. D. Balsdon, Mrs. M. I. Henderson and Professor Alan Watson.

[2] Jones Ch. VI (= *JRS* XL, 1950, 22 ff.). In the end the public *aerarium* disappears, and 'aerarium nostrum' is equivalent to 'fiscus', the state treasury which the emperor controls (e.g. *CJ* X, 10, 4–5, cf. S. Bolla, *Die Entwicklung des Fiscus*, etc., 5, n. 10). Hence classical or post-classical jurists have often substituted 'fiscus' for 'aerarium' in earlier legal texts. One such example, *contra* Jones 104, is *Dig.* XLVIII, 13, 11 (9), 6, where Paul or the compilers have surely altered 'aerarium' in Labeo's text (though not consistently, in view of the later equivalence); I cannot believe that when a proconsul in Augustus' time had returned, but failed to pay in a balance due to the *aerarium*, a claim would have been made against him as a debtor to the local *fiscus*, or that if a local *fiscus* were meant, it would not be specified as 'fiscus provinciae'.

Journal of Roman Studies, 56 (1966), 75–91.

hence to say that property or income was fiscal may simply denote that it was under the emperor's administration and control, whether in strict law it was owned by the emperor in his private capacity or by the *res publica*. In this sense we may call the 'fiscus' the imperial treasury, without implying that it was ever a single chest in which coin or bullion was kept.

Millar is quite right to emphasize 'the importance of the emperor's private wealth in the running of the State'. And not only his private wealth: we should add the staff he employed for its management both in Rome and in the provinces. I shall suggest that it was the employment of this staff to administer public as well as private property and revenue that helped to promote the confusing, and confused, usage of the term 'fiscus'. The same persons handled the emperor's public and private financial business, and, as the emperor very soon ceased to render account for the public monies with which he was entrusted, it became easy and natural for public and private monies (or properties) to be amalgamated. This process, which was doubtless gradual (though we can rarely trace any of the stages), not only had the effect of placing public revenues and property, which strictly belonged to the state, at the free disposal of the emperor, but also, more curiously, of assimilating his own income and property to the public income and property which he administered; thus, for instance, the private patrimony passed from emperor to emperor as such, without regard to the rules of inheritance in private law. This was a necessity in the imperial financial system, precisely because the empire depended so much on the imperial patrimony. I shall try to show that it is only by admitting that this process took place that we can understand how, for instance, *bona caduca* and *bona damnatorum* came to flow into the 'fiscus'; Millar himself gives evidence for this, but his theory does not explain how such *bona*, which ought to have belonged to the state, could be treated as fiscal. Indeed, on my view, Millar is wrong in denying that the proceeds of some (and probably in the end nearly all) taxes went to the 'fiscus', and it seems intolerable to me to suppose that they | were ever legally the private income of the emperor. In the later legal writings indeed 'fiscus' certainly means the public treasury, and this is explicable as the ultimate result of the process I conceive to have occurred.

I

For the sake of clarity, I shall begin by citing the well-known evidence for the use of 'fiscus' in the first three senses mentioned above.

Fiscus, Fisci as Private Funds

Quite literally, 'fiscus' is a basket in which money may be kept. The proceeds of property sold by the state may be deposited in sealed 'fisci'; it is in 'fisci' that Verres sent money to Rome to bribe jurors, that Germanicus kept his cash on campaign and that Claudius put money to reward any one who would assist when a great fire broke out at Rome.[3] A private person, too, 'fiscos parat', 'puts money in his purse', before crossing the sea as a trader.[4] In such texts there are no juristic implications. But just as we may say that a man pays something from his own pocket, meaning that he does so from his capital or income as a whole, so a Roman could say that he paid 'ex suo fisco'.[5] In this sense the 'fiscus' is his property, and it is thus that Seneca uses it of the emperor when he writes: 'Caesar omnia habet, fiscus eius privata tantum ac sua; et universa in imperio eius sunt, in patrimonio propria' (*de benef.* VII, 6, 3). This text is, of course, the foundation of Millar's theory, and wherever 'fiscus' occurs, he makes it accord with the meaning it has here. Unfortunately, 'fiscus' has other senses too.

'Fisci' as Provincial or Departmental Chests

When Cicero represents Verres as saying to himself about certain monies, 'Ego habebo et in cistam transferam de fisco', he means, as the context proves, that Verres was going to transfer them from a public chest into his private purse.[6] 'fiscus' *tout court* is the provincial chest, containing public monies. Jones is surely right in holding that every governor had such a 'fiscus' in account with the *aerarium*, and that the *tamieia* on which the lex Gabinia authorized Pompey to draw were such 'fisci'.[7] The 'fisci' of which Augustus' *breviarium* gave account were evidently public and may be identified with these local treasuries.[8] Under Tiberius we learn of a 'fiscus Gallicus provinciae Lugdunensis' in which imperial slaves were employed; they presumably received taxes and made public disbursements under the procurator.[9]

Inscriptions mention *advocati fisci* attached to various provincial *stationes*:[10] Narbonensis (*CIL* VIII, 1578), tres Hispaniae (*ILS* 9016; *AÉ* 1930, 148) or Baetica (*CIL* VIII, 9249), Alpes Maritimae (*AÉ* 1888,

---

[3] Cic., *Verr.* I, 22; Tac., *Ann.* I, 37; Suet., *Claud.* 19.

[4] Sen., *ep.* 119, 5. [cf. Juv. XIV, 259.]

[5] Val. Max. VI, 2, 11.

[6] *Verr.* II, 3, 197.

[7] Jones 101 ff. [cf. Lucilius 429 M.]

[8] See text to n. 94.

[9] *ILS* 1514 = EJ 158. [cf. *CIL* II, 3271.]

[10] *ILS* 1347 mentions an *advocatus fisci* of eleven provinces.

132), Alexandria, all Egypt and Libya Marmorica (*IGR* IV, 1624), and even to the bureaux of particular taxes or administrative posts: thus we have a *fisci advocatus XL Galliarum* (*ILS* 1411), and another 'at fusa per Numidiam' who also served 'at vehicula per Transpadum et partem Norici' (*ILS* 9018). Now the *quadragesima Galliarum* was undoubtedly one of the public taxes, and the cost of obtaining *vehicula* was a proper charge on public funds.[11] The 'fisci' of these departments should then have been public, though both departments had come under the control of the emperor's officials, the procurators of the *XL Galliarum* and the *praefecti vehiculorum* in the second century. This being so, there is no need to suppose that the provincial 'fisci' enumerated contained only the emperor's private funds and not the proceeds of the taxes levied in the provinces concerned: probably they comprised both.

Admittedly all these inscriptions belong to the third century, when 'fiscus' had certainly acquired a 'public' connotation, but in Asia and Phrygia such *advocati* of a provincial *fiscus* are attested under the Antonines (*IGR* IV, 819: *Forsch. Ephes.* III, 138, 53: *AÉ* 1940, 205), and other *advocati fisci* are known from the second century (Pflaum 1033: 1103) at | Rome itself or in an office unspecified; and, as will appear later, we find one of them pleading before the *praefecti aerarii*, under Marcus; I see no good reason to think that the third-century evidence cannot be used to confirm the existence of provincial 'fisci', handling state funds, in an earlier period.

It is true that we also hear of 'fisci' with their *advocati* which are purely patrimonial, for instance, 'advocati fisci patrimoni tractus Karthaginis' (*CIL* VIII, 24064; 1578; *ILS* 9016; 9018).[12] But it is significant that in the last three of these four instances the persons in question had also been advocates for the 'fisci' of Narbonensis, the three Spains and the vehicular service respectively. The fact that they specify that their post in Africa was patrimonial makes rather against the view that elsewhere it had the same character. We also know of a 'fisci advocatus stationis hereditatium et cohaerentium'.[13] The *hereditates* are admittedly the private inheritances of the emperor (but cf. *infra*), but what are the 'cohaerentia'? Hirschfeld plausibly argued that in the time of Hadrian the *procuratores hereditatium* took over the administration of the *bona caduca* and *bona damnatorum*, and if my later contentions are accepted, these properly belonged to the state and the emperor was merely their administrator or trustee.[14]

---

[11] In the fourth century one could speak indifferently of *cursus publicus* (*ILS* 5905–6) or *cursus fiscalis* (ib. 755).

[12] cf. *KV* 141 and H. Dressel, *CIL* XV, 2, 491 f.; 560 ff. on the 'fisci rationis patrimoni provinciae Baeticae' (or 'Tarraconensis').

[13] *ILS* 1430–1; cf. 5017 (= *CIL* IX, 2565; cf. VIII, 1439).

[14] *KV* 113 ff.

In and after the Flavian period we also know of 'fisci' at Rome.[15] Of these the nature is sometimes obscure (Asiaticus, Alexandrinus, castrensis), but the 'fiscus Iudaicus' received the special capitation tax imposed by Vespasian on all Jews (cf. Suet., *Dom.*, 12, 2); and this was a public revenue. Similarly, the 'fiscus frumentarius' presumably contained the cash at the disposal of the *praefectus annonae*;[16] and the cost of feeding the Roman *plebs* normally fell on public funds, as is clear from the mere fact that some emperors took credit for subsidizing it from their own resources in emergencies. On the other hand, the 'fiscus libertatis et peculiorum', which is attested even before A.D. 69, was surely in Jones' words 'derived from the *peculia* of deceased slaves of Caesar, from the sums with which slaves of Caesar bought their liberty, and no doubt also from the inheritances of imperial freedmen'.[17] These sources of income belonged to Caeser in his private capacity as master or patron.

Thus a 'fiscus', qualified by descriptive words, showing it to be a departmental or local chest or account, may be either public or private. The provincial 'fiscus' is, however, surely both, at least in an imperial province, where the same procurator handled both public and patrimonial funds, and where these funds were probably fused in the course of time. And when 'fiscus' is used without qualification in a provincial document, or by a provincial writer referring to finances within a province, it may always refer to the provincial 'fiscus', to which the provincials made payments, rather than to any empire-wide treasury, whether of Caesar or of the Roman people.[18] Provincial references to 'the most sacred treasury' can be understood in the same way. The epithet 'most sacred' indicates of course that it was viewed as the emperor's, but to provincials who were less familiar with legal niceties than with political realities, the emperor was the state; they were thinking of his control, and their expressions are of no value in determining the question who owned the funds appertaining to the 'fiscus' or 'most sacred treasury' of which they write.[19]

[15] Jones 110 f. His own explanation is conjectural. Herodian III, 13, 4; IV, 4, 7 (cf. *KV* 4) shows that by the Severan period, and probably much earlier (cf. perhaps *ILS* 309), there were actual treasuries at Rome, under the emperor's control, other than the *aerarium Saturni* and *aerarium militare*.

[16] cf. *ILS* 7267 for 'fiscus stationis annonae' at Rome.

[17] Jones 109. M.'s formulation (30) seems less accurate. [Note Suet., *Vesp.* 23, 1.]

[18] All Egyptian texts cited by M. in his nn. 32; 51; 53; 67; 124; 169 *may* thus be explained, as also texts cited in his nn. 46 and 119 (Achaea); 138 (Lycia); 143 (Crimea); so too the evidence cited by M. on 'fines and penalties' (37 f.).

[19] Thus no juristic weight need be assigned to the evidence of Strabo (M., n. 91), Josephus (nn. 21; 56; 101; 113; 118), Dio Chrysostom (n. 41), Plutarch (n. 123) and Eusebius (ib.). Legal texts and documents, e.g. *FIRA* I², no. 105 (where the procurator of Vipasca sells 'nomine fisci'); 104 (1) and (3) (for share of products belonging to 'fiscus'), speak of property going to the 'fiscus', not to Caesar; and where 'fiscus Caesaris' is used, the genitive need not denote ownership.

'Fiscus' as the Imperial Treasury

When the term 'fiscus' is used by Romans in the Principate, however, without qualification and without any local context to which it can be confined, it clearly refers to | the imperial finances as a whole. For Seneca it apparently represents the funds of the 'patrimonium' (*supra*), and both Tacitus and Pliny more than once contrast it with 'aerarium'.[20] Originally then, it referred to the private wealth of the emperor. It is significant that though every man could at one time have his own 'fiscus', the term is now appropriated to Caesar's. So too one may surmise that the Silani were not the first or only private Romans to designate their accountants 'a rationibus', but by Nero's time it could be held that it was an usurpation of the imperial prerogative for a private person to give his own servants that title.[21] The emperor's accountant was becoming, or had become, a public official—I shall argue later that public property and income were already under his control—but enough remained private in origin to make the contrast between 'fiscus' and 'aerarium' not wholly meaningless. By the time of the classical jurists and in lay writings after the second century 'fiscus' is a mere equivalent of 'aerarium'.[22] This development has to be explained.

Patrimonium and Hereditates

Even the vast patrimony of the emperors, constantly augmented by inheritances and legacies, accrued to them in part because of their public powers. Gaius and other tyrannical rulers compelled private persons to leave them legacies on pain of annulling their wills, with what formal justification (if any) it is hard to determine.[23] Moreover, though in private law a legacy was void if the legatee predeceased the testator, Gaius claimed legacies left to Tiberius by those who outlived him (Dio LIX, 15). This innovation was doubtless cancelled on his death (Dio LX, 6), but the irregularity of one reign would become the norm later, and it was the rule under so good a constitutional ruler as Pius that 'quod principi relictum est, qui antequam dies legati cedat ab hominibus ereptus est, successori eius debetur' (*Dig.* XXI, 56). This rule

---

[20] E.g. *Ann.* II, 47 (cf. Jones 194); IV, 20; VI, 2; 17; Plin., *Pan.* 36; 42; cf. Front., *de aqu.* 118; Suet., *Vesp.* 16, 3.

[21] *Ann.* XV, 35; XVI, 8. cf. Ps.-Quint., *Declam.* 353: 'servum . . . supra rationes positum.'

[22] See, e.g. *Dig.* XLIX, 14, 13 and 15. I doubt if we need assume that the texts of the classical jurists in these passages have been altered by the compilers, though either Callistratus or the compilers must have changed 'populus' into 'fiscus' in the fragment of Labeo in XLIX, 14, 1, 1: cf. n. 2.

[23] For the facts, R. S. Rogers, *TAPA* 1947, 140 ff. For an attempted explanation in juristic terms, J. Gaudemet, *St. Arangio-Ruiz* III, 115 ff.

is the more remarkable, as the successor of a deceased Princeps was not necessarily his heir in private law. Even if the property that came to the emperor under both these practices was 'private', it is evident that it accrued to him in virtue of his imperial position.

There is indeed other evidence which shows that the patrimony, however acquired, came to be indissolubly attached to the Princeps as such. Augustus did indeed divide his property between Tiberius and Livia, whose share reverted to the emperor only on her death.[24] But when Tiberius made Gaius and his young grandson, Tiberius Gemellus, co-heirs, the senate in deference to Gaius' wishes set the will aside, so that Gaius might inherit the whole estate.[25] Claudius' will was also suppressed, perhaps because he had left part of his property to Britannicus.[26] The annulment of Tiberius' and Claudius' wills may be reasonably taken to do no more than illustrate the tyranny of Gaius and Nero: it is more significant that later emperors seem to have given up the practice of making wills, even when they could depend on the good-will of their successors. At least we have no record of any emperor making a will after Claudius, except for a statement in the late and unreliable *Historia Augusta* that Pius did so (SHA, *Pius*, 12, 8). And that may be doubted, considering that Dio tells us that Pertinax divided all his existing belongings among his children *on accession*,[27] as if he would not feel free to devise his property by will, and that this testimony lends credence to other statements in the *Historia Augusta* that both Pius and Marcus provided for their children by gifts 'inter vivos',[28] out of their own personal property, i.e. that which had not come to them as emperors. This suggests that custom had hardened into a rule by which the most conscientious emperors considered themselves to be bound, that the income from the patrimony, so essential to the solvency of the state, could not be alienated from the income that an emperor as such enjoyed. Indeed Pertinax recognized that he held the fiscal property as a trust when he forbade his own name to be inscribed on 'the | imperial possessions' (those which had come to him as emperor) and declared them to be the 'common and public possession of the empire'.[29]

In fact the Julio-Claudian property passed into the possession of the Flavians, and all that they had into the possession of Nerva and his descendants by adoption,[30] and Pertinax in turn secured all the

---

[24] *Ann.* I, 8.

[25] Suet., *Gaius* 14; cf. *Tib.* 76.

[26] Suet., *Claud.* 44; *Ann.* XII, 69; Dio LXI, I.

[27] Dio LXXIV, 7, 3; cf. HA, *Pert.* II, 12.

[28] HA, *Pius* 7, 9; 12, 8; *Marc.* 4, 7; 7, 4. cf. *Pius* 4, 8.

[29] Hdn. II, 4, 7, on which cf. *KV* 12 against Mommsen, *StR.* II³, 999, I.

[30] E.g. Vedius Pollio's *piscinae* in Campania (Dio LIV, 23; Pliny, *NH* IX, 167; *CIL* VI, 8584); *horti Serviliani* (*Ann.* XV, 55; *Hist.* III, 38; Pliny, *NH* XXXVI, 23); *horti Sallustiani* (*Ann.* XIII, 47; *Dig.* XXX, 39, 8); cf. *StR* II³, 1007, I, for Vibius Pansa's tile-works and for transfer of 'ius patronatus' to successive emperors.

Antonine estates, as did Severus after him, despite the fact that Pertinax left a son who rose to the consulship (*PIR*² H 74). The acquisitions by their successors of the property of Nero, Domitian and Commodus might be regarded as special cases of the practice whereby *bona damnatorum* went to the emperor; for all were posthumously condemned. (The property of Domitian and Commodus could not be treated as *vacantia*, since under praetorian law in default of a valid will Domitian's estate should have gone to his widow, and Commodus' to his *cognati*.) If the patrimony of these emperors was, none the less, treated as the private property of their successors, it can have been so only in a Pickwickian sense; for it was only in virtue of their public position, not of any rules of private law, that the successors had title to it.

Doubts might indeed arise about the purely private character even of parts of the patrimony of Augustus. Millar notes (p. 30) how Augustus came into possession of Cleopatra's balsam plantations near Jericho. He suggests that they became his private property 'perhaps as spoils by analogy with *manubiae*'. It is no objection to this view that there would have been no Republican precedent for assimilating real estate to movable booty, which could be treated as *manubiae*, for the history of the imperial 'fiscus' is in many respects unique. But Mommsen at least thought that though the victorious general was entitled to 'retain booty and the money realized from its sale, if he wished, in his own administration', without accounting for it to the *aerarium*, he was expected to use the proceeds in the public interest, precisely as Augustus did use his *manubiae* himself and required his generals to do.[31] If this analogy is pressed, the income from such estates as the balsam plantations remained in some sense public. The question must arise, however, whether Augustus, in taking over such estates into his own administration, did deny (as Mommsen held) that he was accountable for them. The greater part of the old royal land in Egypt was made public, the property of Rome, not of Augustus (see text to nn. 106–9). Nor do we know, as Millar assumes (p. 31), that later emperors treated mines they exploited as private. The fact that they appointed procurators to manage them, and other estates, is irrelevant; they had procurators to administer revenues which Millar himself seems to recognize as public (cf. nn. 84–5 below), and rightly.

Bona Caduca

Under Millar's theory it is particularly hard to explain how the emperor in his private capacity came to possess himself of *bona vacantia*

----

[31] *StR* I³, 241 (cf. Mommsen, *Röm. Forsch.* II, 443); see esp. Cic., *de leg. agr.* I, 12; II, 59).

and *caduca*. In cases where there were no validly instituted testamentary heirs (or none who would accept the inheritance) and no persons who were entitled to intestate succession or to *bonorum possessio* under praetorian rules (or none who would claim the estate) the *bona* were *vacantia*, and '*populo* bona deferuntur ex lege Iulia caducaria' (Ulp., 28, 7).[32] Ulpian is referring to the rules of the Augustan marriage laws under which inheritances or legacies to persons debarred from receiving them in whole or part went in the first place 'liberis et parentibus testatoris usque ad tertium gradum' (ib. 18), and then, in default of such beneficiaries, to the people; by the lex Julia 'bona caduca fiunt et ad *populum* deferri iubentur . . .' (Gaius II, 150, cf. III, 62). The effect, if not the motive, of these provisions in the early Principate was to enrich the *aerarium* (*Ann.* III, 25), the treasury of the people; their justification that if citizens would not do their duty and procreate children it was right to provide 'ut . . . velut parens omnium *populus* vacantia teneret' (ib. 28). However, in Ulpian's own day, *caduca* and *vacantia* went to the 'fiscus'; 'hodie ex constitutione imperatoris Antonini omnia | caduca fisco vindicantur, sed servato iure antiquo liberis et parentibus' (17, 2).[33] *Prima facie* it might appear, if we took account only of these texts, that Caracalla had for the first time transferred *caduca* to the 'fiscus', and therefore that references to the 'fiscus' as beneficiary in earlier juristic texts must be regarded as interpolations; but it will become clear that the 'fiscus' had inherited in some cases long before Caracalla, and that the emphasis in the text just cited from Ulpian must be placed on 'omnia'; henceforth the 'fiscus' was to take *all* 'caduca'.

Until the time of Vespasian *caelibes* and *orbi* could evade the restrictions on their rights to take under wills by receiving *fideicommissa*, but in his reign the SC Pegasianum applied the same rules to *fideicommissa* as to inheritances and legacies, with forfeiture 'ad populum' (Gaius II, 286–286a). (Under Hadrian the same rules were applied to *fideicommissa* for *incerta persona* and *postumus alienus* (ib. 287).) A new mode of evasion was then found. Instead of binding the fideicommissary expressly in his will to hand over such and such property to such and such a person, the testator asked him in his will merely to do something which he had previously requested, and defined the nature of this request in a separate document (*chirographum*) or in a 'nuda pollicitatio'.[34] These *tacita fideicommissa* were declared void by Trajan and penalized by the forfeiture of the property, if the fideicommissary carried them out. Trajan, however, provided that the beneficiary

---

[32] cf. Papin. IX, *resp.* 13 (*FIRA* III, p. 443). But Julian, unless *Dig.* xxx, 96, 1, is interpolated, refers to 'fiscus'.

[33] So too a fine for selling or buying fugitive slaves; '*hodie fisco vindicatur*' (*fr. de iure fisci* II, 9).

[34] *Dig.* XXXIV, 9; 10 *pr.*; XLIX, 14, 3 *pr.*; 14, 40.

under such *tacita fideicommissa* might take half of the property that would have accrued to him, provided that he denounced himself 'ad aerarium' before any other delation took place (*Dig.* XLIX, 14, 13 *pr.*). A *senatus consultum* of Hadrian's time enacted that it was for the *aerarium* to sequester the property and hand over half to the self-delator (XLIX, 14, 15, 3). Jurisdiction lay with the prefect of the *aerarium*, and the term used in the mid-century for 'sequester' is still 'publicare' (XLIX, 14, 42). However, the transmitted texts of classical jurists, reporting on and interpreting these rules, freely use 'fiscus' in the same context as 'aerarium' and as a mere synonym. They or later redactors may have altered 'aerarium' or 'populus' into 'fiscus' in accordance with the practice of their own day, but the variations may be due to the undoubted fact that even in Trajan's time, and earlier still, the 'fiscus' as well as the 'aerarium' benefited from *bona caduca*.

In his *Panegyric* Pliny clearly distinguishes between the 'fiscus', which is Trajan's, and the 'aerarium' (ch. 36). He also says: 'locupletabant et fiscum et aerarium non tam Voconiae et Iuliae leges quam maiestatis singulare et unicum crimen eorum qui crimine vacarent' (ch. 42). Thus the 'fiscus' shared already both in *bona caduca* and in *bona damnatorum*. Even earlier, if Tacitus' language is exact, the property of Aemilia Musa who had died intestate had been 'petita in fiscum', though Tiberius handed it over to a member of the same *gens* (*Ann.* II, 48). Moreover some legal texts which mention the rights of the 'fiscus' to *bona caduca* are not easily to be suspected of interpolation, for instance, a *senatus consultum* of A.D. 129 apparently quoted verbatim in *Dig.* V, 3, 20, 6, and the statement of Gaius III, 285 that under another *senatus consultum* of Hadrian *fideicommissa* to *peregrini* were forfeit to the 'fiscus'; this testimony is the more impressive, as Gaius uses 'populus' a few lines later. The fact that both Callistratus[35] and Paul wrote treatises 'de iure fisci et populi' suggests that in part of the Severan period, perhaps until the constitution of Caracalla mentioned earlier, the 'populus' as well as the 'fiscus' still had claims to certain property.

Some light on this strange phenomenon seems to be provided by two reports we have of a case decided by Marcus Aurelius (*Dig.* XXVIII, 4, 3; XXXIV, 9, 12). Marcellus, who was present at the hearing, gives us in one of these reports an extract from the *procès-verbal*. 'Marcus ruled: "Inasmuch as Valerius Nepos changed his intention, cut open his will and erased the names of the heirs, his estate in accordance with the enactment of my divine father does not seem to belong to those whose names were written in the will." He then said to the *advocati fisci*: "You

---

[35] See *Dig.* XLVIII, 20, 1; elsewhere it is cited as 'de iure fisci'; to the compilers 'fiscus' comprised the public rights.

have your judges." Vibius Zeno said: "I beg you, lord emperor, to hear me patiently; what will you decide about the legacies?" Antoninus Caesar said: "Do you think that the testator wished his will to be valid, when he erased the | names of the heirs?" Cornelius Priscianus, the advocate of Leo [evidently a legatee], said: "it was the names (only) of the heirs he erased." Calpurnius Longinus, *advocatus fisci*, said: "No will can be valid without an heir." Priscianus said: "He manumitted certain persons and granted legacies." Antoninus Caesar cleared the court and after deliberating and ordering every one to be admitted, said: "The present case seems to admit of the more humane interpretation, viz. that we should suppose Nepos to have intended only those provisions to be void which he erased."' Thus, as Marcellus observes in his introduction, was resolved the long-debated question whether legacies were to be paid under a will voided by erasure of the names of the heir or heirs. Now it is clear from the presence of the *advocati fisci* that the 'fiscus' had a possible claim to the estate as *caducum*. The invalidation of the will in itself did not make the estate *caducum*, as there might still be 'liberi parentesve' with a prior claim to that of the 'fiscus' (*supra*). In order to secure the estate (less payment of legacies) for the 'fiscus', the *advocati fisci* still had to make good the fiscal claims before other judges. Our second allusion to this case shows that they were the *praefecti aerarii*. Papinian refers to 'the judgment of the divine Marcus in the case of the man whose name the testator had erased after completing his will' and adds that 'he sent the case to the *praefecti aerarii*, though the legacies bequeathed remained valid'.

Now, according to Pliny (*Pan.* 36), Trajan had adopted the practice for which Tacitus praises Tiberius whereby the emperor's *actor* or *procurator* had to submit fiscal claims to a judicial tribunal, presumably instead of determining them arbitrarily himself, as had no doubt been the custom under Domitian. What sort of tribunal? Pomponius writes (*Dig.* 1, 2, 2, 32): 'adiecit divus Nerva (praetorem) qui inter fiscum et privatos ius diceret.' He was writing in the middle of the second century, and he gives no indication that such a praetor (for whom we admittedly have no other evidence) was no longer appointed in his day.[36] It is then plausible to suppose that the tribunal to which Pliny refers was that of this praetor, and that it still existed in the middle of the second century. It may be of course that his jurisdiction had been transferred to *praefecti aerarii* by the date of Marcus' decision; but another possibility exists. We might believe that Nerva's praetor decided suits arising from administration of property by the 'fiscus'[37]

---

[36] Pomponius, l.c., does not fail to note that Titus reduced the number of praetors who heard cases involving *fideicommissa* from two to one.

[37] They are also concerned in fiscal suits in *Dig.* XL, 5, 4, 20, and XLIII, 8, 2, 4 (cf. *StR* II³, 1023, n. 4), which indeed refers to a different kind of case; probably in II, 15, 8, 19, which suggests that procurators had similar jurisdiction (probably outside Italy).

and that the *praefecti aerarii* were concerned with claims to *bona caduca* made by the 'fiscus'. In any event the mere fact that *fisci advocati* appear before the administrators of the state treasury seems to me to show that the 'fiscus' should, in one of its aspects, be regarded as a department of the 'aerarium'. And this is the only view which seems to account juristically for the development whereby claims that by statute belonged to the people were transferred to the 'fiscus'.

Bona Damnatorum

Originally they too went to the people; consequently the proper term for 'confiscate' was at first 'publicare' (e.g. Sall., *Cat.* 51, 43). But as early as 26 B.C. the senate voted that the property of Cornelius Gallus should go after his conviction to Augustus. This may indicate that the first steps in the process by which the 'fiscus' appropriated estates that ought to have belonged to the people, or at least administered these estates, were taken by authority of the senate, and that *senatus consulta* provided precedents for a practice which became in course of time general, and was adopted without express sanction in each particular case. Of the condemnation of C. Silius under Tiberius Tacitus writes: 'liberalitas Augusti avulsa, computatis singillatim quae fisco petebantur; ea prima Tiberio erga pecuniam alienam diligentia fuit.'[38] Two comments may be made on this: first, that there is no indication in legal texts that a private donor was entitled to recover his gifts from a person convicted on a criminal charge (in this case *repetundae* and *maiestas*): and second, that even if the emperor, or more probably the senate, now made new law to the effect that | the emperor might recover such gifts from one who could be held to have shown him ingratitude, that could not constitute a justification in law for the emperor annexing the whole property of the man concerned, as in other and later cases Tiberius himself did. Thus, on Sejanus' fall, his property was 'taken away from the *aerarium* and transferred to the *fiscus*, as if it mattered' (*Ann.* VI, 2), and after Sex. Marius' death 'aurarias argentariasque eius, quamquam publicarentur, sibimet Tiberius seposuit' (VI, 19).[39] In stating that Tiberius set these mines aside for himself, Tacitus uses a verb also employed for Augustus' administration of Egypt (*Ann.* II, 59): and as Egypt was in some sense 'public' (*infra*), we are not obliged to hold that the mines ceased to be in public ownership; Tiberius simply decided to manage and exploit them through his own agents.[40] There was perhaps

[38] *Ann.* IV, 20; Gallus' case (Dio LIII, 23) might also be so explained. The rules of private law under which donor (but not his heir) could recover gifts on grounds of ingratitude (see, e.g. Buckland, *Textbook of Roman Law*[2] 253 f.) are plainly inapplicable.

[39] *Ann.* VI, 2; 19; cf. 17: 'tot damnatis bonisque eorum divenditis, signatum argentum fisco vel aerario attinebatur'.

[40] Philo, *Flacc.* 150 (M. 37) may also be thus explained.

nothing new in this; when it had been proposed that part of Cn. Piso's property should be sequestered ('publicandam'), Tiberius had over-ruled the motion and allowed it to pass to Piso's son, Marcus, and Tacitus' explanation that he was 'satis firmus adversus pecuniam' (*Ann.* III, 18) strongly suggests that had he not done so, he would have been the gainer from the sequestration.

In Domitian's time convictions for *maiestas* and probably for other offences still enriched the *aerarium* as well as the 'fiscus'.[41] But in the course of time (as it would seem from the classical jurists) the 'fiscus' became the sole beneficiary; as Millar says, 'the consequence of *publicatio bonorum* was the reception of the goods by the Fiscus'. This development, however, even if we allow for the importance *senatus consulta* may have had in promoting it, can hardly be explained except on the hypothesis that the 'fiscus' was not, as Millar holds, a merely private fund of the emperor, but that it was itself a kind of department of the *aerarium*, of which the emperor was the administrator. The fact that 'publicare' is still used synonymously with 'fisco vindicare' tells the same way.[42] Certainly it will not do to invoke Hellenistic precedents.[43] A Ptolemy or a Seleucid was himself the state; Caesar was not. Nor could the institutions of Roman law be determined by those of subject peoples.

Other 'fiscal' Properties

In his own provinces, and ultimately in senatorial, the emperor seems to have administered the old *agri publici*.[44] In Italy itself it was tactful for the emperors not to amass too much property in their own hands. 'Rari per Italiam agri' says Tacitus in praise of the early part of Tiberius' reign (*Ann.* IV, 6). It was a count against Domitian that he seemed to seek almost a monopoly of landed wealth in Italy (Plin., *Paneg.* 50), and Trajan sedulously sold off the estates he had confiscated. And even under Domitian some escheats went to the *aerarium*—probably in Italy. The magistrates, probably in this period the *praefecti aerarii Saturni*, could arrange for public lands to be let on long leases.[45] However, Vespasian is reported to have sold *subseciva* for the benefit of the 'fiscus', although they were 'velut communis iuris aut publici'

---

[41] Pliny, *Pan.* 42, 1; cf. 55, 5. HA, *Hadr.* 4, 7; *Marc.* 24; *Albin.* 12 (but cf. Jones, *Later Roman Empire* 426); *Alex.* 46 allege continued sequestration for *aerarium*—unreliably (cf. below, n. 62).

[42] See, e.g. *Dig.* XLVIII, 20, 7, 5; 20, 8; 21, 3, 8; 'fisco vindicare' is the usual expression.

[43] M. 35.

[44] The evidence is indeed meagre, *KV* 139 ff.

[45] 'Populus' as well as 'Caesar' or 'imp. n.' owned estates in the territory of Veleia and the Ligures Baebiani, *CIL* IX, p. 229; long lease, Hyginus 116 L, cf. *KV* 139 ff.

(*Gromatici* 282 L).[46] And in the end the imperial estates in Italy grew to immense size,[47] and the emperors secured the management of the remaining *agri publici*, if the Severan *procurator vectigaliorum populi Romani, quae sunt citra Padum* was charged with collecting rents from these lands.[48] But the development in Italy was probably slower than in the provinces.

Fines

Millar is puzzled by the frequent practice (the legal basis of which is in any event obscure) whereby private persons prescribe penalties to the 'fiscus' for violation of contracts or tombs. Now it may be noted that in and near the city of Rome and to some extent | in Asia, a senatorial province, sepulchral fines are due to the *aerarium Saturni*.[49] Even in Egypt they were payable εἰς τὸ δημόσιον.[50] It is then clear that where 'fiscus' appears, it has taken the place of the Roman people. The practical reason for the substitution is easy to surmise; the 'fiscus' had agents zealous in collecting its dues, and the *aerarium*, except perhaps in Italy, had none. The purpose of private persons in prescribing such fines was to enforce the sanctity of the contracts or burial places concerned, not to enrich the state or emperor, but they naturally chose to give an interest in the enforcement to the 'fiscus', because it was most capable of intervening.[51] (In Egypt τὸ δημόσιον was synonymous with the imperial administration, and the same effect was obtained.) It is even more obvious that 'fiscus' has replaced 'populus' or 'aerarium', when fines were payable under state laws.[52] Here we have other cases in which the 'fiscus' has absorbed what is strictly due to the state, a phenomenon which could never have been justified unless the 'fiscus' itself had been public except in administration.

Taxes

Millar's attempt to show that the 'fiscus' has nothing to do with public revenues is thus open to serious objections, even if we restrict inquiry to 'fiscal' property. Moreover Millar himself finds evidence of extraordinary taxes being paid into the 'fiscus'.[53] Of these *aurum coronarium*,

---

[46] M. n. 101 (cf. Suet., *Dom.* 9, 3; *FIRA* I, no. 75).
[47] Hirschfeld, *Kl. Schr.* 544 ff.
[48] *ILS* 1396 (see Pflaum 765 ff.). Cf. *KV* 142.
[49] *KV* 15, n. 2; cf. *Dig.* xviii, 1, 52.
[50] M. n. 130.
[51] On the legal puzzle see F. de Visscher, *Le Droit des Tombeaux rom.*, 1963, 112 ff.
[52] M. n. 125.
[53] M. 38 f.

which in origin was a voluntary contribution to a victorious general
and of which he had apparently as much right to dispose as of *manubiae*,
but no more, may perhaps be accommodated with his theory, despite
the fact that it became compulsory. But it is much harder to believe
that citizens and even subjects could be required to pay other extraordinary taxes into a merely private fund of the emperor. And what of
the regular taxes, such as tribute and *portoria*? Millar has adduced three
texts which seem to show that these taxes too might go to the 'fiscus',
and which therefore do not suit his views. The last of these need cause
him no difficulty, if we suppose that in the papyrus cited the provincial
'fiscus' of Egypt is meant (cf. n. 18). But the first two are more
intractable, and Millar's efforts to explain them away strike me as
incredibly forced.

　　Suetonius records that Augustus refused citizenship to a tributary
Gaul but offered to exempt him from tribute at the cost of the 'fiscus'
(*Aug.* 40, 6).[54] It would be easier to accept the suggestion that he
proposed to pay the man's taxes out of his own funds, as he once paid
the Asian taxes to the public treasury from his own pocket, if the
language Suetonius used had been as explicit as Dio's (LIV, 30, 3) in the
instance alleged to be parallel. Nor can 'fiscus' without qualification be
easily interpreted as standing for the provincial 'fiscus'. Millar's
objection to the natural signification, that 'fiscus' stands for the public
funds administered by Augustus, derives its strength only from the
absence of other direct testimony that public revenues even from
imperial provinces went to the 'fiscus' in the first two centuries of the
Principate.[55] But he also finds little evidence that *hereditates* went to the
'fiscus', though he is rightly sure that they did (p. 34). The argument
from silence has no weight, as to my knowledge no evidence from the
period in question tells us where the direct taxes did go, [except that in
Augustus' time revenue from Egypt went to the *aerarium* (Vell. II, 39,
2)]. But if we look beyond these chronological limits, we find that the
'fiscus' did receive tribute.

　　Dig. II, 14, 42 (Papinian). Inter debitorem et creditorem convenerat,
　　ut creditor onus tributi praedii pignerati non adgnosceret, sed eius
　　solvendi necessitas debitorem spectaret. talem conventionem quan-
　　tum ad fisci rationem non esse servandam ,respondi: pactis etenim
　　privatorum formam iuris fiscalis convelli non placuit.

　　　　XLIX, 14, 46, 5 (Hermogenianus). Ut debitoribus fisci quod fiscus

---

[54] No need to think that Suetonius is quoting Augustus verbally.

[55] My impression is that the destination of taxes is rarely given in late texts; in *CJ* x, which
abounds in references to taxes, a reference (19, 6) to revenues 'qui ad arcam pertinent
praefecturae' is exceptional.

debet compensetur, saepe constitutum est, excepta causa tributorum (*codd.* 'tributoria') et stipendiorum.[56] |

L, 4, 18, 26 (Arcadius). Decaproti et icosaproti tributa exigentes ... pro omnibus defunctorum (pro nominibus defectorum, *Cuiacius*) fiscalia detrimenta resarciunt.

L, 15, 5 (Papinian). Cum possessor unus expediendi negotii causa tributorum iure conveniretur, adversus ceteros, quorum aeque praedia tenentur, ei qui conventus est actiones a fisco praestantur ...

It is just the same with the *portoria*. Ulpian defines publicans as 'qui publico fruuntur ... sive fisco vectigal pendant vel tributum consequantur' or as 'omnes qui quid a fisco conducunt' (*Dig.* XXXIX, 4, 1, 1). Even if here and elsewhere (XXII, 1, 17, 5,; L, 6, 6, 10) the *vectigalia* collected for the 'fiscus' were to be restricted to rents from imperial estates (as in XLIX, 14, 47), the use of the term 'publicanus' for a collector of imperial rents and the application to such publicans (or 'conductores') of the old provisions of the praetor's edict which had been designed to govern the farming of state contracts would be significant of the essentially public status of the 'fiscus'. But the restriction suggested would be improper, at least for the reign of Severus and Caracalla, who ruled that when the publicans had secured acknowledgment of liability to customs-duty but not obtained payment on the goods, the goods were not forfeit, 'cum poterit satisfieri fisco ex bonis publicanorum vel fideiussorum' (XXXIX, 4, 16, 12, Marcianus); this shows that the publicans or their sureties were liable to the 'fiscus'. If a text of Ulpian is authentic (*Dig.* L, 16, 17), 'publica vectigalia' are those the 'fiscus' receives, and include *portoria* ('vectigal portus'). In these circumstances it is unnecessary to evade the natural interpretation of the elder Pliny's statement that the 'fiscus' sold 'maris Rubri vectigal' as a reference to the 25 per cent customs duty at Red Sea ports.

According to Gaius, in provincial soil 'dominium populi Romani est vel Caesaris', or again 'stipendiaria sunt ea (praedia) quae in his provinciis sunt, quae propriae populi Romani esse intelleguntur; tributaria sunt ea, quae in his provinciis sunt, quae propriae Caesaris esse creduntur' (II, 7; 21). Jones' explanation of this doctrine as 'a conveyancer's phantasy' may be accepted;[57] the distinction between the people's provinces and Caesar's remains significant. Gaius, a jurist, asserts as precisely as any author whom Millar can invoke for his interpretation of the 'fiscus' that some provinces belonged to Caesar.

---

[56] For the right to offset debts to the 'fiscus' with sums due from the 'fiscus', cf. *Dig.* XVI, 2, 12; *CJ* IV, 31, 1.

[57] Jones ch. IX.

Granted that this is an incorrect juristic construction, how did the distinction come to seem plausible? It seems reasonable to me to suppose that it did so because the direct revenues of the imperial provinces were paid into the 'fiscus', which was in some sense Caesar's.

Fiscal Litigation

The duty of *advocati fisci* was to represent the claims of the 'fiscus' in judicial proceedings; in and after the third century (if not earlier) it was prescribed that they must be present and heard before a court adjudicated on any matter in which the 'fiscus' had a claim.[58] If Millar is right in contending (p. 33) that 'a *privatus* could, but the *res publica* (or any part of it) could not, litigate and engage an advocate', it follows of course that 'fiscus' must stand for the emperor's private estate wherever we find an *advocatus fisci* employed. However, the mere fact that advocates are attached to the *fiscus XL Galliarum* shows that Millar's rule will not hold. In the late empire it certainly did not. We have a late inscription of an 'advocatus fisci summe rei' (*ILS* 6502), and the department of the *res summa* was concerned with the public taxes.[59] Similarly, a constitution of A.D. 383 provides: 'Rationales privatae rei causis vel *sacri aerarii praesidentes* examen, praesente fisci advocatione, suscipiant'; appeals lie (as the case may be) either to the *comes rerum privatarum* or to the *comes sacrarum remunerationum* (more usually styled *comes sacrarum largitionum*); in other words *advocati* are concerned, whether the claims relate to the *res privata* (which embraced what had once been the imperial *patrimonium*) or to public taxes, | for which the *comes sacrarum largitionum* was responsible (*Cod. Theod.* XI, 30, 41). I see no reason to think that these activities of *advocati fisci* were innovations of the late empire. An emperor such as Trajan earned commendation for taking his suits to the courts,[60] but to the subjects it would have seemed an artificial distinction if he had restricted this practice only to those suits in which he was interested as a private person and excluded claims arising from the administration of public funds which he controlled no less absolutely than his private income. And *advocati fisci*

---

[58] Hadrian ruled that a *causa liberalis* affecting fiscal interests should be decided 'praesentibus et agentibus etiam his qui negotiis fisci solent intervenire', evidently the *adv. fisci*, as Callistratus proceeds: 'et huiusmodi liberales causae si, non interveniente fisci advocato, decisae sint, in integrum restituuntur' (*Dig.* XLIX, 14, 3, 9); cf. ib. 14, 7: 'si fiscus alicui status controversiam faciet, fisci advocatus adesse debet. Quare si sine fisci advocato pronuntiatum sit, divus Marcus rescripsit nihil esse actum et ideo ex integro cognosci oportet'. These texts do not warrant M.'s statement (text to n. 21) that *adv. fisci* could give judgment themselves. Cf. *CJ* II, 36 (37), 2 (A.D. 226); X, 11, 5 (335); *CTh.* X, 15 passim; X, 10, 32; XI, 30, 41.

[59] Jones, *Later Roman Empire* I, 411; 427 ff.

[60] Plin., *Pan.* 36; cf. *Ann.* IV, 6; 15, on Tiberius.

certainly appeared in claims to *bona caduca* in which in my view the emperor was only the representative of the state (*supra*).

The partly public character of the 'fiscus' (in Jones' final and most general signification) also seems to me to explain the privileges it obtained in litigation.[61] By submitting fiscal claims to judicial decisions even when those claims accrued to them as the representatives of the state, some emperors no doubt abjured certain advantages they might have enjoyed if they had decided them administratively; in return they obtained privileges even for their claims as private persons. Public and private funds in their possession are assimilated, the one to the other. As the imperial 'fiscus' is an unique institution, it is useless to look for parallels or precedents. But it may be noted that when the emperors had constituted a new department for their private property known as the *res* or *ratio privata* (or, once, *patrimonium privatum*),[62] they secured for it the same privileges, and that jurists in stating these privileges imply that the 'fiscus' was not simply private. 'Loci fiscales *vel* publici religiosive' are contrasted with 'Caesaris possessio' and 'quodcumque privilegii fisco competit, hoc idem et Caesaris ratio et Augustae habere solet.'[63]

The Legal Status of the 'Fiscus'

The 'fiscus' drew its income partly from sources which could more or less plausibly be regarded as private, partly from revenues which were properly the state's. Even in the third century the *aerarium* still had funds of its own,[64] and there was still some public property which the emperor did not administer.[65] But in the main the public resources were amalgamated with the emperor's own patrimony; all came under

---

[61] M. 33 f.

[62] Jones 112 ff. But it is now known that the *ratio privata* is at least as early as Marcus and probably goes back to Pius (Pflaum 1005 f.). The reason for its institution, and the nature of its distinction from the 'fiscus', are still obscure. In the late empire it claimed *bona caduca* and *damnatorum* (Jones, *Later Roman Empire* 412 ff.). This marks the final stage in the process whereby the emperor came to be the state. The confusion of later writers is well exemplified in HA, *Sev.* 12, which incorrectly ascribes to Severus the institution of the *ratio privata*; the author successively states that the properties of Severus' enemies were made public and '*aerarium* auxerunt' and that Severus 'magnam partem auri per Gallias, per Hispanias, per Italiam *imperatoriam* fecisset'. '*Aerarium*' seems also to be used for 'fiscus' in the lives of *Marcus* 24, 9 (cf. Jones, *op. cit.* 416), and *Alexander Severus* 46.

[63] *Dig.* XLIX, 14, 3, 10; 14, 6, 1; cf. Jones 113.

[64] *KV* 17.

[65] M. n. 176. But the distinction is one with hardly a difference in *Dig.* XLIX, 14, 3, 10, and the same procurator manages 'opera publica et fiscalia' in *AÉ* 1945, 80. It had probably become a mere matter of history; some property, long administered by the emperor, was fiscal; what was only now being taken into his hands still counted as public.

the control of the 'fiscus'. The 'fiscus' sometimes litigated (under the better emperors) like a private suitor and partly under the procedures and principles of 'ius commune'; but its suits were in some reigns determined by imperial procurators under a sort of 'droit administratif',[66] and even when it appeared as a suitor in the public courts, it was represented by officials, the *advocati fisci*, who were publicly employed, and it enjoyed privileges that derived from Caesar's public functions. Fiscal cases could therefore be contrasted with both public and private cases (*Dig.* III, 6, 13), or with one or the other.[67] |

Preoccupied mainly with private law, and averse to definition and abstraction,[68] the classical jurists never formed or stated any clear concept of this hybrid institution. But it is surely significant that the 'fiscus' as such, rather than Caesar, is constantly said to be selling or leasing or inheriting property, to be making or meeting claims,[69] and that even in the heyday of Severan absolutism, Ulpian could say that 'res fiscales *quasi* propriae et privatae principis sunt' (*Dig.* XLIII, 8, 2, 4);[70] he could hardly have endorsed Mommsen's view that the fiscal revenues were the emperor's private income, nor Millar's, which is in principle the same, though it differs in detail in erroneously denying that any of the taxes had become fiscal. The 'fiscus' was in fact what we should call a legal person, but this was a concept the Romans never evolved in explicit theory.[71] But it is unprofitable to define it or classify it as public or private, aiming at a clarity that is not found in the sources; we should look rather to the recorded facts and describe it as what it really was, the complex of properties and revenues (and their administration) of which the emperor was in absolute control. Some, probably most, of these properties and revenues were in strict law public, and we must now inquire how it came about that the emperor could treat them as 'res quasi proprias'.

---

[66] [See ch. 8.]

[67] 'Fiscus' and 'res publica' are distinguished in *Dig.* XXXVII, 1, 12. A rule in XLIX, 14, 37, that the 'fiscus' is not to lose 'ius commune privatorum' does not imply that it is merely 'private'. It is contrasted with a private creditor in XXII, 1, 17, 5, cf. XL, 15, 1 *pr.* ('neque privatim neque fisci nomine'); in XLIX, 14, 35 (Julian) the 'ius fisci' is equated with 'publica causa', cf. *CJ* VII, 49, 1 (Caracalla), where 'causa privata' is set against 'causa publica sive fiscalis'. In *Dig.* XLVIII, 13, 1, *peculatus* is said to be embezzlement of 'pecunia sacra religiosa publicave'; in the same title 'fiscus' is interpolated by Paul or the compilers in texts of Labeo (11 (9), 3 and 6) and occurs in words ascribed to Marcellus in 14 (12); in Paul, *Sent.* v, 27, the crime applies to fiscal property. I do not believe that this development is later than the Severan period.

[68] F. Schulz, *Principles of Roman Law* ch. II.

[69] Common in *Digest*, cf. n. 19 [first attested in Pliny, *NH* VI, 84; XII 113, 123].

[70] Cf. p. 351; H. M. Last, *JRS* XXXIV, 1944, 57–8. P. W. Duff, *Personality in Roman Private Law* 55, remarks that 'quasi' *can* mean 'in law, though not strictly in fact'. This is clearly true; but other considerations set out above seem to show that it means 'in fact, though not strictly in law'.

[71] cf. Schulz, *Class. Roman Law* 71; 86 ff. Observe the anomalies in the treatment of *municipia* and *collegia*; neither public nor private law was applied purely and logically. Similarly the rules on *societas* were not fully applicable to the publicans, cf. L. Mitteis, *Röm. Privatrecht* 403 ff.

II

In the Republic financial control belonged to the senate, in the Principate to the emperor. But it is not likely that the realities of the new monarchy were at once disclosed. In 27 B.C. Augustus professed to have restored the Republic, and Tiberius, repudiating the appellation of 'dominus' for himself, addressed the senators as his 'bonos et aequos et faventes ... dominos' (Suet., *Tib.* 27; 29). He could afford to style them his masters, precisely because they were 'faventes', and would do what he advised. The emperor was not only the chief executive; he was also the leading senator, who could be 'auctor', or as Tiberius preferred to phrase it, 'suasor', of the decisions the senate might take in its constitutional but more and more fictitious role as the great council of state, which was still supposed to preside over the fortunes of the revived Republic.

Formally then the functions of the senate in controlling finance should not have been abridged at first, and it is no surprise to find that Augustus consulted it on the form of taxation which he deemed it necessary to impose on Roman citizens for the support of the *aerarium militare*, or that Tiberius sought its advice 'de vectigalibus et monopoliis' (Suet., *Tib.* 30); some would even suppose that the young Nero proposed the abolition of *portoria* to the senate and accepted its objections, though this is a view I cannot share.[72] Augustus, Claudius, Nero, Vespasian and Nerva all set up senatorial commissions to deal with important financial problems, and I do not doubt that each was appointed under a *senatus consultum*, but on the motion of the emperor.[73] As in the Republic, it was to the senate that the provinces at first addressed petitions for relief from taxes, and it was the senate that granted remissions to distressed cities.[74] Dio says that provincial governors were not permitted to increase taxes without the sanction of either emperor or senate (LIII, 15, 6). It is significant | that even in his

---

[72] Tac., *Ann.* XIII, 50. The senate would not have dared reject a proposal formally made to it by Nero, and if it had, Tacitus would have stressed so remarkable an instance of *libertas*. But 'senatores' (unlike 'patres') is not a normal equivalent of 'senatus' and may be rendered '(some) senators'; I doubt if emendation is required. Nero's eventual decision was, I presume, endorsed by a *senatus consultum*: *Ann.* XIII, 48–52, seem to depend on the *acta*.

[73] Dio LV, 25, 6; LX, 10, 4; Tac. *Ann.* XV, 18, 3; *Hist.* IV, 40 (cf. 9); Pl., *ep.* II, 1, 9 and *Pan.* 62, 2; cf. Dio LXVIII, 2, 3. Tacitus and Dio, attentive to political realities, speak of action by the emperor; but *Ann.* XV, 18–22, I seem as a whole to depend on *acta senatus*, and Nero's commission was doubtless set up by *SC*, like Nerva's (as we know only from the lucky survival of Pliny's letters).

[74] Petitions for relief to the senate from senatorial provinces, *Ann.* I, 76; from imperial, II, 42 (apparently from *acta senatus*). Remissions, II, 47 (Tacitus speaks at first of action by Tiberius, but the appointment of a commissioner *ex senatu* proves that the senate was involved); IV, 13; XII, 58 (*acta senatus*); 62–3 (senate explicitly involved); these texts concern senatorial provinces, except for IV, 13 (Achaea—recently imperial).

day the senate still retained co-ordinate authority at least in name, and one might surmise that in the earliest period of the Principate it was the senate alone that had formal power to vary the rates of tax. With scrupulous and evidently surprising attention to old-world etiquette, Marcus Aurelius even sought authority from the senate to draw money from the *aerarium* (Dio LXXI, 33); in the Republic only the consuls could do so without the senate's consent (Polybius VI, 13). But the realities were very different. In A.D. 70 the treasury was empty and the emperor far away. The praetors of the *aerarium* urged that a limit should be set on public expenditure. The consul elect moved that the problem be left to Vespasian; the burden was heavy and a solution hard to find. Only Helvidius Priscus held that the senate had the duty to act (Tac., *Hist.* IV, 9). It was such conduct that earned him the reputation of a republican, despite the respect which he showed at this time to Vespasian (ib. 4).

The senate had indeed never displayed initiative or independence on financial questions since Augustus' time. Even then it had been unable to face the problem of raising new revenues for the *aerarium militare*.[75] Acting, if at all, only on the emperor's advice, it came to acknowledge him as the arbiter in financial questions. In A.D. 118 the senate and people officially thanked Hadrian as the first and only *princeps* who in remitting 900,000,000 HS due to the *fisci* had by this liberal act rendered secure not only the living citizens but their posterity as well. Dio says that he had remitted arrears both to the 'imperial' and to the public account. Whatever this may exactly mean, it is clear that the senate itself recognized the emperor's right to release citizens from debts to the state.[76.] Yet, when, in 28 B.C. Octavian had cancelled obligations to the state dating back before Actium (Dio LIII, 2, 3), this was one of his last acts before fully 'restoring the Republic'. Hadrian was admitted to have powers of a kind Augustus affected to surrender. In the *Panegyric* (ch. 36) Pliny acknowledged Trajan's control of the *aerarium*, whose officials had long been the emperor's nominees. Autocracy was avowed.[77]

Even in the earliest days of the Principate the emperors had exercised control over much of the work of assessing and collecting taxes and over the central financial administration at Rome itself.

Augustus instituted provincial censuses which provided a realistic basis for the assessment of taxes; as peace brought prosperity, higher

[75] Dio LV, 25; LVI, 28.

[76] *ILS* 309; cf. SHA, *Hadr.* 7, 6; Dio LXIX, 8, 12 (cf. LXXXI, 32, 2, on Marcus' remissions). See M. 32.

[77] Plin., *Pan.* 36, 3, on imperial control of *aerarium*.

yields could be expected.[78] As early as Tiberius' reign, we find that a proconsul of Narbonensis is also '[leg. a]d cens. accip. et dilect(us)'; it is by the emperor's authority that he takes the census and levies troops. Later too, the emperor sends his own agents, senatorial or equestrian, even to senatorial provinces to take the census.[79] Everywhere the emperor had his procurators, private agents managing his own estates or other business interests; sometimes they were his freedmen, and all had imperial slaves and freedmen to assist them. In senatorial provinces their functions were at first purely patrimonial,[80] and even in Dio's time the proconsuls seem to have been responsible for supervising the collection of the direct taxes.[81] But in the imperial provinces these procurators were charged from the start with the administration of the direct taxes and with making public disbursements—for instance, paying the troops.[82] Even in the Republic a slave or freedman of the governor could be used in important public business;[83] what was new in the Augustan system was the scale of the operations the | emperor's private agents performed. The system was developed as the work of government grew, and procurators with specialized functions were appointed to relieve the provincial procurators of part of their burdens. Thus in provinces where the emperor had come into possession of mines or great landed estates, he appointed procurators to administer these alone. Even if some of these procurators were no more than managers of his private property, others cannot be so described— the procurators who at first supervised the publicans collecting the *vicesima hereditatium* and later, if the orthodox view is sound, collected it themselves,[84] and those who from the second century administered the

[78] *Per.* Livy 134; 138-9; Dio LIII, 22, 5; *ILS* 212, 35 ff. (Gaul); Jos., *AJ* XVII, 355; XVIII, 2 and 26; *ILS* 2683 (Syria and Judaea); *CIL* x, 680 (Lusitania); Luke II, 1-3.

[79] *ILS* 950; cf. 5955 with Stat., *Silv.* I, 4, 83 ff. (Africa); *ILS* 1395 (Africa); 1046; 1395 (Macedon); 9506 (Bithynia).

[80] *Ann.* IV, 15, 2; Dio LVII, 23, 4-5. For the role of *procuratores Asiae* in the early Principate, cf. *Ann.* XIII, 1, 2: they are 'rei familiari principis impositi'; this expression, unlike references to 'fiscus', unambiguously relates to the emperor's private fortune.

[81] Dio LIII, 15, 3: πλὴν καθ' ὅσον τοὺς φόρους οἱ ἀνθύπατοι παρ' ὧν ἄρχουσιν ἐσπράσσουσιν.

[82] Dio LII, 28 ('Maecenas'); LIV, 21, cf. last note; Str. III, 4, 20. The Hama inscription, now conveniently printed in McCrum and Woodhead, *Docs. of Flavian Emperors* n. 466, suggests that they were also responsible for military transport and supplies (cf. *JRS* 1956, 46 ff.), functions later sometimes discharged by *praefecti vehiculorum* and occasionally by special officers concerned with the annona for armies (Pflaum III, pp. 1040, 1052, 1064, 1080). Presidial procurators combined the general work of government with financial duties, cf. *ILS* 3528 (Graian Alps): 'dum ius gubernor remque fungor Caesarum'; this is best attested for the prefect of Egypt.

[83] e.g. Statius, Cic., *ad Qu. fr.* I, 2, 1.

[84] Publicans, Plin., *Pan.* 37, 6; *ep.* VII, 14, 1. Procurators, first attested in Achaea under Claudius, *ILS* 1546 (freedman); in Rome from Domitian (Pflaum III, 1026), also in Italy (ib. 1036 ff.), and both imperial and senatorial provinces from the mid-second century (ib. 1048 f.; 1054 ff.; 1074; 1077; 1081; 1083; 1086; 1097). The record for all posts is very fragmentary and the first documentation of a post may be long after its creation. [See pp. 402-6.]

collection of the *portoria.*[85] They were undoubtedly concerned with public revenues. Similarly the procurators who assisted in taking the census, and the *praefecti vehiculorum* (cf. n. 82) were acting on behalf of the state. In all these ways the emperor's own staff assumed public duties, in senatorial as well as in imperial provinces, in connexion with the raising of taxes or with public requisitioning or with the expenditure of public monies. To a very large extent the financial administration of the empire came into the emperor's hands.

The usurpation by the emperor of control over property such as *bona caduca, bona damnatorum* and *agri publici,* which properly belonged to the state, can be explained in terms of administrative convenience. Millar suggests that 'the Fiscus normally retained property it confiscated (in contrast to the Aerarium, which sold such properties)'. In fact, the 'people' did retain some lands at least in Italy (nn. 45; 65), and the 'fiscus' is often mentioned selling property,[86] no doubt because it needed ready money,[87] or more generally, in cases where it would have been uneconomic to exploit an estate for its own account, for instance *subseciva* in Italy or other small farms isolated from a complex of imperial lands. But Millar's suggestion points the way to a plausible view.[88] Only the emperor had, throughout the empire, a large and experienced staff with the competence to see either to the sale or to the management of property belonging to the state. It was, for instance, convenient for the *procuratores hereditatium,* we may think, to sell or take possession of *bona caduca,* though their original function was simply to enter upon property bequeathed to the emperor as a private person (cf. n. 14). Provincials recognized this when they made sepulchral fines payable to the fiscus, which alone had agents to collect them. It was perhaps easier for the administrators of the *aerarium* to deal with public properties in Italy itself, and this may be one reason why the growth of fiscal estates seems to be somewhat delayed there.

Despite the greater efficiency in tax-administration which Augustus

[85] Such equestrian procurators are found in Gaul and Africa from Hadrian (Pflaum III, 1052; 1093), in Illyricum from Commodus (1065, cf. 1058 f.), in Asia only in the third century (1073; 1077); but some supervision by imperial freedmen and slaves is earlier, cf. S. J. de Laet, *Portorium* 373 ff. [See pp. 406–20 below.]

[86] M. 37. (I think he misinterprets Philo, *Flacc.* 150: the few parts of Flaccus' estate which did not go to the *fiscus* were probably left to him, cf. ib. 168.) Estates which had been 'in formam patrimonii redacta' were not usually sold (*Dig.* xxx, 39, 10), any more than 'horti qui principalibus usibus deserviunt' (ib.), which were doubtless assimilated to '(loca) publica, quae non in pecunia populi sed in publico usu habeantur, ut est campus Martius' (xviii, 1, 6 *pr.*). But there are many allusions to sales of fiscal property, e.g. xxii, 1, 16, 1; xxvii, 9, 2; xlix, 14, 3, 5; 14, 5; 14, 22 *pr.*–1; 14, 36; 14, 50; *CJ* 11, 36 (37), 3, 1; x, 1, 3; 3–5.

[87] e.g. Dio lvi, 8, 4; Pliny, *Pan.* 50. Cf. 'Maecenas' advice in Dio lii, 28.

[88] So H. Dessau, *Gesch. der röm. Kaiserzeit* 1, 198. Hirschfeld plausibly argues that *procuratores hereditatium* took over *bona vacantia* (cf. *Dig.* xlix, 14, 32), *KV* 114 ff.

introduced, public revenues were still inadequate and Augustus supplemented them with grants amounting in all to 2,400,000,000 HS,[89] a
sum perhaps seven times as large as the total revenues of the state in 62
B.C.[90] Other emperors such as Nero copied his munificence,[91] or like
Tiberius and Pius accumulated reserves to be used by their successors
in emergencies or simply squandered.[92] Indeed in time the state must
have become more and more dependent on the wealth that emperors
treated as their own, for the size or number of imperial estates was
always growing. The emperors drew income in the form of rents from
Italy itself, which paid no direct taxes; and in the provinces their
tenants might owe them | thirds of produce, when *stipendiarii* paid at a
different and probably lower rate.[93] Land in the possession of the
emperor was thus more productive of revenue than if it were left in
private hands.

For the central management of his private property Augustus
naturally needed a staff of clerks and accountants at Rome, and like
any other Roman gentleman, he found them among his own slaves and
freedmen. This experienced staff under his own control could be, and
was, used to assist him in supervision of the public treasury, just as his
provincial agents were assigned public as well as patrimonial duties.

As the chief executive of the state, Augustus was responsible for
collecting much of the public revenue and spending large sums from
public funds. But as the total public revenue was so inadequate for all
the expenditure he thought it necessary to incur that he felt obliged to
subsidize it from his own pocket, he could not be certain that he would
be provided with resources sufficient for the proper discharge of his
executive functions unless in his other capacity as the chief citizen he
watched with care over the general finances of the state. He therefore
had to exercise a kind of budgetary control. It was this supervision that
enabled him in 23 B.C. to hand over to the consul Piso an account of the
forces and the public revenues and indeed to issue periodic 'rationes
imperii'. At his death he left a 'breviarium totius imperii', similar to
that which he had given Piso, describing 'quantum militum sub signis
ubique esset, quantum pecuniae in aerario et fiscis et vectigaliorum
residuis'—'how many soldiers were under the standards in each
province, how much money there was in the *aerarium*, and in the
(provincial) chests, and how much was due from (the publicans who

---

[89] Appendix to *Res Gestae.*
[90] Plut., *Pomp.* 45, 3.
[91] *Ann.* xiii, 31, 2; xv, 18, 3.
[92] Suet., *Gaius* 37, 3; Dio lxxiii, 8, 3. No evidence that Vespasian accumulated 4,000,000,000
HS, as he wished (Suet., *Vesp.* 16, 3 amended).
[93] *FIRA* i², no. 100, 1, 25 ff.; cf. ii, 8 ('octonarium agrum', probably land paying eighths, rather
than 8 denarii per iugerum).

collected) the *vectigalia*'. And he added the names of the freedmen and slaves from whom a detailed account could be obtained.[94] We are not indeed actually told that these freedmen and slaves also handled his private accounts, but considering how Augustus had often subsidized the state, we may reasonably assume that he found it convenient that the chief clerks in his office should be able to acquaint him with all the resources, public or private, which might be called on to meet any urgent need.

Here is the origin of the office *a rationibus*. It is an illusion, unsupported by a single text, to suppose that Claudius either created it or invested it with more closely defined or more extensive financial powers. Pallas was certainly not the first incumbent. We know of other freedmen, some earlier than him, others perhaps coevals but subordinates who are styled *a rationibus*.[95] One such clerk was apparently in receipt of a salary from the *aerarium* under Tiberius.[96] That proves that he was acknowledged to be performing a public duty. Pallas himself, on retirement, successfully demanded that his accounts should be deemed to be in balance with the *aerarium* (*Ann.* XIII, 14,1). He presumably wished to safeguard himself against a charge of peculation ('ne cuius facti in praeteritum interrogaretur'), but it is hard to see how this could have been brought unless he had actually had public monies in his hands which he was able to embezzle. We may conjecture that just as procurators (who were sometimes imperial freedmen) paid the troops in imperial provinces, so officials in the department *a rationibus* made the emperor's public disbursements in Rome where he had no such procurators (for instance, pay for the praetorians).[97] But at the same time Pallas was described in the *senatus consultum* Pliny copied as 'custos principalium opum' and as one of those who were 'praepositi rerum (Caesaris)' (*ep.* VIII, 6, 7, and 13): presumably then he managed the emperor's private wealth. In all this there need have been nothing new. From his predecessors (as indeed from his successors) he was distinguished only by the magnitude of his political influence, manifest in his 'praetoria ornamenta', and by the scale of his venality and wealth.

The budgetary duties of the *a rationibus* are poetically and of course

---

[94] Dio LIII, 30; Suet., *Aug.* 101 with *Ann.* I, 11; Dio LVI 33; Suet., *Gaius* 16, 1, with Dio LIX, 9.

[95] P. R. C. Weaver, *Proc. Camb. Phil. Soc.*, 1964, 89, cf. 82.

[96] *CIL* VI, 8409c = EJ 153, where 'delat.' = 'delato ad aerarium', on the public pay-roll because employed on public business, cf. Front., *de aq.* 100. I see no reason to think this merely honorific, *contra* Millar, *JRS* 1964, 38.

[97] [G. Boulvert, *Esclaves et Affranchis Impériaux*, 1970, 106 urged *contra* that no *dispensator* or *arcarius* is known in the department *a rationibus* (or in that of the *patrimonium*). But *tabularii*, who are attested, could also make payments, and an argument from silence is dubious.]

incompletely indicated in a famous passage of Statius.[98] Under Domitian he has to estimate

> quantum Romana sub omni
> pila die quantumque tribus, quid templa, quid alti|
> undarum cursus, quid propugnacula poscant
> aequoris aut longa series porrecta viarum:

in other words, the costs of the armies, the grain-distributions, the temples, the fleets and the roads. These are all public expenses. In addition he has to advise how much coin is to be issued. But he must also consider 'quod dominis celsis niteat laquearibus aurum', and the embellishment of the imperial palace is a strictly household expenditure; he is involved in both the public and private budgeting of the emperor. Naturally he has to forecast revenues as well as 'magni impendia mundi'. He must know how much is to come from the mines of Spain and the Dalmatian quarries, from the harvests of Africa and Egypt. As the emperor had appropriated mines to himself, had large estates of his own in Africa and is often supposed to have regarded the whole of Egypt as his personal estate,[99] it has been held that these are all specimens of the emperor's private income. But it is too restrictive an interpretation to make Statius exclude the produce of the African *stipendiarii* and think only of imperial tenants; and in Egypt too, as will be shown later, the greater part of the land was 'public'. In any event it is unreasonable to suppose that the *a rationibus* attended only to the emperor's private income, when he certainly had to estimate his public expenses.

In order to present 'rationes imperii' Augustus must have ensured that his freedmen and slaves had access to the records of the *aerarium Saturni*, to which proconsuls, and probably he himself, presumably continued to render account. The younger Cato, after holding the urban quaestorship, had set his slaves to copy the records there day by day,[100] and with his pre-eminent *auctoritas* Augustus can have had no difficulty in securing sanction for the mode of supervision that he evidently adopted. Although in my view it must once have been the duty of the quaestors or other administrators of the *aerarium* to furnish the senate with sufficient data for decisions on financial policy to be taken,[101] I do not doubt that this work was done more efficiently under

---

[98] *Silv.* III, 3, 85 ff.

[99] *Hist.* I, 11, 'domui retinere' rightly indicates that it was administered by the emperor's own staff. Philo, *Flacc.* 158 looks at the realities. Neither text has any juristic value.

[100] Plut., *Cato Min.* 18, 5.

[101] *Contra* Millar, JRS 1964, 38. Given the nature of our evidence his argument from silence has no weight. [And note *ad Herenn.* I, 21.]

the new system, and that the administrators of the treasury had no need to duplicate the labours of the emperor's private staff. They remained of some importance, so that Claudius thought it worth while to substitute his own nominees for officials chosen by lot, and Nero to appoint ex-praetors who had more experience than the Claudian quaestors.[102] But they must have been confined to administrative routine, receiving and paying out public monies and checking the accounts of proconsuls.[103] They also had some jurisdiction over treasury claims, as shown earlier.[104]

The better emperors recognized that they were not 'supra leges', if only by securing dispensation from laws which they found it inconvenient to observe.[105] In law they must therefore have been no less accountable for the public monies at their disposal than the magistrates and promagistrates. 'Divus Augustus ... paene idem, facta Aegypto stipendiaria, quantum pater eius Galliis, in aerarium reditus contulit' (Vell. II, 39). Whether this means that Egyptian revenues surplus to local expenditure were actually paid into the *aerarium* may be doubted; but the least we can suppose is that they were treated as notionally due to the *aerarium*, and that Augustus was in account with it. This need surprise only those who think of Egypt as a private estate of the emperor. But both Augustus and the senate held officially that it had been brought under the *imperium* of the Roman people.[106] The powers of the prefect were granted by a *lex*,[107] and the claims of the Idios Logos were regulated in part by *senatus consulta*.[108] Most of the soil became δημοσία and the fellahin, once βασιλικοί, were henceforth δημόσιοι. The use of the novel term δημόσιος, here and elsewhere, signified that Egypt was originally at least deemed to be subject in form to the Roman | people.[109] In the edict of Ti. Julius Alexander the 'fiscus', the 'public account' and the 'account of Caesar' are equivalent terms.[110] Naturally to the subjects the power of Caesar obscured the

---

[102] Jones 106.

[103] Millar, *JRS* 1964, 39; cf. also for payments out of *aerarium* Dio LIV, 2, 3; LV, 26, 5 (*vigiles* in Dio's day); LVIII, 18, 3 (praetorians, A.D. 32, obscure); LIX, 15, 5 (roads, cf. EJ 287); Frontinus, *de aqu.* 116; 118; Dio LXXI, 33, 2 (Marcus Aurelius). Payments into *aerarium* of damages in *repetundae* suits, Plin., *ep.* II, 11, 19–20 (cf. for Republic, *FIRA* I², no. 7, vv. 59 ff.).

[104] Millar, *JRS* 1964, 36.

[105] Dio LVI, 32, 1; LIX, 15, 1, cf. *Ann.* XII, 5–7; *ILS* 244, 22 ff. Dio LIII, 28, 2 (cf. 18, 1–2) is an anachronistic misconstruction of some special exemption, probably from the law *de ambitu*, based on the doctrine of his own time (*Dig.* I, 3, 31).

[106] *RG* 27, 1; EJ 37 = Macrob. I, 12, 35. [See further ch. 10 n. 1, and *JRS* 1983, 61–3.]

[107] *Dig.* I, 17, 1, cf. Jones 121.

[108] *FIRA* I², no. 99, preamble. Cf. *CJ* IV, 31, 1, for senatorial regulations of fiscal rights.

[109] Examples of δημόσιος in index to S. R. Wallace, *Taxation in Egypt*, cf. Wilcken, *Grundz.* 30 f.; 288; H. I. Bell, *CAH* x, 284 f., 292 f. In Egypt, as elsewhere, the emperor had private domains, *ousiai*, on which see Bell 293 f.

[110] See vv. 18–25 (cf. 13, 30) of edict, with the comments of G. Chalon, *L'Edit de Tiberius Julius Alexander*, 1964. The various terms used—αἱ κυριακαὶ ψῆφοι, ὁ κυριακὸς λόγος, τὸ τῶν δημοσίων ὄνομα, ὁ φίσκος, ὁ δημόσιος λόγος, ὁ τοῦ Καίσαρος λόγος—seem indistinguishable.

Roman state of which he was formally the agent; that does not affect the legal status of the province. Administratively Augustus jealously reserved control to himself; 'Aegyptum seposuit' (*Ann.* II, 59). If none the less he recognized his financial accountability for his administration, we may assume *a fortiori* that he did so for other provinces. Indeed, as late as Pallas' retirement, a financial official of the emperor is still accountable to the state (*supra*). After Nero's fall an attempt was made to recover the sums he lavished on his favourites, presumably on the ground that they had been misappropriated from public funds.[111] But no means could be devised of bringing to account an autocrat who held power for life. Domitian diverted the proceeds of a water-rate at Rome from the *aerarium* 'in suos loculos'; it was only on his death that Nerva could restore the revenue to the public treasury.[112]

Indeed there was also no means of discovering how the emperor applied the revenues entrusted to his care. It is plausible to suppose that Augustus was authorized to use the revenues of his vast province in the first place to pay for the public disbursements he incurred, that he was at most obliged to pay into the *aerarium* any surplus and to account for the rest, and that if indeed it was envisaged that these revenues would not suffice for his needs, he received in addition a block grant from the *aerarium*.[113] Always anxious to conciliate public opinion and carry it with him (as he showed, for instance, in his marriage legislation), Augustus published 'rationes imperii', but Tiberius discontinued the practice and Gaius resumed it only temporarily (n. 94). Henceforth the imperial finances were shrouded in secrecy. If an emperor laid his hands on a source of revenue which had previously fed the *aerarium* (like the water-rate), that would be known; but no one could tell how he spent these or other funds. How much of the provincial taxes went to the building and adornment of Nero's Golden House? No one could say. Alternatively, how much did a more conscientious ruler contribute from his private resources to meeting the essential requirements of the state?[114] That too was unknown. The enormous growth of the patrimony makes it likely that its income played an ever larger part in balancing the budget, a part that became indispensable. If this was so, may it not be that the different accounts for which the same personnel might be responsible both in Rome and in the provinces were inextricably entangled?

[111] *Hist.* I, 20; cf. 90. On the view of *fiscus* taken here, Tacitus' words 'reliquias Neroniarum sectionum nondum in fiscum conversas' do not imply that the sums recovered were to go to the private cashbox of the emperor.

[112] Frontinus, *de aq.* 118.

[113] Jones 102–3.

[114] Nero's account of his own subventions of the *aerarium* (n. 91) could hardly have been checked.

Already to Tacitus the distinction was unimportant (*Ann.* vi, 2). The reason was no doubt that he shared Dio's view that the emperor was equally controller of his own monies and the people's (LIII, 16, 1). If confiscated property was made over from the *aerarium* to the 'fiscus', this was merely a matter of administrative convenience (*supra*). In Dio's day the distinction still subsisted, and he was on occasion able to record that an emperor had remitted debts to both *aerarium* and 'fiscus' or had drawn money from the *aerarium*. But in general he did not know whether an emperor met particular expenditure from public or private funds (LIII, 22, 3–4).[115] The obscurity which he found in his sources was not, I suggest, merely to be attributed to their vagueness: it soon (though after Augustus and by a process whose history can never be written) ceased to be clear which funds were public and which were private, and even if jurists had been able to make a sharp distinction in principle, the amalgamation of imperial and public funds in administration and the secrecy of the accounts divested such a distinction of practical importance.

[115] M. n. 171. If M. (n. 152) is right in preferring Suet., *Vesp.* 18, 1 to Dio LVI, 12, 1a, the latter's mistake illustrates his difficulties.

8

Procuratorial Jurisdiction

In A.D. 53 Claudius secured from the senate a grant of jurisdiction to his procurators. Who were the procurators concerned? What kind of jurisdiction did they receive? Was the Claudian innovation permanent?

Tacitus' account (*Ann.*, XII, 60) has been recently the subject of renewed discussion, notably of two important articles by Mr. Fergus Millar, with whose conclusions I am not in full agreement.[1] He is, however, right in my judgement in holding in his first article that when in the last sentence of the chapter Tacitus mentions *libertos quos rei familiari praefecerat* he is again referring to jurisdiction, and not to the political power of the great freedman secretaries; the expression used would suit only the *a rationibus*, not the *ab epistulis* or *a libellis*, who were not in charge of the *res familiaris*. On this interpretation Tacitus implies that jurisdiction was granted even to freedmen, if they held the post of procurator. Numerous freedmen are in fact recorded with the *title* of procurator in the first and second centuries. [Some appear to have been the chief assistants of equestrian procurators, notably those, nearly all post-Flavian, who are styled procurators of provinces, and we may perhaps suppose that in so far as the non-presidial procurators of provinces exercised jurisdiction, it was to the *equites* that it was committed.] But we cannot be sure that in the early Principate freedmen did not hold provincial procuratorships later reserved to *equites*, just as they held posts in the imperial secretariat at Rome which later passed into equestrian hands. It is hard to believe that Augustus' freedman, Licinus, was not the principal procurator in Gaul | (Dio, LIV, 21). Under Tiberius a freedman, Hiberus, was acting prefect of Egypt (Dio, LVIII, 19, 6), and Claudius appointed Felix governor of

---

[1] D. Stockton in *Historia*, 10, 1961, p. 116 f.; R. Seager in *Historia*, 11, 1962, p. 377; F. Millar in *Historia*, 13, 1964, p. 180 f. and 14, 1965, p. 362 f. which I cite as Millar (1) and Millar (2). I agree with Millar that the problems of *Ann.*, XII, 60 cannot be resolved merely by analysis of Tacitus' language. The classic discussion is by Mommsen, *St.R.*, II³, p. 1021 f. On freedmen procurators see P. R. C. Weaver, *Familia Caesaris*, 1972, ch. 21, cf. G. Boulvert, *Esclaves et Affranchis Impériaux*, 1970, 374–419. In revision I have also been much helped by T. Spagnuolo Vigorita, *Secta Temporum Meorum*, 1978, esp. 57–65. Insertions are in square brackets.

Latomus, 25 (1966), 461–87.

Judaea. Felix [had obviously been] given equestrian status; but that did not impress Tacitus, who did not forget his servile origin: *ius regium seruili ingenio exercuit* (*Hist.*, V, 9). Tacitus certainly classed Felix, and any others who were similarly elevated, as freedmen, not as *equites*; and from the social standpoint this was fully justified. Not that Tacitus had Felix in mind in writing of Claudius' measure; as governor of Judaea, Felix would have had jurisdiction irrespectively of any grant of judicial power to the non-presidial procurators (*infra*). [But at all times freedmen procurators could be in charge of imperial estates, and as such we later find them possessed of jurisdiction (n. 71). If Claudius granted it to patrimonial procurators as such,] it would have been awkward to have excluded from the grant any such procurators who happened to be freedmen; and if he had done so, Tacitus' comment would be gravely misleading.

However, this is a subsidiary matter of no great consequence; the majority of procurators were *equites*, and Tacitus, here probably following Claudius himself,[2] treats the new measure as the culmination in the rise of equestrian jurisdiction, which he traces in a rather muddled passage. He points out that Augustus had had magisterial jurisduction conferred on the prefects of Egypt, and that later the juridical powers of praetors had been widely granted to *equites alias per prouincias et in urbe*. The reference to the city presumably implies that the prefects of the praetorian guard, of the *annona* and of the *uigiles*, or some of these officers, had already acquired in some degree the jurisdiction which is otherwise attested only at a much later date.[3] | The chance allusion shows how little we know of the machinery of government in the early Principate, and how unwise it is to lay weight on *argumenta e silentio* in this field. As for the provinces, it cannot have been in *all* the provinces other than Egypt that *equites* had already received jurisdiction;[4] for in most of them the only equestrian officials were financial procurators, and had all these possessed jurisdiction, there would have been nothing left for Claudius to do. We must therefore assume that Tacitus means that *equites* had received jurisdic-

---

[2] R. Syme, *Tacitus*, p. 705; cf. D. Stockton, n. 13. C. Lécrivain in *Mél. d'Arch. et d'hist.*, 1886, p. 91 f. in an article on *La juridiction fiscale d'Auguste à Dioclétien*, which remains useful, had already suggested that the reference came from Egypt from Claudius' argumentation.

[3] For the *praefecti praetorio*, Mommsen, *St.R.*, II³, p. 969 f.; 897; 1120 (the earliest evidence seems to be from Marcus' reign, *C.I.L.*, IX, 2438). [See further O. Behrends, *Die röm. Geschworenenverfassung*, 211–24; H. Galsterer, *GGA*, 1973, 37 n. 1.] For the *praefectus annonae*, *St.R.*, II³, p. 1034 f.; *praefectus uigilum*, *ibid.*, p. 1057 f. Similarly the jurisdiction of the *praefectus urbi* grew far beyond its original limits (*Ann.*, VI, 10); chance allusions in *Ann.*, XIV, 41; *Hist.*, II, 63; Statius, *Silvae*, I, 4, 47 show that its full development, first attested in the classical lawyers, was in process during the first century, cf. Mommsen, *St.R.*, II³, p. 1063 f.

[4] D. Stockton, *o.c.*, p. 118: '*alias*, not *ceteras*'. There is often ambiguity in Latin, owing to its lack of a definite or indefinite article.

tion only in *some* other provinces in addition to Egypt, i.e. in those which, like Egypt, were actually governed by *equites*. [From Claudius' time these equestrian governors, outside Egypt and at times Sardinia, bore the title of procurators.[5] But earlier they seem to have been called prefects, an appellation accorded even in the Republic to equestrian officials in the service of the state.[6] From the first these prefects, or presidial procurators, commanded troops and performed all the tasks that fell to a governor. Jurisdiction was one of these tasks, and it is no surprise to find that the very first equestrian governor of Judaea had the right even to impose sentence of death (Josephus, *B.J.*, II, 117). General probability and the testimony of Tacitus suggest that all these prefects were vested with the same powers. But so long as they bore the title of prefect, it was easier to distinguish them from the financial procurators whom the emperor sent out to the provinces governed by senators.

These procurators were properly no more than private agents of the emperor, and in proconsular provinces they were originally charged only with the management of his personal property. Tiberius declared in the senate that to Lucilius Capito, procurator of Asia, *non se ius nisi in seruitia et pecunias familiares dedisse: quod si uim praetoris usurpasset manibus-que militum usus foret, spreta in eo mandata sua*, and Dio, after recording the same statement, adds that at *that* | time those who administered the emperor's property were expected only to collect his patrimonial revenues and to submit disputes to the ordinary courts on an equality with private persons.[7] It is, however, risky to assume that even in this period the same limitations were imposed on procurators in imperial provinces. They too must have been administrators of the emperor's *res familiaris*, but they also performed public duties, collecting direct taxes, paying the troops and probably organizing the commissariat.[8] For the first of these duties they must in case of need always have had soldiers at their disposal, as in Bithynia in Pliny's time (*Ep.*, X, 27–8). On the death of Herod in 4 B.C., Sabinus, procurator of Syria, assumed that Augustus would claim the royal property and tried to take possession of it with the help of soldiers, as well as of freedmen and slaves under his control; when his action provoked a rising, he defended himself with

---

[5] The governors of Sardinia are often styled *proc. Aug. et praef.* (or *praeses*) *Sardiniae*. Other provinces governed by *equites* were Corsica, various Alpine districts, Raetia, Noricum, Thrace, Cappadocia, Judaea and the two Mauretanias; see lists in H.-G. PFLAUM, *Les carrières procurator-iennes équestres*, p. 1044 f.

[6] A. N. SHERWIN-WHITE in *P.B.S.R.*, 15, 1939, p. 11 f.; A. H. M. JONES, *St. in Rom. Gov. and Law*, pp. 58–63 and ch. VII. *A.E.*, 1963, 104 now proves that Pontius Pilate was styled *praefectus*. [Cf. BRUNT, *JRS*, 73, 1983, 55–7.]

[7] *Ann.*, IV, 15; DIO, LVII, 23. Probably Lucilius was convicted of *uis publica*, cf. ch. 4 n. 18.

[8] DIO, LIV, 21 (Gaul); STRABO, III, 4, 20, p. 167c (Tarraconensis): οἱ διανέμοντες τὰ χρήματα τοῖς στρατιώταις εἰς τὴν διοίκησιν τοῦ βίου where χρήματα probably means supplies as well as *stipendium*.

the legion which the legate had stationed at Jerusalem and which apparently considered itself under his command. In fact he seems to have behaved much as did the procurator, Catus Decianus, in Britain under Nero when Prasutagus, king of the Iceni, died; Catus too had centurions as agents in his confiscations.[9] In the imperial provinces procurators took the place of quaestors, who were magistrates of the people and who had jurisdiction, both independent and delegated by the proconsul, of which all too little is known.[10] Perhaps procurators in the imperial provinces were from the first given similar judicial rights.

Moreover even under Tiberius the procurators may have gained in power. In praising his early administration (*Ann.*, IV, 6), Tacitus suggests that as time went on, it deteriorated. At the end of his reign, C. Herennius Capito, procurator of an imperial domain at Jamnia in Palestine, could send soldiers to collect a debt owed to the *fiscus* by the young Agrippa. We cannot be sure that *he* would have incurred the same censure as Lucilius Capito. The abuse of | one year might become the established custom of a later time.[11] In A.D. 46 Claudius authorized his friend Iulius Planta to investigate and determine his claims to certain lands in the Alps, *adhibitis procuratoribus meis quique in alia regione quique in vicinia erant* (*I.L.S.*, 306). These procurators at least constitute a judicial *consilium*. The *senatus consultum* of A.D. 53 defined the jurisdiction of procurators *plenius quam antea et uberius*. By implication they, or some of them, were already recognized as possessing judicial powers. We might suppose that *all* procurators had acquired *some* jurisdiction before 53, or that the jurisdiction already vested in *some* of them, presumably those in imperial provinces who exercised public functions, was now extended to *all*. Tacitus makes it explicit that jurisdiction now belonged to procurators *quos rei familiari praefecerat*, that is to say, even such officials as Lucilius Capito who were at first no more than managers of imperial property.

The distinction between *equites* who served the emperor in his private capacity and those who were his governmental agents was hard to maintain. The imperial patrimony provided revenues from which the emperor subsidized the public purse. In the provinces governed by *equites* the prefects administered the imperial patrimony besides performing their strictly public duties.[12] In those governed by legates the

---

[9] JOSEPHUS, *B.J.*, II, 16–19; 41 f.; *Ann.*, XIV, 31 f.; cf. F. MILLAR (2), p. 362.

[10] F. MILLAR (1), p. 182 f.; esp. GAIUS, I, 6.

[11] For Herennius, *P.I.R.²*, H, 103. An analogous development perhaps in the greater power of the freedmen by the end of Tiberius' reign, cf. JOSEPHUS, *A.J.*, XVIII, 145; 181; DIO, LVIII, 19, 6 (and perhaps, *Ann.*, IV, 70, 1) with *Ann.*, IV, 6, 4: *modesta seruitia, intra paucos libertos domus*, where the general context suggests that they were not only few but kept under firm control.

[12] Cf. the words of a presidial procurator of the Graian Alps: *dum ius guberno remque fungor Caesarum* (*I.L.S.*, 3528). The fullest documentation is naturally for the prefect of Egypt.

procurators were responsible for public taxes and disbursements as well as for imperial rents. It was artificial to segregate posts that required much the same qualities of their holders; men move freely in careers from one kind of post to another.[13] [As early as Tiberius a man may be simultaneously procurator in a senatorial province, Narbonensis, where his business was purely patrimonial, and in an imperial, Aquitania (*C.I.L.*, X, 3871).] The confusion is apparent once equestrian governors for the most part themselves bear the title of procurator. The first known instance comes very early in Claudius' reign; in 44 the governor | of Mauretania is *proc. Aug. pro leg.* (*A.E.*, 1924, 66). No doubt the addition *pro legato* makes clear the public character of his post; but in future, it is seldom found, and under Claudius himself a governor of Noricum is styled simply *procurator*;[14] henceforward, this designation no longer means (and had probably already ceased to mean) that the man so styled was merely a private agent of the emperor. By the third century, and probably much earlier, all imperial procurators were held to be in the service of the *res publica* (*Dig.*, IV, 6, 32; 6, 35, 2).

The measure of 53 conferred then no new powers on presidial procurators, previously called prefects, but consolidated or enhanced the jurisdiction of financial procurators. Millar has classified these in four groups. But two of these groups might well be amalgamated; the provincial procurators in provinces governed by legates (though they also administered the *res familiaris*) and those concerned with particular taxes and the like (Millar's third group) both unquestionably performed public functions at all times. By contrast, the procurators of senatorial provinces were originally only concerned with the *res familiaris*, and in so far as this remained true, they were not in principle distinct from procurators of imperial estates, including mines (Millar's last group), who were probably appointed only in cases where imperial properties were so extensive that the provincial procurator could not supervise them by himself. (Similarly the multiplication of procuratorships with specialized public functions was doubtless intended to relieve provincial procurators of excessive burdens.)

On the interpretation of Tacitus adopted by Millar and myself even patrimonial procurators received juridical powers in 53. But it would be odd if procurators performing public functions did not also acquire them, unless indeed they possessed them already. Yet Millar says that

[13] A. N. SHERWIN-WHITE, *o.c.*, holds that this development began with Claudius, but I am not convinced by this argument *e silentio*, especially as the most natural interpretation of a dedication by the Tarraconenses to an Augustan prefect of Egypt remains that he had been procurator in their province (*I.L.S.*, 1335).

[14] *I.L.S.*, 1349; cf. *A.E.*, 1936, 83.

'Tacitus does in fact *mean what he appears to say*, that Claudius gave to imperial procurators ... the power to make decisions and exercise jurisdiction *within imperial domains*',[15] and even in his second article he seems disposed to restrict the grant of jurisdiction by Claudius to the domains.[16] But though Tacitus | refers specifically to *libertos quos rei familiari praefecerat*, we are no more justified in deducing from this that the only procurators henceforth vested with jurisdiction were domanial than that they were all freedmen. And Tacitus does not suggest any limitation to jurisdiction within the domains; the general context with its allusions to the civil jurisdiction of the praetors and to the criminal *quaestiones perpetuae* indicates rather that he is asserting that all procurators received the fullest possible grant of powers (*Claudius omne ius tradidit ...*). In all probability he is here guilty of exaggeration or misconception, but his language certainly does not support Millar's interpretation.

In fact Millar seems to have reached his original conclusion on the basis of a review of other literary and documentary evidence for the powers of procurators in the pre-Severan period. Very little of the evidence of this kind which he assembled in his first article and has added to in his second relates to jurisdiction at all. What there is might seem to support his thesis. [But even if documentary evidence revealed no procuratorial jurisdiction except within imperial domains, we could not safely infer that it was so restricted.] This type of argument from silence is surely unsound in principle. The survival of documents is so much a matter of chance that while they can serve to confirm statements in literary authorities the mere absence of such confirmation is no proof that such statements are false. In non-legal literary texts again we cannot expect to find much mention of legal processes (except of political trials at Rome), and even when we turn to the jurists, the great bulk of the surviving texts is from or after the time of Severus, and there is little relating to the fiscal or administrative processes with which procurators were certainly concerned, except in the Codes, which refer almost entirely to conditions from Severus' time onwards. Gaius is not interested in these matters in his *Institutes*, and though some classical jurists wrote treatises on them,[17] what they had to say was of little relevance in the time of the compilers, when the administrative and fiscal system had undergone considerable changes; in particular, procurators were no longer employed in the collection of taxes, while the procurators of the *res priuata* were apparently quite humble officials, though some of the old patrimonial procurators had

[15] F. MILLAR (1), p. 187 (my italics).
[16] F. MILLAR (2), p. 367.
[17] F. SCHULZ, *Roman Legal Science*, 1946, p. 139; 242 f.

been upgraded with the title of *rationales*.[18] It must have been by oversight that a few | antiquated allusions to the judicial or other duties of procurators were left by the compilers in the *Digest* and the earlier *constitutiones* of the *Codex Justinianus*. It is also the less surprising that we know so little of fiscal jurisdiction, as there is an extraordinary paucity of information on the taxes levied in the Principate, their rates, the methods of collection employed and so on.

None the less, it is on sparse juristic fragments, nearly all Severan or later, that our knowledge of procuratorial jurisdiction is founded, and it is reasonable to consider these first and then to ask how far back we can push the conclusions that may be elicited from them, and whether the system we find in the early third century originated with Claudius' innovation. In his second article Millar has recognized the necessity for pursuing this course; he has now himself set out the chief evidence, and partially modified his earlier theory to accord with it. But some points concerning the juridical powers of procurators still need clarification or have been missed by Millar.

Non-presidial procurators[19] had in general only fiscal jurisdiction (*infra*), though they were authorized to hear other types of case by mandate from the governor.[20] As a rule they were not entitled to hear capital charges, not even undefended charges of murder.[21] Severus Alexander declared that it had often been ruled that they had no right to impose fines,[22] though this right had apparently belonged to the procurators of the Vipasca mine in Hadrian's | day.[23] [Probably Alexander's rescript has only a specious generality, and answered a petition concerning a fine imposed by the court of a fiscal procurator who had

---

[18] A. H. M. Jones, *Hist. of Later Rom. Empire*, 1964, p. 412–17 (*rationales* and procurators employed in *res priuata*); in the collection of taxes (p. 427 f.; 448 f.) *rationales* (not procurators) are found only in the *sacrae largitiones*.

[19] Original jurisdiction of presidial procurators, e.g. *F.I.R.A.*, I², 49, 43 (c. AD 176). They are excepted from restrictions on jurisdiction of other procurators, *Dig.*, XLIX, 1, 23, 1 (Papinian); *Coll.*, XIV, 2, 2 (Ulpian); *C.J.*, IX, 47, 2 (AD 212). *Procurator Caesaris*, tout court, means a financial procurator (F. Millar (2), p. 364).

[20] *F.I.R.A.*, I², 39, 43 recognizes jurisdiction (in cases no longer fiscal) *procuratoribus maximorum principum quibus rector prouinciae mandauerit.*

[21] *Coll.*, XIV, 3, 3 (Ulpian) says that they do not *usually* hear capital cases; see n. 27 for exceptions; for the rule cf. *C.J.*, III, 26, 1 (AD 197—undefended murder); IX, 47, 2 (AD 212—exile); *Dig.*, I, 19, 3 *pr.* (Callistratus—deportation, a capital penalty, cf. Mommsen, *R. Strafr.* p. 957 f.). *C.J.*, X, 13, 1 (AD 313) need not mean that the *rationales* Baeticae could impose sentences of deportation.

[22] *C.J.*, I, 54, 2 (AD 228); X, 8, 1 (216) which reads: *nec enim multam tibi procurator meus inrogauit, ultra quam placitum est, sed poenam te iussit inferre*; the procurator could not impose a fine (that was *ultra quam placitum*) but had the right to collect a fine imposed by the competent court. This could involve jurisdiction, since certain claims of creditors took precedence of the *poena*, cf. *Dig.*, XLIX, 14, 37 (Papinian); *C.J.*, X, 7, 1 (224), and these claims might have to be proved, presumably in the procurator's court. See nn. 40 f. with text.

[23] *F.I.R.A.*, I², 104(5)–(7).

usurped a governor's jurisdiction, but had no relevance to the limited powers of domanial procurators over residents on the estates they administered. Again in civil law procurators might not appoint a *iudex in lite privatorum*, a rule re-affirmed by Gordian, except that, by a rescript of Caracalla, they were free to do so if the litigants had agreed to accept their jurisdiction.[24] As late as Decius they were forbidden to decide *causae liberales*, even though these might concern fiscal interests; for example, the property sequestered after criminal conviction or liable to be sold for fiscal debts might include alleged slaves, for whom a claim was made that they were entitled to freedom on the basis of either *ingenuitas* or manumission; though it was in general the duty of the procurator to settle disputes as to the property which it was legitimate to confiscate, the status of such individuals was for the governor's adjudication, at any rate until Diocletian, who authorized the *rationales* to decide claims to freedom by manumission but not those made on the plea of *ingenuitas*.[25] Evidently these restrictions were prompted by attempts some procurators had made to usurp wider juridical powers, as illegal as the action of procurators in the *saltus Burunitanus* in flogging those *coloni* who were Roman citizens. The fact that should be familiar, that Roman laws were often not observed by officials, is irrelevant to deciding what the laws were.[26] Under Caracalla the judicial encroachments of procurators were indeed partially successful: both in Rome and in the provinces they had usurped capital jurisdiction under the lex Fabia on kidnapping; this was at first forbidden and reserved to the *praefectus urbi* or to governors, but Caracalla gave the procurators the right to try charges under this law and to hold a *quaestio*, perhaps the examination of slave witnesses under torture. Gordian, however, reversed the former decision.[27]

None the less the procurator was also a *iudex* (*C.J.*, II, 1, 7, A.D. 223), with *iudicandi potestatem intra certas personas* (n. 24). There is nothing to show that such persons were only those resident on an

---

[24] *Dig.*, XLIX, 1, 23, 1 (PAPINIAN); *C.J.*, III, 3, 1 (Gordian, cf. IV, 57, 5, 2); contrast III, 13, 1 (Caracalla), where the exception is grounded on the fact that the procurator has *iudicandi potestatem intra certas personas*; for the principle implied cf. *Dig.*, V, 1, 1 (ULPIAN), L, 1, 28 (PAUL); it is not contradicted by *C.J.*, III, 13, 3 (AD 293): *privatorum consensus iudicem non facit eum qui nulli praest iudicio*.

[25] *C.J.*, III, 22, 2 (250). MOMMSEN, *R. Strafr.* p. 1029 n. 4 seems to be mistaken in saying that the procurator had jurisdiction when the *fiscus* claimed a person as a slave until the time of Diocletian (cf. *C.J.*, III, 22, 5, contrast VII, 21, 7); the texts he cites (*Dig.*, XLIX, 14, 3, 9 and 14, 7), to which *Dig.*, XL, 1, 10 might be added, merely show that fiscal interests in some *causae liberales* might have tempted him to assume it.

[26] *F.I.R.A.*, I², 103. 'The imperial rescripts with their constant reiteration of theoretically unquestionable rules show, like the pictures drawn by the historians, how intolerable practices subsisted side by side with tolerable principles' (MOMMSEN, *St.R.*, II³, p. 1024).

[27] ULPIAN, *Coll.*, XIV, 3, 1–3, cf. *C.J.*, IX, 20, 4 (Gordian). See the full discussion by SPAGNUOLO VIGORITA (n. 1) 60–5.

imperial domain he administered, and in fact some of the restrictions on his competence, e.g. in the case of capital crimes, or concerning his lack of a right to decide suits between private ligitants, appear to cover such residents as well as all other Roman subjects: Gordian's re-affirmation of the latter rule (*C.J.*, III, 1, 1) was actually addressed to *vicani*, perhaps within an imperial domain. In these domains he had the kind of jurisdiction which belongs to a police magistrate; apart from this it is normally those concerned in fiscal cases who were subject to procuratorial jurisdiction.] We hear in the *Digest* (Papinian in II, 14, 42; cf. Paul in XL, 1, 10) of *ius fiscale*, and of a distinction between fiscal cases and both public or criminal and civil cases;[28] the former are evidently those heard *apud fiscum*, a phrase to which *apud procuratorem* seems to be an exact equivalent;[29] the procurator then determined suits in which the *fiscus* was either plaintiff or defendant, and indeed, as will be seen, suits between third parties, which arose out of fiscal claims. It was from his decisions in such cases that appeals might go to the emperor,[30] but not, by a ruling of Caracalla, to the governor (*C.J.*, II, 46, 1). It is true that the proconsul was also competent, as in every type of case[31]—and the same could be said of all governors[32]—but in the same breath that he asserts this Ulpian adds: *sane si fiscalis pecuniaria causa sit, quae ad procuratorem principis respicit, melius fecerit si abstineat.* Millar rightly says that this is no more than advice, but it was advice that prudent governors, like Agricola *procul a contentione aduersus procuratores* (*Agr.*, 9, 4), surely adopted. What then was *fiscalis pecuniaria causa*?

---

[28] III, 6, 1, 3 (ULPIAN); *C.J.*, VII, 49, 1 (AD 212).

[29] *Apud fiscum, Dig.*, [XLVIII, 17, 3 (MARCIANUS)] XLIX, 14, 45, 7–8 (PAUL); cf. XLVIII, 19, 9, 2 (ULPIAN): *apud legatum* (sc. *proconsulis*) *uel procuratorem*; II, 15, 8, 19 (ULPIAN): *transactiones alimentorum etiam apud procuratorem Caesaris fieri possunt : scilicet si a fisco petantur alimenta.* The rule was that when it was proposed that *alimenta* left e.g. to freedmen should be compounded by payment of a lump sum the question was to be decided at Rome by a praetor, in a province by a governor (who may not delegate jurisdiction in this case) *cognita causa* (II, 15, 8, *pr.*, with 17–18); but the procurator can decide where the obligation falls on the *fiscus*. The right of the procurator to agree to compositions for *alimenta* is presumably (*libro primo ad legem uicensimam hereditatium*) an exception to Macer's rule, [p. 385. n. 101]: *nulli procuratorum principis inconsulto principe transigere licet*; alternatively Macer is writing only of the *uicesima* and perhaps means that the procurators of that tax might not accept any part of the estate in lieu of the money due. *Fiscus* and *procurator* are equivalent terms in many cases; both can be said to sell up property (XLIX, 14, 22, *pr.*, with 14, 36), summon a defendant (XLIX, 14, 47, 1, with 14, 3, 8), or question a person's free status (XL, 1, 10, with XLIX, 14, 7).

[30] DIO, LII, 33; *Dig.*, XLIX, 1, 25 = *P. Oxy.* 2104 (ALEX SEVERUS), [which shows that procurators had tried to obstruct appeals, presumably on fiscal matters].

[31] *Dig.*, I, 16, 9, *pr.*; cf. I, 16, 7, 2.

[32] *Dig.*, I, 18, 11 (MARCIANUS); I, 8, 12 (PROCULUS). The governor has to repress illicit exactions, I, 16, 9, *pr.* (ULPIAN). The duties of governor and procurator often overlapped; thus *conductores uectigalium fisci* were exempt from municipal liturgies; and either governor or procurator might prevent them from volunteering, if they had not discharged their liabilities to the *fiscus*, L, 6, 7, 10 (CALLISTRATUS).

Millar holds that it has nothing to do with tax disputes. This belief rests on a | restricted interpretation of *fiscus*; I am convinced that the public revenues at least in the imperial provinces went from an early date to the *fiscus* (chapter 7).

That liability to tax was sometimes disputed needs no proof; it is curious and unfortunate that even when the legal texts allude to or imply such disputes, they generally state what the law was without specifying the tribunal which was to apply it, perhaps because statements made on this subject by the classical jurists were omitted by the compilers, as inapposite in Justinian's day. We have therefore hardly any testimony to the jurisdiction of *either* procurators *or* governors, in these matters.

Take first the *portoria*. Nero enacted that the praetors in Rome and the governors in the provinces were to hear charges against the publicans 'extra ordinem' (Tacitus, *Ann.*, XIII, 51). Presumably they were also to hear suits brought by the publicans. The praetor's edict at Rome defined the law affecting the collection of *portoria* in some detail, and this part of the edict is still quoted by Gaius and Ulpian.[33] But it would be risky to assume that the *procedure* remained unchanged, any more than we can argue to the continued existence of *quaestiones perpetuae* from the fact that laws under which they were set up were still cited by classical jurists as containing the *substance* of the relevant criminal law. A letter of Severus and Caracalla gave the procurators the task of deciding in court (*cognoscere*) in accordance with certain principles the question whether *a servus inprofessus* was to be held for the benefit of the *fiscus* or returned to his master on payment of his estimated value.[34] This strongly suggests that procurators had acquired jurisdiction in disputes arising from the collection of the *portoria*.

This conclusion was reached on other grounds by S. J. de Laet.[35] He argued that it was found inconvenient to entrust jurisdiction in disputes arising from the *portoria* to provincial governors, since the circumscriptions of the *portoria* were not coterminous with pro | vincial boundaries; this consideration is plainly not decisive. He also appealed to an inscription of C. Sextius Martialis in the late second century which records that he was *procurator Aug. inter mancip(es) XXXX Galliarum et negotiantis*.[36] But this man's title makes it very unlikely that he was *procurator XXXX Galliarum* or that it can be inferred that procurators normally designated by the latter title decided cases arising between the tax-farmers and the merchants from the collection of the

---

[33] *Dig.*, XXXIX, 4, 1, 5 and 12.
[34] *Dig.*, XXXIX, 4, 16 *pr.* and 1.
[35] *Portorium*, p. 445 f.; cf. p. 391.
[36] *I.L.S.*, 1410; for dating, cf. H.-G. Pflaum, *Les carrières procuratoriennes équestres*, n° 204.

quadragesima; more probably, Martialis was a special commissioner appointed to make new regulations which would reduce the number of disputes occurring.

Liability for *tributum* and for *uicesimae hereditatium*[37] could also obviously give rise to litigation, not only between the tax-payer and the authorities, but also between two tax-payers, e.g. owner and usufructuary of land [or between heir and legatees].[38] There is no clear evidence in the classical jurists on the identity of the courts which heard such cases but one text is worth quoting. Papinian wrote: *cum possessor unus expediendi negotii causa tributorum iure conueniretur, aduersus ceteros quorum aeque praedia tenentur ei qui conuentus est actiones a fisco praestantur, scilicet ut omnes pro modo praediorum pecuniam tributi conferant* (*Dig.*, L, 15, 5 *pr.*); ['when to expedite the business a single owner is pursued in the court for liability to tribute, the *fiscus* cedes to him its actions against the rest of those whose properties are equally liable, for the obvious purpose that all should pay tribute proportionate to their properties.' These actions would probably be heard by the procurator, the owner to whom the fiscal actions are ceded having the same right of *protopraxia* as the *fiscus*. It may be suggested that Caracalla's statement that the procurator has jurisdiction *intra certas personas* (n. 24) means that it extends to cases which themselves arise from fiscal claims. Another obscure text (*Dig.*, II, 8, 13), discussed in chapter 17 (pp. 384 f.), suggests that procurators also decided claims of the *fiscus* to inheritance tax.]

Millar concedes that procurators had jurisdiction in 'disputes | between the imperial estate and *priuati*'. [On his view, discussed in chapter 7,] the imperial estate included not only the patrimony and *hereditates* of the emperor but *bona caduca*, *bona damnatorum* and some miscellaneous revenues. This allows wide scope for procuratorial courts. This can be confirmed. Numerous legal texts which refer to the right and duty of the procurators to sequester property for the *fiscus*, to sell it, to require the payment of monies due to the *fiscus* or to collect fines imposed by another authority must indeed be excluded from consideration, since they might be taken to give the purport of directions issued to procurators in an executive rather than in a judicial capacity.[39] Enough remains to illustrate their judicial powers.

---

[37] The allusions to this tax cited from Aemilius Macer's book on it (cf. O. HIRSCHFELD, *Die kais. Verwaltungsbeamten*, p. 100, n. 2) unfortunately give no explicit information about the courts which decided disputes; the existence of his book shows the need for interpreting the law created by such disputes.

[38] *Dig.*, VII, 1, 53 (JAVOLENUS); 1, 7, 1 (MARCELLUS). Some other legal points are found in II, 14, 12 (PAPINIAN); L, 15, 5, 2 (PAPINIAN). Charges of false census returns (V, 1, 53) are also relevant. Cf. further XXXIX, 4, 7, where the *vectigalia* are apparently rents from imperial estates.

[39] E.g. *Dig.*, XX, 4, 21, 1 (SCAEVOLA); XL, 1, 10 (PAUL); *C.J.*, III, 3, 1 (AD 213), 3 (239) and 4 (290); often in *Dig.*, XLIX, 14. Cf. *C.Th.*, X, 8, 1–2 (CONSTANTINE); 9, 1 (AD 369); 10, 5 (340).

Although procurators were not authorized to try capital charges or sequester the property of the accused before he was condemned (*supra*), after condemnation it was their duty to sequester it.[40] The phrase *fisco peti*, used in this connexion (e.g. *C.J.*, III, 26, 1, from 197), shows that this might be not simply a matter of executive action but of a hearing in court. The explanation of this lies in the fact that not all the property of a person convicted on a capital charge was necessarily confiscated; the patron and his children (*Dig.*, XLVIII, 20, 7, 1; 20, 8), his own children, including adoptive children (*Dig.*, XLVIII, 20, 1; 20, 7, 2–4), his son-in-law in respect of his daughter's dowry (*Dig.*, XLVIII, 20, 8, 4–20, 10) and even other third parties (*Dig.*, XLVIII, 20, 11) might have valid claims. The accused might commit suicide before sentence, and it was then important to determine his motive; only if it could be shown that he had acted from fear of a capital condemnation, was his property forfeit (*Dig.*, XLVIII, 21, 3; XLIX, 14, 45, 2, [cf. XLVIII, 1, 6]). In precisely such a case, according to a ruling of 207 (*C.J.*, III, 26, 2), it fell to the procurator to inquire and decide, and the hearing was not to be | transferred to the governor's court, for *iam non de crimine aut poena mortui sed de bonis quaerendum est*.[41]

In Italy, at least during the second century, fiscal claims to *bona caduca* seem to have come before the *praefecti aerarii*.[42] As Hadrian wrote to provincial governors on the subject of fiscal claims, it would appear that in his reign they remained competent in these cases.[43] It was, however, conjectured by Hirschfeld that the greater importance from Hadrian's time onwards of *procuratores hereditatium* indicates that they became responsible for the acquisition by the *fiscus* of *bona uacantia* and *caduca* in the provinces.[44] In confirmation of this he appealed to a rescript of Marcus and Verus to the effect that *bona obsidum* were not to be confiscated in accordance with the general rule, if the *obsides* concerned had conducted themselves in life as Roman citizens; this rescript is addressed to the *procuratores hereditatium*.[45] Once again, we cannot be certain whether the procurators are receiving administrative

---

[40] E.g. *Dig.*, XLVIII, 20, 1–2; 21, 2; XLIX, 14, 22, *pr.*; *De iure fisci*, 14; *C. Th.* IX, 42, 3 (AD 357). Cf. also *C.J.*, III, 26, 3 (AD 215): the procurator *sicut exigere poenam desertae accusationis potest, ita iudicare, ut ea inferatur sententia sua, non potest*. Such a *poena* was usually a fine (MOMMSEN, *R. Strafr.*, p. 499 f.); for exaction of fines by procurators, cf. n. 32.

[41] Cf. *C.J.*, III, 26, 1 (197): *plane defunctis homicidii reis apud procuratores quoque causam agendam esse ratio permittit.*

[42] References in F. MILLAR in *J.R.S.*, 54, 1964, pp. 36–7; cf. pp. 143–5 above.

[43] *PIR²*, A, 987; *Dig.*, XLIX, 14, 2, 1 (addressed to Flavius Arrianus). B. D'ORGEVAL, *L'Empereur Hadrien*, 1930, p. 190, assumes that Arrian was then *praefectus aerarii* and that XLIX, 14, 42, *pr.* conflates him in this capacity with Severus, his colleague as consul and probably as *praefectus aerarii*, but for an Arrianus Severus, cf. *PIR²*, A, 180.

[44] *Die kais. Verw.*, p. 113 f.

[45] *Dig.*, XLIX, 14, 31–2.

instructions or a rule of law to be applied in their own courts. But when we hear of imperial decisions on the action already taken by procurators in sequestering property or exacting payments to the *fiscus*,[46] it seems likely that the cases had gone to the emperor on appeal, and this is perhaps the best explanation of the rescript on *bona obsidum*. The use of the phrase *conueniebatur a procuratoribus* (XLIX, 14, 47, 1) might suggest that the procurators were no more than plaintiffs on behalf of the *fiscus* in another court, for *conuenire* is a verb constantly used by the jurists to mean 'bring an action against', when the plaintiff is a private person. We have to remember, however, that the *fiscus* and its agents were at least quasi-public, and that in Roman administrative law the representative of the state was also the judge.[47] | Further the *fiscus* itself can be the subject of *conuenire*, and we know that cases could be determined *apud fiscum* (n. 29). Moreover in court the interests of the *fiscus* were pleaded by the *aduocati fisci*, not by the procurators;[48] and this fits the assumption that the procurators were actually the judges. A reference to a woman who was *condemnata a fisco* to confiscation of an inheritance (*Dig.*, XLIX, 14, 48, 1) surely means that she was condemned by a procurator.

Other allusions to procuratorial jurisdiction in fiscal cases are more explicit. Thus the emperor rules in 213 that an appellant must try to prove to the procurator that his property was sold by the *fiscus* without due authorization or formalities, and that he is to recover it if he succeeds, and in 239 that if the wife of an appellant can show even without documents that she has paid the price for a house to the *fiscus* and has acquired *dominium*, the procurator will not allow her to be disturbed (*C.J.*, X, 3, 1 and 3). [Again in 215 it is provided that if a man sold a farm before he fell into debt with the *fiscus* the procurator will decide (*cognoscet*) that the purchaser is not to be disturbed in his possession by fiscal claims (*C.J.*, VII, 73, 4).] Such *sententiae* of the emperor may require interpretation from the procurator, and an appeal to the emperor lies against his interpretation.[49] Thus again, if *bona obligata fisco* have been fraudulently sold by officials at too low a price, under a ruling of Gordian the procurator will order their restoration to the original owner, provided that he pays what is due to

---

[46] *Dig.*, XLIX, 14, 47–50 (PAUL).

[47] MOMMSEN, *St.R.*, I, p. 169 f.

[48] [SPAGNUOLO VIGORITA (n. 1) 129–30.]

[49] *Dig.*, XLIX, 1, 4, 1: *ab eo, qui sententiam male interpretari dicitur, appellare licet, si tamen is interpretandi potestatem habuit, uelut praeses prouinciae aut procurator Caesaris: ita tamen ut in causis appellationis reddendis hoc solum quaeratur, an iure interpretatum sit; idque etiam diuus Antoninus rescripsit.* It is evident that the *sententia* must be that of a higher court than that of *praeses* or procurator. *Praeses* would be concerned in non-fiscal cases.

the *fiscus* (*C.J.*, X, 1, 3); whether the price paid was too low is a question for the procurator's interpretative judgment.

As with disputes arising from payment of *tributum*, this fiscal jurisdiction gives rise to judgment between third parties. For instance, in the case last cited, the procurator plainly had to hear the plea of the purchaser of the property as well as of its original owner. In 233 it was laid down that some one who has bought property from the procurator may sue those on whose mandate he made the | [purchase for the price and for the interest due to the *fiscus*, and sue before the procurator (*C.J.*, III, 26, 4). Gordian ruled that the procurator might hear claims by a creditor of those who acknowledged liability for debts to the *fiscus* (IV, 15, 3). Philip refused to reverse the *sententia* of a procurator, against which no appeal had been lodged (presumably in due time), which had transferred property from the principal debtors of the *fiscus* to their sureties, on condition that the latter indemnified the *fiscus* (VII, 45, 5). (We may suppose that it was only to the emperor that appeals would lie from a procurator's judgment (cf. n. 49), not to the governor, in matters on which the procurator was competent; at any rate, a rescript of Caracalla bars the proconsul from granting *restitutio in integrum* with the effect of upsetting such a judgment (III, 36, 1), though the *fiscus* itself, i.e. a procuratorial court, would under a Severan rescript respect the rules for granting *restitutio* (II, 36, 1). Alexander Severus, however, ruled (II, 37, 2) that a petition for *restitutio* affecting fiscal interests should be heard jointly by governor and procurator. The Pauline *Sententiae* say that a person sued by the *fiscus* for the debt of another (in general a surety) could, after discharging the liability, recover from the principal debtor, 'and it is customary for him to be assisted by the office' (*Dig.*, XLIX, 14, 45, 9). I take this to mean that he acquired fiscal *protopraxia* and that, if necessary, he could take proceedings in the procurator's court. This is analogous to Papinian's *responsum* on payment of tribute (L, 15, 5) discussed on p. 173.)

The procurator also hears cases against the *fiscus*. One instance may be given. If property is sold up to satisfy fiscal claims, prior claims of private creditors secured on the property *iure pignoris* must be met. If the procurator has sold it without regard to their claims (perhaps in ignorance of the facts), then 'he will order the money which has been proved to be due to the private creditor to be paid to him'. It is to be presumed that the proof has to be provided in his own court.[50]

The general principle which seems to underlie these details is clearly expressed by Constantine: *ad fiscum pertinentes causas rationalis decidet.*[51]

---

[50] *Dig.*, XLIX, 14, 22, 1 (rescript of SEVERUS and CARACALLA).
[51] *C.J.*, III, 16, 5.

But it is implicit in Ulpian's reference to *fiscalis pecuniaria causa quae ad procuratorem principis respicit*, and in Dio's remark that in Tiberius' time procurators still had resort to the ordinary courts (n. 9), a comment that would have been pointless if it had remained true in his own day. And, as we have seen, these fiscal cases which it rested with the procurator to decide included cases between parties that arose from fiscal claims. But procuratorial jurisdiction did not normally extend, at the time of the classical jurists, to criminal cases, nor to civil suits in which the *fiscus* was in no way concerned.

It remains to consider whether on these points the law of the early third century had been the law since Claudius' time. It is customary to assume this without question. But the assumption is precarious. In the practices of Roman government there is not to be found an invariable progress, or continuity; the tide may ebb and flow. Much depended on the personality and policy of the despot.

It is conceivable therefore that Claudius actually gave his procurators more power than the later legal sources attest. But improbable; despotic as he was, we can hardly think that he was more disposed to vest power in his personal agents than the Severi.[52] | One might even wonder if Tacitus has not misconceived the purport of what Claudius really said, in writing: *parem uim rerum habendam a procuratoribus iudicatarum, ac si ipse statuisset.* This is reminiscent of Ulpian's statement: *quae acta gestaque sunt a procuratore Caesaris, sic ab eo comprobantur, atque si a Caesare gesta sunt* (*Dig.*, I, 19, 1, *pr.*), a statement which he then modifies by pointing out the limitations on the procurator's right to alienate property belonging to Caesar. As the chief instance of the procurator's representative function Ulpian gives the fact that the procurator can make Caesar heir of an estate by ordering an imperial slave *adire hereditatem* and *miscendo se opulentae hereditati* (cf. XXIX, 2, 25, 2). But this is executive, not judicial action. May it be that Claudius, while certainly granting new juridical rights to his procurators, at the same time promised to be bound by their executive decisions as if he had made them himself? To follow up Ulpian's illustration, this would mean that once a procurator had taken over an inheritance in Caesar's name Caesar would also inherit the debts of the estate.[53]

However this may be, we cannot be sure that any new juridical powers Claudius granted to procurators remained intact in each succeeding reign. If Nero's initial undertaking to separate *domus* from *res publica* (*Ann.*, XIII, 4) meant anything, it should have involved a

---

[52] At this time the emperors were making more use than ever of *equites*, cf. *C.A.H.*, XII, p. 26 f. (S. N. MILLER); [H.-G. PFLAUM, *Les procurateurs équestres*, 134–9].

[53] However, the emperor would not inherit litigation, *Dig.*, XLIX, 14, 22, 2 (rescript of PIUS); XXVIII, 5, 92.

withdrawal of jurisdiction from mere procurators of the *res familiaris.* Suetonius says that Nero had cases transferred *ab aerario ad forum ac recuperatores,* and ruled *ut omnes appellationes* (perhaps only in these cases) *a iudicibus ad senatum fierent* (*Nero,* 17). *Prima facie* the first statement means that it was the administrators of the *aerarium Saturni* who lost jurisdiction in claims affecting the treasury to other courts; but confusion between *aerarium* and *fiscus* might perhaps be suspected. Alternatively a measure, by which even the public treasury was no longer to be judge in its own cause, would suit a policy that *also* deprived the *fiscus* of similar advantages given it by Claudius.[54] Nero also reserved to the praetor at Rome and the governors in the provinces the right | of determining disputes between the publicans and the taxpayers (*Ann.,* XIII, 51). Though reason has been given for thinking that procurators ultimately acquired jurisdiction in such disputes, the development may have been slow in coming. A series of decisions on the immunity of Histria from the claims of publicans to collect *portoria* on fish caught locally emanated from legates of Moesia between Claudius' reign and Trajan's.[55] As late as 201 Severus wrote that the people of Tyra were to enjoy immunity from the Illyrian *portoria,* and his letter was published by the legate of Moesia to whose discretion he left the decision whether the grant was to apply to all persons to whom Tyra should thereafter give its citizenship. The letter was, however, addressed not to the legate but to the procurator, with a copy to the legate.[56] Both officials were apparently held to be concerned, the procurator perhaps because of the fiscal interests affected, the legate because the privileges and internal affairs of the city were under his supervision. A dispute between an individual taxpayer and the tax-collectors, in which city rights were not involved, might well have been left to the procurator alone.

In imperial provinces the procurators could still act under Nero, as if they were not fettered by the legate's jurisdiction. If Tacitus has correctly presented the causes of Boudicca's revolt (n. 9), it could be said that in Britain there were two kings *ex quibus legatus in sanguinem, procurator in bona saeuiret* (*Agr.,* 15, 2); this may presuppose exactly the relation between their spheres of jurisdiction that we have observed in the third century. If procurators were responsible for army supplies (n. 8), the abuses in Britain which Agricola terminated (*Agr.,* 19, 4) may

---

[54] Similarly Trajan discouraged delation on behalf of both *aerarium* and *fiscus* (PLINY, *Paneg.,* 36).

[55] *A.E.,* 1919, 10 = ABBOTT AND JOHNSON, *Munic. Admin. in Roman Empire,* no. 68, cf. PIPPIDI, *Epigr. Beitr. zur Gesch. Histrias,* 1962, p. 132 f.

[56] *I.L.S.,* 423. Heraclitus, to whom the letter is addressed, should be *Aur. Heraclitus proc. Augg.* sc. of the Illyrian *portorium* (*A.E.,* 1944, 100 cf. DE LAET, *Portorium,* p. 218).

be ascribed to them rather than to his own predecessors. In Spain, Galba felt impotent to check the procurator's exactions (Plutarch, *Galba*, 4). In Galatia the procurator is at least associated with the legate in determining the boundaries between the city of Sagalassus and the village of Tymbrianissus. Even though there is no direct testimony that that village was | in an imperial estate, I feel that the procurator's presence must be explained on the hypothesis that it was; it was the fiscal interest that brought him in.[57] Frontinus noted that territorial controversies of this kind were very common when imperial estates adjoined city lands (p. 53 L).

All this does not mean that Nero went back on his undertaking, since in imperial provinces procurators were public officials by the nature of their responsibilities and may have possessed jurisdiction even before A.D. 53. And when we find a procurator restoring *praedia publica* to the city of Gortyn in Crete, a senatorial province, we could suppose that he was acting as mandatory of the proconsul.[58] [However, Seneca says that a procurator in Sicily could *efficere imperium quod est procuratio* (*N.Q.*, IV, *pr.* 1–2), and this need not be mere rhetoric.] And it is likely that later, as Nero's rule grew more tyrannical and his financial needs more exorbitant, he gave his procurators free rein. Towards the end of his reign, we are told, he gave no one office without saying: *Scis quid mihi opus sit* or *Hoc agamus, ne quis quicquam habeat* (Suetonius, *Nero*, 32, 4). If these instructions were addressed especially to procurators, he was only reverting to the methods of Gaius who is said to have told his procurators that they had *ius in omnium hominum bona* (Suetonius, *Gaius*, 47).

The exactions of Vespasian were noted,[59] and though some of his agents were senators, the story that he used to promote his most rapacious procurators in order to condemn them after they had accumulated great wealth (Suetonius, *Vesp.*, 16, 2), whether it be true or false, could hardly have arisen unless in his reign they had opportunities for growing rich, which might best be explained if they had jurisdiction of their own. It was under Vespasian too that Agricola was careful not to quarrel with procurators, and Vespasian was the inventor of the *fiscus Iudaicus*, the procurators of which seem under Domitian to have exercised jurisdiction in Africa or perhaps in Italy

---

[57] *O.G.I.S.*, 538. The principle, that the procurator must at least share in a judicial decision when fiscal claims arise, comes out much later in Alexander Severus' ruling (*C.J.*, II, 36, 2) that persons claiming *restitutio in integrum* must apply to the governor, but if their claim is *aduersus fiscum*, both the governor and the procurator: the *aduocatus fisci* must also be at the hearing.

[58] ABBOTT AND JOHNSON, *o.c.*, no. 55. Cf. perhaps *AE* 1952, 132 (Vesp.) n. 19.

[59] TACITUS, *Hist.*, II, 84, 2; 95, 3; DIO, LVI, 2, 5; 8, 2–4; SUETONIUS, *Titus*, 8, 5; JOSEPHUS, *B.J.*, VII, 443 f.; PLINY, *Paneg.*, 35, 4.

itself.[60] It was also perhaps under Domitian that a pro | curator of Dalmatia fixed the boundaries *inter prata legionis et fines roboreti Fl. Marc.* [but this was in an imperial province].[61]

We have more solid evidence of procuratorial jurisdiction under Domitian from Pliny's laudation of the very different practices of his successors. After celebrating *aerarium silens et quietum, et quale ante delatores erat*, Pliny proceeds in his praise of Trajan: *At fortasse non eadem seueritate fiscum qua aerarium cohibes: immo tanto maiore quanto plus tibi licere de tuo quam de publico credis. Dicitur actori atque etiam procuratori tuo: "in ius ueni, sequere ad tribunal". Nam tribunal quoque excogitatum principatui est par ceteris, nisi illud litigatoris amplitudine metiaris. Sors et urna fisco iudicem adsignat; licet reicere ... Eodem foro utuntur principatus et libertas ... Ingens hoc meritum, maius illud, quod eos procuratores habes, ut plerumque ciues tui non alios iudices malint. Liberum est autem discrimini suo locum eligere. Neque enim illam necessitatem muneribus tuis addis, ut qui scias hanc esse beneficiorum principalium summam, si illis et non uti licet* (Paneg., 36).

It is clear from this that there was now in existence a tribunal for hearing fiscal suits, presumably that of the praetor first appointed by Nerva *qui inter fiscum et priuatos ius dicit* (Dig., I, 1, 2, 32); the praetor, whose court was *par ceteris*, constituted a jury of *recuperatores* by the normal procedure of *sortitio* and *reiectio*.[62] By implication the procedure had been very different under Domitian, when the *princeps* evidently did not avail himself of the ordinary courts (*oedem foro*). The reference that follows to Trajan's procurators not only implies that they were men of greater impartiality than Domitian's but that in Domitian's day citizens had no choice but to submit their disputes with the *fiscus* to the judgement of the procurators. Indeed it is earlier suggested that it was novel for the procurators to follow any legal process at all; this is surely an exaggeration, based on the premises that *ius* administered by procurators was not *ius*, and that their tribunal was not truly a court of justice. Pliny is naturally concerned with Rome and Italy, and we are therefore bound to take the view that even there fiscal cases had been heard in procuratorial courts. Who these procurators were I do not know; perhaps the officials known simply as *procurator patrimonii* | or *procurator hereditatium* or *procurator XX hereditatium*, whose duties may have been mainly concerned with imperial properties and inheritances and the estates duty in Italy itself rather than with oversight of the

---

[60] SUETONIUS, *Dom.*, 12 on which see F. MILLAR (2), p. 363.

[61] *I.L.S.*, 5968; for date cf. *PIR²*, B, 103. For other *terminationes* by procurators cf. nn. 57–8 and *A.E.*, 1939, 178 (Syria, AD 102). Millar, who cites these, has overlooked *I.L.S.*, 4966 (late) and 5974.

[62] *F.I.R.A.*, I², 8, 37 (*lex agr.*); 21, *cap.* 95 (*lex Urson.*); 67, 65 f. (*edictum Venafr.*).

provincial *procuratores patrimonii* or *hereditatium* or *vicesima*[63]. I doubt if any of the procurators Pliny had in mind were freedmen, or he would surely have mentioned this as an additional count against Domitian's administration.

Millar (who has not fully seized the importance of this passage) suggests that in the final sentences Pliny need not mean that under Trajan citizens might select the procurator's court, when litigating with the *fiscus*, but that they "would accept the demands of an imperial procurator as just, and not contest them". This seems to me a less natural interpretation of *locum eligere* (a phrase which indeed rests on conjectural emendation); and the last sentence quoted is extraordinarily banal, if it means only that persons faced with a fiscal claim did not need to take it to the courts at all; more probably it shows that they could accept the judicial decision of the procurator rather than go to the praetor, a course which might involve more cost. If this view be right, Trajan did not abolish procuratorial jurisdiction in Italy itself, but provided (like Nerva) an alternative to it. It is curious that in legal texts relating to fiscal claims under Trajan, Hadrian and the Antonines we hear nothing more of the jurisdiction either of the fiscal praetor or of procurators, but only of the *praefecti aerarii* (pp. 143–5).

If procurators had decided fiscal cases in Italy under Domitian, we can conclude *a fortiori* that they had done so in the provinces. The "good" emperors from Nerva to Marcus Aurelius did not necessarily deprive them of this jurisdiction outside Italy, which would have given less offence to traditional susceptibilities. The danger always inherent in procuratorial jurisdiction is evident; it was vested in officials whose prospects of advancement might appear to be dependent on their success in filling imperial coffers. But this danger was itself less under the emperors named, who were conscious of their good intentions and did not fail to proclaim them | [to officials and subjects; as Pliny said, *saepius vincitur fiscus, cuius mala causa numquam est nisi sub bono principe* (*Paneg.*, 36). The difficulty in which even an upright procurator must often have found himself of being at once advocate and judge of fiscal claims was mitigated by Hadrian's creation of *advocati fisci*,[64] who at any rate by Marcus' reign (*Dig.*, XLIX, 14, 3, 9 and 14, 7) were probably

---

[63] Equestrian officials with these ranks are attested before or under Domitian, *I.L.S.*, 1447–8; 1418. Equestrian procurators of imperial estates in Italy are not attested till much later, *I.L.S.*, 1401; 1427; 2768; *C.I.L.*, IX, 784, together with the *procuratores rei priuatae* listed by H.-G. Pflaum, o.c., 1036–40.

[64] [The attribution to Hadrian in *H.A. Hadr.* 20 may be right: they are not found earlier. On these *advocati* see n. 48 and Brunt, *J.R.S.*, 73, 1983, 73 f. They still had the same role in the late empire, cf. *C.Th.*, XI, 30, 4, 1 (383): *Rationales rei privatae causis vel sacri aerarii praesidentes examen praesente fisci advocatione suscipiant*, cf. X, 15, 4 (367); X, 10, 32 (425); X, 8, 5 (435). In 365 the governor is to decide suits against the imperial estate *rationali praesente* (II, 1, 5).]

to appear whenever such claims were to be decided, and who should thus have relieved the procuratorial judges of the burden of pressing them.

It may be too that before the Severan period governors were better able to check the conduct of procurators. They may not yet have been unable in practice to exercise concurrent jurisdiction in fiscal cases. Perhaps the subjects could still appeal to them against the decisions of procuratorial courts. Later, this was probably barred. At least Caracalla would not permit the proconsul to invalidate them by *restitutio in integrum* (*C.J.*, III, 36, 1), though under a Severan rescript (II, 36, 1) the *fiscus* itself, i.e. the procuratorial courts, had to respect the normal rules for *restitutio*. The appeals on points of law, which were allowed both from governors and procurators (n. 49), would go to the emperor. Severus Alexander found it necessary to warn both governors and procurators not to obstruct appeals by the use of force (*Dig.*, XLIX, 1, 25). He was responding to a petition from the Bithynian *koinon*, but copies of his rescript found in Egypt (*P. Oxy.*, 2104, 3106) indicate that the warning was issued throughout the empire.]

Governor and procurator could also be concerned in the same case. Pliny in Bithynia was authorized to hear the claim of Nicaea to succeed to the property of Nicaeans who died intestate, at the expense of the *fiscus, adhibitis Virdio Gemellino et Epimacho, liberto meo, procuratoribus* (*ep.* X, 84); the procurators (of whom one is a freedman) were to be present clearly because of the fiscal interest (cf. n. 57), but apparently only as assessors;[65] the privileges of a city could be decided by no one below the governor.[66] Similarly both governor and procurator are somehow concerned in a Delphic case in Trajan's reign.[67] It is hard to be sure how far jurisdiction is implied in many other allusions to procurators which Millar has collected.[68] Nor is their indepen|dent activity as judges clearly documented in this period, but I suspect, without being able to prove, that many imperial decisions on fiscal claims were given on appeals from their judgements; and was not the institution of

---

[65] Cf. Domitian's *decretum* in *F.I.R.A.*, I², 75: *adhibitis utriusque ordinis splendidis uiris.*

[66] Diocletian, however, instructed a *rationalis* to seize *bona uacantia* without regard to pretended rights of cities to succeed to their intestate citizens and to refer to himself any cases in which cities had already taken possession of such properties, *C.J.*, X, 10, 1. Perhaps this needed stating, just because it was a novelty.

[67] Bourget, *De rebus Delphicis*, 1905, 70; the relevant part is also quoted by E. Groag, *Die röm. Reichsbeamten von Achaia*, 1939, p. 49–50. [In *O.G.I.S.*, 502 (Hadrian) the procurator is merely requested by the proconsul to assist in implementing an imperial decision. Other cases of joint jurisdiction: *Dig.*, L, 1, 38, 1 (p. 186); *C.J.*, II, 37, 2 (Alex. Sev.).]

[68] For instance, as regards the inscriptions cited by F. Millar (2), p. 363 from J. H. Oliver, *Sacred Gerousia*, no. 24, I do not see that we can go beyond Oliver's own conclusion that 'at least in certain questions, perhaps in ordinary questions of financial policy, the imperial procurator ... was the competent authority to assist or guide (the gerousia)' (p. 5).

aduocati fisci otiose, if the procurators themselves and their staff had to present the case of the *fiscus* in the governor's court? But even in Ulpian's day (n. 31) their fiscal jurisdiction was in theory only concurrent with that of the governor, and we cannot be confident that as yet it was in practice exclusive or that they were not subject to control by governors. The powers they enjoyed in the Severan period *may* represent an accretion to their independence. Once they had acquired these powers, which they constantly sought to extend, the gravest abuses could occur. Herodian tells how under Maximin the procurator of Africa imposed sentences of every form of cruelty and especially confiscations, and he comments that at that time even the few decent financial officials were obliged in their knowledge of the emperor's avarice to follow similar courses.[69] The revolt that their exactions stimulated has its parallel (in my view) in the risings in Gaul and elsewhere against Nero (pp. 29 ff); and Maximin perhaps did no more than revive the policy of Gaius, Nero and Domitian.

There remains the question of procuratorial jurisdiction within the imperial estates. It is clearest in the documents pertaining to the Vipasca mine, of which one is certainly Hadrianic and the other may be of the first century.[70] In this latter inscription the procurator is expressly authorized to fine the lessee of the bath monopoly if he fails to provide the service required under his contract. In the Hadrianic document he may beat a slave and have him sold under such and such conditions or confiscate the property of a free man and exclude him from the mining districts if he is found guilty of theft of ore or of contravention of various mining regulations. The power of banishment thus granted is reminiscent of Callistratus' statement[71] | that though procurators may not impose sentence of deportation, they may by a rescript of Pius prohibit any one *quasi tumultuosum uel iniuriosum aduersus colonos Caesaris* from entering an imperial estate.[72] The documents also mention or imply other issues which might have to be decided in court, e.g. breaches of monopolies sold by the procurator or disputes between partners in a mining concession. It is not expressly stated that the procurator would determine such issues in his court, but it seems probable. It is even more likely that he would have the right to impose

---

[69] VII, 4, 2–3. Similar statements in *S.H.A., Max.,* 14, 1; *Gord.,* 7, 2, have little value in themselves; and that in *Pius,* 6: *procuratores suos et modeste suscipere tributos iussit et excedentes modum rationem factorum suorum reddere praecepit,* though credible, probably does no more than reflect the author's view of the conduct of a good emperor.

[70] *F.I.R.A.,* I², 104 (HADR.) and 105. [Cf. pp. 398–400.]

[71] [He is a freedman, cf. BOULVERT (n. 1) 217 f., 417. Cf. nn. 76 f.]

[72] *Dig.,* I, 19, 3, 1. It was necessary to enact specifically that fugitive slaves could be pursued even in imperial estates, *Dig.,* XI, 4, 1, 1; cf. 4, 3 (rescript of MARCUS).

a fine in circumstances where a fine is said to be due to the *fiscus*, or to declare the nullity of a gift of a mining concession by a *colonus* in debt to the *fiscus*. None of these powers is very extensive. Some have an analogy with the jurisdiction of municipal magistrates.[73] Cities could apparently inflict corporal punishment on free men (provided that they were not Roman citizens), whereas the procurators of mines could only beat slaves. Cities again could impose fines and, in certain circumstances, confiscate property. Paul and Barnabas were expelled from the Roman colony of Pisidian Antioch (*Acts*, XIII, 50); the magistrates at Philippi, another colony, flogged Paul and Silas and ordered their expulsion, but on hearing that they were Roman citizens, they apologized for the flogging and translated their command to leave into a simple request (XVI, 35 f.). The right of municipal magistrates to beat and issue orders of expulsion against itinerant seers and soothsayers, attested by Paul's *Sentences* (V, 21, 1), may have existed much earlier with the proviso that it did not apply to Roman citizens. And there is no indication that the free *coloni* of Vipasca were citizens. On the mining estates then these documents show procurators vested with the same kind of powers that municipal magistrates possessed. Since many imperial estates, doubtless including the mines, were extra-territorial to the cities,[74] we should | expect their administrators to enjoy jurisdiction similar to that which city magistrates possessed within their territories.

The inscriptions from the African estates are less informative on jurisdiction.[75] But it is plain from the petition to Commodus from the *coloni* of the *saltus Burunitanus* that it lay with the procurators to decide judicially (*cognoscere*) in disputes between the *coloni* and *conductores* arising from the lex Hadriana under which their obligations were

[73] See A. N. SHERWIN-WHITE, *Roman Society and Roman Law in the New Testament*, 1963, p. 71 f. I have somewhat modified his view on the incident at Philippi.

[74] E. BEAUDOUIN, *Les grands domaines dans l'empire romain*, 1899, ch. 1, lucidly expounds the proof of this given by A. SCHULTEN, *Die röm. Grundherrschaften*, 1896, p. 3 f, 75 ff. Some imperial estates, however, were within city territories, e.g. at Veleia (*C.I.L.*, XI, 1147); Schulten is not always right, I think, in distinguishing which were and which not. R. HIS, *Die Domänen der röm Kaiserzeit*, 1896, pp. 46–7 gives evidence for imperial properties within city territories in the late empire.

[75] *F.I.R.A.*, I², 100–102 and esp. 103. By contrast with the *coloni* of the *saltus Burunitanus* the villagers of Scaptopare had often appealed to governors of Thrace before petitioning the emperor Gordian III (*S.I.G.³*, 888); but there is no sufficient reason for thinking that they were imperial tenants. Similar complaints from imperial *coloni* of Aragua in Phrygia were, however, referred for verification and redress by the emperor to the proconsul (*O.G.I.S.*, 519, AD 244–7). This, we might think, lay in the emperor's discretion; here too the villagers had not approached the proconsul in the first place. The inscription of the early third century from Aga Bey in Lydia (KEIL AND PREMERSTEIN in *Denkschr. der Wiener Akad.*, 57, p. 37 f. = ABBOTT AND JOHNSON, *Munic. Admin. in Rom. Emp.*, no. 142) shows soldiers arresting villagers and ostensibly sending them up to the procurators of Asia for trial, but it is relevant that at the time one of these procurators was acting governor.

prescribed: it does not seem to have occurred to the aggrieved *coloni*, when they found that the procurators were in collusion with the *conductores*, to appeal to the proconsul; their only recourse is to the emperor himself. We cannot, however, conclude that the procurators had any criminal jurisdiction over the *coloni*, as their actions in fettering and beating them are represented as having been violations of law, and this may be true. Thus the only jurisdiction the African procurators are known to have held was, again, very limited.

Millar has also cited the decision by procurators on the liability of Phrygian villagers to angary.[76] Here again we find them taking the place of city magistrates in what was doubtless an extra-territorial estate. The provision of animals and carts for the so-called *cursus publicus* ranked as a *personale munus* (e.g. *Dig.*, L, 4, 18, 4). The assignment of *munera* was a matter for the city councils or magistrates in the later empire (*Dig.*, L, 1, 21, *pr.*; *C.J.*, X, 32, 2) as it had been in Caesar's charter for Urso (*Lex Urs.*, ch. 98). In default of such a local authority, the procurators naturally acted.[77] In cities, it is true, in-dividuals might appeal for immunity to the governor; very probably the *coloni* on imperial estates could not. For the cities imperial regula-tions laid down elaborately the types of cases in which | immunity was granted. Among the classes of persons exempt from city liturgies were the *conductores uectigalium fisci*, who no doubt included *conductores* of imperial estates, *ne extenuentur facultates eorum, quae subsignatae sint fisco* (Callistratus, *Dig.*, L, 6, 6, 10). The question then arose whether they might voluntarily assume the burden of such liturgies. Callistratus holds that either the governor or the procurator may forbid them to do so, and ought to forbid them *nisi si paria fisco fecisse dicantur* (*ibid*). In accordance with the rule we have previously discerned, the governor is concerned because city interests are involved, and the procurator because of fiscal considerations; thus they have concurrent powers. *Coloni* of imperial estates were also exempt from city liturgies *ut idoniores praediis fiscalibus habeantur* (Callistratus, *Dig.*, L, 6, 6, 11). The right of the procurator to exclude from an imperial estate any one troublesome to the *coloni*, e.g. a city official seeking to enforce liturgies upon them, enabled him to enforce this immunity. But for this rule some *coloni Caesaris* would have been liable to municipal burdens as *some* imperial estates did lie within city territories.[78] The rule [is perhaps expressed too absolutely in the text of Callistratus, as we have it, or applied, as

[76] First published by W. H. C. FREND in *J.R.S.*, 46, 46. [BOULVERT (n. 1) 417 stresses the judicial character of the decision of the procurators.]

[77] [They too would be freedman, BOULVERT (n. 1) 416, cf. 218, 292 f.]

[78] See n. 74. Some evidence of attempts by city magistrates to impose liturgies on imperial *coloni* in the Aragua and Aga Bey inscriptions (cf. n. 75).

stated, only when he wrote.] A second-century jurist, Papirius Iustus, cites a rescript of Marcus and Verus whereby *coloni praediorum fisci* may be liable to *munera*, if the *fiscus* suffers no loss; this is for the governor to determine, but *adhibito procuratore* (*Dig.*, L, 1, 38, 1). [And Severus Alexander roundly asserted that *coloni, id est conductores*, of fiscal estates were not exempt from *munera civilia*, with particular reference to *tutela* (*C.J.*, V, 62, 8).]

None of this evidence suggests that procuratorial jurisdiction ever belonged *par excellence* to the procurators of imperial estates. We find them to some extent in enjoyment of juridical powers that belonged to city magistrates within city territories, and to some extent concerned with cases in which there was a fiscal interest. It is only jurisdiction of the first kind that differentiates them from the other procurators, and it is not known to apply to important cases. Later still, when a *colonus* or even a slave of the *res priuata* is accused of a crime, he comes before the governor, though the *rationalis* or procurator must be present (*C.J.*, III, 26, 8, A.D. 358), or has the duty to produce him in court (*C.Th.*, X, 4, 3, c. 370). In a somewhat earlier *constitutio* tenants of the *res priuata* appear | before the governor when litigating in civil cases, though the governor has to refer his decision to the *comes rei priuatae* (*C.J.*, III, 26, 6); by the 370s the *defensor domus nostrae*, i.e. the *aduocatus fisci* had to be present (*C.Th.*, X, 4, 3). But the practice seems to fluctuate; disputes of *dominici coloni et patrimoniales* are reserved in 349 to the *rationalis summae rei*, a rule not limited (as His suggested) to minor disputes (*C.J.*, III, 26, 7); and in 442 all litigation arising in the Cappadocian estates is assigned for decision to the *praepositus sacri cubiculi* (*C.J.*, III, 26, 11). In the view of His there is no evidence in the later law for the jurisdiction of *rationales priuatae rei*, the successors of the former *procuratores saltuum*, before 383 (*C.Th.*, XI, 30, 41).[79] The relevance of these later constitutions to the procedure in use up to c. 300 may be doubted, but in so far as it has any, it cannot be concluded that the procurators of imperial estates had any special juridical powers denied to other procurators. Their status was inferior, and their duties less important, so that precisely the opposite conclusion is more probable. The fiscal jurisdiction which was really most significant belonged especially to those procurators who were charged with the collection of taxes and with the sequestration of *bona caduca* and *bona damnatorum*. And even they were normally denied the right of cognition in criminal cases, and in civil cases in which the *fiscus* had no interest.

The origin of this fiscal jurisdiction seems to lie in Claudius' measure of A.D. 53 (though in imperial provinces, of right, and elsewhere, by

---

[79] See further R. His (n. 74), pp. 113 f.

abuse, it may go back rather earlier). The extent of this measure has certainly been described by Tacitus in a misleading way, perhaps unconsciously; he was writing for readers who knew the facts. If Claudius intended to give his procurators exclusive jurisdiction even in fiscal cases, it is clear that not all his successors followed him. The practice of Domitian and Trajan at least varied widely in Italy. [It is doubtful how safely we can retroject the juristic evidence of the Severan epoch to the Antonine. We have indeed seen various examples of Caracalla conceding more extensive jurisdiction to procurators than his predecessors, but as Spagnuola Vigorita (n. 1) has shown more fully, Alexander Severus and Gordian were sometimes disposed to revert to traditional rules. This illustrates a general truth that it is wrong to assume that there was a continuous line of administrative development from one reign to another, or that measures taken by emperors (of whom Caracalla was one) who flouted the views of the elite were not modified by successors who sought their consent.][80]

[80] Mr. J. P. V. D. Balsdon assisted me in the composition of the first version of this essay. I have not reproduced the original Appendix, the substance of which is taken into this chapter and chapter 17.

9

Conscription and Volunteering in the Roman Imperial Army

At all times in the history of Rome both citizens and subjects were legally liable to military service. Th. Mommsen, who recognized this, also held that after Marius the legions were mainly composed of volunteers, except in the great civil wars of the late. Republic.[1] This opinion has been endorsed by countless other scholars and often generalized to cover all branches of the imperial army. I have tried to show elsewhere[2] that in the late Republic it was not only in civil wars that Italians were frequently subjected to conscription; I now propose to argue that at any rate until the second century AD conscription was far more common in the Principate than the current dogma, endlessly repeated, would allow. That it was normally employed in the fourth century I take to be accepted. It will not be denied that many recruits at all times were volunteers: only the government could not rely on a sufficient supply of such recruits; probably in certain regions conscription was usual; the evidence does not, of course, permit us to determine, however approximately, the proportions of volunteers and conscripts.

In the Republic the terms *dilectus, supplementum* and *conscribere* almost always suggest resort to compulsion;[3] this nuance persists in imperial Latin though some ambiguity must be admitted.[4] Fronto, for instance, can write: *in bello ubi opus sit legionem conscribere, non tantum voluntarios legimus sed etiam latentes militari aetate conquirimus*, a text which shows both that *conscribere* can be used neutrally and that in the mid second century the government did not necessarily rely on volunteers alone.[5] In a letter

---

[1] *Roemisches Staatsrecht* (Leipzig 1887–1888³) 3.298, cf. 2.849 f. R. O. Fink, *Rom. Military Records on Papyrus* (Cleveland, 1971); G. Forni, *Il Reclutamento delle Legioni da Augusto a Diocleziano* (Milano, 1953); A. H. M. Jones, *The Later Roman Empire* (Oxford, 1964); K. Kraft, *Zur Rekrutierung von Alen u. Kohorten an Rhein u. Donau* (Bern, 1951); H.-G. Pflaum, *Les Carrières procuratoriennes équestres* (Paris, 1960) are cited by authors' names.

[2] *Italian Manpower* (Oxford, 1971) ch. XXII. (cited *infra* by title alone).

[3] *Ibid.* Appendix 20 (also for Livy's usage).

[4] See esp. texts cited in nn. 5, 19 f., 31–3, 36, 43 f., 62 f., 67, 79–81, 85. Cf. also *Cod. Theod.* 7.13.9 (380), 7.18. 10 and 20.12 (400); Amm. 17.13.3; 31.4.4; and see n. 107.

[5] 140 N = 2.54H. Cf. texts in n. 45. Fronto 2.206 H. (better than 206 N) is not illuminating.

to Pliny Trajan distinguishes between *voluntarii*, *lecti* and *vicarii*; the *lecti* are plainly con|scripts, and the *vicarii* substitutes provided by men who thereby escaped conscription.[6] The *voluntarii* are said *se offerre*; similarly Severan jurists distinguish recruits who *militiae se* (or *nomen*) *dederunt* from those who are *lecti* or who *se legi passi sunt*; the last phrase may again refer to *vicarii*.[7] By contrast Fronto uses the verb *legere* for enlistment of both volunteers and conscripts, and with some reason, as the recruiting officer had to satisfy himself by *inquisitio* and *probatio* of the qualifications of all recruits alike.[8] But it looks as if in technical language *legere* referred to conscription, and Fronto's use of *conscribere* may also be loose. Persons appointed *ad iuniores legendos* should, like *dilectatores*, have been empowered to enlist recruits by coercion.

They should not have refused to accept volunteers suitably qualified. *Ceteris paribus* they should have preferred willing soldiers. Trajan seems to take it for granted that recruits might be either conscripts or volunteers. Apuleius parodies the activity of a Roman recruiting officer when he makes a robber leader recommend to his comrades: *inquisitioni commilitonum potius insisteretur et tirocinio novae iuventutis ad pristinae manus numerum Martiae cohortis facies integraretur; nam et invitos terrore compelli et volentes praemio provocari posse.*[9] Since his story is based on his knowledge of conditions in Africa, this passage is particularly relevant to levies there, but I do not doubt that he describes the normal conduct of the *dilectus* everywhere. Only an official bent on lining his own pocket would actually prefer compulsion, with a view to extorting ransoms from those unwilling to serve. Given the general standard of official morality,[10] I suspect that such malpractices forbidden by the *lex Iulia de repetundis*[11] were more common than we know and did much to add to what Velleius calls the *trepidatio delectus* (n. 32).

Scholars who claim that conscription was a rarity in the Principate unfail|lingly quote a dictum of the jurist Arrius Menander, who is named as a *consilliarius* by Ulpian (*Dig.*, 4.4.11.2) and who wrote under

---

[6] *Ep.* 10.29 f. with Sherwin-White's admirable commentary (A. N. Sherwin-White, *The Letters of Pliny* [Oxford, 1966]). For *vicarii* cf. Liv. 29.1.

[7] *Dig.* 40.12.29, 49.16.2.1, *h. t.* 4, 1–4 and 8 f.; *h. t.* 8; *h. t.* 16 *pr*; Liv. 4.4.3; *Cod. Iust.* 12.33.1 (Severan), cf. Tac., *Hist.* 2.97.2, 3.58.2. In Liv. 5.10.3 (cf. 2.27.10) and Vegetius, 1.3 men can be forced *nomina dare*.

[8] *Probatio* applies to conscripts as well as volunteers, cf. n. 7 (*contra* Wilcken on *Chr.* 453 = Fink 87). Full description of recruitment partly based on Vegetius by R. W. Davies, 'Joining the Roman Army', *BJ* 169 (1969) 208 ff. (cf. also Watson [n. 71] ch. 2 and A. H. M. Jones, 616 f.); in my view he misinterprets some texts considered below. Both he and Watson repeat virtually without argument that recruits were normally volunteers: ''Tis the song of the Jubjub! The proof is complete, If only I've stated it thrice'.

[9] *Met.* 7.4.

[10] Ch. 4 Part II.

[11] *Dig.* 48.11.6.2, cf. Tac. *Agr.* 13.1: *ipsi Britanni dilectum ac tributa et iniuncta imperii munia impigre obeunt, si iniuriae absint*, nn. 59, 67; p. 205.

Severus or Caracalla (49.16.13.5 f., cf. 49.16.5.4). Arrius certainly
contrasts the present, when *most* soldiers were volunteers, with a former
age, when men who evaded the levy were liable to be sold into slavery;
this is recorded as the old Republican penalty, and Augustus sold a
Roman *eques* for maiming his sons so as to make them unfit for service,
very probably in the crisis of AD 9–10, when he put some men to death
for refusing to serve.[12] The capital penalty, says Arrius, has been
abandoned *mutato statu militiae*; what this may mean will be considered
later. But he does not date the change, and we are not entitled to apply
his dictum to any age before the Severan. Since the extracts from his
first book *de re militari* also illustrate the continuance of the obligation to
military service, I transcribe them, omitting a preliminary discussion of
the conditions under which a man could not legally enlist either as a
conscript or as a volunteer (*Dig.*, 49.16.4, *pr.*–9); he then proceeds:

> 10. Gravius autem delictum est detractare munus militiae quam
> adpetere; nam et qui ad dilectum olim non respondebant, ut
> proditores libertatis in servitutem redigebantur. Sed mutato statu
> militiae recessum a poena capitis est, quia plerumque voluntario
> milite numeri supplentur. 11. Qui filium suum subtrahit militiae
> belli tempore, exilio et bonorum parte multandus est; si in pace,
> fustibus caedi iubetur et requisitus iuvenis vel a patre postea
> exhibitus in deteriorem militiam dandus est; qui enim se sollicitari
> sustinuit (*Mommsen*: se sollicitavit *codd.*) ab alio, veniam non meretur.
> 12. Eum qui filium debilitavit dilectu per bellum indicto, ut inhabilis
> militiae sit, praeceptum divi Traiani deportavit.

Though the units were generally recruited from volunteers and it
had therefore become unnecessary to sell any one who evaded the levy
into slavery (10), the father who tried to withhold his son was liable to
heavy penalties, especially in time of war (11–12); however, even in
peace, he committed a criminal offence, and it follows that a *dilectus*
(which in Arrius' usage clearly denotes compulsion) could still take
place in time of peace. The penalty then applied was a cudgelling; by
the age of Severus this was not imposed on the *honestiores* (senators,
equites, decurions), including even veterans;[13] it may then be inferred
that their sons were not liable to conscription.

Exemption from military service was a privilege recorded in a
number of documents. It was conferred by Octavian on the trierarch
Seleucus, his parents | and descendants (*FIRA* I² no. 55, II 23) and on
some veterans and their children (ibid. 56), though it does not appear

---

[12] *Italian Manpower* 391; Suet., *Aug.* 24.1; Dio 56. 23. 3.
[13] P. Garnsey, *Social Status and Legal Privilege in the Roman Empire* (Oxford, 1970). 136–41; 245–7.

in what is extant of an edict in which Domitian defined the privileges of veterans (ibid. 76). Modestinus cites a letter of Pius, which Commodus had apparently confirmed and which was itself a re-enactment of rules that Hadrian too had confirmed on his accession, conferring privileges on philosophers, sophists, *grammatici* and doctors; these included the right 'not to be enrolled for military service against their will' (*Dig.*, 27.1.6.8). [Evidently the same right belongs to the sons of all *honestiores*.] The mere fact that men were specifically granted this immunity shows that in the absence of such a grant they were liable to serve, but it does not follow that there was much risk of their being actually called up unless exempted; the list of privileges could be tralatician. *Militiae vacatio* was indeed an old Republican immunity.[14]

Forni (28 ff.) argues that 'the Roman state did not dispose of sufficient means to undertake the burden of maintaining an army supplied by a generally obligatory conscription, nor if it had possessed the means, could it have compelled all citizens without distinction to a long term of service, without exposing itself to the peril of subverting the social and economic class order and of having recalcitrant and mutinous soldiers'. Already under Augustus the legionary's term of service lengthened out to 25 years or even more, and thereafter we find that both legionaries and auxiliaries regularly served for 25 or 26 years.[15] As Forni remarks, it was only necessary to raise on average some 5000–6000 men a year to keep the legions up to strength, and though we should substitute a much lower figure for the total number of adult male citizens in Augustus' time than that Forni himself accepted,[16] it is plain that there could be no question of enrolling more than a small proportion of them in the legions, even if the legions had still been recruited solely from citizens by birth. In fact of course provincials were already admitted to them;[17] moreover, the number of citizens was itself continually on the increase with new enfranchisements. As for the *auxilia*, it is no less patent that their numbers did not require resort to universal conscription. Indeed it would be an absurdity to suggest that *all* fit males could have been called up for *long* service. But it is not at all absurd to suppose that individuals were selected by lot or by some other more or less arbitrary criterion to fulfil the obligation of military service that was only in principle incumbent on all. The unfairness of such a procedure is not proof that it was never adopted. On the contrary, to say nothing of modern states, we know

[14] *Italian Manpower* 391 n. 1.
[15] *Ibid.* 401, 332–42; cf. Forni 37 f. and the *diplomata* for the *auxilia*.
[16] He assumed that the Augustan census figures related to adult males. *V. contra, Italian Manpower*, Part I, esp. ch. IX.
[17] Forni ch. IV.

that it was adopted in Republican Rome.[18] | In many years during the first century BC scores of thousands of Italians were conscribed for the army, and some of them served for prolonged terms; and yet of course the majority of Italians remained in civil life. The author of a letter to Caesar ascribed to Sallust commented on this: *ne, uti adhuc, militia iniusta aut inaequalis sit, cum alii triginta, pars nullum stipendium facient* (*ep.* 1.8.6); it matters little for our purpose if the letter were written by Sallust or in the imperial age. Again, it goes without saying that volunteers were always preferred. That does not imply that they were always forthcoming. And the government could hope on the basis of experience that stern discipline would check refractory behaviour on the part of conscripts. Tiberius at least did not think that the few Italians most likely to volunteer would prove better soldiers than men raised by conscription in the provinces (n. 36 *infra*).

In his Panegyric on Rome[19] Aelius Aristides says that the Romans deemed it unworthy of their rule that citizens should be subject to military service and its hardships but saw the imprudence of relying on foreign troops; they therefore formed an army without disturbing the citizens by picking the subjects whose physique was most suitable to perform the 'liturgy'[20] of military service in return for Roman citizenship. Each subject people was required to provide contingents not so large that it was a burden to furnish them, or that any could possess a potentially dangerous force of their own. If we were to attach any value to these effusions of a peaceful *Graeculus*, we might infer that citizens were no longer liable to conscription but that subject peoples were; in Aristides' eyes military service is a burdensome liturgy, and he has no conception that it was relished by any of the subjects. In fact conscription was not unknown among citizens and in Italy itself even in his time (*infra*); [while volunteers may have formed a large proportion] of soldiers provided by the subjects, Aristides was most familiar with Greek cities which provided few recruits,[21] and may have known little of the general practice of recruitment in the empire; [his evidence is of small value]. What Cassius Dio says is another matter: he had experience of government. He makes Maecenas advise Augustus to enrol in the army men of the greatest physical strength and in most

---

[18] Peter the Great instituted life-long selective conscription, later reduced to 25 years [see John L. H. Keep, *Soldiers of the Tsar* (1986)]: a similar system existed in some of the Habsburg dominions in the 18th century. Lot: *Italian Manpower* 628 n. 5, 631; cf. Dio 56.23.2. See Appendix.

[19] 26.74 ff. Hdn. 2.11 thought (wrongly) that Augustus Ἰταλιώτας πόνων ἐξέπαυσε καὶ τῶν ὅπλων ἐγύμνωσε; soldiers were henceforth mercenaries.

[20] Cf. *munus* in Arrius and elsewhere.

[21] Forni gives 9 from Asia, 32 from Bithynia (22 in one Trajanic list of soldiers, n. 66) and 1 from Lycia for the whole period from AD 70. 'Each people' did not bear a fair share of the burden, or sometimes any, cf. Th. Mommsen, *Ges. Schr.* (Berlin, 1905–1913); VI.22 f.

need of livelihood, who would otherwise be most apt to turn to brigandage.[22] As men in need of a livelihood would be most ready to | enlist, this may fit the testimony of Arrius Menander. But Maecenas' speech is notoriously related to conditions in Dio's own time rather than to those of the Augustan age. His allusion to brigandage may well have sprung from his interpretation of the effects produced in Italy when Severus instituted the practice of recruiting the praetorians from provincial legionaries rather than from Italy and to a lesser extent from such relatively civilized regions as Spain, Noricum and Macedonia; in Dio's view (which may have been mistaken) men of the kind who had once joined the guard now took to brigandage and gladiatorial fighting; probably he had in mind the followers of Bulla who plundered Italy for two years.[23] As governor of Upper Pannonia Dio had also learned the fine military qualities of the inhabitants; he explained their bellicosity by their poverty; life in such wretched conditions was hardly worth living. By his time Pannonians provided a high proportion of legionaries as well as auxiliaries on the Danube.[24] But that had only been true since the early second century. Dio's evidence is irrelevant to recruitment for the army at an earlier time. The extent to which conscription had once been used cannot be determined from any of the texts or general considerations so far examined: we must look for more concrete evidence.

Let us first take Italy. In the late Republic and most of all from 49 to 29 BC conscription was usual—and detested (n. 2). Yet at this time soldiers had some claim to be discharged after only six years' service, and if they were fortunate, secured handsome rewards in booty, lands and money. Under Augustus' system all citizen soldiers could count on *praemia militiae*, if they survived the term of service, but these were far less liberal than the luckier among their predecessors had secured,[25] and the term of service had lengthened to twenty-five years or more

---

[22] Dio 52.27.4 f.

[23] Dio 74.2.5; 76.10.1. Recruitment for the praetorians before Severus: 74.2.4 cf. Tac. *Ann.* 4.5.3 (who no doubt rightly ignores provincials, when writing of Tiberius' time), confirmed by data in A. Passerini, *Le Coorti pretorie* (Roma, 1939) 148 ff. (note evidence for volunteering in 143 n. 1; it is also implied in *Edict. imp. Claud. de Anaun.*). The inscriptions similarly confirm the character and permanence of Severus' change, *ibid* 174 ff.; the few Italians attested (173 n. 2) were probably themselves ex-legionaries, since some recruitment for the legions in Italy is attested in and after Severus' reign (nn. 47–50), and Dio then may have exaggerated the social effect of Severus' change. The conduct of the praetorians under Commodus and in 193 (cf. Dio 73.8, Hdn. 2.2.5, 2.4.4) does not suggest that they were to be preferred to the new guards (*contra* Dio 74.2.4–6) but well fits the suggestion that they were drawn from elements in the population that would otherwise have turned to brigandage, not disproved by a few epigraphic instances of praetorians who enjoyed rank and property *before* service, Passerini, 164 f.

[24] Dio 49.36.

[25] *Italian Manpower* 412, cf. ch. XIX, esp. 339–42.

(n. 15), spent often in uncongenial climates and distant lands. Pay was modest, discipline harsh. In AD 14 the legionaries on the Rhine demanded *modum miseriarum*.[26] Of course the men in the praetorian and | urban cohorts were far better off, and were doubtless always volunteers, [though perhaps seldom of high social standing (n. 23). We also know of 35 *cohortes voluntariorum civium Romanorum*, of which one was raised in Campania and two others in Italy; the provenance of recruits for the rest, at the time when they were formed, is not clear. It may be added that there are a few other *cohortes ingenuorum civium Romanorum*, which, together with a *cohors Apula* first attested under Augustus, are not styled 'voluntariorum'; the specification 'ingenuorum' seems designed to differentiate them from the cohorts of freedmen conscribed in the crises of AD 6 and 9,[27] and a recently discovered inscription attests a *dilectus* of *ingenui* held in the city of Rome in one of these years;[28] of course some of those then enlisted may have been drafted into legions, but it seems probable that the *cohortes ingenuorum* were formed and so named at this time. Men serving in auxiliary units composed of Roman citizens, then mostly Italians, received the same donative as legionaries on Augustus' death, and probably their pay and conditions were also the same, and better than those of other auxiliaries.[29] But it can hardly be supposed that service in auxiliary cohorts was more attractive than in the legions, and the fact that volunteers could be found for the former in Italy and presumably also in citizen communities of the provinces should imply that there were men willing to join up in the legions too].

At the same time the practice of enlisting provincials for the legions and giving them citizenship when they joined up, which had begun in the civil wars, appears to have continued, and eventually became normal especially in the east.[30] Yet it would seem that Augustus did not altogether abandon conscription in Italy itself. Livy refers to *dilectus*, held not (as of old) annually but at irregular intervals.[31] Velleius praises Tiberius because *quanta cum quiete hominum rem perpetui praecipuique timoris supplementum sine trepidatione delectus providet;*[32] he could hardly have written thus, if the terror of the levy has not been known since Actium, or known only in the crises of AD 6 and 9, | when there is other

---

[26] Cf. Tac. *Ann.* 1.16 f., 31 f.

[27] Kraft 82 ff., cf. M. Speidel, *TAPA* 106 (1976), 339 ff.

[28] *ZPE* (1974), 161 ff., where I discuss the date. Cf. n. 33.

[29] Tac., *Ann.* 1.8.2. On auxiliary pay see Fink nos. 68–73; M. P. Speidel, *JRS* 63 (1973), 141 ff., arguing that Fink 68 (= *P. Gen. Lat.* 1 recto) shows that foot-soldiers in *auxilia* received five-sixths cf legionary pay, but note A. K. Bowman, *JRS* 66 (1976) 172.

[30] Forni ch. IV.

[31] 6.12.4. Cf. n. 3.

[32] 2.130.2.

evidence that conscription was employed.[33] It was of course precisely in AD 6 that Augustus complained of *penuria iuventutis*;[34] earlier, Livy had suggested that Rome could no longer raise ten new legions in an emergency, as in 349 BC (7.25.9), and in fact in AD 9 Augustus did not replace Varus' three lost legions. Obviously much larger forces could readily have been mobilized by conscription of the kind familiar in the 80s and 40s.[35] It is clear that it was employed but not systematically and universally, by what method or on what principle (if any) we do not know. Conceivably communities were required to furnish small quotas of recruits (*v.* Appendix). In AD 6 and 9 even the urban proletariat and freedmen were called on. Yet there were no mass levies. What was attempted was evidently unpopular. Tiberius preferred to abandon conscription in Italy, and this despite his judgement that men of the right type would not volunteer. In AD 23, to justify a proposed visit to the provinces, *multitudinem veteranorum praetexebat imperator et dilectibus supplendos exercitus: nam voluntarium militem deesse ac, si suppeditet, non eadem virtute ac modestia agere, quia plerumque inopes ac vagi sponte militiam sumant.*[36] Levies were to be held because there were not enough properly qualified volunteers; it is patent that Tiberius assumed the necessity for conscription. But the levies were to be in the provinces, not in Italy, or Tiberius would not have thought or affected to think of leaving Italy. In the event he did not go, but we are not to infer that no *dilectus* took place; they are attested in his reign in Narbonensis (n. 54) and Thrace (n. 80). If Velleius asserts that Tiberius put an end to conscription, it is because Velleius only cared about the Italians.

After Tiberius new legions were raised occasionally, and sometimes, perhaps always, in Italy,[37] when conscription must have been employed, whenever necessary to fill their ranks. Strong arguments have been adduced to show that it was Gaius rather than Claudius who formed XV and XXII Primigenia,[38] | and I would connect with their formation Suetonius' statement that *dilectus ubique acerbissime acti*; probably Suetonius' source or sources would have expressed indigna-

---

[33] AD 6: Vell. 2.111.1, Plin. *NH* 7.149, Dio 55.31; cf. 57.5.4, Tac. *Ann.* 1.31; AD 9: Dio 56.23.2 f; both years, Suet. *Aug.* 25.2; Macr. *Sat.* 1.11.30. [Cf. n. 28.]

[34] Plin. *l.c.*

[35] Dio 56.23.1 is ludicrous.

[36] *Ann.* 4.4.2. Tiberius' objection to *vagi* could probably not be sustained; note their recruitment in late empire, *Cod. Theod.* 7.13.6.1 (altered in *Cod. Iust.* 12.43.1), 7.18.10; 7. 18. 17; 7. 20. 12; 8.2.3 and cf. n. 23.

[37] J. C. Mann, 'The Raising of New Legions during the Principate', *Hermes* 91 (1963), 483 ff. argues that all new legions in normal times were raised in Italy, whether from 'blind conservatism' or to avoid interference with the ordinary process of provincial recruitment for existing units; he finds a little supporting evidence for I Minervia and XXX Ulpia. Cf. nn. 47 f.

[38] Ritterling, *RE* XII (1924) *s. v.* Legio, cols 1244–7; Syme, 'The Northern Frontier from Tiberius to Nero', *CAH X* (1952), 788 f.

tion at the resumption of conscription *in Italy*;[39] in fact about 60% of the soldiers of known *origo* who served in these legions down to 69 came from Italy, and most of the rest from Narbonensis. Nero's *legio I Italica* was certainly raised in Italy, as its *cognomen* shows and Suetonius attests; *conscripta ex Italicis senum pedum tironibus nova legione*; even if no weight is placed on the verb *conscripta*, one might doubt if enough six-foot volunteers could have been obtained.[40] There is no evidence where or how Vespasian formed IV and XVI Flavia, unless we conjecture that the *dilectus* carried out by Agricola early in 70[41] took place in Italy and was connected with their formation; but conceivably recruits were needed at this time rather to strengthen and Romanize the two legions recently formed from 'milites' of the fleets, I and II Adiutrix.[42] Not enough is known of the original recruitment for Domitian's I Minervia and Trajan's II Traiana and XXX Ulpia (but cf. n. 37). But Marcus Aurelius certainly raised two new legions in Italy, as their *cognomina* reveal (II and III Italica); inscriptions also attest *dilectus* throughout Italy about 165, and though the precise dating of the levies is controversial, it cannot be doubted that at the time the defences of the empire seemed so precarious that the government could not have afforded to rely on sufficient volunteers coming forward [cf. Addenda].[43]

In emergencies other levies were held in Italy. Nero tried to obtain recruits from the 'city tribes' for the suppression of Vindex; no volunteers appeared, and he did not resort to compulsion; his authority was breaking down.[44] In 69 Vitellius had more success; men readily gave in their names: *superfluente multitudine curam dilectus in consules partitur*; Tacitus offers a rare example of a *dilectus* in which volunteering is actually attested.[45] Levies under Hadrian in Transpadana and other parts of Italy are to be connected with the Jewish | revolt.[46] Domiciled

---

[39] *Cal.* 43.

[40] *Nero* 19.

[41] Tac. *Agr.* 7.3. So Ritterling *op. cit.* (n. 38) col. 1540.

[42] Of 16 soldiers in II Adiutrix known to Forni 217 as enlisted between Vespasian and Trajan 9 are Italian.

[43] *ILS* 1098 on M. Cl. Fronto *misso ad iuventutem per Italiam legendam* (certainly between 163 and summer 166); *AE* 1956. 123 on Ti. Cl. Proculus Cornelianus (Pflaum, I.401), (*proc.*) *item ad dilectum cum Iulio Vero per Italiam tironum* (*utriusque*) *leg* (*ionis*) *Italicae*. I do not feel confident of the exact date, which cannot be inferred with confidence from such inaccurate sources as *HA. Marc.* 21.6 and 8; Oros. *Hist.* 7.15.6.

[44] Suet. *Nero* 44.1.

[45] Tac. *Hist.* 3.58. Cf. Liv. 5.16.5, 9.10.6 for *dilectus . . . prope voluntariorum*. Suet. *Vit.* 15.1: he promised recruits discharge after victory with the *praemia* of veterans; for a partial parallel see *Cod. Theod.* 7.13.17 (406).

[46] *ILS* 1068: T. *Caesernio . . . Statio Quintio Statiano Memmio Macrino . . . misso ad dilectum iuniorum a divo Hadriano in regionem Transpadanam.* Cf. *Ann. Épigr.* 1955, 238 (partially reproducing an inscription published by Abdullatif Ahmed Aly, *Annals of Faculty of Arts, Ain Shams Univ.* 3[1955] 113 ff., on which see also J. F. Gilliam, 'The veterans and "Praefectus Castrorum"', *AJP* 77

at Rome, the emperor could still raise troops in an emergency most immediately by calling up Italians.

All this did not end in the Severan age. A levy in Transpadana under Septimius may be connected with one of the civil wars or with the formation of new legions for operations against Parthia; there may well have been similar enlistments in other parts.[47] Herodian also attests special measures for enlisting men in Italy as well as in all the provinces for Alexander Severus' Parthian campaign, and an inscription has been plausibly restored to relate to this *dilectus* in Transpadana.[48] Under a system of purely voluntary enlistment we must suppose that recruits were continually coming forward and being accepted for service; if historians record special measures for recruitment, it is natural to infer that they had in mind *dilectus* in which compulsion was applied. It may well have been on this last occasion that IV Italica was raised. Maximinus held a further levy in Italy,[49] and the senate raised troops there for their struggle with him; in their seemingly desperate position, they would not have refrained from conscription.[50]

Certainly or probably, such levies in Italy were all extraordinary.[51] Now it is a long known fact that gradually Italians almost disappeared from the legions. Forni supplies figures which may be summarized thus: |

	Italians	Provincials
Augustus–Gaius	207	128
Claudius–Nero	117	123
Flavio–Trajanic	73	268
Hadrian–c. 300	17 +[52]	1866 +

[1956] 359 ff.); this attests discharge of veterans of II Traiana in 157, including 15 from central Italy, enlisted in 132–3; Mann (n. 37) suggests that they were enrolled by Q. Voconius Saxa Fodus *ILS* 8828 ἐπιμελητὴν ὁδοῦ 'Ουαλέριας T[ει]βουρτείνης καὶ ἐν τοῖς ἄλλοις τόποις στρατολογήσαντα. One third of the 136 veterans came from Africa, none from Egypt. (Numidians had been recruited not only for III Augusta but also for VI Ferrata and another legion outside Africa under Vespasian, *ILS* 9196).

[47] Pflaum 625 ff. supposes that Cn. Marcius Rustius Rufinus was *dilectator regionis Transpadanae* (*CIL* X 1127) just before the war with Albinus. Hdn. 2.14.6 records levies in Italy for the war with Niger. (It is no solid objection to this that they would not have been ready for the one campaign that in fact took place.) Mann (n. 37) would connect the levies with the raising of the *legiones I, II* and *III Parthica* for the Parthian war. The presence of a few Italians in II Parthica (Forni 217) is easily explicable, as it was soon stationed at Alba.

[48] Hdn. 6.3.1; *ILS* 1173: *electo ab op[timo imp. Severo] Alexandro Aug. ad [dilect (um) habend(um)] per regionem Transpadanam*; Ritterling *op. cit.* (n. 38) cols. 1329 ff.

[49] *ILS* 487: he restored a road near Aquileia *per tirones iuventut(is) novae Italicae suae dilectus posterior(is)*'; perhaps the *dilectus prior* was Alexander's.

[50] Hdn. 7.12.1; *CIL* XIII 6763 (better text than *ILS* 1188): ... *missus adv(ersus) h(ostes) p(ublicos) in re[g. Transp]ad(anam) tir(onibus) legendis* ... *CIL* VI 31747: '[misso] ad iuniores legendos per Aemi[liam]* may belong here.

[51] [It would go too far to assert that *no* Italians were enlisted on other occasions, cf. Forni, *ANRW* II, 1, 380 ff.]

[52] Mann (n. 37) eliminates some of these. Forni wrote before discovery of *AE* 1955, 238 (n. 46).

Of course the dating of many of the inscriptions from which these figures derive is not quite certain, and other relevant inscriptions have been discovered since he wrote; moreover for some legions, notably those in the east, we have few epigraphic data, and since those stationed in Egypt were certainly largely provincial from the first and the same may be conjectured for the Syrian legions, it may well be that the proportion of Italians before Hadrian is somewhat too high. The relative contributions to the legions made by particular provinces (with which I am not concerned) can certainly not be determined from our epigraphic evidence, since it is so much more abundant in one region than another, and since a few inscriptions preserve lists of men serving or enlisted in one particular legion and at one particular time, which may be quite unrepresentative. But when every qualification has been made, and whatever changes in Forni's figures may result from subsequent finds or from revised datings, no one can suppose that the general picture that he presents and that others had presented before him can be substantially altered, in so far as it shows the decline in the Italian contribution.[53]

In the provinces where troops were stationed the enlistment of new recruits, whether conscripts or volunteers, must have been entrusted to the governor, who was also their commander. The right to authorize levies belonged in theory to senate and emperor alike, in practice only to the emperor and to those who acted on his orders. His legates and prefects no doubt had standing instructions to fill the ranks of the units under their command, and proconsuls may have received similar permission to recruit men for the smaller auxiliary forces in senatorial provinces. It could only be the emperor who commissioned recruitment within one province for the purpose of strengthening armies stationed elsewhere (n. 27). Under Tiberius a proconsul of Narbonensis is also styled [*leg(atus) a*]*d cens(us) accip(iendos) et dilect(um)*); presumably he held a levy on the emperor's mandate for the Rhine armies. The title is unique, and no doubt later proconsuls who levied troops did not think it necessary to state what every one knew, that they acted on imperial authority, nor even to mention what had become an integral part of their normal duties.[54] The few | *dilectatores* attested in the provinces are men of subordinate rank, who can be assumed to be responsible to the governors;[55] it is the latter who are alone known to 'approve' the

---

[53] [Later evidence collected by Forni, *ANRW* II, i, 366 ff. does not change the picture. Exact statistics cannot be produced, partly because of lack of documentation for the eastern legions outside Egypt, partly because *laterculi* like *AE* 1955, 238 are distorting.]

[54] *ILS* 950. Note *ILS* 2305: . . . *dilecto* (*sic*) *lectus ab M. Silano, proconsul* of Africa under Tiberius; but as commander of III Augusta, he was in a special position.

[55] viz. in Numidia (*ILS* 9195 see n. 46), Aquitania (1454, Hadrianic), an unspecified region ('delectator Augusti', 1341, Hadrianic) and Thrace (*IGRom* I. 824); the first three are numbers

enlistment of individual recruits.[56] In Italy alone we find men of senatorial rank specially commissioned to hold levies; it was evidently not a regular duty for any of the magistrates, and it was by Vitellius' special authority that the consuls were entrusted with it (n. 45). This may mean that it was actually hard for volunteers in Italy to find an official there qualified to enrol them, unless of course they applied to the prefects commanding the praetorian or urban cohorts for admission to those units. Perhaps most of the Italians found in the legions after Augustus' time were then recruited on the extraordinary occasions when levies were held in Italy (which is not to say that they did not include volunteers). It is not at all likely that all of these occasions are known to us; if the Jewish war required a levy in Italy, other emergencies (notably under Domitian) may have had the same result.

Let us now turn to the provinces. In AD 54 Nero *iuventutem proximas per provincias quaesitam supplendis Orientis legionibus ... iubet.*[57] In 58 Corbulo discharged soldiers who were over age or unfit, and *supplementum petivit; et habiti per Galatiam Cappadociamque dilectus.*[58] It is evident that in the east legions (and other units) were under strength in 54. If the government had been relying on volunteers, then the supply was clearly inadequate. The urgent need to make the army effective for the Parthian war made a resort to conscription requisite. It was certainly employed early in Nero's reign in Cyrenaica, where Pedius Blaesus (presumably the proconsul) was condemned for *repetundae*, partly on the ground of *dilectum militarem pretio et ambitione corruptum.*[59] In 65 *dilectus per Galliam Narbonensem Africamque et Asiam habiti sunt supplendis Illyrici legionibus, ex quibus aetate aut valetudine fessi sacramento solvebantur.*[60] Here, once again, it had not proved possible to fill the ranks | with volunteers. That the *dilectus* on this occasion too involved coercion (although there was no grave emergency) is clear from the omission of Italy from the recruiting areas; there could have been no desire to exclude volunteers from Italy, but it remained the policy to spare Italians from conscription.

35a, 106 bis and 113 in Pflaum. Sempronius Caelianus (Plin. *Ep.* 10. 29) *may* be another example. Of two Equites so employed in Italy (nn. 43 and 47) only the second appears to act independently; we now also know of a military tribune officiating at Rome under Augustus and Tiberius (n. 27). See also n. 68.

[56] Cf. *Cod. Iust.* 12.33.1 (Severus and Caracalla): *si militiae nomen dare vultis, offerte vos his qui probandi ius habent.* The prefect of Egypt posts *tirones probatos a me* to their unit, Fink 87 (103), cf. 64 i 31 (156); likewise the legate of Syria (50 i 14) and if restorations are correct, other governors (63 i 30; 66 b i 5–10). Since governors even 'approve' horses for cavalry, ib. 83 and 99, we may suppose that the real work was done by members of their staff. I conjecture that when *dilectatores* were appointed, *probatio* was delegated to them.

[57] Tac., *Ann.* 13.7.

[58] Ibid. 13.35.

[59] Ibid. 14.18, cf. nn. 11, 68.

[60] Ibid. 16.13. *ILS* 986 illuminates the need.

In civil wars rival pretenders were bound to raise forces with all speed, and thus to apply coercion, where necessary. When we read that Galba's new VIIth legion was 'conscribed' in Spain, the word should be given its full force.[61] Vitellius ordered levies throughout Gaul to make good the gaps in the Rhine army created by the despatch of expeditionary forces to Italy; the levies were countermanded after Bedriacum, but apparently resumed in face of the Flavian threat and finally terminated by Petillius Cerealis; that they involved more than the enrolment of volunteers is plain from Tacitus' explicit references to their unpopularity.[62] Similarly an attempt by the procurator of Corsica to win the island for Vitellius had been thwarted by the resentment his levy caused.[63] We must assume that in the same way the new levy of 6000 Dalmatians in the Flavian army included conscripts,[64] and that Vespasian's levies in the east again involved conscription; Tacitus suggests that they were less unpopular than his exactions of money, but it was doubtless only the latter which affected the upper classes, who were more articulate in stating their grievances.[65]

Naturally we must not presume that the practice in civil wars was normal at other times. But it is clear that conscription persisted after 69 and not only in crises. Trajan took it for granted that recruits in Bithynia might be either conscripts or volunteers, including *vicarii* (n. 6). Bithynian soldiers do not often figure in our epigraphic records; if we find no less than 22 out of 98 legionaries in Africa under Trajan who came from Bithynia, can we doubt that this was due to compulsion rather than to a sudden fever for military service?[66] Fronto writes of searches for men who had gone into hiding to avoid the call-up (n. 5). Egyptian papyri not only attest volunteering (for service in Egypt) but also record a village official who was said to have hunted down recruits with dogs (AD 185), in order to extort money for their release. Indeed, if some *tirones probati* were *voluntarii*, others were presumably not.[67]

Dilectus or *dilectatores* are attested in Britain (nn. 11, 85), Gaul | and Germany (nn. 54, 55, 60, 62, 81, 84), Spain (n. 61), Africa and

---

[61] Tac., *Hist.* 2. 11; 3. 22; 25; Suet., *Galba* 10.

[62] *Hist.* 2.57.1, 2.69.2, 4.15.3, 4.19.2, 4.26.1 (*simul dilectum tributaque Galliae aspernantes*), cf. 4.31.1 (*militia sine adfectu*); 4.71.2 (*recepta iuventute facilius tributa toleravere*); and cf. n. 78. By contrast in Africa men were keen to volunteer for Vitellius, *Hist.* 2.97.

[63] *Ibid.* 2.16.2.

[64] *Ibid.* 3.50.2.

[65] *Ibid.* 2.82.1, cf. 2.84.1: *navium militum armorum paratu strepere provinciae, sed nihil aeque fatigabat quam pecuniarum conquisitio.*

[66] *CIL* VIII 18084, cf. n. 21 (Dio Chrys. 43.10).

[67] Fink 65 i 30; volunteers, e.g. *BGU* 423; *P. Mich.* 465; dogs, *P. Lond.* 2.173 f.

Numidia (nn. 46, 54 f., 60), Cyrenaica,[68] Egypt (n. 68), Syria etc. (n. 58), Asia Minor (nn. 6, 58; 60) and Thrace (n. 55; 80). There is also some further evidence in the *Historia Augusta*,[69] the value of which seems dubious, which is commonly held to mean that conscription was a burden on the *Italici* in Spain, though regulated by Trajan, as late as Marcus' reign. They could be members of citizen communities in the peninsula. No doubt they would have furnished recruits for the legions in Spain, but since the Flavian period only one had been stationed there. If these passages are to be taken seriously, Roman citizens in Spain were being drafted abroad for service in a period when local recruiting, long normal for the eastern legions, had apparently been introduced for those on the Rhine and on the Danube. Britain indeed remains, and the composition of the legions there is relatively ill documented; a few Spaniards are attested (in XX Valeria Victrix) before Hadrian. The alleged quotation from Marius Maximus by the writer does nothing to instil confidence.[70]

Since the *dilectus* is so often stated to have been oppressive, there should be no doubt that wherever it is attested, conscription was employed. Indeed this is hardly contested. Instead it is maintained that 'the infrequency with which resort was made to the *dilectus* is remarkable'.[71] But this contention is unjustified. We hear of it infrequently, but that is quite another matter. We do not hear much more often of the exaction of tribute (with which it is sometimes coupled) and which of course went on every year. Nor are there many more officials recorded who were specifically charged with taking the census or with collection of revenue than those who were appointed to levy troops. Both facts are easily explained on the hypothesis that it was the normal responsibility of regular officials in each province to perform all these functions, and that there were special circumstances of which we must profess ignorance when others were called in to do the work or to assist in doing it; [moreover other such posts held by *equites* who did not subsequently attain to higher rank are relatively ill-documented (*JRS*

---

[68] *Ann. Epigr.* 1951, 88 (= E. Birley, *Roman Britain and the Roman Army* [Kendal 1953] 23 ff.): C. *Iulio . . . Karo . . . trib. mil. leg. III Cyr. . . . . centuriones et milites leg. III Cyr. et leg. XXII missi in provinciam Cyrenensium dilectus causa; Ann. Epigr.* 1957, 133: '*tirones lectos ex provincia Cyrenensi*; the first probably (Birley), the second certainly Trajanic. See also n. 59.

[69] *HA. Hadr.* 12.4: omnibus (!) *Hispanis Tarraconem in conventum vocatis dilectumque ioculariter* (!), *ut verba ipsa ponit Marius Maximus, retractantibus Italicis, vehementissime ceteris, prudenter et caute consuluit. Marc.* 11.7: *Hispanis exhaustis Italica adlectione contra Traiani quoque* (?) *praecepta verecunde consuluit;* irrelevant to *dilectus* according to R. Syme, "Hadrian and Italica", *JRS* 54 (1964) 147 f. Speculations in J. Gagé, 'Italici Adlecti', *REA* 71 (1969) 65 ff.

[70] For *verba ponit HA. Hadr.* 12.4 cf. the suspect *Trig. Tyr.* 11.6. I see no reason to think that quotations from Marius must be authentic.

[71] G. R. Watson, *The Roman Soldier* (Ithaca, 1969) 31.

(1983) 71 f.)]. No doubt | Tacitus tends to mention the levy only when
it was necessary for the authorities to exert themselves to an unusual
extent in filling the ranks of the legions, especially in military crises,
[and there is no comparably detailed narrative for events after 70]. It is
not at all surprising that the Syrian legions were seriously below
strength in 54. The legate or legates (Ummidius Quadratus at least)
who had failed to maintain discipline might well have been equally
slack in keeping up the numbers of their forces. Indeed the efficiency of
the central government itself can be doubted, on various grounds, for
much of the period between c. 27 and 70.

If military service was so popular in the early Principate that
volunteers were readily obtained, it is hard to understand why fewer
and fewer Italians are found in the legions. Forni refuted the old view
that they were deliberately excluded by Vespasian and his successors
for political reasons.[72] The proportion of Italian legionaries was
already diminishing before 69, and they still appear, though less and
less frequently, thereafter. This is adequately explained if Italian
recruits were mainly conscripts and enrolled on the relatively rare
occasions on which the government found it necessary, for one reason
or another (often unknown to us), to depart from its normal policy of
avoiding levies in Italy. Forni suggested that this policy was inspired by
a desire to conserve Italian population. But, to say nothing of the fact
that the loss of some 5000–6000 young men a year (given that soldiers
recruited for service abroad were unlikely ever to return) was not
demographically serious, this takes no account of the reason why
Romans valued a large population: it was a guarantee of military
strength.[73] It is far more plausible to suppose that the emperors wished
to escape the unpopularity of imposing a hated burden on the Italians.
But why was it so hated? Forni remarked that young Italians, especially
those of the well-to-do classes, would not readily 'leave fatherland and
family with little likelihood of return, to submit to prolonged service
and lead a hard and comfortless life, garrisoning the most remote
provinces in climates that might be intolerable, without adequate
rewards, with no prospects of a brilliant career, with no guarantee of
their rights, and all this though their fatherland was not in peril'. Some
of this is well said, and explains alike why conscription was hated and
volunteers would be few. But the great majority of Italians cannot
have belonged to the well-to-do classes or have enjoyed comforts at
home or have even thought of making a brilliant career, and if the
material rewards of service were so low under Augustus as to provoke

---

[72] Ch. 5, whence quotations that follow.
[73] *Italian Manpower* 5; and Plin. *Paneg.* 26.

serious mutinies in AD 14, they were notably increased by Domitian (p. 209). Yet it was after Domitian that the disappearance of Italians from the legions but for emergency levies [or the formation of new legions (n. 37)] becomes complete. I suggest | therefore that of the factors Forni describes we should lay most weight on the length and remoteness of service.

But these factors should have been no less discouraging to provincials, so long as the armies were not recruited in the regions where they served. Now, so far as the legions are concerned, such recruiting did not become the rule till the second century.[74] Thus of 39 legionaries serving in Egypt under Augustus or Tiberius only 9 came from Egypt and 24 from Asia Minor. Spaniards are found almost everywhere, though not in Africa, and men from Narbonensis were not used only for the Rhine legions, which were comparatively near. Africans are levied for distant service (nn. 46, 60), though in Africa itself where there was a great number (as in Spain and Narbonensis) of communities with Roman or Latin status, from which legions in the west were as yet mainly recruited, 60% or more of pre-Hadrianic legionaries were on Forni's evidence not of local origin. Auxiliary units were normally posted to regions other than those where they had been raised. Already in the first century new recruits were commonly obtained from the hinterland of their station or from other regions to which they were temporarily transferred, but exceptions still occurred even in the second century; for specialist units, wherever employed, recruits continued to be drawn from the lands where they had been raised and where alone men of the skill required could be found; Thracians, enlisted in large numbers, are found in *alae* far distant from their homes; Britons and Dacians were apparently not used in their own country, to which it was therefore necessary to send men from other parts.[75] And until Trajan's time the legions at least, the kernel of the army, though they had ceased to be mainly Italian in composition, were to an even greater extent than the *auxilia* ethnically mixed, and in the west recruited chiefly from the more Romanized provincial communities. The government had not yet come to trust its subjects to defend their homelands. It is characteristic that in 65 supplements for the Illyrian legions were to be raised in Narbonensis, Asia and Africa. Naturally conscription was unavoid-

---

[74] Generally ascribed to Hadrian. But the Roman government did not usually act *per saltum*. In Forni's lists (182 f.) men from Pannonia and Moesia begin to appear in Danubian legions before Hadrian. I suspect gradual evolution. [Nearly all the innovations credited by modern scholars to Hadrian, merely on the basis that they were not attested earlier, have been proved to be pre-Hadrianic as new evidence has accumulated.]

[75] Kraft 43–68; in the earliest period Gallic and Spanish cavalry were so prized that they too had to be used extensively far from home, 26 ff.

able. A young man from Narbo or Carthage had no greater incentive than one from Bononia to spend twenty-five years on the Danube.

It is sometimes suggested that the Italians, who had so recently conquered the 'world' and had been fighting each other since 49 BC with undoubted courage lost their warlike spirit in the Principate, whereas Rome could easily appeal to the bellicosity of less civilized subjects. Beyond doubt, there was an earnest | desire in Italy, extending to the soldiers themselves in 40 BC,[76] for an end to civil wars. In the Principate there is also evidence that the upper class in Italy had little taste for the military life.[77] Conceivably this distaste spread to all sections of the population. But it would not be convincing to account for this phenomenon (if it occurred) by the level of culture and prosperity in Italy. In modern times relatively civilized peoples, enjoying a far higher level of prosperity, have more conspicuously displayed their proficiency in war than their aversion for it. Patriotism (or some other ideal cause) may afford the explanation. As Forni observed, to Italians in the Principate 'the fatherland was not in peril', at any rate until the third century, when the habit and practice of bearing arms had been lost. But then neither were provincials fighting for their fatherland: most of them were serving far from their own homes and on behalf of a state which they would hardly have regarded as their own until they had lived for generations or centuries under the Roman peace.[78]

In fact it is precisely among the 'fighting peoples' of the empire that the levy caused most trouble. None furnished so many auxiliaries as the Gauls in the Julio-Claudian era, and in 70 we hear of their objection to the *dilectus*.[79] Over thirty auxiliary units were originally raised in Thrace, and after Hadrian Thracians are found in large numbers of legions. Yet under Tiberius the Thracians rebelled *quod pati dilectus et validissimum quemque militiae nostrae dare aspernabantur*.[80] The Batavians enjoyed fiscal immunity in return for accepting an obligation to provide troops; in 69 they furnished eight or nine cohorts and an *ala*, but Civilis was able to induce them to revolt in their resentment at the new levy ordered by Vitellius.[81] In two cases there were indeed special

---

[76] *Italian Manpower* 112, 130, 713; add App. *BC* 5.59–64.

[77] Many senators and *equites* did no military service or the barest minimum.

[78] Lucian is the first Greek writer to refer to the Romans and Roman armies as 'us', J. Palm, *Rom, Römertum u. Imperium* ... (Lund 1959) 54.

[79] Cf. nn. 62 and 75.

[80] Tac. *Ann.* 4.46. Kraft 35 ff. shows that the revolt was caused by the incorporation of Thracian forces as regular units into the Roman army. Note Amm. 26.7.5: *bellatrices Thraciae gentes*.

[81] *Hist.* 4.14, cf. *Germ.* 29 (like the Mattiaci, the Batavians paid no taxes in return for military contingents). See ch. 3 with Addenda.

factors at work. Until Tiberius' reign the Thracians had served under their own chiefs and only in neighbouring lands, *ac tum rumor incesserat fore ut disiecti aliisque nationibus permixti diversas in terras traherentur*; the rumour was doubtless correct, since thereafter the Thracian *auxilia* were to serve in all parts of the empire under Roman officers and the units were to lose their old national character; indeed, like most other auxiliary regiments, | those called Thracian were soon recruited locally. The Batavians in 69 were still under the command of their own chiefs, and their special grievance lay in the conduct of the new levy by Roman prefects and centurions; it is notable that they were not left to enrol recruits through their own *principes*.[82] *Iussu Vitellii Batavorum iuventus ad dilectum vocabatur, quem suapte natura gravem onerabant ministri avaritia ac luxu, senes aut invalidos conquirendo, quos pretio dimitterent*. But these abuses only aggravated the hardship of the levy, which Tacitus regarded as *suapte natura gravem*,[83] and he makes Civilis say: *instare dilectum, quo liberi a parentibus, fratres a fratribus velut supremum dividantur*. Until 68 the Batavian cohorts had been stationed in Britain, a foreign land, whence probably home leave was not given; many would die without seeing friends or family again.[84] It was on the same count among others that the Thracians had revolted against the *dilectus*. Similarly in the *Agricola* Tacitus represents the Britons complaining at the time of Boudicca's insurrection *eripi domos, abstrahi liberos, iniungi dilectus tamquam mori tantum pro patria nescientibus* and Calgacus as declaiming: *liberos cuique ac propinquos suos natura carissimos esse voluit; hi per dilectus alibi auferuntur*.[85]

No doubt the speeches of Civilis and Calgacus are the invention of Tacitus. At least the words are his; it would be too dogmatic to *assume* that he (or his source) had no information about the reasons that prompted revolt or resistance to Rome. Nor can this be proved by the paradoxical contentions that in each passage he is merely using a *topos* and that the parallels, instead of providing reciprocal support and confirmation, are in themselves evidence that all alike spring from the historian's imagination, and *therefore* can have no basis in reality. It must indeed be conceded that Tacitus *may* have drawn on his imagination (or that of a previous writer), and that the conception that men would be reluctant to serve for years far from their homes was familiar

---

[82] *Hist.* 4.14.3 cf. n. 68; no doubt normal for regular units, contrast the way in which the Dalmatians in AD 6 still raised for themselves the troops Rome required (Dio 55.29). Kraft 40 f. conjectures that it was an innovation for the Batavians to be subject to Roman recruiting officers.

[83] Cf. Cic. *Att.* 9.9.1: *dilectus ... ipsa per se molesta sunt*.

[84] Cf. ch. 3 n. 21. The *cohors Usiporum per Germanias conscripta* which deserted in Britain (*Agr.* 28) was doubless trying to get home.

[85] *Agr.* 15.3, 31.1.

to Romans[86] and would readily have occurred to them as an explana-
tion of the discontents | of wild subjects. But even if so much be
granted, must we not add that the explanation was intrinsically and
overwhelmingly probable? Romans had learned to hate long and
distant service in the Republic. Veterans had complained in AD 14
that on discharge they were dragged off to remote lands for settlement.[87] Others, born in the provinces or naturalized there by long
service, had found it repugnant to leave the new homes they had made
there for Nero's colonies in Italy.[88] In 69 the legionaries in Syria, most
of whom were no doubt easterners by birth, were inflamed by a
rumour that Vitellius designed to transfer them to Germany, not only
because service there would be more rigorous but because *plerique
(provinciales) necessitudinibus et propinquitatibus mixti, et militibus vetustate
stipendiorum nota et familiaria castra in modum penatium diligebantur.*[89]
Tacitus' belief that Thracians, Batavians and Britons had a natural
attachment to their own homes was surely right. Julian's army was to
include Germans who had joined him on the pledge that they were
never to be taken south of the Alps.[90]

It will not have escaped notice that the evidence for conscription is,
except for Italy itself, almost entirely pre-Hadrianic and that the
testimony that the army was chiefly recruited from volunteers is
Severan. Now it is precisely within the period between Hadrian and
Severus that it became the rule for the legions as well as most of the
auxilia to be recruited within the province where they were stationed or
in adjoining provinces; Kraft remarks that the area of recruitment for
auxilia tends to become narrower, more strictly local.[91] It is a reasonable conjecture that the adoption of regional recruitment in itself made
it less necessary for the government to resort to conscription. Since
willing soldiers were presumably *ceteris paribus* better soldiers, and since
men might be expected to show more devotion in protecting their own
families and homelands,[92] local recruitment (which also must have
saved transport costs and administrative complexities) was in the
interest of the state, wherever it had become possible to rely on the
loyalty of the subjects. The effect was to spare not only Italy but also
the most Romanized provinces, Narbonensis, Spain and Africa; it was
no hardship for Spaniards and Africans to serve in the small forces in

---

[86] e.g. Liv. 5.11.5 (cf. *Italian Manpower* 641); 29.1.4: service in Africa is *procul domo* for Sicilians.
For another illustration of this surely universal sentiment, see Diod. 18.7.
[87] *Ann.* 1.17.3.
[88] *Ibid.* 14.27.2.
[89] *Hist.* 2.80.3.
[90] Amm. 20.4.4.
[91] Kraft 50 f.
[92] Cf. perhaps Dio 71.3.3.

their own lands, and enough volunteers could surely be found. In all these parts conscription should have become as rare as it had long been in Italy, and as a result we seldom find their natives serving elsewhere. Conceivably the increased number of magnates from these parts in the senate and | the equestrian service contributed to the change, making the emperors more sensitive to local feelings represented by powerful patrons, [but one might doubt if such magnates themselves understood or cared about the feelings of peasant conscripts].

No doubt the government experimented cautiously at first, and found that local recruiting worked well (cf. n. 74). Of course it could not avoid sending soldiers away from their homelands to meet new dangers on another frontier. But for the potential recruit it was one thing to join an army in which he *might* be posted abroad, and another to enlist when he knew in advance that this was bound to be his fate. Some peoples, as we have seen, were still required to serve outside their own homelands; they were a minority, and if (as I think probable) they still had to be obtained mainly by conscription, that would be compatible with Arrius Menander's statement that *most* soldiers were volunteers. In emergencies conscription could always be re-introduced, as in Italy itself, where apart from the urban and praetorian cohorts there were no units stationed before Severus which Italians could join. And if Severus established a legion in Italy, he also denied would-be Italian volunteers the chance to enter the praetorian guard.

The grant of the Roman citizenship to *peregrini* on discharge from the *auxilia* or on enlistment in the legions seems to have made very little difference in the evolution we are considering. In the first century the citizenship was a relatively rare distinction in the provinces, and perhaps of more practical value than later, and the prospect of acquiring it should have been a stronger incentive to volunteering precisely in the period when the evidence points to the prevalence of conscription. It was during or before the time when volunteering is likely to have become more usual that the privileges of ex-auxiliaries were reduced; from 140 their children born in service were no longer to obtain the citizenship. The *Constitutio Antoniniana* naturally altogether removed the incentive to enrolment that the special privilege of citizenship may once have provided. Indeed in the second century more and more recruits to the *auxilia* were citizens before they joined up.[93] (This, incidentally, may suggest that the terms of auxiliary service were not much inferior to those of legionary, cf. n. 29).

Arrius Menander seems to have connected the greater number of

[93] Kraft 69 ff. On the change in 140 H. Nesselhauf, 'Das Bürgerrecht der Soldatenkinder', *Historia*, 8 (1959), 434 ff.; Kraft, ibid, 1961, 120 ff.

volunteers in his day with a change in the *status militiae*. If this is taken
to refer to the legal condition of soldiers, only one change can be in
question: Severus' repeal of the prohibition on soldiers marrying,
which had subsisted since the early Principate.[94] However, in practice
soldiers had always been free to | form permanent unions with women
who in strict law were concubines but who were called wives in
common parlance and even in official documents.[95] The sons of such
unions were legally bastards and Roman citizens [only if both the
soldier and the woman had this status].[96] From the early Principate
such men, born *castris*, were admitted to the legions, and it is often
supposed that they always obtained citizenship on enlistment and that
this was in their eyes the chief attraction of army service. In actual fact
some will have been citizens from birth, indeed a growing number as
the citizenship was more widely diffused among the peoples from
whom soldiers might find their concubines. Moreover in all ages it has
been common for men to follow the calling of their fathers, and no
more specific explanation is needed for the enlistment of soldiers' sons,
whereas desire for the Roman citizenship seems not to have acted as a
decisive incentive towards enrolment (above). The proportion of such
recruits seems to grow in the second century, though it was never so
large as to justify a suggestion that the abundant supply of such
recruits made conscription less necessary.[97] Since units now tended to
remain more or less permanently in or near one place, with relatively
comfortable quarters and sometimes close to towns, including the
canabae which grew up by the great camps, conditions favoured family
life. The government had long condoned the violation of a disciplinary

---

[94] Prohibition: Mitteis, *Chr.* 372,11; Dio 60. 24. Hdn. 3. 8,5 says that Severus τοῖς στρατιώταις
... ἄλλα τε πολλά συνεχώρησε ἃ μὴ πρότερον εἶχον ... καὶ ... ἐπέτρεψε γυναιξί τε συνοικεῖν. P. J.
Garnsey, 'Septimius Severus and the Marriage of Soldiers', *CSCA* 3 (1970) 45 ff., who denies or
doubts that Severus legalized soldiers' marriages, would take this to refer to mere cohabitation,
but that had been tolerated for generations ('concessa consuetudine', *CIL* XVI 122) and required
no innovating constitution. He would also take all legal texts that imply that a soldier could be
married to relate to marriages contracted before service, although (given the freedom of divorce)
we hardly need the testimony of Gaius (*Dig.* 24. 1,61): 'propter militiam satis commode retineri
matrimonium non possit'; he can only reconcile *Dig.* 23.2,35 (Papinian: 'filius familias miles sine
patris voluntate matrimonium non contrahit') with his view by supposing in effect that Papinian
means concubinage by 'matrimonium'; but Pap. clearly means marriage *iure civili*, since the
Roman institution of *patria potestas* is introduced. [See now J. B. Campbell, *JRS* 68 (1978) 153 ff.]

[95] As in the diplomata (*uxoribus quas tunc habuissent cum est civitas iis data*) and *ILS* 9059; *P. Gnom.*
62.

[96] [Gaius 1.75: 'sive civis Romanus peregrinam sive peregrinus civem Romanam uxorem
duxerit, eum qui nascitor peregrinum esse.' Cf. also] E. Weiss, *RE* Bd. 3A2 (1929) s.v. Spurius,
cols. 1889 f., *FIRA* III 4 and 6.

[97] Forni (n. 21) 126–8, giving no statistics, but see Mommsen, *Ges Schr.* VI 29 for soldiers born
castris constituting a third or even half in some second-century lists from III Augusta. However,
R. Cagnat, *L'Armée rom. d'Afrique* (Paris 1912) 298 f. observed that in one such list (*CIL.*
VIII.18087) the proportion sinks to one fortieth.

rule which it could not enforce; Severus finally set it aside. What he did was simply to make the marriage of a soldier valid, *iure civili* or *iure cuiusque gentis*, in such conditions as the marriage of a civilian would have been. But under Roman law, though a marriage could be contracted without *conubium* between a citizen and an alien, the children of such a marriage were aliens (cf. n. 96). | Hence praetorians who formed unions with *peregrinae* still required a grant of *conubium*, which was made only on discharge.[98] Of course the *constitutio Antoniniana* made it less likely that such anomalous unions would occur. Severus' reform no doubt improved the position of the soldier and his family in regard to succession, dowries and the like, but it is hard to believe that it did much to carry further the development of family life of soldiers or to increase the supply of volunteers.

However, Arrius Menander's words may refer simply to a change in the social esteem that soldiers enjoyed, or indeed to the general conditions of army service. Regional recruitment, increased amenities, more family life—all these conditions then become relevant. Pay must also be considered. Domitian increased by a third the pay of legionaries, and Severus seems to have raised it from 300 to 500 denarii, Caracalla to 750.[99] (It is conceivable, though it must not be assumed, that Arrius wrote under the last emperor.) Other branches of the army must surely have benefited proportionately. It is not easy to be sure what these rises represented in real terms. The metal value of the denarius in weight and purity was always declining, but it is hard to determine when there was a consequential increase in prices, at any rate before the inflation of the third century. (Writers on this subject often ignore the huge fluctuations that could take place in the prices of wheat or other foods because of bad harvests.) However, even if the depreciation of the coinage was reflected (and in the end it must have been) in price levels, Domitian's increase of pay should have been equivalent (when made) to one of 20–25% over the Augustan *stipendium*. In the second century further devaluation went on, and became abrupt with Severus; conceivably the increment he gave did no more, perhaps less, than offset rising prices, but that given by Caracalla must

[98] *CIL* XVI.134–56, with few exceptions diplomata for veterans of praetorian or urban cohorts who (as in the past) obtain on discharge *ius conubii dumtaxat cum singulis et primis uxoribus ut etiamsi peregrini iuris feminas in matrimonio suo iunxerint, proinde tollant ac si ex duobus civibus Romanis natos*; the latest is of 298. Here, as always in such documents [if earlier than Severus], the terms *uxores* and *matrimonium* are inappropriate in strict law to the relationship existing before discharge. Since the praetorians were now recruited from the legions, the marriage rights of praetorians cannot have been inferior to those of legionaries.

[99] Brunt, 'Pay and Superannuation in the Roman Army', *PBSR* 18 (1950) Part II; for the subject matter of Parts III and V see n. 29. I no longer feel confident that officers of all ranks received rises proportionate to those of common soldiers.

have made a real and substantial improvement.[100] It is, however, | hard to believe that the soldiers were not much better off under Severus than they had been. We have to allow for donatives, the frequency, amounts and recipients of which are imperfectly recorded, and for allowances in kind.[101] Whether or not Severus instituted the *annona militaris*,[102] one must doubt (especially if everything had in fact become much dearer) if soldiers were still liable to pay, as in the past, for food, clothing and arms. Unless they were now very liberally treated, the testimony of Dio and Herodian that the Severi depended entirely on the troops and pandered to their greed is merely absurd, but even the vague rhetoric of Herodian deserves some respect, and Dio much more.[103]

In their view discipline too was relaxed, always an objective of the common soldiers, as in the mutinies of 14 and civil wars of 69. That did not mean merely that there was less drilling and fatigue duty, but that they were not easily brought to book for misconduct to the civil population. It is no accident that *concussio* and its correlative verb first appear in Latin in Severan writings. Not that the practice was new; we may think of Juvenal's sixteenth satire; provincial governors were hardly more able or willing than the praetors at Rome to repress military outrages, and scattered indications show that they had been well known in provinces before 193. I doubt if many persons of rank and property ever enlisted as privates; those who are attested were, we may suspect, mostly 'black sheep'. If that be right, it is rather sinister that there is much evidence for serving soldiers, not officers, as well as veterans in possession of substantial property; can this generally be attributed to savings from pay, donatives and occasional booty? Especially in the frontier areas, veterans also enjoy an honoured place in local society. Once again, the evidence for soldiers' affluence and dignity tends to increase in volume in the second century and above all in the Severan age. It is then too that we find more and more soldiers occupying administrative posts in the offices of governors and procura-

---

[100] On post-Severan inflation see T. Pekary, 'Studien zur römischen Währungs und Finanzge-schichte', *Historia* 18 (1959); A. H. M. Jones, *Econ. Hist. Rev.* 23 (1953) 295–9, 443 ff. On relation of price rises to soldiers' pay see now R. Duncan-Jones, *The Economy of the Roman Empire* (Cambridge 1974), 7–11.

[101] Fiebiger, *RE* V *s. v.* Donativum, cols. 1542 ff. Severus' payment of 250 den. on entering Rome (Dio 46.46.7) was very low by past standards; but the treasury was bare; it was probably only an earnest of his bounty. In the light of Augustus' practice (Tac. *Ann.* 1.8), which is likely to have been a decisive precedent, I assume that legionaries always received some donative proportionate to that given to praetorians; *HA. Marc.* 7.9 (AD 161) is here surely right. Cf. Dio 77.24.1 (Caracalla).

[102] D. van Berchem, "L'annone militaire dans l'empire romain au III siècle", *BSAF* 80 (1937) 117 ff.

[103] Dio 74.2.3; 76.15.2; 77.3; 9 f.; 77.24.1; 78.3; 78.9.2, 78.11.5, 78.27.1; 78.36.3 etc.; he lays the blame chiefly on Caracalla. Hdn. 2.6.14, 3.8.4 ff.; 4.4 f. etc.

tors. The recruit with a little education had a good prospect of leading a comfortable and very unmilitary life. Indeed never before was advancement to higher posts more accessible to the *caligatus*, but even if few young men think far ahead in choosing a career, opportunities for reasonably good jobs in the army were | plainly visible to all. The social condition of the soldiers was certainly far different from the days when they asked for *modum miseriarum*.[104]

The golden age for the soldiery did not last. For half a century before Diocletian the empire was plagued by incessant civil wars and foreign invasions. Naturally none can have suffered more than the troops, whose unruliness was a major cause of the disasters. Casualties must have been enormous and peaceful amenities greatly reduced. Inflation made pay almost worthless, though of course the soldier obtained subsistence in kind. A career in the army must have lost its old attractions. Diocletian had to tie the sons of soldiers to their fathers' occupation. But that did not suffice. He and his successors actually needed a larger army, and compulsion had to be systematically applied, even though some volunteers were still to be found. It is unlikely that conscription had ever been abandoned at all times and in all places, and it is reasonable to assume that Diocletian built his system on the old. It was now the duty of cities or large landowners to furnish quotas of recruits; I suppose that this had always been true, whenever levies had been held (Appendix). The new system went on to the end of the fourth century, when once more the government could give up systematic conscription of its own people because it relied on barbarian *foederati*. These developments do not concern us.[105]

Professor Eric Birley writes that 'the implication of Vegetius (*epit. rei militaris* II 3) is surely that there were plenty of volunteers in the "good old days".'[106] I can see no such implication in the text cited or in any other,[107] but in any case Vegetius in the judgement of most scholars,

---

[104] This paragraph represents mere impressions. Much evidence and bibliography in R. Macmullen, *Soldier and Civilian in the later Rom. Emp.* (Cambridge, Mass. 1963) esp. chs. 3–5. On property and social status of legionaries see Forni ch. IX. Conscripts might well have some property!

[105] Jones 614–19. In this period of conscription some soldiers were quite well off (646 ff.). Of course illicit military exactions went on.

[106] 'The Epigraphy of the Roman Army', *Actes du Deuxième Congrès int. d'épigr. gr. et lat.* (Paris 1953) 235.

[107] 2.3 insists that the legions should be kept up to strength by continuous recruitment. Vegetius' main discussion of recruitment is in 1.2 ff. In 1.3 he says that rural recruits are to be preferred: *interdum tamen necessitas exigit etiam urbanos ad arma compelli*. Note in 1.4 *pubertatem ad dilectum cogendam*; 6: *qui dilectum acturus est*; the verb *legere* is used *passim*. He certainly assumes that recruiting officers can normally pick and choose; this implies either conscription or a surplus of volunteers. Such a surplus in Egypt would be likely in the second century if Davies and Watson (n. 8) were right in supposing that men needed letters of recommendation to be enrolled. In

including Birley, had in mind the army of the third century. For perhaps a rather brief period | the army did no doubt consist mostly of volunteers. We may reflect with some irony that this was the army that tore to pieces an empire that conscripts had conquered and long protected. The triumph of the voluntary principle was in my judgement the result of local recruiting and a general improvement in the conditions of service, carried furthest by the Severan policy which Septimius allegedly expressed in his dying advice to his sons: 'enrich the soldiers and treat every one else with contempt' (Dio 76.15.2).

APPENDIX

Under Diocletian's system it was the responsibility of the cities or of landowners to furnish recruits each year, though in some years the government chose to exact money (*aurum tironicum*) in lieu of men. See Jones 615; his documentation omits the post-classical allusion of Arcadius Charisius to *tironum productio* as a *munus personale* in cities (Dig. 50.4.18.3) and he cites no evidence earlier than the 370s for *aurum tironicum*, though in its context Lact. *mort. pers.* 7.5 (*Haec quoque tolerari < non > possunt quae ad exhibendos milites spectant*) suggests that the levy was made the occasion for official or illicit demands for money.

Jones shows that the recruits had to be furnished from the rural population. In Vegetius' opinion (I 3) the army had been composed of *agrestes* in the good old days (those of Cincinnatus). There is conclusive evidence that this was true in the late Republic (Brunt, *Fall of the Roman Republic* ch. 5), and the fact that legionaries name cities as their places of origin in the Principate does not of course show that any change had taken place; for cities had *territoria* and most of them were fundamentally agricultural centres.

In the late Republic the *dilectus* in Italy and Cisalpina demanded the cooperation of the local governments (*op. cit.* p. 277; cf. *Italian Manpower* 37, 408, 631–4). In the same way they could be required to furnish money or supplies for military purposes, Caesar, *BC* 1.6.8, 1.15.2, 1.18.4; Dio 41.9.7; App. *BC* 2.34. Augustus obtained *commeatus* in this way probably for operations against the Raetians, Vitr. 2.9.15. In *Italian Manpower* App. 19 I argued that this reliance on the cities for the *dilectus* goes far back in the history of the Republic. It was inevitable since the central government lacked any sort of bureau-

P. Mich. 468 (*CPL* 251) a *classiarius* who hopes to be *transferred* to a cohort says that such letters will be useless, if a man does not help himself. All the supposed allusions to letters of recommendation *for enrolment* are conjectures, asserted as facts, which did not occur to the original editors and seem to me unfounded and implausible. On Vegetius see Watson 26 with bibliography.

cracy. Even under the Principate the number of officials remained small. Provincial governors could not dispense with the aid of local governments. A military officer might be sent to a centre to recruit, but if he could not obtain sufficient volunteers, he was bound to rely on local authorities to produce (*exhibere* or *producere*) men suited for his purpose, or | to resort to the methods of the press gang. The traditions of the Republic make it likely that he was instructed to adopt the former course. [Cf. Addenda.]

In the fourth century it is the liability of landowners to provide recruits, all but the largest forming consortia in which the obligation (*protostasia* or *prototypia*) falls on each in turn; the technical terms first occur in the 290s. Vegetius laments that *indicti possessoribus tirones* are too apt to be the workers the landowner can best dispense with (1.7). But as early as Trajan Frontinus says that provincial cities may claim in territorial disputes with great landowners that they have the obligation *legere tironem ex vico* (53L). In Egypt village officials are concerned with the levy in 185 (n. 67) as in the fourth century. Rostovtzeff, 'Synteleia Tironon', *JRS* 8 (1918) 26 ff. noted that under Gordian the Scaptopareni had to furnish *burgarii*. Now *burgarii* are not regular soldiers, but is it not natural to suppose that whenever the government required conscripts for regular units from communities like Scaptopare it operated in the same way? Rostovtzeff also argued convincingly that an inscription from a Lydian village which refers to τὴν τῶν τειρώνων συντελείαν belongs to the third century and relates to *aurum tironicum*.

In the fourth century the communities or magnates who furnished the recruits also had to fit them out at some cost. Cicero tells of a man who had assisted his neighbours to join up in 43 (*Phil.* 7.24). An inscription from Teos, probably triumviral, seems to commemorate similar munificence (*IGRom* 4.1572). One might suspect that voluntary and occasional liberality of this kind came to be required, and that it was because it was costly to furnish recruits, people would pay not to do so, hence the origin of *aurum tironicum*. (Similarly *aurum coronarium* had its roots in 'benevolences'.) Obviously *lecti* had to pay something to *vicarii* who replaced them.

It is extremely improbable that the recruiting system of the fourth century was entirely new; though it was connected with the capitation system of taxation Diocletian devised, that meant only that the mechanism differed in certain details from anything that could have existed before. [Earlier the provincial censuses instituted by Augustus may, like the Republican censuses of Roman citizens, have assisted in the *dilectus*.] Selective conscription of men drawn mainly from the farms required the co-operation of local councils and landowners and was probably developed from the practice of the Republican government in Italy. We are obliged to guess, for we have no detailed information for the Principate on this and many other such matters (taxation for instance) that matches the Theodosian Code or even the writings of Cicero. The inscriptions that are so abundant seldom illuminate the way in which the administration was actually carried on. Tacitus and Dio are sometimes more revealing.

The Administrators of Roman Egypt[1]

Before AD 70 the prefecture of Egypt was the greatest prize in an equestrian career—three or four praetorian prefects were promoted to it[2]—and thereafter it ranked only just below the praetorian prefecture to which no fewer than fourteen governors of Egypt were advanced between 70 and 235.[3] In the other great provinces of the empire *legati Augusti pro praetore* could leave finance to the procurators, while proconsuls perhaps soon came to retain little of their original responsibility for the collection of taxes,[4] and had no army to command. The prefect of Egypt combined fiscal with military and judicial functions. So did the presidial procurators of such areas as Mauretania or Noricum, but the importance of Egypt and the complexity of its administration set the prefect far above them. Egypt was probably the most populous province in the empire[5] and contributed more than any

[1] Besides usual abbreviations, I use the following in this article:

Chalon   = G. Chalon, *L'édit de Ti. Iulius Alexander* (1964).
Humbert   = M. Humbert, 'La Juridiction du Préfet d'Égypte d'Auguste à Dioclétien', ap. F. Burdeau et al., *Aspects de l'Empire Romain* (1964), 95–147.
Pflaum   = H.-G. Pflaum, *Les Carrières procuratoriennes équestres* (1960).
Reinmuth   = O. W. Reinmuth, *The Prefect of Egypt from Augustus to Diocletian, Klio*, Beiheft xxxiv (1935).
Stein, *Präfekten* = A. Stein, *Die Präfekten von Ägypten in der römischen Kaiserzeit* (1950).
Stein, *Unters.* = A. Stein, *Untersuchungen zur Gesch. u. Verwaltung Ägyptens* (1915).
Wallace   = S. L. Wallace, *Taxation in Egypt from Augustus to Diocletian* (1938).

Prefects are listed and numbered in the Appendix. All dates are A.D., unless otherwise indicated. I am indebted for additions and corrections to Fergus Millar, P. J. Parsons and J. R. Rea; the opinions and errors that remain are my own. I deliberately refer to Egypt as a province, in conformity with all ancient sources (quoted by Stein, *Unters.*, 92 f.), against the opinion of Stein and many others, for which Stein gives two reasons: (i) Egypt had no *koinon* (as if that were not true of nearly all provinces in 30 BC); (ii) it lacked 'die Gliederung nach der Gemeindeorganisation': but even if Egyptian local government is unique, no presupposition about the nature of such government is implicit in 'provincia', for whose derivation and meaning cf. Mommsen, *St. R.*, I³, 51. Cf. p. 160 [and on the reasons for Egypt being under equestrian administration, *JRS* 1983, 61–3].

[2] Appendix nos. 7, 12, 22; cf. the appointment of Macro in 38.

[3] Nos. 26, 30, 33, 36, 41, 46, 53, 58, 64, 65, 75, 77, 83, 84. Cf. n. 20.

[4] Dio liii, 15, 3.

[5] Jos., *BJ* ii, 385 gives Egypt without Alexandria 7,500,000 inhabitants from the poll-tax returns; according to Diodorus i, 31 there were not less than 7,000,000 in Egypt in his day. On my estimate (*Italian Manpower*, ch. 10) Italy had not many more inhabitants under Augustus. We can only guess at the population of most other parts of the empire.

other to the revenues,[6] partly in grain that provided much of Rome's essential food,[7] and its exploitation was a vast public enterprise of which the prefect was the managing director. He also had to do justice not only under Roman law but under the traditional laws of the native Egyptians and of the Greek settlers, among subjects who were both litigious and turbulent. Only defence against external attack was a simpler problem than in other frontier regions.

THE NEED FOR EXPERIENCE

It is evident that ideally the prefect's duties demanded honesty, ability and experience. How far were these demands met? So far as the first two qualities are concerned, perhaps no answers can be given. Only the names of most prefects are known to us, and the careers of some. But the most distinguished career tells us that a man enjoyed the favour of emperors, not that he deserved it.[8] No doubt all emperors, even those most ruthless in | exactions to replenish the treasury or to pay for personal extravagances, did not desire to appoint men who would fill their own pockets; indeed, however 'rapacious' they might be themselves, prudence might make them recognize that the subjects should be sheared, not shaved. So Tiberius informed the prefect, Aemilius Rectus, who did not remain long in post.[9] However, the level of integrity was not uniformly high in the Roman official class,[10] and the best of rulers might have no option but to select its least unprincipled members. He might also not be discerning in his choice. Marcus Aurelius is not likely to have been alone in finding it hard to choose the right agents and advisers.[11] Loyalty was an obvious *desideratum*, yet

---

[6] Wallace, ch. 18. On a minimum estimate the revenue of Ptolemy Auletes (*c.* 55 BC) is given as 36 m. denarii, at a time when Roman provincial revenue amounted to 85 m., or on a more literal interpretation of Plut., *Pomp.* 45, 3, 135 m. But Ptolemy Philadelphus' revenue had been reckoned as equivalent to 88 m., and by more efficient administration (cf. H. I. Bell, *CAH* x, 292, 313) Augustus must have extracted more than Auletes.

[7] Wallace l.c. Jos. *BJ* ii, 383, 386, says that Africa supplied two thirds, Egypt one third of Rome's grain. In fact there were certainly imports from other sources (Pliny, *NH* xviii, 66), and the truth may be only that Africa and Egypt were the main sources at the ratio of 2:1. *Epit. de Caes.* 1, 6 may be wholly unreliable.

[8] Contrast Pflaum, 331 on T. Furius Victorinus (no. 54): 'administrateur financier habile, chef énergique et courageux' (though nothing whatever is known of him but the bare facts of his career), or Reinmuth, 4. cf. 128: 'the prefects of Egypt were, by and large, men of outstanding ability'. As if in proof of this assertion, he notes that several were, or affected to be, men of letters (nos. 1, 23, 40, 47, 60, 62; he might have added 2, 38, 48) or jurists (no. 54; add 68). (Literary gifts do not imply administrative competence, nor of course exclude it.) Balbillus (no. 23) perhaps owed his appointment mainly to Agrippina's influence (Tac., *Ann.* xiii, 21, 6–22).

[9] See n. 64.

[10] pp. 88 f.

[11] Brunt, *JRS* lxiv (1974), 10 f.

Augustus found it wanting in his very first prefect, Cornelius Gallus; Ti. Iulius Alexander not only rebelled against Vitellius but had almost certainly been ready to abandon Nero;[12] Mettius Rufus incurred the suspicion of Domitian, and Calvisius Statianus joined in revolt against Marcus Aurelius. It would be odd if disloyalty were the only offence of which prefects were guilty. True, we know of only two prefects down to 235 who were certainly or probably condemned for maladministration.[13] (The fall of Avillius Flaccus in 38 is not relevant here; whether or not he deserved Philo's biased censures, he perished from the malignity of Gaius and not on account of the complaints of the subjects.) But it was not easy for the subjects (especially in Egypt) to accuse a man in whom, as his very appointment showed, the Emperor had reposed great trust.[14]

Extortion and fraud were endemic in the administration of Egypt among soldiers and officials. We know of this partly from edicts that prefects issued to repress abuses.[15] In 68 Ti. Iulius Alexander covertly imputed certain malpractices to his immediate predecessor, C. Caecina Tuscus. In fact he himself had not dared to prohibit them until Nero was dead, and Caecina may have been no more than he to blame for exactions that were perhaps prompted from Rome.[16] Alexander, and the other governors who sought to impose restraint, deserve credit for good intentions. Many, or most, of the prefects may well have been honourable men.[17] Yet it would be strange if some were not contaminated by the climate of corruption, especially as no other officials can have had so good a chance of impunity.

But if the ability and integrity of the prefects must remain a subject of speculation, or faith, evidence is not lacking about their experience. Once an equestrian *cursus* had been developed, most or all of them had

---

[12] Chalon, 43 f., following Wilcken; cf. E. G. Turner, *JRS* xliv (1954), 60.

[13] C. Vibius Maximus (Stein, *Präfekten*, 52; [cf. Musurillo, *Acts of Pagan Martyrs* vii]; Sherwin-White, *The Letters of Pliny*, 210, 481 disposes of the doubts raised by Pflaum), and the unnamed Severan prefect who was convicted of falsifying his records (*Dig.* xlviii, 10, 1, 4).

[14] Naturally the emperors heard representations from Alexandria, and like Trajan, might show a 'generalized benevolence' (P. J. Parsons on *P. Oxy.* 3022); *P. Oxy.* 3020 also suggests the possibility of complaints against the administration of the Idios Logos, but it was another matter to bring formal charges or complaints against a prefect.

[15] See esp. the edict of Ti. Iulius Alexander, and Chalon *passim*, esp. 239 f.; cf. edicts of 42 (Smallwood, *Docs. illustr. Principates of Gaius* etc. 381), 49 (ib. 382; note reference to edict of Magius Maximus), 54 (ib. 383), 133-7 (Wilcken, *Chr.* 26 and *PSI* 446) and 206 (*P. Oxy.* 1100). The encomium on a Strategus for not taking bribes or resorting to illegal violence illustrates the lowness of prevalent standards during the long prefecture of Galerius, see *SEG* viii 527 = Ehrenberg and Jones, *Documents*, no. 320(a).

[16] See Chalon, pp. 72, 103, 108, 145 and 154 on vv. 14 and 26-32. On Nero's exactions see pp. 27 ff.

[17] It was not my purpose in ch. 4 to deny this, nor to suggest that emperors did not normally prefer such men, when they could find them.

had long and varied official careers. Though the common assumption that continuous employment of Equites was the rule can hardly be proved, a prefect of Egypt could certainly have spent far more years in the active work of government than a consular legate of Britain or Syria, if only because the senate was still in theory the great council of state, and its leading members were therefore required at times to sit idly on its benches at Rome.

In discussing the careers of prefects, Stein thought it enough to point to the posts they had previously held, without asking himself how far the experience they had acquired was relevant to their new duties (*Präfekten*, 180 f.). Yet in Egypt the system of government was unique, and a long official career elsewhere would not necessarily prepare them adequately for novel tasks. Conceivably a man who had grown old in handling problems of | a quite different kind from those which now confronted him might have lacked the flexibility of mind he required. Vice-Chancellors of Oxford University, who are seldom or never quite unfamiliar with the business of their office at the time they take it up, have been known to confess that they were not masters of it in their first year. The prefect's responsibilities were immeasurably more complex and heavy. It is unlikely that he could assert his own control over the administration for some time, unless he possessed transcendent ability or already had some experience of the country.[18] We do not know how many, if any, of the prefects were men of outstanding talents, but (as will be shown) few had any previous acquaintance with the land they were to govern. No doubt their efficiency should have increased with length of tenure. How long were they normally left in office?

LENGTH OF TENURE

The Appendix gives a list of prefects (with what is known of their careers) from 30 B.C. to the eve of the 'military anarchy'; the last prefect named held office till 236, outlasting Severus Alexander. It shows only the dates at which a prefect is actually attested at his post. There are 89 names in all excluding Macro, who was appointed in 38 but never took up the post, and Norbanus (36a), who may have had a very brief tenure under Domitian.

---

[18] No doubt a man who had not been immersed in the routine of Egyptian administration might have examined it with a fresh and critical eye, and made improvements so far as he was permitted. But the edict of Ti. Iulius Alexander, vv. 3–10, indicates that the prefect had little discretion. He was appointed to work the system, not to remodel it. Cf. Chalon 238. *P. Fay.* 21 (p. 239) illustrates the kind of limited administrative reform a prefect could initiate.

If the list were complete, the average tenure would be 3 years. In fact it is evident that names are missing, probably three or four under Augustus (if tenure in his time approximated to three years), and another under Severus Alexander. However, between A.D. 14 and 224 the intervals within which no prefect is attested never extend to three full years and are usually much shorter. It is undeniable that some transient figures, as yet unrecorded, may still be placed in these gaps; we happen to know of 10 men down to 180 who cannot have held the prefecture for two full years (nos. 11, 12, 14, 16, 27, 28, 53, 57, 58, 61), to whom Vernasius (no. 59) should probably be added, if not Norbanus (no. 36a). On the other hand, Reinmuth inferred from *P. Ryl.* 678 that the 6 prefects attested from 133 to 154 held office in succession (he did not know that no. 51 went on beyond 152), with an average tenure of 3·5 years. In many reigns much briefer tenures may be explained by sudden death or by the prefect's recall to meet some unexpected need for his services at Rome. Thus Tiberius who kept C. Galerius at his post for 15 years[19] and Avillius Flaccus (32–8) for the last five of his reign, was plainly unlucky in earlier appointments; Aemilius Rectus (no. 11), who lasted no more than a year, had incurred his disapproval (n. 64), but the short tenure of Sejanus' father (no. 12) was surely, like that of Vitrasius Pollio (no. 14), prematurely ended by death. Of the 4 or 5 prefects who held office in the 9 years of Vespasian's principate one at least died in office, and another may have been recalled to fill the vacancy in the praetorian prefecture which Titus' accession created, after perhaps only a few months' stay in Egypt (no. 31). In the same way Furius Victorinus (no. 53) was rapidly recalled to command the praetorians, like Bassaeus Rufus (no. 58), who had himself succeeded a man with a distinguished career, removed surely by death after less than a year (no. 57); it was a time of pestilence. Again, we may conjecture that Marcus Aurelius did not allow the great jurist, Volusius Maecianus (no. 54), a normal tenure of the prefecture, just because he set so high a value on his legal advice (cf. *Dig.* xxxvii 14, 17, *pr.*). Under Commodus indeed we have 11 prefects attested in 12 years (of whom M. Aurelius Papirius Dionysius perhaps held the office only for a month or two), and similarly we know of 7 in the 11 years from 212–22; the rapid turnover probably illustrates the distrust that the emperors concerned felt for virtually all members of the higher orders; Commodus was also notorious for his frequent removals of praetorian | prefects.[20] It may also be significant

[19] Sen., ad *Helviam* 19, 6 (cf. Stein, *Präfekten*, 25), gives 16 years, presumably reckoning inclusively.

[20] Excluding Cleander, we know 11 praetorian prefects by name from his reign (Passerini, *Le Coorti pretorie* 304 f.), but *HA, Comm.* 6, 6 alleges that he changed them 'per horas ac dies', and

that there were 3 or 4 prefects in the last 7 years of Domitian's rule. The average tenure for the whole period is no doubt much reduced by the fact that it is not more than 2 years between 180 and 236. During that time only two of the known prefects (7 per cent) are known to have been in post for 4 years or more (no. 78 under Septimus and no. 89 under Severus Alexander), whereas we have 14 (22·5 per cent) who are attested in office for almost that length of time, or longer, in the previous 210 years (nos. 6, 13, 15, 21, 23, 26, 37, 40, 41, 42, 44, 45, 46, 47, 51, 60), to say nothing of several others who may have assumed, or demitted, office earlier or later than our extant records as yet prove, and may also have governed Egypt for over 3 years.

It seems to me probable that between 30 B.C. and A.D. 180 no more than half a dozen names of prefects need be lost and that the average tenure was about three years, with a fair proportion holding office longer. From the accession of Commodus the practice changed, and nearly all prefects had too little time in which to familiarize themselves with the special problems of Egypt, if they lacked previous experience there. Until 180, however, most prefects at least had some opportunity of learning their duties *ambulando*. It must remain doubtful whether this was in itself sufficient to ensure good administration, unless they had been prepared by their previous careers for the tasks that awaited them in the Nile valley.

THE CAREERS OF PREFECTS

We may now consider the prior experience prefects had secured. For this purpose I divide them (excluding forty-four i.e. about half of whose previous careers nothing whatever is known) into three classes:

  (i) nine whose careers up to the prefecture are wholly or almost wholly recorded—nos. 39, 44, 49, 50, 53, 54, 58, 59, 68;
  (ii) five or six of whose previous careers much is known—nos. 23, 26, 45 (?), 48, 62, 79.
  (iii) twenty-four to thirty who are recorded in some previous posts—nos. 1, 7, 10 (?), 12, 17, 21, 21a (?), 22, 24, 25, 29, 30, 31, 32, 33, 35, 38 (?), 41, 42, 43, 47, 57 (?), 60, 63, 64, 71 (?), 76, 77, 78, 85 (?).

Naturally the distinction between some members of the last two classes is marginal, while numbers 23 and 48 are excluded from class (i) only

though among those recorded only one ex-prefect of Egypt is found, probably others were promoted to the guard from Egypt; this may help to explain the rapid changes in the government of Egypt.

because it is not certain what higher post or posts immediately preceded their prefectures; by contrast it is the early career of no. 62 that is hidden.

For the whole of the first century we have few '*cursus* inscriptions'. The very first that fully records a prefect's career is that of C. Minicius Italus (no. 39); there are incomplete epigraphic records for only two of his predecessors (nos. 17 and 23), though we know much of the career of Ti. Iulius Alexander (66–70) because he happens to be often mentioned in literary sources. At least four men had been praetorian prefects (n. 1), but it is no less obscure by what path men were promoted to that command; the laconic inscription of Burrus (*ILS* 1321) does not reveal with what justification Tacitus described him as 'egregiae militaris famae' (*Ann.* xii, 42), and the first praetorian prefect whose career can be fully reconstructed from epigraphic and literary sources is Q. Marcius Turbo under Hadrian (Pflaum, no. 94). This dearth of evidence does not mean that there were few equestrian careers to be recorded: rather that Equites were slow to adopt the fashion of having their careers inscribed. That fashion began with senators, and quite late. There had been a senatorial *cursus* for centuries before Augustus' time, yet there are few Republican inscriptions to illustrate it. Even under Augustus and Tiberius senators were less apt to have their careers commemorated than later, if we take the selection made by Dessau as a fair sample not only of career inscriptions now extant but also of all that were ever set up: we find 34, including those which are fragmentary, in *ILS* 880–950 inclusive, which belong roughly to the years 44 B.C. to A.D. 37, as against 26 in *ILS* 954–86 from *c.* A.D. 37 to 69, and 37 in *ILS* 987–1040 from *c.* 69 to 117; the annual rate roughly doubles after | Tiberius. Equites learned gradually to emulate the higher class; freedmen followed the same example later still, and rather infrequently (cf. p. 242).

There were indeed markedly fewer posts available to an Eques under Augustus and Tiberius than a century later. Prefects of Egypt in their day could therefore not have acquired the variety of experience attested under the Antonines. However, they will hardly have chosen men untested by any offices higher than those of the *militiae equestres*, and we may naturally infer from the dedication made by the Tarraconenses to M. Magius Maximus (no. 10) at what was evidently his home town, Aeclanum, that he had previously been procurator of their province, a post that certainly existed in his time (Strabo iii, 4, 20),[21] [though conceivably he was prefect of an auxiliary unit there].

---

[21] Despite doubts of Sherwin-White, *PBSR* xv (1939), 16, n. 34.

PREVIOUS EXPERIENCE IN EGYPT

If only because the prefect of Egypt was equestrian, no senator could be employed as a subordinate to him, and though some such posts later held by Equites may at first have been entrusted to freedmen or natives,[22] Equites are recorded under Augustus and Tiberius not only as commanders of the legions stationed there, but also as Iuridici, Idioi Logoi and Epistrategi.[23] In the very first decade or two of Augustus' reign it may not yet have been recognized that procuratorial posts in general were public offices that qualified their holders for further advancement, and previous experience in Egypt itself may have led on to the prefecture. The first prefect, C. Cornelius Gallus, had probably won Augustus' confidence partly by his success in invading Egypt from the west, especially as Upper Egypt still had to be pacified, and military talent must have seemed to be the primary qualification; like Gallus, the two next prefects both directed military operations,[24] and like Gallus, they may have acquired previous familiarity with local conditions while employed in the country, perhaps as prefects of the legions quartered there. Of course this hypothesis cannot be proved, but it is no objection to it that, later on, commanders of these legions are seldom recorded to have advanced further; in fact, as late as Vespasian, C. Aeternius Fronto (no. 30), who had been *praefectus castrorum* of the Egyptian legionaries engaged in the siege of Jerusalem, did become prefect (cf. n. 23).

At least three of the five prefects Nero appointed had had previous experience in Egypt, Balbillus (no. 23) as head of the Museum and record office etc., Caecina Tuscus (no. 25) as Iuridicus and Ti. Julius Alexander (no. 26) as Epistrategus. This is the more remarkable, as few later prefects seem to have had any previous connection with Egypt.

[22] The first known Epistrategus (Pflaum, p. 1091) is apparently peregrine. Freedmen: Plut., *Mor.* 207 B; Wilcken, *Chr.* 443 with his commentary; Dio lviii, 19, 6. The freedman Hiberus, acting prefect in A.D. 32, must have had a high post, though hardly that of Iuridicus, the substantive rank of acting prefects in 176, 219 (?) and 225 (Appendix).

[23] See Pflaum's lists of the civilian officials, pp. 1083–92; 1107 f. A prefect of XXII Deiotariana (*ILS* 2687) is probably Augustan or Tiberian. Ritterling, *RE* xii, 1490 f.; 1513 f.; 1795 f. lists commanders of legions of Egypt, who are sometimes styled 'praefecti castrorum' or 'pr. exercitus qui est in Aegypto' (cf. *RE* xxiv, 1287 f.). Pflaum, p. 76, says that this post customarily marked the end of a man's career. For this generalization he cites ('surtout') one instance (*ILS* 2696, Claudian); one might perhaps add the anonymous of *OGIS* 586 = *IGR* iii 1015 (Flavian), but he had not certainly ended his career. Contrast not only Aeternius Fronto (my no. 30) but Pflaum, nos. 109, 195 and probably 211; moreover, some equestrian prefects of legions raised by Severus go further. The fact is that there are few of these commanders whose careers are known fully or even in part. It may be significant that after *c.* 100 in the numerous *cursus* inscriptions of men who rose to high rank a legionary post in Egypt occurs only once (Pflaum, no. 109—*pr. ann.*), but such an argument *e silentio* has no force for the Julio-Claudian period.

[24] Stein, *Präfekten* 14–17.

Classes (i) and (ii) include half the twenty prefects who governed between 101 and 169, and of the ten men concerned only Valerius Eudaemon (no. 48) had certainly served in a civil post in Egypt before his prefecture, and only Valerius Proculus (no. 49) and perhaps Baienus (no. 58) are documented in a military or partly military post there. Of course we have a record of no more than one or two offices that most prefects had held. Still, some 80 Epistrategi[25] are known by name and about as many holders of other procuratorial posts in the country; yet apart from the prefects already named | none of these subordinate officials appears in the almost complete Fasti of the prefects. Thus after the Julio-Claudian period previous experience within the country was apparently no recommendation. Other facts may point to a contrast between Julio-Claudian and subsequent practice. Ti. Julius Alexander, and perhaps Balbillus, were the only governors, so far as we know, born in the province. The prefects also include probably four homonymous couples, who were probably each father and son (nos 11 and 18, 14 and 17, 21a and 35, 46 and 57), and one might conjecture that the son accompanied his father to the Nile, just as an Idios Logos under Marcus Aurelius probably held that office in the prefecture of his father (no. 60). But two of the couples are also of the Julio-Claudian era.

SUBORDINATE EQUESTRIAN OFFICIALS

In commenting on the career of Ulpius Serenianus who was Antarchiereus in 160 and perhaps in 162, and Archiereus in 171–8 and (as we have since learned) in 193, Pflaum suggested that the government preferred to keep specialists, of Graeco-Oriental origin, for long periods in Egypt. When he wrote, he was not aware of another perhaps comparable case: Lysimachus, Idios Logos in 69, was probably in the same post in 88, though he had not held it continuously in the intervening years. Moreover, out of 11 Iuridici of whose careers we know something 6 had already served in Egypt in a civil or military capacity (Pflaum, nos. 25, 77, 114, 116, 121, 137), and only 2 had clearly not (nos. 81, 178); in three cases we lack information (nos. 4, 100, 267). Recently it has been shown that of 19 equestrian army officers in Egypt, whose subsequent careers are recorded at least in part, 5 or 6 held civil posts in the country, not counting two who

[25] M. Vandoni, *Gli epistrategi nell'Egitto greco-romano* (1971).

became *praefecti montis Berenicidis*.[26] Perhaps then, the prefect usually had assistance from equestrian officials more familiar with Egypt than he generally was.

However, the samples of careers cited are very small, and much other evidence does not harmonize with this suggestion.

(1) Only 12 men are known to have held more than one civilian post in Egypt, excluding the prefecture (Pflaum nos. 25, 55, 56, 77, 88, 104 bis, 114, 116, 121, 137, 192 bis, 256); to these we may perhaps add a Dioiketes who had once been Arabarch (192).[27] Pflaum gives some details of the previous postings of 4 Dioiketai (ib. nos. 169, 190, 193, 232) and 5 Idioi Logoi (ib. nos. 7, 146, 177 cf. p. 981, 262, 268), but the ex-Arabarch alone had any attested experience of the country. Besides Ulpius Serenianus, and Balbillus, whose responsibilities under Claudius at least overlapped with those of the later Archiereis, we know the career of one Archiereus, L. Iulius Vestinus (Pflaum, no. 105), who probably combined this post with that of head of the Museum; he had no other connection with the country, and went on to palatine duties.[28] Promotion outside Egypt seems to have been usual; of 7 Iuridici, whose subsequent employment is recorded, only Caecina was again in Egypt, as prefect; the other 6 (ib. nos. 25, 116, 121, 137, 178, 250) do not seem to have returned, any more than those Dioiketai whose later posts are known (nos. 169, 193). The prospects of Epistrategi do not seem to have been good; the only one known to have risen to the prefecture, Ti. Iulius Alexander, had a varied career elsewhere. Of the 8 others of whose later postings something is recorded by Pflaum 6 were promoted outside Egypt (nos. 52, 87, 103, 123, 217, 222), and only 2 held higher offices there, the first almost certainly after service elsewhere in the interval (nos. 114, 256). The anonymous figure who had been active in Cappadocia, Pannonia, | Italy and Gaul before becoming 'procurator ad dioicesin Alexandriae', and who then acceded to palatine offices and the prefecture of the corn-supply (Pflaum, no. 271, cf. p. 994), may be as typical, save for his exceptional success, of administrators in Egypt as the Archiereus on whose career Pflaum founded his hypothesis.

---

[26] Pflaum on n. 192 bis; he did not know that the same man appears once more as Archiereus in Feb./March 193, P. J. Parsons, *Chron. d'Ég.* xlix (1974), 135. Lysimachus: P. R. Swarney, *The Ptolemaic and Roman Idios Logos* (1970), 84, cf. pp. 127 f. for up-to-date list of these officials. Military officers: H. Devijver, in H. Temporini (ed.), *Aufstieg u. Niedergang der röm. Welt*, ii, 1 (1974), 452 f., esp. 463 f.

[27] The Arabarch controlled the collection of tolls on the route to the Red Sea (*OGIS* 674), but was not always an Eques, cf. Jos., *AJ* xviii, 159; 259; xix, 276; xx, 100, 147; Schürer, *Gesch. des Jüdischen Volkes*, iii⁴, 132.

[28] G. M. Parássoglou, *Zeitschr. f. Pap. u. Epigr.* xiii (1974), 32 f. lists the Archiereis. He believes the post to be Hadrianic, and therefore excludes Balbillus. [Cf. also Hagedorn, *YCS* xxviii (1985) 167 ff., but over and over again antecedents have been found for supposed Hadrianic innovations.]

(2) None of the equestrian posts, so far as we can tell, was *normally* held for a long period. Thus there were at least 11 Iuridici between *c.* 114 and 147 (Pflaum, p. 1087 f.) with an average tenure of not over 3 years, and at least 41 Epistrategi of the Heptanomia *c.* 114–235 (n. 25), whose average tenure was still briefer since there are obvious gaps in the Fasti. Similarly no fewer than 6 Dioiketai are recorded in *c.* 180–200 (Pflaum, p. 1084). The lists of these officials at other times and of other officials in all periods are manifestly defective, but there is no reason to suppose that the figures given are not typical.

(3) Even in the lowest grade of equestrian posts in Egypt, that of the Epistrategi, Graeco-Oriental *cognomina* hardly preponderate as late as the second half of the second century, when we still find men whose *nomina*, e.g. 'Vedius', 'Lucceius', 'Vettius', 'Egnatuleius' (Pflaum, no. 217), suggest western origin; most Epistrategi have such uninformative names as 'Iulius Quintianus'. Moreover, easterners need not have been specialists in Egyptian administration. All or most may have been as much 'birds of passage' as Ti. Claudius Xenophon (Pflaum, no. 222), Epistrategus in 180, whose varied career was otherwise passed at Rome, in Dacia, Pannonia, Dalmatia, Lower Moesia, Asia and Africa.

(4) What we know of the Archidicasts may also have a bearing on this question. Their jurisdiction was important; whether or not delegated by the prefect or restricted to certain types of case, it extended to the whole country; they could give instructions to Strategi (*BGU* 136; *P. Giess.* 34; *P. Mil. Vogl.* 229). The office was held by Alexandrians of distinguished family, sometimes from one generation to another; some also acted as *hypomnematographoi* or held civic offices at Alexandria. In the second century most of them seem to be Roman citizens, and almost certainly they would then have possessed equestrian census; under Hadrian four of them commanded cohorts both within and beyond Egypt, one twice. Yet none is recorded to have been advanced to higher equestrian posts in their own country. Moreover, though one was in office from 15 to 5 B.C., they mostly seem to have had very brief tenures, some for only a year. Even at this level the government apparently set little value on local experience.[29] [At a still lower level Strategi, who were of course natives, do not seem to have been long in post for the most part nor to have had prior experience as royal *grammateis*.[30]]

[29] On the office and its holders see I. Calabi, *Aegyptus* xxxii (1952), 406 f.; to her list add Ti. Cl. Serenus between 139 and 144 (*P. Mil. Vogl.* 229), Ti. Claudius Alexander, 2nd century (*BGU* 2062), and Calpurnius Petronianus in 225 (*P. Oxy.* 2705). In 120–39, 12 Archidicasts are attested, and in both 143–4 and 159–60, 3. Her doubts on the Roman citizenship of some men who have Roman *nomina* do not seem justified in view of the undoubted equestrian status of the 4 ex-*praefecti cohortis* and the hereditary dignity of some families represented (see e.g. *P. Oxy.* 1434 with commentary). Cf. Devijver o.c. (n. 26), 483–90.

[30] [J. E. G. Whitehorne, *Proc. 16th Int. Congress Pap.* (1981), 419 ff.]

It would then appear probable that most equestrian officials in Egypt had as little prior familiarity with the administration there as most prefects.

PREVIOUS GOVERNORSHIPS OF PREFECTS

As already pointed out, the combination in the prefect's hands of military, judicial and fiscal functions is found elsewhere only in the provinces governed by presidial procurators. If experience in Egypt itself was not deemed to be desirable for a prefect, might he not naturally have been tested out in one or more of these presidial posts? Yet in fact only 8 or 9 prefects are attested in these posts, one in the Maritime Alps (no. 49), one in Judaea under Claudius (no. 26), one or two in Raetia (nos. 57 and 36a, if ever prefect), two in Noricum (nos. 56 and 58), two in Mauretania Tingitana (nos. 57 and 64), [one in Mesopotamia (no. 78)] and one in Sardinia (no. 79); one of the men concerned (no. 57) had governed two of these provinces. Of the 9 prefects in class (i) only 3 had previously governed a province.

PREFECTURES AT HOME

At the end of his reign Augustus appointed a former prefect of Egypt, C. Turranius (no. 5), to be prefect of the *annona*, probably the first holder of the post, but this precedent | was not copied except in bizarre conditions under Commodus (Pflaum, no. 181). Instead, no fewer than fifteen men were advanced from the prefecture of the *annona* to that of Egypt (nos. 30, 32, 33, 35, 39, 41, 42, 49, 50, 53, 54, 57, 63, 68, 78), including 7 in class (i). It seems fair to infer that this was a normal sequence. Now at first sight, in view of the importance of Egyptian corn for the provisioning of Rome, it might seem that *praefecti annonae* as such would have acquired some insight into the administration of Egypt.[31] Yet doubts must supervene. The *praefectus annonae* surely needed to obtain from Alexandria advance notice of the tonnage that he could expect and of the probable dates of shipment, but he did not need detailed knowledge about the upkeep of the irrigation system, the mode of assessing probable yields, the collection of the tax-grain or its transportation to the docks at Alexandria. Nor did the prefect of Egypt need to have been in actual charge of the procurement of grain for Rome in order to be aware that it was one of his most essential duties to

---

[31] cf. G. E. F. Chilver, *AJP* lxx (1949), 16 f.

extract as much grain as possible from the cultivators. Probably it was just because the *praefectus annonae* stood next to the prefect of Egypt in the equestrian hierarchy that he had a claim to fill the first vacancy at Alexandria.[32] If for some reason he were not available, the official who stood next to him in rank, the *praefectus vigilum*, could be preferred; three holders of this office were directly promoted in this way (nos. 43, 44, 58), and one governor of Egypt at least had held both prefectures at Rome (no. 32). Yet there was no natural link between the duties of the *praefectus vigilum* and the administration of Egypt. Of course the tenure of any of these offices is proof that the emperor valued the competence of the holders; but it does not appear that specialized skill or experience was looked for.

MILITARY EXPERIENCE AND DUTIES

The prefect was commander of an army. No doubt most prefects had at least held two or three of the *militiae equestres*. This is true of 7 of the 9 men in class (i). Unfortunately we do not know for how long on average an Eques destined for higher employment retained a legionary tribunate or auxiliary prefecture, or therefore to what extent he may be regarded as a professional expert.[33] In any case, even if we could fix the average, any individual might have served for either longer or shorter terms. In fact some of our 7 men had probably or certainly more than average military experience. C. Minicius Italus (no. 39) had held five equestrian commissions. T. Furius Victorinus (no. 53), who held only three, rose to be prefect first of the Ravenna and then of the Misenum fleet, and was finally to be given command of the praetorians. Q. Baienus Blassianus (no. 57), again after the *tres militiae*, commanded the fleet in Britain, governed two *provinciae armatae* and was prefect of the Ravenna fleet. M. Bassaeus Rufus (no. 58) had governed Noricum and was to be praetorian prefect; moreover he had risen from the ranks of the praetorian guard,[34] through the urban tribunates and the iterated primipilate. At least two other prefects had been tribunes of the guard (nos. 29 and 73), and probably Ser. Sulpicius Similis (no. 41), an ex-centurion, had a similar career. We may also recall that Vespasian appointed a man who had been *praefectus castrorum* of the Egyptian legions (no. 30), and that Tiberius Iulius

---

[32] cf. the promotion of praetorian prefects to Egypt and vice versa, nn. 1 and 2.

[33] E. Birley, *Roman Britain and the Roman Army* (1953), 137 f. argues that 'a period of three or four years' service in each post can have been by no means unusual', but the evidence he cited is clearly too scanty to justify fixing an average.

[34] Dio lxxi, 5, 2.

Alexander was chief of staff to Corbulo, and later to Titus, to say nothing of his procuratorship in Judaea; very probably he had gone through the *militiae equestres*. [Ti. Claudius Subatianus Aquila (no. 78) had actually commanded a more important army in Mesopotamia before his prefecture in Egypt.]

None the less military qualifications were not essential to a prefect of Egypt. Balbillus (no. 23) had perhaps held only an honorary tribunate and certainly had no other experience in the army. Neither Heliodorus (no. 47) nor Eudaemon (no. 48), cultivated Greeks, are likely to have practised arms. The jurist Volusius Maecianus (no. 54) had only held one equestrian commission in the army, and M. Aurelius Papirius Dionysius (no. 68) and L. | Baebius (no. 79) none at all; that can also be conjectured for Commodus' tutor, Sanctus (no. 62).

Augustus would hardly have contemplated appointing mere civilians to command the army in Egypt. The first three governors were all engaged in important military operations (n. 24). At the outset three legions were stationed in the country, together with 3 *alae* and 9 cohorts (Strabo, xvii, 1, 12). But one legion had already been withdrawn before A.D. 23 (Tac., *Ann.* iv, 5) and a second left probably under Hadrian. It was some compensation that the number of cohorts was increased; eight are attested, as well as three *alae*, in a diploma of 83, and in Pius's reign there were twelve. We cannot be sure that we know just how many auxiliary regiments remained thereafter, since there may have been more than those which happen to be recorded. Lesquier, however, guessed that the total force in the country was reduced from 22,800 under Augustus to no more than 17,000–18,000, and perhaps to as few as 11,000 in the post-Hadrianic era; the last figure should perhaps be 13,000.[35] Moreover Egypt was in no danger of a serious foreign invasion; the primary purpose of the legions or legion at Nicopolis was to overawe the unruly population of Alexandria, and elsewhere soldiers were scattered through the *chora* on police duties; officers were often employed in the civil administration.[36] In normal circumstances the maintenance of internal order was within the capacity of a competent civilian, and it may have been his hardest task, as commander-in-chief, to keep the troops disciplined and repress their depredations on the subjects (cf. Philo, *Flacc.* 5). But major revolts or

[35] *L'Armée rom. d'Égypte* (1918), 102 f., brought up-to-date on the number of *auxilia* by H.-G. Pflaum, *Syria* xliv (1967), 339 f.

[36] For their role in jurisdiction cf. nn. 44, 47; in *epikrisis*, *P. Oxy.* xii, p. 149; in the census, Hunt-Edgar, *Select Papyri*, no. 220; police and related duties, see documents listed and transcribed in S. Daris, *Documenti per la storia dell' esercito romano in Egitto* (1964), 153–69. Cf. Mitteis, *Grundz.*, 28–30; 33–6; Wilcken, *Grundz.* 396 f.

inroads necessitated the deployment of additional forces, and then the high command might be placed in hands other than the prefect's. Marcius Turbo (Pflaum, no. 94) was specially commissioned to subdue the Jews at the end of Trajan's reign. Under Marcus Aurelius the legate of Syria, Avidius Cassius, was called in to defeat the Bucoli, shepherds and brigands in the north-west of the Delta.[37] The then prefect, C. Calvisius Statianus, had been *ab epistulis Latinis*; most such secretaries were men with no military experience (cf. n. 43). His inability to suppress the Bucoli without aid was not held against him; he remained in office for the exceptionally long term of six years, till disgraced for his part in Avidius' rebellion. Under Severus Alexander, M. Aurelius Zeno Ianuarius (Pflaum, no. 315), a former governor of Mauretania Caesariensis, operated in Egypt as *dux*, and not (as once supposed) as prefect.[38]

No doubt it was simply impossible for emperors to find men equally qualified for the military and civil duties of a governor of Egypt, and reasonable, given the conditions that generally prevailed there, if they looked primarily for competence in judicial and fiscal business. Hence the choice of men like Bassaeus Rufus, whom Dio (n. 34), while conceding his merits, describes as uneducated, may well evoke surprise: they can hardly have known much law, and came relatively late to fiscal work. Yet in fact legal expertise was still rarer than military proficiency among the prefects.

LEGAL EXPERIENCE AND DUTIES

Like the presidial procurators, the governor of Egypt possessed supreme jurisdiction, both civil and criminal, subject to any rights of appeal to the emperor (*CPL* 237: *P. Oxy.* 2104). Indeed in the view of some scholars all other officials, except the Idios Logos for certain fiscal claims, could only administer justice as his delegates. Whether or not this be so, he obviously had no time to deal with all the cases that might have come before him, and he must have resorted to full delegation on a large scale (cf. nn. 51 f.); alternatively, he could appoint *iudices pedanei* to decide particular suits in accordance with his instructions. Petitioners would try to attract his personal attention by appeals to his pity or to the public interest; this shows that they did not expect him to decide their suits personally | as a matter of course. Still there was no

---

[37] Dio lxxi, 4. Bucoli: *RE* iii, 1013.
[38] Pflaum, no. 315; P. J. Parsons, *Proc. of XIIth Conference of Papyrology* (1970), 389 f.

type of case that he was not in principle competent to hear himself, and might not choose to hear at his own discretion.[39]

And yet only two prefects are known to have been experts in the civil law (nos. 54, 68). Such expertise in officials cannot be assumed in the absence of professional study. It was probably deficient even in most advocates, a class sharply distinguished at Rome from jurisconsults, though no doubt they picked up more knowledge of the law in forensic practice than most gentlemen did in the mere management of their own property.[40] Stein once opined that at least after Hadrian juristic qualifications were required for all higher Roman officials. There is simply no evidence for this. Only a few are known to have studied the law. Most of the subordinate posts Equites filled would not have been provided even empirical training. It is true that in the second century some began as legal *consiliarii* of the emperor or as *advocati fisci*. Hirschfeld, to whom Stein referred, was impressed by this, but to say nothing of the facts that the *advocati* were orators rather than lawyers, and were concerned with a restricted range of cases, it was not common for men of this type to rise to any of the greatest offices; in Egypt only one prefect to our knowledge had been a *consiliarius* (no. 68), and none an *advocatus fisci*.[41]

Fiscal as well as presidial procurators might enjoy some jurisdiction, but it was normally restricted to fiscal matters;[42] and in general nothing had prepared them to exercise even this limited power. Still less were most Equites fitted by previous experience for the presidial posts which

---

[39] Mitteis, *Grundz.*, 24 ff.; Coroi, *Actes du V* *Congrès Int. de Pap.* (1938), 615 f.; Humbert, esp. 100 f., who thinks that only the Idios Logos had jurisdiction independent of the prefect, but argues (109 f.) for permanent delegations to certain officials, cf. n. 52 below. H. Kupiszewski, *Journ. Jur. Pap.* vii/viii (1953/4), 191 f. maintains that the Iuridicus had jurisdiction committed to him by the emperor; Strabo xvii, 1, 2 and *ILS* 2691 strongly suggest this, and all other arguments on each side seem to me indecisive. But no doubt the prefect could overrule the Iuridicus; the Idios Logos too was subject to his authority, cf. edict of Ti. Iulius Alexander, vv. 37–45, and *Gnomon Idiologi*, proem. On the Archidicast cf. n. 30. On petitions, Humbert, 131 f. See, most recently, E. Seidl, *Rechtsgesch. Ägyptens als röm. Provinz* (1974), 93 f.

[40] F. Schulz, *Hist. of Rom. Legal Science*, 108 f. Quintilian argued that the ideal orator should be expert in law (xii, 3), but equally in moral philosophy (ib. 2) and history (4); his ideal had never been realized (x, 2, 9), and it is clear from much that he says that advocates of his day, often appearing before 'imperiti' (ii. 17, 27), relied like Cicero, still the best model for Quintilian, on appeals to plausibility or emotion rather than to juristic arguments. Cicero too had insisted on the necessity of the ideal orator knowing the law (*de orat.* i, 18, cf. 166–201; *Orator* 120; *Part. Or.* 98 f.); in fact it is clear that the views and practice ascribed to M. Antonius (*de orat.* i, 234 f. esp. 248–53, cf. 172) were more typical (cf. *Part. Or.* 100). The ῥήτορες or συνήγοροι of Egyptian trials can be distinguished from νομικοί (*SB* 7696, cf. Seidl o.c. (n. 39), 115 f.).

[41] Stein, *Unters.* 194, citing Hirschfeld, *Kaiserliche Verwaltungsbeamten²*, 428 f. But *pace* Hirschfeld, as Pflaum's lists of imperial *consiliarii* and of *advocati fisci* in Rome and Italy (pp. 1024 f., 1033, 1104) show, very few of them are known to have been promoted except to specialized legal posts; the same is true of provincial *advocati fisci*, who are hardly attested before the third century. Stein also relied on Mitteis, *Reichsrecht u. Volksrecht*, 193 and *Dig.* i, 22, cf. p. 232 below. [*Advocati* as orators: Brunt, *JRS* (1983), 73.]

[42] Ch. 8.

made them supreme judges of all civil and criminal cases; moreover (as we have seen) few of the prefects of Egypt are recorded to have served a sort of apprenticeship as governors of smaller provinces. As *a libellis* or *ab epistulis*, men were certainly concerned with the legal problems referred to the emperor by private petitioners or by officials such as Pliny. But only three of the prefects (nos. 44, 54 and 68) are known to have served as *a libellis*—perhaps it is significant that they included both the jurists—the first (no. 44) for hardly more than a year (p. 236). Only one is attested as formerly *ab epistulis Latinis* (no. 60), three as *ab epistulis Graecis* (nos. 47, 48, 62) and one as *ad legationes et responsa Graeca* (no. 23); three of these (nos. 47, 48 and perhaps 23) seem to have been men of letters and can hardly be credited with legal expertise, which was probably not of much relevance to an emperor's dealings with Greek cities.[43] Caecina (no. 26) had served as Iuridicus in Egypt itself; but that does not make him a professional lawyer; no Iuridicus is recorded to have had legal qualifications, although the very title implies that he was primarily concerned with jurisdiction; two at least (Pflaum nos. 4 and 100) were essentially military men. The other officials to whom the prefects sent down cases for decisions or investigation were equally amateurs; they even included equestrian army officers.[44]

Roman law applied at first only to Roman citizens in the province, though some of its rules were gradually extended to the other inhabitants. For the rest of the population the government naturally had no alternative but to uphold in the main, subject to modifications made in the course of time, Egyptian or Greek laws, or the amalgam of the two that had developed under the Ptolemies, to which their subjects were accustomed.[45] Ideally, the prefect and his delegates needed to be familiar with both Roman and native legal institutions: seldom trained

[43] Of 9 *a libellis* before 235 known to Pflaum (pp. 1021, 1104, cf. 994) 3 were jurists. Yet the freedmen predecessors of these equestrian officials can hardly have been *iurisperiti*, and legal attainments may never have been indispensable. [Cf. Brunt, *JRS* (1983), 49.] Of 14 attested *ab epistulis* or *ab epistulis Latinis* (pp. 1020 f., 1104) 3 again were jurists (Pflaum, nos. 142, 172, 287). Birley, o.c. (n. 33), 142 f., thinks they needed military experience, but on patently inadequate grounds. Of Equites entitled simply *ab ep.*, Pflaum, no. 156 had 'great military experience'; not so all the others whose careers are known, nos. 60, 96, 105, 142, 271 (cf. p. 994), 287. Once again, freedmen *ab epistulis* had been neither lawyers nor soldiers. On rhetors as *ab ep. Gr.* see Pflaum, p. 684. [See generally F. Millar, *The Emperor in the Roman World* (1977), 83–101.]

[44] Mitteis, *Chr.* 84 (Humbert, 110 argues that this *pr. coh.* had a permanent delegation); 90 (trib. as *iudex datus*); *P. Teb.* 488 (tribune); *P. Oxy.* 237, viii, 3, (ἐπάρχῳ στόλου καὶ [ἐπὶ τῶ]ν κεκριμένων τῷ τειμιω[τά]τῳ); 1637 (centurion as *iudex datus*). See Seidl o.c. (n. 39), 102 on *P. Mich.* iii, 159. Cf. n. 36.

[45] Taubenschlag, *Law of Graeco-Roman Egypt*[2] (1955), ch. 1; Seidl o.c. (n. 39), esp. Part iv. J. Modrzejewski, *XIIth Int. Congress of Papyrology* (1970), 317 f. seems to hold that all pre-Roman laws had only the status of customs after the conquest which acquired full legal validity as *Provinzialrecht* only if confirmed by Roman edicts or *decreta*; hence we cannot speak of decisions in

in Roman law and mostly total strangers to the country, few possessed either qualification.

There is some evidence that they could seek guidance from *nomikoi* versed in the local 'laws', but little to show that Roman jurisconsults were available. Provincial governors might have expert *adsessores* at least in the Severan period, but not all *adsessores* were jurisconsults.[46] The papyri show prefects under Vespasian and Trajan discussing their judgements with *nomikoi*, but in the earlier instances the lawyers are Greeks concerned with local laws—the prefects appear to be entirely dependent on them for knowledge of what these laws prescribe—and in the last the issue is elementary. Under Nero the prefect's legal *consilium* consisted of the Iuridicus, the Dioiketes, some army officers and persons who, to judge from their names, were Alexandrian notables; the case related to military privileges, but an army officer also advises on a purely civil issue, just as they could decide such cases as delegates or *iudices pedanei* appointed by the prefect (n. 44).[47] Mitteis suggested that in their *scribae* governors found a staff educated in the law (cf. n. 41): but *scribae* are not attested in Egypt, and there is no evidence that they ever had the qualifications he imputes to them.

It must then remain uncertain how far the prefects had the benefit of professional advice on Roman law. In default of it they could no doubt turn to their archives for texts of the praetorian edicts, and of prefects' edicts in Egypt, for Roman legislation applicable there, for royal ordinances still valid, and for decisions of their predecessors which might serve as precedents.[48] Moreover, some of the more elementary books on Roman law may well have been used by, perhaps devised for, officials (rather than law students), and not only in Egypt;

Roman courts which set aside such customs as violations of law (cf. n. 54). Yet in *P. Oxy.* 2757 a Flavian prefect consults Areius the 'nomikos' about what the (Egyptian) 'laws command'. Obviously both rulers and governed must have started from the presumption that the relevant local 'nomoi' would remain in force, unless and until modified for specific reasons. On Modrzejewski's own showing Roman courts very commonly upheld them (339 f.).

[46] W. Kunkel, *Herkunft u. soziale Stellung der röm. Juristen*[2], 269 f.; 355 f. (add *P. Oxy.* 2757), on jurists in Egypt; ib. 331 ff. on assessors. The *xenokritai* of *P. Oxy.* 3016, whatever they may be, can hardly be relevant.

[47] *Nomikoi*: *P. Oxy.* 2757; 3015 (also for *consilium*); Mitteis, *Chr.* 372, iii, 18. *Consilium* of Caecina Tuscus: *P. Fouad* 21, cf. E. Balogh and H.-G. Pflaum, *Rev. hist. de droit fr. et étr.* xxx (1952), 117 f. The putative Alexandrians might be the archidikast, *hypomnematographos* and *eisagogeus*, for whom see commentary on *P. Oxy.* 1434; the last sits on the *consilium* in *P. Strasb.* 179. A *pr. alae* as *consiliarius* in *BGU* 288. References to the prefect consulting with his *consiliarii*, or employing his 'friends' in judicial functions (e.g. *P. Oxy.* 2754) do not then prove that he had expert jurists on his staff. Seidl o.c. (n. 39) produces no new testimony for his assumption (233) that the prefects had jurists from Rome at their side.

[48] Private collections of rulings on particular legal topics (e.g. Mitteis, *Chr.* 370, 372, 374, cf. also *P. Oxy.* 237, vi, 28; vii, 12 f., Humbert 118) may have been extracted from official archives. On the sources of law in Roman Egypt cf. esp. the proem to the *Gnomon*, and see Seidl o.c. (n. 39), Part I; on the supposed provincial edict, Modrzejewski o.c. (n. 45), 341 f.

in every province the law was, we may think, generally administered by amateurs. The so-called *Gnonom of the Idios Logus* provided guidance to that officer in | imposing penalties for the infringement of administrative regulations.[49] For my present purpose it hardly matters if reliance was placed on lawyers professionally trained or on clerks who would find documents in the archives; in either case the governor and higher officials depended on assistance from below.

According to Philo the Alexandrian Lampon, when an official of the prefect's court, had accepted bribes in both civil and criminal cases, falsified the records and grown rich by encompassing the death or impoverishment of defendants or suitors. These activities clearly antedate the prefecture of Flaccus and must be placed in the long period (16–31) when C. Galerius was prefect (cf. n. 15). Whether or not Philo's charges against Lampon were true, it must at least have been credible that corruption could affect judicial proceedings even under a governor of long experience. Philo in fact explains Lampon's success by the consideration that 'it was impracticable for the governors administering so vast a country, when more and more new business, both public and private, was always flowing in, to remember everything, especially as they were not only administering justice, but were occupied with the accounts for the revenues and taxes, the examination of which took up most of the year'; Lampon could 'trade on the forgetfulness of the judges'.[50]

Officials of his stamp must have had a still better chance of success when a new prefect could not depend at all on his own recollections, but had to rely on such evidence from the files as the officials laid before him. It is significant that in the famous case of Dionysia v. Chaeremon the latter ventured to petition a new governor without reference to the adverse decisions his predecessor had arrived at, though without success; on this occasion the prefect exercised 'his divine memory and unerring judgement' (*P. Oxy.* 237, vi, 8 f.). The fact that so few prefects were initially familiar with the system must also have favoured malpractices; the anecdote in Philostratus' life of

---

[49] Legal textbooks: Schulz o.c. (n. 40), 154 f.; we need not assume that there were not other early works, of which we happen to know nothing. Seidl, *St. Paoli* 659 f., suggests that some prefects' decisions, e.g. *P. Ryl.* 75 (A.D. 150–2) were founded on *regulae*. W. von Uxkull-Gyllenband, *BGU* v, 2, pp. 1–11, points out that the *Gnomon* had nothing on the Idios Logos' administration of land, his chief business. (On this perhaps he needed less guidance than on legal problems.) Fragments of juristic writings on papyri are of late-third-century date, see Taubenschlag, o.c. (n. 45), 36 f.

[50] *Flacc.* 130–4. Lucian, *Apol.* 12 says that he had a high salary for the task of bringing cases to the court (τὰς δίκας εἰσάγειν) and placing them in the right order (τάξιν αὐταῖς τὴν προσήκουσαν ἐπιτιθέναι) and keeping accurate records, especially of the decisions (τὰς τοῦ ἄρχοντος γνώσεις). It is to be noted that Lucian was no lawyer. Whether he held the same post as Lampon—nothing shows that it was equestrian—and what it was called, we do not know. Cf. Stein, *Unters.* 187 f.

Apollonius (v, 36), however unhistorical, about the proconsul of Achaea whose ignorance enabled his assessors and staff to traffic in justice, may yet have the more universal truth of fiction, describing οἷα ἂν γένοιτο, what all his readers knew to be possible, if not common. The preoccupations of the governor of Egypt were certainly greater than those of the governor in Greece; we have to think not only of the complexity of the tax system but of the multitude of petitions on legal and administrative matters which reached him. In under three days a Severan prefect received 1804 in one assize in Arsinoe.[51] M. Petronius Mamertinus (no. 46) refused to hear in the first instance charges or suits brought apparently by Roman citizens, except in a few specified categories, or on appeal, unless the appellants deposited part of the sum at issue.[52] We may conjecture that simple falsification of the records was not the only device of corrupt officials. They might also turn up those documents in the archives which favoured the cause of a particular litigant. They might induce the prefect to decide himself (under their influence), and to give priority to the claims of a litigant who had bought their support, reducing the often long delays of legal process in Egypt, or to select someone to decide the case, who could be counted on to favour that litigant.

The litigation between Dionysia and Chaeremon may reveal some of the defects in the administration of justice. Down to Commodus' reign many, if not all, prefects had repeatedly forbidden litigants to approach them by letter rather than petition. Yet repetition of this rule would hardly have been necessary unless some of them had been prepared to countenance its violation. In fact Longaeus Rufus (no. 65) originally acted in | this particular case on a letter from Chaeremon, a man of some status and wealth, without waiting to hear what could be said in reply.[53] At a later stage, with a new prefect in office (above), Chaeremon was able to claim the right under Egyptian custom to separate his daughter, Dionysia, from her husband against her own will, although (as Dionysia was to show) Roman courts under Hadrian and perhaps under Domitian had decided that paramount consideration was due to the wishes of the wife, at least in conditions which appear to have been fulfilled in her case.[54] Where the law to be applied was not known or was not certain, there were obvious opportunities for officials to manipulate the decisions of the courts.

[51] J. F. Oates et al., *Yale Pap. in the Beinecke Library* (1967), 61.

[52] N. Lewis, *Rev. hist. de droit fr. et étr.* (1972), 5 f.; Li (1973), 5 f. In *P. Ryl*, 74 (probably A.D. 133) the prefect announces that he has no time to hold a *conventus* for the Thebaid, and no need, since most cases have been settled by the local authorities. In one way or another much more judicial business was evidently decided by subordinates than some modern accounts suggest.

[53] *P. Oxy.* 237, vi, 6 f., on which see Mitteis, *Grundz.* 27; 38, n. 3.

[54] Ibid. vi, 17 f., vii, 13–viii, 7. Cf. n. 45 on the 'violation' of Egyptian law.

Again, in a careful review of the types of case the prefect decided personally or delegated to others for investigation or trial, Humbert is unable to detect any clear distinction between them; the prefect tends to take more important cases (cf. Philo, *Flacc.* 4), yet he delegates some of them to others, and deals with some trivia himself.[55] Of course his time was limited, but it may well have been his officials acting in their own interests who induced him to devote it to hearing some claims and not others. Their co-operation was also probably required for the malpractices of the *Eklogistai* forbidden by Tiberius Iulius Alexander (edict, vv. 35 f.): they had been bringing *res iudicatae* over and over again before the prefects, no doubt on various legal pretexts, in order to harass the taxpayers and extort ruinous sums from them. Here again it is evident that this vexatious renewal of fiscal claims was facilitated by changes in the prefecture.

In these circumstances it would be unwise to assume *a priori* that judgements by the prefects or their delegates reflect expertise in Roman law. J. Modrzejewski (o.c. in n. 45, p. 346) suggests that Romanization of Egyptian juridical life affected the law of family and succession more rapidly and completely than contractual relationships. Perhaps the former were institutions of the civil law of which every Roman gentleman had some personal experience, and which the amateur judges therefore understood best.

FISCAL EXPERIENCE AND DUTIES

No doubt justice to private individuals, especially when relatively few of them were Roman citizens, was less important to the government than the extraction of revenue. On Philo's testimony this was the principal care of the prefects (above) and the very name, διαλογισμός, used in Egypt for 'conventus', confirms this. We may therefore think that the emperors appointed so few governors with legal qualifications, because competence in the law was less essential than experience in fiscal administration. Indeed much of the prefect's jurisdiction directly or indirectly affected the revenue; many petitions, for instance, concerned liability to the liturgies through which the collection of the revenue was assured. And it may be thought that in fiscal matters the prefects were generally well prepared for their tasks. At least 22 prefects, including all but the two jurists in class (i), had held one or more provincial procuratorships; probably this was usual from the time of Claudius. A few are also known to have had a part in the central

[55] Humbert, ch. ii.

financial administration, as *a rationibus* (nos. 60, 53, 58, 62, perhaps 49), *procurator rationis privatae* (no. 62), *procurator patrimonii* (no. 45), *procurator hereditatium* (nos. 44, 79) or *procurator vicesimae hereditatium* (no. 50).

We cannot generally tell how long men retained any equestrian offices, civil or military.[56] | Occasionally it is clear that they were transferred so quickly that they may not have acquired more than a superficial knowledge of the duties attached to a given post. T. Haterius Nepos (no. 44), after passing through the *militiae equestres*, became procurator of Armenia Minor, not earlier than 114, when it was temporarily annexed by Trajan; yet five years later he was prefect of Egypt, after holding four other posts. Ser. Sulpicius Similis (no. 41) was still only a centurion, conceivably a *primus pilus*, in Trajan's reign, perhaps at its very outset in 98; he was prefect in 107; we do not know his intervening employments.[57] (Only Dio's testimony shows that he retired into private life on leaving Egypt and re-emerged as praetorian prefect under Hadrian.) Aeternius Fronto (no. 30) had but 7 years to acquire any experience of civil administration. Much earlier, C. Turranius (no. 7) cannot have had a long career when he became prefect under Augustus at about the age of 35, and Balbillus (no. 23) had had only a decade of service before his prefecture. By contrast the official careers of Ti. Iulius Alexander (no. 26), C. Minicius Italus (no. 39), M. Sempronius Liberalis (no. 52) and L. Volusius Maecianus (no. 54) probably or certainly extended for 25 years or more before their prefectures, though it would be a mere assumption that they were continuously employed by the government throughout. Data are lacking by which we could determine the average tenure of a procuratorship, and the Egyptian Fasti indicate that an individual could hold a post for a term significantly more or less than the average.[58] There is,

---

[56] It seems to me clearly impossible, from the evidence and arguments adduced by Birley o.c. (n. 33), 133 f. and by Pflaum, *Proc. Équ.*, 210 f., to determine even the average age at which men entered the equestrian service. No inference is valid from the senatorial offices to which some were advanced, since we cannot tell if they held such offices at the minimum age. Nor do we know whether men whose age at some point of their career is recorded or calculable were typical, nor whether they had been continuously employed. No doubt ex-centurions had usually had considerable service before promotion to equestrian offices, but *ILS* 2641 does not imply that they could not become *primipili* before the age of 50: 'vix. ann. xlix sanctissime et prope diem consummationis primi pili sui debitum naturae persolvit'—this only shows (*a*) that the primipilate was the apex of a centurion's career; (*b*) that *this* individual was 49, when the commission had been issued but not yet taken up. Moreover, centurions 'ex eq. R.' were surely not alone in starting as officers; others of good family, but below equestrian status, may also have done so. Finally, no ruling could bind the emperor to abstain from authorizing exceptionally rapid promotions.

[57] Similarly Marcius Turbo, still an ordinary centurion in 104/5 at earliest, and not *pp. bis* before 109/10, became praetorian prefect in 119 (Pflaum, no. 94).

[58] Some parallels from Pflaum: no. 71 held 5 procuratorial posts, 103 to 117 at latest; no. 73, after *militiae equ.* 102–6, held 3 other posts before the procuratorship of Mauretania Tingitana, attested in 114; no. 104 held 3 military and 4 procuratorial posts, 106–28; no. 106 bis held 8 civil posts in perhaps 22 years; no. 109 rose from a praetorian tribunate through 5 other posts to be *pr.*

however, no reason to doubt that nearly all prefects of Egypt were well acquainted from the start with the general fiscal arrangements of the empire. Unfortunately, the system in the Nile valley was unique.

The Romans never created a system of taxes uniform throughout the empire; but usually adopted that which they found in each land they annexed.[59] Naturally this did not preclude them from subsequent modifications, but even after Diocletian there were still important differences in the taxation of different provinces.[60] In Egypt they inherited the system the Ptolemies had developed in a land where continuous and centralized supervision of irrigation had always been a necessity and had favoured state control of the economy at every point. No other Hellenistic kingdom is known to have had so complex a system which could have been passed on to Rome. Still less could barbarian peoples have evolved such sophisticated practices. It is therefore not surprising that what evidence we have for imperial taxation outside Egypt mostly reveals points of difference rather than of likeness. It must be admitted that the evidence is remarkably meagre, and that we cannot be sure that we can draw up a complete list of imposts collected in, for instance, Asia and Africa; still it remains inconceivable that the diversification of taxes in Egypt was paralleled elsewhere. The early modifications made even in Egypt in the Principate probably tended to accentuate its peculiarities. Thus publicans had already been subjected to close control by the Ptolemies, which the Roman Republic had never attempted, and which the Caesars were only able to introduce gradually elsewhere; yet it was in Egypt that direct collection by state officials began to replace tax-farming long before it was tried out in any other province, [as it is generally held to have been, but see chapter 17.]

In all provinces the land was the chief source of wealth, and therefore of revenue; in some, taxes (or rents due from public and imperial domains) still took the form of quotas of the crops, or cash equivalents, varying with the quality of the soil and the nature of the products, while in others there was a levy on capital as assessed in periodic censuses, covering both immovable and movable property. But in Egypt there was a running survey of the land, which made it possible to fix rents or taxes due from individual cultivators, | varying

---

ann. in probably 18 years (129–47); no. 114 was Iuridicus 21 years after being Epistrategus; no. 116 was *pr. alae* at latest in 117 and held his third procuratorial post (Asia) in 131–2; no. 138 was praetorian prefect 13/4 years after a praetorian tribunate; no. 180 perhaps embarked on the *militiae eq. c.* 160 and became praetorian prefect in 189. I find it hard to generalize from such evidence.

[59] For a brief survey see A. H. M. Jones, *The Roman Economy* (1974), 161 f.; most of the relevant notes there are mine. [Cf. ch. 15.]

[60] Jones, *Later Roman Empire*, 62–4.

with the legal category and normal productivity of each particular holding; the farmer could claim a reduction, or exemption, in a year in which the Nile floods left land waterlogged, or dry, or sanded, and his claim would be approved or rejected after they had been checked by official inspections (*episkepseis*). Grain was collected in kind, and its storage and movement down to the sea for shipment to Italy was organized and controlled by the state. Payments in money were exacted for garden land and vineyards. Numerous additional levies from the farmers were made in cash or kind under a variety of heads.[61]

A house-to-house census was taken in Egypt every 14 years, and kept up to date in the intervals by declarations of births and deaths; these records enabled the government to collect a poll tax on males between the ages of 14 and perhaps 62, at rates which differed from nome to nome; some classes of the population were exempt, while others paid at reduced tariffs. This poll tax may have resembled those collected in other provinces, but there is no known parallel to the so-called *merismoi*, additional capitation taxes, of which Wallace lists twenty, for instance for the upkeep of dykes; if the peasants were too poor to meet their liabilities, or ran away to escape them (a common occurrence), the deficit was 'apportioned' among their fellow villagers. Craftsmen and traders had to pay special capitation fees, or a percentage on their sales. There were also taxes on domestic animals (of which returns had to be made), on transfers of real property, on market sales; state monopolies, for example of salt and oil, and a host of minor imposts; the state took its cut from every lucrative activity of the subjects. Nothing like this is known elsewhere. There were of course burdens that the subjects sustained in other provinces too: duties on goods entering or leaving the country and internal tolls; the requisitioning for public needs of goods and services; taxes that fell on Roman citizens wherever domiciled; or the fiscal claims to *bona vacantia* and *caduca*, which in Egypt engaged the attention of a special procurator, the Idios Logos.

Publicans were used less than in other provinces; most taxes were collected by paid or liturgical officials recruited within the country. In other provinces the Principate never created this kind of bureaucracy; it looked to the local authorities to collect the direct taxes; this was still the practice preferred after Diocletian had enormously increased the number of civil servants.[62] Thus it must have been the task of, say, the procurator of Syria to see to it that the magistrates and council of Antioch furnished the *tributum* due; Antioch would have entrusted the

---

[61] The most lucid introduction to Ptolemaic and Roman taxation in Egypt remains that in Wilcken, *Gr. Ostraka* i, 130–663, cf. his *Grundz.* 169 ff. Wallace's account of the Roman system was exhaustive in its day.

[62] Jones o.c. (n. 60), 456–9; 727 f.; 749; 760 f.

collection from individuals in its territory to its own *leitourgoi* or publicans. But in Egypt only two or three communities enjoyed the autonomy which Rome allowed not only to cities of the Graeco-Italian type but also to the less urbanized *civitates* in areas such as Gaul. Hence the prefect and his staff had to control for themselves the liturgical system. It was no doubt partly for this purpose that they ordered the registration of all property, together with a statement of any legal claims by which it was burdened, so that it might be known which persons, if nominated to liturgical duties, could give adequate security from their own property for the sums they were liable to pay over to the fisc.[63] Here we have one more illustration of the mass and diversity of records that administration in Egypt required. In 134 the prefect ordained that whenever cash, goods or services were furnished in discharge of obligations to the state, documents should be exchanged to record the transaction between the taxpayer and the functionary (*P. Fay.* 21). (This passion for paper obviously presupposes a degree of literacy among the subjects that must have been uncommon in the more barbarous north.)

All these elaborate arrangements were directed and supervised by the prefect. No doubt his discretion was limited. Aemilius Rectus was rebuked, and apparently recalled, by Tiberius when he dispatched to Rome excessive sums in money or grain contrary to | orders.[64] By contrast, under Nero and Severus prefects authorized novel levies, perhaps on instructions from the emperor, perhaps in the belief which Rectus seems to have erroneously entertained, that an increase in revenue, however procured, would earn imperial favour. Once Nero had fallen, Ti. Iulius Alexander felt free to prohibit such levies for the future.[65] Bassaeus Rufus under Marcus could decrease the assessment of a nome, presumably for capitation taxes, to take account of

---

[63] Reinmuth, 75-7, see esp. Hunt-Edgar, *Select Papyri*, no. 219.

[64] Dio lvii, 10, 5: Αἰμιλίῳ γοῦν Ῥήκτῳ χρήματά ποτε αὐτῷ πλείω παρὰ τὸ τεταγμένον ἐκ τῆς Αἰγύπτου ἧς ἦρχε πέμψαντι ἀντεπέστειλεν ὅτι "κείρεσθαί μου τὰ πρόβατα, ἀλλ' οὐκ ἀποξύρεσθαι βούλομαι."' Wilcken, *Gr. Ostr.* i, 497, and others, infer that the emperor 'fixed, apparently each year, the total sum to be produced from Egypt ... which the prefect could not vary downwards, nor at least under good emperors as in this case upwards'. But though it would have been useful for the emperor to know a year in advance the yield of the Egyptian revenues, and though that of the land taxes and rents could have been roughly estimated on the basis of annual *episkepseis*, some revenues e.g. from customs and sales-taxes, would inevitably have varied; if they proved exceptionally buoyant, the prefect cannot have been forbidden to give the benefit to the Roman treasury, and would hardly have been instructed, in case of a short-fall, to make up τὸ τεταγμένον by additional levies. That phrase can mean 'what is prescribed' rather than 'what is assessed'. Probably Rectus did take credit for keeping up revenues, by unauthorized levies, in a year in which the harvest was poor and the people therefore less able to meet demands of all kinds. cf. n. 66.

[65] Edict of Ti. Iulius Alexander, vv. 4; 45-51; *P. Oxy.* 899; 916.

depopulation or impoverishment.[66] The prefect, again, can hardly have enjoyed the right to grant total or partial exemption to whole categories of persons from taxes or liturgies; yet in practice he alone could interpret the extent and application of the immunities emperors had approved, and maintain them, or let them lapse, when the subordinates engaged in tax collection tried to set them aside, in order to line their own pockets or at least to minimize a liability to the fisc, which they might otherwise incur themselves. To order the annual *episkepseis*, or the house-to-house census, or the registration of property, was a routine operation, but the edict of Mettius Rufus in 89 shows that the instructions his predecessors had given for such registration had not been observed; and similar orders had to be made by many later prefects (n. 63).

Reinmuth somewhat depreciates the arduous nature of the prefect's task by asserting that 'administrative procedure within the country was highly organized, well regulated, and almost self-operating', that the prefect only had 'to exercise a supervisory control' and that 'all of Egypt was much like a modern, well-organized business corporation, the functions of whose executive head consist largely in receiving the well-digested reports prepared by his subordinates from innumerable memoranda, from which he can assure himself that all phases of the organization are functioning properly'. This picture leaves out the frequent occurrence of illegal violence, peculation and graft among those very subordinates at every level. Reinmuth himself remarks, 'that this machine did not operate so successfully at times as it might was not the fault of the machine'.[68] In reality the procedures for copious documentation and checking of accounts were of no avail, unless they were exactly followed and their working closely scrutinized. Constant vigilance was needed to keep the machine working smoothly, with at any rate no more exploitation of the subjects than the system in itself entailed. Efficient supervision meant attention to detail. Hence we find prefects giving orders for the building of a nome archive, making repeated inquiries about the taxable status of two small plots of land, demanding to receive a list of persons owing taxes in a particular village, ordering the formalities to be completed for registration of a new vineyard.[69] We cannot suppose that any prefect acquired exact

---

[66] *BGU* 903; the tax in grain would automatically have fallen, in proportion to the land found to be under water or dry, but in these circumstances difficulties would also have arisen in collection of capitation and other taxes from an impoverished peasantry, and Bassaeus no doubt intended to mitigate the normal effects of the μερισμοὶ ἀνακεχωρηκότων or ἀπόρων (Wallace, 137 ff.). The great plague may explain Bassaeus' measure.

[67] Reinmuth ch. iii, cf. 65 f.

[68] ibid. 127 f.

[69] *SB* 7378 (AD 103); *P. Amh.* 68 verso (Flavian); *P. Teb.* 336 (189–90); *P. Oxy.* 1032 (156).

information on all such matters, but then, as in a modern government department, it was evidently considered an appropriate means of ensuring that all subordinates were performing their duties, if the man to whom all were responsible probed here and there, almost at random, into the working of the administration.[70] Above all, the careful auditing of the accounts by the prefect in person was probably indispensable to the uncovering or discouraging of embezzlement. According to Philo it consumed most of his time (p. 233).

Yet almost every incoming prefect must have been handicapped by his unfamiliarity with the peculiar fiscal system of Egypt, with business that Philo described as so manifold | and complex as scarcely to be mastered by men engaged in it from their earliest manhood (*Flacc.* 3). It is true that Philo also asserts that Flaccus very rapidly acquired such a complete understanding of the work that the 'grammateis', who had been his teachers, soon became his pupils (ibid.), and that he was able to make substantial and necessary improvements in the fiscal administration; only in his last year, in terror of Gaius' displeasure, did he cease to attend to his duties (16 f.) and fall under the dominance of Alexandrian notables (20). But Philo admits that he praises Flaccus' earlier conduct in order to make his later villainy more conspicuous (6 f.), and though Flaccus may have really possessed outstanding quickness and grasp, and have deserved Philo's eulogy, the implication of what Philo says is clear and credible: few prefects could be expected to understand the administration at first, and until they did, the real power rested with *grammateis*—not the other officials of high standing, who were mostly as amateurish as the governors. [What Frontinus said, of the inevitability of an inexperienced administrator being dependent on his experienced subordinates (*de aquis pr.* 2) applied not only to the administration of the Roman aqueducts: it was, and is, universally true.]

Who were these *grammateis*, evidently men whose lives were spent in the fiscal administration of Egypt? We can hardly think of the native *basilikoi grammateis* in the nomes, and still less of the scribes of metropoleis and villages, for though largely occupied in the collection of the revenues as paid servants of the state, they were merely local officials, in no position to instruct a prefect. Philo is evidently alluding to members of the prefect's own staff, but not, as the term *grammateis* shows, either to the soldiers who belonged to his *officium* or to such personal *adiutores* as he might bring with him, men as strange to the province as he was himself.[71] He is surely using a non-technical

[70] [I recall the incessant inquiries sent out daily by Sir Cyril (later Lord) Hurcomb, Director-General of the Ministry of War Transport, in which I served for nearly six years.]

[71] A. von Domaszewski–B. Dobson, *Rangordnung des röm. Heeres*, 28 f.; Lesquier o.c. (n. 35), 117. Pflaum n. 56 is isolated as *adiutor*.

expression—'clerks'—for the freedmen and slaves of Caesar, who staffed fiscal departments in every province.[72] Literary sources rarely mention such lowborn persons, and only a minute proportion of them, in Egypt or in any other province, have left any documentary records of their existence; in particular, we have only a score or two of inscriptions which reveal that they too had careers, rising by merit, favour and seniority in a graded succession of posts; it was also in Rome and Italy rather than in the provinces that members of the *familia Caesaris* were most apt to commemorate themselves.[73] These inscriptions show that in the higher grades freedmen might move from one area or department to another, but it is a reasonable assumption that at lower levels they remained long in the same place,[74] just as private soldiers, unlike some centurions, remained with the same unit. Hence imperial freedmen and slaves could acquire the expertise which came with permanence, and which most higher officials lacked.

Strabo (xvii, 1, 12) says that the prefects, Iuridici and Idioi Logoi were 'attended by freedmen of Caesar and by Oikonomoi, who were entrusted with affairs of more or less importance'. His Oikonomoi are clearly slaves,[75] and can be identified with the *dispensatores* found in every province, 'servi quibus permittitur administratio pecuniae' (Gaius i, 122); they were authorized to receive and pay out moneys on behalf of the state, and the trust reposed in them is indicated by the fact that *vicarii*, slaves who belonged to their *peculium*, had a strong claim to succeed them,[76] when they were manumitted and promoted; evidently they were thought the best persons to choose and train their own successors, for whose good conduct as their assistants they could themselves be held responsible. Above them stood the freedmen, procurators, *tabularii* (accountants), *a commentariis* (registrars) etc. Strabo's language shows that some of these men at least had major responsibilities, especially when we compare his rather slighting reference to the Epistrategi, nomarchs and ethnarchs 'who were thought worthy to superintend matters of no great importance' (xvii, 1, 13). In

---

[72] G. Boulvert, *Esclaves et affranchis impériaux* (1970), offers the best account of their functions, and P. R. C. Weaver, *Familia Caesaris* (1972), Part iii, of their careers, Cf. now Boulvert, *Domestique et fonctionnaire sous le haut-empire rom.* (1974), 111–80. Philo was not thinking of officials like Lampon, who were not employed in the fiscal administration (n. 50).

[73] Weaver 8 f. Of 607 dated documents cited in his App. ii only 11 are papyri.

[74] Weaver pp. 244, 246, 249, 253, 276 f. cites inscriptions which mention more than one post. Of 23 *tabularii* (246 f.) only 1 is recorded to have acted as such in more than one province, of 7 *a commentariis* again only one (249); transfers seem to be fairly often attested in higher grades, and never in lower.

[75] A. Świderek, *Chron. d'Ég.* xlv (1970), 157 f.; *SB* 9248 is decisive. She lists nine known documentary references to Oikonomoi. The edict of Ti. Iulius Alexander, v. 22 illustrates their importance, as well as that of (probably freedmen) procurators.

[76] Weaver o.c. (n. 72), 200–23 (though he does not explain why *vicarii* were thus promoted).

the time of Strabo or Flaccus, freedmen may have occupied posts later | reserved to Equites, but in all periods they, and even the imperial slaves, must have retained considerable power, if only because of their relative permanence. The freedmen may have included the *Eclogistai* who were responsible for assessing what was due from the taxpayers, comparing their actual payments with the assessments and bringing defaulters to court; at least in his edict of 48 (n. 15), the prefect Vergilius Capito directs the royal scribes and the scribes of villages and toparchies to furnish information on the illegal exactions made by soldiers to Basilides, an imperial freedman, who was ὁ ἐπὶ τοῦ λογιστ- ηρίου, and to the *Eclogistai*, over whom he presumably exercised control. Yet these very officials were guilty of malpractices which Ti. Iulius Alexander sought to repress; by various devices, the nature of which is not perfectly clear, they had over-assessed taxes for their own profit; probably they received some proportion of the revenue col- lected.[77] Of course it was not only in Egypt that imperial freedmen and slaves could enrich themselves at the expense of the subjects.[78] Ti. Iulius Alexander probably ordered that in future the Strategi in the nomes were not to accept tax lists from them, unless he had certified them as correct (n. 77); in that case, since he could not have hoped personally to do all their work anew, it must have been his intention to examine specimen lists by a random check. As a native of Alexandria, who had at this time been four years in post, he was better placed than most governors to control his staff effectively. But we may doubt with Chalon (239 f.) if his measures had a lasting effect.

CONCLUSIONS

Before taking office most prefects were unfamiliar with government in Egypt. They were seldom men of long military experience, and still more rarely jurists. They had usually held many financial posts, but this would hardly have prepared them for the peculiar complexities of the assessment and collection of taxes, and the maintenance of the irrigation system, in the Nile valley. Most senior, equestrian, officials in the province were initially (so far as we can tell) no less inexpert in Egyptian administration. Until the prefects had spent some time at

[77] Chalon on the edict of Ti. Iulius Alexander vv. 35–40, 51–9.

[78] It was obviously not by legitimate means that Musicus, 'dispensator ad fiscum Gallicum provinciae Lugdunensis' under Tiberius, acquired the wealth to buy plate for which he needed two *vicarii* as *ab argento* (for a parallel cf. Pliny, *NH* xxxiii 145), or that a *vicarius vilici Aug.* could pay for a *teloneum* in Africa (*CIL* viii, 12314). Cf. Smallwood o.c. (n. 15), 408, and for the late Empire *RE* iii, 1295 f. (Seeck).

their post, they were therefore likely, unless men of exceptional ability, to be largely in the hands of underlings, whether they were administering justice or supervising the finances. But on average they did not hold office for over three full years, less after 180. It may well be that for one year or more in three it was not the prefects who were in real control of the country.

The equestrian officials in the Principate have sometimes been represented as an 'imperial civil service'. This description better fits the freedmen and slaves of Caesar, as most Equites served a military apprenticeship, and many alternated between posts that were civilian and others which were partly or entirely military. Moreover, even their civilian tasks embraced a diversity of judicial and fiscal responsibilities. They had little resemblance to modern civil servants, who are so often experts in the special problems of a single department in which they spend their whole working lives.[79]

Such specialism was alien to Roman traditions. The Republic had evolved the Roman system of civil law and conquered the *orbis terrarum* with annual magistrates, who rarely governed a province for as much as three years; they had been accustomed to dispense justice and to command armies, though neither legal nor military talent usually explains their election. The emperors may be supposed to have paid more regard to proved capacity in choosing men for the highest positions, but jurists with little or no training as soldiers could still be appointed as consular legates on the frontiers,[80] and not many senators, however able, were allowed more than about six years in such commands. Prolonged tenures were probably uncongenial to senatorial opinion: they restricted the opportunities of all but the favoured few. Once the equestrian *cursus* had been established, it tended to follow | the senatorial model: Equites who rose in the service must also have desired the best jobs to go round.

Perhaps this amateurism did not do so much harm in general as modern notions might make us too readily suppose. Caesar and Cromwell did not need to learn the general's art in a long, slow progress from lieutenant to field-marshal. Any shrewd, honest man might dispense justice well enough, especially if he had the advice of professional lawyers, which was, however, not demonstrably available to provincial governors.[81] In most provinces the fiscal system was relatively simple. But government in Egypt was a far more complex affair. For those who would like to think that specialization was

[79] [Cf. now Brunt, *JRS* (1983), 42 ff., esp. 47–52.]

[80] C. Cassius Longinus (*PIR²* C 501), Javolenus Priscus (ib. I, 14), L. Neratius Priscus, Kunkel, o.c. (n. 46), 144 f.; Salvius Iulianus (ibid. 157 f.).

[81] By such advice the praetors must have built up the *ius honorarium*.

increasingly favoured in Roman imperial administration Egypt is the test case. It appears to show that the conception is anachronistic.

APPENDIX: THE PREFECTS OF EGYPT 30 B.C.–A.D. 236

The list that follows is now basically that of G. Bastianini, *ZPE* xvii (1975) 263 ff., cf. xviii (1980) 75 ff.; the dates refer to the times when the men concerned are actually attested in office. The list that appeared on first publication was based on earlier compilations and included criticisms of that given by O. Montevecchi, *La Papirologia* (1973), 129 ff., which are now omitted. For evidence on careers readers are in general referred to Stein, *Präfekten* or to Pflaum and relevant articles in *PIR*[2] and *RE*; documentation is offered only when there is something to be added.

B.C. 30–26	1. C. Cornelius Gallus
	He had commanded an army in Cyrenaica, and bore the title of *praefectus fabrum* of Octavian (*AE* 1964, 253, cf. P. M. Fraser, *Ptolemaic Alexandria* ii (1972), 94).
25–4	2. Aelius Gallus ⎫ See S. Jameson, *JRS* lviii
24–2	3. P. Petronius ⎭ (1968), 71 f. on chronology; she has not convinced me that Petronius was in office before 24. [Cf. *P. Oxy.* 2820; N. Lewis, *GRBS* (1975), 295 ff.]
13/12	4. P. Rubrius Barbarus
7 (8. iii)–4 (4. vi)	5. C. Turranius
	Pr. ann. A.D. 14–48, cf. *RE* vii A, 1441 f.
2/1–A.D. 3 (19.ii)	6. P. Octavius
between A.D. 3 and 10/11	7. P. Ostorius Scapula
	Pr. pr. 2 B.C. (only if Dio is wrong on his praenomen).
	8. Pedo.
	PSI 1149, 5 shows that he preceded Magius Maximus, not that he was his immediate predecessor, any more than v. 13 shows that Octavius(?) immediately preceded Aquila. Stein unduly crowded the Fasti from A.D. 10 to 14 by putting Pedo between Aquila and Maximus; he may even belong to 21–7 B.C.	
10/11	9. C. Iulius Aquila

11/14 (after 29. viii)

10. M. Magius Maximus
    Probably former proc. Tarraconensis, cf. n. 21. J. R. Rea, *Chron. d'Ég.* 1968, 365 ff. shows that the text of Philo, *Flacc.* 74, which appeared to show that he was prefect now for the second time is uncertain. Date: G. Wagner, *Bull. Inst. fr. d'Arch. Orient.* lxx (1971), 21 f.

14

11. Aemilius Rectus

15

12. L. Seius Strabo
    Pr. pr. A.D. 14; probably died in office.

16–31

13. C. Galerius

32

14. Vitrasius Pollio (cf. no. 17)
    14a. The freedman, Hiberus, was acting governor on his death in office.

32–Oct. 38

15. A. Avillius Flaccus

(38

15a. Q̣ Naevius Cordus Sutorius Macro, *pr. pr.*, appointed to succeed him, was put to death before taking office.)

38–9 (?)

16. ... ivius

39–41

17. C. Vitrasius Pollio
    Pflaum no. 5. *Tr. mil., pr. eq.*, proc. of Aquitania and Narbonensis under Tiberius. Less probably, this is the career of no. 14.

41 (10.xi)–42 (29.iv)

18. L. Aemilius Rectus

between 42 and 45

19. M. Heius (*P. Oxy.* 3033)

45 (8.viii)–47

20. C. Iulius Postumus

47–52 (24.iv)

21. Cn. Vergilius Capito
    Proc. of Asia (Pflaum 13 bis).

[21a. M. (?) Mettius Modestus
    Attested as a prefect in Suda E 2004 Adler who bought as a slave Epaphroditus, Nero's later freedman; perhaps proc. Asiae (*AE* 1973, 175) and presumably father of no. 35. Omitted by Bastianini.]

54 (29.iii)

22. L. Lusius Geta
    Pr. pr. A.D. 48.

55–9 (11.x)

23. Ti. Claudius Balbillus
    Pflaum, no. 15, identifying him with the homonymous subject of *AÉ* 1924, 78 (from Ephesus); *pr. fabr.* of Claudius, tribune of leg. xx (perhaps honorary), *ad legationes et resp[onsa Graeca]* (under Claudius), *proc. aedium divi Aug. et. ... [e]t lucorum sacro[rumque omnium qu]ae sunt Alexan[dreae*

et in tota Aegypt]*o et supra museum et ab Alexandria bibliotheca et archiereus et ad Hermen Alexandreon* for some years. His final post should probably be restored as *proc. Asiae.* P. rejects this on the ground that the inscription postdates Claudius' death, while in 54 P. Celer held that post (Tac., *Ann.* xiii, 1). But why not a dedication to Balbillus at Ephesus after he had vacated the Asian post? [But K. Rigby, *BASP* xxii 1985, 279 ff. gives stronger grounds for rejecting the supplement.]

60–62 (23. vii)

24. L. Iulius Vestinus

Appointed to rebuild the Capitol in 70. He had been an *amicus*, probably a procurator, of Claudius.

63 (5.ix)–64 (17.vii)

25. C. Caecina Tuscus

Pflaum, no. 16 bis. Iuridicus, 51–2.

66–69

26. Ti. Iulius Alexander

Pflaum, no. 17; his career is fairly fully, but incompletely, known. Epistrategus, 42. Governor of Judaea, 46–8. 'Minister bello (Corbuloni) datus' (Tac., *Ann.* xv, 28) in 63. Proc. of Syria (Nero) *AE* 1978, 819. *Pr. pr.* with army in Judaea in 70; cf. E. G. Turner, *JRS* xliv (1954), 54 f.

70 (before 27. vii)

27. L. Peducaeus Colo(nus)

71/72–72/3

28. Ti. Iulius Lupus (died in office)

74

29. Valerius (?) Paulinus

Pflaum, no. 40. Probably Praetorian tribune ... procurator of Narbonensis probably in 69. See J. R. Rea on *P. Oxy.* 3279.

75–6

29a. [S]ept[imius?] Nu. ...

78–9

30. C. Aeternius Fronto (*PIR* L 287 for his name)

Praef. castrorum of Egyptian legions at siege of Jerusalem in 70. |

perhaps in 79

31. Iulius Ursus

Previously *pr. annonae*, and later (it would seem) *pr. pr.* perhaps on Titus' accession, and then *cos. suff.* 84. *PIR*[2] I 630 prefers to put all his prefectures under Domitian; so too Bastianini.

80/81–82 (12.ii)

32. C. Tettius Africanus Cassianus Priscus

Previously prefect of *vigiles* and *annona.*

83

33. L. Laberius Maximus

Pflaum, no. 43. He had been (financial) procurator of Judaea in 71, was *praef. annonae* in 80, and became *pr. pr.* about 84.

85 (8.ii)–88 (26.ii)   34. C. Septimius Vegetus
89 (spring?)–91/2   35. M. Mettius Rufus
(after 29.viii 91).

Formerly *pr. ann.* (cf. Pflaum, pp. 119 f.) [presumably son of no. 21a] Date: *BGU* 2057.

92 (14. iii)–93 (7. iv)   36. T. Petronius Secundus

Pr. Pr. in 96 as colleague of Norbanus (36a).

91–2 or 93–3   36a. Norbanus

In *Akten des VI. Int. Kongresses für gr. und lat. Epigraphik* (*Vestigia* xvii), 495 f., G. Winkler correctly (in my view) identified the Norbanus of Martial ix, 84 as a procurator of Raetia and as the praetorian prefect of 96 who joined Petronius in conspiracy against Domitian. He also suggested that it was this man who 'confiscated the property of a freedwoman of an Alexandrian citizen who had born children to an Egyptian (sc. on her death), whereas Rufus gave it to the children' (*Gnomon* 50), and supposed Norbanus to have been prefect; Rufus would then naturally be no. 37; it would be plausible that a prefect under Nerva reversed a harsh rule for augmenting fiscal profits that had been introduced by one under Domitian. However, the proem of the Gnomon shows that it was based on rulings by Idioi Logoi as well as by prefects, and Pardalas, named in 23, was Idios Logos under Hadrian. Balogh and Pflaum (n. 47) had identified the Norbanus of the *Gnomon* with an Idios Logos so named under Nero, when severe fiscal exactions would also be expected. There is also little room for Norbanus as prefect after 89, only part of the year beginning Aug. 91, and part of 93/4. Yet cf. p. 220 on the possibility of a rapid turnover of prefects under Domitian. It might be supposed that Domitian was prompt to promote an officer who had displayed signal loyalty in 89, perhaps in succession to no. 35 who was removed as a political suspect, but then soon felt the need to place him in command of the praetorians. Cf. no. 59. [Bastianini omits Norbanus.]

94(1. vii)–98 (24.vi)   37. M. Iunius Rufus

98 (4. ix)–100 (14.ii)   38. C. Pompeius Planta
   Probably proc. of Lycia in 75 or 76 (Pflaum, no. 58).

100/101–3 (19.v)   39. Minicius Italus
   Pflaum, no. 59. Five equestrian military posts in Lower Germany, at least the last under Vespasian, proc. of the provincia Hellespontus, proc. of Asia where he acted as governor on the death of the proconsul, probably in 88, proc. of Lugdunensis, Aquitania and Lactora, *pr. ann.*

103 (30.viii)–107 (26.iii)   40. C. Vibius Maximus
   Pflaum, no. 65, cf. A. N. Sherwin-White, *Letters of Pliny*, 210. He had apparently been prefect of an *ala* in Syria and in 95 *proc. Dalmatiae*, thereafter, perhaps, *pr. vig.* and *annonae* (R. Syme, *Historia* vi (1957), 480 ff.). He appears to have been condemned for maladministration. Cf. n. 13.

107–112 (21.iii)   41. Ser. Sulpicius Similis
   A centurion, perhaps *primipilus*, as late as Trajan's reign. He was *pr. ann.* before and *pr. pr.* after governing Egypt, retiring in 119.

113 (28.i)–117 (5.i)   42. M. Rutilius Lupus
   Attested as *pr. ann.* at a date between 103 and 111.

117 (Aug.)–119 (May)   43. Q. Rammius Martialis
   Pr. vig. 111 and 113. |

120–124 (10. vii)   44. T. Haterius Nepos
   Pflaum, no. 95. Prefect of cohort, tribune of soldiers, prefect of *ala* (all unspecified), *censitor* of British tribes, proc. of Armenia maior (not earlier than May 114 or later than spring 117, probably 114–15), *proc. ludi magni*, *proc. hered. et a censibus*, *a libellis*, prefect of the *vigiles*. Date: J. R. Rea, *Chron. d'Ég.* xliii (1968), 367 f. See no. 71

126 (20.iii)–133 (spring) 45. T. Flavius Titianus
Pflaum, no. 99 identifies him with a man of the same name whose partially preserved career records procuratorship of Galatia-Pontus, the patrimonium and Lugdunensis and Aquitania and no. 57 with the homonymous procurator of Noricum; this is not certain.

133 (11.xi)–137 (26.v) 46. M. Petronius Mamertinus
Pr. pr. at least in 139–43.

137 (before 8.ix)–142 (18.ii) 47. C. Avidius Heliodorus
Pflaum, no. 106. Previously *ab ep. Gr.*

142 (18.vii)–143 (11.ii) 48c. Valerius Eudaemon
Pflaum, no. 110. Proc. *ad dioicesin Alexandreae*, librarian at Rome, *ab ep. Gr.*, proc. of Lycia etc., *proc. hered.*, and probably at the same time proc. of Asia, proc. of Syria. It is not known what posts he held between this and his prefecture.

144 (12.v)–147 (April) 49. L. Valerius Proculus
Pflaum, no. 113. Prefect of a cohort in Syria and of a legion in Lower Moesia, prefect of the Alexandrian fleet and of the 'potamophylacia', proc. of the Maritime Alps, *dilectator*, proc. successively of Baetica, Cappadocia etc., Asia and of 'three provinces' (the names are lost), perhaps a *rationibus, pr. ann.* (attested in 144).

147 (29.viii)–148 (11.xi) 50. M. Petronius Honoratus
Pflaum, no. 117. *Pr. coh.* and *tr. mil.* in Lower Germany, *pr. alae* in Mauretania Caesariensis, proc. successively of the mint, of the XX *hered.*, of Belgica and the two Germanies, *a rat., pr. ann.*

150 (17.iv)–154 (2.iii) 51. L. Munatius Felix
Date: *P. Oxy,* 2961.

154 (29.viii)–159 (Jan.) 52. M. Sempronius Liberalis
Probably *pr. alae* in Mauretania Tingitana, between 120 and 132 (Pflaum, p. 251).

159 (10.vii)–160 (28.ix) 53. T. Furius Victorinus
Pflaum, no. 139. *Pr. coh.* in Britain, *tr. mil.* in Lower Pannonia, *pr. alae* in Dacia, proc. in Gaul and then in Spain (the details are doubtful), *proc. ludi magni,* prefect first of the Ravenna and then of

the Misenum fleet, *a rat.*, *pr. ann.* He left Egypt to become *pr. pr.*

161 (13.ii–15.xi)

54. L. Volusius Maecianus
Pflaum, no. 141, cf. W. Kunkel, *Herkunft u. soziale Stellung der röm. Juristen*[2], 174 f. *Pr. fabr.*, *pr. coh.* in Britain, *adiutor operum publ.*, *a libellis* to Pius as Caesar (138), *pr. vehic.*, *a studiis* and librarian, *a libellis et censibus*, *pr. ann.* After leaving Egypt, he entered the senate and became *praef. aer. Sat.* and consul, cf. nos. 61, 62, 76, 85.

161 (11 Dec.)/162–164 (2.iii)

56. M. Annius Syriacus.
Date: *BGU* 2058.

164 (Aug.)–167 (24.vi)

57. T. Flavius Titianus
Pflaum, no. 154 identifies him with a governor of Noricum (before 161), see on no. 45.

167 (Aug.)–168 (21.ii)

58. Q. Baienus Blassianus
Pflaum, no. 126, cf. p. 974; F. Zevi, *Acts of Vth Epigraphic Congress* (1967), 193 f. He was prefect of the cohors II Asturorum—one unit so named was in Egypt, another in Britain—tribune of a legion in Upper Moesia, *pr. alae* probably in Cappadocia, where he was then *proc. ad. census*. He then became successively prefect of the fleet in Britain, governor of Mauretania Tingitana and Raetia, prefect of the Ravenna fleet, *proc. Lugd. et Aquitan.*, *pr. ann.* No doubt he died in Egypt. Date: A. Świderek, *Proc. of XIIth Intern. Congress of Papyrol.* (1970), 461 f. [From July/Aug. 167, Bastianini o.c., 297.] |

168 (3.viii)–169 (3.iv)

59. M. Bassaeus Rufus
Pflaum, no. 162. A poor rustic (Dio lxxi, 5), who had presumably risen from the ranks of the army, to be *pp. bis.* After the urban tribunates he became proc. of Asturia and Gallaecia, of Noricum, of Belgica and the two Germanies, *a rat.*, *pr. vig.* (an office he held still on 10 March 168) and left Egypt to be *pr. pr.* from 169 until at least 176.

169 (4.viii)–175 (not later than 24.v)

60. C. Calvisius Statianus
   Pflaum, no. 166. He had been *ab. ep. Lat.* within the years 161–9. His son was Idios Logos before 173 and presumably under him.

176

60a. On 1 April C. Caecilius Salvianus, Iuridicus, is acting governor. Calvisius had taken part in Avidius Cassius' revolt.

176–179 (11.iii)

61. T. Pactumeius Magnus
   Probably consul in 183, cf. no. 54.

178–80

62. T. Aius (? Taius) Sanctus
   Pflaum, pp. 1002 ff.; on the *nomen*, see J. R. Rea, *P. Oxy.* xxxvi, p. 41. *Ab ep. Gr., proc. rat. priv., a rat.* After leaving Egypt, he entered the senate and became *praef. aer.* and consul, cf. no. 54.

180–1 (before 14.x 181)

63. T. Flavius Piso
   W. Seston, *Chron. d'Ég.* xlviii (1973), 152 f. Present at Marcus' *consilium,* 177. *Pr. ann.* 179.

181 (4.vii)–183 (May)

64. D. Veturius Macrinus
   Pflaum, no. 179 bis. *Proc.* of Mauretania Tingitana on 13 Oct. 180. He was to become *pr. pr.* under Didius Iulianus. Date: *BGU* 847.

185 (Jan.–Oct.)

65. T. Longaeus Rufus
   He became *pr. pr.* under Commodus. Date: *P. Petaus* 9.

186 (1.i)–187 (Sept.)

66. Pomponius Faustinianus

188 (9.i–12.viii)

67. M. Aurelius Verianus, cf. note on 68.

188

68. M. Aurelius Papirius Dionysius
   Pflaum, no. 181. Legal *consiliarius* at 60,000, then at 100,000 HS under Marcus, *pr. vehic.* etc., probably 178–80, *a libellis et cognitionibus* of Commodus, *pr. ann.* Apparently recalled from Egypt to resume that post and was then put to death in 189. Attested as prefect in 188 (*P. Oxy.* 1110), but *P. Oxy.* 2762 (cf. J. R. Rea ad loc.) and 2800, which in themselves would suggest that no. 69 was the immediate successor of no. 67, indicate that his tenure was very brief.

189 (23.viii)–190 (28.viii)

69. Tineius Demetrius
   Cf. note on no. 68. Date: *P. Oxy.* 2968.

190 (25.ix)

70. Claudius Lucilianus? (but see Bastianini, *ZPE* xxxviii. 84)

Under Commodus?

	71. Petronius Quadratus
	Perhaps identical with Quadratus, *proc. Achaeae*, 179–80 (*Hesperia* ii, 167). [But not if Bastianini 284 rightly places his prefecture between nos. 44 and 45.]
192/3 (before 8.iv 192)	72. Larcius Memor |
193 (6.iii)–194 (21.iv)	73. L. Mantennius Sabinus
	An ex-tribune of the praetorians.
195 (11.iv)–196 (25.ii)	74. M. Ulpius Primianus
197 (1.ii)–199 (2.iii)	75. Q. Aemilius Saturninus
	Later *pr. pr.*
200 (13.v)–203 (25.ii)	76. Q. Maecius Laetus
	Pflaum, no. 219. Formerly proc. of Arabia. *Pr. pr.* in 205. *Cos.* II and *pr. urbi* under Caracalla. Cf. no. 54.
204 (Nov.)–205/6	77. Claudius Iulianus
	Pr. ann. 201 (*IGR* i 380; *ILS* 1346). Date: *BGU* 2024.
206 (Oct./Nov.)–210 (23.vii)	78. Ti. Claudius Subatianus Aquila.
	[Previously the first *praef. Mesopotamiae* under Severus (*Anat. St.* 1977, 191 f.), and not, as has been supposed, the Epistrategus of 169 (*P. Oxy.* 2708), who was probably his father (D. L. Kennedy, *ZPE* xxxvi (1979), 255 ff.).]
212–213 (29.i–Nov.)	79. L. Baebius Aurelius Iuncinus
	Pflaum, no. 251. No military posts, but after subordinate offices at Rome, *pr. vehic.*, governor of Sardinia, probably before Caracalla became joint Augustus in Jan. 198, *proc. hered.* His later posts are not known. Date: *BGU* 2056.
215 (March–Nov.)	80. Aurelius Septimius Heraclitus
	Probably killed in office.
215/6	80a. Aurelius Antinous, probably Iuridicus, is acting prefect.
216 (5.vi)–217 (7.iii)	81. L. Valerius Datus
	Executed by Macrinus.
218	82. Iulius Basilianus
219?	82a. Callistianus [[executed after Macrinus' fall]], Iuridicus, is attested as acting prefect, *P. Oxy.* 3117.
219 (13.viii)–220 (4.iii)	83. Geminius Chrestus
	Pr. pr. in March 222.
222 (6.i)	84. L. Domitius Honoratus
	Pr. pr. in 223.

222 (3.xi)–223 (early)	85. M. Aedinius Iulianus
	Pflaum, no. 297. By 223 he was a senator, later *pr. pr.* Pflaum's view that he was acting governor of Lugdunensis, when procurator there before 222, is disputable.
223/4 (?)	86. ... alerius
224	87. M. Aurelius Epagathus [a freedman; cf. Dio LXXVII 21, 2, LXXX 2]. Cf. *P. Oxy.* 2565: *JRS* 1976 p. 155.
225 (12.i)	87a. Ti. Claudius Herennianus was Iuridicus and acting prefect.
229/30	88. Claudius Masculinus
231/2 (Dec./Jan.)–236 (20.xi)	89. Maevius Honoratianus
	Date: X. Loriot. *Zeitschr. f. Pap. u. Epigr.* xi (1973), 147 f.

Did Imperial Rome Disarm
her Subjects?

In his *Roman Social Relations 50 B.C.-A.D. 284* (New Haven and London 1974) Professor Ramsay Macmullen presents a sombre picture of the condition of the lower orders in the Roman empire, which in general appears to me to represent the truth only too well. But among the many suggestions he throws out which provoke reflection, at least one may challenge dissent. In his sketch of Roman taxation he urges that the resistance movements it caused 'reveal in rough outline a common pattern of desperation: first, initial conquest by the Romans; next, the rapid confiscation of all hidden weapons'; and then assessments and 'recurrent spasms of protest against the weight of tribute harshly calculated and still more harshly exacted'. His belief that even in the early empire taxation was heavier than is commonly assumed seems to me justifiable, but that is not my subject here. Is it right that disarmament, indeed rapid disarmament, was normally the first act of the conquerors as a prelude to taxation? Macmullen founds this claim on (a) a few texts relating to the disarmament of particular peoples and (b) an interpretation of the law or laws *de vi*, which in his judgement show that disarmament was universal.[1] By implication, it was also permanent. There is perhaps some risk that this view will gain credit, unless rebutted. A fuller survey of the evidence suggests to me that disarmament was far from normal and, where attempted, without lasting effect.

(a) Macmullen cites a statement of Strabo that 'the Gauls had laid down their arms and were now compelled to practise the arts of cultivation'.[2] But these words, taken along with other passages

---

[1] 35, with n. 26. Macmullen goes on to contrast the prosperity of the 'cities' with 'the less happy rural world.' But he can hardly mean that only rural dwellers paid taxes (which would be false) and were disarmed; cf. his argument under (b).

[2] οἱ δ' ἄνδρες μαχηταὶ μᾶλλον ἢ γεωργοί. νῦν δ' ἀναγκάζονται γεωργεῖν, καταθέμενοι τὰ ὅπλα, 4.1.2 Cf. 4.1.5 on Massilia's neighbours: ἐξημερουμένων δ' ἀεὶ τῶν ὑπερκειμένων βαρβάρων, καὶ ἀντὶ τοῦ πολεμεῖν τετραμμένων ἤδη πρὸς πολιτείας καὶ γεωργίας διὰ τὴν τῶν Ῥωμαίων ἐπικράτειαν; 4.1.11 on the Cavari and neighbouring peoples, who are no longer 'barbarians' but are mostly Romanized

---

Phoenix, 29 (1975), 260–70.

in which Strabo cele|brates the civilizing effect of the Roman peace, need mean only that the conversion of the Gauls to agricultural pursuits was a necessary consequence of that peace, not that they had been forcibly disarmed; there is abundant proof that they had not (*infra*). Macmullen also adduces two references in Dio to the disarmament of defeated enemies of Rome by Tiberius under Augustus in Pannonia[3] and by Claudius in Britain,[4] and Tacitus' report that Ostorius Scapula took away arms from Britons who were suspected of hostility to Rome.[5] Such testimony merely shows the procedure Rome might follow with peoples whose submission was not assured: it need not have been part of 'a common pattern'. At the same time as he disarmed the hostile Pannonians, Tiberius 'sold most of the men of military age into slavery outside the province'; clearly this was not the way in which Rome regularly treated the conquered. Moreover, Tiberius had been aided in his victory by the Scordisci, who were equipped in the same way as the enemy, likewise dwelt in Pannonia, and were obviously not rewarded for their services by being disarmed. Finally, Macmullen invokes the order made by the prefect of Egypt, Avillius Flaccus, apparently in A.D. 34–5, for the confiscation of arms in Upper Egypt, an order perhaps prompted by apprehension he had felt on a recent visit to the district.[6] According to Philo, a large fleet was required to transport the weapons found down the Nile. If 'the rapid confiscation of all hidden weapons' had been ordered after the conquest, over sixty years earlier, the effect had not been permanent. Philo tells us that Flaccus' measure was justified by suspicion that they would revolt, 'as they had done on many past occasions', presumably with some sort of arms. Here again it is refractory subjects who are disarmed, and a general prohibition on subjects retaining arms cannot legitimately be deduced.

---

in language, in modes of life and sometimes in institutions; 4.1.14 on the Gauls of Narbonensis generally, who nowadays ἄγοντες σχολὴν ἀπὸ τῶν ὅπλων ἐργάζονται τὴν χώραν ἐπιμελῶς καὶ τοὺς βίους κατασκευάζονται πολιτικούς. The parallel texts show that Strabo is thinking of a natural process of civilization resulting from peace (for converse process cf. 3.3.5). Cf. also his account of a similar development in parts of Spain; 3.2.15; 3.3.8 Admittedly this had not gone so far in Gallia Comata, though even there παραπεισθέντες ... εὐμαρῶς ἐνδιδόασι πρὸς τὸ χρήσιμον, ὥστε καὶ παιδείας ἅπτεσθαι καὶ λόγων (4.4.2).

³ Dio 54.31.3 (12 BC): καὶ σφᾶς ὁ Τιβέριος, πολλὰ μὲν τῆς χώρας πορθήσας πολλὰ δὲ καὶ τοὺς ἀνθρώπους κακώσας, ἐχειρώσατο, τοῖς Σκορδίσκοις (cf. Fluss, *RE* IIA [1921] 831 ff.), ὁμόροις τε αὐτῶν καὶ ὁμοσκεύοις οὖσι, συμμάχοις ὅτι μάλιστα χρησάμενος, καὶ τά τε ὅπλα σφῶν ἀφείλετο καὶ τῆς ἡλικίας τὸ πλεῖον ἐπ' ἐξαγωγῇ ἀπέδοτο.

⁴ 60.21.4 f. (AD 43): κἀκ τούτου συχνοὺς τοὺς μὲν ὁμολογίᾳ τοὺς δὲ καὶ βίᾳ προσαγαγόμενος ... καὶ τὰ ὅπλα αὐτῶν ἀφελόμενος ...

⁵ 12.31.2 (47–51): *detrahere arma suspectis ... parat.*

⁶ Philo *in Flaccum* 92 f., dated by a fragmentary letter of Flaccus, quoted and discussed by H. Box *ad loc.*

It is curious that Macmullen has not mentioned the search for arms that Flaccus also carried out in the houses of Jews at Alexandria. Philo alleges that none were discovered, but clearly implies that it would have been criminal for the Jews to have been found in possession of either weapons or defensive armour.[7] Flaccus' suspicions were perhaps not unwarranted. The Alexandrian Jews were able to arm themselves a few | years later, and in 66 they again appear to have possessed arms.[8] Of course this is no proof that they were entitled to do so. But once again it does not follow that a prohibition operative in the turbulent city of Alexandria had universal applicability. Two legions were quartered close to that city, to maintain order, a precaution unique in the empire.

(b) Before reviewing some other evidence relevant to particular provinces, I may now turn to Macmullen's argument that there was a universal rule for disarmament. He finds it in a provision of the Julian law *de vi*. He cites a fragment of Marcianus, writing in the early third century, *Dig.* 48.6.1: *Lege Iulia de vi publica tenetur, qui arma tela domi suae agrove inve villa praeter usum venationis vel itineris vel navigationis coegerit*. In section 3 of the same title Marcianus also says: *in eadem causa sunt, qui turbae seditionisve faciendae consilium inierint servosve aut liberos homines in armis habuerint. Eadem lege tenetur, qui pubes cum telo in publico fuerit*. Now in the first fragment Marcianus attests that it was an offence not to possess arms but only to collect or accumulate them (*'coegerit'*). Moreover, he admits certain exceptions. The list given in the fragment is not exhaustive. For instance, the *saltuarii* whom great landowners employed to protect their estates must surely have been armed, and legitimately.[9] However this may be, Scaevola (*h.t.* 2) explicitly attests two other exceptions: *Excipiuntur autem arma, quae quis promercii causa habuerit hereditateve ei obvenerint*. Both are of some significance. The first allows a trader in arms to possess a store of them. But there could be no true disarmament of subjects if they were free to sell (and presumably to manufacture) arms.[10] The second absolves any person of criminal liability if the store of arms in his possession came to him by inheritance; evidently, the fact that he had not himself accumulated

---

[7] *Ibid.* 86–91; 94–6.

[8] Jos. *AJ* 19.278; *BJ* 2.487 ff.; note 495: τοὺς ἄμεινον ὡπλισμένους.

[9] M. Rostowzew, *Philologus* 18 (N.S.) (1905) 297–307. There is not, I think, any explicit testimony that on private domains they were armed, but common sense demands it.

[10] Macmullen himself collected evidence on arms-traders in the Principate (*AJA* 64 [1960] 24–40); cf. A. H. M. Jones, *The Later Roman Empire* (Oxford, 1964) 66, for state arms factories established by Diocletian; however, it was Justinian who made the manufacture a state monopoly, and forbade private citizens to make or sell arms (*ib.* 671; cf. *Novellae* 85.3). *ILS* 7047 = *CIL* 13.2828 (probably third century) shows that Aeduan "*opifices loricarii*" worked "*sub cura*" of a centurion; he may only have determined standards and specifications.

them was construed to show that he had no criminal intent in possessing them. Likewise there was no such intent if the arms had been amassed for the use of the owner in hunting (cf. Ulpian *h.t.* 10 pr.) or for his protection on journeys by land and sea. Indeed it must be doubted if the law absolutely forbade the carrying of arms in public, since Ulpian (*h.t.* 10 pr.) is reported as saying that it was an offence under the law to | be armed *dolo malo in contione . . . aut ubi iudicium publice exercebitur*, and it is hard to see why these specific locations should be named at all, if the mere carriage of arms in public was criminal *per se.* Similarly under the *lex Cornelia de sicariis* it was an offence to go about armed *hominis occidendi furtive faciendi causa* (*Dig.* 48.8.1 pr.); here again what made the bearing of a weapon criminal was intent, *dolus malus.*

What then was the criminal intent that the Julian legislation *de vi* was concerned with? (For our purpose it does not matter if there was one law, or two covering *vis publica* and *vis privata* separately, or whether the legislation was the work of Caesar or Augustus.) In the first place, the mere fact that there was a *lex rogata* shows that it was originally designed to apply to citizens in Italy; provincials could have been restrained by the *imperium* of governors, and edicts would have been sufficient. No doubt the inclusion of the rules in the imperial codes indicates that at some stage the law, like other such statutes, became applicable to all Rome's subjects, but it cannot have been its original purpose to repress revolts against Rome. Obviously the Julian legislation superseded, and extended, the *lex Plautia* which had been in force in Rome and Italy during Cicero's lifetime. That law does indeed seem to have been intended to repress seditious violence which threatened public order and the proper working of republican institutions, but even a Catiline or a Clodius was not attacking the rule of Rome. Moreover numerous juristic statements cited under the rubric of the Julian legislation *de vi* show that it had also become the object of that legislation, to some extent perhaps as a result of later development and interpretation, to restrain the use of violence for private rapine. In general, so far as they are known, the rules relate mainly to disturbances of the peace, never to actual or incipient revolts against Roman power.[11] No one has shown more graphically than Macmullen the continuing need for repression of such violence or the inadequacy of

[11] Cf. generally M. Balzarini, *Ricerche in Tema di Danno Violento e Rapina nel Diritto Romano* (Padua 1969) 181 ff., esp. 192 ff. with bibliography; for relevant conditions in Italy before Augustus see A. W. Lintott, *Violence in Republican Rome* (Oxford 1968); P. A. Brunt, *Italian Manpower 225 B.C.–A.D. 14* (Oxford 1971) Appendix 8. Cf. *Dig.* 48.6 and 7 *passim*; *CJ* 9.12; *CTh* 9.10; Paulus *Sent.* 5.26; *Inst.* 4.18.8. The provisions of the legislation are conveniently arranged under rubrics in S. Riccobono, *Acta Divi Augusti*, 1945, 129 ff.; they include sanctions against breach of *provocatio* and imposition of new *vectigalia* (sc. by Roman officials, not by subjects), as well as breaches of the peace.

the measures taken.[12] But rebellion was a more serious matter, and was naturally dealt with under the provisions of the law *de maiestate*.[13] Yet | even what is known of that law does not include any express prohibition on the possession of arms.[14]

In any event the possession of military equipment by such individuals as could afford to purchase it was less potentially dangerous to Rome than the existence of stores of arms at the disposal of subject communities, whose local governments were best able to organize a formidable revolt. Yet such stores of arms under local control undoubtedly existed.

The persistence of violence must have made it actually desirable for loyal local governments to have armed men at their disposal, especially in the vast areas where no Roman troops, except perhaps for a few scattered *stationarii*,[15] were quartered. It is hard to believe that the existence of armed police forces, like the *diogmitae*[16] in some parts of Asia Minor, was confined to *civitates*, where they happen to be attested, or where there were special magistrates appointed to keep the peace (irenarchs, *praefecti arcendis latrociniis*, and the like). Although Vienna is not one of those *civitates*, it certainly possessed a stock of arms in 69, which it was forced to surrender to the Vitellians (Tac. *Hist.* 1.66.1). Admittedly, Vienna was no ordinary subject city but a titular Roman colony. The Aedui too, whose *electa iuventus*, with some assistance from the Vitellian troops, put down a popular rising led by Mariccus (*ib.* 2.61), were conceivably privileged as allies and 'brothers' of the Roman people (*Ann.* 11.25.1). But the need for some kind of local militia or police subsisted everywhere, and there was no good reason for Rome to impose disarmament on any subject communities whose local governments could be counted on to show fidelity.

It is indeed quite clear that throughout Spain and Gaul communities as such were not disarmed. In A.D. 15 *ad supplenda exercitus damna certavere Galliae Hispaniae Italia, quod cuique promptum, arma equos aurum offerentes. quorum laudato studio Germanicus, armis modo et equis ad bellum sumptis, propria pecunia militem invit* (Tac. *Ann.* 1.71). I take '*Galliae Hispaniae*' to

---

[12] Chs. 1 and 2. Cf. also his *Enemies of the Roman Order* (Cambridge, Mass. 1966) 255 ff. on brigandage.

[13] Paulus *Sent.* 5.29.1: *lege Iulia maiestatis tenetur is, cuius ope consilio adversus imperatorem vel rem publicam arma mota sunt.* Cf. *Dig.* 48.4.1.1.

[14] I doubt if it is significant that in the summary of, or excerpts from, juristic accounts of the tasks of provincial governors (esp. *Dig.* 1 16 and 18) there is no mention of a specific duty to seize arms in private hands, though it is stressed that he must maintain order.

[15] On state and municipal police forces see O. Hirschfeld, *Kl. Schr.* 576–645 (= *S B Berl* 1891, 845 ff.; 1892, 815 ff.; 1893, 421 ff.).

[16] Amm. 27.9.6 (368) calls them *semiermes*, cf. perhaps *H A Marc.* 21.7 (*armavit et diogmitas*), but for 'their usual arms' cf. *Mart. Polycarpi* 7.

be a comprehensive term for the *civitates* in the Gallic and Spanish provinces. For Gaul there is still further evidence.

Tacitus' account of the Gallic uprising under Tiberius is relevant. An initial revolt among the Turoni was easily repressed by Roman troops with some help from '*Galliarum primores*', including Sacrovir, its secret | instigator; these men were certainly armed (*Ann.* 3.41). Next, Florus raised a rebellion among the Treveri; *aliud vulgus obaeratorum aut clientium arma cepit* (*ib.* 42). To judge from what follows, Florus' adherents may not have possessed proper weapons and armour, for we hear that among the Aedui Sacrovir had had 'legionary' arms manufactured secretly, and even so had not enough to equip more than a fifth of his 40,000 followers; the rest had to make do with hunting spears and knives; they also included a few gladiators (*ib.* 43). It cannot, however, be inferred that the production or possession of arms was forbidden to the *civitas Aeduorum*, then any more than in 69 (*supra*). It was not the *civitas* through its local government that planned the revolt; Sacrovir seized on the capital, Augustodunum, precisely with the object of securing the persons of the children of the ruling class, who were at school there, and forcing their fathers to join his cause; but since the Aedui still preserved their privileges under Claudius (*supra*), the Roman government must have absolved them of complicity. Of course, even in the absence of a Roman prohibition on the manufacture or possession of arms, it would have been taken as proof of treason if a private person had openly ordered equipment for 8,000 soldiers.

Again it would be extremely hard to believe that the forces with which Vindex besieged Vesontio and faced the Rhine legions were wholly armed with hunting or agricultural implements, the kind of '*vilia arma*' possessed by the peasantry of Albintimilium (Tac. *Hist.* 2.13.1), who were Roman citizens and virtually defenceless, not because they had been disarmed, but because they were poor (*inopes*) and could not have expected any occasion to arise on which they would need weapons of war. Vindex had mustered his army rapidly, obviously with the co-operation of the *civitates*. He was indeed easily defeated, but that was natural in any event, since his men were untrained. In the same way the Helvetii could offer no effective resistance to the Vitellians, but they were certainly not disarmed; they manned a fort with their own militia (*Hist.* 1.67), and if they lacked military training and fighting spirit, we can contrast their neighbours, *ipsorum Raetorum iuventus, sueta armis et more militiae exercita* (*ib.* 68). In the Maritime Alps (2.12.3) and in Noricum (3.5.2) the *iuventus* could similarly be called up for local defence; in the former case again want of practice and discipline, not of arms, made them useless against regular troops.[17]

Tacitus' account of the story of the *imperium Galliarum* in 70 also fails | to hint that the Gallic *civitates* were disarmed. He does not make Vocula discount the danger of the rebellion on the ground that the Gauls simply had not the equipment to fight (*Hist.* 4.58), nor was this argument, which might have been decisive by itself, if it had been founded in fact, deployed by the Remi in preferring *pax* to *libertas* (69 cf. 67.2). A 'tumultuary band' of the Baetasii, Tungri, and Nervii, which at first resisted the insurgents, was armed with swords (66). The Lingones invaded Sequanian territory and were defeated in battle (67). The *plebs* of the Treveri cast away their arms only after they had been routed by Roman cohorts (70.4), but a large band remained in the field and were able to assail the legions with missiles, though in hand to hand encounter they were soon overcome (71.4 f.). Once again, it is evident that raw provincial levies were no match for regular troops but also that the Gauls were not at the mercy of the Romans, simply because they had not the arms to fight with.

No doubt it is highly relevant that the emperor Claudius was convinced of the loyalty of the Gauls, proven, he alleged with some exaggeration, by the experience even in crises of a whole century (*ILS* 212, 2.33 ff.). Equally no apprehensions could be felt about the submissiveness of African cities. Hence in the anarchy of 69–70 Oea and Lepcis could fight a private war; admittedly the Lepcitani were no match for the wild and unsubdued Garamantes, whose assistance Oea invoked (Tac. *Hist.* 4.50.4). The government could hardly have been as sanguine about the docility of some other provincials. In A.D. 36, a tribe in Cappadocia, annexed nineteen years before, revolted and its men took to the hills; it is unlikely that they were unarmed (*Ann.* 6.41). The very same tribe gave more trouble in 52 (12.55). So too in Britain, whether or not Claudius' measures in 43 and those later taken by Ostorius Scapula (nn. 4 and 5) betoken that the government's policy was one of systematic disarmament, not only the Iceni, who (it could be argued) had not been affected by such measures, as they had been ruled by their own 'king,' but the Trinovantes and other peoples 'not yet broken to slavery' were able to take arms under Nero (14.31.2) and to rout a Roman legion (14.32). There was still danger of revolt from *homines dispersi ac rudes eoque in bello faciles* in the 70s, and Agricola's plan was not to deprive the Britons of weapons for war but to seduce them

---

[17] The peasants who took part in the African rising under Maximin were armed with clubs and axes, Hdn. 7.4.3. Men of the better classes concealed daggers under the clothes, to assassinate the procurator, but they also possessed swords (7.4.5 and 7.5.3).

with the pleasures of peace (*Agr.* 21). Sporadically attempted, disarmament had proved ineffective as a means of pacification. Indeed the very frequency with which at all times brigandage is attested in certain areas shows how impossible it was for the government to deny to its most refractory subjects the use of arms.

Judaea is a case in point, well documented thanks to the survival of Josephus' works. The Roman administration was continuously plagued by the *sicarii*; they carried daggers under their clothes, whence it might reasonably be inferred that it was an offence in that province to bear arms | openly.[18] Josephus does make king Agrippa argue against revolt, as no one seems to have argued in Gaul, by alluding to the Jews' lack of arms (*BJ* 2.361); the point is not stressed (one phrase in a long speech), and would have been valid, even if the Jews were not totally unarmed, since the relative superiority of the Romans was enormous. The rebels in 66 were able to equip themselves in part at least by breaking into Herod's armoury at Masada (2.434, cf. 7.299), which had been held by a Roman garrison (2.408), and with the arms of Roman troops massacred at Jerusalem (cf. 2.450) or captured in Cestius' defeat (554 f.); only then did they proceed to manufacture missiles and suits of armour (649); previously they had had to rely primarily on missiles (542 ff.), of which, however, there seems to have been no shortage.

Indeed, at all stages in the fighting, we hear most of their use of missiles (cf. for instance 4.424). However, it may be noted that they had been able to charge Cestius' army and actually to break its ranks (2.517); this indicates that they were already not totally unequipped with swords or spears. Probably, these weapons were more readily available in rural areas than at Jerusalem itself; according to Josephus' *Vita* (28) the magnates at Jerusalem were afraid that their unarmed supporters would be no match for the 'brigands and revolutionaries' of Galilee, who had an abundance of weapons, if they were to come up to the city, and in the later struggle of Ananus' followers against the Zealots and Idumaeans, the former, though more numerous, were at a disadvantage because of their inferiority in arms and training (*BJ* 4.197 ff., cf. 243), Josephus estimates the number of the Zealots and Idumaeans at 23,400 (5.248 ff.). We hear now of shields (4.290; 5.120; 6.174) and of a 'phalanx' (5.312). Some still bore clubs as well as swords (5.102). The catapults and *ballistae* the Jews possessed during the siege were certainly, in large part at least, spoils from Cestius' army (4.583; 5.13 ff.; 267; 359; 6.121), and it was only gradually that they acquired skill in their use. We must not of course exaggerate the extent

---

[18] *AJ* 20.186 (cf. 164: *BJ* 2.255) calls their weapons ξιφίδια; they were curved, resembling Persian ἀκίνακαι and, more closely, Roman *sicae*. But other weapons are also mentioned, cf. *BJ* 2.471 (ξίφος); Mark 14.47 (μάχαιρα).

to which the Jews were, at any time, well armed. In Galilee (2.512; 3.15; 3.477), and presumably elsewhere, they evidently lacked defensive armour and were the more vulnerable to Roman attacks. We may doubt whether Josephus' claims to have had 'hoplites' under his command can be taken literally. In his narrative of operations in Galilee in the *Bellum*, he has undoubtedly exaggerated both the number of his troops, as can be seen from the *Vita*, and the training he was able to give them (2.577 ff.). But it is notable that he seems to stress Roman superiority in training and discipline (cf. 3.475 ff.) rather than in equipment (though he describes Roman arms in detail in 3.93 ff.), | and it is clear that a substantial number of the Jewish rebels had at least swords or spears and shields. (Similarly, Cestius was able to obtain armed auxiliaries from Syrian cities, 2.502.) We may also remark that one of the rebel leaders in Galilee actually had a fortified villa (βᾶρις) 'just like an acropolis' (*Vita* 246), so little care had the Roman government taken to deprive turbulent subjects of means of self-defence.

Even the experience of the revolt of 66–70 did not prompt the Roman government to impose effective and durable disarmament on the Jews within or outside Palestine. This is shown by the seriousness of their later rebellions (cf. e.g., A. Fuks, *JRS* 51 [1961] 98–104). The strength of the rebels in Egypt in 115–17 was such that the prefect was unable to repress them with the forces usually garrisoning the country, no doubt weakened by the detachment of some troops to take part in Trajan's Parthian war, and that eventually Marcius Turbo had to be sent for the purpose with a fleet and army; it is now known (*contra* Fuks) that he was not himself prefect (cf. H. G. Pflaum, *Les Carriè|res procuratoriennes équestres sous le Haut-Empire romain* [Paris 1960] 199 ff.). In the interim native Egyptians had been employed to fight the Jews (Wilcken, *Chr.* 16 f.). O. W. Reinmuth, (*The Prefect of Egypt* 126) says that 'the native population was armed under the command of the strategi'. But this statement is not warranted by the evidence. There is no more reason to suppose that the fellahin needed to be armed than the Jews themselves. Weapons were lacking to neither. Under Hadrian the Jews in Palestine had actually kept for themselves and were able to use in their revolt arms they had been required to furnish to the Roman army (Dio 69.12.2).

The practical difficulties of permanent disarmament are obvious enough. Everywhere, even in remote villages, there will have been skilled smiths with materials at their disposal which were needed for the production of the tools used in fields, houses and workshops; both craftsmen and materials could rapidly be turned over to making weapons and armour. In 149 B.C. Carthage was obliged to surrender all its military equipment; not a catapult or javelin or sword was left; yet the apparently defenceless citizens, after rejecting Rome's last demands, set to work to replace what they had given up at the daily rate of 100 shields, 300 swords, 1000 missiles for catapults, and 500 javelins and spears (App. *Pun.* 80; 82; 93), and they held out for three years. We may compare the prolonged resistance of Jerusalem. Moreover, if, as is probable, there were as yet no state armaments factories (n. 10), the Roman army itself had to be supplied by private manufacturers. With the high cost of transport, it was most economic to order supplies from the nearest sources. No doubt prudence suggested that stores of arms produced for Rome's own purposes should be kept in supposedly safe places, like Masada. Thus in 69 on Vespasian's instructions *destinantur validae civitates exercendis / armorum officinis* (Tac. *Hist.* 2.82.1 cf. 84.1). The cities appointed were doubtless fortified, but few, if any, will have been garrisoned. Vespasian will have relied on the loyalty of the city authorities. That must have been the normal policy of the imperial government.

Indeed, as already pointed out, the city governments needed the means to maintain local order and could hardly have been left without arms. In large areas no troops were stationed, and the central government had no police force and in the Republic and early Principate no attested spy system. It was bound to look to the local authorities to keep the peace internally and to ensure that the manufacture of arms, which could not be prevented and on the whole suited Rome's own interests, was not directed to the support of treason and revolt.

But the local authorities themselves, however well disposed, also had not the means to exercise a thorough control. Stores of arms might be kept under public guard, but there was no way of preventing the production of weapons for nefarious ends in scattered village smithies. Robbers and brigands could not be denied the tools of their trade, and a Gallic notable could even organize the secret manufacture of equipment for 8,000 men. Clearly this was exceptional; in general the notables were loyal, and it was a misfortune for Rome that this conspirator was not restrained by the timely delation that might have been expected.

Scholars were for long so prone to idealize Roman imperial rule that it is a welcome reaction when they draw attention to the persistence of exploitation and to the misery of the masses. But there was no novelty in these conditions. Most of Rome's subjects must have lived wretchedly before they were conquered, and probably more wretchedly; the Roman peace must have brought some benefits to all. Nor is it likely that in general they were consciously hostile to their conquerors (the Jews are of course exceptional); rather, they acquiesced in their fate. Macmullen himself recognizes this when he writes (119) that 'the rural lower classes ... accepted their lot without thinking much about it. ... So much we may infer from their passivity, silence and deference.' Perhaps nothing can be properly inferred from their silence: the illiterate cannot speak to us. But there is a more decisive reason for affirming that they gave a measure of consent to Roman rule. As early as the first century A.D., and to an increased extent thereafter, the frontiers were defended by subjects, mostly recruited from the rural lower class in the provinces nearest to the army camps. And yet it was in these provinces that the people were relatively warlike. Here, if anywhere, revolts could be dangerous, and permanent and universal disarmament would be easiest to comprehend. Still, it would be an odd view that Rome sought to disarm the peoples from which her soldiers were enlisted. A few units of specialized fighting men always drew recruits from the territory where they had been first | raised. And that was surely because there young men were still trained in the use of their traditional arms and fighting skills.[19]

When Roman conquest deprived a people of 'liberty,' the loss affected not so much the masses as the old ruling class: we must, however, remember that most of Rome's subjects had been previously under the control of some other king or *hegemon*, and that relatively few of the provincial *civitates* had any real sovereignty to lose. Whatever political loss they did sustain was compensated from the first by the blessings of peace and by Rome's readiness to uphold their local dominance, and in course of time by an increasing share in the imperial government. The notables were in the best position to discern the difficulty or impossibility of successful revolt, and to enjoy the benefits of order, civilization, and actual participation in Roman power. Without the leadership they alone could give, resistance to Rome could not be effectively organized and had even less change of success. The rise of provincials in the imperial service and the endless panegyrics they pronounced on Rome's beneficence alike attest the growth of active consent to Roman rule among the subjects who mattered most, if that rule was to endure. It was by winning over the magnates and not by disarming the masses that the Roman government secured submis-

---

[19] Perhaps the *collegia iuvenum*, attested from the second century at least in some western provinces as well as in Italy (*Diz. Ep. s.v. Iuvenes*) should be mentioned, as the *iuvenes* are generally held to have been drawn from the upper class and to have received some military or pre-military training, cf. M. Rostovtseff, *Soc. and Econ. Hist. of Roman Empire*[2] 47, 103, 107, 128, 326, 429 f. with his notes. But I suspect that he, and others, exaggerate the military, as against the social and religious, significance of these *collegia* and their value to the Roman military system. Thus, C. Jullian (Daremberg-Saglio *s.v. Iuvenes* 784) took Tacitus' allusions to the *iuventus* of the Aedui, Raeti etc. to refer to the young men trained in these *collegia*; in the light of Tacitus' usage of the word elsewhere (Gerber-Greef, *s.v.*), e.g., *Agr.* 27.2.; 29.4, this is unwarranted.

sion and internal peace. Disarmament was neither practicable nor necessary as a systematic rule of policy; it was a mere expedient of no more than temporary utility, to be employed against some peoples at the moment of surrender or when there was some particular reason for apprehending disturbances. The 'common pattern' is quite different; the local ruling class is left to control the masses and share in their exploitation, and Rome adapts the warlike proclivities of her subjects by giving them arms to protect and maintain her own empire.

The Romanization of the Local Ruling Classes in the Roman Empire

I

In his Panegyric on Rome Aelius Aristides claimed that the Roman empire was the first that rested on consent and not on force. No troops were needed to hold down the cities, because the most powerful of the local citizens, men to whom Rome had granted equality of rights, kept each of them loyal. It was for this class in Asia that Aristides spoke; he was himself the son of a landowner who had received the Roman citizenship[1]. Of course in the West the citizenship was far more widely diffused. Only there did many whole communities possess it, and there too more individuals could win it as a reward for military service, since over two thirds of the Roman army were raised and stationed in the western provinces[2]. As a consequence, in the west there were far more provincial citizens of low social status. My concern here, is however, with members of the local ruling classes, men of good family and property. They too more often secured Roman rights in the west, where there were numerous communities of Latin status, not found at all in eastern provinces; in these cities the magnates could obtain the citizenship by serving as local magistrates, or sometimes as councillors, quite automatically. Yet in the east individual grants had also become

[1] Aristides XXVI 22 f. (Persia); 43–57, esp. 52 (Athens and Sparta); 57–67 (Rome). In 39 and 65 f. he claims that Rome maintained equality and protected the poor, which was flagrantly false, cf. n. 21; naturally he had no sympathy with or understanding of the masses; for his own background cf. C. A. Behr, *Aelius Aristides and the Sacred Tales*, Amsterdam, 1968, ch. 1.

[2] Distribution of legions: Ritterling, *RE* XII 1362 ff. Recruitment: G. Forni, *Il Reclutamento delle Legioni de Augusto a Diocleziano*, Milan, 1953, with revisions in H. Temporini (ed.), *Aufstieg u. Niedergang der röm. Welt*, Berlin, 1974, II 339 ff. From Hadrian's time, when local recruitment for the legions had become normal, not more than one third of the legions were stationed in the east. G. L. Cheesman, *Auxilia in the Roman Army*, Oxford, 1914, shows that of auxiliary units whose names reveal their original ethnic composition only one quarter were raised in the east (including Thrace) and that the same proportion holds for units whose station is known in the early and century; I assume that evidence not known when he wrote cannot have significantly changed these ratios.

Sixth International Congress of Classical Studies, 1974; pub. in *Assimilation et résistance à la culture gréco-romaine dans le monde ancien* (1976), 161–73.

more and more common. The distinction, though important, is one of degree. Everywhere it was the Roman policy to win over, and to enfranchise, the local leaders.[3] |

Enfranchisement implied, in some sense, Romanization. This took a cultural form where Latin was the language of government and education. The elder Pliny conceived it as the mission of Italy to unite and also to civilize mankind, giving them a common speech. More cynically, in describing how Agricola promoted the adoption of Roman ways in Britain, Tacitus suggests that the amenities of a civilized life might accustom warlike tribes to docile submission.[4] Whatever its purposes, the government could do no more than encourage a process which, with no system of public education, it lacked the means to impose. Provincials Romanized themselves. In some regions Italian settlers or Latinized veterans supplied them with models to imitate. Everywhere knowledge of Latin must have made it easier for them to influence Roman officials, and to take part in trade beyond their own region. Assimilation might win favours. Thus Gades in 61 BC invited Caesar to revise her laws and, in Cicero's words, 'to remove a kind of ingrained barbarity from her customs and institutions'; it was perhaps partly on this account, and not only for the services that Balbus and his fellow-citizens later rendered to Caesar, that Gades became the first provincial city to obtain Roman status.[5] But imitation of Rome need not have been prompted only by material considerations. Just as the literature and arts of Greece had long exercised a powerful attraction on less developed peoples, the Romans among them, so now Rome opened to many of her subjects a new world of thought and beauty and enjoyment. This was surely one reason why in western towns letters and arts, the buildings and the social life they sheltered, as well as the names of gods and men, and laws and institutions, assumed a Roman dress. (No motives of imperial pride restrained the subjects, as it had once restrained the Romans, from submerging their own languages and traditions in those of the superior culture.) Once the conquered had recognized that further

---

[3] See A. N. Sherwin-White, *The Roman Citizenship*[2], Oxford, 1973, Part II and the important new discussions in Part III. He amply refutes the strange notion of C. Saumagne, *Le droit latin et les cités rom. sous l'empire*, Paris, 1965, that provincial *municipia* were always Latin. But, despite p. 350, F. Vittinghoff, *Röm. Kolonisation u. Bürgerrechtspolitik: Abh. Akad. Mainz*, 1951, 29; 43 ff. was patently right that Latinity was not normally a stage in a community's progress to Roman citizenship, which most Latin cities did not obtain earlier than other subjects under the 'Constitutio Antoniniana'; it was its essential function to reward the local upper class. On viritane grants in the east see Sherwin-White 310 f. A complete collection of evidence is wanting.

[4] Pliny, *NH* III 391. Tac. *Agr.* 21, cf. *Hist.* IV 64. 3. Italian writers in general say nothing of Romanization.

[5] Cic. *Balb.* 43, cf. Brunt, *Italian Manpower*, Oxford, 1971, p. 602.

resistance was futile, they could gradually come to see that assimilation had its own rewards and charms.

By contrast, where Greek was already the language of culture, of government, and of inter-regional trade, the Romans carried further the process of Hellenization.[6] Although they brought with them their own laws which, eventually, modified by Greek legal practices, were to be codified for the Byzantine empire,[7] and although their love of gladiatorial games and beast hunts found too ready a reception among Greeks,[8] in general what was specifically Latin in the common civilization of the empire made little impact in the east. There Greek remained the language in which Rome communicated with her subjects, and Greeks rarely learned Latin, except for the few who entered the army or imperial adminis|tration; of its literary merits they were usually content to be ignorant.[9] The form of the local institutions was rarely changed.[10] Yet this phil-Hellenism, as well as the material benefits that Rome's protection assured, must surely have helped to win the political attachment of her Hellenic subjects, or at least of those who were politically conscious and articulate. It was a long process. Lucian is the first Greek writer to refer to Roman troops as 'our soldiers',[11] and after his time Greeks continued to treat the Romans as aliens, however benevolent.[12] Still, in the end, they were to call themselves Rhomaioi. Romanization in sentiment triumphed at last.

No doubt the cultural difference of the Greek world explains why Roman citizenship was for long less widely extended there. Yet here too it was not denied to the local magnates: why? Characteristically the Romans never explicitly formulated any criteria by which it was bestowed. But Marcus Aurelius declared that it was a reward due only

---

[6] A. H. M. Jones, *The Greek City*, Oxford, 1940, ch. II and XXI, and *The Later Roman Empire*, Oxford, 1964, ch. XXIV.

[7] L. Mitteis, *Reichsrecht u. Volksrecht*, Leipzig, 1891: further bibliography in D. Norr, *Imperium u. Polis in der hohen Principatszeit*, Munich, 1969, to which add R. Taubenschlag, *The Law of Greco-Roman Egypt. . . .?*, Warsaw, 1955. Egypt naturally provides the most copious evidence.

[8] L. Robert, *Les Gladiateurs dans l'Orient Grec*, Amsterdam, 1971 (reprint).

[9] Plut. *Dem.* 2 f., is striking especially in view of his residence in Rome, and close connexions with Romans, cf. C. P. Jones, *Plutarch and Rome*, Oxford, 1971, esp. ch. IX; he concedes that Latin literature had merits, but he had no leisure to master the language to the extent required for literary appreciation. Only the transfer of government to the east in the fourth century led to a temporary vogue for Latin in court and governmental circles there, cf. A. H. M. Jones, *The Roman Economy*, Oxford, 1974, 104 f., which was deplored by Libanius and never spread to cultivated Greek Churchmen (see G. Bardy, *La question des langues dans l'église anc.*, Paris, 1948). In the ninth century the emperor Michael II could call Latin 'a barbarous Scythian tongue' (P. Charanis, *Dumbarton Oaks Papers*, 1959, 23 ff.).

[10] Jones, *op. cit.* in n. 6, ch. XI.

[11] J. Palm, *Rom. Römertum u. Imperium in der gr. Lit. der Kaiserzeit*, Lund, 1959, 54 f.

[12] D. Norr, *op. cit.* in n. 7, 94 ff. However, he was wrong to accept the suggestion that Byzantium fought against 'the Romans' under Severus: that was merely Severan propaganda, treating all adherents of Pescennius Niger as 'hostes'.

'maximis meritis'.[13] Service to Rome was the primary consideration. The enfranchisement of provincial soldiers is only the most conspicuous illustration of this principle.[14] But hardly any class of men rendered more important services to the Roman state than those charged with local government. While most Roman troops were defending the frontiers, it was largely their task to preserve internal order. No large administrative bureaucracy ever existed under the Principate, except in Egypt, and the local magnates were even left to collect the direct property tax, the main source of imperial revenues.[15] The empire could hardly have survived without their loyalty or acquiescence.

Cicero had commended his brother as proconsul of Asia for ensuring that the cities were administered by the *optimates*.[16] This was a traditional and enduring maxim of Roman government, which Dio incorporates in Maecenas' advice to Augustus.[17] In the west the charters of Roman | and Latin towns, models for less privileged communities, themselves embodied the essentially oligarchic practice of the Roman Republic.[18] In Gaul, where Caesar had found his most determined opponents among magnates like Dumnorix and Vercingetorix who appealed to the masses,[19] the aristocracy retained control, and it is significant that they were mostly true to Rome when a few nobles under Tiberius raised a sort of *jacquerie* in revolt.[20] In provincial cities assemblies long continued to elect the magistrates, but their choice was limited to men of property. They could not legally initiate policy, and Rome could be expected to stamp on sedition. Roman

[13] *Tabula Banasitana*, cf. W. Seston and M. Euzennat, *CRAI*, 1971, 468 ff.; A. N. Sherwin-White, *JRS* 1973, 86 ff.

[14] Cic., *Balb.* 22–4. Cf. also the grants to the Anauni and Volubilis, printed in e.g. Riccobono, *FIRA²*, nos. 70 f., and the regulations governing manumission of slaves in the Principate and the promotion of Junian Latins to full citizenship, on which see Sherwin-White, *op. cit.* in n. 3, 322 ff., cf. my *Italian Manpower*, 239 ff. For adoption of Roman culture as a secondary criterion for enfranchisement the case of Emporiae (Livy XXXIV 9) is particularly instructive.

[15] Jones (n. 9) pp. 164 ff. Pre-Severan evidence is scanty, but before c. 200 the central government had no better means of collecting *tributum* with its own officials than afterwards.

[16] *Ad. Qu. fr.* I 1. Cf. *de Rep.* II 39; *Flacc.* 15–18 for Cicero's own sentiments.

[17] Cf. Dio LII 30, and see also nn. 1; 18–21; 35.

[18] The Roman principle that the magistrates should be 'quasi ministri' of the senate (Cic. *Sest.* 137) is written into the Spanish charters, see esp. *Lex Ursonensis* CXXIX; *Lex Malacitana* LXVII.

[19] Dumnorix, *BG.* I 3, cf. 17 f.; Indutiomarus, V 3; Vercingetorix, VII 4; perhaps Ambiorix, cf. V 27. See generally II 1 on opposition to Rome by over-mighty nobles, who could mobilise private armies, partly by demagogic appeals, cf. Posid. *FHG* no. 89, F. 15. Caesar sometimes stresses the presence of needy vagabonds etc. in hostile armies, III 17; V 55; VII 4; VIII 30. Naturally, among some peoples there was more or less united resistance to the Roman conquest; Caesar put to death the whole Venetic 'senate', III 16. He could also appoint kings, IV 21; V 25; or confer power and wealth on his own plebeian partisans, *BC* III 59. 2.

[20] Julian, *Hist. de la Gaule*, IV, Paris, 1920, 332 ff.; Tac. *Ann.* III 40–6, esp. 40, 2; 42, 2 f., cf. *Hist.* II 61.

officials were indeed also supposed to prevent the oppression of the people by the 'potentiores'. But the officials had the same social and economic interests and attitudes as the local oligarchs. In the second century at latest the *humiliores* were being subjected under Roman criminal law to treatment once reserved for slaves. Later, in the interest partly of the landowners, the peasants were to be bound to the soil like serfs. The masses could not look to Rome for effective protection against their local masters.[21]

Of course, in many or most subject communities oligarchic rule was no novelty and wherever it had existed previously the oligarchs would seem to have been the losers, in so far as Roman conquest terminated local sovereignty. Hence in the early stages of Roman expansion some aristocrats took the lead in resistance. But in fact true independence had been rare in the past: most communities had been controlled by kings, or by some other neighbouring state, and had at best been left to manage their internal affairs. Liberty in this sense the local oligarchs retained, or acquired, under Roman rule, if only because governors, even when entitled to intervene in the cities at their discretion, seldom had leisure or staff| for continuous and systematic interference.[22] Only in the second century did the central government begin to attempt a closer supervision. Though this must have been resented by the local magnates, they had by then long come to accept Roman domination as inevitable, and precisely in this period they began to enjoy not only the benefits of peace and security for their possessions and privileges, but also increasing opportunities for sharing in the imperial administration itself.[23]

Rich and educated men, who knew most of the world about them, could see that a single commune was too weak by itself to challenge

---

[21] Jones, *The Greek City*, ch. XI. Dio Chrys. XLVIII shows how at Prusa a proconsul under Trajan suppressed the assembly, probably for rioting, and that it had no power, when restored, to punish magistrates it distrusted; hence there was danger of renewed disorder. Although Plutarch's *Praecepta Reip. Ger.* is mainly related to contemporary problems (Jones, *o.c.* in n. 9, ch. XII), I cannot believe that Rome would have permitted confiscation of private property, or even any substantial distribution of public lands or funds (818), cf. *SIG³* 684; demagogic proposals of this kind, as his examples indicate, belonged to the past. Protection of the masses: Ulp., *Dig.* I 18, 6, 2; Dio LII 37; cf. Cic., *de offic.* II 85; and see n. 1. *Humiliores:* P. J. Garnsey, *Social Status and Legal Privilege in the Roman Empire*, Oxford, 1970, with my remarks in *JRS* 1972, 166 ff. Colonate: see e.g. Jones (n. 9) ch. XIV; M. I. Finley, *The Ancient Economy*, London, 1973, ch. III.

[22] Thus Pliny in Bithynia-Pontus, a large area, with poor communications, was assisted by one legate (ep. X 25), his *cohors amicorum* (84, 2, cf. VI 22), the officers of more than one cohort (21; 106 f.)—for *stationarii* cf. 74. 77 f.—who could be used for civil administration (86b)—in Egypt also in judicial business, e.g. Mitteis, *Chr.* 84: 90; *P. Oxy.* XII p. 1492; in addition there were the procurator and his freedman assistant (27 f.; 83 f.) and the *praefectus orae Ponticae* (21 f.; 86a), and the clerical officials described by A. H. M. Jones, *Studies in Roman Government and Law*, Oxford 1960 ch. X, cf. now G. Boulvert, *Esclaves et Affranchis Impériaux*, Naples, 1970.

[23] Cf. M. Hammond, *JRS* 1957, 77 (for the senate); A. Stein, *Der röm. Ritterstand*, Munich, 1927, 412 ff.; H. G. Pflaum, *Les procurateurs équestres*, Paris, 1950, 170–94.

Rome. At the same time co-operation with fellow-subjects was impeded by the persistence of old jealousies and rivalries.[24] Even within one province or region there was little or no consciousness of a common nationality, which in modern times has militated against the growth of loyalty to an imperial power.[25]

Among all the subject peoples religion did not operate as a divisive force except for the Jews; the subjects accepted the gods of Rome, at least in name, and Rome gave many of their own deities the franchise of the imperial city. Few peoples possessed a literature to keep proud memories of the past alive. Of course in this respect the Greeks as well as the Jews are exceptions. But the Greek traditions enshrined the ideal not of the political unity of a nation, but of the freedom and autonomy of each *polis*, great or small; (it may indeed be said that if even a Greek city had succeeded in unifying the Greeks politically, that would in itself have destroyed the basis of Greek achievement). Under Roman rule most Greek *poleis* possessed as much, or as little, freedom and autonomy as in earlier times. The Jews did indeed remain less tractable, perhaps because the Scriptures and memories of the Maccabees held out hopes of divine aid, by which they might triumph over the Gentiles.

Yet even in Judaea upper class Jews seem mostly to have opposed revolt, or to have sought to sabotage it, not only because (as Josephus makes king Agrippa urge) in their judgement it was certain to fail, and it was folly to 'kick against the pricks', but because Rome guaranteed the social order; the revolt of 66 was almost as much directed against native | landlords and usurers as against the heathen rulers. At least most of the high priests and rulers incurred the hatred of religious fanatics, partly perhaps because they were too prone to favour peace and submission.[26] Outside Judaea, with no religious sentiment to countervail material interests, men of rank and wealth were still less likely to resist an empire that maintained peace, peace which brought most benefits to those with most to lose, and secured them in their

[24] I collected some examples in ch. 4 nn. 89–91, cf. Norr (n. 12) 48–50. The institution of *concilia* or *koina* in the Principate shows that it was not then Rome's policy to 'divide and rule'.

[25] Cf. H. Dessau, *Gesch. der röm. Kaiserzeit*, Berlin, 1930, II 1, 448 f. 460 ff. on Spain, and Spanish Latin authors; 482 ff. on Gaul. Gallic nationalism was in my view nascent in Caesar's time but did not persist as an anti-Roman factor in the Principate, cf. ch. 2, esp. Part II; ch. 3 p. 33 f. Cf. Sherwin-White, *o.c.* in n. 3, 446 ff.; also R. MacMullen, *Enemies of the Roman Order*, Cambridge (Mass.), 1967, ch. VI, and against theories that heresies disguised nationalist movements in Africa, Egypt and Syria, see Jones (n. 9), ch. XV.

[26] See ch. 13. On absence of vernacular literature, cf. Excursus I. H. Kreissig, *Die sozialen Zusammenhänge des judäischen Krieges*, Berlin, 1970, 90 ff. questions the testimony of Jos. *c. Ap.* II 204 to the frequency of literacy among the Jews, but stresses oral tradition. Still, this was more easily preserved, when supported by Scriptures (Jesus 'the carpenter' would not be a counter-instance to Kreissig, if 'carpenter' stands for 'scholar', G. Vermes, *Jesus the Jew*, London, 1973, 21 f.)

property and local dominance; the Roman legal system too favoured the *beati possidentes*. At a council of Gallic notables in 70 Iulius Auspex, 'e primoribus Remorum', expatiated convincingly on the overwhelming power of Rome and the blessings of peace.[27]

Moreover it was not the poor who went to schools and learned the tricks of rhetoric;[28] indeed it seems clear that among the lower class, and especially the peasants, centuries passed before Latin or Greek supplanted the native languages, and in some areas, even in Spain, they never did. At least in the west, the few with means and leisure for education learned from their Latin classics that it was by divine providence that Rome ruled the civilized world: 'his ego nec metas rerum nec tempora pono; imperium sine fine dedi'.[29] We can only surmise how much this teaching reinforced their loyalty; certainly the Romans did not bring with them, like British or French imperialists, ideas of liberty, equality and national sovereignty that were subversive of their own dominion.[30] And Roman ideas undoubtedly permeate the works of writers born in Spain or Gaul, like Seneca or Quintilian, the late panegyrists or Rutilius Namatianus.

Without the leadership and organization which the local magnates could alone, or best, provide, rebellions were rare. Continuous resistance did not keep the embers of disloyalty burning. Time and habit promoted the acceptance of Roman rule. Aristides' ancestors had already been subjects for nearly twice as long as British rule endured in large parts of India.

The Roman citizenship, which symbolized, rewarded and fortified the loyalty of the magnates, also prepared the way for the final step in Romanization: their admission to a share in imperial government, which removed the distinction between rulers and subjects. It was the easier for Rome to offer this concession and for the magnates to accept it, | because in education and economic interests provincial magnates closely resembled the old Italian ruling class. I have never been able to discover that the promotion of leading provincials had any effect on Roman policy, or on the ideas of emperors, senators or Equites. They were apparently uncritical of the established order; the right of the city

[27] Peace; see e.g. Dessau (n. 25) 452 f. (Spain); 497 ff. (Gaul), cf. Tac., *Hist.* IV 69: Iulius Auspex e primoribus Remorum, vim Romanam (NB) pacisque bona dissertans; *OGIS* 458 and *SEG* IV 490 (Asia). Legal system: F. Schulz, *Classical Roman Law*, Oxford, 1951, 544 f. on *locatio—conductio*, 203 ff. on elaboration of law of succession and 26 f. on *addictio* for debt; Garnsey, *o.c.* in n. 21.

[28] Plut., *Sert.* 14; Tac., *Ann.* III 43, 1; *Agr.* 21, 2. Cf. Jullian, *Hist. de la Gaule* VI 140 ff.; VIII 265.

[29] Dessau (n. 25) I 509. For knowledge of Virgil in even the least Romanized provinces cf. S. Frere, *Britannia*, London, 1967, 313 f. and 338; Mócsy, *RE* Suppl. IX (Pannonia) 768; *JRS* 1968, 60 ff. (Egypt).

[30] See ch. 6 Part III.

of Rome to be fed and amused at the cost of provincial taxpayers was never impaired, and Italy was allowed to retain immunity from the heaviest taxes until about 300.[31] Indeed in the reign of the first provincial emperor public money was first provided for the poor of all Italy, and of Italy alone; and provincial senators were required to invest in Italian land, so that they might regard Italy as their real *patria*. Some provincial families, like those of Pius and Marcus Aurelius, obviously became naturalized there. Still, in so far as provincials involved in the central government retained connexions with their original homes, this must have served to attach their peoples still more firmly to Rome. By the time that the eternal city celebrated its millennium under an Arab Caesar, its dominion had virtually ceased to be foreign to the men of rank and property. To a Severan jurist Rome was 'communis nostra patria'. The concept was not alien to Aristides.[32]

II[33]

Of course it had a much earlier origin. Cicero had contended that every Italian had two fatherlands, the municipality of his birth and Rome, the 'communis patria' of all alike. This may remind us that the Romanization of the provinces had its counterpart and model in that of Italy. It was with Italian arms that Rome had conquered the empire she now maintained with provincial troops. The peoples of Italy had been only less diverse ethnically and linguistically than her subjects overseas, and some had fought no less strenuously for their independence. Yet in Italy too Rome had ultimately won the consent of her subjects, and by methods which determined the tradition that the emperors were to follow. Like almost everything that was most valuable in the Roman achievement, the secret of imperial success was discovered in the Republic, before the spirit of innovation at Rome had been depressed, or destroyed.

The peoples of Italy had also been governed by *domi nobiles*, who generally received, and reciprocated, Roman support. Naturally this generalization admits of exceptions which do not disprove it; aristocrats were occasionally popular leaders, and anti-Roman.[34] But the protection | Rome gave to the lords of Volsinii against their serfs in 265 BC,[35] and the refusal of Campanian Equites on two occasions to

---

[31] Victor, *Caes.* 29.31, cf. Jones, LRE I 64. [See pp. 515–17 f.]

[32] *Dig.* XXVII 1, 6, 11, cf. Cic., *Leg.* II 5: Aristides, XXVI 61. cf. Norr (n. 7) 99 ff.

[33] Much of Part II is founded on my article in *JRS* 1965, 90 ff. [now revised in my *Fall of Rom. Rep.*, 1988, ch. 2.]

[34] A. J. Toynbee, *Hannibal's Legacy*, Oxford, 1958, 149 f. See Excursus II.

[35] Harris, *Rome in Etruria and Umbria*, Oxford, 1971, 82–4; 91 f.; 115–18.

join anti-Roman movements,[36] are surely typical of the connexions between Rome and local magnates, which were cemented by relations of *hospitium* and even intermarriage between great Roman and Italian houses.[37] The latter were left to manage their own local affairs; in my judgement this was true before 90 BC no less of towns that already possessed Roman citizenship than of those which still lacked it.[38]

The franchise itself was occasionally granted to these *domi nobiles*, and already by Gaius Gracchus' time it went automatically to the magistrates of Latin towns.[39] Before the Hannibalic war Rome had incorporated many entire communities in her own citizen body.[40] But even such mass enfranchisements were probably of most advantage to the local magnates. Their wealth made it easier for them to visit Rome and vote, and it also gave weight to the votes cast at elections in the timocratic assembly of the centuries. No doubt they could procure all sorts of favours in return for their electoral support. Some could rise to high offices themselves. Within at most two generations after the enfranchisement of his town, a Tusculan became consul in 322 BC and founded the dynasty of the Fulvii.[41] This phenomenon was certainly not unique, and perhaps commoner than we can ever detect; the origin of most new consular and praetorian families is unknown. Probably there would have been little astonishing in Marius' career if he had advanced no further than the praetorship.[42]

Cicero traced Rome's liberality with the citizenship back to the rape of the Sabine women and the synoecism of Romans and Sabines under Romulus. He claimed that since that time Rome had never intermitted a practice, which was the chief source of her power (*Balb.* 31). He chose to forget the narrow and exclusive policy followed for over a century before the Social War. But he could well have argued that that war, the gravest crisis Rome had faced since Hannibal, fortified his case. It was brought on because Rome had departed from her own tradition. However, that tradition worked for Rome's advantage, precisely because of the aristocratic structure of society and political institutions. Tacitus makes Claudius contrast the readiness of Rome to enfranchise

---

[36] Livy VIII 11, 16; XXIII 31, 10; XXIV 47, 12.

[37] Toynbee I 326–43, cf. Wiseman (n. 42) ch. 3.

[38] *Italian Manpower* App. III.

[39] Brunt, [*Fall of Rom. Rep.* 511 f.]

[40] Toynbee I ch. III provides the clearest full account of this, and in general of Rome's organization of Italy before 90.

[41] Münzer *RE* VII 237 f., cf. Toynbee I 126; 196 f. Other Tusculans in office at Rome, ibid. 324 f. Only a few 'inquilini', like the Perpernas, can be detected by their non-Latin names. However, K. J. Beloch, *Röm. Gesch.*, Berlin 1926, 338 ff. was in my view justified in criticising some of Münzer's speculations on the origin of particular noble plebeian families.

[42] See e.g. Harris, Appendix I; T. P. Wiseman, *New Men in the Roman Society*, Oxford, 1971 ch. 2.

her subjects with the illiberality of Sparta and Athens, who were ruined because 'victos pro alienigenis arcebant' (*Ann.* XI 25). Now in the last crisis of the Peloponnesian war Athens did bestow her citizenship on the loyal Samians | (*IG* II² 1). But what benefit could the Samians really have received? At Athens all major decisions were taken by an assembly in which majorities rested simply on counting by heads: a few Samian visitors would have been overwhelmed by the mass of poor citizens from the city and the Piraeus. By contrast the Roman citizenship gave influence and the prospect of political advancement to those who controlled their home towns.

In 90 the Italians demanded the citizenship and rebelled when it was refused. Rome's allies, unlike those of Athens, did not desire to free themselves from foreign dominion, but to share in the political rights of a state they were ready to acknowledge as their own. Even the bitterness of a bloody war did not prevent fusion with the old citizens, once their objective was attained. Naturally, it was the 'principes' who had demanded the franchise in 90, and the chief beneficiaries were the 'boni et locupletes' from all over Italy. Claudius said that it was the wish of Augustus and Tiberius that they should be admitted to the senate; many had been there even before Caesar's dictatorship.[43]

This political assimilation corresponded to a cultural Romanization, the progress of which it is hard to trace but which again must have owed much to Roman settlement and to service in a Latin speaking army, and which culminated in the first century BC not only in the adoption of Roman laws and institutions but in the virtual disappearance from the literary or epigraphic records of all languages but Latin. Of course it is the upper classes who have left us these records; we do not know when Virgil's humbler countrymen in Mantua began to speak his tongue.[44]

From first to last Roman society and politics were aristocratic. The Princeps himself was most secure when he ruled with the consent of the upper orders. At every stage in Rome's history the aristocrats who ruled at Rome found it most natural to support men like themselves elsewhere. Community of interests and sentiments made it easier to admit them to their own circle. It was only the non-democratic institutions of the Roman Republic that made the extension of the citizenship a suitable instrument for winning the consent of the Italians

---

[43] *ILS* 212, II 1 ff. Cf. Wiseman (n. 42) passim, esp. Appendix II. Many of Wiseman's conclusions on the *origo* of senatorial families are highly speculative, but it is improbable that after Sulla doubled the senate, its lower ranks in particular were not largely composed of *municipales*; for Caesar's senate, still further enlarged, cf. Cic. *Phil.* III 15.

[44] For the general reasons given in Excursus I we must be wary of assuming that vernacular languages did not continue in common use long after they disappear from written records.

by giving substantial political rights to the *domi nobiles*, and it was the well-tried success of this policy that suggested to the autocrats its further extension; they built on Republican experience. In this way they fostered and rewarded the growth of an empire-wide loyalty to Rome, if only among the men who were the natural leaders of provincial subjects. We can never know how deeply that loyalty penetrated the masses. They do not speak to us on parchment or stone. The eloquence of an Aristides illustrates what men of rank and education thought: for the rest we have to make dubious inferences from the actions of Illyrian peasants whose valour saved the empire | in the third century[45] or of Bagaudae who sided with barbarians and helped to disrupt it.[46] Yet perhaps the former fought primarily for pay, and the latter in blind discontent with their miseries; Rome may have meant little to both, whether for good or ill. And Rome would be remembered not for what these inarticulate peasants thought of her, but for what the privileged few said in reiterated laudations.

EXCURSUS I: VERNACULAR LANGUAGES

Surveys of the persistence of vernacular language in the empire are to be found in Jones, *Later Roman Empire*, 991–7; R. MacMullen, *AJP* 1966, 1 ff., cf. Bardy, *o.c.* in n. 9, esp. on COPTIC and SYRIAC (cf. F. Millar, *JRS* 1971, 5–8). For AFRICA see F. Millar, *JRS* 1968, 126 ff. (with extensive bibliography, not merely relating to that region), cf. P. Brown, ib. 85 ff.; note *CIL* VIII 8500 (Sitifis) for Greek and Latin as 'utraque lingua'. For ANATOLIA and THRACE P. Charanis, *o.c.* in n. 9, adds something to K. Holl, *Hermes*, 1908, 240–54. For GAUL see C. Jullian, *Hist. de la Gaule*, VI ch. II; VIII 265 ff.; P. M. Duval, *La vie quotidienne en Gaule*, Paris, 1952, 46 ff.; G. Dottin, *La langue gauloise*, Paris, 1918, collected the evidence for Celtic and the Gallic inscriptions. On BRITAIN see K. Jackson, *Language and History in Early Britain*, Edinburgh, 1953, cf. S. Frere, *Britannia*, 1967, 305, 311–14. For SPAIN see A. Garcia y Bellido, in Temporini (n. 2) I 1, 462 ff. As for the DANUBIAN PROVINCES, in the absence of positive evidence for vernacular languages in Upper Moesia and Pannonia, the illiteracy or absolute unintelligibility of Latin in many inscriptions, even when

---

[45] See A. Alföldi, *St. zur Gesch. du Weltkrise des 3 Jahrhunderts nach Christus*, Darmstadt, 1967, 228 ff. (not free of learned phantasy). Of special interest is the reverence professed for Roman traditions in *Coll.* VI 4 and XV 3 by Diocletian and Maximian, cf. Galerius' edict in Lact. *de Mort. Persec.* 34. These emperors were all, it is said, of humble 'Illyrian' origin. But are the ideas, any more than the bombastic style, of their pronouncements, those of Illyrian peasants?

[46] E. A. Thompson, in M. I. Finley (ed.), *St. in Anc. Society*, London, 1974, ch. XIV, and in *JRS* 1956, 65 ff. On brigands cf. R. MacMullen (cited in n. 25) ch. VI and Appendix B.

set up by *curiales* in urban centres, and the fact that 80% of the Latin inscriptions come from the most urbanized 8% of the area of Upper Moesia, speak volumes (cf. A. Mócsy, *Gesellschaft u. Romanisation in der röm. Provinz Moesia Sup.*, Amsterdam, 1970, 199 ff., cf. *RE Suppl.* IX 766–70 on Pannonia).

Evidence is meagre for various reasons. (1) Even ancient ethnographers display little interest in barbarous tongues, cf. J. Sofer, *W. St.* 1952, 138 ff.; Garcia y Bellido, *op. cit.*, Part II. Cf. the neglect of Latin by Greek writers, and of Italic languages by Roman (and note Gell. XI 7,4). Most Latin allusions to Punic come from Augustine (Millar, *JRS* 1968, 130); and he shows a perhaps unusual pride in a region's past (Brown, *o.c.*); Jullian, VIII 383, cites parallels for regional 'patriotism'. (2) Most vernaculars had no written literature. Even Coptic and Syriac only became literary tongues, for religious purposes, after AD 200, though Syriac is a | branch of Aramaic in which parts of the *OT* were written, and Jones puts its rise, or renascence, too late. The lays of Celtic bards were soon forgotten in Gaul (cf. H. Dessau, *Gesch. der röm. Kaiserzeit*, Berlin, 1930, II 2, 484), though apparently not in Britain (Jackson, *o.c.* 116 f.). Many peoples (non-Semitic of course) only learned to write with the advent of Greeks or Romans, and the languages of their masters as well as their alphabets may soon have conquered the few who became literate; even when they continued to speak in the vernacular, they did not choose to write it. (3) Inscriptions were not put up by the very poor, or the illiterate peasants; even funerary monuments were not cheap (cf. R. Duncan-Jones, *The Economy of the Roman Empire*, Cambridge, 1974, 79 f.; 129 f.). Moreover, they do not necessarily reflect the language actually in common use, see Jackson *o.c.* 99 f., Jullian VI 111 n. 1; we could not tell from inscriptions that Getic was common in Tomi in Ovid's time (*Tristia* V 7, 51; 12, 58; *Ex Ponto* IV 13, 17 ff., etc.) or Syriac round Antioch as late as the fourth century.

In the absence or dearth of explicit testimony to vernacular languages, onomastic evidence is important, despite the doubts of Jullian, VI 112. Thus in Gaul itself Celtic names round Trier become commoner, the further one goes from the centre; and we know from Jerome (cf. esp. J. Sofer, *W. St.* 1937, 148 ff.) that Celtic was still spoken there in his day. It is significant that with the renascence of Coptic Egyptian peasants are less apt to take Greek names or 'aliases'. See for exemplary use of such evidence in tracing the diffusion of Latin G. Alföldy, *Noricum*, London, 1974, 133–5; 139, 193 f. Cf. also for instance, R. Thouvenot, *Essai sur la province rom. de Bétique*, Paris, 1940, 185–8.

The survival of vernacular tongues in Anatolia, sometimes almost

1000 years after the people had been first subjected to Hellenization, the emergence after the Roman period of Albanian, Vlach, Basque, the various descendants of British (Welsh, Cornish and Breton), and (*pace* Millar) Berber, and the earlier revival as written languages of Syriac and Coptic, prove beyond doubt that the impression we get from literature and inscriptions that Greek and Latin were wholly dominant is false. If Celtic held out so long near Trier, which was in a frontier zone where the presence of a Latin speaking army should have had some effect, and which had latterly been a great imperial centre, we must suppose *a fortiori* that it was the common speech in most of the hinterland. In Spain too a vernacular language was still in use near the Romanized east coast as late as the fourth, or more probably the sixth, century (Garcia y Bellido, *op. cit.*, Part VII).

It is a reasonable assumption that it was in the towns (not very numerous in the north) that Latin or Greek made most progress among the masses. Onomastic evidence often supports this. Thus the scraps of Latin scrawled by artisans in Britain do not show that it was intelligible to the peasants. The dialect of Coptic that was to prevail was that of Upper Egypt, where Greek settlement had been thinnest and the native language had doubtless always remained most common. In Africa 'Punic' was spoken in the country, but was evidently unfamiliar to many in an urban congregation of Augustine's time. It was indeed long before the Church evangelized the peasantry. Holl observed that translation into vulgar tongues was never initiated by the Church itself, but where it occurred, | e.g. in Syriac, Coptic and Gothic, was the work of bi-lingual individuals. Why individuals conceived the idea of producing translations in some vernaculars and not in others, and how the Gospel was ultimately conveyed to the peasants in (say) Gaul, if they knew little or no Latin and the preachers little or no Celtic, are questions to which I have found no answer. But perhaps in Gaul and Spain, once Latin had become the language of salvation as well as that of landlords and tax-collectors, it had a new and decisive appeal to the masses.

Even among the upper classes some must have remained able to converse in the local vernacular, at least with their tenants, servants, etc. In some places Latin or Greek may not have been the ordinary vehicle of communication at any level. Much of the evidence is late, but naturally probative, *a fortiori*, for earlier times. Ausonius' father, a distinguished doctor in the prosperous town of Bordeaux, was not fluent in Latin (Aus., *Epic in patr.* 9). Ulpian allows the use of Punic, Gallic, Syriac or other languages for certain legal transactions under Roman law (Millar, *JRS* 1968, 130 f.); these were of chief interest to men of property. Some Churchmen who wrote in Syriac or Coptic

were men of Hellenic culture. Jackson shows the influence of a correct
Latin learned by the upper classes in British schools (as distinct from
the vulgar Latin used wherever Latin became the normally spoken
language) on the development of the British language. It is obvious
that small men in the towns had still greater need to communicate with
the peasants who came in to market. On the other hand, in so far as the
upper classes and the urban populations had little of the native
tongues, the villages might easily have become linguistically isolated
from each other, since peasants do not travel far or often, and
dialectical differences could have been accentuated, until only Greek or
Latin as the *lingua franca* remained as a general mode of communication within a region, cf. W. M. Calder, *JHS* 1911, 164, commenting on
neo-Phrygian inscriptions of the empire and adducing the conditions
among Greek speakers in the villages of Turkey at the time. This would
have tended, in the very long run, to promote the triumph of Greek or
Latin. It would also have meant that local languages did not provide a
unifying regional factor, which could have supported 'nationalism'
against Rome.

EXCURSUS II: ROME AND OLIGARCHIES IN ITALY AND GREECE

E. Badian, *Foreign Clientelae*, Oxford, 1958, 147 f. pointed out that
Livy's generalization, that everywhere the local senates favoured
Rome in the Hannibalic war, whereas the *plebs* was in conflict with the
best people (XXIV 2), does not fit his own account of events at Locri,
Arpi and Tarentum; he might have added evidence that *principes* in
Etruria were suspected or convicted for disloyalty (XXVII 24, 2;
XXIX 36, 10–12; XXX 26, 12), but cf. Harris (n. 33), ch. IV, esp.
131 ff. But as Latin has no definite or indefinite article, 'principes' in
such texts (cf. XXIII 30, 8 on Locri, XXIV, 47, 6 on Arpi) can mean
some, not all, 'principes': it is made clear that at Locri they belonged to
one faction, and could be described as 'levissimus quisque' (XXIV 1, 7;
XXIX 6, 5); in any oligarchic state, as at Rome itself and Capua
(XXIII 2, 2), some | aristocrats might woo the *plebs*. The blame for the
revolt at Arpi was laid exclusively on one wealthy man, perhaps a
would-be *tyrannus* (XXIV 45; 47, 10). On the other hand at Capua 70
principes senatus were executed for a revolt they had failed to prevent
(XXVI 16, 6), cf. the treatment Cleon proposed for the *plebs* at
Mytilene. Badian seems to be right on Tarentum, but one exception
does not invalidate a general rule.

Recently J. Deininger, *Der politische Widerstand gegen Rom in Griechen-
land*, Berlin, 1971, has protested against the common view that in

second century Greece oligarchs favoured Rome and democrats were for resistance. He points out that democratic institutions were ubiquitous, though the actual government was in the hands of 'principes', and that the 'principes' themselves were commonly divided. He acknowledges, however, that the anti-Roman 'principes' usually had popular support, and cites numerous instances of this; in the last stages of resistance, the Achaean war and the Athenian revolt of 88, it was the masses who formed its mainstay, led by a very few members of the ruling class. Livy's generalizations about the anti-Roman attitude of the *plebs* at the time of the second and third Macedonian wars (XXXV 34, 3; XLII 30, 1) are thus amply justified, even though the 'principes' (as Livy admits in the second passage) were not all of one mind. It remains more significant than Deininger allows that Flamininus imposed timocratic arrangements in Thessaly in 194, and that Rome took similar measures more generally in and after 146 (for which see A. Fuks, JHS 1970, 78 ff.). The upper classes were more likely to be conscious of Rome's overwhelming might, and were probably averse to the financial sacrifices that war made necessary, as in 147/6 among the Achaeans. Deininger also forgets that in every Greek democracy, the Athens of Pericles, Cleon and Demosthenes not excluded, the *politeuomenoi* were inevitably men of some affluence. In fourth-century Athens no one avowed oligarchic sympathies before the Lamian war. But 'principes' like Phocion were very ready to accept power under an undemocratic regime imposed by Antipater. So were 'principes' in Thessaly in 194 and in Achaea in 146. It is no great distortion to call those upper-class politicians democrats who had the support of the masses, and those oligarchs who were ready to override the sentiments of the people, and if occasion offered, to take office under an oligarchic régime, established by a foreign conqueror, which at least guaranteed peace and the preservation of their material interests. Cf. also J. Briscoe, *St. in Anc. Soc.* (ed. M. I. Finley), London, 1974, ch. III.

13

Josephus on Social Conflicts in Roman Judaea

In chapter 12 I had occasion to observe that 'even in Judaea upper class Jews seem mostly to have opposed revolt or to have sought to sabotage it, not only because (as Josephus makes king Agrippa urge) in their judgement it was certain to fail, and it was folly to "kick against the pricks", but because Rome guaranteed the social order; the revolt of 66 was almost as much directed against native landlords and usurers as against the heathen rulers.'

For a justification of this statement it might seem enough to cite the valuable work of H. Kreißig[1] with some supplementary material in S. Applebaum, JRS 1971, 156 ff.; both cite earlier works, some in Hebrew. A full analysis of social conflicts in Roman Judaea and of the conditions which generated them can clearly only be offered by scholars who have at their command the evidence of the Dead Sea Scrolls and the Rabbinic writings. Lacking this qualification, I cannot assess with confidence the views of those who can handle all the material. Kreißig himself complains that in general scholars have underrated, or ignored, the social tensions in Roman Judaea. This complaint is justified of accounts he does not castigate, e.g., of Mommsen, Schürer (even in the revised English version[2]), and Dessau. Even Rostovtzeff[3] makes little of evidence that he could well have used to support his thesis of conflict between city bourgeoisie and peasants. A. Momigliano did indeed clearly note the contribution made by social tensions to the troubles in Roman Judaea, but only in a sketch[4] in which full documentation was not permitted. Yet even in our principal source, Josephus, the importance of these tensions appears so startlingly clear that it must evoke surprise that little attention has been paid to them. So far as I am aware, the relevant passages have never

[1] H. Kreißig, Die sozialen Zusammenhänge des judäischen Krieges, Berlin 1970.
[2] The History of the Jewish People in the Age of Jesus Christ I, Edinburgh 1973.
[3] M. Rostovtzeff, Social and Economic History of the Roman Empire, Oxford [2]1957, 270.
[4] CAH X, 850.

Klio, 59/1 (1977), 149-53.

been assembled, not even by Kreißig and Applebaum, and it may therefore be useful if I give them here, with a minimum of comment, to show that an explanation of the revolt of 66, and its antecedents, in exclusively religious, or religious and political terms, is actually inconsistent with that suggested by Josephus himself.

Josephus continually characterizes the faction (οἱ στασιασταί and the like) of revolutionaries (νεωτερίζοντες etc.) as brigands or *sicarii*; they are the scum of the earth (BJ IV 241, V 27, 444). At times he includes in this category both the Zealots, whose | villainy belied their honourable name (VII 268 f.), and (if they should be distinguished, which is unlikely) the sect founded in AD 6 by Judas of Galilee,[5] and still led by his descendants as late as 70, who held that obedience to God excluded allegiance to any Gentile ruler and that God would help the faithful who resisted Rome and took vengeance on Jews who disobeyed His law by submission; it was their teaching and conduct that in his view led on to the great revolt (AJ XVIII 2–25; BJ II 117–19, VII 253 ff.). For full documentation see M. Hengel,[6] note also his cogent protest (146 ff.) against viewing these religious fanatics as 'nationalists'. With this party Josephus continually contrasts the high priests and rulers, the 'first men', the notables (γνώριμοι or ἐπίσημοι) or magnates (δυνατοί), who even included Roman Equites (BJ II 308; cf. Vita 32 for the pro-Roman Iulius Capella at Tiberias), and with whom he himself, well-born and evidently rich (Vita 1–16), associated at Jerusalem in 66 (17 ff.). From AD 6 onwards men of this class were almost always advocates of submission, cf. AJ XVIII 3, XX 120–3 (with BJ II 237, under Cumanus), 178 (under Felix), notably at the inception of the great revolt (BJ II 315–25, 331 f., 338, 410–22). It is true that very soon the high priest, Ananus and other men of note took control, and it was they who sent Josephus to Galilee. But Josephus avows that he was opposed to the revolt, knowing it was bound to fail (Vita 17 ff.; cf. BJ III 131, 135 ff.), as did Ananus (IV 320)—the arguments imputed to Agrippa (II 345 ff.) and his agent at Gamala (Vita 59) represent their views—and that he was always anxious to surrender to Rome (ib. 175, cf. 72 and 78), like Ananus (BJ II 651). The instructions he received, to disarm the revolutionaries, a task that proved impossible (Vita 77), and to arm the 'best people' (29), already suggest that Ananus' party had no heart for the war; in Acrabatene, too, they were engaged in

---

[5] Applebaum 162 argues that Judas' resistence to the census of Quirinius can be explained in both economic and religious terms. On the weight of Roman taxes and of religious dues cf. 169; however, we have no warrant for the suggestion that Roman taxes were 'now collected directly by Roman officials', cf. BJ II 405, 407 and A. H. M. Jones, The Roman Economy, Oxford 1974, 165, with my notes there.

[6] M. Hengel, Die Zeloten II, Leiden–Cologne 1961.

suppressing the 'brigands', *i.e.*, the most resolute opponents of Rome
(BJ II 652). The protection Josephus initially afforded to pro-Roman
Sepphoris (Vita 30 f.) and his association with the leading men in
Galilee (220, 228, 266, 305), just the sort who were ready to submit
(131, 386), bear out his own version of his secret intentions (cf. the
analysis of the Vita by M. Gelzer[7]). Ananus later acknowledged that he
himself preferred the Romans to the Zealots (IV, 151, 160, 177–84).
Both Josephus (Vita 129 ff.) and Ananus (BJ IV 216 ff.) were charged
with treason, not unreasonably (pace IV 226, 250 f.), and Ananus and
other high priests paid for their duplicity with their lives (IV 314 ff.).
For other advocates of submission cf. II 649 f., IV 128. Desertions were
frequent (II 556, V 420 ff., VI 14 f.), though not entirely confined to
the rich and moderates (V 448 f., VI 229 f.), as well as killings of
suspects (infra). Cf. VII 409 ff. for the opposition of Jews of distinction
at Alexandria and the first men of the *gerousia* to the *sicarii*.

Josephus' vilification of the anti-Roman party as brigands and *sicarii*
derived plausibility from their persistent attacks on the property and
persons of all who would not join them in resistance. This began in AD
6 (AJ XVIII 7) and continued, spreading from rural areas to
Jerusalem under Felix, (BJ II 253–65, 271–9), | and reaching a cres-
cendo during the revolt (II 426–8, 441, 652, IV 134–46, 168, 181,
314 ff., esp. 327, 334 ff., 365, 560, V 424, 439, 527 ff., VII 254, Vita 77).
Josephus often makes it explicit that the rich were their chief targets.
Under Felix the notables used their power on local councils to arrest
the terrorists (II 273); by contrast, humble villagers could be regarded
as their accomplices (II 253), in 66 they were clearly dominant in
Galilee outside the towns, and their influence with the plebs at
Jerusalem is attested before the revolt (AJ XX 120 f.). Josephus says of
the élite at Jerusalem in 66 that 'they desired peace for the sake of their
possessions' (II 338), and that the leading men at Gadara offered
surrender 'from a longing for peace and because of their property' (IV
414, cf. 416).[8] If we built on this evidence alone it might seem enough
to say that the upper class in Judaea opposed resistance because it was
futile and they were bound to suffer economically from the costs of war
and from Roman reprisals, little as they can have loved foreign rule,
and that it was simply on this account that they incurred the wrath of
the extremists, whereas the common people, with less to lose and less
knowledge of Roman strength (BJ IV 126 f.), were naturally readier
for resistance. Even this analysis of the parties in Judaea bears out my

<hr />

[7] M. Gelzer, Kleine Schriften III, Wiesbaden 1964, 299 ff.
[8] The greater number of the Jews in Gadara fled rather than surrendered; Josephus estimates
the number of refugees who were killed and captured in the pursuit at far more than 17,000 (IV
435 f.).

initial statement about the attitude of the local ruling class in Judaea. But it does not do full justice to Josephus' own interpretation.

Josephus also ascribes the conduct of the revolutionaries to sheer greed (AJ XVIII 7; BJ VII 256, cf. 264). No doubt they included criminals whose purpose was simply to enrich themselves by robbery. But this is not all. He speaks of a universal sickness in Judaea from AD 6 which led the powerful to oppress the masses and the masses to plunder the rich (BJ VII 254-62). In AJ XX 180 f., 206 f., 213 f. he gives some instances of such behaviour; the first of these texts again depicts something like a class struggle. In 66 revolutionaries at Jerusalem burned down the record office, 'in order to destroy the bonds of the money-lenders and prevent the collection of debts, and so to win over the mass of grateful debtors and to make the poor rise against the rich with impunity' (BJ II 427). Thus they did not rely solely on men's religious sentiments. There was a similar incident at Antioch in 70, for which Jews were not responsible (VII 61). Animosity against the rich in Judaea was thus not due simply to their rejection of the ideals of religious fanatics, but partly to conditions which had analogies elsewhere. In Galilee the villagers were hostile to the towns (Vita 375), especially to Sepphoris (cf. 99, 124, 392) and Tiberias (99, 384); we may suppose that many of the peasants were burdened with debts to urban landlords and money-lenders. Naturally enough, Sepphoris was never loyal to the rebel cause (*contra* BJ II 574) and went over to Vespasian at the first opportunity (Vita 104, 123, 232, 340 f., 375 ff., 394, 411; cf. BJ II 511; III 30 ff., 61). Similarly at Tiberias the respectable people favoured peace—it was they who made repeated overtures to Agrippa (Vita 155, 381)—and it was the 'sailors and poor' that formed the war party (ib. 32 ff., cf. 66; BJ III 445-61). For Gadara cf. supra; at Tarichaeae the Romans distinguished between the urban population of the latter place, pacific 'because of their properties and city', and the immigrants who resisted its capture (III 492 f., cf. 532 ff.). At Gischala, too, the townsfolk, though themselves workers in the fields, favoured peace (IV 84, 120). There may even be some truth in Josephus' reiterated contention | that the people of Jerusalem itself really came to want peace (II 445, 449, 525, 538-40; IV 193, 197, 205 ff., V 27 ff., 53, 65) and that the city was controlled by the 'brigands' who had poured in from the countryside (IV 135-8); Ananus' party, we are told, was superior in numbers, but outclassed in arms and training (IV 197, 205 ff.). However, it was the urban plebs that had first risen in revolt.

Jesus and his early disciples were poor men. It is then significant that hatred of rich oppressors of the people comes through some texts of the *NT.*, *e.g.*, Luke I 52 f., VI 20 and 24 f., XVI 19-31; Mt XIX

22 f., XXI, 33–42, perhaps XXIII 6. But see above all James II 5 f., V 1–5.[9]

According to Josephus, during the great revolt every 'city', and even families and friends, were divided (BJ IV 131 f.). This is what we should expect in a revolutionary situation, especially when religious differences were compounded by social conflicts. Some of the 'brigands' no doubt deserved that appellation, and we need not wonder that they could be used by a procurator or by unscrupulous magnates for their own nefarious ends (AJ XX 163, 180, 213 f.). It is also comprehensible that individual magnates, from conviction or ambition, placed themselves at the head of the revolutionaries (BJ II 274), notably Eleazar, son of the high priest, Ananias (II 409); this set him in opposition to his own father and brother (418, 426 ff.), though he was soon fighting the Zealots after they killed his father (441 ff.). H. Drexler[10] could not believe that the family did not act as one, but such divisions are not unknown in civil wars.[11] Some persons of rank remained passively at Jerusalem (*e.g.*, IV 571 ff., VI 114 f., 201 f.), where many were to perish for suspected disloyalty; others, as we have seen, like Ananus and Josephus, provided half-hearted or insincere leadership for the rebels; the ambiguity of their intentions and the complexities of their predicament inevitably involved them in inconsistencies; Josephus had to act at times against his natural friends (*e.g.*, at Sepphoris) and even to fight the Romans. Josephus' bête noir, Justus of Tiberias, was probably another of the same kidney (cf. Vita 175 f., 390–3), like the Earl of Clare in the great English Civil War, of whom Lucy Hutchinson wrote that 'he was very often of both parties, and, I think, never advantaged either'. Even John of Gischala was initially for submission, until incensed by Gentile attacks on his town (ib. 43–5); men may go further in revolutions than they first designed. The Zealot faction led by Eleazar, son of Simon, included some persons of distinction (V 6); religious fervour might outweigh economic interests (cf. also VI 280, 356; Vita 191). But the extremists took most of their leaders from the lower orders, like John of Gischala (II 585); they chose as high priest, by lot, an ignorant rustic (IV 147–55); characteristically, poor Jews in Cyrene were seduced into a revolt by a weaver

[9] L. E. Elliott-Binns in Peake's Commentary on the Bible, London 1962, 1022 ff., takes the Epistle of 'James' to be addressed to Galilaean Christians from a very early period. The reminiscences of various prophetic books in chapter V are unlikely to be merely conventional; rather, they show that the greed and oppression of rich landowners denounced by Isaiah, Jeremiah, Amos, and Micah were the subject of complaint in the author's own day.

[10] Klio 19 (1925), 277 ff.

[11] *E.g.*, the Pierreponts in England in 1642, see Lucy Hutchinson's Memoirs of Col. Hutchinson.

(VII 437 ff). The general social complexion of the war and peace parties is quite clear in Josephus's account.

On his interpretation hostility to the rich clearly helped to swell the support the | extremists obtained, particularly among the peasants. Since Josephus was an apologist both for the Romans and for his own apostasy from the independence movement, it may well be that he emphasized the element of social conflict, precisely in order to convince Jews who read his work either in Greek or in the earlier Aramaic version of the *Bellum Iudaicum* that the victory of Rome best served their own interests.[12] (Naturally only the better educated would have read the Greek, and Kreißig 90 ff. questions if literacy was common, even in Aramaic, among the masses.) Even so, it seems unlikely that his interpretation had no basis in the facts, which must have been well known to contemporary readers in Palestine. Moreover, on occasions Josephus shows a certain degree of impartiality, criticizing the oppressiveness of the magnates as well as the violence of the reprisals taken against them. Of course we need not deny that religious fanaticism, Messianic delusions and the desire for freedom from foreign rule[13] played a larger part than economic considerations in the conscious motivations of many or most of the actors. Moreover, very probably the peasants were not more oppressed in Judaea than elsewhere[14] yet it was only in Judaea that their discontent issued in a formidable insurrection. Still, if we knew more of conditions and sentiments there, controversy on the basic causes of the revolt might be as acute as, for instance, on those of the Puritan revolution in England.

---

[12] BJ IV 508 alleges that Simon bar Giora offered freedom to slaves. This may be true, but the allegation was a familiar way of discrediting political opponents.

[13] Applebaum 161 f.

[14] Cf. the *émeute* at Antioch (BJ VII 61).

14

Laus Imperii[1]

I. THE NATURE OF THE EVIDENCE

My purpose in this paper is to explore the conceptions of empire prevalent in Cicero's day. What Romans thought is often best ascertained from their institutions and actions, and some use will be made of this kind of evidence; it is necessarily inferential, and there is always a danger of reading into the actions of Greeks and Romans motives of too modern a kind. However this may be, I propose to draw principally on actual statements by Romans, as the clearest indications of what was most explicit in their own consciousness; how far this reveals the true driving forces in their imperial conduct is another matter, which may be left to bolder inquiry.

Only two authors supply much material: Cicero and Caesar. It may indeed be remembered that Virgil, Horace and Livy all matured in Cicero's lifetime, and that Livy may often reflect the views of annalists of this or of a still earlier period; moreover I believe that the imperial ideals of the Augustan age were much the same as those of the late republic.[2] Still, citations of these writers will be subsidiary. It remains, however, to ask how far the utterances of Cicero and Caesar can be regarded as representative of their time. Any assumption that they actually held typical views themselves may appear unwarranted and indeed implausible.

Cicero's own personal opinions can be properly elicited only from his intimate letters and those theoretical writings in which he speaks *in propria persona* (as in *de officiis*) or through an interlocutor in a dialogue who can be identified as his own mouthpiece, like Scipio and Laelius in his *de republica*, or Cotta in *de natura deorum*. It is astonishing that certain

---

[1] This is an enlarged and revised version of the paper read to a Cambridge seminar. References to modern works are necessarily sparse and often hardly reveal my debt to them. See Bibliography at end for citations: otherwise standard abbreviations are used. [See also ch. 18 n. 1.]

[2] See chapter 5; cf. also W. Schmitthenner, *Gnomon* XXXVII (1965), 152 ff.; Wells (1972)—though the archaeological evidence he examines naturally cannot attest Augustus' ultimate intentions.

P. D. A. Garnsey and C. R. Whittaker (eds.), *Imperialism in the Ancient World* (Cambridge, 1978), 159–91.

scholars freely quote from speeches, or from his exposition of those
Stoic theories, which he may have been inclined to adopt but in later
years could never quite accept,[3] as if they are sufficient to attest his true
beliefs. Even the grand statement of a political programme in his | de-
fence of Sestius (96–139) can only be safely taken as sincere because it
agrees so closely with what he says in other works, where he had no
reason to veil or distort his real views. But for our present purposes the
speeches are actually of prime value. The skilled and successful orator,
such as he was, had to persuade his audience and, therefore, to play on
their beliefs and feelings.[4] We know that Cicero could for this end
express views he was far from sharing, for instance in the ridicule he
cast on the study of civil law and on Stoic tenets in his speech for
Murena (26–9, 60–7). His appeals to religion may in some degree be
comparable (see below). Whereas his own genuine beliefs about the
empire might in principle be treated as unique or unusual, his public
utterances should tell us by implication what was widely thought by
those who heard him. Orations delivered before the senate or upper-
class juries would have mirrored the opinions of senators and equites,
and *contiones* those prevalent in other strata of society.

Unfortunately we cannot overhear Cicero on the *rostra*; with one
exception the published versions of the speeches we have were not
verbally identical with those he delivered, and may sometimes have
differed significantly in substance; some indeed had no spoken proto-
types.[5] But it may surely be assumed that when Cicero published
speeches he had delivered, as well as those he had not, his purpose was
either to influence opinion or to immortalize his eloquence,[6] if not to do
both. In the former case his speeches are evidently indicative of what
others thought. The reading public must indeed have consisted only of
men of education and therefore of wealth. It might then seem that the
published versions of speeches delivered to the people *may* tell us little
of what he said to them and consequently can provide no certain
evidence of their sentiments. But this need not be true. In so far as his

---

[3] *de nat. deor.* 3.95. In *de offic.* he adopts the practical morality of the middle Stoa, but all his last
philosophical works show that he could no longer accept the metaphysical basis for ethics and
politics which he had taken over from the Stoa in *de leg.* book 1 with 2.15 f.

[4] See e.g. *de orat.* 1.219–23; 2.30, 131, 178 and 206. All these passages are put into the mouth of
Antonius, whose conception of the orator's role certainly falls short of the ideal, expressed in the
dialogue by Crassus, and by Cicero himself in his own person in his *Orator*, but Antonius'
conception is treated as only inadequate, and the views cited are not contradicted elsewhere; cf.
also *Brut.* 184–9; *pro Cluent.* 139.

[5] On the relation between actual and published speeches see esp. L. Laurand, *Ét. sur le style des
discours de Cicéron*[2] (Paris, 1925) 1 1 ff.

[6] *ad Att.* 2.1.3 seems to me to show that when he sent his consular speeches to Atticus, surely for
publication, his aim was to perpetuate the fame of the Roman Demosthenes, not to disseminate
pamphlets relevant to the political situation in 60; cf. n. 8.

aim was to give permanence to specimens of his oratorical skill, he had good reason not to omit any of the sophistries of persuasion that he had actually employed and that connoisseurs of the art would enjoy. Although Cicero sometimes equated the perfect orator with the wise statesman,[7] statesmanship was to be judged by the ends pursued and the adoption of means appropriate to those ends, and he had no reason to fear that his readers would think less well of him as a politician, if it appeared that he had | pandered in words to the mob for such laudable purposes as defeating Rullus' land-bill or Catiline's conspiracy.[8] Such speeches in fact 'ring true', and surely reveal the popular sentiments on which Cicero found it expedient to play.

As for Caesar's *Commentaries*, I take it for granted that, however truthful they may be as a record of events, they were written partly at least in order to depict Caesar's conduct in a way that would win the approval of his readers. Thus Caesar too betrays the attitudes common in the whole upper class, to whom he is addressing an apologia.

II. ROMAN AND ATHENIAN VIEWS OF THEIR EMPIRES

It will appear that the Romans themselves liked to believe that they had acquired their dominions justly, by fighting for their own security or for the protection of their allies. Victory had conferred on them the right to rule over the conquered, and they were naturally conscious that this right was profitable to them, nor were they ashamed of the booty and tribute they exacted. However, they preferred to dwell on the sheer glory of empire, which made Rome specially worthy of the devotion of her citizens (*de orat.* 1.156). Much of this thinking is reminiscent of the interpretation Thucydides put on Athenian imperialism, in the speeches he ascribes to Athens' spokesmen. Like all other

---

[7] This view is asserted, and repeated against objections, in *de orat.* 1.29–34, 202; 3.55–60 and 133–42, but virtually abandoned in *Orator* (despite continued insistence on the need for philosophic knowledge) and *Brutus*.

[8] Contrast references to the Gracchi honorific in his *contiones* (*de leg. agr.* 2.11, 31 and 81; *pro Rab. perd.* 14), hostile in speeches to the senate (*in Cat.* 1.3 ff. and 29, 4.13; *de leg. agr.* 1.21). In 60 he was engaged in protecting the interests of Sullan *possessores* by amendments to Flavius' bill without objecting to the purchase of lands for distribution (*ad Att.* 1.19.4); in 63 he had shown his care for the former class in the senate (*de leg. agr.* 1.12), but railed at Rullus for protecting them before the people (*de leg. agr.* 3 *passim*), and he had protested against purchase of lands from willing sellers (1.14, 2.63–72). Knowing readers would have perceived the insincerity of his reproaching Rullus for speaking of the urban plebs *quasi de aliqua sentina* (ibid. 70; cf. *ad Att.* loc. cit.), and would have smiled at his pose as a true *popularis* and at his skill in representing the optimate ideals, of which in 60 he was an unashamed champion, as genuinely popular (1.23 ff., 2.6–10; cf. *pro Ses.* 97 ff.), and in invoking popular conceptions of *liberatas* against the professedly popular tribunes, Rullus and Labienus (e.g. *de leg. agr.* 2.15–22; *pro Rab. perd.* 10–17), all in the interest of senatorial control.

peoples, the Athenians had been led to acquire their empire by considerations of security, profit and prestige (1.76), but it is on the undying fame that Athens had won by reducing the greatest number of Greeks to subjection (2.64) that he seems to lay the greatest weight, and it was the power of the city that should inspire the affection of her citizens and make them glad to sacrifice themselves in her service (2.43). To Romans the glory of their empire was even greater than that which Pericles could claim for Athens, because they had come to think that it properly embraced the whole world. Moreover, this dominion was ordained by the gods, whose favour Rome had deserved by piety and justice, and it was exercised in the interest of the subjects. It needs no proof that Thucydides did not look on Athenian policy in the same light. But less impartial or less cynical observers could go almost as far in justifying her imperialism. We can see this from Isocrates' *Panegyricus*, which certainly reflects ideas already current | in the fifth century, though it would take me too far afield to demonstrate this here. The Athenians too had liked to see themselves as protectors of peoples unjustly threatened or oppressed, and as benefactors of their subjects; it seems very doubtful if many of them acknowledged publicly or in their own hearts that their empire was a tyranny and unjustly acquired. What was most novel in the Roman attitude to their empire was the belief that it was universal and willed by the gods.

III. THE GLORY OF IMPERIAL EXPANSION

In the political programme Cicero sketched in his defence of Sestius (96 ff.) he maintained that all good men should seek *otium cum dignitate*. *Otium* must have included security from external attack (*de orat.* 1.14), and *dignitas* suggests, among other things, the glory of the whole state (*pro Sest.* 104); *provinciae, socii, imperii laus, res militaris* are expressly named among the *fundamenta otiosae dignitatis*. Much of Cicero's programme can have had no appeal to the poor either in Rome or in the country, but the urban plebs at least could apparently be moved by the glamour of imperial glory; in his speech for the Manilian law Cicero enlarges on the dishonour Rome had suffered from the pirates and from Mithridates, and on the necessity of entrusting the eastern command to Pompey, in order to restore 'the prestige of the Roman people which has been transmitted to you by our ancestors and whose greatness appears in every way and above all in the military domain' (6; cf. 7–11, 53 ff.). No other people, he says there, had ever had such an appetite for glory, and we know that in his own judgement this had been a dominant motive for the old Romans (*de rep.* 5.9). He can argue for the propriety or wisdom of any practices which have in the past served to aggrandize the empire (*pro Rosc. Am.* 50, *Phil.* 5.47), or which its long existence in itself justifies. Both Pompey and Caesar are lauded for making its boundaries coterminous with the *orbis terrarum*,[9] a boast that Pompey made for himself on a monument recording his deeds in Asia (Diod. 40.4). The speech *de provinciis consularibus* is particularly significant in this connexion. As an encomiast of Caesar in 56, Cicero was in a delicate position. Both he and the majority of the senate had recently been in opposition to Caesar. However, he finds it plausible to assert that Caesar's achievements in Gaul | had changed their attitude, and rightly changed it, hence the extraordinary honours the senate had already voted to the conqueror (25; cf. *in Pis.* 81). In the long letter he wrote to Lentulus in 54, which was probably intended as an apologia for a wider public, Cicero exculpates his own change of course in much the same way: it is now, he claims, the triumvirs who are doing most to secure *otium cum dignitate*, and Caesar's conquests are part of his case (*ad fam.* 1.9.12–18 and 21). It seems to me highly improbable that these sentiments, however insincere on the lips of Cicero, whose correspondence in the 50s, even with his brother Quintus in Gaul, betrays little interest and no pride in the conquests, were not genuinely felt by Romans, with less than Cicero to lose from the dominance of the triumvirs, or that Caesar himself was untruthful in recording that in 49 the councillors of Auximum, in Pompey's homeland of Picenum, declined to exclude from their town *C. Caesarem imperatorem, bene de republica meritum, tantis rebus gestis* (*BC* 1.13).

There is abundant evidence for the value individual Romans set on *gloria*,[10] but, as Cicero says in his defence of Archias, they could win no greater renown than by victories in war, renown in which the whole people shared (21 ff.; cf. 30). In *de officiis* Cicero admits that most men rank success in war above achievements in peace (1.74), and that it had been the most natural and traditional objective for a young aristocrat (2.45); in public he declared that military talent had brought eternal glory to Rome and compelled the world to obey her commands and that it was to be more highly valued than the orator's eloquence (*pro Mur.* 21 ff.). He scoffed at the Epicurean Piso's professed disdain for a triumph as preposterous and incredible (*in Pis.* 56 ff.), and for all his own rational expectation to be immortalized as the Roman Demosthenes (cf. n. 6) and perhaps as the Roman Plato, he magnified his own petty exploits in Mount Amanus in hope of the honour.[11] The triumph,

---

[9] E.g. *in Cat.* 3.26; *pro Sest.* 67; *de prov. cons.* 30, 33; *pro Balb.* 64.

[10] *pro Arch.* 12–32 is the *locus classicus*. Much evidence in U. Knoche's paper, reprinted in H. Oppermann (1967), 420–46. On the old Roman *virtus*, manifest in services to the state, see Earl (1961), ch. II.

[11] See esp. *ad fam.* 15.4–6. Cicero retained the title of *imperator* at least till May 49 (ibid. 2.16).

properly granted only to the general who had slain 5,000 of the enemy in a single battle (Val. Max. 2.8.1), was itself the institutional expression of Rome's military ideal. According to Cicero (*de rep.* 3.24) the words *finis imperii propagavit* appeared on the monuments of her great generals; in his speeches he takes it for granted that victory and the extension of empire are the objectives of any provincial governor (*de prov. cons.* 29, *Phil.* 13.14), and at his most theoretical he | prescribes that wise statesmen should do their utmost in peace and war *ut rem publicam augeant imperio agris vectigalibus* (*de offic.* 2.85), thus accepting in 44 B.C. a principle of statecraft that no contemporary had done more to fulfil than Caesar, whom at this very time he was concerned to vilify (1.26, 2.23–8, 3.83 etc.). In *de oratore* 1.196 he roundly asserted that no fatherland deserved so much love as Rome, *quae una in omnibus terris domus est virtutis, imperii, dignitatis.*

IV. *VIRTUS, FORTUNA* AND THE WILL OF THE GODS

Thus Cicero could not free himself from the militarism of the traditions he revered, which appeared in the old prayer of the censors for the aggrandizement of Rome (Val. Max. 4.1.10), in the rule that the *pomerium* might be extended only by those *qui protulere imperium* (Tac. *Ann.* 12.23)—among them was Sulla—and perhaps in the alleged predictions of *haruspices* that the wars with Philip V, Antiochus and Perseus would advance *terminos populi Romani*. If these predictions recorded by Livy (21.5.7, 36.1.3, 42.30.9) are not annalistic fabrications, they cast doubt on the view that any of these wars were merely defensive in motivation, but even if they were invented by Valerius Antias or Claudius Quadrigarius (if not earlier), they still illustrate the imperialistic conceptions dominant in the time of their invention, and accepted by Livy, in whose work *belli gloria* is naturally a pervasive theme. In particular, the legend of Marcus Curtius, for which our earliest source is a contemporary of Cicero, Procilius, enshrined the truth that it was *arma virtusque* that guaranteed Rome's perpetuity (7.6.3). In Livy's view it was the number and valour of Rome's soldiers and the talents of her generals—elsewhere he also stresses military discipline, to which Cicero only once alludes (*Tusc. disp.* 1.2)—which with the help of fortune had made Rome unconquerable.[12]

---

[12] Cf. Livy 1.16.7, 8.7.16: *disciplinam militarem, qua stetit ad hunc diem* (340 BC) *Romana res;* 9.17.3: *plurimum in bello pollere videntur militum copia et virtus, ingenia imperatorum, fortuna per omnia humana, maxima in res bellicas potens; ea et singula intuenti et universa sicut ab aliis regibus gentibusque, ita ab hoc quoque* (Alexander) *facile praestant invictum Romanum imperium;* 9.17.10 (discipline); *praef.* 7: *ea belli gloria est populo Romano ut cum suum conditorisque sui parentem Martem potissimum ferat, tam et hoc gentes*

It was, however, not only military qualities that were thought to have made Rome great. Wise policy was another factor (*de rep.* 2.30). Like Polybius, Cicero clearly laid great weight on Rome's balanced constitution.[13] Most Romans were not political theorists, but traditions counted heavily with them; as Cicero's innumerable allusions in speeches to ancestral wisdom[14] indicate; in his defence of Murena (75) he casually refers to *instituta maiorum quae | diuturnitas imperi comprobat*, and we may conjecture that a widely shared conviction that these institutions had contributed to the acquisition of empire was one reason why Augustus felt it necessary to veil the extent to which he had subverted them.[15] In one speech Cicero suggested that Rome's readiness to share political rights with other peoples, even with defeated enemies, had been of the highest importance in her aggrandizement (*pro Balb.* 31); more was to be made of this theme by Livy, and by Dionysius who doubtless drew the idea from Romans he met or from the annals he read.[16] Posidonius too was obviously following Roman mentors when he extolled the frugality, simplicity, good faith and piety of the old Romans in a passage in which he is acounting for Rome's rise to power:[17] *moribus antiquis res stat Romana virisque*. Sallust and others apprehended danger to Rome from the degeneration from those pristine standards which they detected in their own day.[18]

Romans themselves acknowledged that fortune as well as virtue had assisted them; for instance the situation of the city, and the centrality of Italy within the Mediterranean world, had favoured expansion, and Italy's natural resources were actually exaggerated.[19] But the Roman

---

humanae patiantur aequo animo quam imperium patiuntur. (The idea that subjects accept an imperial power as 'deserving' to rule because of military prowess is in Thuc. 2.41.3.) Drexler (1959) cites many other texts from Livy on the concept of military glory.

[13] *de rep.* 2 *passim*; cf. Polyb. 6.50, [and notably 3.6.2.]

[14] See Roloff (1938).

[15] F. Millar, *JRS* LXIII (1973), 50 ff. and E. A. Judge in J. A. S. Evans, ed., *Polis and Imperium: Studies in honour of E. T. Salmon* (Toronto, 1974), 279 ff., may be right in denying that Augustus officially claimed to have 'restored the Republic' in so many words, but Vell. 2.89 (and much else) shows that such a claim would well have summarized the official view of his settlement; it is significant that Velleius, a new man himself, is so concerned to stress that *prisca illa et antiqua rei publicae forma revocata (est)*. [See Brunt, *Biblioteca di Labeo* 6 (1982), 236 ff.]

[16] Livy 4.3 ff. (whence Claudius' speech in *ILS* 212 and Tac. *Ann.* 11.24); 8.13 (*voltis exemplo maiorum augere rem Romanam victos in civitatem accipiendo? materia crescendi per summam gloriam suppeditat*); Dionys. *Ant.* 2.16 ff.; 14.6; cf. Brunt (1971), 538 f. Cf. Cic. *de offic.* 1.35 and p. 316.

[17] Jacoby, *FGH* 87 F 59. 111b (military discipline) and 112. I would ascribe Diod. 37.2–6 to Posidonius, who also deplored the decay of the old standards; cf. n. 18.

[18] E.g. Sall. *Cat.* 6–13; Cic. *pro Marc.* 23; *Tusc. disp.* 1.2; Hor. *Odes* 3.6 and 24, etc. Hampl (1959) cites further texts and argues that such complaints (cf. also n. 17), which are just as common in classical Greece, have no basis in history and may actually betoken a heightened moral consciousness in the ages when they are made; I agree.

[19] Cic. *de rep.* 2.5–11; Livy 5.54 (site of Rome); Vitruv. 6.1. 10 ff.; Strabo 6.4.1 (strategic centrality of Italy). *Laudes Italiae*, a theme dear to Varro: Brunt (1971), 128 ff.

conception of fortune tended to be that of which Cicero speaks: *divinitus adiuncta fortuna* (*de imp. Cn. Pomp.* 47). The gods were the guardians of city and empire.[20] It was Roman piety that had earned their goodwill. In Propertius' words (3.22.21), *quantum ferro tantum pietate potentes stamus.* Virgil's Aeneas, *pietate insignis et armis*, was the prototype of the people aided and destined by the gods to conquer. In public Cicero gave the most eloquent expression to the notion, which we can trace from a praetor's letter of 193 B.C. to the time of Augustine, that 'it was by our scrupulous attention to religion and by our wise grasp of a single truth, that all things are ruled and directed by the will of the gods, that we have overcome all peoples and nations'.[21]

It may be doubted if Cicero himself had firm religious convictions. There is no hint of personal devotion in his intimate letters; above all, he never expresses hope of assistance from the gods in moments of the deepest distress or anxiety.[22] But he held that it was expedient to imbue the citizens with religious faith, in order that they might be deterred by the fear of divine retribution from infringing oaths and treaties, and from crimes in | general. If men ceased to think that the gods took no care for mankind and to pay them due honour, good faith, social co-operation and justice would surely be extinguished. Polybius had already traced the high moral standards of old Rome to the prevalence of a scrupulous fear of the gods.[23] The ideal system of sacred law Cicero sketches in the second book of *de legibus* is expressly modelled on the Roman (2.23). He lays great emphasis on the powers of the aristocratic priesthoods, 'for it helps to hold the state together that the people should always need the advice and authority of the *optimates*' (2.30). Cicero unhesitatingly approved the abuse of priestly authority for obstructing 'seditious' proposals.[24] The truth of beliefs implicit in

---

[20] E.g. *in Cat.* 2.29, 3.18–22 (a remarkable testimony to popular superstition); *de dom.* 143; *pro Sest.* 53; *in Vat.* 14; *pro Scaur.* 48; *pro Mil.* 83; Sall. *BJ* 14.19.

[21] *de har. resp.* 18 ff., with particular reference to the skill of the *haruspices* in advising on the placation of the gods. Cicero was bound, if he was to persuade senators who credited this nonsense, not to let his own scepticism appear. Cf. *de nat. deor.* 2.8 ('Stoic'); *SIG³* 601; Hor. *Odes* 3.6.1 ff.; *Mos. et Rom. Leg. Coll.* 6.4.8. (Diocletian); Aug. *Civ. Dei*, books 4 and 5 *passim*.

[22] K. Latte (1960), 285 f. Goar (1972) ascribes a more sincere religious belief to Cicero, but his candid analysis of the letters yields a similar result.

[23] *de leg.* 2.15 ff.; *de nat. deor.* 1.3 ff., 77; Polyb. 6.56; cf. Posidonius (n. 17). Cicero also suggests that Athenians and Romans were civilized respectively by the Eleusinian Mysteries and by Numa's rituals (*de leg.* 2.36; *de rep.* 2.26 ff.). It is hard to see how Roman religion was ever thought to deter men from wrong-doing. Goar (1972) notes that Cicero only twice threatens his enemies with punishment after death (*in Cat.* 1.33; *Phil.* 14.32); see Latte (1960), 286 ff., for lack of belief in an after-world, cf. esp. *pro Cluent.* 171. *de leg.* 2.25 suggests that religion makes men fear immediate punishment by the gods, but *de har. resp.* 39, *de leg.* 1.40 that they merely afflict the wrongdoer with *furor*, to which *de leg.* 2.43 ff. adds posthumous infamy.

[24] *de leg.* 2.30–4, 3.27; *post red. sen.* 11, etc.; cf. Goar (1972), 48 ff. Yet, as Latte (1960), 299, justly remarks, Bibulus' *obnuntiatio* had no effect even on the masses.

the ancestral rituals was irrelevant to their utility. In the same way Varro adopted the view of Q, Mucius Scaevola that philosophic views on religion were unsuited to the masses and that traditional rites should be kept up for their benefit. Varro indeed held that there was a basis of truth in the old religion, which he reconciled with Stoic pantheism.[25] In *de legibus* Cicero adopted a similar standpoint.

In this work he accepted the Stoic justification of divination; it was at least credible in principle, though Cicero already denied that the augurs of his own day (he was one himself) any longer enjoyed knowledge of the future,[26] and insisted above all on their political importance. By the end of his life he had come to reject every kind of divination. Yet in the very treatise, *de divinatione*, in which he discredits belief in the supernatural power of *haruspices* and augurs as mere superstition, he reiterates that for political reasons the old practices should be maintained.[27] This work is a sequel to his *de natura deorum*, in which his mouthpiece, Cotta, refutes all Stoic teaching on divine providence in a way which could be said *deos funditos tollere* (*de div.* 1.9). Cotta is actually made to say that experience throws doubt on the very existence of gods, though as a pontiff, bound to maintain the cults, he would never avow this *in contione* (*de nat. deor.* 1.61). It is true that at the end Cicero makes Cotta indicate that he would like to be convinced that the Stoics were in the right (3.95), and declare that no philosophic reasoning could induce him to question the truth of ancestral beliefs on the worship of the gods, and that Rome could never have achieved such greatness but for her supreme care in placating them | (3.5 ff.; cf. 14). Strictly this means that Cotta accepts on authority all the traditional *beliefs* including those which Cicero was to ridicule in *de divinatione*. I suspect that Cicero has gone further than he really intended here, and that he should have made Cotta say merely that all the ancient *practices* were to be preserved, irrespective of their truth.

Whatever Cicero's personal convictions may have been, they are primarily of biographical interest; we cannot properly generalize from a single individual. But the cynical manipulation of the official religion for political ends is itself one piece of evidence for the decay of belief in it among the controlling aristocracy. Of course it does not stand alone: at this time many cults were neglected, the calendar was often in

---

[25] Varro, who himself accepted Stoic theology (Tert. *ad Nat.* 2.2), regarded it as superstition to fear the gods, disapproved of images and thought sacrifices futile (Arnob. 7.1), none the less held that the state religion was better than that of philosophers for the people, whom it was expedient to deceive; though he would not have instituted the old Roman religion in a new city, it was the duty of the priests to keep up the cults *ut potius (deos) magis colere quam despicere vulgus velit* (Aug. *Civ. Dei* 4.31; cf. 4.11.13 and 27; 6.5 f.). Cf. Latte (1960), 291 ff.

[26] *de leg.* 2.32 ff.; cf. *de div.* 2.75. On Appius Claudius see Latte (1960), 291.

[27] *de div.* 2.28.70 and 148.

disarray, priesthoods were unfilled, temples were falling into disrepair, the pontifical law was no longer studied, and in public and private life auspices were not duly observed.[28] Can we then suppose that the conception that the empire depended on divine favour really had much influence on men's minds?

The answer is surely that Cicero and other highly educated aristocrats were not representative figures. It is significant that Cicero in his speech *de haruspicum responsis* (18) finds it necessary to deny that his philosophical studies have alienated him from the old religion. The frequency of his public appeals to religion is surely proof that belief was still widespread.[29] There can be no doubt that superstition was rife among the ignorant masses.[30] But Cicero was just as apt to play on religious sentiment when addressing members of the higher orders. To take only one example, *religiones* and *auspicia* come first in the *fundamenta otiosae dignitatis* as a part of the programme that was to enlist the support of all *boni et locupletes* throughout Italy (*pro Sest.* 98). I do not suppose that they were meant to think only of the opportunities for political obstruction which the old religion furnished. The so-called religious revival that Augustus was to attempt may well have appealed to the old-fashioned municipal gentry, who were already playing a larger part in the political life of Cicero's time and whose support he sought, like Augustus after him.[31] It may be noted that the incest of Clodius in 62 aroused indignation first among the lower ranks in the senate, a body of which probably under | thirty per cent belonged to noble houses.[32] Most Romans may well have retained the conviction that it was to the gods that they owed their empire, an empire that was said to be coterminous with the *orbis terrarum*.

V. THE CONCEPTION OF WORLD EMPIRE

Virgil's Jupiter was to bestow on Rome a dominion without limits in space or time (*Aen.* 1.277 ff.). Cicero and his contemporaries, and

[28] Latte (1960), ch. X; F. Schulz, *Roman legal science* (Oxford, 1946), 80 ff.

[29] They are collected by Ursula Heibges, *Latomus* XXVIII (1969), 833–49. I do not accept her assumption that Cicero shared, as well as adapted himself to, the vacillating beliefs of his contemporaries.

[30] See W. Kroll, *Kultur der ciceronischen Zeit* (Leipzig, 1933), I ch. I, who in my view overestimates the continuing strength of the traditional religion even in educated circles.

[31] Tac. *Ann.* 3.35, 16.4; Pliny, *Ep.* 1.14.4 apply *a fortiori* to this period, cf. Cic. *pro Rosc. Am.* 43–8; it is reasonable to believe that piety was as much valued as other ancient virtues.

[32] This is based on analysis of the list of senators in 55 in P. Willems, *Le Sénat de la République rom.* (Paris, 1878), ch. XV, which, though antiquated, will serve for a rough estimate; I assume that *novi* preponderated among the *ignoti*. Clodius' *incestum: ad Att.* 1.13.3; cf. 12.3, 14.1–5, 16.1–9. I can see no evidence that Cicero or the other *principes* acted from outraged religious feeling.

perhaps Virgil's, were somewhat less confident. More than once Cicero avers that Rome had no external enemies to fear, but that her eternity could only be assured if she remained faithful to the institutions and customs that had made her great.[33] On the other hand he constantly speaks, and sometimes in quite casual ways with no rhetorical inflation (e.g. *de orat.* 1.14), as if Rome already ruled all peoples or the whole *orbis terrarum*.[34] This conception also appears in an admittedly rather grandiloquent preamble to a consular law of 58: *imperio am[pli]ficato [p]ace per orbe[m terrarum confecta]*. A century earlier, Polybius had held that by 167 B.C. the whole, or virtually the whole *oikoumene*, or its known parts, had come under Roman dominion. His true meaning is better conveyed in other texts in which he ascribes to Rome mastery over land and sea of concern to us (*kath'hemas*), or of those which had fallen under inquiry (*historian*); evidently these did not embrace all the parts of the world that geographers had described but only those which formed Polybius' political universe.[35] *Orbis terrarum* was often used in the same restricted sense (cf. n. 34).

Even so, it is obvious that in the time both of Polybius and of Cicero Rome did not herself administer the whole of this political universe. Both must then have conceived that her dominion extended beyond the provinces to the kings, tribes and cities who were bound to Rome by alliances, even if the terms of the treaty, as with little Astypalaea,[36] affected a formal equality between the High Contracting Parties which harsh reality rendered meaningless, or who were linked by the looser tie of *amicitia*, which within Rome's own society was often a courteous synonym for clientage.[37] In form the status of such allies and friends of Rome beyond provincial frontiers was no different from that of others like Massilia whose territories constituted enclaves within a | province. In reality the degree of their dependence was determined by the advantages or disadvantages that might induce Rome to punish or overlook disobedience to her will.

Augustus was to regard all *reges socios* as *membra partisque imperii* (Suet. *Aug.* 48). Owing their thrones to recognition, if not to appointment, by

---

[33] *in Cat.* 2.11; *pro Rab. perd.* 33; *pro Sest.* 50; *de rep.* 3.41. Cf. Hor. *Epodes* 16; Livy 9.19.17.

[34] Vogt (1960) assembles texts and interprets the meaning of the phrase. *ad Her.* 4.13 is the earliest extant instance in Latin. Alternatively, Cicero speaks of Rome's power over all peoples, II *Verr.* 4.81; *de leg. agr.* 2.22; *de dom.* 90; *pro Planc.* 11; *Phil.* 6.19. Cf. n. 67.

[35] *SEG* 1.335 [for better text cf. C. Nicolet etc., *Insula Sacra, Collections de l'École fr. de Rome* (1980)], cf. Cic. *ad Att.* 4.1.7 (consular law of 57 *de annona*); Polyb. 1.1.5, 1.3.10, 3.1.4, 6.50.6; for his true meaning 1.3.9, 15.9.5 with 2.14.7 and 4.2.2. A gloss in Vell. 1.6.6 shows that Aemilius Sura dated Rome's world dominion to the defeat of Antiochus III; some hold that he wrote before 171, see Swain (1940). Polybius' conception was then perhaps shared by Romans in his own lifetime.

[36] Sherk (1969), no. 16.

[37] Badian (1958), part I *passim*.

Rome, they were not necessarily scions of an established royal house nor even drawn from the people they ruled; normally they now enjoyed Roman citizenship, a symbol of their function as creatures and agents of the suzerain. Augustus naturally included his dealings with them in his record of the deeds *quibus orbem terrarum imperio populi Romani subiecit*. In his view Armenia was in revolt when it rejected the princes he named. He justified by ancestral practice his decision not to annex that country; Lucullus and Pompey had in fact already reduced it to vassalage.[38]

Under his more efficient regime 'client' states were perhaps more closely controlled than in the republic, but Cicero had already included all kingdoms and *liberae civitates* in the *orbis terrarum*, where every Roman in virtue of his citizenship should be safe from arbitrary punishment (II *Verr.* 5.168), and in 47 B.C. an attack on king Deiotarus could be construed as a violation of *populi Romani ius maiestatemque* (*B. Alex.* 34). In Cicero's phrase Rome was *dominus regum* (*de dom.* 90), and when Tacitus declared it to be an ancient and long-approved practice of the republic to make kings *instrumenta servitutis* (*Agr.* 14), he was echoing Sallust, who represents Mithridates as telling how Eumenes of Pergamum had been reduced by Rome to the most wretched slavery (*ep. Mith.* 8; cf. *BJ* 31.9). Sallust too makes Adherbal recall to the senate that his father, Micipsa, had enjoined on him *uti regni Numidiae tantummodo procurationem existumarem meam, ceterum ius et imperium eius penes vos esse*.[39] From the second century such rulers had had to look to Rome for recognition, and like free cities and friendly tribes, they were expected to conform their policy to Rome's will, to furnish military aid and money or supplies, when occasion demanded; some were actually tributary. In return they had a moral claim to Rome's protection (e.g. *BJ* 14, *B. Alex.* 34). In 51 B.C. king Ariobarzanes of Cappadocia plainly depended wholly on Rome to defend him against Parthian attack or the internal discontent, fostered no doubt by the exactions required to meet the usurious demands of Pompey and | Brutus. Modern descriptions of such client kingdoms or peoples as 'buffer states' is never adequate and often quite misleading. Analogies with the princedoms of British India or the system of 'indirect rule'

---

[38] Cimma (1976) gives the fullest recent treatment of 'client' kings. Citizenship: *PIR²* A 900; H 153; I 65, 131 f., 136, 149 f., 175 f., 274–7, 472, 512–17, 541, 582, 637, 644, 651–3. Armenia: *RG* 27. Lucullus had overrun Armenia; Pompey received the humble submission of Tigranes and recognized him as king, friend and ally of Rome (Cic. *Sest.* 58 ff.; Plut. *Pomp.* 53, etc.). When Corbulo proposed *parta olim a Lucullo Pompeioque recipere* (Tac. *Ann.* 13.34), he designed (as the context shows) to force the Parthian nominee on the throne to recognize, like Tigranes, the suzerainty of Rome: there was no thought of annexation.

[39] *BJ* 14.1; cf. Livy 42.6.8 (Antiochus IV, see n. 80); 45.44.19 (Prusias I); also the Rhodian speech in 37.54.

in British Nigeria would be more to the point.[40] A recent writer has drawn a distinction between the Roman empire *stricto* and *lato sensu*, the former comprising only territory under Rome's own administration and the latter the subordinate states as well. This is clearly a useful tool of analysis, but it does not correspond to Roman usage.[41]

VI. UNLIMITED EXPANSION

The duty acknowledged by the Romans (but not invariably performed) of protecting their friends and allies could involve them in wars with peoples who had hitherto lain beyond their orbit. Victory made these peoples in turn Rome's subjects. Thus the limits of the *orbis terrarum* within which she claimed dominion were continually advancing. There was no point at which such expansion could halt, so long as any independent people remained. Indeed, as P. Veyne has argued, the very existence of a truly independent power was viewed at Rome as a potential threat to her own security.[42]

The early treaties with Carthage, and perhaps one with Tarentum, had bound Rome to keep out of certain lands or seas.[43] There is no certain evidence that she ever accepted such a restriction after the war with Pyrrhus. Livy indeed says that under the pact with Hasdrubal the Ebro became *finis utriusque imperii* (21.2.7), but Polybius that it simply forbade the Carthaginians to cross that river, and there is no hint that Hannibal contended that Rome had infringed its terms by intervening on behalf of Saguntum.[44] At one time Flamininus offered Antiochus III a line of demarcation between his sphere of authority and Rome's, but the treaty of Apamea certainly set bounds for Antiochus, without debarring Rome from interfering beyond them.[45] Caesar would not accept either Rhine or Channel as limits to Roman power. Whatever the practice of earlier ages, his attitude was characteristic for his own time.

[40] In 47 Caesar required the kings and dynasts near Syria to protect that province as friends of Rome (*B. Alex.* 65.4). But most of them had territories that did not lie *between* Syria and Parthia. Ariobarzanes: Cic. *ad fam.* 15.1–4 *passim*; *ad Att.* 6.3.5. Tribute: Livy 45.18.7 f.; Badian (1968), ch. VI.

[41] Liebmann-Frankfort (1969), 7 ff. and *passim*.

[42] Veyne (1975) is no doubt right that in the third and early second centuries, with which he is concerned, 'Rome ne songe pas encore à dominer le monde, mais plutôt à être seule au monde', but 'defensive' wars fought for this purpose were bound to appear aggressive to others and to be interpreted in the light of the dominance Rome attained, which in turn created the ideal of world rule.

[43] Polyb. 3.22–5 (the last renewal was in 279) for Carthage; App. *Bell. Samn.* 7.1 (Tarentum); the clause was perhaps ambiguous.

[44] 2.13.7 (cf. Walbank, ad loc., for varying views); 3.15, 3.20 ff. and 28–30.

[45] Livy 34.58; see Badian (1958), 76 ff.; Livy 38.38.

It is true that according to Orosius (6.13.2) the Parthian king complained that Crassus' crossing of the Euphrates was an infringement of 'treaties' made by Lucullus and Pompey; Florus (3.11.4) refers instead to 'treaties' made with Sulla and Pompey. | Many scholars suppose that one or more of these generals had in fact recognized the Euphrates as a boundary delimiting the Roman and Parthian spheres of influence or at least as one which neither party was to cross in arms. Yet, since Crassus was patently launching an offensive against Parthia, the Parthian king was perhaps merely reminding him of previous pacts of friendship, which need have comprised no such precise stipulation. Certainly none is recorded in the other texts, admittedly meagre, which relate to the negotiations between these generals and the Parthians.[46] Lucullus was actually quartered far east of the Euphrates at the time, having overrun much of Armenia. Pompey too invaded Armenia, reduced king Tigranes to vassalage, and sent troops into Gordyene. Acording to Plutarch (*Pomp.* 33.6) Phraates then proposed the Euphrates as a frontier, but Pompey merely replied that he would adopt the just boundary. That was manifestly an evasion. In his monument he claimed to have 'given protection to' not only Armenia but Mesopotamia, Sophene and Gordyene (Diod. 40.4), and if he was unwilling to fight the Parthians, who did indeed forbid him to cross the Euphrates again (Dio 37.6), for Tigranes' right to Gordyene, he successfully offered Roman arbitration between the rival claims there of Tigranes and Phraates (Dio 37.6 f.). It is significant that he denied Phraates the title of 'king of kings' (Dio 37.5; Plut. *Pomp.* 38), which might have suggested that his state was on a parity with Rome. He entered into friendly relations with the rulers of Osrhoene, Media Atropatene and even Elymaitis,[47] as well as Armenia; when and if it suited Rome, she could intervene to defend her friends beyond the Euphrates against Parthia.

When Crassus did cross the river, he was received as a liberator from Parthian oppression at least by many Greek cities (Dio 40.13, Plut. *Cr.* 17), and he had the support of the vassal king of Armenia (Dio 40.19), while the ruler of Osrhoene pretended to be friendly (ibid. 20).

Although Cicero denied that Crassus had any justification for war (*de fin.* 3.75), and our authorities all represent him as the aggressor, perhaps condemning him, as Plutarch suggested (*comp. Nic. et Cr.* 4), only because he failed, we can easily surmise that he had excuses for intervention, on behalf of peoples with whom Rome had already

---

[46] Ziegler (1964), 20 ff.; Liebmann-Frankfort (1969), 171 ff., 237 ff., 263 ff., 276 ff., 296 ff., 308 ff. for evidence and discussion. Of course there was never any formal treaty ratified at Rome, and perhaps no more than a vague understanding; cf. Dio 37.5.

[47] Plut. *Pomp.* 36; Dio 37.5–7; 40.20.1.

entered into friendly relations, as plausible as | Caesar for his Gallic
offensives. It is, moreover, significant that even though Romans could
see the disaster at Carrhae as divine retribution for an unjust and
undeclared war, just as Cicero ascribes the 'destruction' of Piso's army
by pestilence to the judgement of heaven on Piso's alleged aggressions
(*in Pis.* 85), they continued to assume down to 20 B.C. that it was right
for them to punish the Parthians and even to conquer them, in order to
vindicate Rome's honour and secure her eastern dominions.

Whatever the provocation they had received, foreign peoples which
attacked Rome could at best be said to wage a *bellum prope iustum* (*de
prov. cons.* 4). It would be hard to say how far the conviction that the
gods had destined them to rule the world predisposed Romans to treat
as legitimate *casus belli* which the uncommitted observer would have
thought nugatory.

VII. RELUCTANCE TO ANNEX TERRITORY

As Romans regarded 'friends' and 'allies' as virtual subjects, it is quite
mistaken to deny that Roman policy was imperialistic whenever it did
not result in outright annexation. Until the first century B.C. Rome
was notoriously slow to annex territory.

Gelzer explained this on the ground that the Roman state absolutely
lacked an organ for carrying through far-reaching plans of expansion;
annual magistrates whose choice rested on the caprice of the electorate
were often incapable, and in any event could not assure continuity in
policy, while the senate met only when summoned by a magistrate to
consider such matters as he referred to it.[48] It seems to me that he
unduly depreciated the real power of the senate to initiate and make
decisions, and that the fluctuations in its policy did not differ significantly from those we find in the policy of imperial states governed
either by absolute rulers or by parliamentary democracies; for instance, no change in senatorial foreign policy was more marked than
that which occurred when Hadrian succeeded Trajan.

Badian, while rightly insisting that at any rate after 200 Rome was
determined 'to dominate whatever was within reach and to build up
strength to extend that reach' and practised what he calls 'hegemonial
imperialism', argues that the Roman governing class was reluctant to
resort to annexation, because it early became conscious 'that large
increases of territory could not easily be administered | within the
existing city-state constitution'. I know of no evidence for such

---

[48] Gelzer (1963), 15 ff. (first published in 1940).

consciousness, and I doubt if it be true that 'under the Roman Republic no real system of administering overseas territories was ever evolved'.[49]

As Gelzer observed, we must not think in terms of a modern bureaucracy when we speak of Roman government. But this applies almost as much to government in the Principate as in the republic. Pliny actually had not so many high officials to assist him in governing Bithynia and Pontus under Trajan as Cicero in Cilicia.[50] The activities of government were far fewer than they are today, and they were largely left to local authorities; at most these were gradually subjected by the emperors to somewhat closer supervision. It was only rarely under the Principate that even barbarous tribes were directly governed by Roman military officers; the centralized administration of Roman Egypt was always exceptional.

Nor was there anything unusual by ancient standards in Roman practice. In the Persian empire Greek and Phoenician cities had been left to manage their own affairs; so had the Jews, and doubtless most other unurbanized peoples of whom we know nothing; it is immaterial that the Persian kings, like Rome, sometimes installed local rulers on whose loyalty they could count. Athens and the Hellenistic kings (except again in Egypt) had followed the same practice. The Romans had no reason to think that they were less able than other ruling powers to administer subjects in this loose way. The only puzzle is that they did not always choose to demand tribute (as distinct from heavy war indemnities, which could ultimately be paid off), outside the frontiers of a province; the first known cases are those of Macedon and Illyria in 167 (Livy 45.18.7 f.).

In the republic the tasks of provincial government may be classified under four heads.

(a) *Taxation.* Collection of taxes was left to publicans or to local authorities; a host of officials employed by the central government was not needed. This long remained true under the Principate.[51]

(b) *Jurisdiction.* The governor was omnicompetent, outside privileged communities, but we need not assume that he as yet possessed that monopoly of jurisdiction over serious crimes which may be inferred from evidence of later centuries, and in civil cases he may generally

---

[49] Badian (1968), 9 ff.

[50] Cicero had a quaestor, four legates, a *praefectus fabrum* (*ad fam.* 3.7.4) and other equestrian prefects, of whom he sent one to do justice in Cyrpus (*ad Att.* 5.21.6). Pliny had only one legate (*Ep.* 10.25); there were also an equestrian procurator with one or two freedmen assistants—Epimachus perhaps succeeded Maximus—and the prefect of the *ora Pontica* (21 ff., 27 ff., 83–6a). Both could call on a *cohors amicorum*, and on military officers, of whom there were far more in Cicero's province. No doubt the procurator had more clerical staff than Cicero and his quaestor.

[51] A. H. M. Jones (1974), ch. VIII for a brief survey. [Cf. chs. 15, 17.]

have limited himself to suits in which Romans were | concerned. A *lex provinciae* might actually lay down rules that reserved many types of case to local courts. In Cilicia such rules evidently did not exist, and Cicero makes out that it was his innovation to let the Greeks settle their own disputes in local courts under local laws, but I suggest that he did no more than *guarantee* this 'autonomy' to them, whereas his predecessors had been ready to assume jurisdiction if ever they saw fit, perhaps to the advantage of influential magnates and to their own pecuniary gain.[52]

(c) *Supervision of local government.* Cicero praised his brother for ensuring that the Asian cities were administered by the *optimates*. This was normal policy (chapter 12), though in Asia, for instance, popular assemblies were allowed to retain some power,[53] and Caesar on occasion installed kings in Gallic *civitates*.[54] In general local rulers, whether or not Rome had placed them in control, were left to administer their own communities with little interference. Cicero indeed must have spent much time in checking municipal accounts and unveiling corruption, but the mere fact that he examined accounts for the past ten years indicates that within that period no proconsul had thought this a task necessary to perform.[55]

(d) *Internal order and defence.* Here lay the governor's inescapable obligation. Spain, Gaul, Macedon and some parts of the east nearly always required legionary garrisons. As Badian saw,[56] this was costly to the treasury and burdensome to the Italian peasantry.[57] Generations of war in Spain might well have made the senate apprehensive of assuming military responsibilities that could be shifted on to reliable vassals. Even with the threat of a Parthian invasion in 51, the worthy consul, Servius Sulpicius, vetoed a *supplementum* for the weak forces in Syria and Cilicia.[58] The elder Cato is said to have opposed annexation of Macedon in 168 because Rome could not afford protection (*HA Hadr.* 5.3).

It may be thought that this aversion to assuming the task of military defence ill fits the Roman passion for military glory. But we have to

---

[52] Cic. II *Verr.* 2.32; *ad Att.* 6.1.15, 6.2.4. I am not convinced by D. Kienast's rejection in *ZRG* LXXXV (1968), 330 ff., of the orthodox view that grants of *libertas* did not give cities exemption from the governor's jurisdiction.

[53] *ad QF* 1.1.25; cf. A. H. M. Jones (1940), 170 ff., [G. E. M. de Ste Croix, *Class Struggle in the Ancient Greek World* (1981), 518 ff.].

[54] *BG* 4.21, 5.25 and 54; but Commius (4.21) ultimately turned against the Romans, and the native leaders most dangerous to Rome were sometimes kings or aspirants to kingship backed by popular support (1.3 ff., 7.4; cf. the case of Ambiorix, 5.27, 6.31).

[55] *ad Att.* 6.2.5.

[56] Badian (1968), ch. I.

[57] Brunt (1971), 432 ff., 449. Conscription: ch. XXII.

[58] Cic. *ad fam.* 3.3.1. Cicero's army: Brunt (1971), 689.

reckon, as Badian argued (cf. n. 56), with the prevalence of mutual jealousy among the Roman aristocracy. Provincial commands gave particular individuals better than average chances of augmenting their personal glory and wealth, and their influence at home. This jealousy is manifest in the *leges annales*, in the normal restriction of provincial commands to a single year, and in the | strength of the objection in the late republic to extraordinary commands. In 57–6 no agreement could be reached on the restoration of Ptolemy Auletes to the Egyptian throne, whether by Pompey or any one else; success would bring too much honour even to such a respectable figure of the second order as Lentulus Spinther. Moreover, once a commander was in the field, it was hard for the senate to exercise any control over him. For over two years (57–5) the proconsul L. Piso did not so much as send a single despatch to Rome, though Cicero claims that this was abnormal. The provisions that appeared in Sulla's law on *maiestas* and in Caesar's on *repetundae*, and in many older enactments, forbidding governors *exire de provincia, educere exercitum, bellum sua sponte gerere, in regnum iniussu populi Romani ac senatus accedere* (*in Pis.* 50) were clearly unenforceable.[59] Both in order to restrict the opportunities for individuals to attain pre-eminence and to preserve its own authority, the senate had good reason to frown on annexations. And that was not all. Just because annual commands were preferred, there was always the danger that incompetent nonentities would sustain ignominious defeats, while it was hard for generals to carry through a systematic course of expansion or pacification; hence it was not until Augustus' time that order could be established throughout Spain, though it is hard to believe that the complete subjugation of that country can ever have seemed undesirable.

VIII. THE THEORY OF THE JUST WAR

Following Panaetius, Cicero implied that states as well as individuals should respect the just principle of *suum cuique*. Men should not only abstain from doing wrong themselves but so far as possible prevent

[59] See also the Cnidus inscription published in *JRS* LXIV (1974), col. III 5 ff. Despite Cicero's *plurimae leges veteres*, the prohibition might have been introduced first in Saturninus' *maiestas* law, as a result of recent disasters incurred by aggressive proconsuls. But were all provincial frontiers clearly defined? And was a proconsul debarred either from striking first at an enemy force mustering outside the province, or from pursuing it after repelling an incursion? In Cicero's Cilicia the land route from the Phrygian *conventus* to Cilicia Pedias actually passed through the Cappadocian kingdom; he went outside his province three times in a year. Caesar felt no inhibition in attacking Ariovistus, etc., and there is no indication that his apparent violations of his own rule were censured even by his enemies except in one instance (cf. n. 81). [Cf. pp. 495 f.]

wrong-doing by others (*de offic.* 1.20–4). Wars should therefore be fought only *ut sine iniuria in pace vivatur*, and as a last resort, if diplomacy failed; they were, however, justified not only in self-defence but also for the protection of friends and allies against injury.

Cicero claimed that Numa had implanted in the Romans a 'love of peace and tranquillity, which enable justice and good faith most easily to flourish', and in rebutting an argument, which had been advanced by Carneades on his visit to Rome in 155, that all men necessarily followed their own interests without regard to justice, | and that Rome had naturally pursued a policy of aggrandizing her own wealth and power, he maintained that her wars had been just: in particular, it was by defending her allies that Rome had secured world dominion. (Sallust propounds a similar view.) According to Cicero, by strict observance of the old fetial procedure, or of a procedure modelled on it, under which war had to be formally declared, and was to be declared only when reparation had been sought and refused, with the gods invoked to punish unjust demands, Rome had demonstrated her respect for the rights of others. Cicero's insistence that every war must have a *iusta causa* was certainly not peculiar to himself, but corresponded to Roman practice or propaganda since at least the third century.[60] Nor, despite lamentations on the supposed decay of moral standards, was the principle less observed in Cicero's own time. Caesar followed it with as much, or rather as little, scrupulosity as the senate had done in the second century. Augustus was later to boast that he had pacified the Alps *nulli genti bello per iniuriam inlato* (*RG* 26).

In fact the primitive fetial procedure was certainly formalistic and permitted the enforcement in arms of demands that had no equitable basis. Livy, to whom we owe the preservation of what he took to be the ancient ritual (1.32), put into the mouth of the Alban dictator the cynical observation that though both Romans and Albans were putting forward claims for reparation *ex foedere*, 'if we are to say what is true rather than what is plausible, it is lust for empire that rouses two kindred and neighbouring peoples to arms' (1.23.7). For Livy himself the two cities were contending for *imperium servitiumque* (1.25.3); as Drexler observed, we are in a world where there can only be rulers and

---

[60] *Iustae causae* and fetial law: Cic. *de offic.* 1.34–6 and 80: *de rep.* 2.31 (cf. 26 on Numa), 3.34 ff., part of the answer to Furius Philus' speech, 8 ff., which derives from a discourse of Carneades (Lactant., *div. inst.* 5.14 ff.), delivered at Rome in 155; cf. Capelle (1932) and Walbank (1965), 13; it is immaterial here whether Panaetius supplied the answer (*contra*, Strasburger (1965), 45). See also Sall. *Cat.* 6.5; *or. Lepidi* 4; Drexler (1959) collects much material from Livy. For adaptation of fetial procedure in the middle republic, see Dahlheim (1968), 171 ff.; but see now J. W. Rich, *Declaring war in the Roman Republic period of transmarine expansion* (Collection Latomus CXLIX) (1976), ch. III. Neither its origins, cf. Hampl (1957), nor Roman practice, when documented, can warrant Cicero's claims that Rome observed a distinctively high moral standard.

subjects, not equal independent powers. It was particularly hard for others to concede that Rome were merely fighting in defence of her friends and allies if (as was sometimes the case) she admitted states to her friendship and offered them protection at a time when they were already threatened or under attack; it was all too obvious that she was then acting for her own interest,[61] and of course victory would give her control of the conquered *iure belli*, and justify mass-enslavements, heavy indemnities or annexation, at her own discretion. Moreover, even Cicero adopted a wide formulation of the rights of a state to defend itself and its friends: 'we may ward off any disadvantage that may | be brought to us' (*si quid importetur nobis incommodi propulsemus, de offic.* 2.18).

To an enemy like Perseus (Livy 42.52.16), and even to so sympathetic an interpreter of Roman policy as Polybius (1.10.6), it could appear that Rome took the mere existence of a powerful and potentially dangerous neighbour as such a disadvantage, and Cicero's principles were quite compatible with Cato's argument for finishing Carthage off: 'the Carthaginians are our enemies already; for whoever is directing all his preparations against me, so that he may make war on me at the time of his own choice, is already my enemy, even if he is not yet taking armed action' (*ORF*[2] fr. 195). In all cases the Romans were in Hobbes' words 'judges of the justness of their own fears'. In retrospect Lactantius could aver that 'it was by using fetials to declare war, inflicting injuries under cover of law and unceasingly coveting and carrying off what belonged to others that Rome obtained possession of the world' (*de div. inst.* 6.9.4). Roman reactions to the possibility of a threat resembled those of a nervous tiger, disturbed when feeding. It is hardly surprising that Polybius concluded that Rome had persistently and deliberately aimed at extending her dominion.[62]

Cicero himself casually refers to Roman wars like those waged with Italian peoples, Pyrrhus and Carthage, the purpose of which was empire or glory. Such a purpose was hardly consistent with Panaetius' general account of justice, and I take it that it was Cicero who inserted

---

[61] Witness the cases of Saguntum, and of the Greek cities in Asia, whose freedom Rome professed to protect against Antiochus III, while perfectly willing to abandon it in her own interests, Badian (1958), 75 ff.

[62] 1.3.6 ff., 1.6, 1.10 with 20; 1.63.9, 2.31 with 21; 3.2.6, 3.3.8 ff., 6.50.6, 9.10.11, 15.10.2. For Greek views of Roman imperialism, see also 5.104, 9.37.6, 11.5; Livy (P) 31.29.6. Polybius' general judgements deserve attention although they conflict with the details of his narrative perhaps derived from Roman informants, which fit a defensive interpretation of Roman policy (Walbank (1963), with a different explanation of the apparent inconsistency). See also Walbank (1965) on his cynicism in analysing many Roman actions after 168. Perhaps his experience of contemporary Roman conduct and knowledge of the actual consequences of earlier wars made it hard for Polybius to credit that Rome's policy had ever been so defensive as the information he accepted in his narrative naturally suggested. [Cf. now P. S. Derow, *JRS* (1979), 1 ff.]

the reference to them, half-conscious that Panaetius' doctrine did not after all permit the justification of all Rome's wars. He does indeed hasten to add that just causes must be found even in such cases.[63] But a just cause is now nothing but the 'decent pretext' that Polybius (36.2) thought the Romans were right to look for, after deciding on war for reasons of self-interest; it might be as legalistic and inequitable as those adduced for the Third Punic War.

Polybius thought that Rome needed them to impress the world, i.e. the Greek world, and it may be that as late as c. 150 the senate still had some regard for Greek public opinion, such as it had shown in the previous generation. This sort of consideration | is certainly ascribed to the Romans on other occasions,[64] and their propagandist assumption of the role of protector of Greek liberty finds an analogy in Caesar's attempt to parade himself in 58 as the champion of the freedom of Gallic peoples against Germn invaders (*BG* 1.33 and 45); indeed his relations with the Gauls in a single decade offer a sort of telescoped parallel to those of Rome with the Greek cities between 200 and 146.

But Polybius may have been both too cynical and too inclined to overrate the importance in Roman eyes of his own fellow-Greeks. We must not forget that for Romans a just war was one in which the gods were on their side. The very formalism of Roman religion made it possible for them to believe that this divine favour could be secured, provided only that all the necessary ceremonies and procedures had been duly followed. Drexler suggested that the Romans fought better because they were convinced in this way of the rightness of the cause, even in cases when it does not seem morally defensible to us.[65] However Machiavellian the *principes* may have been in directing policy, they had perhaps to think of the morale of the common soldiers. Dio at least supposed that the near-mutiny at Vesontio in 58 was inspired not only by fear of Ariovistus but also by the suspicion that Caesar was entering on a campaign out of personal ambition without a just cause (38.35).

[63] *de offic.* 1.38, 3.87. On the Hannibalic war see Lucret. 3.836 ff.; Livy 22.58.3, 27.39.9, 28.19.6 ff., 29.17.6, 30.32.2. Unlike some Stoics (Cic. *de fin.* 3.57), Panaetius probably allowed some value to glory, but could hardly have regarded its pursuit as condoning injustice.

[64] Polyb. 36.2 and 9, on which see Hoffmann (1960); for a parallel, 32.9 and 13. There is nothing peculiarly Roman in insistence on a *iusta causa* for a war prompted by very different motives, cf. Thuc. 6.93 and 105; 7.18 (Sparta); 6.6 and 8 (Athens); Polyb. 3.6 and Arr. *Anab.* 2.14 (Macedon). For public opinion, Drexler (1959) cited Livy 3.72.2 ff., 30.16.8 ff., 45.18.1.

[65] Drexler (1959) cited Livy 5.51 ff., 31.9.5, 45.39.10 and many other texts. Cf. Thuc. 7.18 (Sparta).

IX. CAESAR IN GAUL

The most remarkable document of Roman imperialism is Caesar's *de bello Gallico*. Sallust thought that he hankered for a new war in which his *virtus* would shine out (*Cat.* 54.4). Suetonius was later to write of his shameless aggressions and ascribe them principally to greed (cf. n. 81). Conquest was clearly bound to fill his purse and enhance his fame.

Plutarch said that by crossing the Channel he carried Roman supremacy beyond the *oikoumene* (*Caes.* 23.2), just as Claudius later boasted of extending the empire beyond the Ocean (*ILS* 212.1.40), that encompassing stream which Alexander had done no more than reach. According to Sallust (*Hist.* 3.88), Pompey had sought to emulate Alexander from his youth; his assumption of the *cognomen* 'Magnus' suggests this, and Cicero could refer to him as 'invictissimus' (*in Pis.* 34), just as Alexander had been honoured as the 'unconquered | god' (Hyperides, *c. Dem.* 32). There is indeed little reason to believe that Alexander was much in Caesar's mind,[66] and even Pompey had had no such freedom as the autocratic king to carry his arms whithersoever he would. Still it was Alexander who had first conceived, or so it was generally supposed, the ideal of world conquest, which figured in the contemporary appearance of the globe on Roman coins, a symbol that became more common under Caesar's rule,[67] and which was voiced in the imperialist language of Cicero; he extolled Pompey for making the Roman empire coterminous with the limits of the earth and sky, and found it necessary to praise Caesar in almost similar terms (cf. n. 9). A writer so friendly to Caesar as Nicolaus held that at the end of his life he was bent on subduing not only the Parthian empire but India and all lands up to the marge of the Ocean.[68]

However that may be, before Caesar had attained absolute power, he could, like Pompey whom he was no doubt intent on rivalling, pursue only limited objectives. He did not even start with the project of conquering Gaul. His original purpose must have been to operate in Illyricum; he was diverted by the accident of the Helvetian migration.[69] But he seized every opportunity to extend Roman dominion. He assumes the sympathy of his readers. Every forward step he took

---

[66] Weippert (1972) is exhaustive and judicious on imitation of Alexander in the republic.

[67] M. H. Crawford (1974), index s.v. 'globe'.

[68] Jacoby, *FGH* 90 F 130.95; cf. Plut. *Caes.* 58; Weippert (1972), 171 ff.; also 209 ff. on Antony. [See pp. 449–51.]

[69] Illyricum, not Transalpina, was his province under the lex Vatinia. Early in 58 three of his four legions were at Aquileia (*BG* 1.10), a suitable base for an Illyrian offensive, for which such incidents as are described in 1.5.4 and 5.1.5 would have provided pretexts. As late as 56 he still desired *eas quoque nationes adire et regiones cognoscere* (3.7); the same verbs are used of his plan to invade Britain (4.20). Cf. App. *Bell. Ill.* 12. The task had to be left to his adoptive son.

could be said to conform with the peculiar Roman conception of defensive war, which covered the prevention and elimination of any *potential* menace to Roman power. The *Commentaries* candidly reveal that *casus belli* were subsidiary at least to that end. Though they voice no grandiose aspirations for world conquest, world conquest, if attainable at all, could be attained only by stages, and as opportunities offered. It would be unwise to affirm that belief in Rome's mission to rule the world did not underlie Caesar's own attitude, and that which he expected in his readers.

Beyond the narrow confines of the province it is convenient to call Narbonensis, Rome had recognized the freedom of Gallic peoples such as the Arverni, whom she had defeated c. 120 B.C., and had established ties of friendship with some of them, for instance the Aedui. Her policy had, however, been largely one of non-intervention. She had not sought to arbitrate in wars in which her own friends were involved. The Sequani had called in bands of Germans under Ariovistus to aid them against the Aedui, apparently in | 72, and inflicted a heavy defeat on that people, only to find themselves gradually reduced to submission by their own *condottieri*. So far from answering an Aeduan appeal for protection in 61, Rome at Caesar's own instance honoured Ariovistus with the name of friend in 59 allegedly at his own request.[70] None the less, the ties of friendship formed outside the province gave the Romans what they could regard as a just cause for intervention, whenever it suited them.[71]

In 58 the Helvetii sought to migrate from Switzerland to Saintonge. Very naturally, Caesar refused them passage through Narbonensis (*BG* 1.5–8). But he was also resolved to resist their movement by any route. They were (he claims) a fierce, warlike people, who had destroyed a Roman army in 107, an event Caesar harps on;[72] they evidently had no peaceful relationship with Rome. He contends that whereas they were useful in their old home, as a buffer between north Italy and the Germans, their presence in Saintonge would endanger the security of Narbonensis (*BG* 1.10). They designed to march through the lands of the Aedui, whose appeals gave Caesar a *iusta causa* to fight and hinder or punish their depredations.[73] But he leaves no room for doubt that he

[70] See generally *BG* 1.1–4 (cf. Cic. *ad Att.* 1.19.2 and 20.5), 31 (cf. 6.12), 35, 36.7, 40.2.

[71] Rome's *amici*: *BG* 1.33.2 and 35.4; probably too the peoples under Aeduan hegemony, cf. 43.7–9; I take it that the friendship with a former Sequanian king (1.3.4) did not mean that his people were still *amici* of Rome in 58. But the Arverni may have been: until 52 they took no known part in resistance, and they retained a privileged position after their revolt (7.90.3; Pliny, *NH* 4.109).

[72] 1.7.4, 1.10.2, 1.12–14 and 30.

[73] 1.11; later Caesar told the Aedui that he had undertaken the war for their sake *magna ex parte* 16.6.

had decided to bar their migration simply because of the danger so strong a people might constitute in Gaul to Roman interests.

Meantime Ariovistus had been bringing more Germans into Sequanian territory. Not only the Aedui but the Sequani were encouraged by Caesar's victory over the Helvetii to seek his aid against the German intruders (*BG* 1.30–2). Caesar says that, recalling the Cimbric invasion of Gaul, he thought the presence of this growing German power there a threat to Rome, and considered it disgraceful *in tanto imperio populi Romani* that the Aedui, as friends and brothers of the Roman people, should be in servitude to Germans (*BG* 1.33). Yet their plight must have been well known to him when he had procured Ariovistus' recognition as king and friend of Rome. He presented Ariovistus with the demands that he should settle no more Germans across the Rhine, restore the Aeduan hostages and make no wrongful attack on the Aedui and their allies. Ariovistus, on Caesar's own showing, found these demands inconsistent with Rome's previous neutrality and his own position as her friend. He retorted that Caesar had no better right to | interfere in his part of Gaul then he in the Roman province; both had acquired legitimate dominions *iure belli* (*BG* 1.34.4; cf. 44). Caesar obviously intended his readers to take this as proof of what he calls the German's insolence. Ariovistus was told that Rome expected from her friends dutiful compliance with her will. Of course compliance would have dissipated his own prestige and power. War inevitably followed. It was clearly not the consequence of Aeduan appeals which had hitherto been disregarded, nor of any German aggression—Caesar lays no stress on the fact that the Germans actually struck the first blow (*BG* 1.46)—but of Caesar's decision to destroy a potential menace to Rome, and to aggrandize Roman dominion.[74]

He claims that by his success in 58 he pacified all Gaul, evidently in the restricted sense of that term, excluding Aquitania and Belgica.[75] This meant in effect that its peoples were now Rome's subjects. Like so

[74] 1.34–6, 1.40, 1.42–5. Ariovistus' insolence: 1.33.5, 1.46.4 (paralleled by similar Roman criticisms of the Aetolians and Rhodians in Livy 33.11.8, 37.49.2, 44.14.8; cf. Dahlheim (1968), 269 ff.); his duty of respect as *amicus*: 42.2 ff., 43.4 (with his reply, 44.5). Dio makes Caesar answer the charge that he was bringing on the war for personal ambition by maintaining that it was Rome's tradition not only to protect subjects and allies but to seek aggrandizement (38.36–8), that she must anticipate inevitable attacks (38.40), and that Ariovistus' contumacious conduct proves his hostile intentions of which Caesar had been unaware in 59 (38.42–5). The speech is invention and often echoes imperialist speeches in Thucydides, but gives a perceptive interpretation of Roman imperialism in general and of Caesar's conduct in 58, or rather of his apologia for it.

[75] 2.2. 'Gallia' is used in contradictory senses here, as in 1.1.1 and 6, and often: the Remi are outside in 2.3 and inside in 6.12. K. Christ (1974) argues that Caesar exaggerates the unity of Gaul, to justify his policy of subduing the whole land. That policy is enunciated by Cicero (*de prov. cons.* 32), not in the *Commentaries*. Caesar had not conceived it before early 58 (n. 69 and text), but in retrospect he could claim to have carried it out, and this representation of his actual achievement is implicit throughout from the first chapter of book 1.

many others who had sought Roman protection, they had become *subiecti atque obnoxii* to the Romans (Livy 7.30.2). The legions wintered in Sequanian lands (*BG* 1.54), and henceforth even the Aedui were bound to obey Caesar's directions, to submit like other friendly peoples to interference in their internal affairs, and to send contingents to his army.[76] In his reply to Ariovistus Caesar had said that the victory over the Arverni in 121 had already given Rome the best title to rule over the Gauls, and that it was an act of grace on her part to allow them freedom, an act that also debarred any one else from taking it away from them (*BG* 1.45). It soon appeared that Rome rather than the Germans would deprive them of liberty.

In 57 the Belgae already feared attack and 'conspired' to anticipate it. Caesar took this as a justification for striking first. He does not bother to suggest that a Belgic raid on the territory of the Remi, who had voluntarily submitted to him, was the warrant for his offensive operations.[77] One by one the Belgae were forced to surrender. If such peoples took up arms again, it was rebellion and a breach of faith.[78] In 56, without so much as an allegation that any attack on Roman territory was brewing, Roman troops invaded Aquitania, where the people could be treated as hostile because they had assailed Roman forces in the Sertorian war (*BG* 3.20). |

In 55 Caesar first crossed the Channel on the plea that Britons had assisted his Gallic enemies in almost every war; this hitherto unmentioned assistance cannot have been significant. Some *civitates* were forced, or induced, to promise obedience to Roman orders, and the second invasion could then be justified, either to hold them to their undertakings or to protect them against still independent neighbours.[79] Tribute was imposed (*BG* 5.22.4); this must have been Caesar's general practice in Gaul, whenever he had met and subdued resistance (cf. *BG* 7.76.1); in 51/50 he was careful to impose no *new* burdens (*BG* 8.49).

---

[76] 2.14, 5.5–7, 7.32 ff. Caesar also interfered in the internal affairs of other peoples, before they had taken up arms against him (5.3.25 and 54).

[77] 2.1–6. Sherwin-White (1957) notes an exact parallel in Pompey's preventive war against the Iberians (Dio 37.1).

[78] 3.10.2, 4.30.2 and 38.1, 5.26.1, 6.8.8, etc. Livy 8.14.4 speaks of the *crimen rebellionis*. As Timpe (1972) shows, Gallic peoples normally came under Caesar's control by *deditio*, even if they had not previously been at war with him; for earlier examples, see Dahlheim (1968), 52 ff. For the consequences, cf. n. 80. The *dediti* had a claim to protection (2.28.3, 32.2, etc.). Timpe argues from 2.35 that Caesar would not accept *deditio*, if he felt unable to guarantee this; cf. also 4.21.6 and 27.5. In the last cases at least it seems to me clear in the context that Caesar did accept the offers made. He is often less explicit about the settlements he made than Timpe presumes. According to Timpe no Gallic *dediti* became *foederati* or *amici*. But Caesar does not mention the *foedus* with the Helvetii (Cic. *pro Balb.* 32), and he does let out that the Treveri were *amici* (5.3.3); cf. 4.16 (Ubii).

[79] 4.20.1, 21.5–8, 27.1, 30.2, 5.20–2.

,ples which had voluntarily submitted were required to send
ı. y contingents and in general to obey Caesar's will.⁸⁰

Again in 55, after refusing to allow some German tribes to settle
peacefully west of the Rhine, in the fear that they would combine with
disloyal Gauls against him (*BG* 4.5 f.), Caesar attacked and massacred
those who had crossed. The preventive action he took was no different
in principle from his previous offensives, of which his enemies at Rome
do not seem to have complained, and he no doubt expects his readers to
infer that his Machiavellian detention of the German chiefs who had
come to him as ambassadors, while he cut their leaderless followers to
pieces in time of truce, was warranted by an earlier violation of the
truce on the part of the Germans (*BG* 4.11–14; cf. 8.23.3). At Rome, as
usual, supplications were voted for his victory, though Cato urged that
for his perfidy he should be delivered up to the Germans.⁸¹ Both in 55
and 54 Caesar went further, crossing the Rhine himself, to punish
German inroads and spread the terror of the Roman name. Once
again he had clients (the Ubii) to protect beyond the river, whom he
characteristically treats as subject to his orders—and that made it
absurd in Roman eyes if the Sugambri claimed that the Rhine was the
frontier of the Roman empire. But Caesar does not conceal the fact
that his German campaigns were essentially designed for the security
of Roman dominion in Gaul.⁸²

Caesar's account of these transactions is self-exculpatory only in a
certain sense. He undoubtedly intends his readers to think that it was
not for personal greed or glory that he undertook his campaigns, but he
has no need to insist on their justice. Though he never claims to have
planned the conquest of Gaul, it is implicit in | the *Commentaries*, from
the very first sentence, that this was what he had achieved. Few
Romans besides Cato needed to be convinced of the propriety of any
measures he took to this end. In his speech of 56 *de provinciis consularibus*,
without troubling himself about the niceties of Caesar's treatment of

---

⁸⁰ 3.11; 4.6; 6.5. Once the Ubii sought his protection, he considered them subject to his orders,
though *amici* (4.8 and 16, 6.9). The Treveri, who had sought his aid (1.37) and sent him cavalry
(2.24), were treated as hostile in 54, because *neque ad concilia veniebant neque imperio parebant*; such
obedience was part of the *officium* of *amici* (5.2–4); cf. n. 74. In 173 Antiochus IV had promised to
obey Roman orders *quae bono fidelique socio regi essent imperanda; se in nullo usquam cessaturum officio*
(Livy 42.6.8).

⁸¹ Plut. *Caes.* 22; *Cato Minor* 51; *comp. Nic. et Crassi* 4. Suetonius presumably reflects contemporary criticisms in asserting that his campaigns were unjust and inspired by lust for glory and wealth
(*Caes.* 22, 24, 47, 54), but it was surely in 54 that the senate voted to send a commission to enquire
into charges of aggression (ibid. 24), if indeed it ever did; more probably this was only a hostile
proposal. There is no evidence that his earlier offensives had been challenged at Rome, and as
noted by Timpe (1965), the supplications decreed in his honour, e.g. in 57 (*BG* 2.35), gave them
retroactive approval.

⁸² *BG* 4.4–19; cf. 5.9.2, n. 80.

this or that individual Gallic people, Cicero argues flatly that Caesar was performing the highest service to the state by conquering the whole country, since there was no other way of providing permanently for Italy's security; it made no difference that Caesar had mastered peoples whose very names had never been heard at Rome before.[83] On this sort of principle no war that Rome could fight against foreign peoples who might some day be strong enough to attack her could be other than defensive. There is no indication in the speech that this view was contested. Those who wished to relieve Caesar of his command at this time evidently argued not that his campaigns had been unjust or unnecessary, but that the war was already over.

Of course this was far from true. Caesar's greatest crises were yet to come. In 52 he had to contend with an almost pan-Gallic rebellion. It may be that he actually exaggerated Gallic unity on sundry occasions (n. 75), thus making it plausible that Rome could not stop short of subduing the whole nation and implicitly excusing operations against any one *civitas* whose offence was solely that of not having submitted. Caesar himself allows that his opponents were fighting for liberty, 'for which all men naturally strive'. Roman writers were never reluctant to recognize this motive for resistance and revolt.[84] But they did not concede that their subjects or dependants had any right to be free of Roman rule. Liberty was the privilege of the imperial people, as Cicero boasted to the Quirites: *populum Romanum servire fas non est, quem di immortales omnibus gentibus imperare voluerunt.*[85] Caesar's admiration for Vercingetorix is easily to be discerned, but as the great rebel, he still merited death.[86]

X. ROMAN 'CLEMENCY'

Wherever necessary, the most brutal methods of repression were therefore in order. Death or enslavement was the common penalty for freedom-fighters. Caesar was alleged to have made a million slaves in Gaul;[87] he himself casually refers to a load of captives he shipped | back

[83] *de prov. cons.* 19–36; *in Pis.* 81; *ad QF* 3.6(8).2. See Collins, *ANRW* I 1, 922–66.

[84] *BG* 3.10.3; cf. 3.8.4, 4.34.5, 5.7.8, 5.27.6, 5.29.4, 5.38.2, and often in book 7 (1.5–8, 4.4, 14.10, 64.3, 76.2, 77.13–16, 89.1), 8.1.3. Similarly he makes Gauls refer to Roman acts of injustice, 5.38.2, 7.38.10. Gelzer (1963), 7 gives other examples of Roman writers putting the anti-Roman views, e.g. Sall. *ep. Mithr.*; *BJ* 81.1; Tac. *Agr.* 30. The Romans could pretend to free subjects from the rule of kings—under whom they wished to live (Livy 45.18; Strabo 12.2.11).

[85] *Phil.* 6.19.

[86] Yet in 46 he no longer needed to satisfy his troops' lust for vengeance, as in the war itself (7.28.4, 8.38).

[87] Plut. *Caes.* 15; App. *Celt.* 2, misinterpreted by Westermann, *Slave Systems of Greek and Roman Antiquity* (1955), 63, though naturally unreliable. Note *BG* 7.89.5.

from Britain in 55 (*BG* 5.23.2), the only kind of booty, Cicero had heard (*ad Att.* 4.16.7), that could be expected from this poor island; he was delighted at Quintus' promise to send him some of them (*ad QF.* 3.7.4). Caesar did all he could to extirpate the Eburones (*BG* 6.34 and 43). On one occasion, like Scipio Aemilianus, that paragon of Roman *humanitas* (App. *Iber.* 94), he had the right hands of all his prisoners cut off (8.44). Yet he speaks, as does Hirtius, of his clemency.[88]

It was characteristic of Romans as early as Cato (Gell. 6.3.52) to boast of what Livy calls their *vetustissimum morem victis parcendi* (33.12.7). Once again Cicero held that Roman practice conformed to Panaetian laws of war; especially when wars were fought for glory, the conquered were to be treated with mercy. Only the destruction of Corinth had perhaps marred Rome's record. Not indeed that Cicero considered that mercy was always proper; it was not due to enemies who were themselves cruel or who were guilty of violating treaties, Rome naturally being the judge, nor when Rome's own survival was at stake. He does not make it clear how he would have justified the destruction of Numantia, which he approves.[89] But Numantia had rebelled; to Romans rebellion was in itself proof of perfidy. Polybius reports Flamininus as saying in 197 that the Romans were 'moderate, placable and humane', since they did not utterly destroy a people the first time they fought them (18.37). By implication repeated resistance might call for severity, which was also regarded as a virtue. When Virgil defined Rome's mission as *parcere subiectis et debellare superbos*, he was in effect dividing mankind into two categories, those too insolent to accept her god-given dominion, and those who submitted to it. The latter were to be spared: what of the former? Germanicus was to set up a monument boasting that he had 'warred down' the Germans, after exterminating one community with no distinction of age or sex (Tac. *Ann.* 2.21. f.).

Naturally this was not the practice Romans preferred. We may readily believe Augustus' claim that it was his policy to preserve foreign peoples who could safely be spared rather than extirpate them (*RG* 3). After all, the dead paid no taxes. Moreover it was usually more expedient to accept the surrender of an enemy, offered in the hope or expectation of mercy, rather than to incur the expense of time, money and blood in further military operations, and | then to fulfil that expectation, if only to encourage others not to prolong their own resistance. Hampl found a precedent for Rome's normal conduct in

---

[88] *BG* 2.14.28 and 31 ff., 8.3.5, 21.2. In 8.44.1 and 3.16 note apologies for special severity; but cf. Cic. *de offic.* 3.46.

[89] Cic. II *Verr.* 5.115; *de offic.* 1.33–5, 1.82, 2.18, 3.46. Numantia: see Astin (1967), 153–5 on App. *Iber.* 98.

Hittite inscriptions. It was not motivated primarily by humanity, but by rational consideration of self-interest.[90]

It is true that Cicero connected with Rome's supposed clemency to the vanquished her liberality with the franchise. In degree, if not in kind, this was undoubtedly a practice for which we can find no parallel in the policy of other city states. But for Cicero himself it was not altruistic generosity, but a device by which Rome had extended her empire (see p. 294). In early days it must have been prompted by self-interest, however enlightened, and it was not always welcome to beneficiaries such as the Capuans, if they did not attain to full equality of rights in the Roman state. By the time that Roman citizenship had come to be an object of the subjects' aspirations, it was a privilege granted reluctantly and sparingly. In Cicero's youth the Italians had had to wrest it from Rome by force of arms. Few now wished to go further and add to the numbers of *Romanos rerum dominos gentemque togatam*. All efforts to enfranchise the Transpadani failed until Caesar could carry the measure by military power in 49.[91] It was Caesar too who began to extend citizenship to provincial communities. More often he was content to bestow the Latin right, as to the Sicilians. They were Cicero's old clients, whose loyalty to Rome he had extolled in fulsome terms in 70; none the less, he regarded this grant as 'insufferable'.[92]

XI. JUSTICE FOR THE SUBJECTS

In general Cicero speaks with contempt of provincials. Thus the most eminent of Gauls are not to be compared with the meanest of Romans; they were an arrogant and faithless people, bound by no religious scruples, the true descendants of those who had burned down the Capitol (*pro Font.* 27–36). Conceivably there might be Sardinians whose testimony a Roman court might believe, but most of them were mere barbarian half-breeds, more mendacious than their Punic forebears, and not one community in the island had earned the privileges of friendship with Rome and liberty (*pro Scaur.* 38–45). Even the Greeks, to whom Rome owed her culture, as Cicero often allowed,[93]

[90] Hampl (1966) adduces early atrocities to disprove the fable that the Romans became less humane to enemies in the late republic. *Deditio*: Dahlheim (1968), ch. 1. Especially significant on Roman motives for clemency: Livy 42.8.5 ff., 44.7.5 and 31.1; Jos. *BJ* 5.372 ff. Cf. generally Livy 30.42.7: *plus paene parcendo victis quam vincendo imperium auxisse.*
[91] Cicero sought to arouse prejudice against L. Piso, *cos.* 58, because his mother was Insubrian, in *Pis.* fr. 9–12 (OCT); *post red. sen.* 15.
[92] *ad Att.* 14.12.1. Contrast II *Verr.* 2.2–8.
[93] *pro Flacc.* 62; *ad QF* 1.1.27 ff.; *de rep.* 2.34; *Tusc. disp.* 1.1–7 (but stressing Roman moral superiority).

were now for the most part degenerate,[94] yet they stood at a far higher level than such peoples as Mysians and Phrygians (*ad QF.* | 1.1.19), who constituted most of the population of the province of Asia. Jews and Syrians were 'nations born for servitude' (*de prov. cons.* 10). Admittedly in most of the passages cited Cicero was trying to discredit witnesses hostile to his clients, and he could speak, when it suited him, honorifically of provincial magnates and communities, but none the less such statements are eloquent of the prejudice he could easily arouse, and some of his private remarks even on Greeks are disdainful (e.g. *ad QF.* 1.2.4).

The '*ideal* of inclusiveness' which Last treats as an 'outstanding feature of the political technique devised by the Roman Republic' had not in fact emerged.[95] The third book of Cicero's *de republica* preserves traces of an argument in which imperial dominion seems to have been defended as just in much the same way as the rule of soul over body or masters over slaves; men who were incapable of governing themselves were actually better off as the slaves or subjects of others.[96] The theory naturally did not imply that any actual slaves or subjects belonged to this category, but a Roman could easily persuade himself that experience showed the subjects to be unfitted for independence.

Under Roman private law the master was entitled to exploit his slaves as he pleased, and the *iura belli*, accepted throughout antiquity, allowed similar rights to the victor in war. Beyond doubt Romans took it for granted that Rome was justified in profiting from her empire. Yet in Panaetius' theory, which Cicero adopted, just as masters were bound to give slaves just treatment (*de offic.* 1.41), so an imperial power had a duty to care for the ruled, which Rome had faithfully discharged in the 'good, old days' before Sulla (2.27). Good government was due even to Africans, Spaniards and Gauls, 'savage and barbarous nations' (*ad QF.* 1.1.27).

Many or most of Rome's subjects had come under her sway, not always after defeat, by *deditio*, which involved the surrender of *divina humanaque omnia* (Livy 1.38) and the extinction of the community concerned, but Rome regularly restored to the *dediti* their cities, lands and laws, often recognized them as her friends and sometimes concluded treaties with them; they thus acquired rights, which *fides* or *religio* bound Rome to respect. In practice Rome left them all to

---

[94] *pro Flacc.* 9, 16, 57, 61; *ad QF* 1.1.16, 1.2.4; *pro Sest.* 141; *pro Lig.* 11. He found it necessary to differentiate the Sicilians (who were almost like old Romans!) from other Greeks, II *Verr.* 2.7.

[95] *CAH* XI 437.

[96] *de rep.* 3.37–41, whence Aug. *Civ. Dei* 19.21, cf. Capelle (1932), 93: note there *ideo iustum esse, quod talibus hominibus sit utilis servitus et pro utilitate eorum fieri, cum recte fit, id est cum improbis aufertur iniuriarum licentia, et domiti melius se habebunt, quia indomiti deterius se habuerunt.*

manage their own internal affairs, at most ensuring that they were administered by persons loyal to the sovereign.[97] |

Indemnities or taxes might be demanded from defeated enemies as *quasi victoriae praemium ac poena belli* (II *Verr.* 3.12), and provinces could be described as virtual estates of the Roman people (ibid. 2.7), yet Cicero at least felt it necessary to argue that taxation was in the interest of the provincials themselves: armies were required for their protection, and revenue was indispensable to pay them (*ad QF.* 1.1.34). Thus taxation of the subjects was justified by the benefits conferred on them. Precisely the same argument was to be advanced by Tacitus.[98] There was not even anything new in Tiberius' celebrated dictum that he would have his subjects sheared, not shaved (Suet. *Tib.* 32): Cicero rebutted Verres' claim that he had acted in the public interest by selling the Sicilian tithes at unprecedentedly high amounts, by observing that neither senate nor people had intended him to act in such a way as to ruin the farmers and jeopardize future returns (II *Verr.* 3.48). This, however, is only a question of rational exploitation of the subjects, not of justice towards them.

We may indeed ask how far Cicero spoke for many more than himself in advocating justice to the subjects. Here I attach some significance to his denunciations of the misgovernment prevalent in his time, in the Verrines written for an upper-class audience, in his speech before the people on the Manilian law, and even in a despatch from Cilicia to the senate.[99] He assumes that his own sentiments are generally shared. He actually tells the senate that because of the oppressive and unjust character of Roman government the *socii* are too weak or too disloyal to contribute much to defence against Parthia. About the same time he wrote to Cato that it was his principal object, given the lack of adequate military resources, to provide for the protection of his province by his own mild and upright conduct that would ensure the fidelity of the *socii*, and he later claims that he had reconciled the provincials to Roman rule by the excellence of his own administration.[100] It was indeed a commonplace of ancient political thinking, doubtless based on oft-repeated experience, that in Livy's words *certe id firmissimum longe imperium est quo oboedientes gaudent*;[101] it recurs, for instance, in discussions of absolute monarchy, which teach

---

[97] Dahlheim (1968), chs. I and II.

[98] *Hist.* 4.74. Dio makes Maecenas add that taxation should be levied on all alike (52.28 ff.). That was still not the case when he wrote.

[99] See esp. II *Verr.* 3.207 (in 2.2–8, 5.8 he implausibly claims that the Sicilians loved their masters, but treats them as exceptional); *de imp. Cn. Pomp.* 65; *ad fam.* 15.1.5.

[100] *ad fam.* 15.3.2 and 4.14; *ad Att.* 5.18.2.

[101] Cf. Polyb. 5.11, 10.36; Sall. *BJ* 102.6; Cic. II *Verr.* 3.14; Livy 8.13.16.

the king to show justice not only for its own sake but in order to secure the affection of his subjects and make his rule more secure.[102] |

However, Cicero's letters from Cilicia and his advice to his brother in Asia (*ad QF.* 1.1) do not suggest that good government was to be practised purely for this prudential reason. Cicero tells Atticus, for instance, that his integrity as a governor afforded him the greatest intrinsic satisfaction of his life. It mattered to him, he says, more than the fame it brought (*ad Att.* 5.20.6). But the allusion to fame should also be marked. 'Fame' he says in the first *Philippic* (29) 'is demonstrated by the testimony not only of all the best men but by that of the multitude.' It was in this sense that he expected his reputation to be enhanced by his virtues as a governor. So too he surely supposed that denunciations of misrule would evoke indignation—Pompey in 71, he tells us (I *Verr.* 45), had actually roused the people in this way—and equally that there would be a popular response to his laudation of Pompey, not only as a great general but as one whose upright behaviour won the hearts of the subjects (*de imp. Cn. Pomp.* 36–42); he does not add in this encomium that his behaviour would strengthen Roman rule. In the same way Caesar in his *Civil War* digresses to excoriate the cruelty and rapacity of Metellus Scipio and his officers in the east (*BC* 3.31–3); this was in part a propagandist work, and Caesar evidently hoped that his readers would condemn his enemies for their ill-treatment of provincials. The author of the *Bellum Africum* also contrasts Caesar's care for African provincials (3.1, 7.2) with the depredations, and worse, of his adversaries (26).

Perhaps the constant use of the term *socii* to describe provincials in itself indicates something about Roman attitudes to them; it could hardly have been totally divested of the nuance imparted by its other senses. Much more striking, however, is the history of *repetundae* legislation. At least from the late third century the senate had been ready to hear complaints from the *socii* against Roman officials and to provide for reparation or punishment.[103] The statutes on this subject passed between 149 and 59 were the work of politicians of varying complexion, but according to Cicero (*de offic.* 2.75) each enactment made the law stricter. It is notable that the clause authorizing recovery of money from third parties who had benefited from the governor's extortions, a clause that could affect equites and was apparently often

---

[102] E.g. Sen. *Clem.* 1.3, 8.6 ff.,11.4, etc., as in Polyb. 5.11.

[103] Toynbee (1965), II 608 ff. Particularly significant are the activities of the elder Cato in seeking to redress or punish wrongs done to subjects (*ORF*² frs. 58 ff., 154, 173, 196–9); note also the indignation that Gaius Gracchus tried to arouse at ill-treatment of the Italians (Gell. 10.3). Even if personal or political feuds explain why some or most charges were brought, it would remain true that injustice to subjects was a suitable pretext for assailing personal adversaries.

invoked, was introduced by Glaucia, who sought their political back-
ing, and was | simply adopted in later statutes (*Rab. post.* 8–10). Cicero
briefly characterizes Sulla's law as *lex socialis* (*div. in Caec.* 18). Caesar's
statute, comprising no less than 101 clauses (*ad fam.* 8.8.3), and
approved by Cicero (*pro Sest.* 135; *in Pis.* 37), remained in force until
Justinian's time and formed the basis of the law throughout the
imperial period.[104] Our accounts of the eventful year in which it was
passed are fairly full, yet they do not allude to its enactment. It was
probably uncontroversial. Like earlier *repetundae* laws, it was concerned
only with the wrong-doing of senatorial officials. The governor himself
was supposed to protect subjects in his courts against publicans and
usurers. On paper even Verres promised heavy damages against the
former, if they were guilty of illicit exactions (II *Verr.* 3.26), and some
governors gave the provincials real protection.[105]

No proof is needed that provincials found insufficient remedy
against extortionate governors in the *repetundae* laws, *quae vi, ambitu,
postremo pecunia turbabantur* (Tac. *Ann.* 1.2), or that many governors, for
prudence or profit, connived at or participated in the rapacity of tax-
gatherers and moneylenders. Personal or political connexions could
also distort the conduct of senators who, like Cicero, had no wish for
their own part to pillage the subjects.[106] In practice the provincials
were usually at the mercy of the proconsul, who was virtually absolute
in his province, *ubi nullum auxilium est, nulla conquestio, nullus senatus, nulla
contio* (Cic. *ad QF.* 1.1.22). Their best hope lay in his probity and
courage. In general he was restrained from indulging in or permitting
extortion only by his conscience, or regard for his own reputation.
Cicero enjoins upon Quintus and claims for himself, and for Pompey,
such virtues as justice, mercy, accessibility and diligence. No quality is
more often commended than that elementary honesty for which the
most revealing Latin term is *abstinentia*.[107] The very frequency with

[104] See ch. 4, part I.

[105] On the duty of governors and its delicacy, Cic. *ad QF* 1.1.32–6; *ad Att.* 5.13.1. Posidonius
held (with some anachronism) that equestrian control of the courts made governors too fearful to
restrain Equites in the provinces (Jacoby, *FGH* 87 F 108d and 111b). There were certainly
exceptions like Q. Mucius Scaevola and L. Sempronius Asellio (Diod. 37.5 and 8 from Posid.),
Lucullus (Plut. *Luc.* 20) and perhaps Gabinius in Syria (Cic. *de prov. cons.* 10; *ad QF* 3.2.2); Cicero
adopted Scaevola's edict on the publicans, while that of Bibulus in Syria was overtly still stricter
(*ad Att.* 6.1.15, but see *ad fam.* 3.8.4).

[106] From Cilicia Cicero pressed administrators of other provinces to comply with Roman
moneylenders' demands (e.g. *ad fam.* 13.56 and 61) in terms perhaps not very different from the
pleas on Scaptius' behalf that he resented. Despite his condemnation of Appius Claudius' conduct
as governor (e.g. *ad Att.* 5.15 ff. and 6.1.2), he did what he could to hinder his conviction at Rome
(*ad fam.* 3.10.1; *ad Att.* 6.2.10), and showed his displeasure with hostile witnesses from Cilicia (*ad
fam.* 3.11.3). Similarly in 70 L. Metellus had reversed Verres' *acta* in Sicily (II *Verr.* 2.62 ff., 138–
40, 3.43–6, 5.55) but obstructed his prosecution (2.64 ff., 160–4, 3.122, 152 ff., 4.146–9).

[107] *ad QF* 1.1 (a letter presumably intended for publication) commends *aequitas, clementia,
comitas, constantia, continentia, facilitas* (for the meaning of which see *de imp. Cn. Pomp.* 41; *ad Att.*

which it is ascribed, whether truly or falsely, to individuals shows how little it could be assumed as a common characteristic of officials (cf. n. 110). Still, we must not too lightly treat a Verres or an Appius as typical of republican governors. Others are known to have been men of personal integrity, or, like Scaevola, Lucullus and perhaps Gabinius (n. 105), to have protected the subjects against usurers and publicans. Scaevola remained an exemplar; Cicero took his edict as the | model for his own (cf. n. 105). In 50 Cicero tells Atticus that he had heard only good reports of all but one of the eastern governors; they were behaving in conformity with the high principles of Cato, *a quo uno omnium sociorum querelae audiuntur*,[108] and, incidentally, with those which Atticus had himself repeatedly recommended to Cicero.[109] The standards of good government were already recognized and approved in the republic, and the only change that came about in the Principate in this regard was that they were somewhat better observed, an improvement that it is easy to exaggerate.[110]

When Cicero included *provinciae, socii* among the *fundamenta otiosae dignitatis*, I feel sure that he meant among other things care for their welfare (cf. *de leg.* 3.9). But *aerarium* is another of the *fundamenta*, and in his day it was the provinces which supplied most of the revenue. It was probably not until the nineteenth century that any imperial power scrupled to tax subjects for its own benefit; the Romans were not ashamed to do so, and I imagine that most of them would have thought Cicero's justification of the practice, which I cited earlier, as superfluous. In one way or another senators and equites, soldiers and grain recipients at Rome all profited from the empire. In addressing the people Cicero can refer to 'your taxes' and 'your lands'.[111] He did not forget in advocating the Manilian law to argue that it served the interests of the treasury and of Romans with business in the east (*de imp. Cn. Pomp.* 14–19). Pompey boasted of the enormous accretion of revenue his conquests had brought (Plut. *Pomp.* 45). Nor must we overlook what Romans seldom mentioned, that victorious wars helped to stock Italian estates with cheap slaves.

6.2.5), *gravitas, humanitas, integritas, lenitas, mansuetudo, moderatio, severitas, temperantia*. Several of these virtues (also *fides, innocentia*) recur in Cicero's eulogy of Pompey (*de imp. Cn. Pomp.* 13, 36–42) and in the claims he makes on his own behalf in 51–50 BC (*ad Att.* 5.9.1, 15.2, 17.2, 18.2, 20.6, etc.; *ad fam.* 15.4.1 and 14), along with *abstinentia* (for whose meaning see also *ad Att.* 5.10.2, 16.3, 21.5; *continentia, innocentia, integritas, temperantia* are more or less synonymous), *iustitia* and *modestia*. See R. Combès, *Imperator* (Paris, 1966), ch. VIII.

[108] *ad Att.* 6.1.13; *ad fam.* 15.4.15.

[109] *ad Att.* 5.9.1, 10.2, 13.1, 15.2, 21.5 and 7. Conceivably in pressing Scaptius' case, Atticus did not know all the facts.

[110] See ch. 4, part II.

[111] *de imp. Cn. Pomp.* 4 ff., 7; *de leg. agr.* 2.80 ff.

I will add only one further point [cf. pp. 515–7]. Under the Principate the worst features of republican misrule were obliterated; above all peace and order were better preserved. But exploitation did not end. Italy benefited as much as the provinces from the Roman peace, yet until c. AD 300 the land there was immune from tax.[112] While contributing less than the provinces to the common needs for expenditure, Italians continued, as late as the third century, to enjoy a share of the higher posts disproportionate to that of provincials, if we simply equate Italy with an area in the provinces of like size and population.[113] Moreover provincial revenues were spent lavishly on feeding and amusing the inhabitants of Rome and beautifying the | city, to say nothing of court expenditure. These privileges were not challenged by provincials in the senate or on the throne. Equality as between Italians and provincials was not attained, until all were sunk in equal misery.

BIBLIOGRAPHY

Astin, A. E. (1967). *Scipio Aemilianus*. Oxford.

Badian, E. (1958). *Foreign clientelae*. Oxford.

Badian, E. (1968). *Roman imperialism in the late republic*. 2nd ed. Oxford.

Brunt, P. A. (1971). *Italian manpower 225 B.C.–A.D. 14*. Oxford.

Capelle, W. (1932). 'Griechische Ethik und römischer Imperialismus', *Klio* XXV 86–113.

Christ, K. (1974). 'Caesar und Ariovist', *Chiron* IV 251–92.

Cimma, M. R. (1976). *Reges socii et amici populi Romani*. Milan.

Crawford, M. H. (1974). *Roman republican coinage*. Cambridge.

Dahlheim, W. (1968). *Struktur und Entwicklung des römischen Völkerrechts*. Munich.

Drexler, H. (1959). 'Iustum bellum', *RhM* CII 99–140.

Earl, D. C. (1961). *The political thought of Sallust*. Cambridge.

Gelzer, M. (1963). 'Die Anfänge des römischen Weltreichs', *Kleine Schriften* II 3–19.

Goar, R. J. (1972). *Cicero and the state religion*. Amsterdam.

Hampl, Fr. (1957). 'Stoische Staatsethik und frühes Rom', *HZ* CLXXXIV, reprinted in Klein (1966).

Hampl, Fr. (1959). 'Römische Politik in republikanischer Zeit und das Problem des Sittenverfalls', *HZ* CLXXXVIII, reprinted in Klein (1966).

Hoffmann, W. (1960). 'Die römische Politik des 2. Jahrhunderts und das Ende Karthagos', *Historia* IX 309–44, reprinted in Klein (1966).

---

[112] Aurelius Victor, *Caes.* 39.31. [See p. 515.]

[113] G. Barbieri, *L'Albo senatorio da Severo a Carino* (Rome, 1952), 441, found that forty-three per cent of senators whose origins were known or probable were Italian. H.-G. Pflaum, *Les Procurateurs équestres* (Paris, 1950), 193, assigned an Italian origin to twenty-six out of ninety-one third-century procurators.

Jones, A. H. M. (1940). *The Greek city from Alexander to Justinian*. Oxford.
Jones, A. H. M. (1974). *The Roman economy*. Oxford.
Klein, R., ed. (1966). *Das Staatsdenken der Römer*. Darmstadt.
Latte, K. (1960). *Römische Religionsgeschichte*. Munich.
Liebmann-Frankfort, T. (1969). *La frontière orientale dans la politique extérieure de la République romaine*. Brussels.
Meyer, H. D. (1961). *Die Aussenpolitik des Augustus und die augusteische Dichtung*. Cologne.
Oppermann, H., ed. (1967). *Römische Wertbegriffe*. Darmstadt.
Roloff, H. (1938). *Maiores bei Cicero*. Göttingen.
Sherk, R. K. (1969). *Roman documents from the Greek East*. Baltimore.
Sherwin-White, A. N. (1957). 'Caesar as an imperialist', *G&R* IV 36–45.
Swain, J. W. (1940). 'The theory of the four monarchies: opposition history under the Roman empire', *CPh* XXXV 1–21.
Timpe, D. (1965). 'Caesars gallische Krieg und das Problem des römischen Imperialismus', *Historia* XIV 189–214.
Timpe, D. (1972). 'Rechtsformen der römischen Aussenpolitik bei Caesar', *Chiron* II 277–95.
Toynbee, A. J. (1965). *Hannibal's legacy*. Oxford.
Veyne, P. (1975). 'Y a-t-il eu un impérialisme romain?', *MEFR* LXXXVII 793–855.
Vogt, J. (1960). *Orbis*. Freiburg im Breisgau.
Walbank, F. W. (1963). Polybius and Rome's eastern policy', *JRS* LIII 1–13.
Walbank, F. W. (1965). 'Political morality and the friends of Scipio', *JRS* LV 1–16.
Weippert, O. (1972). *Alexander-Imitatio und römische Politik in republikanischer Zeit*. Diss. Würzburg.
Wells, C. M. (1972). *The German policy of Augustus*. Oxford.
Ziegler, K. H. (1964). *Die Beziehungen zwischen Rom und den Parthenreich*.

15

The Revenues of Rome*

LUTZ NEESEN, *UNTERSUCHUNGEN ZU DEN DIREKTEN STAATSABGABEN DER RÖMISCHEN KAISERZEIT* (27 *V.CHR-*284 *N.CHR.*). Bonn: Habelt, 1980. Pp. XIV + 311.

This doctoral dissertation, the first comprehensive treatment of its subject since J. Marquardt, *Röm. Staatsverwaltung* II² (1884), examines *tributum soli* (19–98) and *tributum capitis* (117–34), rents on public and imperial property (99–103), the *vicesima hereditatium* and *vicesima libertatis* (135–41), and extraordinary levies in kind (104–16) and cash (142–8); the introduction reviews the Republican inheritance, and a final chapter sums up Neesen's conclusions and looks forward to the system of the late empire (149–80). The notes which follow cite most of the evidence, and (perhaps to excess) the views of earlier scholars on every point treated; only for Egypt is N. content to summarize standard works; here the student will still turn particularly to Wilcken's *Gr. Ostraka* I (1899), for its incomparable lucidity, and to the briefer and sometimes modified account Wilcken gave in his *Grundzüge* (1911), and for fuller detail to S. L. Wallace, *Taxation in Egypt from Augustus to Diocletian* (1938), with the *index locorum* in *ZPE* 16 (1975)). Some years ago I tried to collect and analyse the non-Egyptian evidence; the results of this investigation, now long suspended, appear in the notes and appendixes to A. H. M. Jones' admirable survey in *The Roman Economy* (1974), ch. VIII (cited as Jones, *Taxation*), and now enable me to supplement N. on some matters he has not fully considered, and to venture on certain criticisms of his views on the census and on *tributum*. At the outset I must make it clear that his lucid, cautious and accurate work must be regarded as fundamantal. The *index locorum* will facilitate its use.

* I am indebted to Dr. A. K. Bowman for discussion of an earlier version of this review article. [I have made a few corrections in the original text. The new numbered notes refer to sections of the Addenda to this chapter.]

THE REPUBLICAN HERITAGE

N. rightly begins with a brief but clear and well-documented survey of Republican practices, from which imperial developed, as he insists. Cicero attests the diversity of direct taxes (ii *Verr.* 3, 12–15). In Sicily the Romans extended to the whole island the tithe-system that had existed in the dominions of king Hiero of Syracuse. They took over what was familiar and in operation. Tithes had also been levied in some regions once under Persian rule (Ps-Arist., *Oec.* 1345b 28 ff.), perhaps too by the Attalids: C. Gracchus may have done no more than entrust their collection in Asia to Roman publican companies. But in some other provinces Rome, like Athens, simply demanded lump sums from subject communes, assessed no doubt on a rough estimate of their capacity to pay. Presumably the communes could then collect those sums at their own discretion. So too, when quotas were due to publicans, communes which made *pactiones* with the publicans were probably free to raise the sums required under these *pactiones* by imposing local taxes, which could also be levied to meet their own needs, or to satisfy extraordinary Roman demands (e.g. App., *Mithr.* 83). *Tributum* in Republican usage denotes a tax levied by a city (including Rome) on its own citizens (cf. ch. 17 nn. 2 f.); only in the Principate does it come to mean, like *stipendium*, a tax imposed by the imperial power. (N. 9 f.; 25 ff. discusses with care the use of these terms.) In particular, local capitation taxes disappear, and imperial *tributum capitis* comes in: the practice perhaps began with exactions in civil wars (cf. Caesar, *BC* iii, 32), though in Africa a capitation tax was imposed from 146, according to Appian (*Lib.* 135). Censuses, which some communes had taken for the purposes of assessing local imposts and of determining property qualifications for office (N. 34), are now ordained by Rome. Eventually the communes even in Italy, where no *tributum* was paid, were debarred from imposing their own taxes without imperial sanction (*ILS* 2666A: 5874: 5876: 6092: Pliny, *Ep.* x, 24; Severan rescripts in *CJ* iv. 62. 1 f.; *Dig.* xxxix. 4. 10).

THE PERSISTENCE OF DIVERSITY

There was however, still no uniformity; indeed diversity in direct taxation persisted after the reforms of Diocletian and Constantine (Jones, *Later Roman Empire* 62–8). In some provinces quotas were still levied, fifths and sevenths in the second century (Hyginus, 205 L), though other rates are probably attested (Jones, *Taxation* 182); one may compare the way in which *portoria* levied on trade *within* the empire in different circumscriptions range at least between two per cent and five per cent *ad valorem* (S. J. de Laet, *Portorium*, esp., 242–5). It would be rash to assume that with tax quotas in kind *adaeratio* was never practised. In other provinces there was a tax expressed in money on the assessed value of land (Hyginus, l.c.), or perhaps of all capital (*infra*). Again, we must beware of supposing that then the taxpayers could never fulfil their obligations by payment in kind. For instance, Caesar originally assessed Gallic tribute in cash (Suet., *Caes.* 25), but very little money | circulated in parts of Gaul in the early first century A.D. (D. Nash, in *Scripta Nummaria Romana*, edd. R. A. G. Carson and C. M. Kraay (1978), 21 ff.); the government could hardly have obtained payment in cash and moreover, the Rhine armies required large supplies. Thus the tribute in kind exacted from the Frisii (Tac., *Ann* IV, 72) need not be an isolated case. The model constructed by K. Hopkins of the effects of taxation on the economy (*JRS* 1980, 101 ff.) could be adjusted accordingly.

In Egypt the land tax was certainly different again: on land under grain the government took neither quotas nor cash payments but fixed quantities of grain. The rate of tax on private land ranged from less than 1 to 2 *artabae* per *aroura*, but rents on public land from $1\frac{1}{2}$ to $14\frac{1}{2}$ (Wallace, ch. 11). The variations in rents can be explained by the varying fertility of different parcels, but the possessors of private land were, as in the Ptolemaic period, privileged. So too citizens of Rome and Alexandria paid no capitation tax (ib. 407 n. 24), and some Egyptians (those who were better off) paid at lower rates than others, but even the privileged paid 20 drachmae in the Arsinoite nome, 12 in the Oxyrhynchite and 8 in the Hermopolite, and in different quarters of Thebes the unprivileged paid from 10 to 24 (Wallace ch. VIII).

Not all these variations can be explained. No doubt in richer areas the state could take a higher proportion of production, since there was a greater surplus available. Privilege too was rampant in the empire; one may think of the immunity from *tributum* enjoyed by Italy and by favoured provincial communities (N. 207 ff.), and, to judge from a fragment of Ulpian, *de censibus* (*Dig.* 1. 9. 12, clearly interpolated), by consulars or perhaps all senators. The saying that 'unto every one that hath shall be given, and he shall have abundance, from him that hath not shall be taken away even that which he hath' made good sense in the Roman world. But some diversity (as N. thinks) must surely be ascribed to the Roman preference for not changing practices they found in operation or had once established. Of course exceptions occurred; important changes were made by Caesar and Augustus in particular. However, N. 204 is not entitled to infer from Pliny, *NH* III, 88–91 that either man substituted fixed *stipendia* in place of tithes on the

Sicilian cities; the texts he adduces (217), especially Cic., *Balb.* 24; Vell.
II, 38 f., show that Pliny's use of 'stipendiariae' need not have this
precise meaning. It may be that the change was made, and that *ILS*
7193—5 can be explained, as suggested e.g. by G. Rickman, *Corn Supply
of Ancient Rome* 84 f., but we do not know (cf. p. 389) and it is at least
certain that the quota-tax system was not abolished everywhere, and
probable that payments in kind continued where they suited the
government or were almost necessitated by a dearth of money.[1]

THE SPECIAL CASE OF EGYPT

It is only in Egypt that papyri and receipts on ostraka yield relatively
abundant, though still defective, documentation on the Roman tax
system. The diversity of taxes in different provinces is, however, in
itself enough to deter us from generalizing from the Egyptian evidence,
unless there are at least hints suggesting that it has a wider application.
Certainly Egypt was unique in at least two respects. (1) The land was
the gift of the Nile; the productivity of different plots varied, even from
year to year, with the extent of inundations or sand-storms, and taxes
or rents were therefore based on a land survey, brought up to date
(where necessary) by annual inspections. The Ptolemies inherited this
system and transmitted it to Rome. (2) The centralization of government in Egypt, which the maintenance of the irrigation system has
always required, had enabled the Ptolemies to create a bureaucratic
machinery unparalleled elsewhere, which in great part the Romans
took over; if Rome eventually substituted liturgical for salaried officials and for tax-farmers, the difference was the less in that the
Ptolemies too had imposed a personal liability for a shortfall of revenue
on all concerned in its collection. They had exploited the whole
economy by an extraordinary diversification of direct and indirect
taxes, monopolies and licences. In principle this system was adopted by
Rome. Even what seem to be Roman innovations may have been
anticipated by the later Ptolemies, for whose practice we are less well
informed than for the third century B.C. Most Roman taxes in Egypt
have a Ptolemaic origin. Some have discerned an exception in the
Roman poll-tax (cf. C. Préaux, *L' Économie royale des Lagides* 380 ff.),
but the Ptolemaic *syntaxis* seems to have been a capitation tax based on
an enumeration of the inhabitants or *laographia*, and the fact that from
Augustus' time *laographia* has become the usual name for the poll-tax is
perhaps best explained by the hypothesis that it had been levied so long
that the term for the census on which it was based had been transferred
by custom to the tax itself. Thus, even if it was a novelty that the

Romans took a census every fourteen years, to facilitate levy of the poll-tax to which males became liable at the age of fourteen (Wallace 105), the principle was not new; the house-to-house declarations required in the Roman census presumably developed out of Ptolemaic *apographai* (cf. Wilcken, *Grundzüge* 173–5).

N. is then clearly right in treating Egypt separately from all other provinces. He does indeed allow for some probable influences of Egyptian practice on Roman taxation elsewhere (97 ff.), for instance in cadastral and census operations. But the peculiarities of the Nile valley made the Egyptian land survey an inappropriate model, and accustomed as they were to centuriation even outside Italy, | the Romans hardly needed to obtain from Egypt the concept of surveying provincial lands; while their use of local forms of measurement (Hyginus 121–3; 206 L, cf. N. 30 ff.) may suggest that in such surveys no single procedure was employed universally. Augustus took the first provincial censuses only a year after he had completed his first census of Roman citizens, and the form of the old Roman census, which unlike the Egyptian involved registration of property as well as of persons, corresponds more closely than the Egyptian to that 'forma censualis' which Ulpian describes (*infra*). Roman practice then probably provided Augustus with the inspiration, and a pattern to be followed or adapted, though again wherever the communes had already taken censuses, he could adopt or modify local procedures. In other cases where N. conjectures an Egyptian origin for Roman practices we may be content to note mere resemblances.

We must not indeed assume that everything in the Egyptian system was unique. The use of liturgical officials corresponded to practice elsewhere, especially after Severus gave the Egyptian *metropoleis* city status and imposed on their councils communal liability for the taxes. In Egypt the poll-tax was payable in full or in part on those who had died within the year (Wallace 124 f.); we find the same rule operating in Bithynia under the Tetrarchy (Lact., *Mort. Pers.* 23, 7), and by making Boudicca complain that even the dead had to pay tax, Dio (LXII 3) indicates that he supposed it to have applied in Britain, or perhaps everywhere. At Andros *bouleutai* were liable (*IG* XII, 5, 724), but the incidence of the tax in Egypt warns us not to assume that they paid so much as humbler persons (cf. Jos. *AJ* XII, 142 for Seleucid Palestine), or indeed that rates were uniform in different provinces. In Egypt, apart from a variety of levies made, on a capitation basis, from the fellahin, craftsmen paid what were in effect licences to perform their trades (Wallace, chs. IX, X, XII). Ps-Aristotle, *Oec.* 1346a 4, shows that such *cheironaxia* had been familiar in other parts of the Persian empire, and a Hellenistic observer was perhaps surprised to find none levied in India (Diod. II, 41). It would be imprudent to assume that Rome imposed them only in Egypt. Josephus alleged that in Africa there were all sorts of taxes (*BJ* II, 383). A sales tax there is mentioned only in *Passio S. Scill.* 19 (A.D. 180): 'siquid emero, teloneum reddo', cf. Wallace ch. XIII, for Egypt. A Hadrianic inscription from Aphrodisias (J. M. Reynolds, *Aphrodisias and Rome* (1982), Doc. no. 15) alone attests a tax on nails collected by Roman publicans. We know of a Roman tax on prostitutes in the Tauric Chersonese (*IGR* I, 860); for Egypt cf. Wallace 209–11. Most of the taxes in Egypt itself are documented only by papyri and ostraka; this shows how little we can rely on arguments from silence for the levy of similar taxes elsewhere. The facts that Augustus imposed unpopular taxes in Italy itself, the 5 per cent estates duty, the 1 per cent sales tax and the 2 per cent tax on the sale of slaves, and that Gaius and Vespasian invented tiresome imposts payable in Rome (Suet. *Gaius* 40; *Vesp.* 23, 3) make it unlikely that the imperial government neglected any source of provincial revenue which might have relieved the purses of Italians and which it had been a local custom to levy; the introduction of the poll-tax, or its transfer from municipal to imperial purposes, is in itself significant.

THE PROVINCIAL CENSUS

The greatest innovation of the Principate, due to Augustus, was the institution of the provincial census. (See Table at end for summary of evidence.) N. rightly doubts the reliability of very late sources that he had the whole empire systematically surveyed, and denies (39 ff.) that a census was taken simultaneously in all provinces, as Luke (2, 1) supposed. He also thinks it unproven that censuses were in fact held everywhere and at regular intervals, especially in senatorial provinces, or that they always involved a complete registration of all property and persons. Certainly there was no uniform type of census. In Egypt, with its house-to-house declarations required every fourteen years, its land survey annually revised, and other declarations of moveable goods, there was nothing like the *forma censualis* described by Ulpian (pp. 336 f.). Nor, as N. points out (34 ff.), was there any need for the registration and valuation of property in this *forma* in provinces where the land tax consisted in the exaction of quotas of produce: what was then required, as in Republican Sicily, was an annual record of the cultivators, whatever their title to the land (*subscriptio aratorum*), and of the acreage under particular types of cultivation (*professio iugerum*). But it does not follow that no kind of census would then have been necessary. As in Egypt, if there were capitation taxes, the persons liable must have been registered, and so must urban real estate and move-ables, if they were also subject to tax. Moreover, Roman citizens, wherever resident, were liable to the *vicesima hereditatium* and the government had to know what they were worth. The old census of Roman citizens provided this information (*infra*). So far as we know, such a census of citizens was taken after A.D. 14 only by Claudius and Vespasian, but it may well be that citizens were also listed with their assets in provincial censuses; certainly they had to be reported in Egypt (Wallace 103), and under Hadrian Phlegon drew particulars of centenarians from the census records alike for Italians, citizens of Roman colonies, e.g. Philippi which possessed *ius Italicum*, and for non-Roman provincials (*FGH* no. 257, F37). Hence, the fact that Ulpian's *forma censualis* cannot have been universally applicable does | not prove that some kind of census was not taken in every province. Luke's error would in fact have been more natural if the practice had already been universal in Augustus' time.

We know by chance of censuses in Gaul and perhaps in Spain in 27 B.C. (Dio LIII, 22, 5), and of later censuses under Augustus in Gaul, Lusitania and Syria. The annexation of Judaea by Augustus, of Cappadocia by Tiberius and of Dacia by Trajan were all followed by censuses. It is significant that Tacitus explains the rising of a Cappado-cian tribe 'quia *nostrum in modum* deferre census, pati tributa adigeba-tur' (*Ann.* VI, 41). All these provinces were imperial, but Augustus' first Cyrene edict (*FIRA* I² no. 68) seems to me to imply that the property of all residents in that senatorial province was registered; it is no objection that the records were not accessible to Augustus at Rome, for they would have been kept locally, as in Gaul (Dio LIX, 22, 3). Under Tiberius the proconsul took a census in Narbonensis, admittedly by special authority from the emperor (*ILS* 950): that illustrates the general supervision he could exercise over finance in virtue of his *imperium maius*. (N.'s suggestion, p. 27, that the distinction sometimes drawn between *tributum* in imperial provinces and *stipendium* in senator-ial indicates that the emperor more closely controlled collection of taxes in the former, is speculative.) The Table indeed shows that there is no testimony to a census in some senatorial provinces but that is true of some imperial provinces; no reason can be given why a census should have been taken in Macedon but not in Lycia, in Pannonia but not in Moesia. It is mere chance that we have any evidence, direct or indirect, for the practice in any province, and apart from Gaul, the documen-tation is not significantly greater for imperial than for senatorial provinces. A fragment of Ulpian *de officio proconsulis* (*Dig.* XLVIII. 18. 1. 20) shows that the proconsul had jurisdiction 'in causa tributorum', which must surely refer to fraudulent census returns (p. 337). The intimate connection between census and direct taxation in the minds of provincials in Judaea appears from the fact that *kensos* can be used as equivalent to *phoros* (Matt. 22, 17 and Mark 12, 14 with Luke 20, 22), just as in Egypt *laographia* meant poll-tax. A constitution of 213 (*CJ* VIII. 14 (15). 1) runs: 'universa bona eorum qui censentur vice pignorum tributis obligata sunt'; here 'qui censentur' surely designates 'all persons liable to tribute'. So, too the fact that Ulpian and Paul wrote treatises *de censibus* shows how vital was the census for taxation law. Ulpian's work ran to at least six books; its length is hardly intelligible unless censuses involved complexities and probably diversities from one province to another, which the scanty fragments do not reveal.

Another piece of evidence points to the universality of the census: Nero's ruling 'ne censibus negotiatorum naves adscriberentur tributumque pro illis penderent' (Tac., *Ann.* XIII, 51). In the course of an argument that *tributum* was probably assessed only on land and its appurtenances, N. suggests (p. 59) that this refers to ships 'quae exportandorum fructuum causa parantur', which were part of the *instrumentum fundi* (*Dig.* XXXIII. 7. 12.1). The context rebuts this suggestion; Tacitus' immediately preceding words state that 'temperata apud transmarinas provincias frumenti subvectio', and show that he has in mind a privilege analogous to those recorded in *Dig.* L. 6. 6 etc, conferred not on landowners exporting their own produce but on shipowners employed in the Roman grain trade, especially but no exclusively from Africa and Egypt (cf. G. Rickman, *Corn Supply of Anc!. Rome*, ch.v), whose ships had previously, at any rate if not owned by Italians or perhaps if not based on Italian ports, been assessed for tribute in provincial censuses. [See n. 3.]

Column I of the Table cites the few literary texts that refer to particular censuses, column II epigraphic testimony to census officials, and column III other documentation: allusions to *tributum capitis* which clearly imply registration of persons, as well as direct testimony to registration of either persons or property, and references by Ulpian and Paul to the *ius Italicum* or immunity of certain cities, which would not have been relevant to their works *de censibus* had not the tribute paid in the provinces where those cities were situated been based on censuses. Not indeed that we must infer that the census did not extend to these privileged communities; *ILS* 1146 shows that it was taken at Lugdunum, and Phlegon proves this for Philippi, though both possessed *ius Italicum*.

This has a bearing on the clause we find in a contract for sale of half a house at Alburnum Maius in Dacia (*FIRA* III, 90, A.D. 159), in which the vendor agrees to pay 'tributa' on it till the next 'recensus'. Von

Premerstein may well have been right that Alburnum enjoyed *ius Italicum* (*RE* x, 1243) and that 'tributa' must refer to a local impost (cf. *Gromatici* 349, 8 L). It is no objection that Alburnum is not in Ulpian's list of privileged Dacian communities, since we cannot be certain that the compilers of the *Digest* excerpted his list in full even for certain provinces; in excerpting Paul's list for Syria, for instance, they omitted Emesa, which he like Ulpian must have included, and in the fragment of Ulpian they left the status of Palmyra unclear. (Of course comparison of the two excerpts shows that neither covers all provinces, and therefore that both together are not comprehensive; at least they omit the Liburnian communes in Dalmatia, cf. Pliny, *NH* III, 139.) But, though Premerstein's view is unproven, it may still be that 'recensus' refers to the Roman census and implies that it took place at regular intervals; and naturally the vendor would not have undertaken an indefinite liability.

Regularity, as in Egypt, was surely necessary for the exaction of a capitation tax; in Syria we | should expect registration to have taken place at least every twelve years, since there females (who were exempt in Egypt) became liable on reaching the age of twelve (Ulpian, *de censibus* II; *Dig.* L. 15. 3). And the evidence for *tributum capitis* is so chancy and so scattered that it is hard to believe that it was not universal, though not of course uniform in incidence. Intervals of ten years are apparently presupposed in Ulpian's account of the *forma censualis* (Dig. L. 15. 4 *pr.*): periods of some kind are perhaps implied in *Dig.* x. 1. II; XXII. 3. 10. No doubt the sytem broke down in the anarchy of the third century. Only one census official (in Noricum) can be dated after 250 (*ILS* 9478, cf. Pflaum, *Carrières* no. 357). Diocletian revived the system, perhaps with rather simplified forms; as it had become unfamiliar a Gallic orator could speak of 'novi census enormitas' (*Pan. Lat.* v (VIII) 5). Lactantius (*Mort. Pers.* 23) and Eusebius (*HE* x, 8, 12; *Vita Const.* I, 55, cf. IV, 3) dilate on its horrors, but the rigours of tax assessment had probably been paralleled in earlier days (see Jones, *Taxation* n. 118, where one should read G. Chalon, *L'Édit de Tib. Jul. Alex.*, Part III *passim*). Once again, the census should have been systematically and regularly revised, but evidence from Egypt shows that it was not (Jones, *LRE* 454 f.), and it may be suggested that the *ad hoc* re-assessments of particular dioceses, provinces, cities or individuals which are attested cast light on the appointment in the Principate of commissioners who took the census only in certain *civitates* (*ILS* 1338, 1380, 1395, 2740, 9501; *AE* 1962, 183a; *CIL* VI, 1463; VIII, 19428); here too we might have partial revisions of the census. But this explanation of such appointments is not necessary (*infra*), and in Egypt at least, where the fourteen-year cycle of house-to-house declarations was maintained from Augustus' time to A.D. 258 (M. Hombert and C. Préaux, *Recherches sur le recensement dans l'Égypte rom.*, 1952), the government was in this respect more efficient than in the later empire: why not in other provinces too?

Column II cites the epigraphic evidence for census posts in senatorial (25) and equestrian (31) careers. The Equites, if not procurators conducting the census in provinces they governed, Mauretania Caesariensis (Pflaum 262a) and Thrace (*AE* 1973, 485, cf. W. Eck, *Chiron* 1975, 365 ff.), are either *adiutores* of senators (*ILS* 1392; *AE* 1939, 60) or operated only within part of a province (e.g. *AE* 1931, 36), or within particular *civitates* (*supra*), or are mere *sexagenarii*, who cannot have been responsible for taking the census in the whole of a province or group of provinces, a task for which high-ranking senators were normally appointed, and must be regarded as their subordinates.[2] This applies even to the Severan official, who was the first Eques to be honoured with a statue by the three Gauls for his work in taking the census (*ILS* 1390, cf. Pflaum 272), since in and after the Severan period consulars were designated to take the census in each of the Gallic provinces, in accordance with past practice (F. Jacques, *Ktema* (1977) 285 ff). On a rough calculation I estimate that we know about 10 per cent of the procurators of Tarraconensis and the Gallic provinces; if we were to assume that special commissioners, usualy senatorial, with considerable staff of Equites, were appointed to hold provincial censuses, we should have to conclude that the paucity of such attested *censitores* (to use one of the titles which these officials bear) is proof that the census was taken except perhaps in Gaul (for which there is most evidence) only at long intervals, and in other provinces very rarely and in some perhaps never. However, the initial assumption need not be right.

In Egypt it was the duty of the prefect to take the census (Hombert and Préaux 53 ff.). We know of occasions when it was taken by senatorial governors in the imperial provinces of Syria (Sulpicius Quirinius), Arabia (n. 7), Galatia (*ILS* 1039), Tarraconensis (*ILS* 1145; *AE* 1939, 60) and Lower Germany (*ILS* 1020) and equestrian in Mauretania Caesariensis and Thrace (*supra*). In Narbonensis a proconsul under Tiberius was simultaneously '[leg. a]d cens. accip. et dilect.' (*ILS* 950). Under Hadrian the *censitor* of Macedon, D. Terentius Gentianus (*ILS* 1046), is known also to have governed the province *extra ordinem* as consular legate. Perhaps the consulars who took censuses in Lugdunensis, Aquitania and Belgica as 'legati Aug. pro pr.' also took over the government which normally belonged to praetorians. The governor of Mauretania (Pflaum 262a) mentioned above (Octavius Pudens) is described in one inscription simply as 'praeses', in two inscriptions simply as 'procurator a censibus', and in two others also as governor. It follows that a man designated only as *censitor* (like Terentius) or the like might also be governor, and that one recorded only as governor (like Octavius in one instance) might also have taken the census. If it was a routine duty for a governor to take the census in the appropriate year, we should not expect this task to be mentioned in career inscriptions. It may be that it was usually mentioned only in special circumstances, e.g. if for the purpose of taking a census a man was appointed governor as a consular legate in a province normally governed by a praetorian legate or by a proconsul. Such appointments may have been made when there was more to be done than a mere revision of the last census returns. Rutilius Gallicus conducted cadastral operations in Africa, not as proconsul but as consular legate of Vespasian (*ILS* 5955), and Statius (*Silvae* I, 4, 83) suggests that he was concerned with the assessment of tribute and therefore with a census. Such operations could at times have resulted from disputes between | contiguous cities on the delimitation of their territories 'propter exigenda tributa' (Hyginus 114, 12 L), and no doubt, as with disputes between cities and the possessors of extra-territorial *saltus* (Frontinus 53 L), over the incidence of civic *munera* and of extraordinary Roman levies. Or again, whereas the ordinary census may have involved no more that the registration of persons and property, there may have been occasions when a systematic revaluation was ordered. Perhaps only in such circumstances did governors receive special *mandata* for the task, and were provided with senatorial or equestrian officers to take over the work or assist them in it; for such a senator see *ILS* 1135 (an ex-praetor who was 'leg. Aug. cens. acc. Hisp. Cit.', cf. G. Alföldy, *Fasti Hisp.* 98). One senator (*ILS* 1145) and three Equites (1391; 9011; *AE* 1975, 849) were twice employed, and may have been thought expert. We have instances (*ILS* 2683; *CIL* VI, 1463, cf. perhaps Wilcken, *Chr.* 202) of army officers being used to assist; another officer was detained for the Cappadocian census when about to retire (*AE* 1931, 36). For Diocletian's time see *OGIS* 612. R. MacMullen, *Soldier and Civilian in the later Roman Empire* (1963), ch. III, gives evidence for the Principate too on the use of soldiers in civil administration. If assistance with the census was a duty not uncommonly devolved on army officers, it would like any other which they performed seldom be mentioned in career inscriptions.

At a lower level we have only two known cases of slave clerks concerned with the census; the staff of the provincial procurators no doubt kept the records. But most of the work of registration was surely done by magistrates or *leitourgoi* of the *civitates*, perhaps by *quinquennales* in cities of the Roman type. For the east there is a little possible evidence for censuses and census officials (A. N. Sherwin-White, *Letters of Pliny* 672 ff.; *IGR* 1,769; III, 204; IV, 445 f.; Dio Chrys. XXXIV, 23); for the late empire cf. Arcadius Charisius, *Dig.* L. 4. 18. 16; *CTh.* XIII. 10.1). What titles such local officials bore we cannot in general tell; were it not explicit in the documents, we should not know that at Messene *mastreiai* were charged with the task (*IG* v, 1, 1432 f.; *pace* A. Giovannini, *Rome et la circulation monétaire en Grèce* (1978), 115 ff., probably of the early first century B.C.); Salvian shows that in the fifth century *curiales* were charged with both assessment and collection (*Gub. Dei* v, 15–44), and it is clear that collection was in the hands of local men in the Principate (p. 339), though again the evidence is meagre. The local magnates seldom paraded their functions as agents for the Roman treasury. In Egypt the role played by local liturgical officials is beyond doubt, and again because we are not wholly dependent on literary and epigraphic texts; if we were to trust arguments *e silentio* in relation to Roman taxation, we should have to conclude that there were provinces in which Rome extracted not a single penny from her subjects!

It follows that the dearth of evidence on provincial censuses does not in itself make N.'s agnosticism plausible; general considerations make it probable that in some form they were universal and regular in the Principate.[3]

THE NATURE OF *TRIBUTUM SOLI* AND *CAPITIS*

The Romans distinguished between *tributum soli* and *tributum capitis*. N. 117 ff. argues that there is no non-Egyptian evidence that the latter was other than a poll-tax, but there is at least no proof that the term cannot have also embraced the *cheironaxia* attested in Egypt. There owners paid poll-tax for their slaves, and if this was the practice elsewhere (as we might presume), it was an impost which affected traders and manufacturers as well as landowners. *Tributum soli*, to judge from its name, was simply a tax on land, though N. is willing to suppose that, where it took the form not of quotas of produce but of some kind of levy on the assessed value of a *fundus*, it might be assessed on the *instrumentum fundi* as well, i.e. everything required for the exploitation of the estate, such as slaves, animals, equipment for cultivating and processing crops, farm buildings, storage vessels, waggons, boats, grain stored for seed or maintenance of the *familia* (Steinwenter, *SB Wien* 1942). He sees no proof that *tributum* affected urban real estate or moveables (except in so far as they were part of the *instrumentum fundi* or subject to *tributum capitis*). In principle this could be true, and N. is not dogmatic. In Sicily and probably in most provinces in the Republic

Rome had been content to levy only a land tax, *scriptura* and *portoria*; only in Africa do we hear even of a capitation tax (App., *Lib.* 135). Land was the chief source of wealth (but cf. now K. Hopkins, in Abrams and Wrigley, *Towns in Societies*, 1978). Jones seems to have shown the relative unimportance of the *collatio lustralis* imposed by Constantine on the capital owned by traders and manufacturers (*Roman Economy* 35 ff.; one might wonder, however, about the extent to which freedmen traded with capital borrowed from patrons).

None the less in the old Roman census the imperial government had a model for the registration of property which could have been applied in the provinces and which would have permitted assessment and taxation of all capital: Roman citizens had been obliged to declare not only Italian land and the equipment for farming it, but also cash, debts due to or from others, clothing, jewels, slaves of all sorts (Festus 50; 322 L; Cic., *Flacc.* 79 f.; Livy VI, 27, 5; 31, 2; XXXIX, 44; Gell. VI, 11, 9, cf. generally *FIRA* I² no. 13, 146 ff.; Cic., *Leg.* III. 7) and *aedificia* (*FIRA* I² no. 8, 8), and to | estimate the value of their property apparently in accordance with formulae laid down by the censors (e.g. Festus 51 L). Provincials too had to make such estimates for the property they returned (*infra*, cf. Jos. *AJ* XVIII, 3), no doubt again in accordance with formulae. Thus in Pannonia lands were classified as 'arvi primi, arvi secundi, prati, silvae glandiferae, silvae vulgares, pascuae' (Hyginus 205 L, fully discussed by N. 44 ff.); a somewhat similar classification survived in the late empire in Syria (*FIRA* III pp. 795 ff.) and in Asia (A. Déléage, *La Capitation du Bas Empire*, ch. IV). Naturally it is not significant that Hyginus, whose concern is with land surveying, has nothing on the classification of non-landed property. But the allusion in *CIL* VIII, 23956 to 'praetium servi ex forma censoria' surely indicates that there were prescribed scales for valuation of slaves in the census. We have more information in excerpts from Ulpian, *de censibus* III, on the *forma censualis* (N. 48 ff.). It must be premised that as the census must have taken different forms in different provinces (*supra*), the compilers of the *Digest* (L. 15.4) would have misled us, if we were to think that Ulpian was describing a procedure followed in all parts. Moreover, they have clearly abbreviated and not merely transcribed.

As the fragment stands, it tells us (*pr.*) that possessors had to declare their lands (*agri*), specifying acreage in arable cultivation, number of vines and olives, acreage under olives (but not under vines!), acreage of meadow land and of *pascua*, and *silvae caeduae* (presumably acreage again, but this is not stated); one misses a reference to other fruits besides vines and olives. Flocks and herds would presumably often be pastured on lands that were not in possession of the stockbreeders, and

we should expect them to be taxed on the number of animals, the basis
for *scriptura* (e.g. Varro, *RR* II, 1, 16); hence animals too should have
been declared (cf. for Egypt, Wallace, ch. VI), and we may infer that
this requirement has been omitted in the fragment from the statement
in § 9 that 'all things born or acquired subsequently to the census
declaration may (must?) be declared before the work of taking the
census has been completed', though in the present state of the text
'nata' can refer only to slaves. Possessors must also declare 'lacus
piscatorios' and harbours (§ 7) and 'salinas' (§ 8); why not also any
lands exploited for non-agricultural purposes, e.g. the production of
clay for bricks, pottery or fulling? In § 5 we are told that in declaring
slaves they must state, evidently for valuation, their nationality, age,
employment and skills, but if they have to declare all slaves, in their
possession, why not moveables in general, or if the excerpt is only
concerned with the *instrumentum fundi*, why not animals, waggons, etc?
'Si quis inquilinum vel colonum non fuerit professus, vinculis censualibus tenetur' (§ 8); this refers back to a lost statement regarding
penalties for false declarations of all kinds. Minor regulations in §§ 1-5
also suggest how much detail has been omitted in the account of the
basic requirements. 'Omnia ipse qui defert aestimet': N. is uncertain
whether the possessor is to estimate the extent or value of his holdings,
but as this prescription supplements the requirement that he is to
declare how many *iugera* he has under this or that kind of cultivation, it
must refer to value. But how is the value to be assessed, or checked by
the *censitor*? Ulpian must have made this clear with juristic precision
and in the detail to be expected in a long and thorough work on the
census. N. inclines to suppose that the excerpts relate only to declarations of a *fundus* and its *instrumentum*; if this were so, we could not
conclude that Ulpian did not elsewhere deal with declarations of other
property, but 'inquilinus' naturally suggests a lodger in a house, and we
are reminded that in Egypt the subjects of Rome had to declare all who
lived in the same house (Wallace, ch. VII). It is most likely that the
owners of estates and houses were required to return their tenants and
lodgers, in order to facilitate the levy of the poll-tax (as in Egypt), but
there is clearly a possibility that a house was assessed for tax on the
basis of rentals (cf. Wallace 75 f. on the Egyptian *enoikion*). For
declarations by Roman citizens in Egypt of houses and their furnish-
ings see Wilcken, *Arch. f. Pap.* 1973, 75 ff.

False declarations gave rise to delations; the action was penal, and to
attempt the corruption of the delator was proof of guilt (Ulpian, *de
cens. ap. Dig.* XLVII. 15. 7; XLIV. 7. 26). Slaves implicated in the frauds
would suffer death, and evidence they gave when tried might impeach

their owners; Severus ruled that they could be examined against their owners for census frauds, as for *maiestas* and adultery and for no other crime (*CJ* IX. 41. I. cf. *Dig.* V. I. 53; XLVIII. 18.I. 19 f.). In Egypt conviction probably led to confiscation of one fourth of the property or to the loss of slaves undeclared (*Gnomon Idiologi* 44; 58–63). Now it must have been relatively hard to disguise the extent or quality of landholdings as compared with what at Athens, where (as in Messene) personal as well as real property was assessed for *eisphora* (for doubts see Busolt-Swoboda, *Gr. Staatskunde* II², 1213 n. 2), was called ἀφανὴς οὐσία, for instance cash hoarded or money on loan; it was to uncover such concealments that it was indispensable to make an exception to the general rule that the evidence of slaves was not to be received against their masters. Tertullian's reference (*Apol.* 42, 9) to the loss the state sustained from fraudulent declarations is probably relevant.

It is not surprising that legal texts generally refer to *tributum* only on *fundi* or *praedia*, since they must have constituted the larger part of taxable wealth, but *praedia* can include urban real estate and *solum* all that is attached to the soil (*Oxf. Lat. Dict. s.v.* 4b). *Aedificia* on public lands had | evidently been a source of revenue in the Republic (Cic., *leg. agr.* I, 3), and extraordinary levies were laid on private buildings in the Principate (*Dig.* L. 4. 6. 5): why not tribute too? Herod Agrippa, on becoming king of Judaea, abolished a tax on houses at Jerusalem (*AJ* XIX, 299); *pace* N. 59 this looks more like a Roman tax than one levied by the local priestly government. Ulpian takes 'census' to denote all that a man has (*Dig.* XXXVI. I. 17 (16) *pr.*); Eusebius (*HE* III, 20, 2) may indicate that cash had to be declared in Judaea. Scaevola reports that when a man had received usufruct of one third of a testator's *bona* the question was raised whether 'tributa praeterea, quae vel pro praediis aut moventibus deberi et reddi necesse est' should be deducted from the sum due to him; however, no certain inference can be drawn from this fragment, since 'praeterea' is misplaced and 'deberi' corrupt; Mommsen read 'tributa quaeve praeterea . . . dari et reddi necesse est' (*Dig.* XXXIII. 2. 32. 8 f.). However, the registration and assessment of ships in provincial censuses (p. 164) is decisive proof that moveables were [sometimes] declared and taxed.

Thus N.'s hesitation in allowing that tribute was levied on anything but persons and real property, perhaps land alone, seems to me unjustified. But of course there is a puzzle. Moveables (if we except the *instrumentum fundi*) cannot be brought under *tributum soli*. We must then infer that *tributum capitis* had a wider connotation than N. admits, and that *caput* must have meant something like 'personality'; for analogies we may think of its sense as 'civic status' or of its use in the late empire as a unit of taxable wealth, equivalent to *iugum*. This might perhaps explain why Titus *construed* immunity from *tributum capitis* as comprising immunity from *tributum soli* (*Dig.* L. 15. 8. 7), and why *caput* acquired its later sense in the tax system.

INDIVIDUAL AND COMMUNAL LIABILITY FOR TRIBUTE[4]

N. does not examime the relation between individual and communal liability for tribute and the related question of its collection by communal officials.

An Asian testament of the early Principate assumes that the possessor of an estate will owe the *fiscus* a fixed payment *per iugerum*, to be paid to the city of Nacrasus (*SB Wien* 1969, 7 ff.). The individual is liable to his city, the city to the Roman government. Collection within city territories was normally in the hands of local magistrates or liturgical officials, see Jones, *Taxation* 165, where in n. 83 *IGR* III, 86, 7 should be read, and L. Robert, *Ét. Anatoliennes* 136 f. added, together with *Dig.* L. 4. 1. 1 (Hermogenianus) and L. 4. 18 *pr.*, 1 and 26f., where Arcadius Charisius (early fourth century) cites the late Severan jurist, Modestinus. It is true that we hear occasionally of imperial slaves as *exactores* (*ILS* 1519a; 4258; *CIL* III, 349) and once of an equestrian officer with this title (*ILS* 2705 cf. perhaps 1330); they were perhaps appointed *extra ordinem* to collect arrears (cf. *BGU* 8 II. 9); for parallels in the late empire see Jones, *LRE* 456 ff. Even then, with an enlarged bureaucracy, the government relied in the first instance on curial officials, and so *a fortiori* it must have done in the Principate, wherever the use of publicans had been discontinued, except perhaps in the most barbarous areas, where military agents could be employed (cf. Tac., *Ann.* IV, 72; perhaps Dio LXVII, 4, 6; D. Sperber, *Latomus* 1969, 186–8). Curial officials cannot, however, have been employed to collect tribute from the private possessors of extra-territorial *saltus* (Frontinus 46, 5; 53 L), nor rents from the lands of the Roman people or emperor. Here the government may have relied usually on tax-farmers, publicans or *conductores*, cf. Ulpian's classification as publicans of all who 'fisco vectigal pendant vel *tributum* consequantur' (*Dig.* XXXIX. 4. 1. 1). Scaevola reports a complicated case (XIX. 1. 52 *pr.*, on which see Mommsen, *Ges. Schr.* III, 172) of the *conductor saltus* (cf. XLIX. 14. 3. 6) selling a *fundus*, for supposed non-payment of *tributa*, a term which here seems to cover rents on lands held on emphyteutic tenure, as in the imperial estates of Africa (*FIRA* I² nos. 100–3); the *conductor* who must himself have been liable to the *fiscus* was entitled to sell up the defaulting possessor, as no doubt were the city officials within their territories.

The *pecunia phorica* in the hands of publicans in Asia under Augustus (*AE* 1968, 483) came perhaps from rents on public or imperial lands; the term *phoros* was so used in Egypt (Wallace 71). Or for another suggestion see p. 390. The texts N. cites (24) do not warrant his claim that in the Principate public lands paid only a trifling *vectigal*; the reverse was certainly true in Egypt.

Many legal texts (cf. also *ILS* 6953) illustrate the liability of the individual possessor, including the usufructuary (*Dig.* VII. 1. 7. 2; 1. 52; XXXIII. 2. 32. 9), passing on death to his heir (XXX. 39. 5; XLI. 1. 34); tribute on land is 'onus fructuum' (XXV. 1. 13), and though vendor and purchaser, debtor and creditor may make private arrangements between themselves on liability, 'pactis privatorum formam iuris fiscalis convelli non placuit', and in fiscal law the possessor has to pay in the first place, though he may recover from a third party under his contractual rights (II. 14. 42; XIX. 1. 21. 1; 1. 52; 5. 24). Similarly Pius ruled that a *fideicommissarius* was liable, though after payment he might recover from the beneficiary of the trust (L. 15. 5). Tribute is a first charge on an estate against all other debts (v. 1. 50. 1) and indeed on all a man's assets (*CJ* VIII. 14 (15). 1). He may not set off payments due to him from the *fiscus* against his liability (XLIX. 14. 46. 5). A text of Papinian, which I | find obscure, envisages that for convenience the *fiscus* may sue one possessor for a liability that falls on several and after obtaining the whole sum from him transfer to him its rights of action against the rest (L. 15. 5), presumably with *protopraxia* (cf. Chalon, op. cit., 131 ff.). Here too we find that an estate may be sold up, if payment has not been made on the appointed day; in this case a legatee is liable and may not plead for delay on the ground that the heir and 'is qui tributis recipiendis praepositus fuerat' are solvent. This seems to imply that if but only if his own property did not cover his liability, the *fiscus* could have recourse to the heir (cf. XXX. 39. 5) and the tax collector. Cf. *supra* for the sale of a *fundus* by the *conductor saltus*.

On the other hand we hear of communal assessments under Augustus (Strabo x, 5, 3; XIV, 2, 19; Dio XLIX, 34, 2). In accordance with Ulpian's *forma censualis* a possessor must declare an estate 'in ea civitate, in qua ager est; agri enim tributum eam civitatem debet levare, in cuius territorio possidetur' (*Dig.* L. 15. 4. 2). This seems to imply that a *civitas* owed a lump sum to the state (this might also be true of a *Koinon* like the Thessalian, L. Robert, *Hellenica* v, 29 ff.), and that its burden would be less heavy, the more taxable property lay within its territory. Dio Chrysostom also suggests that a city benefited, the more tribute it had to collect from the peasants (XXXVIII, 26; XXXV, 14; XL, 10). This in part explains the territorial controversies mentioned above, and also the fact that it was apparently a disadvantage to pay tribute through another city (id. XL, 10, cf. *ILS* 6091, from the time of Constantine). A man who served his city as legate 'ad census accipiendos' (Hermogenianus, *Dig.* L. 4. 1. 2, cf. perhaps Robert, op. cit.) was more probably an ambassador appointed to negotiate the communal liability than an official responsible for census assessments. Does not all this suggest that the total communal liability was often less than the sum of the liability of individual possessors and that the community could appropriate the balance to its own uses?

Communal liability explains why the government would grant remissions of tribute to cities as such which had sustained natural disasters or losses from warfare (e.g. Tac., *Ann.* II, 47; XII, 63; H. Kloft, *Liberalitas Principis* (1970), 118 ff. for collection of evidence), although it is obvious that not all the individual taxpayers will have suffered equally, if at all, in such circumstances; by contrast in Egypt it was the individual farmer who was relieved in a season when the Nile had left his land dry or under water. One might wonder if the cities were then allowed to collect what they reasonably could from the individual taxpayers in their territory and use the sums themselves, e.g. for repairing damage done by earthquakes. Occasionally grants of imperial revenue for local purposes are attested (*SIG*³ 837, on which see A. H. M. Jones, *Cities of Eastern Roman Provinces*² 84; *JOAI* 1954, 110 ff.); *HA Alex. Sev.* 21 is, however, at best evidence that this practice was familiar to the fourth-century author (cf. W. Liebeschuetz *Antioch*, 151 ff.). Communal liability is also implicit in the readiness of the government to allow payment of tribute from communal revenues (*IG* XII, 5, 946, perhaps *SIG*³ 800) or from benefactions (*OGIS* 565 with notes; *IGR* IV, 181; *ILS* 6960); one magnate paid *tributum capitis* for the whole province of Macedon (*SEG* XVII, 315).

Publicans who collected tribute guaranteed to the state the sums of money which they were bound by contract to pay (whatever they actually collected) and for which they had to give security. Communal liability meant that even if the assets of individual taxpayers were insufficient to meet their tax obligations, the state could look to the whole commune, or to the tax collectors the communes appointed, to make up the deficit. In Egypt arrears of *laographia* which could not be collected from the destitute or from peasants who had fled were distributed by *merismoi* among the remaining villagers (Wallace 135 ff.). There liturgical tax-collectors were not only liable themselves for the taxes they were appointed to gather but were appointed at the risk of their communes, and in post-Severan times at that of the *boulai* of the metropoleis (Wilcken, *Grundzüge* 210–18, cf. 41 f.; 339 ff.; Wallace, ch. XVII). Outside Egypt too, the Severan jurists show that the 'munus exigendi tributi' was a liturgy that fell on those whose patrimony provided the government with security, especially on decurions (*Dig.* L. 1. 17. 7; 4. 1; 4. 3. 10 f.; 4. 6. 4 f.; 5. 7, cf. XLIX. 18. 2). Since tax-collection also involved personal activity, Modestinus preferred to class it as a 'mixed' liturgy (*Dig.* L. 4. 18. 26); women, minors, the aged and decrepit, however large their patrimony, could not have performed the actual work, but must have employed agents, a practice known in Egypt (*Grundzüge* 216). It seems unlikely that this system did not exist in every province from the time that the use of publicans was discarded. Already in the triumviral period, when Roman exactions were probably oppressive, immunity from the duty of tax-collection was a valued privilege (*Inscr. Syriae* 718, 33 f.; *FIRA* I² no. 56). It is not indeed specified among the onerous liturgies from which privileged persons were exempted by first and second-century emperors (*FIRA* I² nos. 73; 76; *Dig.* XXVII. 1. 6. 8); perhaps exemption was sparsely granted; Aelius Aristides seems to have claimed it with success (*Orat.* L, 96–9). The statement of Hermogenianus (*Dig.* L. 4. 1) that *decemprimi* acted at their own risk as collectors might in itself be interpreted restrictively, as implying that their property was security only against their negligence or fraud (cf. for later times *CTh.* XII. 6. 9), but Arcadius Charisius says that the city collectors 'pro omnibus | defectorum (Cuiacius: 'defunctorum' codd.) fiscalia detrimenta resarciunt', and he is apparently repeating a dictum of Modestinus (L. 4. 18. 26); in particular they had to pay the tax on deserted lands (ib. 27). The enactment of Aurelian making the *curiales* liable for such lands (*CJ* XI. 59 (58). 1) may not have been novel; the principle is the same as that operating in the Egyptian *merismoi*. Cf. also p. 340 for Papinian, *Dig.* L. 15. 5. 2.

In Egypt, where some at least of the liturgical collectors seem to have received remuneration, they were none the less tempted to oppressive exactions, partly no doubt because of their liability for deficits (see e.g. Chalon, op. cit., ch. xv). Here it is surely the documentation, not the conditions revealed, which makes Egypt a special case. Cf. *CJ* II. 11. 2 (197) and Ps-Ulpian, *Opiniones, Dig.* I. 18. 6 *pr.*–6, a work that can be dated before constitutions of Philip (cf. *Dig.* L. 4. 3. 3 with *CJ* X. 64. 1) and Severus Alexander (cf. *Dig.* XLIX. 18. 2 with *CJ* X. 44. 1). It is sinister that outside Egypt tax-collectors could boast of their justice and humanity (*IGR* III, 488; 739 II), and perhaps that men so rarely took credit for performance of this liturgy, by contrast with the gymnasiarchy and the like. We may surmise that their humanity was most evident in behaviour to men of their own class, who were also best able to protect themselves. 'Decernunt potentes quod solvant pauperes': the complaints of Salvian (*Gub. Dei* v, 15–44, cf. *CTh* XIII. 10. 1, A.D. 313) might probably have been voiced earlier, had there been a comparable spokesman for the poor. In general, we must beware of supposing that malpractices in administration were much more rampant in the late empire than in the Principate: for the earlier period we simply have far less evidence, but there are for instance hints that the abuses of the *cursus publicus*, amply documented in *CTh.* VIII. 5, were familiar both in Egypt and elsewhere from the first century onwards (Jones, *Taxation* 179; see now S. Mitchell, *JRS* 1976, especially 111–15 for full collection of the evidence).

It is indeed true that the remission of large tax arrears by Hadrian and Marcus Aurelius (*ILS* 309; Dio LXIX, 8; LXXI, 32) is proof that the government did not systematically sell up defaulters or tax-collectors who were in deficit. Similar remissions were granted in the late empire, and Salvian's allegation that it was the rich who benefited is confirmed by the testimony of emperors (Jones, *LRE* 120; 205 f.; 466 f.). Pressure on the city magnates was perhaps not so harsh in times of prosperity, especially if the communal liability could be met without enforcement of the full sums due from every individual; in that case remissions may have done little more than secure the 'potentes' from delation for non-payment of taxes which the treasury had in fact foregone without serious effect.

THE BURDEN OF TAXES: TRANSITION TO THE LATE EMPIRE

The burden of taxation in the Principate is hard to assess. Hopkins has recently re-stated the commonly held view that it was not heavy (*JRS* 1980, 116 ff.). See *contra* Jones, *Taxation* 183–5; neither Domitian nor Marcus seems to have shared this modern view. N. rightly stresses that taxation was regressive. In this connection it is well to remember that so far as the relative equity of quotas (Jones 174) is concerned, the large landowner might be compensated for a poor harvest by the high prices he could get for his diminished surplus (especially if he could hold back sales), whereas the small farmer might not have enough for subsistence and seed, and might have to buy in the market after paying his quota to the state. Even in the early Principate complaints of the burden are recorded (Tac. *Ann.* I, 76; II, 42; XII 63), before Vespasian had raised and sometimes doubled the rates (Suet, *Vesp.* 16), and taxation was one cause of revolts (Tac., *Ann.* III, 40; IV, 72; VI, 41; XII, 34; *Agr.* 30–2; Strabo XVII, 1, 53; Dio LV, 29, 1; LVI, 16, 3; 18, 3; LXII, 3; LXVII, 4, 6), though we cannot tell how far it was resented as a mark of subjection, or because assessment or exaction was unjust and brutal (cf. *Ann.* IV, 6, 4), rather than because it was intrinsically onerous. It is generally assumed that it was much heavier in the late empire, because of far higher public expenditure, but see C. R. Whittaker and A. K. Bowman, in C. E. King (ed.), *Imperial Revenue, Expenditure and Monetary*

Policy in the Fourth Century A.D. (1980), and on the size of the army R. MacMullen, *Klio* 1980, 451 ff. If we hear more of the burden of taxation after Diocletian, the explanation may be in part that our evidence is far more copious.

In the Principate it was certainly increased at times by extraordinary levies with which Nero is said to have exhausted the provinces (Suet., *Nero* 38). To the evidence on these levies collected by N. add *AE* 1956, 90 (apparently Flavian); *CJ* viii. 13. 6; Hermogenianus, *Dig.* L. 5. 11. Contrasting Trajan's rule with Domitian's, Pliny says of the provincials: 'nec novis indictionibus pressi ad vetera tributa deficiunt' (*Paneg.* 29, 4). Modestinus' phrase (*Dig.* xxvi. 7. 32. 6) 'onera annonarum et contributionum temporariarum' suggests that we have here the origin of the *annona militaris*. It is significant that under Diocletian 'indiction' came to be the term for the regular tax on property, while additional levies were henceforth called superindictions. Thus, as N. says, the later tax system developed out of the irregular exactions on which the government relied increasingly in the third century. The depreciation of the coinage then made it preferable to require taxation in kind rather than in cash, but there had been precedents for additional levies in earlier periods, especially no doubt when emperors | had failed to accumulate or conserve the reserves which prudent rulers like Tiberius (Suet., *Gaius* 37, 3) and Pius (Dio LXXIII, 8) laid up, in the same way as the Persian kings and imperial Athens, to meet extraordinary expenses. (This was the ancient equivalent to the modern device of public borrowing.)

We can then glimpse the way in which the tax-system of the late empire evolved from that of the Principate. In his last chapter N. offers observations on the development and on the differences of the two systems. They do not call for dissent so much as for doubts; the evidence is so meagre, especially for the Principate, that the relations between taxation and the economic and social structure, and the changes therein, are hard to assess.

Table (cf. n. 2): EVIDENCE FOR PROVINCIAL CENSUSES

For explanation see p. 331. Pflaum = H. G. Pflaum, *Les Carrières procuratoriennes équestres* (1960-61)

	I	II	III
SICILY	—	—	—
SARDINIA	—	—	—
BAETICA	—	—	—
LUSITANIA		EQUES: *CIL* x, 680.	*Dig.* L. 15.8; Phlegon, *FGH* no. 257, F 37, 1 and 62ff.
TARRACONENSIS	—	SENATORS: *ILS* 1135; 1145; *AE* 1939, 60. EQUITES: *AE l.c.; CIL* vi, 1463; viii, 19428.	*Dig. l.c.*; Pliny, *NH* iii, 28. *Tr. capitis* (?): *ILS* 6960.
GALLIA COMATA	27 BC.: Livy, *Per.* cxxxiv; Dio liii, 22. 5. 12 BC.: Livy, *Per.* cxxxviii, cf. *ILS* 212, ii 35ff. A.D. 14-15: Tac. *Ann.* i, 31; 33; ii, 6. A.D. 61: *Ann.* xiv, 46 (cf. *AE* 1972, 175). A.D. 83: Front, *Strat.* i, 1, 8. Archives: Dio lix, 22, 3.	SENATORS: *ILS* 1024; 1040; 1077; 1128 (?); 1145; 1185; *AE* 1924, 74; 1929, 158; 1957, 161; 1972, 153 and 175. EQUITES: *ILS* 1380; 1390; 1391; 1392; 1393; 8850; 9011; 9501; Pflaum no. 52; *AE* 1962, 183a; 1975, 849. (*Pace* Pflaum p. 1054, *CIL* xiii, 2924 is suspect). SLAVE *dispensator: ILS* 1511.	*Dig. l.c.*
NARBONENSIS	—	SENATOR: *ILS* 950	*Dig. l.c.*
LOWER GERMANY	*Contra* N. 40, Dio lvi, 18, 3f. does not attest an Augustan census.	SENATOR: *CIL* iii, 10804 (cf. Alföldy, *Fasti Hisp.* 24ff.) EQUES: *ILS* 1394.	*Dig. l.c.*
UPPER GERMANY		SENATOR: *ILS* 1020.	—
BRITAIN	—	EQUITES: *ILS* 1338; 2740; 9011; 9013.	*Tr. capitis:* Dio lxii, 3; Tac., *Ann.* xii, 34.
RAETIA	—	—	—
NORICUM		EQUES: *ILS* 9478.	—
DALMATIA	—	—	—
PANNONIA	—	SENATOR: *CIL* x, 3852.	Hyginus 205 L.
MOESIA	—	—	—
THRACE	—	SENATOR: *IGR* I. 796. EQUITES: *ILS* 1391; *CIL* v, 7784; *AE* 1974, 583 (cf. *Riv. di Fil.* 1974, 454ff.); 1975, 849.	—
DACIA	Under Trajan: Lact., *Mort. Pers.* 23, 5.	SLAVE ab instrum. censualibus': *ILS* 1513.	*Dig.* L. 15. 1; *FIRA* iii, no. 90 (?).

EVIDENCE FOR PROVINCIAL CENSUSES—*Continued*

	I	II	III
MACEDON	—	SENATOR: *ILS* 1046 (cf. Groag. *RE* VA 660). EQUES: *ILS* 1409.	*Dig.* L. 15. 8. Phlegon *l.c.* F 37, 47ff. *Tr. capitis: SEG* xvii, 315; *Jahreshefte* 1954, 110.
ACHAEA	—	—	*Tr. capitis: IG* xii, 5, 724; 946.
BITHYNIA-PONTUS	—	EQUES: *ILS* 9506.	*Dig.* L. 15. 1. Phlegon *l.c.* F 37, 55ff.
ASIA	—	—	*Dig.* L. 15. 8. Hyginus 206 L (?); *Tr. capitis: IGR* iv, 181; 259.
LYCIA-PAMPHYLIA	—	—	—
GALATIA	—	SENATOR: *ILS* 1039. EQUES: *AE* 1924, 82 (Pflaum no. 336 quite uncertain).	*Dig.* L. 15. 8.
CAPPADOCIA	Under Tiberius: Tac., *Ann.* vi, 41, 1.	EQUITES: *AE* 1931, 36; Pflaum no. 126, cf. *AE* 1974, 583. (No. 93 is too hazardous to list.)	—
CILICIA	—	—	*Dig.* L. 15. 1; App., *Syr.* 50 implies registration of property.
CYPRUS	—	—	—
SYRIA (including JUDAEA)	A.D. 6/7: Jos., *AJ* xvii, 355, xviii, 2 and 26, cf. Luke ii, 1, 3; *ILS* 2683.	SENATOR and EQUES: *ILS* 2683.	*Dig.* L. 15. 1 and 8.; App., *Syr.* 50; Euseb. *HE* iii, 20, 2; Ulpian, *Dig.* L. 15. 3. *Tr. capitis ib.* 15. 8. 7.
CRETE and CYRENAICA	—	—	Probably implied in Augustus' first Cyrene edict.
AFRICA	—	SENATOR: *ILS* 5955 (?) EQUES: *ILS* 1395.	*Dig.* L. 15. 8; *Tr. capitis:* App., *Lib.* 135; Tert., *Apol.* 13, 6.
MAURETANIA Caesariensis	—	EQUES: Pflaum no. 262a.	—
Tingitana	—	—	—
UNKNOWN	—	SENATORS: *CIL* vi, 3842; viii, 2754; 5355; xiv, 2927. EQUITES: *ILS* 1408; Pflaum nos. 126 (?); 157 bis.	—
ARABIA³	—	SENATORIAL GOVERNOR (*P. Yadin* 16, A.D. 127).	—

16

Remarks on the Imperial *Fiscus*

In *JRS* 56 (1966), 75 ff. (chapter 7), I restated the thesis of A.H.M. Jones that the term *fiscus* can refer either (1) to the private funds of an individual, including the emperor, or (2) to a chest, provincial or departmental, containing public monies, or (3) in the Principate to 'the whole financial administration controlled by the emperor', that is to say the properties and revenues of the state which he administered as well as his private domains. The second usage seems now to be illustrated in the document published by P. Herrman and K.Z. Polathan, *SB Wien* 1969, which show that tribute in the province of Asia went to the provincial *fiscus*. My essay was usefully supplemented by P. Baldacci, *Parola del Passato* 24 (1969), 349 ff. The article on *fiscus* by Ürögdi in *RE Suppl.* 10 (1965), 222 ff., is most helpful for its collection of texts on fiscal privileges. It is not clear to me from F. Millar, *The Emperor in the Roman World*, 1977, ch.IV, how far, if at all, the author has resiled from his contention in *JRS* 53 (1963), 29 ff., which I sought to refute, that whatever was fiscal in the Principate was in law the property of the emperor. This view, essentially that of Mommsen, is dogmatically reasserted by E.Lo Cascio, *Annali del Istituto per gli Studi Storici* 3 (1971/2), 55 ff., who does not meet the objections that to me seem decisive. For a balanced account see F. de Martino, *Storia della Costituzione Romana* IV 2², 1975, 868–930. He concludes that the emperor could eventually have been thought to possess fiscal assets (of the kind that had properly once been public) not as a private proprietor but 'as an organ of state' (912). What follows is merely designed to reinforce my thesis.

I adduced texts to show that taxes levied under the supervision of imperial procurators were considered to be public revenues (p. 149). It is no objection that the term 'procurator' originally designated a man's private agent: the emperor's procurators performed public functions from the first in imperial provinces and very soon in senatorial, and were recognized as state officials (*JRS* 73 [1983], nn. 64–77 with text). In 1966 I failed to remark that some revenues whose collection they supervised are expressly called public: the *publicum*

Liverpool Classical Monthly, 9/1 (1984), 2–4.

portorium vectigalis Illyrici and the *quattuor publica Africae*, which are in my view rightly taken to have comprised the *portorium* in Africa, the taxes on the sale by auction and manumission of slaves, and the 5% duty on the estates of Roman citizens (see Vittinghoff, *RE* 22, 368 f.). A fragment of Ulpian's tenth book on the edict (*Dig.*50.16.17.1) should have been fully quoted: *'publica' vectigalia intellegere debemus, ex quibus vectigal fiscus capit: quale est vectigal portus vel venalium rerum, item salinarum et metallorum et picariarum.* Ulpian was of course giving illustrations, not providing a complete list. The first two examples he offers confirm what we can learn from the titles of the Illyrian and African texts: the last three provide specimens for rents or dues from domain lands, public or imperial. There can be no legal distinction between such revenues from e.g. mines and those from agricultural or pastoral lands.

Some domains, as I argued before, which had come to the emperor by inheritance or bequest, could be properly viewed as his private property; but others belonged to the patrimony of his predecessors, to whom he did not succeed by right of private inheritance; and they also included *agri publici* which had come under his administration, viz. (a) *bona caduca, vacantia, damnatorum* which were forfeit strictly to the state; (b) former royal estates and the like which had been appropriated by the Republic after inheritance or conquest. Even in the Principate such estates continued to pass in form to the people and not to Caesar. Thus, even in Egypt 'royal' land became 'public' (p. 160; cf. p. 215 n. 1). We now know from the Tabula Banasitana (republished by A.N. Sherwin-White, *JRS* 63[1973], 87 ff.) that under Marcus *tributa* and *vectigalia* were due from Mauretania to both *fiscus* and *populus*; I take this to imply that they paid *vectigalia* in part for the use of royal lands which had become the property of the people when Gaius annexed Juba's old kingdom, or that of lands which before the period of Roman rule had not been appropriated for the exclusive enjoyment of private persons. Payments could of course have been made in Mauretania only to imperial officials. In general the emperor must have taken over the administration of public domains. The process was probably gradual. Under Claudius it was found that private persons had encroached on the royal lands of Cyrene bequeathed to the Roman Republic, and a senatorial commissioner was appointed to recover them; Vespasian had to take similar action (Tacitus, *Annals* 14. 18; Hyginus 122 L., cf. Luzzato, *Epigrafica Giuridica Greca e Romana*, 1942, 189); it looks as if no imperial procurator was yet available there to preserve public claims. I cannot guess why very occasionally the recollection that lands administrated by procurators were public creeps into our documents, e.g. not only in *ILS* 1396 (cited in chapter 7, n. 48) but in 9017 (Pflaum, *Carrières Procuratoriennes* no. 274): *res populi per tr[actum] utriusque Numidiae.*

Lo Cascio reposes his case principally on two famous texts in which Gaius asserts that *in provinciali solo dominium vel populi Romani est vel Caesaris* (2.7), and distinguishes between provincial estates which were *stipendiaria* and *tributaria* on the basis: *stipendiaria sunt ea, quae in his provinciis sunt, quae propriae populi Romani esse intelleguntur; tributaria sunt ea, quae in his provinciis sunt, quae propriae Caesaris esse creduntur* (2.21). No confidence can be felt in this distinction. It is contradicted by usage of the terms elsewhere.

In Republican authors indeed *tributum* seems to denote either (a) the property tax at one time levied on Roman citizens or (b) similar taxes levied by subject communities, often to supply funds required to meet Roman exactions, but not directly payable to Rome, see Cicero, *2 Verr.* 2. 131; 3.100; *Flacc.* 20 & 44; *Rab.Post.*31; *Q.fr.*1.1.20; *Fam.*3.8.5, 15.4.2. Provincials who paid tax to Rome are *stipendiarii*, e.g. Africans, Sardinians, Sicilians and Spaniards (*Balb.*24 & 41; | *Div.Caec.*7; *Verr.*4.134) cf. *Prov.Cons.*10 (Syrians); *Pis.*98 (Macedonians); in *Verr.* 3.12 Cicero merely distinguishes the *vectigal certum, quod stipendiarium dicitur* imposed on Spanish and many African *civitates* from the quotas levied in Sicily. *Vectigal* itself can be a generic term for Roman taxation (*Q.fr.*1.1.33), as later in Tacitus (*Hist.*3.8.2), though it may be contrasted with *tributum*, as in *Annals* 1.11.4; in that case *tributum* no doubt refers to land and capitation taxes, and *vectigal* to any other kind of public revenue, though Pliny can imply that the 5% duty on the estates of Roman citizens is both *vectigal* and *tributum* (*Paneg.*37.1). Caesar uses *tributum* for extraordinary levies exacted by the Pompeians in Asia (*BC* 3.32), but *stipendium* is what the victors normally imposed on the vanquished (*BG* 1.44.2, cf. 36.3, 7.54.3), and which Rome may refrain from demanding in Gaul (1.45.2); Suetonius (*Caesar* 25.1) says that he required from Gaul an annual payment of 40 million sesterces *stipendii nomine* (Caesar himself calls the annual tribute he demanded from the Britons a *vectigal, BG* 5.22.4). This Republican usage of *stipendium* which we find for Africa in the *lex agraria* of 111 (*FIRA* 1² no.8, 77 f.) and in a late Republican or early imperial inscription (*ILS* 901) reappears in parts of Pliny's *Natural History* which derive principally (as all agree) from Augustan *formulae provinciarum*, and is applied indifferently to communities in the senatorial provinces of Baetica (3.7), Sicily (3.91) and Africa (5.29) and the imperial of Tarraconensis (3.18) and Lusitania (4.117); he does not use *tributum*. In his survey of Roman expansion Velleius (2. 38f.) refers to the imposition of *stipendium* on Gaul, Egypt, Danubian regions (where he had served) and Cappadocia; on the other hand he describes Asia as *tributaria*.

All this seems to show that until the early Principate *stipendium* was the normal term for direct taxation imposed by Rome on her subjects in all provinces alike. But later it fell out of favour. It is not used by

Tacitus, except where he calls the Gauls (under imperial rule) *stipendiarii* (*Annals* 4.20.1); he prefers *tributum*, and though (as it happens) he is generally writing of taxes in imperial provinces, he can apply it (like Velleius) to senatorial (4.13.1; 12.58.2, 63.3. cf. Suetonius, *Claudius* 25.3). The older usage became so obsolete that Eutropius (6.17.3) in paraphrasing Suetonius' statement on Caesar's taxation of Gaul substitutes *tributum* for *stipendium*. The Flavian cadastre of Arausio in a senatorial province refers to tributary *solum* (*JRS* 32[1942], 65 ff.). Two legal texts which refer to *stipendium vel tributum vel solarium* (*salarium* codd.) and *neque· stipendium neque tributum* (Ulpian in *Dig.*7.1.7.2; 25.1.13) appear to make a distinction without a difference, Pomponius regarded the words as synonyms (*Dig.*50.16.27). Frontinus appears to have used them indifferently: he says that in Italy *nullus ager est tributarius*, whereas in the provinces some lands are *stipendiarii*, and the possessors are subject to *tributum* (35 f.L. = 23 Thulin: the text is in part corrupt, but so much is certain). Gaius' curious statement is best explained by the hypothesis that the older term lingered in use in some provinces known to him which had been annexed at a relatively early date and which were senatorial. In general, texts in the *Digest* refer only to liability to *tributum*, and it is hard to suppose that the texts concern only subjects in imperial provinces. I conjecture that *tributum*, formerly used to designate direct taxes collected by subject communities for their own account, was now applied to Roman direct taxes, because they too were collected from the individual taxpayer by those communities, now acting as agents of the Roman state (cf. p. 339).

The contrast between provinces of the people and those of Caesar, though found in Strabo (17.3.25) and Tacitus (*Annals* 13.4), is also unworthy of the jurist who could more correctly describe all Rome's subjects as *qui sub imperio populi Romani sunt* (1. 53), seeing that Caesar was no less than a proconsul the representative of the people, from whom in law he derived his *imperium* (*JRS* 67[1977], 107 ff.), and that the people did not directly govern any province, and exercised no more control over proconsuls than over the emperor. Thus, even if *dominium* were taken to mean 'sovereignty' (a common sense in non-legal writers) rather than 'ownership' (its natural juristic significance), Gaius' language would be inappropriate both to the law and the reality. It is indeed plain from the context that (as we should expect) he is writing of ownership, since he is trying to explain how it was that title to provincial land did not permit of its conversion to *solum religiosum* or to alienation by mancipation. However, provincial land could be *pro religioso* with exactly the same effect as if it were *religiosum*, and could be alienated by *traditio*; the possessor was protected as well as if he had acquired ownership by mancipation (cf. Lenel, *Edictum Perpetuum*[2],

188 f.); Diocletian did not scruple to speak of *dominium rei tributariae* (*Fr. Vat.*315, cf. 316). Gaius has produced a legal construction for which, as his use of *creduntur* may suggest, he had no authority, to explain the fact that some 'concepts and processes' of the *ius civile* were through formal conservatism thought inappropriate to *solum peregrinum* (cf. A. H. M. Jones, *Studies in Roman Government and Law*, ch. IX). Frontinus, who makes the same point as Gaius about mancipation, also suggests that provincial taxpayers could only 'possess' their lands *quasi fructus tollendi causa et praestandi tributi condicione* (*loc.cit.*). Here again we have a mere theory, which purports to account for Roman taxation. It can be contrasted with that advanced by Cicero (*Q.fr.*1.1.34), Tacitus (*Hist.* 4.74) and Dio (52.29) that Rome had to secure revenue for the good of the subjects, a *topos* to which Menander adverts (περὶ ἐπιδεικτικῶν p. 90, ed. Russell & Wilson); their explanation also covered imposts on Roman citizens even in Italy.

There indeed the old property tax (*tributum*) was no longer levied after 168 B.C. except probably in the disturbed years that followed Caesar's death, but it may be doubted if it was ever formally abolished, and whether the immunity of Italian land was more than a fact of actual experience. But the practical difference between the immunity of Italian land and the taxation of provincial land evidently gave rise to Frontinus' notion that the provincial property tax was a form of rent, confusing sovereignty with some kind of 'eminent domain'; this was a mere inference from | the fact that Rome chose, where she had the power, to raise revenue in particular ways, and not the true explanation, nor the best defence of provincial taxation (which is that given by Cicero etc.). No further consequences were deduced from the notion; in reality it was possible to own private lands in the provinces by a title that differed only technically from *dominium* in Italy. The theories of Gaius and Frontinus do not make the true distinction between domains of the people or emperor on which the tenants paid rent and the lands, e.g. in the city territories, which were subject to direct taxation, but which had all the other characteristics of private property. But even if we grant that Rome claimed 'eminent domain' over all provincial land, we still cannot believe that the so-called 'public land' of Egypt or the estates of the people in Numidia and Mauretania were vested in Caesar, except for purposes of administration.

Lo Cascio also interpreted Ulpian's statement that *res fiscales quasi propriae et privatae principis sunt* (*Dig.*43.8.2.4) in accordance with his thesis, whereas I had taken it to prove the opposite; his discussion only convinces me that no consensus will ever be reached on its implications. However, I showed that the jurists at times contrast fiscal rights either with public or private rights or with both (p. 152 f.), and argued that their views are incoherent, as a result of the development by which the *fiscus* represented the emperor both as an administrator of public property and interests and as a private owner. The fusion of estates which strictly belonged to the people with those which were parts of his patrimony, both managed in the same way and both entitled to fiscal privileges in law, meant that it was in practice hard and futile to distinguish their original statuses. To provincials the emperor was in fact the state; he had absolute control of his provinces, and it is therefore not surprising that Philo (*Flacc.* 158) and Josephus (*BJ* 7. 217) treat Egypt and Judaea respectively as his private possessions, though there is no better reason to accept this as technically correct in the latter case than in the former. But even jurists could blur the distinction between imperial property and public property under imperial administration because it made no difference in process of law.

As the patrimony of each emperor was amalgamated for administration with other lands which were properly public, and as he acquired fiscal privileges for the former as well as the latter, the patrimony was also assimilated to the public land he administered; it became 'Crown' land rather than his personal property. In the second century some emperors, whose personal property would thus naturally have become Crown land on their accession, seem to have tried to provide for their own families by gifts *inter vivos* (140 f.). The institution of the *ratio* or *res privata* (discussed at length by Lo Cascio) may have had a similar origin; it was once attributed to Severus on the strength of the *Historia Augusta* (*Severus* 12), but we now know that it went back to Marcus (Pflaum, *Carrières* II. 1002 ff.), and Pius, and perhaps beyond (cf. H. Nesselhauf, *Bonner Historia-Augusta-Colloquium* 1963, 76 ff.; I am not convinced by P. Baldacci's interpretation of an inscription in *Atti Centro St. e Doc. sull'Italia Romana* 1 [1965/70], which makes it Hadrianic—the words *ad Caesaris praedia dividenda* must mean 'dividing up the lands of Caesar' by assignation; in the next line read *comprobanda in ...*, with uncertain sense).

The attested procurators of this department in Italy (Pflaum pp. 1036–1040) and in a very few provinces (id. pp.1073, 1079, 1093[?], 1095, 1097, cf. *ILS* 1330) are all Severan or later, but as shown in my article in *JRS* 73 (1983), Appendix I, the Fasti of procurators (especially *sexagenarii*) are extremely defective, and many more such posts probably existed. The very name of the department indicates that the property was regarded as private in some sense in which other property under imperial administration was not, and in *ILS* 1330 the later praetorian prefect, Timesitheus, combines, or alternates between,

patrimonial posts and those of the *ratio privata*; by implication the
patrimonium was Crown property. Now it is a curiosity that Marcus
appointed a man as procurator of the *patrimonium* in Narbonensis (*AE*
1962, 183, on which see Pflaum, *Bonner Jahrb.* 171 [1971], 349 ff.). G.
Alföldy (*Chiron* 11 [1981], 169 ff. at n.34) has recently inferred that he
was therefore subject to the same constraints as a procurator of
patrimonial property in Asia under Tiberius; see Tacitus, *Annals* 4.15,
and Dio 57.23.5, who implies that these would not have applied in his
own day. But both earlier and later procurators in this province are
simply styled *proc. Narbonensis* (*ILS* 2726 & 1386), and I can see no
reason why Marcus' nominee should have had more limited powers
than they, or why the procurators of Narbonensis should not have
acquired like all procurators in senatorial provinces the more extensive
functions with which they are generally credited in the time after
Tiberius. Perhaps the land under imperial administration in Narbonensis was chiefly patrimonial in origin, but it may also be that for once
patrimonium was introduced into the official's title to differentiate him
from another local procurator concerned with the *ratio privata*. Pius'
family came from the province, and he may well have instituted such a
post there, to administer those estates which had descended to him by
private inheritance. It must of course be admitted that the *ratio privata*
lost the character which I conjecture it first had, and began, perhaps
under Severus, to absorb escheats, which strictly fell to the state as
such, cf. Millar, 171 ff.; this was certainly true in the fourth century,
see Jones, *Later Roman Empire*, 410 ff.. No hypothesis explaining this
development can be more than conjectural.

17

Publicans in the Principate[1]

I. INTRODUCTION

The Roman Republic had few civil servants, and none collected its revenues. The property tax (*tributum*) paid by Romans themselves until 167 BC was collected by citizens of substance (*tribuni aerarii*); they doubtless discharged the task as a compulsory public service, a *munus* corresponding to the Greek 'liturgy', and their property was probably pledged to the treasury for due performance;[2] we do not know what arrangements were made for collection of the extraordinary levies imposed on citizens between 43 and 29 BC. In some provinces Rome demanded lump sums from the local communities, presumably assessed on a rough estimate of their resources, which they were free to raise by their own imposts and through their own agents, including local publicans.[3] For the collection of direct taxes in other provinces, of indirect taxes, and of rents or fees for the use of public domains, both in Italy and in the provinces, Rome relied on private contractors working for profit, as it did for the construction and upkeep of public buildings and the provision of supplies for armies and fleets.[4]

[1] Conceived when I was working on the role of Equites in the Principate for my article in *JRS* (1983), this essay arises from scepticism about the orthodox theories of Rostovtzeff, Hirschfeld, and de Laet, though it could never have been written without the benefit of their investigations; in many points I follow Maria Rosa Cimma, the value of whose work on the imperial period is not impaired by some errors concerning the Republican (for which see E. Badian, *Gnomon* (1984), 54 ff.; his own treatment of that period is the best), but my account modifies or amplifies hers. I cite by the names of authors the relevant works of these and other scholars as follows: E. Badian, *Publicans and Sinners* (1972); M. R. Cimma, *Ricerche sulle società di publicani* (1981); W. Eck, *Die staatliche Organisation Italiens* (1978); O. Hirschfeld, *Die kaiserliche Verwaltungsbeamten²* (1912); F. Kniep, *Societas publicanorum* (1896); S. J. de Laet, *Portorium* (1949); H.-G. Pflaum, *Les Carrières procuratoriennes équestres* (1960); M. Rostowzew, *Gesch. der Staatspacht* (1902); F. Vittinghoff, *RE* xxii. 346 ff., s.v *Portorium*; S. Wallace, *Taxation in Egypt from Augustus to Diocletian* (1937) (with *index locorum* in *ZPE* 16 (1975)); *ESAR* = T. Frank, *Econ. Survey of Anc. Rome* (1933–40). I am indebted to A. K. Bowman for comments on an earlier draft, but any remaining errors are my own.

[2] C. Nicolet, *Tributum* (1976).

[3] Cic., *Verr.* ii. 3. 12. Local taxes (e.g. *tributa*): ib. 2. 131; 138; 3. 100; *Fam.* iii. 8. 5; *Qu.fr.* i. 1. 25; *Att.* v. 16. 2; *Flacc.* 91 (cf. Broughton, *AJP* lvii (1936), 175 ff.), cf. Livy xxxiii. 46. 9. Local publicans: *Qu. fr.* i. 1. 33; in Principate: *lex Irnitana* (*JRS* (1986), cf. pp. 212 f., 218 f.) J and LXIII f. (= *FIRA* i². LXIII f.); *AE* 1962. 288; *Dig.* xxxix. 4. 10. 1 (Hermog.), 4. 13. 1 (Gaius); Palmyra, de Laet 357 ff.

[4] Contracts were leased by magistrates at Rome (Cic., *de leg. agr.* i. 7, ii. 55), e.g. in 75 tithes on Sicilian fruits (*Verr.* ii. 3. 18), Sicilian *portoria* and *scriptura* (2. 169 ff.), and rents on Sicilian *ager*

In Republican usage these contractors, operating on behalf of the *res publica*, could all be styled *publicani*. In the Principate the term has a somewhat more restricted meaning. Ulpian defines publicans thus: 'those who enjoy the use of what belongs to the people—hence their name—whether they pay a *vectigal* to the people or gather in *tributum*' (which now denotes direct taxes on property and persons in the provinces, Italy being exempt) 'and all who lease anything from the *fiscus* are rightly called publicans'; the definition includes both those who leased from the state the right to collect taxes (*vectigal* and *tributum*) and those who rented certain public (or imperial) domains, but excludes contractors for buildings and army supplies.[5]

Farming of the revenue was of course the common practice in Greek cities and kingdoms too, as in many European states in the early modern period; it was also adopted by municipalities in the Roman empire (n. 3). The sums involved in some of the Republican contracts were vast, and the contractors were then organized in companies to perform them; the standing and riches of the members and the importance of their functions to the state gave them great political influence. On this account, and also because their own staff was small, Republican magistrates at Rome and governors in the provinces were often unable or unwilling to control the activities of publicans in accordance either with the laws and contractual rules, or with the interests of the treasury and taxpayers, which the law and contracts were designed to protect.

Undoubtedly there were changes in the Principate. Local governments were normally charged with the collection of the *tributum* within their territories. In my view, though this is disputed, this practice was established generally or universally by Caesar. All other revenues were, however, still farmed at first. Publican companies too continued to exist, though we no longer hear of their political influence. The emperors gradually created a kind of civil service consisting of their own freedmen and slaves, who were able, under the direction of

publicus (ii. 3. 13, cf. 5. 53), which also paid *decumae* on grain (*ESAR* iii. 329–33); Sicilian *decumae* on grain, by an exception to the rule, were leased by the governors in the province, ii. 3. 14 and 104 ff.

⁵ For earlier usage cf. Livy xxv. 3. 12; xxxix. 44. 8; xlv. 18. 4. The publican companies whose importance and organization Polybius vi. 17 describes were principally concerned not with taxes, but with public works and revenues from public domains (cf. my *Fall of Rom. Rep.* (1988), 148–50), probably also with army supplies, on which note Ulpian, *Dig.* xxii. 5. 19 *pr.* on a privilege enjoyed both by publicans and by 'is qui quid exercitui praebendum conduxerit'. He writes: 'publicani autem sunt qui publico fruuntur (nam inde nomen habent) sive fisco vectigal pendant vel tributum consequantur; et omnes qui quid a fisco conducunt recte appellantur publicani' (xxxix. 4. 1. 1) and 'publicani autem dicuntur, qui publica vectigalia habent conducta' (4. 12. 3); cf. n. 132 and on the meanings of 'vectigal' App. III.

generally equestrian procurators, to control the publicans more closely than had been possible under the Republic. In course of time special bureaux were set up for particular revenues derived either from taxes or domains. Since some of these revenues were still farmed at least for a time after the institution of these bureaux, it is certain that initially their task was that of supervision and not of collection. Supervision would have become the more necessary if there was a change in the mode of tax-farming, whereby publicans received a percentage of what they collected, instead of taking the gross proceeds in return for lump sums payable to the treasury under their contract (s. IV). Some scholars also think that in the second century companies were often displaced by *Einzelpächter* or *fermiers-généraux*, individuals who might have one or two partners, but who were no longer organized in companies. In the end this unquestionably occurred; the law applicable to the old companies had become obsolete and unfamiliar when Justinian's codes were compiled. However, companies still survived as late as the Severi.

On the orthodox view, at a further stage in the second century the procurators and their staffs assumed the task of collection for many taxes. Whether or not this is demonstrable or probable in the cases for which evidence has allegedly been found, we must beware of arguing from analogy that the change also affected taxes for which there is no evidence at all. In principle tax-farming was never rejected; it remained important when the Severan jurists were writing. The fact that in the late empire local governments were still responsible for levying the direct taxes on persons and property, despite the immense growth of the bureaucracy which had then occurred, shows that collection of the revenues by employees of the state was never accepted as the normal procedure. If in specific instances officials took the place of tax-farmers, we must surely suppose that there were specific reasons to account for the adoption of a new expedient. Unfortunately dearth of evidence precludes us from determining what these reasons were.

It is impossible to insist too strongly on the paucity of documentation for the imperial fiscal system. What there is has survived only by accident. This makes it in general most imprudent to rely on arguments from silence. Many illustrations of this will appear in what follows. Suspension of judgement is nearly always advisable. Standard accounts of tax collection are often constructions marked by excess of dogmatic certitude. Maria Rosa Cimma has done well in challenging orthodox doctrine on the pace and extent of the changes they postulate (n. 1). But her exposition admits of both reinforcement and modification. I propose therefore once again to review the imperial evidence on the operations of publicans, and in particular on the persistence of companies with a corporate status. Hints provided in imperial sources may attest the continuance of practices of which there is more explicit evidence for the Republic. I must begin by summarizing so much of the Republican system as is required for explication of the imperial.

II. THE REPUBLICAN BACKGROUND

In the Republic state rents and taxes were normally farmed at Rome (cf. n. 4) by the censors under a *lex censoria*, which was so described even if other magistrates (e.g. consuls) acted in their place. The content of each such *lex*, which constituted the contract between the state and the publicans and which must have varied in details for different types of operation, was evidently in the main tralatician, though clauses could be added or amended by the magistrate at Rome responsible for any particular lease. So too as governor of Sicily Verres was apparently not acting *ultra vires* when he introduced modifications, however outrageous they were, in the terms of the contracts for the Sicilian corn tithe, which were leased in the province by the governors, though traditionally regulated by the so-called *lex Hieronica*, derived from the practice of king Hiero of Syracuse.[6] In the Principate censors ceased to function; it is not clear in most cases which magistrates or other officials now leased the contracts; some were probably leased locally by procurators (p. 377), others by the prefects of the *aerarium Saturni*.[7] A juristic fragment (*fr. de iure fisci* 18) of imperial times treats a *lex censoria* as still valid; this presumably means that a standard form of contract devised in the Republic was still in use, not necessarily without alteration.

The terms of such contracts might also have been in part determined by statute laws, like that passed by Gaius Gracchus which governed the leasing of the Asian tithes.[8] Tacitus, in a context that relates to *portoria*, writes of 'numerous tax companies established in the Republic by consuls and tribunes', and this suggests that legislation promoted by these magistrates, of whom the tribunes could never have performed

---

[6] Cic., *Verr.* ii. 2. 32; 3. 14 f. Verres' edicts which 'destroyed' the *lex* (3. 24) did not exceed his competence, and were not *per se* grounds for his condemnation, unless it could be shown that they had furthered his illegal enrichment (ib. 40); similarly a so-called *lex provinciae* was strictly no more than an edict of a governor (normally issued on the advice of *legati* despatched by the senate), and his successors were not legally bound to observe it, see B. D. Hoyos, *Antichthon* (1973), 49 ff. *Leges censoriae: FIRA* i². no. 36. 35; Cic., *Verr.* ii. 1. 143 (magisterial amendments); 3. 18; *Prov. Cons.* 12; *Nat. Deor.* iii. 49; Varro, *RR* ii. 1. 6; Alfenus Varus (*cos. suff.* 39 BC) in *Dig.* l. 16. 203; Pliny, *NH* xxiii. 78; Kniep 112–43. Alfenus also cites a *lex locationis* prescribed by 'Caesar' (*Dig.* xxxix. 4. 15). Cf. *fr. de iure fisci* 18 for a *lex censoria* still valid in the Principate.

[7] Eck 115. Consuls still acted in Ovid's time (*ex Ponto* iv. 5. 19, 9. 45), as in 75 (*Verr.* ii. 3. 18).

[8] *Verr.* ii. 3. 12; Schol. Bobb. 157 St., cf. *Qu. fr.* i. 1. 35 for *lex censoria* regulating the Asian taxes.

the executive act of leasing out contracts, had in some way sanctioned the creation or regulated the organization of *societates* as a condition of their taking leases.[9] In the Principate both senate and emperor acquired legislative power, and the jurist Gaius says that corporate status had been granted to some publican companies by *leges*, decrees of the senate, and imperial constitutions (n. 53); this will be discussed later. In the Republic the senate had assumed the right to vary the contractual obligations of publicans; we may suppose that in the Principate this right was also exercised by the emperor.

The rights and duties of the collectors of revenues in relation to the taxpayers were regulated by the praetor's edict at Rome and by the edicts of governors in the provinces. The *Digest* preserves part of the praetor's edict, stereotyped by Hadrian, which prescribed the actions that could be brought against publicans for wrongdoing; the 'title' need not have been very much changed since the late Republic. Presumably the edicts of provincial governors were, so far as possible, modelled on the praetor's. The edicts were supplemented by imperial constitutions; juristic commentaries on the edicts cite rescripts of Hadrian, Pius, Marcus, and the Severi; Tacitus tells how Nero introduced reforms by edict. A fragment of Gaius shows that the rights given to taxpayers by the praetorian and provincial edicts to sue the collectors of state taxes had been extended, probably by imperial constitutions, to persons wronged by the lessees of state properties and by municipal publicans.[10] However, the emperors were probably shy of innovations: Paul writes that with virtually all taxes custom is commonly observed, and that this is actually prescribed in imperial constitutions (*Dig.* xxxix. 4. 4. 2). It may well be that many rules were never defined in either laws or contracts; for example the levy of the *scriptura* in Italy probably conformed to immemorial practice (Pliny, *NH* xviii. 11).

Cicero says that in Italy and virtually all provinces publicans had the right to sue and take pledges but not to seize and appropriate the taxpayer's property. The meaning of this statement is unclear. In Italy they had once been authorized by the *lex censoria* to take pledges from

---

[9] *Ann.* xiii. 50. 3: 'plerasque vectigalium societates a consulibus et tribunis plebis constitutas acri etiam tum populi libertate'. C. Gracchus 'nova instituebat portoria' (Vell. ii. 6. 3), clearly by statute.

[10] *Dig.* xxxix. 4 *passim*; for the extension see 4. 13 from Gaius' work on the provincial edict. (Conceivably this was the edict of the province where he resided; there is no explicit evidence for a provincial edict applying to all provinces, and this seems unlikely, given that conditions varied from one to another, and that to judge from the case of Egypt Rome never imposed her own law unmodified on peregrine subjects, without regard to their own practices. Still, the praetor's edict probably served as a model wherever possible for provincial ordinances (cf. Cic., *Att.* vi. 1. 15), and uniformity was most likely in matters of administrative law.)

the goods of defaulters, and this right still belonged (*c.* AD 100) to the lessees of public monopolies and various dues at the mining settlement of Vipasca in Spain, and to their partners. However, according to Gaius, in place of the right to take pledges they had been given an action for the value of what they might have taken, in effect for a fine on default or slowness in payment.[11] They still had sharper remedies at their disposal in the Principate. They could lead off animals grazing on the public pastures for any alleged breach of the relevant tax-law by the graziers.[12] They could with certain exceptions impound goods which had not been declared for customs-duty.[13] This right could have been one source of the extortions which Nero tried to check; presumably he did no more than circumscribe it. For default in payment of direct taxes or rents on public land, they perhaps had no alternative but to sue in the courts. Equally they could themselves be sued for wrongful exactions. Their rapacity was notorious in the Republic and as late as Constantine.[14] The praetor's edict gave the taxpayer double damages if they, or their employees, seized goods by violence and did not restore them; this part of the edict went back at least to the time of Labeo (Augustus) and presumably to the Republic.[15] Gaius' commentary on the provincial edict evidently showed that the same rules could be applied in provinces.[16] In the Republic too Verres had actually promised eightfold damages to the wronged taxpayer in his edict, though in practice they could expect no redress in his court. Gabinius allegedly refused even to hear suits brought by the publicans in Syria. Both Cicero and Bibulus devoted parts of their provincial edicts to litigation in which the publicans were involved. The rights and obligations of tax-farmers and taxpayers were of course defined by the relevant statutes and *leges censoriae*, and the courts should have enforced them, but Cicero intimates to his brother governing Asia that it would

---

[11] *Verr.* ii. 3. 27; Gaius iv. 28, 32; *FIRA* i². no. 105. 16, 41, 45, 48; Steinwenter, *RE* xx. 1238.

[12] *Dig.* xlvii. 8. 2. 20 (Ulpian citing Labeo), best interpreted as concerning the publican who had farmed a *scriptura* (cf. Varr. *RR* ii. 1. 16).

[13] *Dig.* xxxix. 4. 7. 1 (Papirius Iustus); 14 (Ulp.); 16 *passim*, but cf. text to nn. 102 f.

[14] e.g. Cic., *Qu.fr.* i. 1. 33; *CJ* iv. 62. 4 (Constantine). Tax-farmers have been hated in all times and lands; the Jacobin government in France guillotined them. It is odd that M. Goodman, *Ruling Class of Judaea* (1987) 131 f., finds it unaccountable that Jews assimilated them to sinners. Official or liturgical tax-collectors might also make illegitimate gains, but only publicans were as such getting their living from profits made at the taxpayers' expense. Roman publicans escaped odium in Roman society, as he remarks, but only when their victims were subjects; the abolition of Italian *portoria* in 60 BC evoked jubilation because of their rapacity (Dio xxxvii. 51).

[15] *Dig.* xxxix. 4. 1–4 (Ulp. with a citation of Labeo). Another clause of the edict provided a special remedy for thefts by publicans, *h.t.* 12. 1. See Lenel, *Edictum perpetuum*³, 333 f., 387 ff. The reference in [Paul] *Sent.* (*h.t.* 9. 5) to triple damages and penalties *extra ordinem* in cases of illegal seizures by force appears to represent post-Severan development.

[16] *Dig.* xxxix. 4. 5, cf. n. 10.

be politically expedient if he persuaded the provincials to pay the publicans more than strict obligation demanded.[17] Nero ordered that the praetor at Rome and the governors in the provinces should determine complaints against the publicans 'extra ordinem'; that probably meant that they were to give them priority, and perhaps to decide them rapidly by *cognitio*, personally or through their delegates, not of course that praetor or governors had hitherto lacked jurisdiction.[18]

III. *SOCIETATES VECTIGALIUM*

Tax-farming in the Republic was generally in the hands of companies (*societates*). Tacitus attests their survival in the reigns of Tiberius and Nero (n. 9). It will appear that they still existed under the Severi. How far, if at all, had they changed in character or been replaced by individual publicans or salaried officials? We must first briefly examine what is known of their organization in the Republic. Certain technicalities must be introduced whose relevance will become plainer as we proceed.

In the most common Republican usage the contractor who obtained the right to collect taxes or rents for the state was said to purchase this right. He was termed the *manceps*. The same name could be given to one who 'purchased' the right to exploit public lands in return for a rent. Festus defines the *manceps* as 'qui quid a populo emit conducitve'.[19] The second verb indicates that as the right he purchased did not give him ownership but merely enjoyment for the period stated in the contract he could be regarded as the lessee rather than the purchaser. The language of leasing is already applied to this kind of contract in Republican texts. In the Principate it becomes more frequent, and is

---

[17] Verr. ii. 3. 26; *Prov. Cons.* 10; *Att.* vi. 1. 5; *Qu. fr.* i. 1. 35.

[18] *Ann.* xiii. 51. 1. The praetor's jurisdiction in cases concerning publicans is surely earlier, cf. Labeo (n. 15), but in the Republic censors and consuls (cf. Vell. ii. 92) had also possessed it in certain circumstances. Suetonius' statement (*Nero* 17) that Nero transferred such cases from the *aerarium*, i.e. presumably from its administrators (*Ann.* xiii. 29), 'ad forum et reciperatores' is puzzling: it suggests that before his reform the latter had usurped magisterial jurisdiction and decided suits themselves by *cognitio*. Had they acquired powers analogous to those which Claudius conferred on procurators (ch. 8)? Even on this hypothesis we might expect their jurisdiction to have been restricted to cases in which the treasury had a direct interest, viz. disputes between the treasury and the publicans, or disputes involving the taxpayers only if the proceeds of the tax went direct to the treasury, as was probably true of the *vicesima hereditatium* (cf. s. IV). Has Suetonius confused the *aerarium militare*, which benefited from that revenue, with the *aerarium Saturni*? In my view he fell easily into that sort of inaccuracy.

[19] *Manceps*: Festus 137 L; *TLL* s.v.; Steinwenter, *RE* xiv. 987 ff. Note Hyginus 116 L (cf. 117) on leases of municipal *agri vectigales*: 'mancipibus ementibus, id est conducentibus'. See Kniep 93 ff.

preferred by jurists.[20] The term *manceps* is still found,[21] but more usually we hear of a *conductor*. Like the lessee of private property, the man who rents public lands is a *conductor*, but so is the lessee of the right to collect public revenues. Hadrian assimilated them.[22] The term is applied in the second century to the publican who farms *portoria*, for instance in Gaul. But an inscription of this period refers to the *mancipes* of the Gallic *portoria*; they can only be the publicans who are more generally styled *conductores*.[23] Or again, minting operations are said to have been farmed sometimes to a *manceps*, sometimes to *conductores*,[24] and both terms can be used of the lessees of the sulphur mines at Agrigentum.[25] The equation is made explicitly in a rescript of the early fifth century: 'mancipum, id est salinarum conductorum'.[26]

The *manceps* might be an *Einzelpächter*, an individual contractor acting without any partners. The *manceps* had to satisfy the state that he could fulfil his obligations, by providing sureties (*praedes*) and, when the contract was made at Rome, securities (*praedia*) in Italian land.[27] But he might be his own surety. He would presumably be accepted as such if his own resources could cover his potential liabilities, especially when the sum at stake was small. Some contracts were in fact petty affairs, and the *mancipes* little men.[28] But even in such cases of *Kleinpacht*, there might be partners (*socii*). If a *manceps* had to find others to go surety for him, or to pledge their own lands on his behalf, kinsmen or friends might conceivably oblige, out of sheer goodwill or in fulfilment of prior obligations to him, but in general he would have had to offer them a share in profits. Thus in practice *praedes* would commonly be partners as well.

The *mancipes* who contracted to collect the tithes of a Sicilian city were *Einzelpächter*; when Cicero refers to them in the plural, he is not implying that they formed a collective body.[29] But at Rome public contractors had been organized in companies at least as early as the

---

[20] Cic., *Att.* i. 17. 9; *de leg. agr.* i. 7; ii. 55; *FIRA* i². no. 8. 87 on the magistrate who 'vectigalia fruenda locabit vendetve' and no. 36. 25 etc. for the *lex locationis* (ὁ τῆς μισθώσεως νόμος); *Dig.* xxxix. 4. 9 *pr.* ('locatio vectigalium'); *lex Irnitana* (n. 5). Cf. nn. 5, 19, 130.

[21] Cimma 115 n. 87, 136 n. 169, 155 ff. It can be synonymous with *redemptor*, the contractor for public buildings etc.

[22] *Dig.* xlix. 14. 3. 6.

[23] *ILS* 1410 (Pflaum no. 204); *conductores*: 1854, 5884; *AE* 1930. 29.

[24] Hirschfeld 185.

[25] *ILS* 8712 a–e.

[26] *CJ.* iv. 61. 11. Cf. Rostovtzeff, *Diz. ep.* s.v. *conductor* 579.

[27] Cimma 64 ff. assembles and discusses the texts. The requirement for security in Italian lands (Cic., *Flacc.* 80) would not apply to taxes leased in provinces, e.g. Sicilian tithes.

[28] *ILLRP* 465 (2 of 3 *mancipes* for roads are freedmen); Cic., *Verr.* ii. 1. 130–2 (upkeep of buildings; one contractor is 'homo de plebe Romana', 151). *Mancipes* in *Att.* vi. 1. 5, *Fam.* v. 20. 3 are men of no standing.

[29] e.g. Cic., *Verr.* ii. 3. 67, 75.

Hannibalic war, as texts of Livy show (p. 364). According to Polybius large numbers of Romans were involved, not only as purchasers (*mancipes*) and sureties (*praedes*) but as parners (*socii*); he also mentions that others had investments in these joint enterprises, apparently rather like the shares of modern stockholders; their position is so obscure that I shall say no more about them, except that the distinction drawn between them and the *socii* suggests that the latter, unlike the holders of shares, must have taken an active part in the business and not merely contributed capital.[30] Now Cicero and Livy write as if the *societates publicanorum* were as such the contractors.[31] In strict form the contract was purchased or rented by the *manceps*, whom Festus calls 'auctorem emptionis', but the *socii*, like those in a merely private business, must have contributed working capital, or services as managers, or both; they would normally have included the *praedes*, who placed their entire substance at risk, and those who pledged particular *praedia* as security, and all would have shared the profits and losses in proportions agreed among themselves.

We can see why their assistance was often required. For large undertakings substantial capital and, in particular, a numerous personnel, chiefly slaves and freedmen, who would need supervision at a higher level, had to be employed. We hear of the huge *familiae* of tax-farmers in the late Republic.[32] No doubt it was after Gaius Gracchus' time that the operations of publicans reached their apogee (n. 30), but to consider some of the types of contract to which Polybius refers, in the state mines near New Carthage 40,000 workers were employed surely by publicans (n. 140 with text), and some of the constructional work at Rome was very costly; above all the Marcian aqueduct cost 150 million sesterces (Front., *de aqu.* i. 7). No individual could assume the risks and liabilites of such operations. Moreover it was in the interest of the state to ascertain that an adequate organization would be available before the contract was leased to any would-be *manceps*. It was not enough to require him to put up sufficient *praedes* and *praedia*. Take the case of contracts for buildings or the provision of military supplies. The state presumably made payments to the contractor initially and in stages thereafter; if the work was not satisfactorily

---

[30] Polybius vi. 17. 3 f. (see esp. C. Nicolet, *Irish Jurist* (1971), 163 ff., cf. Brunt, *Fall of Rom. Rep.*, 148–50). The *lex Irnitana* (n. 3) also distinguishes *socii* from holders of *partes* in municipal undertakings. Polybius specifies contractors for public buildings and for revenues from public domains including mines and *portoria*: only after the Gracchi were contracts for collecting provincial tribute leased at Rome.

[31] e.g. Cic., *Att.* i. 17. 9; Livy xxiii. 49. 1.

[32] Cic., *de imp. Cn. Pomp.* 16; Caesar, *BC* iii. 103. 1. The personnel was required for *portoria* and *scriptura* and for collection of tribute outside city territories, within which the cities raised the sums due to the publicans under *pactiones* (s. V).

performed, it could then seek to recover its disbursements by selling up the *praedes* and sequestering *praedia*. But if in the meantime the army or fleet had not got its supplies, the result might have been disastrous, and it would have been at least inconvenient if a building erected had been liable to collapse. In the case of revenues it might be said that if the publicans failed to remit the agreed sum from the proceeds of collection the treasury might make good the deficit from the *praedes* and *praedia*; still at best, there would be delay, and at worst it might not be possible to realize enough from the assets at assessed values; in a given state of the property market there might be no sufficient demand. Hence it was in the public interest to give a contract in the first place to a *manceps* who had the backing that would make it likely that the work would be done efficiently. Whether or not the *manceps* was legally the mere representative of a *societas* already formed, the reality was that which Cicero and Livy represent it to have been.

It may be said that the state entered into a direct legal relationship only with the *manceps* and *praedes* and with such other persons as obligated *praedia* to the treasury, and that the *socii* were involved only indirectly as a result of the rights and obligations determined by private contracts with the *manceps* and *inter se*. In support of this contention it would be possible to cite provisions in the standard form of charter for Latin *municipia* in Spain, which is often modelled on Roman institutions. The local magistrates who let municipal contracts are bound to register and publicize the names of the contractors and of their *praedes* and the *praedia* pledged on their behalf, but not the names of *socii*. Persons in certain categories are debarred not only from entering into such contracts but from being partners (*socii*) of the contractors or taking any share in the enterprise (just as senators were excluded from public contracting at Rome), but breaches of this rule can apparently be uncovered only by private delations of the offenders.[33] A contract for construction of a wall costing 1,500 sesterces at the colony of Puteoli in 105 BC was given to C. Blossius, who was his own surety ('idem praes'); four names follow his, but they may be those of other *praedes* rather than of mere *socii*.[34] On the other hand even in so small an affair as the purchase of sequestered property at Rome the purchaser registered the name of his partner.[35] We may suppose at least that wherever it was necessary for the *socii* themselves to be actually engaged in tax collection (p. 365 f.), they must have been registered.

It is clear that in large contracts the magistrates took cognizance of

[33] Cimma 59–64, 95–8, cf. *lex Irnitana* (n. 3) J and LXIII f.
[34] *FIRA* iii. no. 153 at end. Mommsen, *Ges Schr.*, i. 361 f. took them to be *praedes*, *contra* Badian 68.
[35] Cic., *Quinct.* 76. *Socii* were registered in Ptolemaic Egypt (App. I. 2).

the identity of the *socii*. In the Hannibalic war the state granted exemption from military service to the nineteen members of three companies which were to furnish army supplies. This privilege was stipulated by them as a precondition of their taking on the task.[36] The censors of 169 excluded from the auctions for public works and for the collection of taxes all who had been *socii* in such contracts in 174.[37] Verres as urban praetoi acted in a similar fashion. His conduct was evidently not illegal, though Cicero represents it as outrageous that he thereby excluded a bidder who could provide adequate security. Cicero, however, indicates the defence that Verres could have made. He could claim that the bidder could not efficiently maintain the temple of Castor, the work to which the contract related. Cicero brushes this aside with the remark that it lay with Verres as praetor to inspect the work and give or withhold his approval; in other words, the contractor could be compelled to make good any deficiency.[38] But it would have been reasonable for the magistrate to give the work in the first place to whoever appeared most competent to perform it; it was much less satisfactory to exact reparation later. The fact that it was remarked that the censors of 184 accepted the highest bids for the collection of revenues and the lowest for the construction of public work also implies that magistrates were not bound to follow this practice.[39] Verres seems to have done nothing illegal in refusing the highest bid for the tithe of Leontini, though, as Cicero alleges, he was no doubt in collusion with the successful bidder.[40] In principle the magistrate letting out a contract had to have regard to the presumed efficiency of the competitors, to the capital and personnel available to them, and in some cases to the standard of past performance; the state did not necessarily benefit from accepting what seemed prima facie the most attractive financial terms. When the magnitude of the work to be performed required the co-operation of *socii*, it therefore had to be satisfied that they were to be found and were fit for the task.

It was because the collection of revenue was in fact farmed in most cases to a *societas* that the plural *publicani* is normally used rather than the singular to denote the collectors; probably indeed there is little significance in the use of the singular, which could be deemed to include the plural. The praetorian edict, which in its imperial form may well have been the same as in the late Republic, prescribed actions for wrongs done either by the *publicanus* or by the *familia publicanorum*; it is obvious that no significance attaches to the use of singular or plural here. The *familia* was deemed to comprise all employees of the

---

[36] Livy xxiii. 49. 1–4.
[37] Livy xliii. 16. 1 f.
[38] *Verr.* ii. 1. 143 f.
[39] Livy xxxix. 44. 7 f. Cf. n. 202.
[40] *Verr.* ii. 3. 147–51.

publicans, who could be deemed its *domini*, whether or not they were slaves owned by them (n. 65), and the *domini* include the 'socii vectigalis'.[41] When we read in the *lex agraria* of 111 BC of payments due 'publicano' for the enjoyment of public lands in Italy and Africa, we are surely not bound to infer that the farmer of the revenues concerned was an individual contractor rather than the member of a company. A *senatus consultum* of 73 BC shows the senate adjudicating on a claim by the temple of Amphiaraus in Oropus for immunity from rent on public land payable under the *lex locationis*; the claim is resisted by 'the publicans', though the *lex* apparently used the singular, perhaps referring to the *manceps*; in reality the farmers were evidently member of a *societas*. Presumably it was a *manceps* who offered the formal bid for the Asian tithes, but Cicero characteristically writes of 'Asiam qui de censoribus conduxerunt' and of 'publicani'. In his usage 'publicani' occurs frequently to denote both a *societas* at Rome itself and its provincial representatives (cf. n. 47), and *publicanus* seems often to mean simply a person engaged in the public contracts in any capacity.[42]

Under the law governing private partnerships, partners shared in agreed proportions in the profits or losses of all the activities of any of them pursuant to the common enterprise, and their reciprocal obligations were enforceable by actions in the courts, the bringing of which, however, automatically dissolved the partnership. 'In general the *socii* were, as against third persons, so many individuals: a man who had contracted with one *socius* had no right or liability as against the others.' As a rule too each was alone liable for his own delicts committed in the course of the common operations. There were certain exceptions, in the case for instance of partnerships for slave dealing and banking. The *socii* who took up public contracts, even if they were not organized in the great companies to which some sort of corporate status might be granted, and were merely engaged in *Kleinpacht*, appear to be another exceptional category. They might divide up the administration among themselves, and in this case they must surely all have been registered in public records. The interdict that secured the lessee of public land in its enjoyment was also available to a parner. At Vipasca the right to seize pledges belonged not only to the lessees of various petty monopolies but to their *socii* and *actores* (n. 11). A person

---

[41] *Dig.* xxxix. 4. 1 *pr.*; 4. 1. 5 ('familia' cf. n. 65); 4. 1. 6 and 4. 3. 1 ('domini'); for *socii* cf. also *h.t.* 4. 6 and 9. 4 (all Severan or post-Severan texts); they are not necessarily partners in a corporate *societas*, for which cf. n. 53.

[42] *FIRA* i². 8. 20 and 83 etc; i. 36; Cic., *Att.* i. 17. 9, cf. 18. 7. An individual is entitled 'publicanus' in *Verr.* ii. 1. 135, *Flacc.* 11, *Rab. Post.* 3, Varro, *RR* i. 2. 1, Ascon. 47 C.

wronged by the *familia publicanorum* can sue any of the *socii vectigalis*, and if successful he can obtain compensation from any.[43]

If we turn to the great companies, we find that in the Republic their decisions were not taken by the *manceps* or by the *socii* as such, but by their *magistri*, probably appointed annually, and in one instance by a mysterious body of *decumani*, some sort of board of directors.[44] Like *collegia*, which also had *magistri*, these companies could in Cicero's time pass 'decrees'.[45] In the provinces they were represented by *promagistri*, who are also attested in the Principate.[46] It must have been they who made *pactiones* with the cities, i.e. bargains fixing what the cities should pay the companies, irrespective of what was strictly due under the *lex consoria*, and who brought or accepted suits on behalf of their companies in the governor's court.[47] Since the title *promagister* surely indicates a relationship to *magister* analogous to that of proconsul to consul, it seems safe to assume that at Rome *magistri* performed the same functions as *promagistri* did locally, and this assumption is corroborated by a fragment of Ulpian alluding to the capacity of the *magister* of a *societas* to make a *pactum* binding on the *societas*;[48] this must surely relate to a publican company, since no *magistri* are attested for ordinary business partnerships. Though few, the imperial references to *magistri* and *promagistri* indicate the survival right down to the Severan period of the kind of organization of publican companies best known from Cicero's writings.

This inference is supported by other allusions to these companies in the excerpts from classical jurists preserved by the Justinianic compilers of the *Digest*. Now it has long been accepted that the text of all such fragments has often been interpolated, i.e. altered, by the compilers, if

---

[43] *Dig.* xliii. 9. 1. 2 (interdicts); *FIRA* i². 105. vv. 16, 35, 42, 46, 53 (cf. n. 144). The quotation is from Buckland-Stein, *Textbook of Roman Law*³ 510. For slave dealers and bankers ib. 512. 'Socii vectigalis' (*Dig.* xxxix. 3. 1, cf. 9. 4 for common administration, an obscure fragment on which see Cimma 226), liable for each other's delicts, ib. 6.

[44] Cimma 70 based on *Verr.* ii. 2. 182 and *ILS* 1862, cf. *Verr.* ii. 3. 147 f.; *Planc.* 32; *Fam.* xiii. 9. Badian ch. IV is best on organization of the Republican companies. Ps-Ascon 196 St., a poor authority, thought the *mancipes* 'principes publicanorum'; perhaps they often were, but not necessarily as *mancipes*. The *manceps* effected the formal act of 'purchase' ('auctor emptionis', Festus 137 L), but when Cicero describes Cn. Plancius as 'maximarum societatum auctor, plurimarum magister' (*Planc.* 32), his specific role is that of 'magister', while 'auctor' means merely the principal member (cf. *Oxf. Lat. Dict* s.v. 4b). The *manceps* might be a mere agent (*Fam.* v. 20. 3).

[45] e.g. *Verr.* ii. 2. 177; *Sest.* 32 (also mentioning *decreta* of *collegia*, cf. *ILS* 7216–21; they too had *magistri*, ILS 1924, 7215a etc).

[46] *Verr.* ii. 2. 169; *Fam.* xiii. 65. 1; for Principate see nn. 125, 143, 156, 186.

[47] Cic., *Qu.fr.* i. 1. 35 (Asia), cf. *Att.* v. 13. 1; 14. 1; vi. 1. 16 (Cilicia); *Prov. Cons.* 10 (Syria). *Fam.* xiii. 65 seems to show that in Bithynia cities also made bargains for the *scriptura*, perhaps on behalf of their citizens who grazed animals on public domains. In Sicily the *decumani* made bargains with individual farmers, *Verr*, ii. 3. 36 f., 112.

[48] *Dig.* ii. 14. 14.

not already in revised editions of the treatises which they excerpted, principally in order to adapt it to subsequent developments in the law. No doubt some scholars were too prone to detect 'interpolations' everywhere, but no one can doubt that they may be found. It seems to me clear that all or nearly all the fragments relating to publican companies have suffered such alterations, though in this case they were not made to bring the texts up to date. Tax-farming persisted, but in the form of *Kleinpacht*. Hence, though old rules governing the reciprocal rights and obligations of tax-farmers and taxpayers could still be relevant, and duly appear in the *Digest*,[49] the compilers had no need to excerpt anything from the classical jurists on the special status of tax companies and their relationship with the treasury, since these companies had vanished (s. XI). None the less, working in haste, they occasionally left all sorts of traces of practices and institutions which had become obsolete. Thus few allusions to the companies survive in extracts they made from treatises which the classical jurists began to compose in the second half of the second century on public and administrative law, and in which the most systematic discussion of the companies had probably been offered, since the questions that arose hardly belonged to private law.[50] However, in writing on the private law of *societas*, the classical jurists had also from time to time found it necessary to refer to distinctions between ordinary business partnership and *societates vectigales*. The compilers failed to eliminate a few of these references, but since they were indifferent to and unfamiliar with the special status of these *societates*, which no longer existed in their own day, it seems to me that they abbreviated the texts, and thereby garbled them, to an extent that defies conjectural emendation,[51] while leaving enough to reveal, however dimly, that these *societates* exhibited peculiarities that conform to what we know or might expect to have been true of the publican companies in the Republic. Cimma cautiously remarks that we cannot be sure that their status had not

---

[49] *Dig.* xxxix, 4 *passim*; the edict was supplemented by imperial rescripts of Hadrian (*h.t.* 4. 4), Pius, Marcus, and the Severi (*h.t.* 6, 7. 1, 16). The rules apply especially to *portoria* and forfeitures of undeclared merchandise (*commissa*): *h.t.* 4, 1, 8, 9. 7, 11. 1–4, 14, 16, but also to *vectigalia* from domains: 7 *pr.*, 11. 1, 13 *pr.*, 15, though it is not easy to see how lessees of domains could commit delicts of the kind the praetor envisaged. Gaius says that the edict had been extended to cover municipal publicans (13. 1).

[50] F. Schulz, *Hist. of Rom. Legal Science*² (1946) 139; *Class. Roman Law* (1951), 88 f. Treatises *de iure fisci* would have discussed fiscal claims against publicans, and also against taxpayers, in so far as taxes were collected by officials or by publicans taking only a percentage of the proceeds; Hadrian's rescript cited in n. 198 comes from Callistratus, *de iure fisci*; cf. also the *fr. de iure fisci* cited in n. 6. Ulpian mentioned persons debarred from leasing taxes in *de officio proconsulis* (*Dig.* xlviii. 19. 9. 9). Macer wrote at least two books on the *vicesima hereditatium*.

[51] I shall therefore not enter into detailed discussion of the texts to be cited, on which Cimma reports diverse views (see her index of sources).

changed in the Principate, since of the relevant juristic fragments none
comes from a jurist earlier than Gaius.[52] But this *caveat* has little force.
The compilers seldom drew on Republican works on law, and indeed
made few extracts from any writings (except Julian's) earlier than
Gaius. Statistically it is to be expected that the few references to
societates vectigales should be Severan; actually in one of them Ulpian
cites Labeo (n. 53).

Of particular importance is a fragment of Gaius, which is certainly
not verbally correct and which has probably been much abbreviated,
but which at least tells us that in general a *societas* or *collegium* was not
entitled 'corpus habere', but that the right had been granted in a few
cases, e.g. to the 'vectigalium publicorum sociis', to those engaged in
the extraction of gold, silver, and salt (the list, to judge from another he
gives elsewhere (Dig. xxxix. 4. 13 *pr.*), is illustrative, not exhaustive),
and to certain *collegia*; it was clearly a privilege, not necessarily
appertaining to all *societates* of publicans any more than to all *collegia* as
such. The matter was regulated by *leges*, decrees of the senate, and
imperial constitutions; if any of the *leges* he had in mind affected
publican companies, they must surely be either the *leges censoriae*,
standard contracts under which they farmed the *vectigalia*, which (as
we have seen) were of Republican date, or statute laws enacted not
later than the reign of Augustus, since thereafter hardly any statutes
were passed and new legislation almost always took the form of decrees
of the senate and imperial constitutions.[53] The title in the *Digest* which
preserves this fragment is devoted to actions which may be brought
against or on behalf of an *universitas*, a corporate body, primarily a
municipality, and Gaius explains what is meant by the right 'corpus
habere' by reference to the model of a municipality ('ad exemplum rei
publicae'); a *societas* with this status can hold property in common with
a common chest and take action like a municipality through an *actor* or
syndicus. He does not say that it was assimilated in all points to a
municipality.

The statement that corporate companies could have property in
common with a common chest must be understood in the light of the
words 'ad exemplum rei publicae'. Any two or more citizens, whether
or not associated in a private partnership, could jointly own property,

[52] Cimma 95 f.

[53] *Dig.* iii. 4. 1 (cf. xxxix. 4. 13 *pr.*); I agree in general with Cimma 219 f., but would add (*a*)
that the translation of *societas* in the *Basilica* as *hetaireia* and not *koinonia* (p. 187) may spring from
ignorance of the institution to which Gaius refers, and (*b*) that the genuineness and meaning of
the text imputed to Papinian in xviii. 2. 82 (cf. Cimma 203) are too uncertain to permit any
conclusion on the common funds of tax companies (for which see Cimma 161, Badian 77). It
seems to me that there are other allusions to companies with corporate status in Ulpian, ii. 14. 14
(n. 48), xxxvii. 1. 3. 4, xlvii. 2. 31 (citing and endorsing Labeo) and Florentinus, xlvi. 1. 22.

but at any time they had the right to demand that it be shared out, whereas a municipality owned property 'zur gesamten Hand', i.e. the *municipes* had the right to use it for common purposes but not to divide it among themselves; nor were they, as citizens, liable individually for municipal debts.[54]

However, the municipal analogy cannot have been complete. Municipalities existed in perpetuity, tax-companies for the duration of their contract. At its termination, unless it were renewed, the common funds would indeed have been distributed. Nor is the mere fact that they had common funds, as we know for the Republic from Cicero, and for the Principate from epigraphic references to their *arcae and arcarii* (n. 53), proof in itself that they were held even for the duration of the contract *zur gesamten Hand*. It is practical considerations that make this a necessary assumption. At any given moment these funds must have included, besides sums due to the state and to private persons (for instance those who banked with them), cash that was needed for the current costs of the enterprise. No doubt under the terms on which the *socii* contracted *inter se* there were annual distributions (dividends), but whereas in a private partnership that was a matter to be settled by the *socii* among themselves, in the case of a public contract it may well have been thought necessary to regulate it in the *lex censoria* itself; the members cannot have been entitled to withdraw capital needed for carrying on the work, nor to insist on the sale of slave employees owned in common and the distribution of the proceeds; indeed, if any of them had placed his own slaves at the company's disposal, he might well have been debarred from recalling them. As for liability to the state, that of the *manceps* and *praedes* was unlimited, and that of other *socii* determined by the extent of the *praedia* they might have pledged; but all must also have had obligations *inter se* for a share in costs and debts proportionate to their stake in the business, just like partners in private law.

Very probably the great companies were able to renew their leases over and over again. A rival firm which sought to displace the company in possession, by outbidding it when the contract came up for renewal, might have been unable to operate efficiently without the experienced slaves in the service of its predecessor, and would then have had little option but to purchase them at the vendor's prices.[55] It might therefore

[54] Ulpian applies this generally to any *universitas* (*Dig.* iii. 4. 7. 1). Corporate companies would presumably not have had the rights which municipalities enjoyed to manumit and receive legacies, granted first by Marcus to authorized *collegia* (*Dig.* xxxiv. 5. 20, xl. 3. 1). See in general Schulz, *Class. Rom. Law*, 86 ff.

[55] Admittedly Cic., *Att.* i. 17. 9 implies that there had been keen competition for the Asian tribute in 61 BC.

often have seemed the best course for those who wished to engage in the business to buy their way into the old company. This may explain why 'very many companies' farming taxes in AD 58 could be described as 'having been constituted in the Republic by consuls and tribunes': Tacitus' expression is vague but suggests not only that the farm was regulated by consular or tribunician laws but that companies active in AD 58 had had a continuous existence since Republican times.[56]

It may have been this degree of factual permanence that made it seem reasonable to grant them corporate status. It was also convenient that they should be capable of appointing persons to manage their funds, who could sue and be sued as their legal representatives. Gaius uses the terms 'actor' and 'syndicus', which are found in municipal contexts and are also attested for publicans.[57] We need not, however, assume that one of these *names* was necessarily given to every legal agent of a *corpus*. The management of municipal funds and property lay with the magistrates, and they could be sued for municipal debts.[58] The *magistri* and *promagistri* of publican companies in Cicero's time must have performed a similar role. Both are still attested in the Principate (nn. 46, 48), and presumably *promagistri* as well as *magistri* (n. 48) could bind their *societates* by *pacta*.

The corporate status which at least some tax-companies enjoyed in Gaius' time also appears to be implicit in a few fragments of Florentinus, who wrote under Marcus or later, and of Ulpian (n. 53). In that case such companies still existed in the period in which it is held that tax-farming by companies had commonly been replaced by collection either by officials or by *Einzelpächter* (individual lessees). One fragment of Ulpian seems to me to make strongly against the view that in his day taxes were generally leased to individuals with perhaps only one or two partners: 'no one' he says 'can be ignorant of the audacity and boldness of the factions of publicans.' 'Factions' implies combinations, and it is more likely that such combinations could display the audacity for which Ulpian impeaches them if they were organized in companies of the old style. Although I think it probable that many tax-contracts were now leased in the provinces, some must still have been leased at Rome, for it is conditions at Rome of which 'no one can be ignorant'.[59] However, in the time of the compilers, tax-farming invariably assumed the form of *Kleinpacht* (section XI), and this may be why the juristic

---

[56] *Ann.* xiii. 50, which also refers to some later companies; we may think of those constituted to collect the *vicesima hereditatium* and *portoria* in newly annexed or organized provinces, e.g. in Illyricum.

[57] *CIL* x. 1913; *AE* 1930. 87; 1947. 180 (AD 174); we have a procurator in *ILS* 1876. For municipal *actores* see *lex Irnitana* (n. 3) LXX f. with the editor's commentary.

[58] *Dig.* xliv. 7. 35. 1.

[59] *Dig.* xxxix. 4. 12 *pr.*

fragments in *Digest* xxxix. 4 refer only to claims that may be brought against an individual publican or publicans and his or their heirs, sureties, and partners; allusions to the possibility of suing a company through its legal representative have dropped out.[60] So too the compilers represent Callistratus as recording separately the exemption from municipal burdens enjoyed by *conductores* of fiscal revenues (who of course *might* be *Einzelpächter*) and by *collegia* of craftsmen to which corporate status had been granted in the public interest, but not the exemption of tax-companies with like status.[61]

No doubt Cimma is right in discounting the view that a publican company ever had a 'legal personality' in the same sense as corporate bodies may have it in a modern legal system.[62] This is in any case a question of more concern to the comparative lawyer than to the historian. She casts doubt on recognition of their corporate entity by remarking that the term *socii* is used in preference to *societas* in most literary and epigraphic texts. If this argument had any validity, it would prove too much on her own view; she does not deny the authenticity in substance of the fragment of Gaius just discussed. However, it takes no account of the proclivity of Latin for designating a collectivity not by a collective noun but by the plural of its members. A *res publica* such as a *municipium* or colony unquestionably had corporate status, but the praetor's edict contained rubrics 'quibus municipum nomine agere liceat' and 'quod adversus municipes agatur'; jurists and the draftsmen of municipal charters commonly employ the same mode of expression.[63] This normal preference for the collective plural makes it all the more significant that both Cicero and the jurists occasionally use the collective noun *societas* to designate a tax-company. It also appears in at least one inscription.[64] Cimma claims that the slaves who belonged to such companies are said to belong to the *socii*, not to the *societas*; in fact what we usually find is the abbreviation 'soc.', which can be supplemented in either way. And municipal slaves are sometimes called 'servi municipum' though more often 'servi municipii'. We also have a number of inscriptions of the form 'pub[lici] [vicesimae] lib[ertatis] servus'. In one case the stone commemorates the burial place of the *familia* of the tax. This may

---

[60] In *Dig.* xxxix. 4 see 1. 4 and 3. 1 (Ulpian), 4 *pr.* (Paul, citing Labeo), 6 (Modestinus), 13. 3 f. (Gaius), 16. 12 (Marcian). 'Publicanus' and 'publicani' alternate, *h.t.* 16. 10–14. Perhaps in the jurists they are used in the same way as in Republican texts, cf. n. 42.

[61] *Dig.* l. 6. 6. 10 and 12.

[62] Cimma 95 f. and ch. IV.

[63] *Dig.* iii. 4. 2 and 7 *pr.*, cf. *lex Irnitana* (n. 3) LXX and *passim*. *Collegia* may be designated as such or as *corpora* or by collective plurals (*ILS* 7268, 7287–9; in 7259 usage alternates).

[64] Cic., *Verr.* ii. 3. 165, 187 f., *Fam.* xiii. 9. 3, *Brut.* 85; *Dig.* ii. 14. 14 (n. 48); xlvii. 2. 31 (n. 53); more often *societas* denotes for jurists the legal relationship between *socii*; *CIL* xv. 7916.

recall the juristic definition of the 'familia publicanorum' as comprising all the employees, free as well as slaves, who were actually engaged
in the collection; it excluded slaves of the publicans who were not so
employed, but included the slaves of other owners who were. The
inscription evidently uses the term *familia* in this way; one of those who
shared the burial ground was in fact a free man. No doubt the majority
of the *familia* belonged to the company that farmed this tax.[65] Of
course a tax could own nothing; the genitive denotes not possession or
ownership but attachment, just as a 'miles legionis primae' is attached
to that legion.[66]

Some legal texts treat a *societas vectigalis* or *vectigalium* as a special
category of partnership. It is obvious that the use of the term *societas*
implies that it had something in common with private partnerships,
especially no doubt with that variety of parnership described as
'societas alicuius negotiationis', e.g. banking. Under these consensual
contracts each partner undertook to bring capital or services into the
common enterprise and was to share in its gains and losses in an agreed
proportion; that must also have been true for the publican companies.
Like other Romans who had no contractual relationship with each
other, partners might own assets (including slaves) in common, but
each was free at all times to require their division. They might act
through procurators, or through slaves operating as *institores* or trading
with their *peculium*, but a partnership was not a corporate entity with its
own representatives, who could sue and be sued on its behalf. A *societas
vectigalis* indeed differed from other *societates* even when it had not been
granted that status. As we have seen, any *socii* who farmed taxes were
liable for each other's delicts. Other differences from ordinary partnerships arise from the rules that the latter are dissolved by the death or
withdrawal of any one of the partners or by litigation between them;
on such dissolution all the partners, and the heirs of one deceased, were
entitled to their due shares in any net profits accruing from previous
transactions and liable for any debts already incurred, and the
common assets could, if any of them wished, be divided. They were
also free to enter into a new partnership in which the heir of a deceased
partner might share.[67] These rules were unsuited to the importance of
the functions publicans performed for the state, and seem to have been

---

[65] *ILS* 1864–72 ('familia', 1870), cf. de Laet 395 n. 3; *Dig.* xxxix. 4. 1. 5 f; *h.t.* 12; l. 16. 195. 3.
Municipal slaves: *ILS* iii. pp. 699 f.

[66] Cimma 141 refutes Rostovtzeff's thesis that the attribution of slaves to a tax shows that it was
no longer farmed but collected by officials, referring to *ILS* 1862 where a slave of the *quadragesima
port(oriorum) Asiae* appears in the Greek version as slave of the κοινόν (*societas*) or κοινωνοί (*socii*).

[67] Besides any textbook of Roman law see above all F. Wieacker, *SZ* (1952), 302 ff. and 488 ff.

varied in their case, whether or not they were accorded corporate status.[68]

Suppose that in public contracts the state had a legal relationship only with the *manceps*, even though the capital and services of the *socii* were essential for performance. In that case, if he were to die (he could hardly withdraw) before fulfilment of his obligations, the state could require compensation from his sureties and heirs, but the work would be intermitted until a new contract was made with a new *manceps*; the operations, of building, or furnishing military supplies, or collecting the taxes, would be suspended; even though *socii* were actually doing the work, they would cease to have any authority to proceed. This would have been absurd and unnecessary. This is a sound reason for concluding that the *manceps* was no more than the agent of the *socii*, who must also have been under obligation to the state. It would have been no less contrary to the public interest, had the death or withdrawal of any one of the *socii* entailed the dissolution of the *societas*, given that the survivors were still able to fulfil the contract, and that their co-operation was needed for its fulfilment. These considerations apply less when little men contracted locally, perhaps with partners, to collect minor imposts within a limited district; a new contract could have been made in a relatively short time. Contrast the confusion that must have resulted from the premature termination of a contract let for five years at Rome for the collection of the taxes of an entire and distant province. The relevant *lex censoria* may have actually prohibited the withdrawal of any of the *socii*, whose capital and services might have been indispensable, but in any case we must suppose that neither the death nor the withdrawal of any of them affected the continuance of the *societas*. The heir of a deceased *socius* could surely be required to succeed to his obligations, to remove any danger that the *societas* would lack essential capital (including slave personnel). The stipulation for sureties and securities in land for fulfilment of the contractors' obligations was no doubt a valuable guarantee against fraud or negligence on their part, but it was no safeguard for the public interest in the contingencies just considered. Indeed the state would have suffered indirectly in another way if the tax-farming companies had been liable to dissolution by the death or withdrawal of any of the members, and if the state had then had no option but to exact pecuniary compensation. This would have exposed every participant to unforeseeable risks and incalculable liabilities, and would therefore

---

[68] For special position of *societates vectigales*, besides nn. 69 and 71 see *Dig.* xvii. 2. 5 *pr.*, and 2. 33 (on which cf. Cimma 207; I do not understand it, but it does not bear on what follows).

either have deterred men from venturing on the public contracts at all, or led them by way of insurance to take them only on terms far less favourable to the state than it could otherwise have obtained.

The differences between a *societas vectigalis* (or *vectigalium*) and private partnerships, obscurely indicated in juristic texts, support this reasoning. Pomponius is quoted as writing in *ad Sabinum:*

'It is so abundantly clear that a partnership is dissolved by the death of a partner that we cannot so much as initially agree in the contract that even the heir should succeed to the partnership. He [Sabinus?] applies this to private partnerships: in one concerned with the taxes the partnership still continues even after the death of a member, but subject to the condition that the share of the deceased be attached to the person of the heir in such a way that it must be transferred to the heir too; this has to be determined in accordance with the circumstances of the case. What in fact is to happen, if the deceased is the person through whose effort the partnership was principally formed and without whose co-operation it could not be carried on?'

The excerpt supplies no answer; it has therefore plainly been cut off at the end, and it seems to me that the preceding sentence is abbreviated beyond intelligibility. But Pomponius surely laid down at least that a tax-farming company was not dissolved by the death of any member (including of course the *manceps*), and that subject to certain rules the heir succeeded to the share of the deceased. Again, Ulpian, after stating that in the event of the death of a partner the heir is entitled, in a private partnership, to the decedent's share in profits accruing from common transactions within his lifetime, is represented as adding that 'with regard to all partnerships including tax partnerships, we observe the same rule, viz. that the heir should not be a partner, unless co-opted, but that he has a title to all accrued profits and should acknowledge any liability that arises, whether incurred in the lifetime of the tax-partner *or thereafter*, a rule that does not similarly apply in a voluntary partnership'.[69] This too is so unclear that it must have been at least abbreviated, but the second part seems to show that the heir shares in the liabilities, and therefore we must presume in all the profits, of a tax-company, including those arising after the death of the decedent, and not merely, as in other partnerships, in those which had already accrued; and that agrees with what Pomponius appears to state. On the other hand, the fragment as it stands categorically asserts that the heir does not himself become a partner, unless co-opted; hence he would not automatically take part in the administration, or have a

---

[69] *Dig.* xvii. 2. 59 (Pomp.); 63. 7 f. (Ulp.). For Egypt see App. I. 2.

voice in the meetings that passed *decreta*. It is obvious that the heir might be a minor, or unfit in some other way to be admitted to an active role in the business; on the other hand, the assets that he had inherited might be vital for the continuance of operations, and would be retained in the business.

Another text affirms, without making any exception for a *societas vectigalis*, that no one in making a contract for *societas* can make it a condition that his heir should succeed.[70] This is not incompatible with the fragment previously cited, if that is understood to show that the heir is admitted to partnership only by co-optation when the time comes. In any event it is evident that unlike other partnerships a *societas vectigalis* was not dissolved by the death of a partner, nor, as another fragment tells us, by litigation between the members.[71] We may infer that for the same reasons of public interest it could also not be dissolved, within the period for which the public contract ran, by amicable agreement among them.

It must surely be supposed that a *societas vectigalis* was excepted from general rules appertaining to partnerships by the terms of the contract made with the state. We have already seen reason to suppose that the state concerned itself in the composition of a publican company and probably registered the *socii*. We might conjecture that if the *socii* had the power to co-opt a new partner, such as the heir of a deceased member, their decision required public sanction. Manifestly it was the state which conferred on some such companies the corporate privileges to which Gaius refers. These must have seemed necessary in the public interest, precisely because the responsibilities that some publican companies assumed, for the collection of tribute or other revenues throughout one or more provinces, or for the exploitation of rich mines, required a large organization; they also had to hold big sums in cash, and might be involved in litigation far from Rome. The conditions that explain why publican companies were distinguished in law from other partnerships as late as the Severi, and why some at least had corporate status in Gaius' time, and probably in Ulpian's, had existed in the late Republic, and it can hardly be doubted that what the classical jurists tell us was already true then; in so far as their special status conduced to their own benefit, as well as to that of the state, it could most easily have been obtained at the time when they possessed the greatest political influence. But though their power as a pressure group waned after the establishment of the Principate, and though (as will be seen) they lost the function of collecting tribute within city

---

[70] *Dig.* xvii. 2. 35, cf. 2. 65. 9.
[71] *Dig.* xvii. 2. 65. 15, contrast 65 *pr.* (Paul).

territories, they were still employed to gather in other revenues of great importance to the treasury, notably *portoria* and the *vicesima hereditatium* instituted by Augustus. The considerations of public interest which are sufficient to account for their special status remained valid, and it is not surprising that *societates vectigales* still differed significantly from other partnerships in the Severan period; some probably retained the corporate status which Gaius attests for the mid-second century.

It is indeed hard to see why the state should have ever preferred, or how it would have been practicable, to lease revenues to individual contractors without partners when their collection necessitated substantial investment and a large organization. Even in cases of *Kleinpacht* we find that the lessees may have partners. They were surely indispensable in contracts for the collection of, for example, the *portoria* throughout circumscriptions which embraced the whole of Gaul, or all the Illyrian provinces, or most of the Anatolian, or a combination of taxes in Africa (nn. 90–2). In fact we shall find in the cases of Gaul and Illyricum that the lessees sometimes called *conductores* were not single individuals. They could have formed a *societas vectigalis*, perhaps a corporation. The use of the term *conductor* should not in itself compel us to suppose that any of them was an *Einzelpächter*. On the other hand its very meaning precludes Rostovtzeff's strange view that they were semi-officials (*Halbbeamten*).[72]

The fact that there were still tax-farmers under the Severi is naturally no proof that they had not in certain instances been displaced by official collectors. Wherever this occurred, if it did, there would have been the possibility of claims by the subjects for extortion or by the *fiscus* for failure to pay what was due. If there was any discussion of such matters in juristic texts, it would have been found in treatises on administrative law, and has been neglected as obsolete by Justinian's compilers.

It remains to examine the evidence or arguments for the supposed substitution of *Einzelpächter* for companies and of officials for publicans as collectors in regard to each particular type of revenue, but first it will be helpful to enquire into possible changes of another kind in the modes of leasing, and to review the character of the evidence available for investigation.

[72] De Laet 284 with bibliography dismissed it.

IV. POSSIBLE CHANGES IN TAX-FARMING UNDER THE PRINCIPATE

Except for the tithes of Sicilian cities, in the Republic revenues were farmed at Rome.[73] In the Principate there was certainly leasing in the provinces of petty imposts (*Kleinpacht*), as in Egypt or at Vipasca. It is possible that eventually important taxes were also leased by procurators in the provinces. There is no direct evidence for this; but the functions of procurators are known only in part, from scattered bits of evidence. The hypothesis may explain a puzzling passage of Tacitus (pp. 389–93). Such a transfer of responsibility from the centre to the provinces would have made it easier for provincials to bid for the contracts. Some of the known *conductores* of *portoria* appear to be provincials, and a fragment of Ulpian shows that it was common for proconsuls (and doubtless other provincial governors) to impose as a penalty disqualification for leasing public revenues; conceivably this might refer to *Kleinpacht*.[74]

Can we detect other changes in the mode of tax-farming? In the Republic the farmers of both the Sicilian and the Asian tithes, and presumably of all other revenues undertook to pay fixed sums in cash or kind to the state; the surplus, if any, that was lawfully collected (to say nothing of illicit exactions) was to cover costs and provide profits, while the deficit, if any, would be their loss.[75] When the contract was for a quinquennium (as in Asia), they must have been bound to pay in instalments. Quinquennial leases are still envisaged in rescripts of Hadrian and Alexander Severus;[76] much later, Constantine referred to a minimum period of three years.[77] Hermogenianus says that *conductores* who failed to pay instalments when due lost their contracts or could be charged with interest.[78] Some inscriptions mention publicans in the *n*th year of their operations: in my view this need not mean that their contracts were annual, but only that they had been active for so many years.[79] However, in Egypt the Ptolemies had farmed taxes on an annual basis, and there the Roman government may have done the same (Appendix I. 3). The Sicilian tithes had also been leased annually. Very probably there was no uniformity in the Principate. At any given moment publicans would have in their hands sums due to the

---

[73] Cic., *de leg. agr.* i. 17, ii. 55.

[74] *Dig.* xlviii. 19. 9. 9, where 'vectigalia publica' should refer to state, not municipal, revenues, cf. l. 16. 15 f.

[75] Cic., *Verr.* ii. 3. 110; *Att.* i. 17. 9.

[76] *Dig.* xlix. 14. 3. 6; *CJ* iv. 65. 7.

[77] *CJ* iv. 61. 4.

[78] *Dig.* xxxix. 4. 10. 1.

[79] See texts cited in nn. 156, 178, 209, cf. de Laet 237 ff. on *CIL* iii. p. 958 XXIII; *ILS* 1861.

state, the 'vectigaliorum residua' noted by Augustus in AD 14 (Appendix I. 4). Farming of taxes for lump sums is also known for harbour
dues in fifth-century Athens,[80] and in Ptolemaic Egypt. There, however, the proceeds of revenue went direct to the state, and the publicans
received in arrears any balance due to them under the contract
between the amount collected and the amount they had undertaken to
pay, though they were also entitled to a substantial bonus (*opsonion*) for
fulfilment of their obligation (Appendix I. 4). This bonus has some
analogy to the additional fees which the tithe-farmers in Sicily had
been accustomed to levy before Verres' time without lawful authority
and which Verres legitimated, to the surcharges publicans had also
imposed on the Sicilian *portoria*, and probably to the fortieths and
fiftieths of the *portoria* which the publicans in Italy had been wrong-
fully exacting until they were prohibited by Nero.[81] In Roman Egypt
surcharges persisted (Appendix I. 6).

It may be observed that we are relatively well informed about the
mode of tax-farming in Egypt under the Ptolemies, whereas for the
Roman period we can only say that the meagre evidence is compatible
with the assumption that in so far as tax-farming continued in Egypt,
the Romans followed the practices that they found in use, just as they
adopted the *lex Hieronica* in Sicily.[82] In the same way the emperors are
unlikely to have altered the Republican mode of tax-farming unless
they saw some special need or advantage in doing so.

What did a state gain or lose from adopting this system? Firstly, like
any mode of tax-farming, it supplied the deficiency of public officials.
In ancient cities men did not think of creating a civil service, nor for
that matter a professional army. Even under the Principate the
number of officials multiplied very gradually, and apart from the
imperial freedmen and slaves they tended to alternate between varying
civil and military posts in such a way that few can have become experts
in any branch of the administration (chapter 10). As a consequence
states lacked officials not only to collect the revenues but also to
forecast their gross proceeds.

Hence there was a second advantage in farming collection for lump
sums; it guaranteed the income the state could expect to receive.
Against this could be set the risk that the farmers might be entitled to
take under the contract a quite excessive proportion of what was due
from the taxpayers, to say nothing of the temptation to extortion for
their own profit. In principle it was possible to audit their accounts and

---

[80] Andocides i. 133.

[81] Cic., *Verr.* ii. 3. 70–118 (see tabulation in A. H. M. Jones, *Roman Economy* (1974), 120);
portoria: ib. 181; Tac., *Ann.* xiii. 51.

[82] *Verr.* ii. 3. 12–15. Variations in provincial tribute (pp. 325 f.) may be thus explained.

ascertain what their takings had actually been and by publishing the results, to stimulate competition at the next auction. How far most ancient states adopted this practice, we cannot say; most of them, including Republican Rome, probably had no administrative means of exercising this sort of control, but the Ptolemies employed it, and the growth of the procuratorial service in the Principate may have enabled Rome to follow suit.

There was a third potential advantage, taken for example in England by the government of Charles II, that the farmers could be forced to lend money in advance on the security of the revenues farmed,[83] but I know of no instance of this in antiquity.

A fourth is discerned by Claire Préaux in the case of Ptolemaic Egypt. She suggested that there the publicans would be able to provide cash, when the circulation of money was such that the taxpayers could not do so. For all we know this may sometimes have been true in the Roman empire. But even when the government wished to received dues in kind, for instance in grain, the contractors could perform a useful role. In Egypt the peasants had to bring their grain to public threshing floors and storehouses which seem to have existed in each village, and there was an elaborate organization for the transport to Alexandria of that part of it which was due to the state, under the supervision of paid or liturgical officials. This was a system that could hardly work except in a land where there were easy communications as well as a highly developed bureaucracy. Conditions must have been quite different elsewhere, for instance in Africa. There it would have been impractical to impose on the peasants themselves the obligation to arrange delivery of taxes or rents in grain at a perhaps distant point where it was required by the government, nor were there officials to collect small quantities from innumerable holdings and transport them all to their destination. It was therefore natural to lease the tasks to contractors (cf. Addenda to chapter 15 n. 1).

However, for Préaux herself the Ptolemaic tax-farming was primarily an 'institution of assurance against fiscal risks'. Indeed in her judgement the farmers did not actually collect tax; that was left to public employees: they merely insured the sum fixed in their contracts. I incline to think her wrong in supposing that the collectors were employees of the state rather than of the publicans, but be that as it may, the latter, together with their partners and sureties, certainly guaranteed a predetermined revenue.[84] Roman tax-farmers in the Republic performed the same service. And in so far as they adopted the

---

[83] C. D. Chandaman, *English Public Revenues 1660–1688* (1975) 27.
[84] App. I. 4; Wallace ch. IV.

practice, which in Cicero's time prevailed in the eastern provinces, of entering into bargains (*pactiones*) with cities, under which the cities were to pay them specified amounts in cash or kind and were left to collect them through their own machinery what was needed to meet this commitment, they had become no more than guarantors of the revenue. This made it the easier to dispense with them altogether.

In 47 Caesar made the cities of Asia themselves responsible for the tribute on their territories; at the same time he reduced their burden by one-third. Since he was short of money, and soon had to resort to all sorts of exactions, he can hardly have intended a consequential diminution by one-third in the revenue that the treasury actually received.[85] He surely reckoned that one-third, or probably more, of the gross receipts had previously been going into the coffers of the publicans. The change was administratively easy, since under the *pactiones* the cities had already been collecting the sums due to the publicans. But what of the role of the latter as guarantors of the revenue? I suppose that the collectors appointed by the city were liable for the sum at which it was assessed. This was the case in and after the Severan epoch for the direct taxes, when the cities throughout the empire seem normally to have collected them, (pp. 339 ff.), and whether or not Caesar, as I believe, dispensed with the use of publicans for the tribute in other provinces besides Asia (section VI), it is likely that wherever he did so, he introduced this rule.

In Egypt there were originally only three cities of Greek type, of which Alexandria lacked full autonomy. In the rest of the country the Romans could not delegate the collection of taxes to city authorities. But the Ptolemies had created a bureaucracy such as Rome never developed elsewhere in the Principate. Egyptian officials who saw to the collection of the rents from state lands and supervised the farming of other revenues were remunerated but were liable with their own property for deficits.[86] The Roman government seems to have progressively narrowed the sphere of tax-farming, without (as far as we know) entirely eliminating it; as late as the third century it is still attested. The equestrian officials and the imperial freedmen and slaves employed in the province had no liability for deficits, but the liturgical administrators, *apailetai*, *epiteretai*, *practores*, were compulsorily chosen from men of substance, and their own assets, or those of their sureties, guaranteed the revenues; in the last resort communities were collectively liable for deficits. In other provinces collectors of tribute were nominated by and responsible to the cities for whom they acted, though nominees could

---

[85] Caesar's reform: App., *BC* v. 4; Dio xlii. 6; Plut., *Caes.* 48; his exactions: Broughton, *ESAR* iv. 580.

[86] Préaux *L'Économie royale des Lagides* (1939) 43–7, 444–50; Wilcken, *Grundzüge*, 180 ff.

appeal against appointment, as in the case of other liturgies, to imperial officials, under rules of eligibility which the government had prescribed or approved, whereas in Egypt collectors were designated by officials and agents of the state. Severus' creation of councils in the Egyptian metropoleis in some degree assimilated the Egyptian regime to that which existed elsewhere.[87]

Thus the Roman government had at its direct disposal in Egypt a host of officials or quasi-officials available to collect taxes, which it lacked in other provinces. And yet even in Egypt some tax-farming long persisted. It is implausible that it was still employed there for collection of any tax which had been entrusted to officials in the rest of the empire.

Caesar's reform in Asia was represented as an act of beneficence to the cities, but we may doubt if it would have been introduced unless it had appeared of advantage to Rome. The elimination of the excessive profits of the publicans made it possible to extract the same net revenue as before, or even to augment it, with less burden on the taxpayers, and less discontent with Roman rule; at the same time the cities themselves, or in fact their richer citizens, furnished the security which the publicans had previously provided. But a similar reform, which guaranteed a net yield to the treasury, could hardly be found for other imposts. It is thus not surprising that they were farmed for much longer, or perhaps so long as they existed.

It is, however, possible that a different mode of tax-farming was commonly introduced. In AD 6 and 7 Augustus instituted taxes of 5 per cent and 2 per cent respectively on the estates of deceased Roman citizens (with numerous exceptions) and on the sale of slaves by auction.[88] They were certainly farmed (section VIII). But initially there can have been no data to show the probable yield of either tax. It would therefore have been hard for entrepreneurs to make realistic bids for lump sums satisfactory to the government; more probably they contracted to take a percentage of the proceeds with perhaps the right to levy supplementary charges for costs.[89] This was certainly the way in

[87] Wilcken, *Gr. Ostraka*, 572 ff.; from his lists of taxes farmed and not farmed it is hard to see any principle on which the Roman government acted; taxes of the same type were differently collected in different nomes. Liability of liturgists: *Grundzüge*, 214 ff.; Wallace ch. XVII. Councils: see A. K. Bowman, *Town Councils of Roman Egypt* (1972). Supervision of tax-farmers continued under Roman rule, see e.g. Wilcken, *Chr.* 277 (AD 139). A variety of terms was used for tax-farmers: Wilcken, *Gr. Ostraka*, i. 575–8. It is curious that the collectors of registration fees for transfers of catoecic land were called by various titles, at one time *epitēretai* and in the late 2nd c. *dēmosiōnai*, and were perhaps farmers throughout, cf. L. C. Youtie, *ZPE* 38, 273. Note App. I. 6.

[88] Dio lv. 25; 31. 4; the rate of the second tax was raised to 4 per cent, at latest by 44/3 (*ILS* 203).

[89] Cf. e.g. Hirschfeld 99, and see App. I. 6.

which tolls levied on internal traffic in Egypt were farmed in 139 to *Einzelpächter* (App. I. 5)

Was the same system introduced for taxes which had once been leased for lump sums? This must surely be supposed if we regard as *Einzelpächter* the *conductores* of *portoria* in the extensive Illyrian[90] and Gallic[91] circumscriptions, and of the *quattuor publica Africae*, which seem to have comprised the *portoria* together with the duties on inheritances, manumissions, and sales of slaves by auction;[92] individuals could hardly have provided adequate security for lump sums corresponding to the estimated yield of these taxes, which must have been large. However, in my view this argument is not cogent, since it can be questioned whether these *conductores* were *Einzelpächter*.

However, the multiplication of procurators concerned with specific taxes, such as those mentioned, within the period when they were certainly still farmed, point to the adoption of the percentage system, since the stricter control of publicans, which the creation of these posts was evidently intended to secure, was more necessary in the fiscal interest if the publicans were taking a percentage of the proceeds than if they had simply undertaken to pay lump sums.[93] In the latter case the government only had to ensure that the farmers had furnished adequate security and were apparently competent for their tasks, to enforce payment from them when due, and to adjudicate disputes between them and the taxpayers; it might also examine their accounts, with a view to publicizing the actual yield at the next auction, in the hope of obtaining higher bids. Under the percentage system it would have become advisable to protect the treasury against frauds by the publicans. They would still have had to find sureties,[94] and have themselves been liable to the *fiscus* for the sums due from the taxpayers less their own agreed remuneration. But only by close supervision cóuld the government ascertain that they were not retaining more than their contractual due, or not making corrupt deals with the taxpayers. They might collect 100, on which their proper percentage was 10, but declare only 80, retaining 8 as their due and embezzling 20. Or they might bargain with the taxpayers to receive openly 50 instead of 100,

---

[90] App. II.

[91] We find both *socii* and *conductores XXXX Galliarum*, not of any single district or station (de Laet 377 n. 3; 387 n. 2).

[92] De Laet 247 ff. (though I do not accept every point in his discussion). The absence in Africa of *procuratores XX hereditatium* (cf. n. 171) may be noted.

[93] So Mommsen, *St.R* ii³. 1018 f.

[94] In *Dig.* xxxix. 4. 9 *pr.*, 4. 16. 12 the compilers have perhaps substituted *fideiussores* for *praedes*. The tax-farmers as well as sureties were liable to the *fiscus*, as Marcus exempted them from municipal liturgies in order that their capacity to meet their liability might not be impaired (I. 6. 6. 10).

obtaining another 25 on the side. Such possibilities made it more essential to scrutinize their accounts; comparisons could then be made between the assessed value of taxable objects and the amount on which duty had been paid.[95] This perhaps explains why in Egypt for instance declarations of the value of inheritances are made to officials by Roman citizens (n. 174). *Delatores* were also given the opportunity to expose malpractices.

If the government went over to the percentage system, it lost the advantage of a guaranteed revenue known in advance, and was involved in additional costs arising from the need for greater supervision. Why not go further and commit collection to officials? Vittinghoff (n. 1) held that it was but a small step from the employment of publicans under close control to that of officials (p. 387). But there was a fundamental difference. Publicans always had an incentive to maximize profits, and when they did so under the percentage system, the *fiscus* too directly benefited: in so far as this system was adopted, that was perhaps the main reason for its adoption, though it is also possible that it had become hard to find contractors who would accept the hazards of undertaking to pay large lump sums. Salaried officials had no like incentive, and they could hardly have provided sureties for their operations; who would assume the risks of being sureties without a share in profits? So much did the government rely on the profit motive that it even contracted out the minting of coins at Rome (n. 24), and sometimes allowed imperial slaves, who were obviously operating with their *peculium*, to take leases of state-owned quarries.[96] It is indeed commonly held that the government did in the second century introduce direct collection of many taxes. It will be seen that this can seldom, if ever, be proved, and in any case tax-farming was never entirely abandoned. It was then never rejected in principle, in the belief that the integrity of officials would make direct collection more beneficial to the treasury or the taxpayers or both. That belief would probably have been groundless.

Now a long excerpt from Marcian's *de delatoribus*, which was apparently written after the deification of Caracalla, and which is mainly, if not exclusively, concerned with *portoria*, cites a rescript of Severus and Caracalla under which a procurator is to have jurisdiction

---

[95] However, I do not find it credible that the emperor himself would personally scrutinize publicans' accounts; hence in Fronto 86 N, which refers to the 'ratio' of a 'conductor IV publicorum Africae', I would translate 'quom ratio eius a domino nostro [Pius] tractabitur' by 'when his affair will be handled'; the affair might indeed be a renewal of the contract, in which case the leasing of the contract still took place at Rome under the emperor's own supervision. For 'accounts' one would expect 'rationes'.

[96] Hirschfeld 162–7 (partly conjectural, but *OGIS* 678 is clear).

on a claim that a slave had not been declared for payment of duty.[97]
We also know of an *advocatus fisci* for the Gallic *portoria* under the Severi
or later. But outside imperial domains it was properly to cases in which
the *fiscus* was interested that the jurisdiction of procurators (unless by
consent of the litigants) was reserved (chapter 7), and it was prescribed
in the second century that in such cases an *advocatus fisci* must be present
to plead on its behalf.[98] This evidence then implies that the *fiscus* stood
to gain from the actual yield of the duties in question. This could not
have been so, if they were farmed to publicans with an obligation to
pay the *fiscus* the same lump sum, whatever they actually collected. It
therefore implies either that the *portoria* were farmed on the percentage
system or that they were collected by officials. But the same excerpt
cites rescripts of Pius, Marcus, and Severus and Caracalla which refer
to publicans as collectors.[99] The fact that it is drawn from a treatise on
delators evidently shows that they had a role even in regard to taxes
which were still farmed. *Delatores*, unless prompted by sheer malice,
must as in other matters have been induced to lay information in the
hope of a reward. Presumably they received this from the *fiscus*. It
might have been a share in the value of the merchandise forfeit if they
proved their case. Ownership of forfeited articles (*commissa*) belonged
to the 'res vectigalis'. This expression suggests to me that it did not
appertain entirely either to publicans or to *fiscus*; it denotes the proceeds
of the *vectigal* in which under the percentage system both shared. The
publicans too would have had their share in the value of *commissa*,
forfeited as a result of the intervention of delators, unless of course the
delators had exposed a fraud that they had themselves perpetrated.[100]
Macer, writing about the same time as Marcian, stated in his work on
the *vicesima hereditatium* that a procurator was not entitled to compromise fiscal claims to that tax without imperial sanction. This has been
taken even by Cimma to show that by that time procurators were
responsible for its collection. That need not be so. It might be that they

---

[97] *Dig.* xxxix. 4. 16 *pr.*–1; for procuratorial jurisdiction cf. ch. 8; T. S. Vigorita, *Secta temporum meorum* (1978), 57 ff.

[98] Pflaum no. 282 (*ILS* 1411), cf. *Dig.* xlix. 14. 3. 9 (Hadrian) and 4. 7 (Marcus).

[99] *Dig.* xxxix. 4. 16. 1 f. (Sev. and Carac.), 4 (Pius), 6 (Marcus, referring to *publicani*), 9 (Pius), 11–14 (Sev. and Carac., or Carac. alone, referring to *publicani*).

[100] Delators: *RE* iv. 2427 f. (Kleinfeller). G. Klingenberg, *Commissum: Der Verfall nichtdeklarierter Sachen in röm. Zollrecht* (1977) was wrong to hold that delation had no place where publicans were employed: cf. Wilcken, *Chr.* 273 col. III, and for Ptolemaic practice *P. Hibeh* 29, as well as *Dig.* xxxix. 4. 16. 6 and 12; indeed, though he is right to say that the excerpt from Marcian does not imply *throughout* that the *portoria* were farmed, the references to publicans in a treatise on delators implies in itself that the latter had a role when they were employed, and the specific cases given show that it was not restricted to frauds on the *fiscus* by publicans (which do not happen to be mentioned). *Res vectigalis*: Ulp., *Dig.* xxxix. 4. 14. Very probably rules on delation similar to those for *portoria* applied to the *vicesimae* etc., which were of no concern to Justinian's compilers, since unlike *portoria* they were no longer levied.

simply had jurisdiction between farmers working for a percentage and taxpayers, and were forbidden to rule out claims made for payment in full on the ground that they themselves had agreed to a compromise settlement, unless that had been expressly sanctioned by the emperor. (See also p. 171 n. 29.)[101]

Procurators, who may themselves have leased the contracts to publicans (but cf. n. 95) presumably received for them the instalments due under the contracts. The money must often have been needed to meet government expenditure incurred locally, and for this purpose would be held for a time in their own chests. They would in any event have had to account to Rome for all the sums that passed through their hands, as well as to audit the accounts of tax-farmers, at least if the latter worked for a percentage. For all these purposes they needed accountants, cashiers, scribes, copyists, archivists, messengers, and the like. These are the *arcarii, commentarienses, contrascriptores, dispensatores, librarii, tabellarii, tabularii*, whose precise functions are not always to be discerned from their appellations. *Vilici* (who may have *vicarii* as deputies) and *praepositi* are presumably persons placed at the head of a particular office or a group of other employees, and *actores* persons who are given some power to act on behalf of the administration. Publicans (and other private persons) who also had to keep accounts and records naturally had employees with the same appellations. Hence for any tax that was farmed under procuratorial supervision, the proceeds of which passed from the publicans to the procurators, there would simultaneously have been *arcarii* etc. in the offices of both publicans and procurators. It is curious that as it happens we hardly find outside Egypt employees of either with designations that unambiguously show them to have been concerned with the work of demanding and receiving money from the taxpayers. I know of only four *scrutatores*, whose duty, like that of the *eraunetai* attested in some papyri, was presumably to search out merchandise liable to customs-duties. Two of them are imperial slaves. With this exception, the titles of procuratorial staff furnish no proof that they were engaged in collection rather than in control of tax-collectors.[102]

To summarize this section, it can be plausibly argued that it was necessary from the first to farm the new Augustan taxes on a

---

[101] *Dig.* ii. 15. 13, cf. Eck 144 (*contra* Cimma 143). The dictum was preserved by the compilers evidently because they gave it a general applicability; the *vicesima* itself had been abolished.

[102] On these appellations see P. R. C. Weaver, *Familia Caesaris* (1972), chs. 16–19; *Diz. Ep.* s.v. *arcarius, commentarii, contrascriptor, dispensator, librarius, RE* s.v. *tabularius*. De Laet listed those attested for *portoria* (see his Index), Hirschfeld those in other fiscal departments; they are also found in other public offices and in private establishments. *Scrutatores*, all in Illyricum: *CIL* iii. 1568 (of publicans), 14354, 27 (of *statio*), *AE* 1933. 180 (AD 211), 1974. 485 (both imperial slaves). *Eraunetai*: de Laet 419, see for rummaging of merchandise Wilcken, *Chr.* 273.

percentage basis and that the adoption of this system for other taxes, previously farmed for lump sums, helps to explain why tax-farmers were subjected to closer official supervision; the change must be presumed if the collection of large revenues was ever leased to *Einzelpächter*, though I doubt if that was practicable under any system. The evidence which shows that the *fiscus* had a direct interest in the proceeds of certain taxes is compatible with the hypothesis that they were still farmed, but for a percentage, just as much as with that of direct collection, and the functions of procuratorial staff deducible from their designations might almost always be functions of control rather than of collection. There were certainly reasons why the government would have preferred tax-farming, and it is clear that it was never abandoned altogether. We therefore need to find specific evidence to demonstrate its disuse in any particular case.

V. THE PAUCITY OF EVIDENCE

Our ignorance of Roman finances in both Republic and Principate is profound. No ancient treatment survives.[103] For the Principate there is nothing comparable to the material on the Sicilian tithes found in the *Verrines*, and we owe this material to the accidents that Cicero undertook the prosecution of Verres and published his indictment in order to immortalize his eloquence. We can hardly complain that historians like Tacitus give us little information on taxation; standard histories on a similar scale of modern countries tell no more. It is fortuitous if occasional allusions are found in other literary works preserved for their stylistic merits. Inscriptions are sparse and seldom perspicuous. What is known for one part of the empire need not apply to others. It is demonstrable that direct taxation took different forms in different provinces. The universality of capitation taxes and the liability of moveables to taxes on property can be disputed.[104] The rates of *portoria* were 5 per cent in Republican Sicily, $2\frac{1}{2}$ per cent in imperial Gaul and Asia, 2 per cent, later $2\frac{1}{2}$ per cent, in imperial Spain, 25 per cent on traffic crossing the eastern frontiers; no others are on record, but some impost of 5 per cent was at one time levied in Illyricum.[105] We cannot even draw up a complete list of all imperial taxes. An inscription has recently disclosed an unsuspected impost on nails

---

[103] Unfortunately Appian's book on the subject (*pr.* 15) is lost.

[104] See ch. 15 with addenda (pp. 531 ff.).

[105] See p. 431 for de Laet's speculations on the Illyrian rate. No doubt we can assume that the rates on traffic within the empire were all fairly low, and the rates on traffic with the east may have been much higher than those on other frontiers.

collected by publicans in Asia under Hadrian.[106] Rabbinic texts reveal that in Judaea tax-collectors might enter houses and steal goods from them; this may suggest the existence of some sort of excise duty, of which we know nothing.[107] In Egypt there was an immense variety of taxes. It is supposed that this was peculiar to that province. But it is only in Egypt that papyri and ostraca supply relatively abundant information. The so-called *lex metalli Vipascensis* (n. 144) shows that at least on an imperial domain the government was not averse to levying all kinds of petty imposts (which were farmed out), though perhaps only to meet local expenditure in much the same way as municipal revenues met municipal costs. Even in Egypt the nature of some imposts remains obscure, and some are attested only in a few tax-receipts. As for collection Wallace observed that little is known there of tax-farming in the Roman period.[108] Numerous other examples of our ignorance will be given later. All this should make us very wary of confident dogmas. Arguments from silence have little weight, unless we can give reasons for thinking that the silence is not to be expected. In regard to modes of collection the very contrary is the case.

It is particularly imprudent to infer that publicans were not used, if they are not attested. We hear much of them in the Republic, because they then had considerable political influence, and Cicero, our chief source, was closely connected with them. In the Principate their influence had vanished, at least from sight, and no author whose works survive had any special interest in their operations. Literary allusions are therefore rare. Only the fragments of classical jurists show that they were still important as late as the Severan epoch. The value of their testimony has been minimized by scholars who have constructed theories on the basis of epigraphic material. But the theories rest not so much on the explicit testimony of inscriptions as on questionable interpretations of them, and on deductions from the mere disappearance of epigraphic allusions. Now nearly all the inscriptions which do mention companies or individuals engaged in tax-farming are tombstones or memorials of votive offerings, erected by their freedmen or slaves, who incidentally record their patrons or owners. The fortuitous character of this evidence is shown by the facts that far more of those relating to *portoria* are found in Illyricum, a region not rich in inscriptions, than anywhere else, and more for the *vicesima libertatis* than for the remaining taxes. The relative dearth of data from Africa, where in general inscriptions abound, may also be noted. A few

---

[106] J. M. Reynolds, *Aphrodisias and Rome* (1982), no. 15.

[107] *Hagigah* 3, 6; *Tohoroth* 7, 6 (I rely on H. Danby's tr. of the Mishnah). On tax-collectors in Judaea cf. Rostovtzeff 475 ff., M. Goodman, *State and Society in Roman Galilee* (1983) 132 f.

[108] Wallace 288, cf. App. I.

publicans also appear in their own dedications. But they never made a habit of setting out their careers like officials; some of those who did declare their activity in tax-farming also had official posts to commemorate. According to Suetonius the Asian provincials honoured Vespasian's father in an inscription for his good conduct as a publican; there is only one epigraphic parallel extant.[109] We can well understand that they were not often the subjects of laudatory decrees. The collection of taxes did not win men's hearts. Nor was it anything to boast of. Collectors of *tributum* appointed by cities seldom allude to this function in surviving inscriptions, and then only when they could extol the generosity they had displayed.[110] Even of procurators administering specific revenues only a minute proportion have left any record on stone or bronze, mostly those who later attained higher eminence.[111] Men were perhaps little minded to honour even officials whom they saw as instruments of fiscal exactions. Epigraphic silences can thus never prove that one mode of collection rather than another was in use. Yet they are the chief support for some current dogmas. *Non liquet* is a more judicious conclusion.

VI. COLLECTION OF TRIBUTUM

Meagre as the evidence is, it seems to me sufficient to show that in the Severan period the collection of *tributum* was demitted to local authorities within the territories where their writ ran (p. 339 f.). This must already have been the case in the Republic wherever Rome imposed a 'certum stipendium' on communities. Cicero tells us that the Spaniards and most or very many ('plerique') of the 'Poeni' in Africa were thus assessed.[112] I think it likely that the same practice was observed in the old province of Transalpine Gaul and was extended by Caesar to the Gallic peoples he conquered.[113] Sicily may already have been the only western province in Republican times where tribute from all the communities was collected by publicans. That practice was apparently universal in the east. However, in 47 Caesar eliminated publicans from

---

[109] Suet., *Vesp.* 1; *ILS* 1465.

[110] *IGRR* iii. 488, 739 II (cf. 86. 7), iv. 259; *IG* xii. 3. 226. An emperor commends one man's efficiency, *IGRR* iv. 1441.

[111] Brunt, *JRS* (1983), App. I, esp. 14–20.

[112] *Verr.* ii. 3. 12.

[113] Publicans in Gaul mentioned by Cicero (*Font.* 12, 46) may have collected only *portoria* and *scriptura*; Fonteius demanded grain and money directly from the *civitates* (12, 19, 26). Caesar imposed tribute in Gallia Comata (*BG* vii. 76. 1), but also in Britain (v. 22. 4), where publicans could not have been used. Suet., *Caesar* 25. 1, suggests lump sum assessments, cf. Dio xlix. 35. 2 (35 BC) for Alpine tribes.

the collection of tribute on the cities of Asia and made the cities themselves responsible (n. 85). The same considerations which presumably led him to take this measure in Asia would have applied equally to all the eastern provinces, and it need not be significant that it is expressly attested for Asia alone. In fact it can be inferred from documents preserved by Josephus that he made the same change for the client but tributary state of Judaea.[114]

In Sicily the grain tithe had been farmed locally to *Einzelpächter*. Appian says that in 39 under the agreement made between the triumvirs and Sextus Pompey Sicily was to send to Rome the grain that had long ago been 'assessed' ($\tau\epsilon\tau\alpha\gamma\mu\acute{\epsilon}\nu o\nu$). This word in itself might suggest that Sicily now had to furnish a fixed quantum of grain rather than the tithes of Verres' time. But the phrase 'long ago' makes against this interpretation; more probably Appian simply means that the exportation of the tithes of grain to Rome, intermitted since Sextus had ruled the island, was to be resumed in the traditional way. This, however, would not entail that the tithes were still farmed to publicans. It had always been possible for a city to contract for its own tithe, and the local authorities could have been charged with the task of furnishing their quotas. The agreement was abortive, and in 36, after finally defeating Sextus, Octavian demanded an 'eisphora' of 1,600 Talents from the Sicilian cities. 'Eisphora' should denote a levy on capital, and Octavian might have imposed such a levy, like that which Sulla imposed on the Asian cities in 84 (chapter 1), as a once-for-all indemnity for the loss of Sicilian revenues during Sextus' occupation. This would not imply that he changed the traditional form of annual taxation. On the other hand, there is nothing to show that Caesar's abolition of farming *tributum* had not affected Sicily, subject to the rider that payment was still to be made in grain and not in cash. In fact we know nothing of imperial taxation in Sicily. The 'frumentum mancipale' attested in Trajan's reign may be rent from public domains collected by publicans (n. 125) such as the *ager Leontinus* (n. 117).[115]

In general, whatever may have been the position in Sicily, it seems probable that after Caesar Roman publicans were not used in general to collect *tributum*, where the task could be committed to local authorities, who might conceivably have employed their own (cf. n. 3); at any rate no emperor is credited with creating the system that operated in the third century and thereafter. Communal assessments in Asia are reported under Augustus.[116] However, Ulpian refers to publicans, i.e.

[114] Jos., *AJ* xiv. 201, cf. Rostovtzeff 475 ff. D. C. Braund, *Klio* (1983), 241 ff. refutes the theory that Gabinius had already eliminated publicans from Syria and Judaea.

[115] App., *BC* v. 72, 129, cf. n. 125 with text; on Pliny, *NH* iii. 88–91 see p. 327. Cities contracting for tithes: *Verr.* ii. 3. 72, 77, 99.

[116] Strabo x. 5. 3; xiv. 2. 19; cf. *SB Wien* 1969, 7 ff. (early Principate).

Roman publicans, collecting *tributum* (*Dig.* xxxix. 4. 1. 1). Where might this have been? (1) Perhaps on large estates, private as well as imperial, which lay ouside city territories. The dues exacted from *coloni* on imperial domains in Africa may have represented their liability to tax as well as rent, and they were collected by *conductores*, who ranked as publicans on Ulpian's definition (n. 5); of course in the Republic publicans had collected revenues from public lands in the provinces.[117] So too private owners of estates outside city territories might have paid tax to publicans rather than direct to officials.[118] (2) Perhaps in communities which lacked city status. In Asia for instance we hear of the 'cities, nations and peoples' which comprised the province (e.g. *SIG*³ 760), but it was the Asian *cities* to which Caesar is said to have transferred the collection of *tributum* (n. 85). Not indeed that it was only communities organized on the pattern of Greek or Italian cities that could be entrusted with the task. The priestly administration of Jerusalem was performing it in 66.[119] But if the government expected the local authorities to provide adequate security for payment of what was due, it would naturally employ other modes of collection where this condition could not be fulfilled. In the wildest areas indeed publicans could not act with safety; soldiers seem to have exacted the hides which the Frisians paid as tax under Tiberius.[120] But among more peaceful tribes publicans could still have operated. The progressive elevation of tribal units to city status in Asia[121] may betoken *inter alia* that their governments were considered equal to the task of collecting tribute.

A dedication of AD 6/7 at Ephesus by publicans 'ex pecunia phorica' may then refer to tribute they were still collecting outside city territories, though it is conceivable that the *phoros* from which the fund

---

[117] In Sicily the *ager Leontinus*, which was public and subject to a rent in money leased at Rome (*Verr.* ii. 3. 13, 53; *Phil.* ii. 101; iii. 22), also paid tithes in grain farmed locally (*Verr.* ii. 3. 110 ff.). In Bithynia the former royal domains, now public, were 'enjoyed' by publicans, who presumably collected rents and *scriptura* (Cic., *de leg. agr.* ii. 40, 50). For Africa see n. 124.

[118] Frontinus 46, 5, 53 L for private estates, cf. *Dig.* xi. 4. 1. 1 and 3. A constitution of 366 shows that then large proprietors were charged with collection from their *coloni* (*CJ* xi. 48 (47). 4. 1.). Procuratorial jurisdiction over the inhabitants of some imperial estates (ch. 8) shows that these too might be outside city territories, but the restrictions on the liability of *coloni* on such estates to *munera* in cities (l. 1. 38. 1 and 6. 6. 11) would surely have been needless if all were; the confiscated lands of Hipparchus (*PIR*² C 889) presumably remained within the territory of Athens. In the 3rd c. the *coloni* of a Lydian estate protest against the oppressive behaviour of municipal officials 'on the pretext of magistracies or liturgies' (Abbott and Johnson, *Munic. Admin. in the Roman Empire* (1926), no. 142). Cf. also p. 339 on *Dig.* xix. 1. 52 *pr.* for a *conductor* levying *tributa* on an estate.

[119] Jos., *BJ* ii. 405–7.

[120] *Ann.* iv. 72, cf. p. 339; App. I. 4. It was perhaps chiefly when soldiers were employed that 'corporum verbera', as well as 'ademptiones bonorum' (presumably always the ultimate sanction for non-payment) might occur (*Ann.* iv. 6. 4).

[121] Broughton, *ESAR* iv. 704–6; C. Habicht, *JRS* (1975), 64 ff.

derived was rent on public domains, including *scriptura* on animals pastured thereon.[122] We also have a dedication to a quaestor, Fonteius, by the 'mancup[es] stipend[iorum] ex Africa'. This cannot be dated, except that Fonteius' lack of a cognomen suggests that it is from the Republic or early empire: so it may be pre-Caesarian.[123] It may be recalled that according to Cicero it was only 'plerique Poenorum' who paid a fixed sum as tribute. Perhaps these 'stipendiary' cities farmed out local taxes to their own 'mancupes', the proceeds of which were to meet their liability to Rome. Perhaps African peoples without a civic organization paid quotas of produce through publicans in Cicero's time and later. The *lex agraria* of 111 BC shows that occupiers of public land in Africa paid to publicans *vectigal* or *decumae* or *scriptura*, i.e. either a fixed rent (*vectigal*), plus tithes on arable and *scriptura* for grazing animals on pasture land, or a *vectigal* which consisted in tithes or *scriptura*. These occupiers are distinguished from the *stipendiarii*.[124] However, as the payments they made were equivalent to *stipendium*, the distinction may not have been always observed, and the 'mancup[es] stipend[iorum]' may perhaps have been the farmers of dues paid by the occupiers of the public domains. C. Vibius Salutaris, who flourished under Trajan, was 'promagister portuum provinciae Siciliae item promagister frumenti mancipalis', i.e. he was the local manager of publican companies.[125] The meaning of *frumentum mancipale* is obscure. If it was the Sicilian tithe, then not only had tax-farming of tribute survived in Sicily but it had been transferred from the local *Einzelpächter* of old to a Roman company. But *frumentum mancipale* may be the rent in kind obtained from *ager publicus* (cf. n. 117). The same term appears in two other inscriptions, one from Spain and dated to Pius' reign, where it might be similarly explained.[126] The *decumani* known from two other inscriptions at Rome may have collected tithes either from public domains or from lands outside city territories.[127] At any rate none of these texts proves that the government did not rely for collection of *tributum* on local authorities within their own territiories, in so far as they could furnish security.

What then of Tacitus' statement that in the first period of Tiberius' reign down to 24 'frumenta et pecuniae vectigales, cetera publicorum

---

[122] *AE* 1968. 483, cf. pp. 339 f., but if Broughton 510 f. is right that there was little public or imperial domain land in Asia, the former view may be preferred.

[123] *ILS* 901.

[124] *FIRA* i². no. 8. 82–9, contrast 77–80.

[125] e.g. *ILS* 7193 f.; the Greek rendering of *promagister* as *archones* (cf. also n. 156) refutes the view that Vibius was as such an official, even though later or earlier he held official posts.

[126] *CIL* ii. 1197; *ILS* 1536, see Hirschfeld 141–3. Note also later procurators concerned with *frumentum* from public domains, Pflaum pp. 727 ff.

[127] *CIL* vi 8585 f.

fructuum   societatibus   equitum   Romanorum   agitabantur'
(*Ann.* iv. 6. 3)? He is surely implying that what was true then ceased to
be true either in the latter part of the reign or at any rate by his own
day. This has often been taken to show that Tiberius later abolished or
reduced the farming of taxes, or rather of direct taxes. But what does
his statement of the position down to 24 actually mean? Is he telling us
that equestrian companies farmed all the direct revenues in kind
('frumenta') and cash ('pecuniae vectigales') as well as all other
imposts ('cetera publicorum fructuum')? On this interpretation they
were then responsible for collecting tribute not only in the provinces in
which Caesar had transferred the task to local governments but also in
those where it had never been farmed in the Republic. Caesar's reform
would have been more than undone, and must have been repeated by
Tiberius or some later emperor. No explanation of the changes comes
to mind. There is nothing of them in the sources. Perhaps in this
instance an argument from silence is less hazardous than usual. To
judge from his account of Nero's projected abolition and eventual
reforms of the *portoria*, Tacitus himself would not have passed over so
momentous a measure. It is true that his narrative survives only for
some thirty years of the period between 24 and the time when he wrote,
and that a reform could be placed in one of the gaps. However,
Suetonius, who had some interest in administrative changes is also
silent. Moreover, we must note that there is no warrant for confining
any supposed alteration in the system of tax collection after 24 to the
direct taxes. If Tacitus implies that at some date after 24 equestrian
companies ceased to collect taxes, this should include the indirect taxes
too. But they were certainly farmed in and beyond Tacitus' own
lifetime.

   It may first be observed that there is no clear implication that
Tiberius himself made any change. Not every feature of the early part
of his reign that Tacitus describes altered later; for example there was
no obvious difference in the type of men advanced to the higher
magistracies, and 'sua consulibus, sua praetoribus species' remained
true to the end. Tacitus was perhaps simply enlarging on the point that
after 24 Tiberius' rule gravely degenerated: till then he had observed
all the traditional proprieties. In fact it was Tiberius' general principle
to adhere to the principles and policies of Augustus; he was not a
reformer, and never less likely to have introduced any sweeping change
in the tax system than in the only years (29–31) for which Tacitus'
narrative is lost, and his silence therefore explicable.[128]

   [128] On *Annals* iv. 6. 3 see esp. Mommsen, *St.R* ii³. 1017, Hirschfeld 68 f. Wilcken, *Grundzüge*,
212 f. adduced a trivial change to direct collection in Egypt under Tiberius; J. D. Thomas, *Das
röm.-byz. Aegypten (Aegyptiaca Treverensia)* (1983), 35 ff., does not establish any considerable

Ambiguities often arise in Latin from its lack of definite and indefinite articles. Hence the reference to 'frumenta et pecuniae vectigales' which in contrast to 'cetera publicorum fructuum' surely denotes tribute in grain or cash, does not necessarily mean that *all* the tribute was farmed to companies of Roman Equites but only that *some* was. As we have seen, there is other evidence for such farming long after Tiberius' or Tacitus' time. No doubt the phrase 'cetera publicorum fructuum' implies (as 'alii publici fructus' would not) that all the other imposts were so farmed. (This was of course untrue of Egypt, and there, Roman companies were never involved; of arrangements in Egypt Tacitus probably knew nothing).

Tacitus certainly implies that the traditional practice observed till 24 had been abandoned later, though perhaps only by the time when he wrote. Yet even then tax-farming remained the rule for indirect taxes, conceivably without exceptions; scholars who believe in the introduction of direct collection date it to Hadrian or later. The emphasis must then be placed on 'societatibus equitum Romanorum'. The old companies had been extruded. That suggestion would fit well with modern hypotheses that they were displaced by *Einzelpächter*. If these too are to be rejected, the change at which Tacitus hints may have consisted in the fact that the equestrian monopoly had disappeared. It is certain (n. 28) that in law Equites had never had the exclusive right to participate in public contracts, but in practice they had dominated the companies. This domination might easily have ended, if the contracts were often leased in the provinces, and to provincials; it would be a mere accident, if some of these provincials enjoyed equestrian status. But this change too cannot be attributed to Tiberius: it would seem that for the *portoria* at least the old companies were still functioning under Nero. (n. 56). If it occurred, it may have been a gradual process, which could easily have passed unrecorded.

VII. PUBLICANS AND STATE DOMAINS

Domains owned by the state, which in the Principate came under imperial management (p. 146), or by the emperor, including not only arable, pastoral, and orchard lands but mines, quarries, salt deposits,

replacement of tax-farmers there by liturgical officials in his reign. De Laet, besides ascribing specific reforms to Tiberius, writes of his 'vast reform of the financial organization of the empire' (363 ff.); this is sheer fantasy, and incompatible with Tiberius' generally conservative policy (Brunt, *CQ* (1984), 424–6). His action in depriving many cities of immunity or of the right to raise certain revenues (Suet., *Tib*. 49) is of course irrelevant.

etc., could be exploited in various ways.[129] (1) They might be managed by officials, directing labour owned or hired by state or emperor. This method, unknown in the Republic, became practicable in the Principate, when the emperor, like any private individual, could entrust a domain to the management of procurators, *actores*, and *vilici*.[130] (2) They might be leased to individuals or companies, or left to occupiers, paying dues equivalent to rent or to both rent and tax on a customary basis, under varying degrees of official supervision. The rent or dues might be payable either direct to officials (in Egypt often liturgical) or to publicans to whom collection was farmed out. (3) In the Republic at least it was usual not to grant exclusive leases of pastoral land in state ownership, but to allow graziers to pasture their animals on it, in return for a fee per animal (*scriptura*) collected by publicans.[131]

Rent from public land was a *vectigal*, and on the basis that 'eum qui vectigal populi Romani conductum habet, "publicanum" appellamus' (Gaius), the lessees of some public properties were described as publicans; Ulpian asserts that 'omnes, qui quid ['quod', MSS] a fisco conducunt, recte appellantur publicani'. This was certainly the name given to lessees of public mines in the Republic and later. Yet usage was hardly consistent; the tenants of public lands in Campania in the Republic were, for instance, not so described. Gaius was uneasy about it; he writes 'hi qui salinas et cretifodinas et metalla habent publicanorum loco sunt'.[132] There was no true legal distinction between the lessees of a single farm and a large mining area, and if the latter but not the former were called publicans, it was probably because they were organized in companies, like the collectors of taxes, and because the revenues were comparable in importance to taxes. The 'publicans' concerned could obviously also be termed 'conductores', and this term can be applied in the Principate both to those who rented the right to exploit public domains for their own account, and to those who leased the right to collect dues from persons actually engaged in the farming, mining, etc. (Tenants of small farms on public land are usually called *coloni*, but one may note the phrase used by Severus Alexander (*CJ* v. 62. 8): 'coloni, id est conductores'; the latter term was not strictly inappropriate for any lease-holders.)

Imperial evidence on the methods of exploiting public domains is scattered, often equivocal, and never abundant. It is tempting to use

[129] I shall not distinguish here between the old public domains of the Republic and those of the emperor (whether appertaining to the *fiscus*, *patrimonium*, or *res privata*), on which see D. J. Crawford *ap.* M. I. Finley, *Studies in Roman Property* (1976), 35 ff.

[130] For use of this method in Italy see Crawford (n. 129) 44, 47, 50; Hirschfeld 136 n. 3, 137-9.

[131] *RE* ii A 904 f. (Kübler); Cimma 19 f.

[132] Gaius in *Dig.* l. 16. 16 *pr.*, cf. xxxix. 4. 13 *pr.*, Ulp. in xxxix. 4. 1. 1 (n. 5). Publicans in mining: Livy xlv. 18. 3 f.; Pliny, *NH* xxxiii. 78.

what is known for some particular region or domain to interpret ambiguous indications for others. The temptation should be resisted. Uniformity was never an objective in imperial policy. It is my purpose to question hypotheses that resolve perplexities which ought to leave judgement in suspense.

In Egypt small tenants on domain land paid their rents to officials. This became the normal practice elsewhere in the late empire, but in the Principate outside Egypt the necessary bureaucratic machinery was lacking, especially for the conveyance of rents paid in kind to central points of delivery (p. 379).[133]

On certain African domains of which we happen to be informed the cultivators (*coloni*) paid their dues in kind under a sort of emphyteutic tenure through *conductores*. As they also had to provide the latter with labour for ploughing and harvest, it appears that the *conductores* themselves had their own farms on the domains. Some take them to be tenants-in-chiefs of the *fiscus*, and the *coloni* to be their subtenants; others think that they had leased part of the domains for themselves, together with the right to collect dues from the *coloni*. The latter might be regarded as occupiers rather than tenants in a contractual relation with the *fiscus*; in any event they had specified obligations to the *fiscus* and rights guaranteed by the emperor.[134] The *conductores* on these estates were doubtless *Einzelpächter*. *Conductores* or *misthotai* are attested elsewhere,[135] but we cannot say if they were all of the same type, and never simple tenants of large estates who, like lessees from private proprietors, rented the land from the *fiscus* and cultivated it with slave or hired labour or with subtenants, whose rights and obligations were determined simply by their contractual relation with the *conductores* and not by imperial regulations of the African kind. On the imperial estates in Asia Minor we also find members of the imperial *familia* as *oikonomoi* or *vilici*; perhaps they managed farms with a servile or free labour force for the direct account of the *fiscus*.[136] The attested procurators of domains and their staffs could have supervised the administration of imperial estates under any of these systems. In addition they exercised within them the same kind of governmental authority as appertained to local authorities within the territories of cities (pp. 183 ff.). Their presence, however, is not enough to show that they must have been

---

[133] App. I. 4: Wallace ch. IV; Jones, *Later Roman Empire* (1964), 417.

[134] FIRA i², 100–3. The cultivators of the Lydian estate mentioned in n. 118 were probably not tenants but occupiers on customary terms (note τὸ τῆς γεωργίας δίκαιον). We must beware of assuming that peasants on public or imperial estates in one area had the same rights and obligations as in any other.

[135] *Diz. Ep.* s.v. *conductor* (Rostovtzeff) 587 ff. Cf. *Dig.* xix. 2. 49 (Modestinus); xlix. 14. 3. 6 (rescript of Hadrian); xlix. 14. 45. 13 (Paul); l. 6. 6. 10 (Callistratus).

[136] Broughton, *ESAR* iv. 648–63, cf. 672–4 for *misthotai* of private proprietors.

engaged in precisely the same functions as in Africa. We have no warrant for believing in uniformity from province to province in the exploitation of domains any more than in the modes of taxation.

On pastoral land the survival of the *scriptura* (n. 131) is in my view implied by a fragment of Ulpian (n. 12). Rostovtzeff, however, denied it. We hear of the 'publicani qui pascua conducunt' in Cyrene, and three inscriptions refer each to a *conductor pascui*, associated with *salinae*;[137] he took them to be simply lessees of grazing lands and salt deposits. This interpretation of the Latin terms is not inevitable. When Cicero writes 'Asiam qui de censoribus conduxerunt' (*Att.* 1. 17. 9), he means that the publicans had leased not the possession of Asia but the right to collect taxes there. By analogy the *conductor pascui* could be the lessee of the right to levy *scriptura*. But even if Rostovtzeff were certainly right, four instances would not be enough to establish the universality of the practice he envisages. It would indeed hardly have been practicable except where grazing land could be delimited and parcelled out in such a way as to ensure exclusive rights to the lessees. But that condition could scarcely be fulfilled in areas like the high plateaux of the Apennines, which provided summer pasturage, or the parts of Libya into which nomadic or semi-nomadic peoples moved their flocks. In such cases the continued imposition of *scriptura* was the most natural procedure. Nor can we argue *e silentio* that it was no longer farmed to companies, which like other publicans might have left no epigraphic record in the Principate any more than in the Republic. Dearth of evidence shrouds the whole subject in obscurity. Of course the emperor could pasture his own animals on public land free of tax. He might, like private stockbreeders, have placed his herds and flocks in the charge of his own freedmen and slaves. He certainly did not always choose to do so: he might lease them to *conductores*.[138]

Let us turn to mines, quarries, and the like. Publican companies concerned in mining were among those whose importance in his own day Polybius attests (vi. 17). It may be that he had in mind particularly those operating in Italy, but it was natural for the Republic to extend their use to publicly owned mines in the provinces. We hear of their

---

[137] Rostovtzeff 410 f., citing Pliny, *NH* xix. 39; *CIL* iii. 1209, 1363 (cf. Hirschfeld 150 n. 4); see also *AE* 1937. 141; 1967. 388. Where a *conductor* leased both *pascua* and *salinae*, he might *either* have rented the area in which there were both pasture land and salt deposits, *or* have farmed both *scriptura* and dues from salt extractors; a 'conduc(tor) pascui salinar(um) et commercior(um)' in *CIL* iii. 1209 presumably also levied tolls on local trade. The connection between *conductores salinarum* and contractors who at various times enjoyed a monopoly of the sale of salt (Rostovtzeff 412) is quite unclear. *Socii* collecting a *scriptura* in Africa *may* be attested in *AE* 1912, 209 (Cimma 119 n. 105).

[138] *Dig.* xxxix. 4. 9. 8 (Pauline *Sententiae*): 'fiscus ab omnium vectigalium praestationibus immunis est'. See App. iii.

activity in Gallia Cisalpina, and the famous decision of the senate to close the gold and silver mines in Macedon rather than lease them to publicans who would oppress the natives shows that it was taken for granted that Rome could only work provincial mines by the instrumentality of a company that would be strong enough to be oppressive; this must reflect experience gained elsewhere.[139] Spain rather than Cisalpina is the region where the lesson would have been learned, in view of the abundance of the metals mined there. It has indeed been argued that, as the accounts that we possess of Republican mining operations in Spain, derived from Polybius and Posidonius, do not refer explicitly to publican companies, the pits might have been leased to relatively small operators such as we find in imperial Vipasca (below).[140] I doubt if the regime at Vipasca could have been adopted before imperial procurators were available to administer it. The scale of Republican operations at New Carthage, as reported by Strabo, must have demanded the investment of substantial capital, not least in the purchase of slaves. It is true that all but one of the extant ingots of lead from the area are marked with the names of individual Italians, but they might have been managers or subcontractors of the company. Even if extraction was in the hands of numerous small entrepreneurs, the smelting, transportation, and marketing of the refined product surely demanded a large organization. However, Strabo (n. 140) remarks that in the late Republic the Spanish mines were privatized; it was in the Principate that public ownership of mines in the empire was resumed, probably by a gradual process; municipal or private ownership is still attested.[141] There was then no continuity in the leasing of mines to companies from the Republic to the Principate, at least in Spain.

The existence of such companies in the second century AD is attested by Gaius (n. 53). His reference to *aurifodinae* and *argentifodinae* naturally suggests that they engaged in the actual extraction of ore; one inscription reveals a 'societ[as] argent[ariarum] fod[inarum] mont[is] Ilucr[onis]' (n. 140). Pliny writes of the *locatio*, apparently as single units, of lead mines in Spain for annual rentals of 200,000, 250,000, and 100,000 *denarii*. The gold mines in Asturia, for which large-scale engineering works were required and which according to Pliny produced 20,000 pounds of gold (22,500,000 *denarii*) a year, were also surely leased to one or more companies with the necessary capital for

[139] Pliny, *NH* xxxiii. 78; Strabo iv. 6. 7 (Cisalpina); Livy xlv. 18. 3 f. (Macedon).
[140] J. S. Richardson, *JRS* (1976), 139 ff., citing. Diod. (Posid.) v. 35–8; Polyb. *ap.* Strabo iii. 2. 10 (8 f. may relate to extraction of ore by native Spaniards only); p. 146 for inscribed ingots, one marked 'societ. argent. fod. mont. Ilucr.' (*ILS* 8708, perhaps Augustan).
[141] Hirschfeld 146–50, 158; there was never a state monopoly.

extraction. But we also hear of a company responsible for the refinement of cinnabar after it had been conveyed from Spain or Asia to Rome; it may also have effected the extraction and transportation, but we do not know.[142] In general we cannot be sure of the precise functions of *socii* or *societates* vaguely described as *aerarii*, *argentarii*, *picarii*, and the like; they were not all necessarily involved in extraction as well as in refinement, transportation,, or marketing. In my judgement *conductores*, where attested, as well as *mancipes*, may be connected with either a partnership or a corporation of the kind Gaius mentions, and other individuals named as concerned in the exploitation of mines may also be members or employees of a *societas*; thus we cannot differentiate between the positions of L. Arucanius Verecundus metalli Lutudarensis and Ti. Claudius Tr... Lut[udarensis] Br[itannici] ex arg[entariis], and take the former to be an individual entrepreneur and the latter to be one of the *socii* engaged in these silver mining operations who are explicitly mentioned in other inscriptions.[143]

The extraction of ore might be the business of individual small entrepreneurs called *coloni*, not *conductores*. This is most clearly revealed by two bronze tablets from the mining settlement of Vipasca in Portugal, administered by a procurator who was an imperial freedman, possessed of local jurisdiction. Each tablet is preserved only in part.[144] What remains of one, the so-called *lex metalli Vipascensis*, which has been dated *c.*100, relates to the leasing of various monopolies within Vipasca, e.g. for the upkeep of the public baths, to various *conductores*, who could have partners. It refers (v. 59) to the 'lex metallis dicta', which presumably comprised general regulations for all silver and copper mines in the public domain at least in Spain; there is also an allusion to a 'lex ferrariarum' (v. 34). The second document appears to be part of the former *lex*, amended by Hadrian, in whose reign it was inscribed. It shows that the procurator could assign a pit (*puteus*)

---

[142] Pliny, *NH* xxxiv. 165 (lead), xxxiii. 78 (gold) (cf. for engineering works P. R. Lewis and G. D. B. Jones, *JRS* (1970), 169 ff.; R. F. J. Jones and D. G. Bird, *JRS* (1972), 59 ff.), 118 f. (cinnabar, cf. Vitruv. vii. 9. 4, which shows that the same company refined ore from Asia; *ILS* 1875 f.).

[143] *Aerarii*: *AE* 1971. 181 (connected by Cimma 153 n. 253 with the *flatura* of *aes* for the mint, cf. n. 24, *CIL* vi. 8455, xiv. 3642 and for silver, vi. 791, *AE* 1976. 737). *Argentarii*: n. 140. Lead company in Britain: *ILS* 8711; *JRS* 1941, 146. *Picarii*: *CIL*. xi. 6393. Sulphur producers: *ILS* 8712 f. *Ferrariarii*: Pflaum no. 52 (*CIL* xii. 671) gives a first century *promagister* in the Gallic provinces, i.e. a local manager of the company; cf. xiv. 4326 (slave of 'socior. vect. ferr.'). (*ILS* 8641 shows that a *clarissima*, probably related to Alexander Severus' wife, possessed a 'massa ferrariarum' in Gaul, leased to *socii* for a 'splendidissimum vectigal'; 'vectigal' is an unusual term for private rent, and was perhaps adopted here because the revenue from the mine had been diverted to her from the *fiscus*, and the same system of farming it to *socii* was kept up.) See also n. 153.

[144] *FIRA* i². 104 f., cf. D. Flach, *Chiron* (1979), 399 ff. for better texts with bibliography and commentary. The procurator at Vipasca was a freedman, cf. perhaps *AE* 1933. 273.

producing silver to an individual prospector in return for a down payment of 4,000 sesterces, and presumably less still for one producing copper. In certain circumstances the assignee forfeited his rights, and the pit could then be 'sold'. The *fiscus* retained a right to half the ore extracted. It is curious, since the down payments were apparently made direct to the procurator, that under the *lex metalli Vipascensis* a purchaser also had to pay to monopolist *conductores* percentages on the purchase price (vv. 3, 16), while anyone working a pit had to pay to another such *conductor* a *vectigal* for a certificate of his exclusive right of occupation (vv. 58 ff.). The down payments for each pit were small, but the *lex metallis dicta* envisages (v. 7) that an individual operator might be assigned five pits, which need not be a maximum, and of course he had to find money for equipment and for slaves or hired labour. He might be unable to proceed without partners, whose rights and obligations the *lex* lays out. One has the impression that the *coloni* could be small men, and they and their partners evidently did not constitute a corporate company.

The ore extracted, half belonging to the *fiscus*, has to be moved, with precautions against theft, from the pit-face to *officinae* where it is to be refined (vv. 25 ff.). Who is responsible for the refinement? Or for the transportation of the product to some larger centre and for its marketing? (No doubt the state was the chief customer). The *lex Vipascensis* shows that anyone might crush and refine ore left on slag heaps on payment of a *vectigal* to a *conductor* (vv. 47 ff.). This does not seem to have any bearing on the processing of the ore brought from the pits to the *officinae*, but there is a reference to the slaves and freedmen (not to other hired workers) of the 'flatores argentarii aerarii' (v. 56); the use of the plural may suggest that the process of refinement was leased to a company, and not simply to an individual, who might or might not have partners. It would in any event be unlikely that the procurator undertook it with his own staff. Even at the Roman mint such work was done by a contracting company (n. 143). Again how were the *coloni* paid for their share in the ore refined in the *officinae*? By the procurator? Or did the products of the pits at Vipasca pass, together with products of other pits in the province or peninsula, to *conductores* charged perhaps not only with the processing but with the transport and marketing of the refined metal, and did they pay both *coloni* and *fiscus* for their shares in the ore? Such *conductores* might have acquired ownership of the product in return for lump sum payments to the *fiscus*, or they might have shared the product with the *fiscus*. Many diverse arrangements could be surmised.

The procurator at Vipasca must have controlled a fair-sized staff drawn from the *familia Caesaris*, both for the general administration of the settlement and for invigilation of the mining and smelting in the interest of the *fiscus*; probably it also included soldiers, since they as well as the imperial freedmen and slaves are entitled to free bathing (*lex m.V.* v 23). It could reasonably have been said that the settlement and mining were under his *cura*. This is the expression used to designate the responsibility of some procurators in charge of imperial quarries. We have a number of other scattered testimonies both epigraphic and literary to procurators, Equites as well as freedmen, who administered particular mines or quarries, and to personnel drawn from the *familia Caesaris*. In Egypt and perhaps elsewhere military men acted in place of procurators. The earliest case on record in which we might suspect a regime like that at Vipasca to have existed is furnished by a dedication to a *vilicus* in Gaul by the 'familia Ti. Caesaris quae est in metallis' (*CIL* xiii. 1550). Wherever a mine or quarry required the presence of an imperial administrator on the spot, it was perhaps because he had functions similar to those of the procurator at Vipasca.[145]

It is unlikely that the actual work of extraction was commonly undertaken by employees of the state. In a few instances soldiers were detailed for mining,[146] but there seems to be no clear case of the use of civilian labour owned or hired by the *fiscus* and directed by the procurator. At most in quarrying, where it was important to produce blocks of specific size and quality, soldiers or imperial slaves and freedmen, presumably with the necessary technical qualification, might assume close control of operations;[147] the labour may still have been furnished by private occupiers or tenants, or contractors whose efficiency could be promoted by a profit incentive. As already remarked, an imperial slave could actually be given a lease for this purpose (n. 96). It is true that some convicts, *servi poenae*, were allotted to work in the 'metalla' (including quarries and salt deposits), but they could have been hired out by the *fiscus* to private operators; we know that under Trajan persons condemned to the lesser penalty of labouring on public works could be placed at the disposal of cities, and in the late empire convicts were assigned to work in private bakeries.[148] An official would have been needed to maintain discipline among them, as indeed among slaves employed by private entrepreneurs, and for this purpose he would probably have had some military force at his disposal; we have seen that soldiers were to be found at Vipasca. For

[145] *CIL* iii. 13239 f. (Dalmatian *ferrariae*); ii. 956, 1179 (Spanish copper); 2598 (Galician gold); Galen xii. 234 K, xiv. 7 K (Cyprus copper); quarries: Hirschfeld 164 n. 1. Egypt, ib. 172 f. Cf. perhaps Euseb., *Mart. Pal.* 13. 2 (Judaea).

[146] Tac., *Ann.* xi. 20; S. S. Frere, *Britannia*[2] (1974), 320 ff.; R. MacMullen, *Soldier and Civilian in the Late Roman Empire* (1963), 26 f., 31 f.

[147] Hirschfeld 162 ff.

[148] F. Millar, *PBSR* (1984), 137–43, cf. 132–7 (*opus publicum*), 143 (*pistrinum*).

that matter military protection must be assumed wherever precious metals were extracted, refined, and transported for the direct or indirect benefit of the *fiscus*. Probably it was mainly because of the gold mines in NW Spain that a legion was always retained there. Such protection was also afforded to some toll-stations.[149] It need not imply that private contractors had no part in the operations concerned.

Probably the nearest that the government got in general to public operation of 'metalla' was the allocation of particular pits or quarries to tenants or to occupiers of the Vipasca type under procuratorial superintendence. There is some evidence for such miners in both Moesia and Dacia under the Principate, and A. H. M. Jones held that in the late empire extraction was in the hands of small men, working individually or in groups.[150]

We cannot say if or when this system became universal. The *lex metallis dicta* of Vipasca antedates the writings of the jurist Gaius, in whose time corporate companies could still undertake the extraction of ore. It follows that if the *lex* applied to state mines throughout the empire, there must have been among the lost clauses provisions which either prescribed the rules under which mines were leased to corporations or excepted such cases from its scope. As argued above, the regime at Vipasca also left room for the use of large companies in refinement, transportation, and marketing. Whether the *conductores* of the iron mines in Noricum, sometimes in combination with those of Pannonia and Dalmatia, were representatives of such companies, or were *Einzelpächter*, there is no proof of Hirschfeld's view that their function was simply to collect a *vectigal* from small operators.[151] The various *conductores* at Vipasca, authorized to collect different dues from the *coloni*, appear to be petty local contractors, like those charged with the upkeep of the baths, and the chief payments made by the *coloni* seem to go direct to the local procurator. Nor is it significant that we hear alternatively of a lease of mines and of lease of a *vectigal* from mines, since the rent from mines itself counted as a *vectigal*.[152] The *conductores* mentioned surely contracted for some mining operations throughout the regions designated, and not just for particular pits, though not necessarily for extraction (n. 151). As in the case of the *portoria*, such *conductores* could be supervised by procurators with similar regional

---

[149] De Laet 226 n. 2, 307, cf. his conjectures, 140, 150 f., 153, 194, 208 f.

[150] *FIRA* iii. 150 (where 'conductor' denotes 'conductor operarum', not the lessee of a mine); A. Móczy, *Pannonia and Upper Moesia*, (1974) 134; 216 f. Jones, *Later Roman Empire*, 838 f.

[151] G. Alföldy, *Noricum* (1974), 115 f., who transcribes the Norican inscriptions dated in his view before Marcus; for the Dalmatian, J. Wilkes, *Dalmatia* (1969), 268 (early 3rd century); *AE* 1973, 411–14. Cf. Hirschfeld 152; of course *conductores ferrariarum* are not *necessarily* extractors of ore any more than *conductores pascui* are graziers.

[152] *Contra* Cimma 149 on *CIL* xiv. 4326.

circumscriptions. Thus documentation of *procuratores ferrariarum Galli-carum*, attested *c.*112–231, of *procuratores ferrariarum Dalmatiae* (third century), of *procuratores argentariarum Pannonicarum et Delmaticarum* (from Pius to 274) and *procuratores aurariarum (Dacicarum)*, and of imperial freedmen and slaves in their head offices does not prove in itself that they were superintending local managers of settlements like Vipasca,[153] though this might have been the case, rather than supervising the activities of contractors, perhaps corporations, interested in the entire business of mining throughout the areas concerned. It need hardly be said that such documentation as we have for procurators, companies, or *coloni* largely depends on chance; varying customs determined whether such persons wished to leave memorials of themselves, and accident whether the memorials have survived.[154] Thus no chronological arguments from silence are valid, and the extent and pace of the substitution of small operators for large companies cannot be reconstructed.

From all this it emerges that though the state may sometimes have exploited its property under the operational management of officials, directing a public labour force, it often preferred in one way or another to leave production in the hands of entrepreneurs from whom it collected a rent, and might lease to publicans the right to collect rents or dues from a multitude of small occupiers. All this should not predispose us to expect that it forsook the traditional practice of farming taxes other than the tribute. And tribute too was not normally collected outside Egypt by officials from individual taxpayers.

VIII. FARMING OF THE *VICESIMAE LIBERTATIS*, *HEREDITATIUM*

The silence or ambiguity of our sources on the *scriptura* under the Principate is matched for other *vectigalia*. Apart from some of the *portoria*, we are best informed about the *vicesima libertatis*.[155] We have 16 inscriptions from Italy and about half that number from the provinces which attest collection by publicans. Most were set up by their employees, sometimes free men but normally slaves described as belonging to publicans or the tax (cf. p. 371). *Socii* or a *societas* are

---

[153] *Contra* Hirschfeld 153–9. For lists see Pflaum pp. 1053 (add *AE* 1962. 183), 1062 (add *AE* 1973, 412), 1063, 1065 (cf. 1107).

[154] Cf. Brunt, *JRS* (1983), 68–74. Note that there are no prosopographic data at all for regional procurators for mines in e.g. Britain, Spain, Cyprus; in Spain the procurators of Asturia-Callaecia, documented from 79 to the 3rd c. (Pflaum p. 1047), probably controlled the mines in that region.

[155] Hirschfeld 106 ff. and Eck 114 ff. (for Italy) cite the texts.

mentioned in 5 of the Italian inscriptions. The existence of a *societas* is also implied by the records of two provincial *promagistri*. One, dated between 114 and 116, commemorates a *promagister* of the tax in Achaea and Syria; presumably he held successive appointments in those two provinces. The second, which has also been assigned to Trajan's reign for reasons that are not clear to me, honours Crispinus, who was in his fourth year as *promagister* of the Asian *portoria* and in his third as *promagister* of the *vicesima* in all the provinces of Asia Minor; he might have served a single company which had leased both taxes, or two separate companies.[156] On the former view it might be that the *vicesima* was leased region by region, and that a single company found it advantageous to contract for two taxes in the same area. Petronius (*Sat.* 65) and Epictetus (iv. 1, 33) refer to the *vicensimarii* or *eikostonai* for this tax. In Egypt one office administered the *vicesima libertatis* and the *vicesima hereditatium* in 189 (*BGU* 326). The former tax was still farmed there at least till Hadrian (*P. Oxy* 2265), the latter at least till Pius (n. 167). In another papyrus, datable to the mid-second century, we have a receipt given by an imperial slave for payment of the tax for a slave manumitted *per vindictam* before the prefect of Egypt. Eck has suggested that this type of manumission was relatively rare, and that payment would be made directly to the prefect's office when it was used, while the tax on testamentary manumissions could still have been farmed.[157] Alternatively we might imagine that collection in Egypt was leased to small men operating in their own districts; if at any given time no one could be found to take the contract voluntarily, the government might fall back on deputing imperial slaves for the task. In any case arrangements in other provinces were not necessarily the same as in Egypt. Of the inscriptions mentioned not all can certainly be put before Trajan's death. I see no way, for instance, of dating one from Capua that attests *socii* (*ILS* 1863). Moreover, it seems to me virtually certain that the manumissions tax was comprised in the *quattuor publica Africae* (n. 92), and these taxes were certainly farmed (to a *conductor*) under Pius.[158] Perhaps they were directly collected later (section X), but farming of the tax, which was levied at least till Macrinus but apparently not after Diocletian,[159] is not *known* to have been discontinued.

[156] *AE* 1964. 239; *Inschr. von Ephesus* ii. 517, 517a (transcribed by de Laet 274 f.); Crispinus is designated *archones* in the Greek version, cf. n. 125.

[157] W. Eck, *ZPE* 27, 205 ff., on the text best consulted in *CPL* 171. The *XX hered.* fell on Roman citizens only, but Egyptians also paid taxes on manumissions (Wallace 230); the mode of collection is apparently unknown.

[158] See n. 95. An *eikostones* in Lycia apparently later than Hadrian (*AE* 1976. 671) has been connected with the *XX lib.* rather than the *XX her.* on the unfounded assumption that the latter tax was no longer farmed.

[159] Dio lxxxvii. 9. 4 f., lxxix. 12. 2, cf. Hirschfeld 105, 109.

A conventional though invalid argument for direct collection of taxes is derived from the presence of numerous procurators and their staffs. But Pflaum recognized only two equestrian procurators of the manumissions tax, one Severan, and the other in fact undatable.[160] Three freedmen are also connected with it: one was in charge of the tax in Bithynia, Pontus, and Paphlagonia, again in the Severan period.[161] Pflaum also registers five procurators of the *quattuor publica Africae*, one of whom belongs to the time when they were still demonstrably farmed.[162] It is hardly conceivable that there were not many more such officials, who have left us no memorials of their existence (cf. n. 154). However, their functions could have been merely supervisory. Moreover Eck (n. 155) detects an equestrian procurator for the *vicesima* active in Italy before the destruction of Pompeii in 79, who cannot have performed any other role. If he is right, there was presumably a long line of procurators in Italy, who are unknown to us, and there is no reason to think that at any time they acquired new responsibilities.

The 4 per cent tax on the sale of slaves by auction is known, from only two inscriptions, to have been farmed by a company. One dates from 43/4, and that suggests that it had been farmed from the first. In this case the company was the same as that collecting the tax on manumissions. There is no other evidence; perhaps, as apparently in Africa (n. 92), it was normally combined for collection with another tax.[163]

Nothing is known of the collection of the general 1 per cent tax on sales, which was still raised in the third century (Ulpian, *Dig.* l. 16, 17. 1), but perhaps only in Italy.[164]

The *vicesima hereditatium* too was presumably farmed from its inception, as it was in Trajan's time, when this is certified by chance allusions in the younger Pliny's works. As no inscription mentions earlier farmers of this tax, it has no significance that none expressly refers to them later;[165] at most there may be some indirect epigraphic evidence fo their activity before and perhaps after Pliny's time (n. 173). A number of procurators are recorded; for the central bureau at Rome the list begins with two men who held the post under Vespasion and Domitian, and contains three Trajanic holders;[166] of these the first two at least must have been restricted to supervision, and it is not evident

[160] Pflaum no. 240; *CIL* ii. 1308.
[161] *CIL* vi. 8451 (1st c.), iii. 4827 (after 180), 6753 (3rd c.)
[162] Pflaum p. 1093, cf. n. 192.
[163] Hirschfeld 95 f.
[164] Ib. 93 f. Collection by a company is not established by a dubious supplement in *CIL* xii. 1082.
[165] Pliny, *Paneg.* 37, 39; *ep.* vii. 14. Cf. Eck 125 ff. against Hirschfeld 96 ff.
[166] Pflaum p. 1026; add *AE* 1973. 485 (Vesp.), 1962. 312.

that their successors had other duties.[167] They were assisted by *promagistri*, the first known under Hadrian. Hirschfeld conjectured that the title was borrowed from that held by managers in the company of publicans whose work he supposed procurators to have taken over. But so far as we know, the title of *promagister*, both in the Republic and in the Principate, was borne only by the chief local representatives of publican companies in a province, whereas the heads of the central bureau were *magistri*.[168] Moreover, we also find *promagistri hereditatium* as the principal assistants of the *procuratores hereditatium*;[169] and it is unattested and hardly conceivable that the emperors had ever farmed out their claims to inheritances. We may perhaps surmise that the heads of Palatine bureaux were informally styled *magistri* long before this usage became official in the late empire,[170] and that their chief subordinates could be called *promagistri*. Thus Hirschfeld's argument from titulature has no validity in proving that the procurators had taken over collection from the publicans. At latest in the Flavian period an imperial freedman is attested as procurator of the tax in Achaea (*ILS* 1546); his role too must have been supervisory. But it is impossible to discern why such an official should have been needed in Achaea and not at least in those other provinces in which Roman citizens liable to the tax were as numerous (or more) as in Achaea. We must conclude not that such officials did not exist already elsewhere but that they have left us no memorial (n. 154). In the second century Equites are found in similar posts, not only in provinces but in particular regions of Italy.[171] But this may mean only that the posts had been elevated in dignity, not that they had changed in function. Equestrian officials were more likely to leave records than freedmen. Even the evidence for the former is sporadic and sparse; a very small proportion of all who must have held the posts is known and the lack of documentation for humbler predecessors is thus the less surprising.

Naturally, the procurators had imperial freedmen and slaves as their subordinates,[172] but, as argued previously (p. 385), their titles offer no proof that the procurators were concerned in collection rather than in

---

[167] The bureau at Rome perhaps supervised collection in and near Rome, the domicile of senators and eminent Equites, perhaps also kept central accounts, unless that was the duty of the *praefecti* of the *aerarium militare*, to which the tax was appropriated.

[168] Pflaum p. 1027 lists four. *Promagistri* of publican companies: nn. 45, 125, 156, 186.

[169] Pflaum p. 1026.

[170] This appellation is used for the heads of various palatine bureaux in the 3rd c. (Pflaum nos. 327, 338, 339, 341) and not only for the *proc. XX her.* (no. 317), but was still apparently unofficial (ib. pp. 847, 883 f.)

[171] Pflaum pp. 1036 f., 1040 (cf. 1105) for Italy; 1048 f. cf. *AE* 1972. 250 (Spain); 1053, 1056 (Gaul), 1074, cf. *AE* 1967. 644 (Asia); 1077 (Bithynia), 1081 cf. *ZPE* 34, 257 (Syria); 1083 (Palestine), 1086 (Egypt); none in Africa, cf. n. 92.

[172] Hirschfeld 105 n. 1.

control. In Egypt we have a few declarations made to officials of property liable to the tax (n. 174), and it might be surmised that it was the duty of the officials to check the sums collected by publicans by reference to such returns, as well as to arbitrate on valuations. Four slaves are said to belong to the tax itself; I take them to be slaves of the tax-farmers (p. 371); at least one *tabularius* (*ILS* 1552) is of the period when tax-farming is certain, though the others might be later.[173] In Egypt farming persisted in Pius' reign,[174] yet there it would have been easier to substitute direct collection. The *vicesima* was probably among the *quattuor publica Africae* (n. 92), which were farmed under Pius (n. 92), but perhaps collected by officials later (s. X). No other evidence, for or against the supposed change, can be found. The tax itself, like that on manumissions, survived at least until Macrinus but not in the fourth century (cf. n. 159).

IX. FARMING OF *PORTORIA*

Lastly I come to the *portoria*. De Laet has most fully developed the hypothesis that there were three stages in their collection: (1) until Trajan they were farmed by companies; (2) from Trajan to Marcus by *conductores* who were *Einzelpächter*; (3) in or after Marcus' reign collected by government servants in some regions. He holds that in the second stage special procuratorial posts for the *portoria* concerned were, if not created, at least raised to equestrian dignity; in the third their increased responsibilities were reflected in higher salaries. In order to account for the juristic evidence he allows that publicans were still employed under the Severi in collecting *portoria* in Syria, Judaea, and Egypt.[175] Thus on his own theory the government did not adopt any general principle of abolishing the farming of *portoria*; if it did so in certain circumscriptions, it must have been for particular reasons which applied to them alone, and which we can at best conjecture. So we cannot argue from analogy that a reform attested in one or more circumscriptions also took place in any of those for which evidence is lacking. In fact de Laet's case rests principally on the Illyrian material, which happens to be the most copious, and to a lesser extent on the Gallic and African.

For Britain there is no evidence at all, if we think that the supplementation of certain inscriptions of uncertain date, which would

[173] Ibid. 100 n. 1.

[174] *P. Ross-George* ii. 26. A tax-receipt of AD 250 (*P. Oxy.* 3609) and 3rd c. declarations of inheritances (ib. 3103, *P. Amherst* 72, *P. Ryl.* 109) cast no light on the mode of collection.

[175] De Laet ch. XVII (in general agreement with Rostovtzeff and Hirschfeld), cf. *RIDA* (1949), 215 ff.

show the presence of publicans at London, is imprudent. More strangely, only two relevant inscriptions concern the Spanish *portoria*; one which is undated was set up by the *socii* collecting the tax; the second attests an imperial slave *dispensator* as *praepositus* of the port of Ilipa in Severus' reign; his function, which might be that of superintendent of port facilites, naturally does not imply that the Spanish *portoria* were not still farmed, perhaps to a company. No procurators of the Spanish *portoria* are recorded in any period.[176] In Sicily a *promagister* active about 100 implies the employment of a company; nothing else is known (n. 125). Similarly in Achaea we hear of publicans under Pius; no more.[177]

Even for Asia the relevant evidence is meagre, and does not support de Laet's thesis, as he claims. A publican company is attested in the first century. De Laet supposes that from Trajan's time it was replaced by *Einzelpächter*, two of whom (he thinks) are known from inscriptions. The first of these, Crispinus, whose dating to Trajan's reign seems to be conjectural, appears in a bilingual inscription as *archones* in Greek but as *promagister* in Latin (n. 56). The former term properly corresponds to *manceps*,[178] but, as in another instance (n. 125), it was used here to render the Latin *promagister*, for which there was no Greek equivalent, no doubt because the local manager of a publican company was to the provincials the tax-farmer *par excellence*. As *promagister* Crispinus should have been such a manager, and the Asian *portoria* should still have been farmed to a company. De Laet, however, supposes that Crispinus was himself a *conductor*, and an *Einzelpächter*, although his supposed *Einzelpächter* elsewhere are never styled *promagistri*, partly because he wishes to attribute to Trajan the abandonment of the use of tax-farming companies, partly because he finds another later *Einzelpächter* for the Asian *portoria* in a great magnate of Asia Minor, M. Aurelius Mindius Matidianus Pollio, who held several procuratorial posts under Commodus, and who is recorded to have been *archones* for thirty years.[179] Mindius, whose inscriptions are all in Greek, is not styled *promagister*, and *archones* cannot in his case render that term. With his many other avocations he hardly had leisure to act as local manager of a company farming the Asian customs for thirty years. May he have been the *manceps*? That would not exclude his belonging to a company. But perhaps we should not presume any such technical precision. In Egypt a variety of designations for tax-farmers is found, none of which seems to have any specific signification (n. 87). Mindius would perhaps have

---

[176] Britain: *CIL* vii. 1235, *AE* 1967. 271, 1971. 229. Spain: *ILS* 1462, 1406.
[177] *Dig.* xiv. 2. 9.
[178] Wilcken, *Gr. Ostraka*, 527.
[179] Pflaum no. 193 transcribes the inscriptions.

been described in Cicero's time as 'publicanus', a term which simply indicated that its bearer was concerned in tax-farming. In Mindius' time, to judge from evidence in other provinces, 'conductor' had become the usual term. I shall argue that it does not necessarily mean *Einzelpächter*. Mindius' appellation shows only that he had a leading role in the farming of the Asian *portoria*.

There is nothing to be said for de Laet's contention that he eventually took over the direct collection of the *portoria* as procurator. Two inscriptions honour him as having held four ducenarian posts (which are listed), as a former high priest of the temples of Asia in Ephesus, in which capacity he gave splendid games, as three times *agonothetes* at Ephesus, as Bithyniarch, as Arabarches in Egypt,[180] and as *archones*; one breaks off, but the other shows that he was also *logistes* of three Bithynian cities. A third inscription set up at Halicarnassus by his *pragmateutai*, who embellished the customs house there, describes him as *archones* and procurator (with no specifications), twice Bithyniarch, and Asiarch (without elaborating his services at Ephesus); it ignores his role as *logistes*. Now this inscription must be later than the other two, since only here are we told that he was *twice* Bithyniarch. But it plainly abbreviates his dignities. Hence the title procurator can merely refer to his tenure of the four ducenarian posts, not to his being at the time procurator of the Asian *portoria*, an office which he is not recorded as ever holding. De Laet has a notion that the *pragmateutai* (*actores*), whom he takes without justification to have been Mindius' slaves, were transferred to imperial ownership when the putative change was made from farming by Mindius to direct collection by officials: as he himself admits, this has no warrant in the text. In fact no equestrian *procurators* of the Asian *portoria* can be certainly dated before the third century. This may be chance. But when they do appear, they are merely sexagenarian.[181] (Mindius held no such lowly post.) If they were responsible for collection their rank does not at all fit de Laet's thesis that wherever direct collection was introduced, this is reflected by the up-grading of the procurators, now charged with greater responsibilities. In fact there is no cogent evidence for the leasing of the Asian *portoria* to *Einzelpächter* and none at all for the institution of direct collection in a later stage.

The circumscription of the *quadragesimae portuum Asiae* embraced a

---

[180] On this post see esp. J. Lesquier, *L'Armée rom. dans l'Égypte* (1918), 421 ff.; some take the Arabarch to be a publican rather than an official; for another Arabarch from Asia see *AE* 1973. 517.

[181] Pflaum p. 1073. Pflaum later found a freedman procurator, T. Flavius Asclepias, who could not be later than Hadrian (*ZPE* 18 (1975), 13 f.), but the man could be an Eques of Flavian or any later date.

large part of Anatolia in Crispinus' time and perhaps normally. Few procurators vested specifically with its administration are attested, and none in other Anatolian provinces except Bithynia.[182] For all the other eastern provinces too none are recorded and the evidence for *portoria* in general is extremely scanty. On the eastern frontiers customs-duties were apparently fixed at the high rate of 25 per cent. If it be true, as Pliny states (*NH* xii. 84), that there was an annual outflow of precious metal to the east amounting to 100 million sesterces, 25 millions would have been paid in duty on imports alone. The 'maris Rubri vectigal' which, as he tells us, has been 'bought' under Claudius by one Annius Plocamus, clearly affected this foreign trade. Annius was probably *manceps* of a Roman company rather than an *Einzelpächter*, given the large sums involved. Pliny also refers to publicans who farmed the duties on foreign goods passing through Gaza. The *tetartonai* active at Palmyra in 161 and 174 (local men) were evidently among their successors. Philostratus shows such publicans at work at Zeugma in his romance on Apollonius of Tyana; this might indicate that the tax was farmed when he was writing under the Severi. The publicans found at Dura between *c*.165 and 256 must have been engaged in the same operations.[183] It is plain that no history of the collection of duties imposed on trade across the eastern frontiers can be constructed. The farmers of a mere thirtieth at Berytus, who cannot be dated, were surely collectors of tolls on internal trade, imposed either by the state or by the colony. There is the same uncertainty about the publican at Caesarea mentioned by Josephus (*BJ* ii. 287). The publicans in Galilee notorious from the Gospels must have been farming taxes for the tetrarch or for local authorities, not for Rome. The terms used for 'tax-collector' in Rabbinic texts are ambiguous, and may denote either liturgical officials or tax-farmers, and again it is not always clear whether they were acting for Rome or for a city.[184] In Egypt the

---

[182] Crispinus, described on one inscription as *promagister* of the *quadragesima Asiae* and *vicesima libertatis*, is said in another to have operated, perhaps for the former as well as the latter tax, throughout Asia, Bithynia, Pontus, Galatia, Cappadocia, Pisidia, Lycaonia, Pamphylia, Lycia, Armenia Minor (though one would expect a higher duty than 2½% to have been levied on trade with foreign parts on the upper Euphrates as in Syria and Egypt); if this is right, 'XXXX Asiae' (which also appears in Mindius' title) could be shorthand for a circumscription far wider than the province of Asia; we also know of a Severan procurator for the tax in both Asia and Bithynia (*ILS* 9490). In the early 3rd c. the famous Timesitheus deputized *extra ordinem* as *procurator Bithyniae* for the procurators of the *quadragesima* and of a *vicesima* (*libertatis* or *hereditatium*) in that province (*ILS* 1330). The circumscriptions of procurators administering the Anatolian *portoria* may have changed from time to time, and conceivably Timesitheus was not the only provincial procurator to discharge this function.

[183] De Laet ch. XIII f. with 415 ff.; 25 per cent rate, 306 ff., cf. 335. See Pliny, *NH* vi. 84; xii. 65; *AE* 1947. 179 f.; *SEG* vii. 570, 593, 623; Philostr., *v. Apoll.* i. 20. The relation of the imperial *portoria* to the municipal *octrois* at Palmyra, also collected by publicans (n. 4), is unclear.

[184] De Laet 340 postulates a *societas* at Berytus, *contra* Vittinghoff 389. cf. nn. 107, 183.

farming of tolls on internal trade is sufficiently but not copiously attested. So far as I am aware, none of the documents is certainly later than the second half of the second century.[185]

Thus there is no documentary evidence for tax-farming in Syria, Palestine, or Egypt securely dated to the Severan period, and its survival there is postulated by de Laet, only because he had to find some application for the Severan legal texts which show that it survived somewhere, and his theory had excluded so many other regions. One of these texts refers specifically to duties on eastern spices (*Dig.* xxxix. 4. 16. 7). Naturally this is no proof that only eastern *portoria* were still farmed. I feel virtually certain that they were. De Laet's theories are founded only on the evidence from Illyricum, and to a lesser extent from Gaul and Africa.

Here too the *portoria* were at one time farmed either to companies or to *Einzelpächter*. There are 7 attestations of *socii* for the Gallic circumscription, and 4 for the *quattuor publica Africae*, which are taken to include the *portoria* (n. 92); not all can be dated to the first century any more than the single reference to the company that farmed the Spanish customs (*ILS* 1462).[186] In the Principate there was a toll-station of the Illyrian *portoria* at Aquileia, and we have 2 cases of *socii* there or at Tergeste, given a Republican dating by de Laet, I do not know why; they might be imperial, and they might be farmers of Italian *portoria* (Appendix IV).[187] His theory that leasing to companies ceased under Trajan is of course *compatible* with this evidence, on the assumption that all the *socii* known are pre-Hadrianic, and with the fact that *promagistri*, who should be local representatives of companies, in Sicily and in Asia, are Trajanic.[188] So too all the *conductores*, who in his judgement took their place, *may* be Trajanic or later, but their dating is, once again, not always secure. We have 2 from Gaul, one certainly of the late second century, and 2 in Africa, from about the same time.[189] For Illyricum he lists 11 or 12, of whom one was certainly operating in 100, and 6 under

---

[185] De Laet 415 ff. cites *SB* 7365 (AD 104), *P. Lond.* iii. 1169a (second half of 2nd c.), Wilcken, *Chr.* 277 (AD 139). Cf. also *Chr.* 273 (2nd/3rd c.); *Gr. Ostraka*, ii. nos. 43 (96/7), 150 (129), 801 (107), 806 (114), 1569 (119); no doubt more instances might be found. Farming of other imposts certainly persisted, e.g. *P. Oxy.* 3092 (217).

[186] Africa: *CIL* viii. 1128, 12920; *AE* 1900. 126; 1923. 22 ('promagistri soc.'); Gaul: *CIL* v. 7213, 7264, xii. 724, 2348, 5362, xiii. 1819, *AE* 1916. 55. Cimma 118 and 130 n. 148 transcribes the texts, some of which she takes to be post-Trajanic; if this could be proved, it would destroy one of de Laet's hypotheses.

[187] De Laet 179, cf. 77 on *CIL* v. 792, *ILS* 1851; if these inscriptions are Republican (as he asserts) it was the 'portorium Aquileiense' that the *socii* farmed (Cic., *Font.* 2). Cimma 136 f. adduces also *CIL* iii. 4009, but the imperial *socii* here admittedly need not have been farmers of the Illyrian *portorium*, and v. 798 (AD 165), but this contains no reference to *socii*, and the 'publicanus' mentioned *could* have been a collector of municipal revenue at Aquileia.

[188] See nn. 125, 156, cf. 182, 186.

[189] De Laet 387 (*ILS* 5884 = *CIL* v. 6649 probably does not give a third Gallic *conductor*). For Africa cf n. 95.

Pius and Marcus; but I see no proof that the rest were not active before 98 or after 180.[190] A *manceps* of the *quattuor publica Africae*, also undatable, and the *mancipes*, whose disputes with the merchants in Gaul were the subject of procuratorial arbitration in or after the reign of Commodus, may be equated with *conductores*.[191] Most of the inscriptions which constitute our evidence were set up by slaves or freedmen of the *socii* or *conductores*, as the case may be.

De Laet's argument is essentially this. (1) A *conductor* is necessarily an *Einzelpächter*. Therefore, wherever we find *conductores*, the taxes were no longer farmed to companies. (2) No securely dated allusions to *socii* are later than Trajan's time, and no such allusions to *conductores* are earlier. Therefore all texts relating to companies must be dated to the first period and all relating to *conductores* to the second. The logical fallacy in (2) is apparent, even if the first premiss is accepted, and I regard it as arbitrary (below). Moreover on de Laet's own view we have no imperial testimony to companies farming the Illyrian *portoria*. Thus the appearance of *conductores* for these duties under Trajan (and some *may* be earlier) is no proof of a change in that circumscription; and there is no ground in the facts so far adduced for thinking that it was Trajan who made the putative reform in Africa or Gaul; we can say only that it must have occurred at latest in Africa under Pius (n. 95), and in Gaul under Commodus (nn. 189, 191), in whose reigns *conductores* are attested.

De Laet supposes that the *conductores* were receiving only fees and percentages for their work, and were subjected to closer procuratorial supervision than companies. He thought that equestrian procurators of sexagenarian rank first appear in our records under Hadrian for the *quattuor publica Africae*; till then the procurators had been freedmen. One such freedman contemporary with two former slaves of Nerva might have been in post as late as Hadrian; de Laet adduces two predecessors from the first century, at least one of whom can most plausibly be so dated.[192] But it is now virtually certain that one of the

---

[190] De Laet 385 n. 2. I see no way of dating C. Calcinius Tertianus, Iulius Proclus, T. Iulius Perseus (whose inclusion in the list is conjectural), the *anonymus*, or M. Antonius Fabianus who, like T. Iulius Saturninus and C. Antonius Rufus (Pflaum nos. 150, 151, 174), also had an equestrian public career, before, after or during his term as *conductor*. *ILS* 4225 *suggests* that Rufus was simultaneously *praefectus vehiculorum* (a post which might have been generically designated in other inscriptions as 'procurator') and *conductor*, and Mindius (n. 179) must have farmed the Asian *portoria* while holding procuratorial posts outside that province. On statistical grounds it is doubtless more likely that all these undated inscriptions are later rather than earlier than 100, particularly in the case of Fabianus; to place them all before 180 and contend that consequently leasing of the *portoria* had then ceased is circular.

[191] *AE* 1913. 113; *ILS* 1410 (Pflaum no. 204).

[192] Pflaum p. 1093, but see W. Eck, *Entretiens Hardt* (1987), xxxiii. 216 f. Freedmen; *ILS* 1549 (the man married Iulia Demetrias, probably a freedwoman of a Julian emperor); 1550 (Coccei); *CIL* vi. 8589 (dubious date and supplement).

equestrian procurators belongs to the mid-first century. If the *quattuor publica* included the *vicesima hereditatium*, and if it had been farmed on a percentage basis from the start, strict control of the tax-farmer would always have been appropriate. There may have been no comparative need for it over the Gallic and Illyrian *portoria*, so long as the farmers contracted for lump sum payments. Of course we cannot be sure from what date (if ever) a percentage system was substituted in their collection. For the Gallic *portoria*, no procurators are attested before Hadrian, and for the Illyrian none before Severus,[193] but the evidence for holders of all procuratorial posts is too fragmentary to warrant the assumption that none were appointed much earlier to supervise the farming of these taxes (cf. n. 154).

We may now examine de Laet's conception of the position of a *conductor*. Some *conductores*, e.g. on imperial estates, were undoubtedly *Einzelpächter*; but is this true of all? A Frisian dedication of uncertain date was set up by 'conductores piscatus, mancipi Q. Valerio Secundo' (*ILS* 1461). The fishing rights were perhaps leased by a local community, not by the state; but in any case the text illustrates linguistic usage in the Principate. 'Mancipi' is evidently used in the old sense, of the man who 'bought' the contract. The *conductores* must be his partners, described as such and not as *socii* presumably because in reality they no less than the *manceps* were the lessees, contributing capital and services to the common enterprise. In some other cases, as we have seen, no distinction is made between *manceps* and *conductor*.[194] When either word is used in the plural, it may denote not a number of *Einzelpächter* but partners in a common enterprise. Thus, as the Gallic *portoria* were leased as a unit, the *mancipes* of the inscription cited above (n. 191) must all be partners in their collection. We also have at least one instance under Marcus of a consortium of three *conductores* of the Illyrian *portoria*, and some other lessees are described as 'tpc' or 'trpc', which is most plausibly, though conjecturally, taken to stand for 'tertiae partis conductor'; this would signify in de Laet's opinion not that they had divided up the circumscription geographically, since each had his own slaves acting in diverse parts of it, but that each had a third share in the contract with the government.[195] This interpretation is not necessarily right; we could suppose that partners active in the business divided up the administration, as a rather obscure text in the Pauline *Sententiae* (*Dig.* xxxix. 4. 9. 4) indicates, and on a geographical

---

[193] Pflaum pp. 1052, 1059.

[194] See nn. 23–6 with text. 'Mancipes' collected *octrois* at the gates of Rome at least from Marcus to Severus Alexander (*ILS* 375, cf. de Laet 347 ff.); they may have been partners, or each may have contracted for one gate.

[195] De Laet 236 ff.; 385 n. 2.

basis; the distribution of the inscriptions attesting their operations need only mean they did not each year take the same districts under their control. Nor can we exclude the possibility that there were more than three *socii* as parties to the contract, even if only three were active in the administration. These same men appear in some inscriptions with no reference to their partners; we therefore cannot say that other *conductores* who are only attested individually did not also have partners: the slaves who set up the inscriptions naturally mention only their own masters. Such *conductores* may all have been members of a *societas vectigalis* personally active in the business and styled *conductores* for the same reason as that which explains the use of the term in the Frisian document. (The *conductores* of imperial flocks in Italy (App. III) may be members of such a *societas* or lessees of different flocks.)

De Laet thinks it significant that in Gaul and Africa all slave employees in the period in which we find *socii* belong to them but later to individual *conductores*.[196] But, as shown above, the inscriptions of the *socii* and of several *conductores* in Gaul and Africa cannot be dated. It is a *petitio principii* to assume that these documents do not overlap in time. Even in Illyricum some of the slave employees (again of uncertain date) are not said to belong to individuals; they merely record where they served, or may be said to belong to the tax; this may well mean that they were owned by a company that collected it (cf. p. 371).[197] In fact a *societas vectigalis* (or any other *societas*) might employ slaves owned by one of the partners and, for that matter, hired slaves (n. 41). Now if a slave owned by an individual *socius* wished not simply to name his master but to designate the function of his owner in tax-farming, how should he have done so? How indeed should the publican concerned have described himself? Given that in effect he was one of the lessees of the tax farmed, 'conductor' seems a very natural choice.

Why should companies have been replaced by *Einzelpächter*? De Laet seems to oscillate between alternative explanations: (1) the business was no longer sufficiently lucrative to attract rich investors; (2) the government suppressed the companies. He conjectures that profits had been diminished by Nero's measures. Yet on his own chronology this result of Nero's reforms was retarded, while according to Tacitus their effect was largely transient (*Ann.* xiii. 51. 1). And why should an enterprise so unremunerative that men would no longer undertake it in combination have allured them as individuals? Moreover, Gaius certifies that the government did not suppress all tax companies in the

---

[196] Ib. 392 f.; for slaves of *socii* see Cimma cited in n. 186.

[197] De Laet 395 f.; his list of imperial slaves (411 ff.) includes some unjustifiably assigned to that category.

early second century; why should it have *suppressed* any? Knowing as little as we do about economic conditions in general and public finance in particular, we can imagine that companies farming *portoria* for lump sums could suffer heavy losses, but that would not make it intelligible that their place should voluntarily be taken by *Einzelpächter*.

X. COLLECTION BY OFFICIALS?

I come now to the supposed introduction of direct collection by officials. If this ever occurred, one reason might have been the difficulty of inducing entrepreneurs to make satisfactory bids for the farm of taxes. Some evidence is to be found that this difficulty was encountered at times, though it also indicates that the remedy adopted was to apply compulsion on tax-farmers to renew their contracts.

Under Severus Callistratus declared that compulsion was not authorized, and quotes a rescript of Hadrian: 'it is an extremely brutal custom whereby the lessees of public revenues (*vectigalium*) and lands are forced to continue, if they cannot be leased (to others) at the same rate [as before]; it will in fact be easier to find lessees if they know that they will not be subject to [further] obligation, should they wish to give up at the end of the quinquennium'.[198] The assimilation of lessees of revenues to lessees of public lands suggests that Hadrian had in mind *Kleinpacht* known for example in Egypt, effected by local officials. They had apparently not been acting in accordance with what he announced as imperial policy. However, compulsion was nothing new. In the past cities had applied it to their own publicans; the privilege of exemption from nomination as publicans (*demosionai*) or as purchasers of *tributa*, signifying property taxes imposed by local authorities (n. 3), which Octavian granted to Seleucus of Rhosus and to veterans in general, or at least to those domiciled in Egypt, is proof of this.[199] In 68 the prefect of Egypt, Tiberius Iulius Alexander, acceded to the petition that men should not be forced, as in his predecessor's time, to lease the farming of taxes and public lands; he avers that this was contrary to tradition in Egypt and custom elsewhere, and adverse to the public interest. His professions resemble Hadrian's, and reflect good intentions which were evidently often not realized; Hadrian admits that the abuse was customary. It was certainly common in Egypt to assign domain lands compulsorily to individuals or communities; as usual, we know less of tax-farming. But towards the end of the first century the farmers of two imposts who had lost money on their contracts were prepared to

---

[198] *Dig.* xlix. 14. 6. 6.
[199] Sherk, *Rom. Documents from the Greek East* (1969) no. 54, 34; Wilcken, *Chr.* 462.

abscond rather than renew them; obviously they feared compulsion. No other bidders had come forward. The prefect suggested that the terms of the contract might be made less burdensome; at this point the document breaks off.[200] Much later, the emperor Philip confirmed that lessees and their heirs were not to be retained against their will; it is sinister that he adds that this rule had been stated in many previous rescripts. Yet juristic opinion fluctuated; the Pauline *Sententiae* at one point reaffirm the principle declared by Hadrian and Philip, but at another state that contractors who have made very large profits in the collection of revenue 'are required' to renew their contracts on the same terms, if no one else would offer as much.[201] We may infer that not all emperors set themselves against compulsion on publicans, and that prohibitions proved ineffective. It must have seemed reasonable by analogy with the collection of direct taxes, which had become a liturgical responsibility imposed by the cities or in Egypt by officials. And what other course was open to the official whose own chances of promotion might seem to rest on his success in maintaining the yield of taxes? Still, we must not conclude that tax-farming was normally unprofitable. The Pauline *Sententiae* also tell us that bidders for the contracts might in the heat of auctions offer unusually high prices, which it was imprudent to accept without adequate security.[202] This looks like advice tendered to local officials who had not too much experience.

None the less, I question whether persons of such status as those who farmed the *portoria*, some of whom could secure procuratorial posts (n. 190) were ever compelled to continue their work; this was more likely to be the fate of little men without rank or influence. No doubt in crises there might have been difficulties in letting contracts to big men too. The great plagues under Marcus and Commodus presumably had an adverse effect on trade, mortality could have raised the price of slaves, and the northern wars of Marcus' reign might have produced such insecurity, especially in the Illyrian provinces, that private entrepreneurs might have been unwilling to venture slaves and other capital in the customs-stations there. If such conditions existed, Marcus might well have been obliged to introduce collection by officials.[203] It would

---

[200] G. Chalon, *L'Édit de Ti. Iulius Alexander* (1964), 101 ff. on vv. 10–15; G. Poetke, *Epimerismos* (1969), cf. Wallace ch. IV, Wilcken, *Grundzüge*, 188, 292 ff., *Chr.* 275.

[201] *CJ* iv. 65. 11; *Dig.* xxxix. 4. 9. 1 and 11. 5.

[202] *Dig.* xxxix. 4. 9. *pr.* Préaux, *L'Economie royale*, 455 n. 1 cites comparable evidence for Ptolemaic Egypt; at times tax-farming there was lucrative, at times deficits led to sequestrations of the property of the tax-farmers and their sureties.

[203] De Laet 405 makes Marcus the author of the change in the misapprehension (cf. Pflaum no. 151) that C. Antonius Rufus, *conductor* in his reign, returned as procurator to collect the tax. *CIL* iii. 1568, as supplemented by de Laet 238, 1, which Pflaum overlooks, establishes Rufus' date. See n. 190.

be less easy to guess why the same change should have occurred (if it did) in Gaul, where farming persisted after the end of his northern wars (cf. n. 191), or in Africa. Certainly there was never any decision to terminate tax-farming as a matter of principle: it continued for tolls at the gates of Rome itself (n. 194). What is the proof that the reform was actually effected for the Illyrian or Gallic *portoria* or for the *quattuor publica Africae*?

The Illyrian material is again the foundation of de Laet's case. He lists over 30 slaves and freedmen of the *conductores*, employed as *vilici*, *arcarii* etc., nearly all securely dated between Trajan and Marcus, and rather more members of the imperial *familia* with the same appellations, of whom nearly half served between 182 and the death of Alexander Severus, and none are certainly dated earlier or later.[204] He infers that the emperor's servants had replaced those of the *conductores* in the work of collection, and that the procurators were now directing the operation. I remarked earlier (p. 385) that both *conductores* and *procurators* might have clerks and accountants with identical titles, though in the one case they were employed in collection and in the other in supervision. Hence the titles of most of these imperial slaves and freedmen are not enough to show that they were collectors. However, they include two *scrutatores* whose task was presumably to examine goods liable to duty (cf. n. 99). It might also be doubted if for mere supervision the procurator needed *vilici* and the like at each toll-station, yet imperial slaves are found in these posts with exactly the same designation as employees of the *conductores*. It may reasonably be concluded that between the reigns of Commodus and Alexander Severus they were employed as collectors; thereafter evidence fails us.

And yet is it so certain as de Laet supposes that tax-farmers had been eliminated? Can we be sure that if the *conductores* could not provide staff of their own, the emperor might not have hired out his own servants to them? They rather than the procurators would then still have directed the operations. This would have been a system somewhat similar to that which Préaux postulates in Ptolemaic Egypt (App. I. 4). It might have been introduced rather more gradually than de Laet's presentation of the evidence makes it appear. Some of the *conductores* and their servants cannot in fact be dated before 180 except on the *petitio principii* that de Laet's hypothesis is correct (n. 190), nor can we date the slaves whose ownership is unstated or who are said to belong to the tax (n. 197). Hence we cannot be sure that only imperial slaves were employed after 180. And equally we do not know that none were

---

[204] De Laet 393 ff., 411 ff. gives evidence for Gaul and Africa, but my figures exclude some slaves unjustifiably counted by him as imperial.

employed earlier. No doubt the fact that so large a proportion of the imperial slaves are dated after 180 suggests that in that period they preponderated. And since *conductores* are attested mainly by inscriptions set up by their own slaves, it is not surprising that none of those known to de Laet demonstrably belongs to a period in which few of their own slaves were active in the business.

The Gallic and African evidence is similar to the Illyrian, but less copious (n. 204); and on that account it would hardly create the impression but for the Illyrian that the imperial *familia* entirely took over the work; the documents for either of the two periods distinguished by de Laet are too few for any statistical or quasi-statistical conclusions. It should hardly need saying that a single imperial slave active in Spain as 'dispensator portus Ilipensis' (*ILS* 1406) under Severus is insufficient proof that the putative change occurred in Spain.

According to de Laet (p. 406) 'the sources reveal' that after the reform the procurators with their new responsibilities were raised from sexagenarian to ducenarian rank. This cannot be proved. De Laet relied on two texts. The first expressly attests that M. Rossius Vitulus was ducenarian procurator of the *quattuor publica Africae*. The three known predecessors of this Severan official were certainly of a lower grade, centenarian in Pflaum's opinion. For that of his successors we have no information. Rossius had an exceptional career, and his salary in Africa may have been a favour personal to himself, or there may have been special reasons for the extraordinary appointment of an unusually senior and trusted official to the post. De Laet's second text is a reference in the *Historia Augusta* to a ducenarian post held by Pertinax in Dacia; however, Pflaum summarily and rightly dismisses the conjecture that he was administering the *portoria*.[205]

No known procurator for the Illyrian *portoria* can be securely dated before Severus. Thereafter we know of two *ducenarii* with the title 'procurator vectigalis Illyrici'; on the other hand Ti. Claudius Xenophon was still a *centenarius* when 'procurator Illyrici per Moesiam inferiorem et Dacias tres'; 'Illyrici' stands for 'vectigalis Illyrici'. It is clear that when he held this office the control of the Illyrian *portoria* had been divided, and Pflaum assumes that there was also a centenarian post whose holders covered Raetia, Noricum, Dalmatia, both Pannonias, and Upper Moesia; he then divided the procurators who can be connected with the Illyrian *portoria* into two lists on the basis of the find-spots of their inscriptions. This is quite arbitrary, since (1) there is no evidence that at the time when Xenophon was in post the

---

[205] Pflaum p. 1093, cf. nos. 224 (Rossius), 179 (Pertinax).

circumscription had been divided into only two regions; (2) the full title of any other procurator is not on record, and some of them could have been in charge of the whole area; the division in Xenophon's time might have been quite temporary. (The *cursus* of all these procurators, including two whom Pflaum takes to be successors of Xenophon, is unknown or so imperfectly recorded that we cannot tell whether they too were *centenarii* when administering *portoria*.) The chronological relationship of the ducenarian procurators, who presumably administered the *portoria* throughout the entire circumscription, and those who, like Xenophon, may all have been centenarians administering only a part of it, is also uncertain.[206] It is possible, but not demonstrable, that at some date in the Severan period the ducenarian post was replaced by two or more posts of lower rank for parts of the circumscription, but there are certainly no grounds for supposing that a post covering the whole circumscription had previously been only centenarian.

Though I am far from believing that posts did not exist before their first attestation, perhaps long before it, we might guess that at one time each provincial procurator handled questions connected with the *portoria* that arose within his own province. No doubt the creation of a new specialized post of whatever status would suggest that there had been an increase in the work, which *could* be ascribed to the substitution of direct collection for leasing. But theories cannot be sustained by mere possibilities.

As for Gaul, the Hadrianic procurator of the *portoria* was certainly sexagenarian and the last known (*c.* 242), taken by Pflaum to be centenarian, might in my judgement be ducenarian; I do not think we can venture to determine the salaries of the other three, except that an anonymous figure who *perhaps* held the post and who *may* have served in Marcus' wars could only be centenarian. Thus we do not know precisely when, still less why, the post was upgraded.[207]

I may repeat *ad hominem*, since de Laet holds without any justification that in Asia the customs-duties were collected by officials in the third century, that there the procurators of the time were sexagenarian (n. 181).

Of the Illyrian *conductores* listed by de Laet (385 n. 2) one seems to have farmed in 100 only the customs of the *ripa Thraciae*, which was evidently amalgamated later with the Illyrian *portoria*; the others are most fully described as 'conductores publici portorii Illyrici utriusque et ripae Thraciae' (App. II). But since de Laet wrote, an inscription has been found with the name of P. Aemilius Eutyches, 'conductor VII

---

[206] Ib. pp. 787, 1058, 1059, 1065; Xenophon, no. 222.
[207] Ib. p. 1092; see nos. 331 bis, 217.

et XX ripae fluminis Danuvi'.[208] Since we also know that one C. Titius
Antonius Peculiaris, who may plausibly be identified with a homonymous city councillor of Aquincum after that city had received colonial
status from Severus, was 'vectigalis octavae Pann[oniarum] II
[duarum], anno [conductionis] XII', it is tempting to amend 'VII' in
Eutyches' inscription to 'VIII'; both men then leased a tax of 12½ per
cent.[209] What this *octava* was is a matter for speculation.[210] Eutyches
also on this view leased a *vicesima*, evidently on goods that passed the
Danube. Two other Illyrian inscriptions mentioning a *vicesima*, the first
a dedication by the slave of a *conductor* 'Genio Commerci et negotian-
tium' (*ILS* 1861) and therefore naturally connected with the *portoria*,
were already known to de Laet, and he deduced that in all probability
the rate of the Illyrian *portoria* at any rate on goods imported into or
exported from the empire was 5 per cent; he argued that a probable
reference to a *quinquagesima*, distinguished from the *vectigal Illyricum*, in
an Aquileian inscription (*AE* 1934, 234) could be explained by the
hypothesis that internal traffic paid only 2 per cent.[211] But what may be
most significant in the new text is the reference to the bank of the
Danube. Eutyches is not, like the *conductores* previously known, a lessee
of the *portoria* throughout the Illyrian circumscription. They were then
no longer, as in the second century, leased as a unit (App. II). We may
recall that Ti. Claudius Xenophon was procurator for the tax only in
the three Dacias and Lower Moesia (n. 206). Did Eutyches belong to a
period when tax-farming of the *portoria*, if ever intermitted, had been
resumed, but when the old circumscription had been broken up,
perhaps because no one could be found to undertake contracts of the
former magnitude? Peculiaris too may well have been active as a
conductor octavae in the period when the Illyrian *portoria* were supposedly
collected by officials; whatever the *octava* was, this would show that in
principle tax-farming was not shunned in the Illyrian region in
Severan times, any more than it was abandoned universally.

In conclusion, (1) it is certain that some *portoria* were still farmed
under the Severi; (2) the emergence of *conductores* in the second century
is no proof that by then the tax-farmers were *Einzelpächter*; wherever a
large organization and substantial capital were required, it was in the
government's interest to commit the task to companies, and it is

---

[208] *AE* 1975. 413, I have considered if he could mean that he was *conductor* for 27 years; for
parallel references to length of tenure nn. 156, 179 (Mindius was *archones* for 30), 209; cf. de Laet
237 f. on *CIL* iii. p. 958 XXIII and *ILS* 1861, but one would expect 'vectigalis' or some equivalent
before 'ripae'.

[209] *AE* 1968. 423, cf. *ILS* 7124; *RE Suppl.* ix. 509.

[210] An *octava* is attested in a rescript of Alexander Severus (*CJ* iv. 65.7) and in much later
evidence; de Laet argues that it was a sales tax (463 ff.).

[211] De Laet 242–5, cf. App. IV.

impossible to see why companies should have resiled from a business which individuals found profitable; (3) the introduction of direct collection, if it occurred, was not based on a rejection in principle of tax-farming but must have been occasioned by special circumstances affecting a particular region, and might have been impermanent; (4) it is at most probable that this change was made for the Illyrian circumscription, but even in this instance it cannot be demonstrated; the evidence for any similar change in Gaul or Africa is insufficient, and elsewhere non-existent.

XI. EPILOGUE: THE LATE EMPIRE

In the late empire the government had at last created a large bureaucracy. None the less most of the direct taxes were usually collected by the city councillors, who were collectively liable to the treasury, though officials could often not be restrained from taking a profitable part in the business, and were normally employed to exact arrears.[212] The vast imperial estates appear to have been leased by *conductores* who were tenants of the crown, and not simply collectors of dues owed to the state by the small cultivators.[213] Some of the taxes which had been farmed in the Principate, the *vicesimae hereditatium* and *libertatis*, and the 4 per cent tax on sales of slaves by auction, had disappeared, but we hear of a *gabelle*, of market tolls, and of the *octavae*, which may have been taxes on sales (n. 210), and these were all farmed. So too were the *portoria* from Constantine to Justinian.[214] But they were no longer organized in the extensive circumscriptions of the Principate. Instead we find 'conductores diversorum portuum ac vectigalium'; the latter term may refer to imposts on sales. The publicans (as tax-farmers can still be called in rescripts) are evidently the 'minuscularii' of whom Augustine as well as the emperors speak.[215] They are *Kleinpächter*. A rescript of 323 shows that at that time contracts ran for a minimum of three years (*CJ* iv. 61. 4).

There is no place in this system for the *societates vectigales* of classical law, which were unfamiliar to the compilers of the *Digest*, who none the less included excerpts from classical jurists which concerned remedies available against tax-farmers as such. De Laet himself remarks that in the late empire there is no evidence of direct collection

---

[212] Jones, *Later Roman Empire*, 456–8, cf. 467 f. For exceptions 431 f. (*collatio glebalis*), 435, cf. 432 (*siliquaticum*). The former tax fell on senators alone; officials could easily collect from this limited group, and probably no persons of lower position could have succeeded in the task.

[213] Ib. 417 f.

[214] De Laet ch. XXII, cf. Jones, *Later Roman Empire*, 430.

[215] *C. Th.* xi. 28. 3 (401); Aug., *Civ. Dei* vii. 4.

of *portoria* as distinct from official control of the publicans. And yet it does not strike him as strange that direct collection should have been adopted in a time when the bureaucracy was far less equipped for the task, and have been abandoned when it was fully developed. This consideration alone should make us view with the utmost suspicion claims that tax-farming was progressively eliminated in the Principate. The strongest positive evidence is required to counterbalance the instrinsic implausibility of this theory, and it is not forthcoming; at most we have inconclusive grounds for holding that direct collection was introduced for some of the *portoria*, but if this be true, there were surely special reasons, unknown to us, why the government adopted a practice alien to tradition, and then only in particular cases, and probably as a measure of transient effect. So far as we can discern principles underlying its methods of collection, as distinct from unthinking conservatism, it was guided by the need to secure, so far as possible, guarantors of predictable receipts from the revenue, or by the desirability of giving the tax-collectors a financial incentive for maximizing the proceeds. Naturally it must have been well aware of the cupidity shown by tax-farmers in all ages (cf. n. 14). But we must beware of supposing that it ever decided to abolish tax-farming in a beneficent desire to mitigate the burdens of the subjects. It could not even have had any assurance that officials would prove less rapacious. Complaints abound in the late empire of harsh and illicit extortions to which both imperial officials and curial collectors resorted. The fees pocketed by the former in the west amounted in 458 to about 26 per cent of the sum paid in property tax or nearly one-third of what the treasury received. This was not far short of the profits probably made by publicans in Republican Asia (p. 380). In the east the government was far more efficient in keeping the perquisites of collectors within bounds.[216] Supervision by procurators in the Principate may have done as much to limit the exactions of publicans, though of course the collusion between procurators and the *conductores* of an imperial estate in Africa alleged in a petition of the *coloni* (*FIRA*[2] 103) could have had its counterpart in collaboration between procurators and the farmers of taxes.

SUMMARY

In the Principate, probably from Caesar's time, the direct taxes were collected by the cities within their own territories, in Egypt by liturgical officials. Otherwise tax-farming long persisted. The meagre testimony

[216] Jones *Later Roman Empire*, 468, cf. 457 f.

of literary, epigraphic, and even papyrological sources does not justify the prevalent modern theory that it was progressively eliminated in the second and third centuries, or even that *Einzelpächter* normally took the place of *societates* of the Republican type, whose continued existence is attested by Gaius and implicit in Severan legal fragments. This juristic evidence is the best we possess, although it fails to show precisely which taxes were still farmed in the late second and early third centuries. The silence of other sources is no proof that tax-farming was discontinued in any given instance. Nor is the multiplication of procuratorial bureaux administering particular revenues, since it is certain that they could coexist with tax-farmers; initially their function was supervisory, and specific evidence is needed to show that they moved from control to collection. It can be found only for *portoria* in a few regions, and is inconclusive. The reasons for the reform, if it occurred, elude us. It may well have been transient. Tax-farming was normal for indirect taxes in the late empire (though the *societates* had then disappeared), in the very period when the strength of the bureaucracy would have best enabled the government to dispense with it.

APPENDIX I

Tax-farming in Ptolemaic and Roman Egypt

1.   The foregoing essay contains various incidental allusions to practices in Egypt, but a summary of some of the main features may be helpful. I depend chiefly on Wilcken's exposition of unsurpassed lucidity in *Gr. Ostraka*, 513–69 (Ptolemaic) and 587–601 (Roman), modified in some details in his *Grundzüge* and commentary on *UPZ* 112, cf. also C. Préaux, *L'Économie royale des Lagides*, 450 ff. and other passages cited in her index s.v. *ferme* (influenced by G. M. Harper, *AJP* XIV (1934), 49 ff., 269 ff.), and Wallace ch. XVII. Thanks chiefly to the chance survival of the Revenue Laws of Ptolemy Philadelphus and of *UPZ* 112, we know far more of the Ptolemaic system than of the Roman, for which the evidence is surprisingly scanty. However, the Ptolemaic system is not irrelevant to my theme, partly for the analogies it presents to that of the Roman Republic (from which imperial practice in other provinces derived), and partly because it was presumably the basis of the Roman system within Egypt.

2.   The 'purchaser' of the Ptolemaic farm is the *archones* (Wilcken, *Gr. Ostraka* 527), though there may be joint *archonai* (544 ff.). He *must* provide sureties (548 ff.). He *may* (and frequently does) have partners (*metochoi*), who do not necessarily take part in the operations in the

Ptolemaic period (535 ff.), though even then they may do so; on occasions we find them as well as the principal giving receipts to the taxpayers; this continued in Roman times, when they like the principal are styled *telonai* (590 f.). The Ptolemies required that the partners should be registered when the contract was made; hence by that time the partnership has already been formed (542 f.). Harper suggested that the purpose of registration was to enforce the rule excluding officials from sharing in the contract; as there was an analogous rule at Rome prohibiting the participation of senators, it might be thought that there too registration had a similar object. But these rules could have been enforced by delation, and registration could have served other and more important purposes: (*a*) the qualification of partners who might share in the operations had to be certified; (*b*) in the Ptolemaic system, unlike that in Republican Rome, the partners as well as the sureties were liable to the state for deficits. There is no evidence for corporate tax-companies in Egypt at any time, but a document of AD 153/4 (*P. Paris* 17) shows that the heir of a deceased partner succeeded to the partnership.

3. In the Ptolemaic period and, if we may generalize from *P. Grenfell* ii. p. 41 (AD 46), cf. Wilcken, *Gr. Ostraka*, 587 ff., in the Roman period too, the tax-contract was for a year, unlike leases of domain land, which were of indefinite duration (*Grundz.* 274, 290), though the same contractor might renew it, and also farm several taxes (*Gr. Ostraka*, 515, 518, 521, 587–94; note Wilcken, *Chr.* 275). It might affect a nome, or a single village (520). In the Roman period, under the general control of the the prefect (592), the leases were effected by subordinate procurators and by *strategoi* and *komogrammateis* (*Chr.* 275), obviously when they concerned only small circumscriptions. Wilcken's list of taxes farmed under Rome (575 ff.), which could no doubt be supplemented, suffices to establish that *Kleinpacht* of petty imposts was then common. For example, different persons farmed the customs at particular stations (*SB* 7365; *Chr.* 277).

4. Ptolemaic tax-farmers contracted to pay lump sums; any surplus (*epigenēma*) in the actual proceeds of the tax was theirs, and they had to make up any deficit; they were also entitled to an *opsonion* of 5 per cent, later 10 per cent, on fulfilment of their contracts. Accounting took place each month, perhaps in the Roman period each quarter (cf. *P. Grenfell* ii. 41). Taxpayers (e.g. of the *apomoira*) could deliver what was due directly to the officials of the royal banks or *thesauroi*; in that event what they paid was presumably credited to the publicans' account. Préaux and others persist in the view already rejected by Wilcken (555 ff.) that collection was never the responsibility of the tax-farmers. The Revenue Laws prescribe that the number of collectors (*logeutai*

etc.) had to be agreed between tax-farmers and officials and that they were to be paid from the proceeds of the tax; they argue that this implies that they were state employees. Wilcken had urged that the farmers as well as the *logeutai* etc. are said to exact taxes; moreover the farmers give receipts to taxpayers and obtain them for sums they handed in to the banks or *thesauroi* (569). These considerations seem to me decisive, whereas Préaux's objection can be met. If the cost of the salaries of the *logeutai* etc. was a first charge on the revenue, and the obligation of the farmers was to pay a lump sum subject to deduction of this amount, we can see why the state would have wished to limit their number, as it bore their cost, whereas the farmers could well have wished to increase it, in the hope that the more numerous the personnel, the higher the yield might be, and the greater their prospect of obtaining a surplus or avoiding a deficit. It is they who named and presumably chose the collectors. This too suggests that the collectors were their servants; that being so, it is easier to see why the state needed an official *antigrapheus* to supervise their operations. Officials did indeed step in to collect arrears and fines. So too in the late Roman empire officials exacted arrears of taxes normally collected by *curiales* (A. H. M. Jones, *Later Roman Empire*, 457 f.), as they probably had done in the Principate (p. 339 above). It remains true, however, that under this system, in which publicans would have paid in what they collected each month, they did not retain large sums in their hand for long periods, as the Roman companies did in the republic (Jones, *Studies in Roman Government and Law* 1960, 101–4, cf. Badian 77; add Caesar, *BC* iii. 31. 2; 32. 6; 103. 1), and in AD 14 (Suet., *Aug.* 101. 4, if the 'vectigaliorum residua' are moneys still in their hands).

5. It is clear from Wilcken, *Chr.* 277 (AD 139), that the farmer of Roman *portoria* at Socnopaei Nesus was the actual collector (under official supervision). As he was accused of failing to credit the *fiscus* with duties payable, it appears that he had contracted to remit the sums actually collected in return for a percentage; if his liability had been to pay over a lump sum, he would have gained nothing from the offence imputed to him. The same document also seems to show that a man was not entitled to farm the same tax for as long as four years. It therefore indicates that the Ptolemaic system had been changed in this instance: how far we can generalize from it is uncertain.

6. In Roman Egypt surcharges were imposed on many taxes, both those collected by officials and those which were farmed; see Wallace 324 ff. He observes that 'a surtax is rarely mentioned in receipts for taxes farmed', but admits an exception for the *enkyklion*; for customs duties see de Laet 315–21. The explanation for these surcharges is obscure. Wallace conjectures that they may have met part of the cost of

collection. It is possible that in so far as Roman publicans in Egypt or elsewhere contracted to collect for a percentage of the receipts, they may also have been entitled to levy surcharges for their own account in case the percentage failed to cover their costs. It is remarkable that surcharges are also, and chiefly, attested in Egypt for taxes collected by officials. Here again they may have constituted part or all of their remuneration. We cannot exclude the possibility that those who collected *tributum* on behalf of the cities were compensated in the same way. See also n. 81 with text.

APPENDIX II

The Illyrian Portorium

Appian (*pr.* 6) states that in his day, i.e. under Pius, the Romans leased as a unit (ὑφ ἕν ἐκμίσθουσι) a tax called Illyrian levied throughout the provinces extending from the sources of the Danube to the Black Sea. This is clearly the *vectigal Illyricum* of inscriptions. It is orthodox to identify it with the *publicum portorium (utriusque) Illyrici et ripae Thraeciae* recorded epigraphically and to hold that the evidence relating to its *conductores* under Pius and Marcus confirms what Appian says, as it shows that the circumscription embraced Raetia, Noricum, Dalmatia, both Pannonias and Moesias, the three Dacias, and territory close to the mouths of the Danube; the last area was at first part of Thrace (de Laet 175 ff.; cf. 153–8), and to judge from inscriptions recording a *conductor ripae Thraciae* operating in 100 (*AE* 1919, 10; cf. Pippidi, *Epïgr. Beitr. zur Gesch. Histrias* (1962), 133 ff.; *AE* 1940, 100), had once been a separate unit. The name *vectigal Illyricum* was presumably adopted at the time when Illyricum, divided after the revolt of AD 6–9 into Lower and Upper Illyricum, comprised the later provinces of Dalmatia and the two Pannonias (*RE Suppl.* ix. 583); it was not changed when the new provinces were formed in the region. In the third century it seems that this circumscription was broken up (pp. 417–19 f.). *Stationes*, attested chiefly by the dedications which slave employees of the *conductores* or of the emperors set up, are expressly designated as toll-stations of the *p(ublicum) p(ortorium)*, or of the *vectigal Illyricum*; others whose function is not recorded are conjecturally taken to be toll-stations of the *portorium*. On some of the last there may be room for doubt, but in all other respects the orthodox views seem to me correct, and it would hardly be worth justifying them, but that they have been challenged by P. Ørsted, *Roman Imperial Economy and Romanization* (1985), 251 ff., on the basis of unproven assumptions about the functioning of the *portorium*, which in his view exclude the possibility that all those *stationes*, and particularly most of those explicitly connected with the *vectigal*, were places at which certain tolls were collected. In general I find his book one of inspissated darkness, through which all kinds of errors can still be glimpsed, and for that reason I have been unable to make use of it. It is, however, relevant to some part of my argumentation to establish that the *publicum portorium* of 'Illyricum' was leased as a unit in the second century.

Now we know from Appian that this was true of the *vectigal Illyricum*. The nature of this *vectigal* is indeed not specified by Appian or in any of the relevant inscriptions. *Vectigal* is a generic term for any kind of revenue (L. Neesen, *Unters, zu den direkten Staatsabgaben der röm. Kaiserzeit* (1980), 25–9). In the plural it could thus include all or any of the revenues obtained from 'Illyricum', not only the *portorium* but e.g. the *tributum*, the *vicesimae hereditatium* and *libertatis*, and rents from public domains, notably mines. Ørsted in fact persistently writes of the *vectigalia Illyrici*, and in most documents the words are abbreviated and the plural could be restored rather than the singular. However, in *CIL* iii. 8140 we have 'genio splendidissumi vect. Illyrici', and we should surely accept the usual restorations elsewhere of the singular. I am disposed to take 'Illyricum' to be an adjective, not a genitive. Aurelius Ianuarius, *procurator vectigalis Illyrici* after 195 (Pflaum no. 342), was thus 'procurator of the Illyrian tax', and 'vectigalis' is to be understood in the title of Aelius Faventinus, 'procurator ducenarius Illyrici' (*AE* 1956, 230), and that of Ti. Claudius Xenophon, 'procurator Illyrici per Moesiam inferiorem et Dacias tres' (Pflaum no. 222), as in that of some *conductores*. (The titles of other presumed holders of the procuratorial office in Pflaum's lists (n. 206) are not on record.) Illyricum, as a geographical entity, was not a unit for government except for this one tax. In general the tax administration must have been in the hands of the governors and procurators of the several provinces in the area, save that the mines too had eventually their special procurators, and these, or the lessees, are denominated not as Illyrian, but as Norican, Pannonian, Dalmatian, Dacian. It seems to me inconceivable that collection of the *tributum* was ever removed from the control of provincial governors and procurators and consolidated in one 'Illyrian' unit; moreover, we may presume, in default of testimony, that wherever possible its collection was entrusted, as elsewhere, to local authorities, and not leased, like the tax of which Appian writes. Thus the *vectigal Illyricum* cannot connote either *tributum* or revenue from mines, nor of course any tax like the *vicesimae* levied everywhere in the same form and not in a form peculiar to the Illyrian provinces.

So we are left with the *portorium*, and in fact it is expressly identified by apposition with the *vectigal Illyricum* in an inscription which refers to a 'c[onductor] p[ublici] p[ortorii] vectigal[is] Illyr[ici]' (*CIL* v. 1864) and implicitly in another in which an employee of the *vectigal* offers a dedication to the *numen* of the 'p[ublicum] p[ortorium]'. (*ILS* 1856). Iulius Saturninus, active under Pius and Marcus, who appears several times in dedications of his employees, as 'conductor publici portorii', is named on a wax tablet as 'conductor Illyrici', and on inscriptions he himself set up as 'conductor Illyrici utriusque et ripae Thracicae' (*CIL* iii p. 958, no. XXIII; *AE* 1928, 133; 1934, 107; the introduction into his title after 'conductor' of '[p(ublici) p(ortorii)]', though found in most transcriptions, seems to be unwarranted). The analogy with the appellation of T. Iulius Capito and two partners, Iulius Epaphroditus and Iulius Ianuarius, as 'conductor(es) publici portorii Illyrici et ripae Thraciae' (*ILS* 1463, 1858), is manifest. 'Conductor portorii Illyrici' is also attested (*CIL* iii. 4013; *ILS* 9010). Ørsted, 312 ff. usefully tabulates all the evidence on *conductores* of the Illyrian *portorium*, accompanied by partly fanciful reconstructions of their careers.

Most of this evidence consists of dedications by their slaves, who refer to their owners simply as 'c.p.p.'. From such inscriptions taken singly it would not be possible to deduce that the *conductores* concerned had leased the collection of the tax at any station other than that in which the dedicant was employed. But the titles just cited tell another story. They are naturally read as meaning that Saturninus etc. had leased the collection throughout the entire circumscription. It seems altogether implausible to hold with Ørsted, 324, that their designations merely 'indicate the maximum range of the *portorium* in question' and that each may only have been charged with collection at various stations within that range. In fact particular lessees such as Saturninus are attested as active in such widely scattered places within the circumscription as to confirm the most natural interpretation of their titles. Capito and his partners were honoured by seven cities distributed among the provinces of Lower and Upper Pannonia, Lower and Upper Moesia, and Dacia (*ILS* 1465), all of which must surely have been affected by their operations. Thus the specific evidence on the *portorium* fits Appian's description of the Illyrian tax leased as a unit.

APPENDIX III

The Saepinum Inscription

Under Marcus Aurelius an imperial freedman, Septimianus, reports to Cosmus, *libertus a rationibus*, complaints made by 'conductores gregum oviaricorum qui sunt sub tua cura', that on the *calles* traversed by the flocks in transhumance the magistrates and police of Saepinum and Bovianum had carried off 'iumenta et pastores quos conductos habent', on the plea that they had been stolen, and that in the consequential disturbance 'oves quoque dominicae' had run off; he demands action 'ne res dominica detrimentum pateretur'. Cosmus in turn seeks the intervention of the praetorian prefects 'ut beneficio vestro ratio fisci indemnis sit'. As a result the prefects sent a warning letter to Saepinum, which we have, and presumably to Bovianum too. This famous dossier (*FIRA* i². no. 61), reproduced by M. Corbier, *JRS* (1983), 126 ff., has generally been understood to mean that the *conductores* were lessees of imperial flocks and that losses were being incurred by the 'ratio fisci', inasmuch as this embraced property owned by the emperor (cf. ch. 7). This explanation seems to me correct. It has been challenged by Corbier. One may agree with her that the practice of transhumance was not confined to imperial flocks, and that flocks in private owner-ship might also have been leased to *conductores* and exposed to the outrages described, though Varro, *RR* ii. *passim* took it for granted that owners would manage their flocks through their own slaves as *magistri pecorum*, and it would be rather surprising if all the privately owned flocks supposedly in question had been leased. It is also conceivable that all grazing on public pastures might have been under the general care of imperial officials. But this is not attested, and nothing in the documents suggests that in this instance they were concerned about damage to private interests. The words 'oves *quoque* dominicae' do not imply that there were sheep belonging to persons other than the emperor which had been lost. Septimianus is saying that in seizing on shepherds and pack animals ('iumenta') the municipal agents had brought about the loss of imperial sheep as well. (It would seem that the *conductores* of the imperial flocks had to provide for themselves the necessary human and animal labour needed, which they had hired.)

APPENDIX IV

Italian Portoria

Portoria, which (it is believed) were originally not designed as customs-duties but as tolls for the use of public places such as harbours (Mommsen, *St. R.* ii³. 440), were levied in Italy until their abolition in 60 BC (Dio xxxvii. 51). Caesar, however, reinstituted duties on foreign merchandise (Suet., *Caesar* 43). In 42 the triumvirs revived *vectigalia* (τέλη) previously abolished, besides levying heavy direct taxes on property; Dio expatiates on the discontent that the latter occasioned (Dio xlvii. 16 f.). His vague reference to the restoration of taxes previously abrogated cannot refer to anything but the reintroduction of the Italian *portoria*, presumably on exports as well as on imports, since Cicero, writing in 59, asserted that their abolition had left no domestic source of revenue but the 5 per cent tax on the manumission of slaves (*Att.* ii. 16, 1), and there is no indication that this had ever been discontinued. (Admittedly Cicero overlooked *scriptura*.) There is no indication that the Italian *portoria* were subsequently abolished once more. Dio, for instance, does not mention this in his account of Octavian's benefactions and fiscal reliefs in 31 and 28 (li. 3. 3; liii. 2), and probably he would not have passed over a measure that would have rejoiced everyone (cf. n. 14), while drawing attention to the removal of specific burdens on freedmen. In AD 6 Augustus established the *vicesima hereditatium*; it was resented, and then and later Augustus invited others to suggest, and himself suggested, alternative modes of raising the revenue required, but not *portoria* (lv. 25; lvi. 28). Gaius too devised new imposts, including a tax on foodstuffs at Rome, until it could be said that he could raise no extra revenue in Rome and Italy (Suet., *Gaius* 40; Dio lix. 21. 1), but *portoria* in Italy do not figure among them. The most natural explanation is that they could not furnish a new source of revenue, because they were already among its existing sources.

None the less, de Laet stated flatly that there was no specific circumscription for *portoria* in Italy in the Principate. This would not mean that Italian imports and exports were free of duty. They would pay the appropriate duties within each circumscription from or to which they were shipped. But they would not pay two sets of duty. Now Strabo tells us that eastern merchandise paid duty on entry into Egypt and again on re-export through Alexandria (xvii. 1. 13). We might suppose by analogy that Spanish exports to Gaul paid both Spanish and Gallic *portoria*, and that the same practice was followed for all traffic between different circumscriptions. It is hard to tell how far traffic was also liable to internal tolls imposed by the imperial or municipal governments. Such tolls are attested in Egypt (n. 185), and probably existed elsewhere (n. 184, cf. de Laet 168–70, 219, 268–70, 290, 368 f.); *octrois* were even levied at the gates of Rome (n. 194). Though all the attested rates on trade within the empire were low, the total burden may have been considerable. But on de Laet's view goods whose origin or destination was Italy escaped more lightly than other merchandise. This would have been a privilege analogous to Italy's exemption from *tributum*.

It would be no objection to this thesis that Nero's notion of abolishing the *portoria* and the reforms he actually enacted were prompted by clamours from 'the people' (Tac., *Ann.* xiii, 50 f.). The *portoria* in provincial circumscriptions affected Italian trade, though less severely than inter-provincial trade, and must somewhat have raised prices on imported goods. Nero provided *inter alia* for prompt adjudication of disputes between tax-farmers and merchants in the court of the urban praetor as well as in those of provincial governors. Tax-farmers, including those organized in companies at Rome, could certainly sue and be sued in the provinces where they were operating, and this would be normal, where the other party to litigation resided in the province, but it is easy to envisage circumstances in which that party too was domiciled in Italy, and then, even though the dispute arose out of the collection of provincial *portoria*, it would be tried at Rome, in accordance with the 'forum rei' principle. Rome might also be the forum by agreement between the litigants. Nero's measure then carries no implication that it would be cases arising from collection of Italian *portoria* that would come before the praetor's court. The fact that the praetor in his edict, on which the jurists comment in its stereotyped Hadrianic form (though the relevant part may not have been changed much since the Republic), promised actions in his court to or against publicans, can also be explained on the hypothesis that some disputes arising from the collection of provincial taxes might be tried at Rome, though most of them were probably brought before governors or procurators (imperial interpretation of the law generally took the form of rescripts, which were more probably addressed to these officials than to the urban praetor).

An inscription from Ostia (*CIL* xiv. 4708) attests a *statio* there of the Gallic and Spanish *quadragesimae*. At the relevant time it was presumably possible for importers and exporters to pay there the duties on shipments from or to Gaul and Spain which would otherwise have been levied in Gallic or Spanish ports. (A Severan rescript (*Dig.* xxxix. 4. 16. 12) shows that it was customary to allow payment in arrears on goods duly declared.) This was clearly a convenience to shippers with funds in Rome or Ostia. One cannot see why it should have been denied to those trading with other provinces. Yet this is the only record we have of the arrangement. If it was not short-lived, that might warn us not to trust the argument that if there had been specifically Italian *portoria*, they would have left some epigraphic trace. Yet it is this silence that presumably made de Laet suppose that there were none.

It is not certain that this silence is complete. In north Italy there were unquestionably *stationes* of the Illyrian *portoria* at Aquileia (*AE* 1934, 234), Altinum (*CIL* v. 2136), Glemona (8650), Iulium Carnicum (1864), and Plorucum (*AE* 1923, 46). Their existence does not prove that in one or more of these places there were not also *stationes* of Italian *portoria*, farmed to different contractors who might have had their own separate office buildings. Only by setting this possibility aside can we assign other evidence for unspecified toll-stations in the region, at Aquileia (*CIL* v. 820), Pola (8139), Tergeste (706), and at Tricesimum (1801) to the Illyrian circumscription. Moreover the slave 'vilicus vectigalis Illyrici' in *AE* 1934, 234, was also 'praepositus qq'. Taking 'qq' to stand for 'quinquagesimae', de Laet conjectures that this was the Illyrian rate on merchandise passing from one part of the empire to another, whereas two inscriptions (*ILS* 1861, *CIL* iii. 137798), which mention a *vicesima*, suggest to him that this higher rate was paid on traffic crossing the frontiers (pp. 242–5). But the 'qq' seems to be distinct from the 'vectigal Illyricum', not one of two rates at which it might be levied, and we might suppose some distinction between the functions designated by 'vilicus' and 'praepositus'. The inscription is of Caracalla's reign, i.e. it falls within the period when the 'vectigal Illyricum' seems to have been collected by imperial freedmen and slaves, whether (as de Laet holds) for the direct account of the *fiscus*, or (as I think possible) on hire to publicans. As *vilicus* the slave was no doubt in charge of these collectors, but as *praepositus* he could have been responsible for supervision of publicans and their *familiae*, who might have been collecting a 2 per cent duty on goods entering and leaving Italy. *Praepositi* are also found in the Gallic circumscription (de Laet 135 f., 413 n. 1), and there is one case from Spain (*ILS* 1406); the employment of the imperial *familia* for collection in Gaul is far from assured, and certainly undocumented (unless by this inscription) for Spain. We also have another Illyrian *praepositus* under Severus Alexander (*CIL* iii. 10301), at Intercisa within the sector of the 'ripa Danuvii' when tax-farmers may have resumed their operations, if they had ever been intermitted (p. 419). Other evidence is given in n. 187, which *might* refer to the activities of publicans collecting Italian *portoria* at Aquileia, as under the Republic. Interpretation is inevitably conjectural.

Some taxes were surely still farmed at Rome, and to companies (p. 37). In no case is this practice more likely to have been retained than in that of Italian *portoria*, if there were any. The old system whereby publicans undertook to make lump sum payments to the treasury perhaps never fell into total disuse, and it meant that there was less need for close control than where publicans took a percentage of the gross proceeds (p. 382). We might thus explain why no specialized procurators are known for Italian *portoria*. In Spain too none are on record, nor for the *portoria* levied on the Syrian frontier. And once again it must be stressed that our documentation for imperial taxes is extremely deficient; for example only two chance allusions to publicans collecting the *vicesima hereditatium* (outside Egypt), only one to the farmers of the tax on sale by auction, nothing about the 1 per cent tax on sales, and indeed very little on *portoria* in several circumscriptions, notably in Spain. There de Laet (pp. 286–91) could find evidence for only toll-stations in the peninsula, but in five cases it consists not of local inscriptions but of *tesserae* from Monte Testaccio; there is only one attestation of the tax-farmers (*ILS* 1462), and only one of an imperial slave 'portus Ilipensis dispensator' (*ILS* 1406). De Laet's reliance on an argument from silence has to be set against the consideration advanced in the first paragraph of this Appendix, which may seem to have more strength.

18

Roman Imperial Illusions[1]

In aeternum urbe condita, in immensum crescente
(Livy iv. 4. 4)

I

Vitruvius, writing not long before 27 BC, asserted that Augustus (as he was soon to be known) was possessed of the government of the whole world and had subdued all peoples (i. *pr.* 1). Like Augustus' claim in his own record of his achievements that he had waged wars throughout the world (*RG* 3. 1), and that in the prescript composed posthumously, that he had subdued the world to the *imperium* of the Roman people, this language, which had been commonly used by Romans in the late Republic, appeared to equate the extent of Roman dominion with that part of the earth's surface within which were to be found all lands known to be inhabited, enclosed (so Greeks and Romans thought) by the encircling Ocean, and called by the Greeks *oikoumene* and by the Romans *orbis terrarum*. Of course Greeks and Romans in the first century BC (though ignorant of the true dimensions of Asia and Africa) knew of neighbouring peoples who, as Augustus himself put it, 'did not obey our *imperium*' (*RG* 26. 1), and more vaguely of others like the Chinese with whom they had no contact; in affirming their world dominion, Romans put these inconvenient facts out of mind, or implicitly treated all independent peoples as rightfully their subjects.[2] In 7 BC (i. 3. 4; 7. 2) Dionysius of Halicarnassus, then resident at Rome,

---

[1] This essay complements and sometimes modifies chs. 5 and 14. Much in the latter was subsequently reinforced in various ways by E. Gabba, *Athenaeum* (1977), 49 ff. (on imperialist sentiments in the 2nd c. BC), W. V. Harris, *War and Imperialism in Republican Rome 327–70 BC* (1979) (with which I am in general sympathy), P. S. Derow, *JRS* (1979), 1 ff., and A. W. Lintott, *Greece and Rome* (1981), 53 ff. These works, together with D. Kienast, *Augustus* (1982) (see pp. 274–310 for an admirable outline, with bibliography, of Augustan imperialism) and E. N. Luttwak, *The Grand Strategy of the Roman Empire* (1976) (see my review in *Times Lit. Sup.* (1978), 154 f. and esp. J. C. Mann, *JRS* (1979), 175 ff.), are cited by names of authors. I do not document all statements which can be readily checked in standard histories, or evidence supplementing Augustus' claims in *Res Gestae*, for which see J. Gagé's edition.

[2] J. Vogt, *Orbis* (1960), 151 ff.

could say that the imperial city possessed a universal 'hegemony' over every land within the circuit of Ocean that was not uninhabited or inaccessible (3. 3; 4. 2).

The term 'hegemony' may have been chosen with care to indicate that Rome's empire was not composed entirely of provinces under her direct administration. Even within these bounds allied or free cities constituted enclaves, dispensed by treaties or unilateral grants from control by the governor, though in practice Rome would intervene in their affairs when it seemed necessary, while other communities over which governors had full authority might normally be left in possession of substantial self-government. Beyond the provincial frontiers there were numerous dynasts or peoples which nominally enjoyed Rome's 'friendship', but which were expected to behave as vassals. Polybius had already treated the Hellenistic kingdoms within his purview as comprised within Rome's dominion, and he continually recounts how Rome required their rulers to comply with her will. Writers in Augustus' day could suggest that he had reduced the Arsacid kings of Parthia to the same level as the Seleucids or Ptolemies in the past (p. 437). Vassals were expected to furnish contingents in Rome's wars, and were sometimes obliged to pay tribute.[3] 'Client kings', to use a modern denomination, were appointed by Rome, or at least had to receive Roman recognition. In Augustus' time they had often been made Roman citizens, and as such were indictable in Roman courts.[4] Augustus regarded their realms as 'membra partisque imperii' (Suet., *Aug.* 48).

Naturally they could be recalcitrant, and some doubtless failed to understand the peculiar sense that Romans placed on the term 'friendship'; not all saw themselves as vassals: Ariovistus, for example, had not appreciated that by accepting that appellation he was considered to owe Rome allegiance (chapter 14 n. 74). In realistic terms some might be more independent than men at Rome liked to admit. Luttwak has suggested that in the Principate client peoples on Rome's western or northern frontiers were less susceptible to Roman control than the more organized dynastic states in the east, since they were able to migrate beyond Rome's horizons, while their own rulers had too little stable authority to be efficient instruments for mediating Rome's will.[5] Be that as it may, Roman supervision over client kings or peoples varied from case to case. In the Republic they could flout with impunity commands which the Roman government lacked the energy

---

[3] E. Badian, *Roman Imperialism in Late Rep.* (1968), ch. VI; Lintott 63; on Polybius see Derow.

[4] Ch. 14 n. 38. Trials at Rome: Tac., *Ann.* ii. 42, 67, it is surely mere accident that Archelaus and Rhescuporis are not attested as citizens.

[5] Luttwak 32 f.

to enforce. The contumacy of Jugurtha is a salient instance, and but for popular indignation at his massacre of Italians, a grave affront to the *dignitas imperii,* he might well have been left unscathed.

In general, their independence was the greater, the more remote they were from Rome or from Rome's armies. In distant Pontus Mithridates Eupator could build up his power till he became a formidable enemy. From the official Roman standpoint Cleopatra acted in the same way. The Ptolemies had been vassals for generations, but she (so it was alleged) had so bent Antony to her will that she had established a rival empire, embracing all the provinces east of the Adriatic, the government of which had been entrusted to Antony as triumvir; not only had he given away parts of them to Cleopatra and her children, but he himself was represented as a mere tool in the hands of a hostile ruler. Augustus could therefore boast that in the Actian war he had recovered them from kings (*RG* 27. 3). Since on this view Egypt too had passed out of Roman hegemony, he could say that by its annexation he had added it to the empire of the Roman people (27. 1). His reduction of Armenia to its former vassal status[6] and his subjugation of the country after a subsequent revolt also counted as substantial imperial successes, of which he boasts in the *Res Gestae.* By contrast he makes no mention of his peaceful conversion of the Galatian and Judaean kingdoms into provinces. As no real increase of imperial power was involved, these were not exploits worth commemorating. So too Tiberius, who had adopted the policy of containing the empire within its existing limits, did not think it inconsistent to annex the kingdoms of Cappadocia and Commagene. From one reign to another there was a tendency to bring client states under provincial administration. Direct rule was thus substituted for indirect, if on the demise or deposition of a client king no successor at once compliant and efficient could be found. The particular reasons for such a decision cannot always be discerned. Augustus declared that he might have annexed Armenia but preferred to follow tradition and therefore instituted a new king (*RG* 27. 2). This explanation can hardly be accepted as sufficient, since he did not hesitate to place other former client kingdoms under Roman governors. No doubt he supposed that the Armenians would give less trouble if *their* traditions were respected.

From the Roman standpoint it was thus not necessary, in order to aggrandize the empire, to reduce any region to 'the form of a province' and impose Roman taxation.[7] The Roman 'hegemony' could be

---

[6] Ch. 14 n. 38.

[7] Vell. ii. 38. 1 (cf. 37. 5) thought it worth while to record when each particular people 'redacta in formulam provinciae stipendiaria facta sit'; obviously this meant subjection in its most perfect form. Ti. Plautius Silvanus Aelianus took pride in having (under Nero) made over 100,000

enlarged in other ways. Augustus intended his readers to think that this had been achieved, when he recorded that the Cimbri, Charydes, Semnones, and other German peoples in their neighbourhood had sought his friendship and that of the Roman people (*RG* 26. 4), that Dacian tribes beyond the Danube had been forced to submit to Rome's commands (30. 2), and that 'I often received embassies from Indian kings which had never before been seen with any Roman commander. Our friendship was sought through ambassadors by the Bastarnae, Scythians, and kings of the Sarmatians on either side of the river Don, and by the kings of the Albanians, Hiberians and Medes.' We know of two Indian embassies. In 25, according to Orosius (vi. 1. 19–20), who doubtless drew on Livy, both Indian and Scythian envoys appeared before Augustus at Tarraco with gifts and *supplications*; and in 20 at Samos Indians actually made a treaty of 'friendship' with Rome (Dio liv. 9. 8). Orosius, or Livy, was reminded of the embassies sent to Alexander at Babylon with gifts and petitions from 'almost the entire world' (Diod. xvii. 113). The numerous allusions to these occasions both in contemporary literature and in later accounts of Augustus' reign, meagre as these are, show the impression they made, or at least their significance in Augustan propaganda. Augustus goes on to mention how Parthian, Median, British, and German kings sought refuge with him, how king Phraates of Parthia pledged his own children and grandchildren for 'our friendship', how very many other peoples with whom Rome had had no previous dealings learned of the *fides* of the Roman people when he was Princeps, and how on the request of the Parthian and Median nations he had supplied them with kings (*RG* 32 f.). *Fides* suggested that they entrusted themselves to Roman protection. These chapters of the *Res Gestae* were certainly calculated to suggest that Rome had acquired some sort of lordship over peoples in Germany, across the Danube, in south Russia and the Caucasus, and even in Iran and India.

Strabo saw clearly that vassal states were part of the empire and that there had been a tendency for Rome ultimately to annex them and bring them under direct rule. In a notable chapter (vi. 4. 2) he observes

---

'Transdanuviani' liable to tribute after transplanting them into provincial territory, but his further boasts of his dealings with peoples beyond the river, e.g. that he had prevailed on 'ignotos ante aut infensos p. R. reges' to adore the Roman standards, imply that they too were in a broader sense subject to Roman dominion (*ILS* 986). The term *imperium* was indeed ambivalent; when Suetonius writes of Augustus, 'tantum afuit a cupiditate quoquo modo imperium vel bellicam gloriam augendi, ut quorundam barbarorum principes in aede Martis Ultoris iurare coegit mansuros se in fide ac pace quam peterent' (*Aug.* 21. 2), he plainly restricts it to the territory that Rome governed, but equally Augustus regarded the barbarians concerned as subjects, as argued in the text.

that Rome had once administered Asiatic possessions 'through kings', but had converted their realms into provinces when a dynasty died out (e.g. Pergamum), or when the rulers like Mithridates and Cleopatra had proved disloyal; kingdoms in Africa (i.e. the Numidian and Cyrenaean) had had the same fate. He notes that it was proving less easy to secure the fidelity of the Armenians and of Caucasian and northern peoples through vassal kings; he ascribes this to Roman preoccupation with other affairs; no doubt the German wars, which he had just mentioned as in progress, were in his mind. In the general context of the account he gives here of Roman expansion a reader would naturally suppose that, once Rome was free to intervene with vigour, these peoples would be reduced to full subjection, like other hostile or rebellious peoples in the past. He proceeds to a brief analysis of Rome's relationship with the Parthians. Powerful as they were, they had acknowledged Rome's supremacy; they had restored the trophies of their victories over Rome (i.e. the standards captured from Crassus and Antony), and king Phraates was obsequiously wooing Augustus' friendship by entrusting to him his sons and grandsons as hostages. These words were clearly written before Phraates' death in or not long before 2 BC, but despite his vague allusion in the same chapter to 'some triumphs' over 'Celts' and 'Germans', he supposed the northern wars to be still continuing, and was probably writing before Drusus' and Tiberius' campaigns in the north had reached their apparently triumphal termination in 8 BC; Pannonia was then made into a province (*RG* 30. 1) and Germany between Rhine and Elbe was in Velleius' view (ii. 97. 4) virtually reduced to the same status; the success of these operations helps to explain Dionysius' even more optimistic description of the extent of Roman hegemony in 7 BC.

However, Strabo's next sentence seems to have been appended later; here he refers to frequent Parthian missions to seek a king from Rome, which can only refer to the time of the civil wars in Parthia from *c.* AD 4 to 9, when one party prevailed on Augustus to dispatch Vonones, one of the 'hostages' sent to Rome by Phraates, to claim the throne. Strabo treats this as an indication that the Parthians were almost ready to subject themselves to Rome. He can hardly have thought this after Vonones had been expelled in AD 12 and Tiberius had refused to attempt his restoration. The final sentence which refers to Tiberius' accession must then be a still later addition to the text. It was presumably the relationship between Parthia and Rome in Tiberius' reign that made Strabo elsewhere treat the Parthians as 'in a sense rivals' (ἀντίπαλοι) of the Romans (xi. 9. 2). In Augustus' time he had supposed that they were sliding from formal recognition of Roman superiority into real dependence.

In Strabo's view (iv. 5. 3) the friendship of British kings with Augustus had also made the whole island virtually a Roman possession. It is obvious that only kings in the southern part had entered into this relationship with Rome. But Romans were perhaps apt to identify the part with the whole; Caesar had probably treated the submission of some Gallic peoples as involving the submission of all the rest (ch. 14 n. 75). This way of thinking is relevant to the way in which Romans understood the overtures of Bastarnae, Sarmatians, Indians and the rest to Augustus.

Naturally Augustus and all knowledgeable Romans, perhaps Dionysius too, were aware that Rome had no means to impose her will on the more remote of her 'friends'. But their supposed recognition of her supremacy gave her the right to do so, when and if she had the power, a right which Caesar had exercised in suppressing 'rebellions' among Rome's 'friends' in Gaul, and which justified Augustus' interventions in the kingdoms of Armenia and Bosporus. Might it not also have been thought that Rome could require the obedience of all peoples?

Both Cicero and Virgil, to name no others, declared that Rome had a divine mission to rule the world (pp. 297 f.). Dionysius said that her 'hegemony' was not subject to dispute or protest (i. 3. 5) and was founded on her superior capacity for ruling (5. 2). Dionysius cannot have been ignorant that both subjects and vassals were at times refractory; the former statement presumably means that no protest against her authority was justified, and the latter that she had a natural right to demand universal submission. He was then perhaps not so much asserting an implausible claim that Rome was already mistress of the world, as a right which she was entitled to enforce at her own discretion. Alexander seems to have behaved as if he had such a title to obedience; even beyond the limits of the realm of the Achaemenids, whose legitimate successor he professed to be, he demanded acceptance of his authority, and put down resistance without mercy.[8] Did the Romans act in much the same way? Augustus never made war on any people 'without just and necessary reasons' according to Suetonius (*Aug.* 21), who echoes what Augustus himself says with regard to Alpine tribes (*RG* 26, 3). We may think that such 'just and necessary causes' might not constitute the only or decisive explanations of conquest; Cicero had prescribed that when a war was waged 'de imperio' with 'gloria' as its aim, there ought still to be such causes (i.e. pretexts) to be adduced in its justification (*de offic.* i. 38). And was it perhaps a 'just and necessary cause' for war if any people refused to comply with the wishes of the state entrusted by the gods with world

---

[8] See my Loeb edition of Arrian's *Anabasis*, i. App. XV, ii App. XXIII, 2–5.

dominion? Resistance then called for the utmost severities, massacres, enslavement, extirpation.[9] Dio alleges that in 35 Octavian attacked the Pannonians, though he had no complaint against them, since he treated any measure as just which was directed against peoples of inferior military strength (xlix. 36. 1). Perhaps this is too cynical an interpretation of the mentality which regarded all other peoples as owing obedience to their Roman superiors. It was an offence in Maroboduus, who had indeed been dispatched from Rome to rule the Marcomanni, and who must have had the status of a 'friend' (Strabo vii. 1. 3), that, though not disposed to attack the Romans, he showed himself resolved to resist, if attacked, and it was a *casus belli* that he declined to surrender refugees from Roman dominions (Vell. ii. 108 f.). Augustus would have been astounded if he had been required to surrender princes who sought asylum with him (*RG* 32. 1). Probably he did not think Alpine peoples entitled to levy tolls on Roman traders or publicans.[10] Rights which pertained to Rome might not be conceded to others.

Certainly the Romans, themselves the arbiters of their own cause, could treat the flimsiest grounds as justifying attacks on others. Of course barbarian incursions into their territory often supplied reasonable occasions for their subjugation. But the mere existence of an independent power was menacing in their eyes. No doubt they would have thought that experience vindicated Hobbes's dictum that 'in all times, Kings, and Persons of Soveraigne authority, because of their independency, are in continual jealousies, and in the state and posture of Gladiators, having their weapons pointing, and their eyes fixed on one another'. Subjects too might be encouraged to revolt by the spectacle of adjacent peoples or rulers still independent, and by the hope of the assistance which they might afford in a struggle for liberation. Agricola would think the conquest of Ireland advantageous on the ground that it would promote the final pacification of Britain, 'if Roman arms were omnipresent, and freedom were removed, as it were, from sight' (Tac., *Agr.* 24). (By giving asylum to an Irish prince 'specie

---

[9] On Roman apologies for the justice of their wars see ch. 14 s. VIII. Lactantius' cynical comments quoted there, which doubtless derived from Carneades, are anticipated by Livy ix. 11. 7 and 12; Roman writers, who had learned in the rhetorical schools to state both sides of a question, were capable of expounding views of Rome's policy which her enemies had, or might have, voiced (cf. Caesar, *BG* vii. 77; Sall., *ep. Mithr.*; Tac., *Agr.* 30–2). For Roman *Schrecklichkeit* see ch. 14 s. X. It is characteristic of the partiality of most modern interpreters of Roman imperialism that Gagé treats it merely as an illustration of Roman *clementia* that Augustus avers (*RG* 3. 2): 'externas gentes, quibus tuto ignosci potuit, conservare quam excidere malui'; for the fate of those it was not safe to spare cf. nn. 10, 67, and Domitian's boast that he had extirpated the Nasamones (Dio lxvii. 4. 6).

[10] Caesar, *BG* ii. 1, Strabo iv. 6. 7, cf. for the Salassi, who were mostly enslaved, L. J. Keppie, *Colonisation and Veteran Settlements in Italy 47–14 BC* (1983), pp. 205–7.

amicitiae', whose restoration Rome would demand, if and when convenient, he got ready a pretext for attack.) There could be no security or certitude of peace while any potential enemies remained. Virgil's vision of universal peace would be fulfilled only after the birth of Caesar (Augustus) 'imperium Oceano, famam qui terminet astris' (*Aen.* i. 288–95). The conquest of the world would be of benefit to all its inhabitants, and confer immortal fame on the conqueror.

II

It is conventional to hold that Rome's wars in the Republic, even when they issued in conquests, were normally designed, at least when they were undertaken by decisions of the home government and not by generals in the field, to protect Rome's existing possessions or those of her friends and allies. Yet it is obvious that conquests proved immensely profitable both to the state and to innumerable individuals, especially in the higher orders, and some will allow that economic motives had a subsidiary part in promoting them.[11] The allurement of gain may appear not entirely irrelevant to Augustus' imperial policies; though there was no prospect of enrichment from annexations in the north, the acquisition of Egypt and the pacification of north Spain with its rich mines enormously increased Rome's fiscal resources, and the expedition against the Arabians in 25/4 is said to have been prompted by the hope of large revenues (Strabo xvi. 4. 22); by contrast the idea of conquering Britain could be rejected on the ground that the costs of the operation would exceed the returns (iv. 5. 3).[12] (Suetonius' statement that Augustus disapproved of any battle or war 'nisi cum maior emolumenti spes quam damni metus ostenderetur' (*Aug.* 25. 4) is, however, not to be restricted to calculations of economic gains and losses.) Still in orthodox theory the main purpose of Augustus' plans of aggrandizement was the improvement of imperial defences; to this end (it is held) he pushed forward the frontiers in the north, while abjuring any offensive against the Parthians, with whom a *modus vivendi* could be negotiated. Security and perhaps profit are taken to be aims that can properly be attributed to a statesman prudent and calculating as

---

[11] Harris ch. II; I would, however, minimize the importance of commercial motives (*Fall of the Roman Rep.* (1988), 179–91).

[12] NW Spain: Pliny says that 20,000 lbs. of gold were extracted annually from the mines there (*NH* xxxiii. 78). G. D. P. Jones conjectures that Balbus' expedition against the Garamantes *c.*20 (Pliny, *NH* v. 36 f.) was designed to 'carve a slice in the profitable trade route south to Chad and the Upper Niger'; if so, I would think that it was the prospect of increased revenue from tolls that mattered (see *Bull. John Ryl. Libr.* (1978), 118).

Augustus undoubtedly was, whereas the aspirations of the poets for world dominion are taken to have seemed as chimerical to him as they do to us: the pursuit of power and glory for their own sakes would have been altogether irrational. This is a conception that also appears in modern discussions of Trajan's imperial policies. His annexation of Dacia can be explained by considerations of security, perhaps too by the desire to gain possession of the Dacian gold mines. The conversion of the Nabataean kingdom into the province of Arabia was of course only one more example of the substitution of direct administration for indirect rule through a client prince. But even his offensive against Parthia has been viewed as at least in inception an attempt to establish a better frontier in the east or to seize control of lucrative trade routes. Yet for Dio it was prompted by desire for fame (*doxa*) and emulation of Alexander; no ancient writer suggests other motives. It is characteristic of the prevailing modern outlook that one modern scholar who concedes that Dio may be right renders *doxa* as 'vainglory', and speculates on the possibility that a 'decline in health' impaired Trajan's judgement and produced 'emotional strain'. No man guided by reason could have had such an objective.[13]

This quasi-utilitarian conception of rationality, which hardly accords with the value that modern statesmen profess to set on 'national honour', not to speak of the passion for 'la gloire' that dominated Louis XIV, is surely alien to the mentality of most Greeks and Romans.[14] It is not indeed to be denied that we *can* account both for the expansion Augustus achieved or attempted in the north and for his abstention from embroiling Rome with Parthia by the hypothesis that his imperial aims were primarily defensive. But it does not follow that we *must* do so, when another explanation can be found, more consonant with Augustus' own style in recording and magnifying his achievements and with the ideals prevalent at Rome throughout his lifetime and voiced by the poets who enjoyed or courted his favour. This rival interpretation is admittedly incompatible with the opinions of later writers in antiquity, Suetonius and Dio, but they reflect a different outlook, and they do not expound and probably did not discern the extent to which Augustus in fact aggrandized the empire: their judgement was based on imperfect appreciation of the actual facts (see section VII).

[13] Dio lxviii. 17. 1, 29 f.; F. A. Lepper, *Trajan's Parthian War* (1948), Part II, esp. ch. XII.

[14] For example Thucydides makes Athenian representatives say that men are governed 'chiefly by fear, next by honour, and lastly by profit' (i. 75. 3), and Pericles boast that it would never be forgotten that among Greeks the Athenians ruled over the greatest number of Greeks, held out against coalitions in the greatest wars, and dwelt in a city best provided with all resources and unsurpassed (ii. 64. 3): they should love the power of the city (ii. 43. 1), the main theme of the Funeral Speech from ii. 36. 2 to 41. 3. The usage of φιλοτιμίαι to denote civic benefactions in Roman times shows that they were designed above all to extend and perpetuate the honour of the donors.

The notion that the desire for power and glory is irrational was certainly maintained by some (but not all) philosophers, who taught that the only unconditional good for man is virtue, or pleasure to be found essentially in peace of mind. But their doctrines were hardly less dismissive of the pursuit of such material advantages as security and wealth. Their disciples outside the schools were surely few, and not all of them practised what they professed. The love of military distinction infused Romans of every social class.[15] Above all for aristocrats it was the traditional objective to acquire glory, especially in warfare.[16] Services to the state were rewarded not least by election to the high offices, which were, significantly, termed 'honores'. Moralizing critics of Roman decadence in the late Republic lamented that love of honour had too often been perverted into ambition, the lust for power unrestrained by any care for the public interest. The celebrated funeral rites of the nobility (Polybius vi. 52–4) show how much they were traditionally concerned not only to enhance their reputation in life but to perpetuate it with posterity. It hardly needs proof that Augustus was of this way of thinking. The record of his distinctions and achievements designed for his mausoleum demonstrates his wish for posthumous commemoration. Equally his career was obviously marked throughout by ambition for dominance. Of course he made out, and doubtless believed, that he had also been serving the interests of Rome. But if glory was a proper objective for the individual, it was such no less for the state. *Laus* (*dignitas, gloria*) *imperii* was an ideal which all right-thinking men would cherish. It had come to involve the claim that Rome ruled, or was ordained to rule, all peoples (chapter 14, ss. III, V, and VI). To translate this claim into reality was a proper aim for a patriotic statesman.

> Wider still and wider shall thy bounds be set.
> God who made thee mighty, make thee mightier yet.

The imperialistic ditty, fervently sung at our Conservative Party Conferences, would have been congenial to every Roman ear.

Augustus' sagacity amounted to genius: no Roman was ever more adept at devising effective and often novel means to secure his ends. But that does not show that his choice of ends was that which would occur to men of the type characterized by Burke as 'sophisters, economists and calculators'. Nothing could have been more audacious than his resolve to enter on the political inheritance of Caesar and

---

[15] Harris ch. I.

[16] D. C. Earl, *The Moral and Political Tradition of Rome* (1967), ch. 1 and index s.v. *gloria*; J. Hellegouarc'h, *Le Vocabulaire latin des relations et des partis politiques* (1963), 362–414 on *gloria* and related terms. The *locus classicus* for the Republic is Cic., *Arch*, 26–30. Cf. n. 28.

eventually to make himself master of the state: it was the courses he followed in ensuring these purposes that were gradual, devious, experimental, and generally prudent. Why not think him capable of envisaging world dominion as the ultimate goal of imperial policy, and working towards it in a similar manner?

As I argued in 1964, Augustus was surely sympathetic to the expansionist sentiments expressed by the contemporary poets. He can indeed hardly have believed predictions that he himself would finish the task of world conquest. He could have had no expectation of a long life, and the strategy of expansion which he followed, whatever his ultimate goal may have been, was marked by caution and deliberation that precluded the fulfilment of any such aim within the lifetime of one man, however prolonged. However, in the edict of 2 BC issued on the completion of his forum he announced that he had set up there the monuments of Romans who had advanced the bounds of empire as examples both to himself and to later *principes* (p. 101). It would be their mission to continue or consummate his own work.

In my earlier essay I threw doubt on Hans Meyer's assumption that 'the poets were the heirs of Republican aspirations and the spokesmen of a public opinion which shared those aspirations'. It now seems to me on the basis of considerations advanced in chapter 14 that Meyer was on this point right.

The Republican system had indeed precluded the continuous and planned adoption of policies directed to fulfilment of these aspirations. Since in Roman conceptions the empire was not confined to the provinces, the senate's aversion to annexation, which has probably been exaggerated (n. 17), is not very material to the question. However, the senate was also reluctant to embark on any large-scale military enterprises. Offensive operations, for example in Spain, were commonly initiated by generals in the field, seeking booty and a triumph, whom the senate could hardly control. Only popular clamour constrained it in the end to take measures for the destruction of Jugurtha. With short tenures and armies hardly exceeding 25,000 men, proconsuls in the second century could hardly carry out any coherent strategy of aggrandizement. The great expansion in the first century was due to Lucullus, Pompey, and Caesar, with their prolonged commands and large armies. But what they did could not be part of any general strategy of aggrandizement; Lucullus and Pompey were not in a position to determine the policy of the state, nor was Caesar before he became dictator; but then he did (we are told) make such a plan (below).

Any explanation of the senate's attitude is necessarily conjectural. Possibly it was influenced by the unpopularity of the levy by which citizens were conscribed for the legions. It may have dreaded the risk of humiliating disasters incurred by incompetent generals, such as brought on Rome the danger of Cimbric invasion. Jealousy of the pre-eminence that any one of its members might attain by conspicuous successes was surely a more important factor. In any case a body of 300 or, after Sulla, of 600, rent by constantly changing factions, was probably incapable of clearly formulating and systematically execut-ing any consistent and coherent imperial strategy, once the problems of Rome's external relations had become far more complex than in an earlier time, when it had been an obvious objective to acquire and retain control of Italy itself. In general the senate did no more than react to events and adopt such expedients as they suggested.[17] It even failed to complete the pacification of Spain for nearly two centuries in which Roman armies had been continuously present there, or to afford full protection against barbarian inroads to the inhabitants of north Italy.[18] In 67 pirates had almost closed the seas to commerce, and though Pompey cleared them, no measures were taken to prevent recrudescence of an evil, from which the state had suffered dishonour and fiscal loss, and the Roman plebs deprivation.

In the last instance we can see most clearly that what the senate did and did not do is no guide to what public opinion wanted. I now believe that 'laus imperii' strongly appealed to the 'boni et beati' whom Cicero wished to mobilize in support of senatorial government.[19] It was of course they who dominated the towns throughout Italy. The prayers these towns offered for Pompey's recovery in 50 show how the great conqueror had become in their eyes a national hero.[20] If they evinced little enthusiasm in supporting him against Caesar in 49, it was surely in part because Caesar's well-publicized victories gave him a rival claim on their admiration. To persons like Cicero, devoted to the Republican government in which they themselves enjoyed great influence, the services of a Pompey or a Caesar to the empire counted for less than the danger of their personal dominance, which was accentuated by the wealth and prestige derived from their conquests. Under Augustus, apprehensions of this kind would no longer restrain

---

[17] In ch. 14 s. VII I too readily accepted the orthodox view that the senate was averse to annexations (see Harris ch. III); but I now also think that Gelzer was more percipient than I allowed in doubting the senate's capacity to follow any well thought-out policy. On jealousy of pre-eminence see my *Fall of Rom. Rep.* (1988) 43–5.

[18] Spain: Vell. ii. 38. 4, 90; Justin (Trogus) xliv. 5. 8; *ILS* 103. Alpine regions: Pliny, *NH* iii. 136 f., cf. my *Italian Manpower* (1971), 198 f.

[19] *Sest.* 96–8, 104. On the relation between Cicero's programme and Augustus' policies see my *Fall of Rom. Rep.*, 55–68.

[20] Cic., *Tusc. Disp.* i. 86; *Att.* viii. 16. 1 (implausibly suggesting insincerity); Sen., *ad Marc.* 20. 4; Plut., *Pomp.* 57; Dio xli. 6.

imperialistic sentiments. Though attachment to the Republic was not wholly confined to a narrow coterie, the higher orders in general cared still more for the preservation or restoration of internal order and security for life and property, and principally on this account they had become ready by 27 to accept Augustus' veiled monarchy. Thereafter his prestige, and their loyalty, could only be strengthened, the more he went on to fulfil their imperial aspirations. The poets who voiced them themselves belonged to the upper class, and must have found their readers chiefly within it. The martial spirit of this class, which Augustus sought to encourage, was perhaps dwindling, but they could get a vicarious satisfaction from victories in foreign lands without being obliged to shed their own blood in wars of conquest,[21] nor indeed until AD 6 to open their purses in order to pay something to the costs of the army.[22]

The sentiments of other citizens counted for less. The peasantry who had always supplied the legions had surely had their fill of wars. Conscription, especially for prolonged service far from home, was detested. Augustus thought it necessary to maintain many more legions than the senate had raised except in periods of great wars. The number was little changed after his successors had adopted a defensive posture.[23] Still offensive wars at least offered some chance of booty and glory and to the soldiers themselves might have seemed preferable to long years spent under harsh discipline in remote garrisons.[24] Moreover, the increasing practice of enlisting provincials in *auxilia* and even in the legions progressively lessened the need for conscription in Italy. Even in the crises of AD 6 and 9 it cannot have been at all comparable with the levies of the civil wars.[25] In any event the peasantry had no means of pressing their grievances on the imperial government, as they had occasionally done in the Republic, and they probably had no views to express on questions of state. The urban plebs could by contrast make their feelings known by clamours or riots. An emperor would naturally prefer plaudits to stone throwing. But the city dwellers were seldom called on to furnish recruits for the legions (though this

---

[21] Augustus wished all young men of rank to serve in the camps (Suet. 38. 2), but in course of time patricians usually followed purely civil careers.

[22] On the *vicesima hereditatium* Dio lv. 25; lvi. 28.

[23] It sank after Varus' defeat from 28 to 25, rising to 27 under Gaius, 29 under Vespasian, 30 under Trajan, 33 under Caracalla.

[24] See the complaints of the mutineers in AD 14, Tac., *Ann.* i. 16 (note 'nullis novis causis'), 17; Vell. ii. 125.

[25] Ch. 9 nn. 30–6 with text. The strength of 25 legions, together with praetorian and urban cohorts, would on a realistic estimate have been less that 150,000 men, not all Italians, whereas 200,000 Italians had been under arms in 72 BC and far more in the 80s; the number, reduced in 69–50 to *c.* 60,000–80,000, rose again in the 40s and 30s to nearly 200,000; see my *Italian Manpower*, chs. XXIV–VI.

happened in the crises of AD 6 and 9), and if it was their living conditions with which they were most concerned, and largesses did most to gain their affections, they were probably responsive to jingoistic propaganda, and delighted by festive celebrations of victories.[26] Not that there is any hint that they actually demonstrated in support of imperialist policies. Among the higher orders too there was no powerful pressure for the extension of Rome's dominion: however, once it had been achieved, it would have been valued as the highest service to the state and enhanced the prestige of the ruler, who could take the credit to himself.

III

It would have been quite natural if Augustus shared the sentiments common in the milieu from which he himself came. His personality is hard to seize, but vaulting ambition and political genius are not incompatible with acceptance of quite conventional beliefs or ideals. He professed allegiance to the traditional morality and religion, and his professions may well have been sincere (even if he did not live up to his own moral standards). In private life he was often old-fashioned.[27] It is at any rate certain that he was conscious of the contribution of military glory to the foundation and consolidation of his authority and that he cared deeply for his reputation with contemporaries and posterity and believed it to rest in part at least on his imperial achievements.

Knowing that, as Cicero had admitted,[28] distinction in war made the greatest impression on the minds of Romans, he had from the first pretended to it. His early assumption of the *praenomen imperatoris* betokened a claim that he was uniquely qualified for military command. In the course of his career he accumulated twenty-one imperatorial acclamations for victories won by himself or by generals acting under his auspices.

Enemies told stories impugning his sang-froid on campaign; but to say nothing of his honourable wounds in Illyricum, the audacity with which he assumed Caesar's political inheritance and won over Lepidus'

[26] Z. Yavetz, *Plebs and Princeps* (1969), showed that the plebs in the Julio-Claudian period cared for more than 'panem et circenses', though I can find no explicit testimony for the view suggested in the text.

[27] See my *Fall of Rom. Rep.* 58, and esp. Suet., *Aug.* 40. 5, 64. 2; Augustus' parsimony (72 f., 76 f.) and religiosity (90–3) were old-fashioned traits.

[28] Writing philosophically, or with his own civilian accomplishments in mind, Cicero stresses that *gloria* is acquired by any deeds demonstrating *virtus* in its broadest sense cf. Hellegouarc'h (n. 16) 372 f., but in *Mur.* 24, *de offic.* ii. 45 he recognizes the more typical Roman view.

soldiers in Sicily may make us doubt their veracity. The slanders in themselves show how much a reputation for soldierly qualities was expected to count with public opinion. Officially his *virtus* was extolled together with his *clementia, iustitia,* and *pietas*; in this collocation it cannot bear its most general sense, but rather the more primitive meaning of the manliness which was proper above all to the warrior and general.[29]

At first he was overshadowed as a leader in war by Antony. But in 36 he would boast of clearing the seas of 'pirates' and restoring peace by land and sea;[30] for this he celebrated an ovation. He then proceeded to make conquests in Illyricum, which could be sharply contrasted with Antony's disasters against the Parthians. There followed the Actian war, which resulted in the annexation of Egypt and also, on the official view, in Rome's recovery of all her possessions in the east (above). These victories earned him a triple triumph. Moreover, between 36 and 25 no fewer than twelve of his partisans, who governed provinces in the west, obtained successes which could be treated as occasions for triumphs, whereas only one of Antony's supporters had been allowed the same honour (in 34).[31] All this would suggest how with the collaboration of his agents he had been strengthening the empire, while Antony was diminishing its prestige and territory. It made it plausible to contend in 27 that he alone was fit to be entrusted with the care of the provinces most in danger from revolts or invasions.[32]

Naturally he could not himself command all the armies in these widely scattered provinces, and after a few years he ceased to direct military operations in person even from rear-headquarters; his health was frail, and he doubtless recognized that his talents as a general were limited. The actual command therefore fell to his legates. Some of them obtained notable successes, and it may not have impressed everyone that he claimed the credit on the basis that they were fighting under his auspices; on this ground he denied them triumphs and even imperatorial salutations. But their tenure was relatively brief, and major offensives were entrusted to imperial princes. Indeed, whereas later emperors would take imperatorial salutations for victories that their legates gained, Augustus after 27 accepted them, fourteen in all,

[29] *RG* 34, cf. *ILS* 82, EJ 22 for the *clipeus*; Suet., *Aug.* 8. 2; 10. 4; 13. 1; 16. 2 has anecdotes which impute personal courage or cowardice (cf. Pliny, *NH* vii. 149) to Augustus.

[30] App., *BC* v. 130, cf. *RG* 25. 1. It was rather the result of Augustus' creation of permanent fleets that ensured peaceful navigation for the future, cf. Hor., *Odes* iv. 5. 19, Suet., *Aug.* 98, etc. Of this, and of other measures to promote security for all under Roman rule, Augustus says nothing in *RG*.

[31] EJ pp. 34 f. *sub annis.*

[32] Suet. 47. 1; Dio liii. 12. 2. But for political reasons not Illyricum (until 12 BC), Macedon, and Africa, see Syme, *Roman Revolution* (1935), 314 f., 329 f., 394.

only for successes obtained when he or members of his family exercised personal command; Tiberius as a holder of independent *imperium* shared in some of these salutations, and was allowed to celebrate two triumphs.[33] Thus, so far as possible, the military glory accruing from aggrandizement of the empire was reserved to the reigning house, in furtherance of Augustus' dynastic plans. Supposing that it was Augustus' intention to enlarge the empire only to the extent that would make it 'possible to reduce foreign policy to the protection of the frontiers', Syme suggests that thereby Augustus sought to 'banish at the same time the occasion for warfare on a large scale and its unfailing concomitant or sequel, the menace of intestine strife' (*CAH* x. 340). But this menace was minimized when no private person was given the opportunity to emulate a Pompey or a Caesar. The stability of the regime was strengthened, not imperilled, by warfare on a large scale which enhanced the prestige of the emperor and his family.

In Augustus' lifetime his forum was effulgent with the names of the peoples he had subdued (Vell. ii. 39. 2), which could also be recorded locally on triumphal arches (Pliny, *NH* iii. 137). We know from an edict quoted by Suetonius (28. 2) that he once expressed the hope to be remembered as the author of a lasting system of goverment. But in the great inscription he composed for his mausoleum, which was surely intended to commemorate him to all future ages,[34] though he enumerates his offices and the many extraordinary honours conferred on him, he makes no attempt to indicate the nature of this system, perhaps because it did not lie solely within his own power to guarantee its permanence, nor to enumerate his administrative and legislative reforms: he prefers to preserve against oblivion those achievements which posterity could not take away, his acts of munificence, and above all his successes in waging wars 'throughout the world' (3. 1), in establishing universal peace by land and sea (13), in extending the bounds of every frontier province, in pacifying Gaul, Spain, Germany

[33] T. D. Barnes, *JRS* (1974), 21 ff. E. Badian, *Romanitas—Christianitas* (ed. G. Wirth), 18 ff. esp. pp. 38–42, rejects Dio's statement (li, 25) that Augustus took an imperatorial salutation in 29 for M. Crassus' Thracian victories. It is an obvious difficulty in accepting it that Augustus took no salutations for the successes in these years of other generals who like Crassus were permitted to triumph (n. 31). Badian's solution is to find the occasion in the operations of Cornelius Gallus, prefect of Egypt. But Augustus took no salutation for those later achievements of prefects of which he boasts in *RG* 26. Now Augustus was *imp. VI* after Actium (Oros. vi. 19. 14; *ILS* 79), and remained so according to *ILS* 80, in some part of 29, in which year he was also *imp. VII* (*ILS* 81). If this be so, he took no salutation for the capture of Alexandria, although in the triple triumph of 13–15 Aug. 29 this was distinguished from the victory at Actium (*Per.* Livy cxxxiiii; Dio li. 21; Macrob. i. 12. 35); we should then expect a separate salutation, in 30, and might suppose that 'imp. VI' in *ILS* 80 is an engraver's error for 'imp. VII'.

[34] I cannot understand how Kienast 176 can think that *RG* was designed not to serve Augustus' reputation with posterity but only to represent the new monarchy in the form of a record of achievement.

to the mouth of the Elbe, and the Alpine peoples, in sending a fleet to the Jutland promontory, and armies into Ethiopia and Arabia (26), in annexing Egypt, restoring control over Armenia, and recovering all the eastern provinces (27), in forcing the Parthians to beg for Roman friendship (28), in conquering the Pannonians, advancing the frontier to the Danube, and compelling the Dacians beyond it to submit to Roman commands (30), in accepting offers of friendship from Germans, Indians, Bastarnae, Scythians, and Sarmatians, and very many other peoples which had had no previous contacts with Rome (26. 3, 31; 32. 3), in giving refuge to foreign kings and appointing rulers for foreign peoples, including the Parthians (32 f.). The claim that he sometimes makes in express words, to have been the first to have achieved these successes (26. 4; 30. 1; 31. 1; 32. 3), is often implicit elsewhere in their bare recital. The accent is not on measures for the more effective defence of Rome's existing possessions.

IV

All this suggests that the admiration Augustus expressed for Alexander was genuine,[35] and that he was not indifferent to the example of Caesar. He was the heir of Caesar and *divi filius*. Once he was Princeps, he would make less of this relationship than in his rise to power, no doubt because Caesar had estranged men by ostentatious autocracy, which he was careful not to revive. But he had no like reason to repudiate the ambitions attributed to Caesar 'de tuendo *ampliandoque imperio*' (Suetonius, *Caesar* 44. 3), since they corresponded to beliefs and hopes prevalent in the higher orders.[36]

At the time of his death Caesar had prepared an expedition to be directed first against the Dacians (or Getae), whose aggrandizement in the Balkans under their king Burebista inspired alarm at Rome, and then, through Armenia, against the Parthians.[37] According to Plutarch (*Caesar* 58), he proposed to subdue them, and then to march from

[35] See p. 108. Weippert (ch. 14 n. 66) holds that Augustus substituted his own image for Alexander's on his seal (Suet. 50) not later than 23 BC, as the despotic king was no proper exemplar for the Princeps, and that Alexander ceased to command his overt respect after he himself (supposedly) relinquished thoughts of world conquest in 20, though he shows that imitation of Alexander can be traced in C. Caesar, Drusus, and Germanicus. But, as Kienast remarks (285), it was in 2 BC that Augustus embellished his forum with Apelles' pictures glorifying Alexander (Pliny, *NH* xxxv. 94); if this served any propagandist purpose, it was to keep alive the hope of subduing Iran, however little Augustus was meditating that enterprise at the time. Later both Trajan (n. 13) and Caracalla (Dio lxxvii. 7.) were influenced by Alexander's example.

[36] Syme, *Rom. Rev.*, 317 f. But see Kienast 428. Lucan makes a Republican say of the Parthians, 'gens unica mundi est de qua Caesaris possim gaudere triumphos' (viii. 429 f.).

[37] App., *BC* iii. 25; Strabo vii. 3. 5 and 11; Suet., *Caesar* 44.

Hyrcania, south of the Caspian, through the Caucasus, round (i.e. to the north of) the Black Sea. It must be borne in mind that it was then and long remained the prevalent view, which Strabo, for example, adopted,[38] that the Caspian was not a lake but a gulf of the encircling Ocean, and that the Romans since Pompey's campaigns regarded as their vassals the Albanians and Iberians in the southern part of Caucasia, and the Bosporan kingdom in the Crimea and Krasnodar. Caesar was next to invade 'Scythia', Germany, and surrounding lands. The vagueness of these terms was natural; according to Strabo it was not known how far eastwards the Germans extended or who their neighbours were; 'Scythia' obviously does not refer (as it may elsewhere) to Asiatic lands east of the Caspian but to the peoples such as the Sarmatians adjoining the Bosporan kingdom. Of course, if the attack on the Dacians had been successful, Caesar would already have extended Roman power beyond the Danube. Finally he was to return to Italy 'through Celtic lands', perhaps from what were to be Raetia and Noricum. Plutarch says that as a result the empire would have been bounded by the Ocean. This seems to imply that he was to carry it in some sense not only to the Caspian 'gulf' but also to the northern shore of the Ocean. In that region he might have expected little resistance; Strabo thought that it might not be inhabitable. Nicolaus of Damascus tells that Caesar also hoped to subdue the Indians (F. 130. 95), and that would have been indispensable, to make the Ocean the limit of the empire.

Gelzer, who seems to accept Plutarch's account of his design in relation to Europe, rejects Nicolaus' testimony that he aimed at the conquest of Parthia and India.[39] But that of Parthia is implicit in Plutarch's version too; he was to penetrate to Hyrcania, in the heartland of the Parthian realm. Crassus too, we are told, had hoped without difficulty to reach Bactria, India, and the 'outer Ocean' (Plut., *Cr.* 16. 2). His fate had shown that it was no easy task to vanquish the Parthians, but Carrhae could still be explained in part by his incompetence. The project ascribed to Caesar may too readily be treated as impracticable, merely because Caesar's death prevented the attempt. Had Alexander died soon after Gaugamela, and we had been told that he proposed to subdue Iran, scholars would certainly have been found to deny credence to any report of unfulfilled intentions, which no man

---

[38] e.g. Strabo viii. 2. 4. Later on, Ptolemy knew the Caspian to be a lake, yet his view did not always prevail; see J. O. Thomson, *Hist. of Ancient Geography* (1948), index s.v. Caspian.

[39] *Caesar* 322 f., citing other evidence. For careful discussion of the rationality of Caesar's preparations and probable projects see J. Malitz, *Historia* (1984), 22 ff. It is important for assessment of Augustus' policy regarding Armenia that Caesar designed to invade the Parthian empire through that country, minimizing the danger from the Parthian mounted archers, cf. Suet. 44. 3.

of sense could have entertained. Any suggestion that his successors, though warring among themselves, could hold on to a large part of Iran for generations after his conquest would have seemed still more absurd. We have no better right to deny the possibility that with sufficient resolution the Romans could have done as much as Alexander had done, and the Arabs were to do later, or to assume that Caesar was too level-headed (a presupposition that may itself be questioned)[40] to have conceived so grandiose a plan. Of course he would not necessarily have contemplated the annexation of all the lands he might overrun. He might have thought it enough to enforce recognition of Rome's 'hegemony'. Perhaps too he never committed himself to specific conquests. When he had intervened in 58 against the Helvetii, he had hardly yet set himself to conquer all Gaul, still less to cross the Rhine and Channel. But he had been ready to go as far as opportunity offered. In 44 his primary aims were no doubt to break the Dacians' power and avenge Carrhae, but he would again have pursued any advantage as it occurred. He must at least have let it be thought that he was pursuing the realization of world empire.

In Nicolaus' view it aggravated the guilt of his assassins that they frustrated this project. Nicolaus mentions it in his panegyrical life of Augustus. He could have ignored it, and would surely have done so, had he supposed that it was alien to Augustus' own aspirations. In other fragments he eulogizes Augustus for having ruled over the greatest number of men in human memory and having extended by war and diplomacy Roman dominion to its furthest limits; he had tamed peoples never before heard of and not known to have been subject to any other power; the catalogue that followed is not completely preserved (F. 25). His successes in civil and foreign wars were to be celebrated as well as those in politics (F. 126). Nicolaus doubtless thought that this sort of laudation would earn Augustus' approval.[41]

V

Caesar was 'an old man in a hurry'; Augustus, still only thirty-five in 27, could take longer views. For all his admiration of Alexander, he is said to have criticized him for not seeing the organization of an empire

---

[40] J. H. Collins, *Historia* (1955), 445 ff.

[41] Kienast 224 accepts a date for Nicolaus' work in the late 20s, whereas R. Laqueur, *RE* xvii. 401–6, argued that it post-dated Augustus' death; whichever view is right, we must assume that Nicolaus thought that his encomium would be congenial to the reigning emperor. (Tiberius, while abjuring further expansion, did not venture to deny Augustus the glory of his conquests, as the prescript to *RG* shows.)

as a greater task than its acquisition.[42] This does not imply that in his judgement Alexander would have been wrong, once organization was complete, to undertake new conquests. Augustus certainly devoted years after Actium partly to consolidating his own control at Rome, partly to administrative reforms and pacification within the empire. Within a decade he completed the subjugation of Spain; his own personal part in the preliminary stage of the operations was magnified,[43] but his was the responsibility for ensuring that the task, which the Republican government had so long shirked, was systematically carried out. So too he at last gave north Italy security by reducing the Alpine peoples; this also prepared the way for the more ambitious northern offensives which were to follow.[44] Even within this period the Arabian and Ethiopian expeditions of 24 betray hopes of aggrandizement not prompted by mere considerations of frontier defence.[45] They had little or no result, and Augustus had not committed great resources to them. It was certainly his policy to incur no serious risks for the time in trying to enlarge Roman dominion in the east. A demonstration in force was enough in 20 to obtain a nominal submission from Parthia and to restore Roman suzerainty in Armenia. Rome's honour was satisfied and the danger was minimized of a Parthian attack, so long as he was preoccupied with the great project of conquest in the north.

That began in 13, and the campaigns of 13–8 BC resulted in the annexation of Pannonia and the establishment of Roman suzerainty in Germany up to the Elbe[46] There followed a pause, perhaps designed initially for consolidation, and then possibly prolonged, because the death of Drusus in 9 and the retirement of Tiberius in 6 left Augustus with no members of his own house of the age and experience requisite for high command, and it presumably seemed to him imprudent to allow any one else to win renown from major conquests. It was perhaps in this period that he forbade his commanders in Germany to provoke trouble there by crossing the Elbe; we do not know if the instruction had been cancelled, or was ignored, when L. Domitius Ahenobarbus did so a little before AD 1. A revolt then broke out in that part of Germany which had supposedly been subdued. Its repression was postponed because of the breakdown of the eastern settlement of 20 BC

---

[42] Perhaps a *topos*, cf. Sen., *Suas.* i. 8; Aristides, *To Rome* 24.

[43] Barnes (n. 33) 21.

[44] C. M. Wells, *German Policy of Augustus* (1972), 35–87.

[45] Kienast 276–8.

[46] Syme, *CAH* x. 351–81, remains the best account, though D. Timpe, *Saeculum* (1967), 278 ff., shows that he unduly depreciated the extent of Drusus' apparent success in Germany, through which Tiberius had an easy and rapid passage to Drusus' corpse (cf. Vell. ii. 97. 3; Strabo vii. 1. 3a; Aufidius, *HRR* ii. 96. 3).

(Dio lv. 10a. 3). Augustus was evidently unwilling to precipitate warfare on a large scale simultaneously on two fronts.

Yet he would also take no measures to restore Roman power in the east, which might entail a serious war with Parthia, until the command there could be entrusted to an imperial prince. Tiberius had been designated for this task in 6 BC (Dio lv. 9. 4), but his retirement followed immediately, and Augustus postponed any action until AD 1, when he gave the command to the young Gaius Caesar; he was to be accompanied by mature advisers, but the honour of any success obtained would redound to the imperial house (lv. 9. 20). In fact Gaius was able to reach a new accord with Parthia and to place Armenia under a king of Rome's choice without serious fighting (below). His death facilitated Tiberius' return to public life.

The task of pacifying Germany could now be resumed under Tiberius' command. On Velleius' flattering estimate (ii. 108. 1) his campaigns in AD 4 and 5 left nothing to be conquered in Germany, i.e. up to the Elbe, except for Maroboduus' kingdom in Bohemia. A few years later Varus seems to have been engaged in introducing the forms of provincial government in west Germany.[47] In much the same way after a process of pacification in Augustus' reign, which our sources do not permit us to trace, following the operations of M. Crassus in 29–28 BC, Moesia was evidently to be organized as a province, though not until the principate of Tiberius, who first imposed taxation (App., *Ill.* 30). Augustus' next step was to be the conquest of Bohemia, where Maroboduus, initially a protégé of Rome (Strabo vii. 1. 3), had in effect thrown off his allegiance (Vell. ii. 108 f.). Great forces were mobilized for a two-pronged attack, when the revolt in Illyricum compelled Augustus to reach an accommodation with Maroboduus (Tac., *Ann.* ii. 46. 2). This had no sooner been crushed than Arminius destroyed Varus' army in Germany. About the same time Rome once more lost control of Armenia and was menaced by the possibility of renewed Parthian hostility. As a result the territory supposedly acquired between Rhine and Elbe was to be abandoned, Maroboduus was saved from direct Roman attack, and Tiberius would desist from all further projects of imperial expansion.

This summary narrative serves to expose the facts that Augustus was bent on aggrandizing the empire, that he proceeded cautiously, in stages, as circumstances permitted or required (*festina lente* in its Greek form was a favourite maxim),[48] that he would commit large-scale enterprises only to members of his family, and that he preferred to conquer in the north rather than in the east. The record does not reveal

[47] See ch. 3 n. 15.
[48] Suet. 25; Gell. x. 11. 5.

his motives or ultimate purposes. Velleius, who served in many of the campaigns, offers no explanation at all. Probably he thought that none was needed: the extension of Roman dominion was *per se* an intelligible aim. But in telling that the suppression of the Illyrian revolt led to the abandonment of the projected invasion of Bohemia, he remarks, 'necessaria gloriosis praeposita' (ii. 110. 3); he takes it for granted that the subjugation of Maroboduus would have been a glorious enterprise, which had to be given up because it was necessary to maintain Rome's existing dominion. He does not hint that it was primarily for the security of the empire that any conquests in the north were attempted. Considerations of security would no doubt always have determined when and where offensive operations should be launched for the glory of conquest. Internal pacification was the primary need, together with the protection of Italy itself against external attacks.[49] A show-down with the Parthians could at least be postponed, since at worst it was only outlying parts of the empire that they menaced, and diplomacy accompanied by demonstrations of force could, as it proved, neutralize them for the time. It was more urgent in the interest of security to advance Roman power in the North, but there too glory could be won, perhaps more easily.

It was not enough simply to impose a peaceful life on the Alpine tribes immediately adjacent to north Italy. That could not obviate the danger from *Völkerwanderungen* in Germany and the Balkans. Recollections of the Cimbric irruptions cannot have been extinct. Augustus would tell the senate on the occasion of the Illyrian revolt that in the absence of precautions the rebels might be seen at Rome within ten days (Vell. ii. 111. 1), and Tiberius would allege that Maroboduus, 'an enemy so close to Rome', was more to be feared than Pyrrhus or Antiochus of old (Tac., *Ann.* ii. 63). Some measure of genuine apprehension may have underlain these absurd exaggerations. Moreover, while experience had revealed that the Parthians were formidable adversaries within their own country, it could well have been

---

[49] Syme, *CAH* x. 353, suggests another reason for expansion in the north: it would 'broaden yet further and consolidate still more firmly the western half of the Empire and thereby ensure its preponderance in peace as in war over the East'. But Augustus and his contemporaries surely conceived of the empire as an *Italian* dominion over subject peoples, and I know of no evidence that they (or later Romans) discerned a greater affinity between Italians and Numidians, Celtiberians, Gauls, Germans, or Illyrians than between Italians and Greeks or Hellenized easterners; the contrary is more likely, given Rome's acknowledged debt to Hellenic culture. It could not be foreseen that in the long run Rome would more thoroughly assimilate some (not all) barbarians in the west than Greek speakers, but when this assimilation took place, those affected were esteemed not for western origin but for having become Romans or even Italians (cf. Stat., *Silv.* iv. 5. 45 ff.); moreover, Greek speakers, who came to feel as much loyalty to Rome and would eventually be known as Rhomaioi, would also be admitted to a share in imperial goverment, as freely as western provincials; Augustus would not have envisaged such an advancement for either.

expected that the barbarous peoples in the north could be subdued as rapidly as the Gauls. It had taken Caesar no more than eight years to conquer them, and since 52 BC there had only been sporadic risings among them of no great consequence. It would have been easy to overlook the fact that the more developed economy of Gaul had made it easier for Caesar to solve problems of commissariat than Augustus' generals must have found it in Germany, and that a people dependent on a settled agricultural life might be more submissive than tribes readier to migrate. In fact it is evident that after the operations of 13–8 BC, and again after those of AD 4–5, the Romans overestimated the acquiescence of the Germans in Roman control, just as they overestimated that of the Illyrians; they even relied too much on the active loyalty of troops raised among the conquered peoples, serving under native chiefs.

We cannot gauge Augustus' intentions from what he had actually accomplished at any given moment. If he had died in 14 BC, we should have no inkling that he thought of advancing Roman power to the Elbe and Danube, and if in AD 5, we might not have suspected that he would have conceived of conquering Bohemia. The defensive advantage of improved lateral communications on the Hamburg–Leipzig–Prague–Vienna line, discerned by Syme, if ever apparent in the absence of modern maps, can hardly have been seen until more was known of the interior of Germany than at the time of the offensive of 13 BC; exploration accompanied conquest.[50] Since in the end Augustus was unable to establish the frontier on that line, we cannot be certain that it was the furthest limit he ever envisaged (n. 46). On one view it could never have been satisfactory, since the Elbe ran though the most populated part of Germany, with the strongest German people, the Suebi, bestriding the river.[51] Augustus could never have been confident that no formidable and aggressive power would rise beyond, like that of Burebasta in the past, or Decebalus in the future. A 'natural' barrier would only have been reached, on the geographical theory of the time (n. 38), when Roman arms had been carried as far as the Caspian 'gulf' of the Ocean. At that point the right flank of Roman armies in

---

[50] On the inadequacy at all times of information available to emperors on peoples and geographical features beyond the empire see now F. Millar, *Britannia* (1982), 15–20. Syme, *History in Ovid* (1978), 51 f., taxes me with misinterpreting his 'line Hamburg–Leipzig–Prague–Vienna as a limit', but in fact I never supposed that he conceived this line as a frontier of the Hadrianic sort, and his new formulation ('to annexation a limit could be found, with suzerainty claimed beyond it') still implies that in his view Augustus excluded any design of annexing more territory than was required for control of the river communications that Syme has in mind, and this remains a disputable hypothesis. I do not challenge Syme's view that Augustus attached priority to the subjugation of Illyricum as against that of Germany.

[51] Timpe (n. 48), 292.

the north would have lain on the Caucasus, where the Iberians and
Albanians had been the nominal vassals of Rome since Pompey's
campaigns; their kings were among those who sought Augustus'
friendship, as were the Bastarnae and Scythians, dwelling north of the
Danube, and the Sarmatians 'on either side of the Don'. If it was
Augustus' aim, as Syme supposes, to shorten communications between
armies and make it easier to reinforce whichever was under attack,
such a frontier would have appeared far more defensible than that
which Syme takes to have been his objective. The great rivers that
empty into the Black Sea would have served in place of the Elbe for the
movement of troops and supplies to the far north, where it was
conjectured there were few inhabitants, if any. And it could have been
thought that once this line was reached, it would be easier at last to
strike at Parthia, since the northern frontier would then have been
continuous with the eastern, and control of the Caucasus would have
exposed north-western Iran to invasion. Of course any such design
would have been chimerical, not only because its geographical precon-
ceptions were false, but because Rome lacked the power, or the
tenacity of purpose, to subdue even the German peoples. But it does
not follow that it was not in Augustus' mind.

VI

Nothing has perhaps done more to convince modern interpreters of
Augustus' imperial aims that they were fundamentally defensive than
the unquestionable fact that he refrained from attacking the Parthian
empire, and preferred to negotiate settlements with its kings; they do
not entertain the possibilities that he was merely deferring execution of
Caesar's project in the east until he had sufficiently enlarged the empire
in the north, and that he hoped in the interim to establish some sort of
suzerainty over Parthia. They applaud the moderation and sagacity of
his policy, as they see it, because in their view the Parthians were too
weak to constitute any serious threat to Rome and her possessions, and
had ceased to be aggressive, and at most censure him for insisting on his
right to nominate to the Armenian throne; since the Parthians
regarded Armenia as naturally lying within their sphere of influence,
and the Armenians themselves inclined to the Parthian side, efforts to
maintain Roman influence in Armenia could never (it is contended)
have had any lasting effect, but simply disturbed friendly relations
between the Great Powers. 'Save for this apple of discord, there was no
reason why the two empires should not have lived in peace and amity',
a judgement penned in the heyday of League of Nations Union

idealism.[52] On this view Nero did better, in accepting a compromise under which a Parthian prince was formally invested by Rome as king of Armenia. That was of course a face-saving device; in fact Nero renounced real control of Armenia. As a result Vespasian thought it necessary to station two legions in Cappadocia, in addition to the six which had long protected the eastern frontier (including those in Egypt); this corresponded to a net increase in the legionary establishment, and with the accompanying *auxilia*, the new garrison was a not insignificant extra drain on Rome's fiscal resources, in a period when the weight of provincial taxation was increased.[53] The Roman government could have no faith in the peaceful intentions of the Parthians, and the Parthians could have as little in those of the emperors. There were to be serious wars under Trajan, Marcus, Severus, and Caracalla, and once the Parthian Arsacids had been supplanted by the Persian Sasanids, worse would follow. A Roman emperor (Valerian) would suffer defeat and capture; Syria and other eastern provinces would more than once be overrun; and indecisive but repeated wars weakened both antagonists, none more than the invasion of Chosroes II in the early seventh century, when for a time he made himself master of Syria, Egypt, and much of Asia Minor, only to leave both the Byzantine empire and his own so enfeebled that neither could withstand the onslaughts of the Muslims.

Augustus had no 'divining eyes': how did he and his contemporaries see the Parthians? In lost histories Strabo and Pompeius Trogus, writing in Augustus' time, recounted at some length how the Arsacids, rulers of a small and poor people near the south-eastern shore of the Caspian, had in the last two centuries made themselves independent of the Seleucids and become masters of the heartlands of the Babylonian, Assyrian, and Persian empires, with their western frontier on the Euphrates.[54] Strabo could regard them 'as in a sense rivals of the Romans'; as we have seen (p. 437), this must have been written in

---

[52] J. G. C. Anderson, *CAH* x. 254–9, whose views may still be regarded as representative of common opinion. Kienast 412 also thinks that Augustus knew that he had nothing to fear from the Parthians. Anderson 773 f. also approves of the Neronian settlement, as it 'led to a stable peace on the eastern frontier, which lasted for half a century, disturbed only by an occasional passing cloud'. In fact the policy of Augustus also preserved peace, interrupted only by some military demonstrations or minor operations in Armenia, from 20 BC to AD 52, and at less cost in manpower and money; and Hadrian's return to the Neronian policy did not prevent Parthian aggression in 161 resulting in a war far graver than that waged by Corbulo.

[53] Domitian wrote that 'the provinces can barely meet necessary demands' (*SEG* xvii. 753), cf. p. 343.

[54] Strabo xi. 9. 1 f. summarizes the fuller accounts given in his lost historical works; of Trogus xli f. we have only Justin's epitome, perhaps composed in the early 3rd c. (Kroll, *RE* x. 956–8), to whose probable unreliability the general considerations I advanced in *CQ* (1980), 477 ff. are pertinent.

Tiberius' reign, as Strabo had thought them virtual vassals of Augustus. Trogus' epitomator, Justin, says that 'the two emperors virtually divided the world' and that the Parthians ruled the east (xli. 1. 1), but we cannot be certain that this is not his judgement rather than that of Trogus, who might not have conceded such parity in Augustus' time. Under Tiberius, king Artabanus III would, like the Sasanids in later times, assert his right to the entire dominion of the Achaemenids;[55] and we cannot be certain that this pretension was something new. At any rate for a long period the Arsacids had been conquerors, and there could have been no certainty that their ambitions were satisfied, or their capacity for expansion exhausted.

They must have seemed potentially formidable antagonists. They had inflicted disasters on Crassus and Antony, admittedly in their own lands, repelling Roman invasions. In 40 they had occupied Syria and much of southern Anatolia. Once large Roman forces had been dispatched against them, they had been defeated and ejected, but in the interval the provinces had sustained grave losses from their depredations.[56] It might have appeared doubtful whether the victories of the Romans in 39–38 had decisively proved their permanent superiority. In any case it must have been clear that a substantial army was needed to ward off any renewed attack on the eastern provinces, and still greater forces for a successful offensive in Parthian territory.

However, Augustus must also have been aware of what Trogus made clear (Justin xl. 1. 9): the Parthians were liable to attacks from their northern and eastern neighbours, and had been weakened from time to time by dynastic strife and other internal dissensions (xli. 3, 7–9).[57] There had been, and were to be, frequent struggles over the succession among the Arsacid line. Moreover, the Parthian ruler was literally 'king of kings', that is to say he numbered many other kings among his vassals, among them the kings of Persis (n. 58), ancestors of the Sasanids who were to supplant the Arsacids in the end; it was these kings and other powerful vassals whose retainers constituted the Parthian army, and they were prone to conspiracy and revolt. All this had become patent to Romans in the thirty years preceding the settlement of 20. After the victory at Carrhae, king Orodes executed the hereditary grandee who had been in command on suspicion of

---

[55] Tac., *Ann.* vi. 31, cf. Arr., *FGr.H.* no. 156 F 31; Sasanids: Dio lxiii. 4; Hdn. vi. 2. 1 f.; Amm. xvii. 5. 5 f. If the memory of the Achaemenids was lost in Iranian tradition (L. Raditza in *Cambridge Hist. of Iran* iii (1983), 120, cf. E. Yarshater, ib. 366, 389 f.), it would have been preserved by the Greek sources; the Arsacids were partly Hellenized.

[56] For devastation as far west as Caria see *SIG*[3] 765.

[57] I rely for the political history of Iran under the Arsacids on *RE* xviii. 1969 ff. (Schur) and the *Camb. Hist. of Iran* iii. (A. D. H. Bivar), and on the latter for the Sasanids (R. N. Frye).

treason, and he did not trust his own son and heir enough to allow him to launch a counter-offensive, when Rome had only feeble garrisons in Syria and Cilicia, nor even when these had been removed to serve Pompey in the civil war. It was perhaps on account of internal discontent that king Phraates, so far from exploiting victory over Antony in 35, allowed him with the help of his rebellious vassal Artavasdes, king of Media Atropatene, to occupy Armenia in 34; though in 32 he took advantage of the Roman civil war to expel Artavasdes from both Atropatene and Armenia, the great revolt of his own nobility which followed may well have been brewing long before. The rebels set up another Arsacid, Tiridates, as king. Soon expelled, he was given refuge in Roman Syria, whence he made another attempt to instal himself as king with only short-lived success (26–25), and then once more found asylum in Roman territory. There were intermittent negotiations between Augustus and Phraates concerning the return of the Roman prisoners and standards which the Parthians had captured, and also no doubt on the fate of Armenia. Because of his other preoccupations, it was not until 20 BC that Augustus could mobilize the forces needed to make Phraates yield to his demands, but he had been able to count on Phraates' own insecurity on the throne restraining him from aggression.

In general dynastic conflicts and the disloyalty of vassals would effectively inhibit any aggressive tendencies on the part of the Arsacids in the future too, until they finally succumbed to the Sasanids. From time to time they would seek to install a prince of their own line or choice in Armenia, generally with the support of the native barons, but the Roman emperors, when they chose, could forcibly eject the Parthian nominee and substitute their own, sometimes at the cost of overcoming indigenous resistance, but without determined Parthian opposition. Only in AD 161 did the Parthians initiate general hostilities and invade Syria; in retribution the Romans penetrated to their capital at Ctesiphon and sacked it. It is usual to explain Parthian inertia by the loose feudal structure of the state and its lack of a standing army fitted to sustain offensive campaigns. Something of this was certainly known to Augustus, but it was equally known to him, what modern analyses of the situation ignore, that for many previous generations these inherent structural weaknesses in their system of government had not prevented the Arsacids from enormously extending their power. It is also an admitted fact that in the third century and thereafter the Sasanids proved aggressive and dangerous enemies. The increase in their offensive capacity is commonly ascribed to the centralizing policy they pursued internally. But this centralization had hardly begun in the reign of Shapur I (241–72), who defeated and captured the emperor

Valerian and for a time occupied Syria and part of south Anatolia. For example, like the Arsacids he was suzerain of many kings.[58] Centralization, and above all the replacement of the feudal host by an army raised and paid by the king, seems to have been the work of Chosroes I (531-79).[59] And the Sasanids too were at times diverted from attacks on Rome by wars on other fronts, or weakened by the contests for the succession and aristocratic revolts; in the end, after the ephemeral Persian conquest of Syria, Palestine, Egypt, and much of Asia Minor by Chosroes II early in the seventh century, their empire dissolved into virtual anarchy, which left it at the mercy of the Muslims. All this suggests that the peoples of ancient Iran could always be formidable under a ruler of talent and ambition, whose emergence could hardly be predicted, while their power disintegrated when rulers lacked the personal qualities to retain their loyalty and direct their energies. Centralization itself betokened the vigour of the monarch. We may be reminded of the great conquests made by the Persians under Cyrus, Cambyses, and Darius I, and of the decadence that followed, marked by civil wars and revolts of satraps; in all probability the social structure under the Achaemenids had not been widely different from that which can be discerned under the Arsacids. It is hindsight that permits us to perceive that after a long period of spectacular aggrandizement the Arsacids had in Augustus' time entered on a new age of stagnation or decline. This was naturally beyond his power to foresee.

The later wars between the Roman or Byzantine emperors and the Sasanids were punctuated by peace treaties which gave now to one side and now to the other disputed border areas in Armenia and Mesopotamia and which lasted as long as both were either exhausted or preoccupied with internal troubles or hostilities on other fronts. There was no mutual trust or chance of enduring amity. Similarly Augustus had no reason to confide in the sincerely peaceful intentions of Phraates and his successors, while in view of Rome's pretensions to world rule the Parthian king had as little cause to believe that he would not be attacked, whenever it suited the Romans. Even if we grant that Augustus was simply concerned to secure the eastern frontier, he could not expect the Parthians to observe the terms of any settlement, if an opportunity for aggression presented itself.[60] It was therefore not enough to repair Rome's honour by obtaining the return of the Roman captives and standards: he also needed control of Armenia as a deterrent to the invasion of Syria. Armenia was a potential base for invading, and therefore attempting to subdue, the Parthian empire, if

---

[58] *Camb. Hist. of Iran* (V. G. Lukonin) iii. 729 f., cf. 262 (from *Res Gestae Saporis*).

[59] Ib. 152, 164.

[60] Justin xli. 3. 10: 'fides dicti promissique nulla, nisi quatenus expedit'.

and when the time appeared ripe (cf. n. 39). Must we suppose that Augustus had permanently excluded all thought of such aggrandizement? The Arabian expedition of 25 shows that he was then hoping for expansion in the east. Strabo's account suggests that his objective had been to obtain command of one of the great trade routes to India and the spice lands, duties on which would enrich the Roman treasury (xvi. 4. 22). But it may also have been in his mind that success (which was denied) would have brought Roman dominion to the edge of the Ocean. The same motives could beckon him down the Euphrates and Tigris to the Persian Gulf. Moreover direct taxation in Mesopotamia and Babylonia might have produced returns comparable to those from the Nile valley. Such an enterprise he certainly abjured for the present in 20 BC, but it does not follow that he considered it for ever impracticable. The spectacle of Parthian feebleness in his time might actually have encouraged him to undertake it, all the more as he could not be sure that the Parthians might not one day recover their power and aggressive spirit. His preoccupation with the northern wars is enough to explain why he never did so.

Dio is indeed cited to show that he did permanently rule out all aggrandizement in the east. But Dio's narrative should be examined closely. He tells how in fear of a Roman invasion in 20 BC Phraates at last fulfilled undertakings he had given earlier to return the captives and standards (liv. 8. 1). Augustus treated this as equivalent to military conquest (8. 2). Dio says that he 'commanded' celebrations to be voted, some of which occurred much later (8. 3). It is evident that Augustus at once reported his diplomatic triumph to the senate, and prompted it to vote the celebrations. No doubt, though Dio does not say as much, Phraates also agreed not to resist the subsequent Roman intervention in Armenia. Dio fails to indicate that Roman propaganda represented Phraates as supplicating for peace and accepting Rome's superior status (p. 105).

Dio then proceeds to tell that Augustus administered the subject territory in accordance with Roman practices, while allowing the allied peoples to be governed in their traditional manner: 'he did not think it proper that there should be any addition to the former or any other acquisition; Rome should be content with her existing possessions, and he wrote this in a letter to the senate'. Dio then notes some changes he made among the 'client' principalities, and reports Tiberius' expedition to Armenia, where the anti-Roman king Artaxes had been killed before Tiberius' arrival; he omits to record that Tiberius installed a Roman nominee on the throne, and that the 'recovery of Armenia' was officially regarded as a major success. As we have seen, Augustus himself was to declare that he might have made Armenia into a

province but preferred in accordance with tradition to entrust it to a
king (*RG* 27).

Now the letter to the senate which Dio cites was obviously written
later than that in which Augustus announced the accord with
Phraates; it concerned his subsequent reorganization of affairs in Syria
and eastern Asia Minor. Augustus was not renouncing the conquest of
the Parthian empire; that was not now in question. If Dio correctly
summarized its purport, he was advising against (1) the transfer of any
territory from indirect to direct rule, and (2) any attempt in this region
to enforce suzerainty on princes or peoples who had not yet acknowledged themselves to be Rome's vassals. The former declaration agrees
completely with what he himself tells of his Armenian policy, and the
suspicion must arise that Dio has generalized it. What can be meant by
the vaguer warning against expansion in (2)? Perhaps Augustus had in
mind the position of Media Atropatene. Its king, Artavasdes, had in 35
thrown off his allegiance to Phraates, accepted the friendship of
Antony, and been rewarded with part of Armenia Maior; driven out of
his realm in 32, he had taken refuge with Octavian and been granted
the kingdom of Armenia Minor. He was now dead, and in 20 Augustus
installed Archelaus in that kingdom. But the question may well have
arisen whether any attempt should be made to bring Atropatene as
well as Armenia Maior back into the Roman sphere. Perhaps it was a
quid pro quo for Phraates' abandonment of Armenia Maior that
Rome should not make any such attempt. But, however that may be,
we must surely resist the inference which, in conformity with his
general and erroneous interpretation of Augustus' imperial policy
(section VII), Dio probably drew, and intended his readers to draw,
that the letter to the senate did more than justify the arrangements that
Augustus made in the east at that particular time and that it
unnecessarily laid down principles of foreign policy even in the east for
the indefinite future. Augustus himself would later transfer Paphlagonia and Judaea to provincial administration. The project of expansion
in Arabia would later be resumed (p. 464). It is hardly conceivable that
he wished to bind himself to the status quo, whatever might betide.
The letter Dio cites is relevant only to the course of action in the east
which he thought best in the actual circumstances obtaining in 20.

If the subjugation of the Parthians was not to be essayed by force or
arms, or not yet, there might be other devices for making them
increasingly subservient to Rome. At some date after 13 and probably
before 9, Phraates IV handed over to Augustus' custody all his four
legitimate sons and their families. In Roman versions they were to be
pledges or hostages for his fidelity to Roman friendship.[61] Why did he

---

[61] *RG* 32. 2; Vell. ii. 94. 4; Justin xlii. 5; Oros. (Livy) vi. 21. 29. Strabo xvi. 1. 28 relates some of
the true circumstances (cf. Jos. *AJ* xvii. 39 ff.) and fixes the time as that of Titius' administration

take this step? Tacitus says that he was prompted 'not so much by fear of us as by distrust of his own people' (*Ann.* ii. 2). King Phraates III had been murdered by his own sons in 58, among them his successor Orodes II, the father of Phraates IV, who had in turn killed Orodes and Orodes' other children. In the years between 31 and 26 Phraates had only with difficulty overcome revolts by his nobility; doubtless he had not allayed their discontent, and was apprehensive that with their support one or more of his sons would serve him in the same way as he and his father had served their fathers. Moreover, if we follow Josephus (*AJ* xviii. 39–42), he had become infatuated with an Italian slave girl presented to him by Augustus in 20, and was bent on securing the succession for the bastard son she bore him, Phraataces. Presumably Augustus knew the truth; the sons and grandsons of Phraates in his keeping at Rome were not in any ordinary sense hostages for the king's good behaviour, since nothing would have suited Phraates so well as to be rid of them altogether; but they were potential pretenders to his throne in his lifetime, if he gave trouble, or after his death. Their honourable treatment at Rome, together with the aid that Rome might give any one of them in making good his claim to the succession, might have the result that in due course the Parthian empire would be ruled by a Roman protégé. It turned out that the Parthians would resent all Roman attempts to give them a king who appeared to be a Roman puppet, infected with an alien culture.[62] This could hardly have been foreseen, all the more as the Parthian mentality was probably not understood by Romans. Still the existence of such pretenders did at the least furnish opportunities to enfeeble the Parthian empire with internal conflicts. Certainly the custody of the princes that Rome enjoyed fortified the belief that Parthia was slipping into dependency on Rome, as Strabo (p. 437), and very probably Augustus himself, thought.

In fact it was Phraataces with his mother who murdered old Phraates and then usurped the throne, perhaps in 2 BC. He lent his aid to the anti-Roman party which had already gained control in Armenia. Augustus refused recognition to him unless he withdrew Parthian forces from Armenia. It was now that Gaius Caesar was dispatched to the east. Ovid predicted great victories over the Parthians.[63] Since there had also been a revolt in Germany (p. 452), it is unlikely that

---

of Syria (for which see *RE* vi A 1562), but he too thought that the Parthians were becoming dependent on Rome.

[62] Besides Vonones under Augustus, Tiberius dispatched first Vonones' brother Phraates (who soon died) and then Vonones' son Phraates, and Claudius his grandson Mithridates. Trajan announced on coins REX PARTHIS DATUS, but his nominee Parthamaspates had no better success. Caracalla hoped to marry a daughter of the Parthian king and to succeed him (Dio lxxxiii. 1).

[63] *Ars Amat.* 177–278; *Rem. Amoris* 155 f., cf. Syme, *Hist. in Ovid*, 8. Cf. n. 35 (Apelles' pictures).

Augustus really contemplated conquest in the east, expecially as Gaius had no military experience. The mere threat of Roman attack brought Phraataces to terms. In return for recognition he would abandon his friends in Armenia and his demand for the return of the royal hostages! On an island in the middle of the Euphrates, the pact was solemnized in a personal meeting of 'duo inter se eminentissima imperiorum et hominum capita', as the eye-witness Velleius rather oddly describes it (ii. 103. 3). This looks like a symbolic recognition of Parthian parity, which was perhaps more than Augustus had intended. Gaius once again restored Roman suzerainty in Armenia; Augustus took an imperatorial salutation, and another for operations apparently in Arabia which Gaius conducted and of which we are inadequately informed.[64]

Gaius was posthumously commemorated for campaigning 'ultra fines extremas populi Romani' (*ILS* 140). This indicates that hopes of expansion in the east had not been altogether abandoned. Seneca had read that Gaius was later preparing for a Parthian war (*ad Polyb.* 15. 4). But there was more trouble in Armenia, where Gaius received a wound that was to prove fatal.

Tiberius, now restored to favour, was required for wars in the north. For the next decade the concentration of Rome's military efforts there precluded armed intervention either in Armenia, where the kings nominated by Rome failed to hold the loyalty of their subjects, or in Parthia, where internal revolts led first to the expulsion of Phraataces and then to the assassination of his successor Orodes. Augustus did, however, send one of Phraates' surviving sons, Vonones, to assume the crown in response to a request from the Parthian nobility. If Vonones had been able to establish himself, Parthia would have been ruled by a Roman protégé. In fact just because he had adopted a Roman life-style, he proved unacceptable to his own people, and was soon thrown out by Artabanus III. For a time he then set himself up as king of Armenia, but by AD 15 he had been compelled to flee to Syria, where the governor interned him, to appease Artabanus, who was threatening that province. It remained for Tiberius as emperor to reach an accommodation with Artabanus, on the old basis that Rome should once more invest a prince of her choice with the Armenian crown, while Artabanus desisted from any offensive against Roman territory. Tiberius was certainly averse to all military expansion, and all thoughts of subduing the Parthians remained dormant until Trajan's reign.

---

[64] Syme, *Hist. in Ovid*, 10 sets out the evidence, with undue scepticism; it is quite unlikely that for once Augustus took an imperatorial salutation for a success gained by a legate, cf. n. 33.

VII

Modern interpretations of Augustus' policy as fundamentally defensive are admittedly sustained by the two principal accounts of his life and reign which survive from antiquity.

Suetonius briefly recites his subjugation of various peoples (21. 1), without even summarizing the effect of this work in consolidating the defences of the empire, as Tacitus does (*Ann.* i. 9. 5); he gives rather more space to Varus' disaster (23). He expressly says that Augustus never made war on any people without just and necessary reasons (cf. p. 438) and had no desire for 'aggrandizement or military glory' (n. 7); it was just his reputation for 'virtue and moderation' that led Indians and Scythians to seek his friendship and the Parthians to return the captured standards, hand over 'hostages', and accept a king of his choice (21. 3); the *naïveté* of this explanation of Parthian behaviour is flagrant. Perhaps the biographer has so little to tell of external wars, since Augustus, as he says, only twice commanded in person, and generally conducted them through legates (20); it was natural for him to concentrate on Augustus' personal activities. Still, in the life of Caesar too he had given only the barest summary of military operations! But above all he explicitly denies that Augustus aimed at imperial expansion. We have to remember that he was writing under Hadrian, who had set himself against it. Augustus he plainly regarded as a model for emperors to follow, and it would thus have been tactless to represent his external policy as directed by ambitions of the kind that Trajan had espoused and Hadrian had repudiated. And Suetonius may well have sincerely sympathized with Hadrian's outlook. He was certainly consistent in belittling or condemning imperial expansion. While briefly recounting Caesar's conquest of Gaul and attacks on Britons and Germans (*Caesar* 25), he remarks that Caesar's aim was to procure personal riches and glory (22. 1) and that in Gaul he let slip no pretext for aggression, however unjust (24. 3); his victories enriched him personally (26–8), and thus facilitated his seizure of autocratic power; they seem to evoke in Suetonius' mind no patriotic pride. He notes without disapproval that Tiberius was averse to offensive war (*Tib.* 37); on his own view of Augustus this attitude was not new. Tiberius is criticized in this connection only for alleged inefficiency in providing for imperial defence (41). Suetonius also decries Claudius' invasion of Britain: it was undertaken to obtain an unearned triumph (*Claud.* 17). And it was among the creditable aspects of Nero's reign that he never showed the least impulse to extend the bounds of empire and abstained from evacuating Britain only out of respect for Claudius' reputation (*Nero* 19. 3, cf. 18).

Dio too disapproved of imperial aggrandizement (p. 101). Thus he observes that all the risks and hardships incurred by Roman armies in the Parthian war inspired by Trajan's lust for fame and emulation of Alexander (n. 13) proved absolutely futile (lxviii. 33). Though far from being an unqualified admirer of Hadrian, he clearly approves of his defensive policy: Hadrian's sound military preparations, his abstention from aggression, and his subsidies to foreign peoples ensured the preservation of peace (lxix. 9). After reporting Severus' boast that by the annexation of territory beyond the Euphrates (which formed the new province of Mesopotamia) he had vastly aggrandized the empire and established a bulwark for Syria, Dio comments that in reality the conquest was a source of constant wars and great expense, involving Rome unnecessarily in the internecine conflicts of Iranian peoples (lxxv. 3).

Dio intensely admired Marcus Aurelius (lxxi. 33–6), whose reign was consumed in foreign wars. But on any view Marcus was warding off attacks, first from the Parthians, then from German and Sarmatian peoples in the north. His victories were celebrated in high-sounding *cognomina* of a conventional kind, and an inscription set up on the Capitol declared that he had surpassed all the glories of the greatest of previous emperors (*ILS* 374), but fame was not an objective to which he himself attached any value,[65] and his principle of copying Pius (*Med.* vi. 30. 2) should have meant that he had no desire for aggrandizement as such. It was presumably to improve the defences of Britain that Pius had pushed forward the frontier there, and it was doubtless on similar grounds that Marcus decided to install a Roman nominee, Sohaemus, on the Armenian throne, and to extend Roman control or occupation into parts of northern Mesopotamia,[66] a policy that foreshadowed that which Severus would adopt, and that he planned, if we credit his biography in the *Historia Augusta* (24. 5; 27. 10), to annex the lands of the Marcomanni, Quadi and Sarmatians (Iazyges). Whether or not Dio acknowledged this plan we do not know; there is nothing of it in the surviving extracts and epitomes. What Dio does tell us is that Marcus was so convinced of the bad faith of the Iazyges that he designed their extermination (a procedure that Stoics could approve where wickedness was irremediable), but that the revolt

---

[65] Brunt, *JRS* (1974), 14.

[66] *RE* iii A 798 on Sohaemus (5). Osrhoene and even Adiabene were now client states (Dio lxxv. 1. 2) and Carrhae (*RE* x. 2015) a colony. Hence perhaps L. Verus is called 'propagator imperii' (*CIL* xiv. 106). Marcus and Commodus appear with the same title on a medallion, as remarked by A. R. Birley, *Trans. Archit. and Arch. Soc. of Durham and Northumberland*, iii. 21, who associates it with Marcus' alleged project of expansion in the north; the article (pp. 13 ff.) is a valuable review of expansionist policies from Augustus to Severus.

of Avidius Cassius[67] compelled him to reach an accommodation with them. He seems to have been pursuing somewhat similar methods at the end of his reign with the Marcomanni and Quadi, showing, says Dio, that he sought to punish them without acquiring their lands, and it is perhaps in this sense that we should understand the statement by Dio's epitomator that 'had he lived, he would have subdued all those parts'.[67] Commodus, shirking the hardships of the camp, preferred to accept them as vassals, just as Marcus had ultimately accepted the Iazyges.[68] It may be added that from Dio's standpoint Marcus had done his work well; the offensive power of the Parthians was broken, as it turned out, for ever, and that of the northern peoples for two generations.

Now in writing his account of Augustus Dio was primarily and rightly intent on stressing his momentous work in founding the monarchy, which was in his view Rome's salvation. The fictitious debate between Agrippa and Maecenas, the speech of Augustus to the senate in January 27, and the systematic account of the institutions of the new regime which follows all serve to illuminate the significance of the revolution he effected. For Dio no less than for Suetonius he was the model emperor. To show this he puts a long funeral oration into the mouth of Tiberius and appends his own eulogistic obituary notice. Both are almost exclusively devoted to Augustus' internal measures and to his relations with the ruling class. Another fictitious discussion between Augustus and Livia (lv. 14–22) highlights the clemency he displayed, once *Princeps*, so lamentably wanting in many of his successors, who failed to realize that it was the best means of ensuring the monarch's safety, and therefore internal stability. Dio judges them by the standards Augustus had set. Given his disapproval of imperialist adventures undertaken for glory alone, he must have been disinclined to think of Augustus as concerned to do more than strengthen Roman defences. It is significant that the oration of Tiberius dismisses in a sentence or two his military exploits (lvi. 37. 4–5); it was Augustus' merit to have protected the subjects from foreign attack (40. 2). The contrast is marked with the record that Augustus had composed himself for his mausoleum, and with the prescript affixed to it, evidently approved by Tiberius himself, which magniloquently declared that he had made the world subject to the *imperium* of the Roman people. Dio quotes Augustus' own saying that he had found Rome of clay and left it of marble (30.3), and refers it not to the buildings in the city but to the increased strength of the empire; but of course he did

---

[67] Dio lxxxi. 13. 1, 16. 1, 17. 1. Stoic views: Sen., *de Ira* i. 19. 2, cf. ii. 31. 7.
[68] Dio lxxi. 20, 33. 4²; lxxii. 2.

not equate strength with enlargement. He does not even elaborate on this to the extent of Tacitus' summary: 'mari Oceano aut amnibus longinquis saeptum imperium; legiones provincias classes, cuncta inter se conexa' (*Ann* i. 9. 5).[69]

As we have seen, he probably wished Augustus' dispatch to the senate in 20 BC to be construed as renouncing all expansion; certainly he held that the 'consilium coercendi imperii intra terminos' was a warning against all territorial acquisitions, since they would be hard to protect and would endanger Rome's existing possessions; and he adds that Augustus had himself always acted on this principle and had refused even to make conquests within his power (33). This is the opinion of a man who simply would not recognize facts unpalatable to him. It is significant that he gives the least possible attention to Augustus' wars in his narrative.

His narratives of Republican wars are often fairly detailed, even if seldom perspicuous, but of those waged after 27 he furnished only brief notices. Oddly enough he has more to tell of Marcus Crassus' feats in the Balkans in 29 and of the destruction of Varus' legions than of the successes of Augustus' generals. It is characteristic that he reports Aelius Gallus' Arabian expedition without explaining its purpose or indicating its failure (liii. 30). He does not even make it clear, like Velleius (ii. 38. 4, 90), that the operations in Spain from 26 to 19 BC (liii. 22. 5; 25–6; liv. 5 and 11) at last completed the pacification of the peninsula. The stages of the subjugation of the lands south of Danube are obscure in his narrative, all the more as he says that Pannonia was conquered in 34 (xlix. 36 f.). Since he cared so little to expound, and perhaps did not comprehend, what Augustus had actually done, we can hardly look to him for guidance on what Augustus had hoped or essayed to do.

VIII

The last years of Augustus' reign did indeed inaugurate the period in which Rome ceased, except intermittently, to pursue the aim of indefinite expansion, and in which some like Suetonius and Dio would disapprove of attempts to resume it. Yet men would still speak of Rome's world empire, and not all were content with the defensive posture that most emperors maintained. Nor is it certain that Augustus even at the end of his life, after the partial failure of his designs for the

---

[69] Millar (n. 50) 19 f. adduces other evidence for the conception of the great rivers as frontiers; Hdn. ii. 11. 5 wrongly thought that Augustus had fortified these as barriers. They were more useful as lateral communications.

extension of Roman power in the north, envisaged that there should be an end to all future aggrandizement.

The revolts in Pannonia and Germany both illustrated the danger of relying on troops raised from peoples recently subdued and serving in or close to their own countries under local chiefs. Arminius had been commander of such an auxiliary unit (Vell. ii. 118. 2; Tac., *Ann.* ii. 10), and very probably the Pannonian regiments, who rebelled in AD 6 (Vell. ii. 105. 5), were serving under native officers. These soldiers had learned something of the Roman art of war without being imbued with devotion to the Roman emperor or state. Tiberius was to try to obviate future risks of the same kind by transferring the units recruited among the Thracians to distant lands under Roman officers (p. 204). Augustus had evidently felt it necessary to resort to such levies in order to minimize the burden of military service on Italians. He did not venture to replace the three legions lost by Varus. Moreover, in order to make enlistment in the legions more attractive, he had had to promise liberal bounties to be paid on discharge. The heavy cost had compelled him to impose a tax on the Italian propertied class, which was resented (n. 22). Even so, the promises could not be kept. Legionaries were detained in service beyond the fixed term.[70] This was one cause of the mutinies of AD 14. They threatened internal stability: 'defuit qui contra rem publicam duceret, non qui sequerentur' (Vell. ii. 125. 2). The difficulty of pacifying Illyricum and Germany had also turned out to be far greater than had probably been foreseen. All this must have contributed to Augustus' decision to call a halt to northern expansion. He authorized punitive campaigns beyond the Rhine, but only to redeem Roman honour, not 'cupidine proferendi imperii aut dignum ob praemium' (*Ann.* i. 3. 6). Tiberius communicated to the senate his posthumous 'consilium coercendi imperii intra terminos'.

In these words of Tacitus the advice is opaque and ambiguous, and Dio's version, which is explicit, may be distorted by his own misinterpretation of the policy that Augustus had pursued hitherto. We may doubt if Augustus, always an opportunist himself, would have thought it sensible to recommend to his successors a rule for them to follow indefinitely, whatever the circumstances. More probably he was expressing a judgement that it was inexpedient to attempt expansion for the present. This was especially pertinent to the German war still in progress, but of course applied *a fortiori* to the east.

Conceivably Tiberius had inspired the advice. As a general in the field, he was cautious (Vell. ii. 115. 5); he was also by ancient standards already old; he was to show himself averse to any more campaigning in

---

[70] Brunt, *Italian Manpower*, 33–5.

person, and though he had two princes of age to hold great commands, Drusus lacked experience, and Germanicus did not possess his trust: and neither lived long. In any case it was his principle to treat all Augustus' words and deeds as having the authority of law (Tac., *Ann.* iv. 37). Under his long tenure of the Principate Rome adopted a defensive posture. To save appearances, Germanicus was to triumph in magnificence, as if he had successfully finished off the German war (ii. 41). In fact the Germans were to be left to quarrel among themselves (ii. 26. 3; 62. 1). Maroboduus was subverted by intrigue. Tiberius preferred bloodless victories (ii. 64. 1). Diplomacy and threats would also induce Artabanus III of Parthia to let Germanicus once again invest a Roman nominee with the crown of Armenia. The work had to be done all over again at the end of the reign. Artabanus was then menacing Roman possessions in the east; Tiberius, preferring 'consiliis et astu res externas moliri' (vi. 32), put up survivors from Phraates' brood of 'hostages' as pretenders to the Parthian throne, and this sufficed to promote another peaceful restoration of the Augustan settlement on the eastern frontier.

No later emperors can have thought Augustus' advice binding. But only a few of them were to depart from it. Why was this? Were they all indifferent to the traditional attractions of military glory? Had they, each in turn, with one or two exceptions, convinced themselves that Rome lacked the necessary resources for expansion, or that, if practicable, it would be unprofitable, and that the empire could best be made secure within its existing bounds? Or can any other explanation be offered?

One possibility may be considered. For two centuries and more after Tiberius' death most emperors had had no service in the field, or virtually none, before their accession. The exceptions are Galba, Vespasian, Titus, Trajan, and Hadrian; even Severus, though in 193 recently appointed legate of Pannonia, had done no fighting. And none except Vespasian could turn, as Augustus had done, to a member of his own family qualified for great commands: Vespasian did confide to Titus the task of quelling the Jews. It is not surprising that, in the aftermath of civil wars and revolts, Vespasian and Titus had no thought of undertaking large-scale offensives in their brief tenure of power.

From great victories great glory would accrue to the commander; it was imprudent to give any subject the chance to secure it. Claudius wished to appropriate to himself the credit for the successful invasion of Britain, by appearing on the scene in person. Nero gave Corbulo only restricted scope during his long command in the east. In Britain legates with brief tenures were allowed in the first century to push the frontier forward in stages, but perhaps Tacitus was not wrong in believing that Agricola, who had been exceptionally favoured in the length of his command, was recalled by Domitian, just when and because he could report that he was about to complete the subjugation of the whole island. When Domitian had initiated an important offensive on the Rhine, limited indeed to annexing and fortifying territory for the better protection of Gaul, he had assumed the command himself, despite his inexperience in warfare, as he did later for major operations in the Danubian theatre, though these were still more purely defensive in nature. Similarly Marcus and Verus directed in person the great wars in the east and north which were forced on them by foreign attacks. Not only Trajan but Severus and Caracalla took command in great offensives. In the third century it was normal for emperors to place themselves at the head of armies they concentrated for the most serious wars. But emperors conscious of their unfitness for the role of general, or more attracted to civil administration or to mere frivolities, would naturally prefer not to precipitate wars demanding their own presence.

It may be doubted whether any of them between Tiberius and Hadrian deliberately and rationally formulated a policy that required the renunciation of aggrandizement. Neither in that period nor later were emperors indifferent to military glory. Most of them relished imperatorial acclamations, honorific *cognomina* for the victories of their armies, sometimes triumphs, even when they had not been earned.[71] None publicly declared that it was enough to provide merely for the better protection of the empire.

Claudius boasted, in a context where the boast was irrelevant, of the glory of extending the empire beyond the Ocean. (He had surpassed Alexander!) There is no evidence that he invaded Britain out of apprehension of British raids on the coast of Gaul. In fact, though he could hardly have foreseen this, no frontier within the island would be reached as satisfactory as the Channel.[72] The considerable Flavian extensions of Roman territory beyond the upper Rhine improved the defence system in that region, but may have been generally seen as a stage in the conquest of Germany. Tacitus would complain: 'tam diu

[71] J. B. Campbell, *The Emperor and the Roman Army*, (1984), 120–57. A striking example of the wish to magnify military achievements is the mendacious boast on the Arch of Titus that the capture of Jerusalem had never before been attempted or carried out (*ILS* 264). Both Claudius and Vespasian extended the *pomerium* 'auctis populi Romani finibus' (ib. 213, 248).

[72] *ILS* 212, I 39 (cf. Dio lx. 19. 2!). Claudius, whose 27 imperatorial salutations betray his zest for specious military glory, took 4 of them in 43, presumably for the British campaign (cf. Dio lx. 21. 4), for which he also triumphed. Collingwood's conception, pervading *CAH* x. 790–802, that the conquest of Britain was seen as essential for the defence of Gaul, is a flagrant attempt to find an explanation that suits his modern ideas of rationality, but conflicts with the evidence.

Germania vincitur' (*Germ.* 37); the task was taking unduly long to finish, but it had not ostensibly been abandoned. Trajan resumed expansion in the grand style. The annexation of Dacia has indeed been represented, and justified, by some modern writers as designed only for the effectual protection of the other Danubian provinces.[73] This may be questioned. Dacia constituted a vulnerable salient in Roman defences which on poor authority Hadrian is said to have thought of abandoning (Eutropius viii. 6) and which Marcus, who had found it hard to maintain, perhaps hoped to remove by annexing the lands of the Iazyges to the west (p. 466). It was the first province to be surrendered, once Rome was exposed to severe pressure from without, and by an emperor (Aurelian) justly proud of his military achievements in 'restoring the empire'. Its strategic value is thus at least arguable: it is a certain fact that it was a source of gold that would enrich the treasury.[74] This enhanced the intrinsic glory of conquest. In the east again there was much to be said on purely defensive grounds for Trajan's annexation of Armenia, and of northern Mesopotamia up to the Khabur–Jebel Sinjar–Tigris line,[75] but Trajan went as far as the Persian gulf; the conversion of Adiabene into a province shows that he intended to hold on to the valleys of the lower Euphrates and Tigris, and they would hardly have been tenable, unless the heartland of the Parthian kingdom had been reduced to subjection; even though his immediate device was to nominate a vassal king (n. 62). Again, Trajan may have been influenced by the prospect of additional revenue, but it is hard to reject Dio's view that he was motivated above all by the desire for glory (n. 13). Writing surely in his reign, and not under a successor who had given up his eastern conquests,[76] Tacitus castigates Tiberius as 'princeps proferendi imperii incuriosus (*Ann.* iv. 32. 3); he was among those to whom Trajan's purposes were congenial. It was during this most imperialistic phase of his reign that the senate officially conferred on him the appellation of Optimus.

However, since Tiberius' reign a new kind of defence system had been evolving. By Hadrian's accession only 3 of the 30 legions remained in the pacified interior provinces, one in Spain and two, soon reduced to one, in Egypt. Others had been transferred to vulnerable frontier areas in response to strategic needs perceived on particular occasions. It was probably by a process that began with other

[73] Luttwak 97–104.

[74] J. Carcopino, *Points de vue sur l'impérialisme rom.* (1934), ch. 1, cf. J. Guey, *Mél. Carcopino* (1966), 445 ff.

[75] Luttwak 107 f.

[76] I do not find Syme's dating of the *Annals* (*Tacitus* (1958), ch. XXXV) convincing. It is only one objection that Tacitus would hardly have ventured on even an oblique criticism of Hadrian (whom senators must have mistrusted), if writing in his reign.

improvised expedients that on frontiers where natural barriers did not interpose between settled areas under Roman rule and potentially hostile peoples beyond the frontiers, a network of forts, watchposts, and roads were created, first in south-west Germany, to hinder or cut off raids on Rome's subjects. Luttwak has described this 'grand strategy' in admirably comprehensible terms.[77] Yet it may be doubted if any emperor before Hadrian was fully conscious of this strategy and deliberately adopted it. Hadrian, though proficient in the arts of war, as Tiberius had been, but unlike Tiberius still in the prime of life and unwearying in travelling round the empire, sometimes marching at the head of his troops, was almost ostentatious in rejecting expansion of the empire, and made it virtually certain that his policy would be continued after his death by designating as his successor an elderly senator who had no military experience at all. Pius in turn did not even see any need to give his heirs the opportunity of commanding an army, and if Marcus and Verus were obliged to spend years in the camps, it was to repel the gravest attacks that had been made on the empire since the Principate had been established. Of their successors Severus and Caracalla did initiate offensive operations,[78] but thereafter frequent usurpations, civil wars, and foreign invasions were to make it hard for the short-lived emperors before Diocletian to prevent the total disintegration of Roman power.

Hadrian's policy was at once revealed when he refused to try to retain any of Trajan's eastern acquisitions. Widespread revolts had broken out in Trajan's rear. It is a common opinion that Trajan had overstrained Rome's strength and that it would have been folly to have persevered in the attempt to expand Roman dominion so far from the centre of imperial power. We are too apt to treat what occurred as natural and what did not occur as inconceivable. Republican conquests of the lands scattered all round the shores of the Mediterranean had been excessive on the reasonable premiss that the proper aim of Roman strategy was then simply to ensure the efficient defence of Italy. The later annexation of lands in north Europe and the Balkans might be said to have stretched beyond its natural limits an essentially Mediterranean empire. If the revolt in Gaul of 52 BC, which separated Caesar from the greater part of his army, had led him to abandon any further efforts to subjugate the whole country, it would have been judged that that enterprise had been doomed to failure from the start.

[77] Luttwak ch. II *passim*. For reservations on his valuable interpretation of the different phases of imperial strategy see reviews cited in n. 1. Cf. also Millar (n. 50) 2 f.

[78] Severus often appears on inscriptions as 'propagator imperii', see Birley (n. 66), citing H. U. Instinsky, *Klio* (1942), 212 ff., esp. *ILS* 425; he annexed Mesopotamia and probably aimed at completing the subjugation of Britain.

Since Hadrian did not put to the test the possibility of holding on to Trajan's acquisitions, we cannot tell whether he could initially have succeeded, nor how long Roman rule might have endured in Mesopotamia. Must the Romans have failed in an enterprise in which, at least for a time, Macedonians and Arabs succeeded? Apart from a tenuous claim on the allegiance of the princes of Osrhoene, Hadrian chose to revert to the Euphrates frontier. The Parthian invasion in Marcus' reign, foreshadowing Sasanid aggressions, was to show that there could be no reliance on the durability of peaceful relations with the masters of Iran, and that Syria needed better protection. Hence Marcus thought it necessary to extend Roman territory or control within the adjoining region of northern Mesopotamia (n. 66), and Severus would push the frontier forward to the more defensible Khabur–Jebel Sinjar–Tigris line, which later rulers sought to retain, or regain, in their ever recurring wars with the Sasanids. It seems questionable whether Hadrian had not resiled from Trajan's annexationist policy beyond the limits of prudence.

Withdrawal from Britain would have been more rational (in the modern sense). The island can never have repaid the costs of occupation. Moreover the garrison of over 50,000 men, perhaps an eighth of Rome's forces, was stationed in an extremity of the empire: time was needed to reinforce it in case of need, or to remove troops to other theatres where they were more urgently required; the partial occupation of Britain weakened Rome's defences everywhere. Commitments elsewhere forced Trajan himself to relinquish the territory Agricola had gained in Scotland. It is conventional to say that in north Britain the land and its inhabitants were too wild to admit of pacification. But in Spain, in the Alps, in Anatolia, the Romans had overcome at least equal difficulties. The analogy with Spain is notable. In Britain the imperial government showed a lack of insight, or tenacity, or both, similar to that of the Republican government in the northern part of that peninsula. There the pacification undertaken by Augustus required an unusual concentration of forces, but once it was completed, the garrison could gradually be reduced until, a century later, it numbered only some 8,000–9,000 men, retained perhaps chiefly to guard the rich mines in the north-west. Of course Augustus' methods were ruthless in the traditional Roman manner. It was always considered legitimate to exterminate intractable peoples if necessary; in Spain prisoners were sold into slavery, crucified, their hands cut off.[79] The tribesmen were also deported to serve in distant Roman armies; 70 or more auxiliary regiments were raised in Spain, mostly in the north-

---

[79] Strabo iii. 4. 18; Florus ii. 33. 52; Dio liii. 29. 2; liv. 11. 2.

west, as compared with about 20 in Britain.[80] By contrast, in the forty years of relative repose which the empire enjoyed under Hadrian and Pius, no such systematic and resolute efforts were made to complete the conquest of Britain. Instead, Hadrian chose to fortify the existing frontier, and Pius with no lasting success to push it forward to a new fortified line. The independence of hostile tribes beyond these lines fomented serious risings behind them. The walls of Hadrian and Pius are monuments of Roman failure. If we believe Dio (lxxvi. 13. 1), Severus at the end of his reign was hoping to subdue the Highlanders; on his death Caracalla gave up the project. It seems that a long period of relative peace followed, but still at the cost of immobilizing a large army in north Britain, comparable to that which protected the rich Gallic provinces on the Rhine. From the quasi-utilitarian standpoint it would always have been rational to evacuate the island, if it could not be entirely subjugated. But imperial honour, as Appian thought (p. 476), precluded emperors after Nero (p. 465) from so much as considering the surrender of a possession for which the Romans had been fighting for over seventy years at Hadrian's accession.

IX

It is remarkable that under the Antonine peace Florus chose to compose what is entitled in the Bamberg manuscript of his work an epitome drawn from Livy of all the Roman wars over 700 years going down, as he says himself (i. *pr.* 7), to Caesar Augustus, 'when the whole world was pacified' (cf. ii. 34), and that Appian chose to arrange his far more detailed account of Rome's history under the wars fought against different nations and the civil wars of the Republic (though he added a book (*pr.* 15), of which nothing remains, describing the system of defence, taxation, etc. that obtained in his own day). Both of them looked back to the imperial expansion of the Republic as to Rome's heroic age, when Rome struggled first for independence, and 'mox pro finibus, deinde pro sociis, tum gloria et imperio, lacessentibus usque-quaque finitimis' (Florus i. 3. 6); Florus gave an inadequate sketch of Augustus' wars, and Appian did not go beyond the conquest of Egypt. In Florus' view for almost 200 years since Augustus Rome 'inertia Caesarum quasi consenuit atque decoxit, nisi quod sub Traiano principe movit lacertos et praeter spem omnium senectus imperii quasi reddita iuventute revirescit' (i. *pr.* 8). No doubt he alludes to Trajan's

[80] G. L. Cheesman, *Auxilia of Rom. Army* (1914), App. II; the figures are probably not up to date.

conquest of Dacia; when remarking on the campaign of Cn. Lentulus beyond the Danube in Augustus' reign he wrote, 'Dacia non victa, sed submota atque dilata est' (ii. 28). On the other hand he seems to think that the Sarmatians, whom Lentulus also attacked, were not worth subduing: 'nihil praeter nives pruinasque et silvas habent; tanta barbaria est ut nec intellegant pacem' (ii. 29). His account of Augustus' German wars which follows (ii. 30) might lead his readers to draw the same conclusion concerning the Germans. He concludes his work by referring to the numerous embassies to Augustus from foreign peoples, showing their reverence for 'victorem gentium populum Romanum', and to the settlement with the Parthians in 20 BC; hence 'ubique certa atque continua totius generis humani aut pax fuit aut pactio' (ii. 34).

One might have thought that with this felicity attained and destined to continue there was no sufficient reason for complaining about the 'inertia' of Augustus' successors. But it is common enough for men to entertain contradictory conceptions simultaneously, and that seems to have been Florus' condition. Appian, on the other hand, offers a rational justification of 'inertia'. In the 200 years since the foundation of the Principate the city of Rome had been embellished, its revenues had grown, and prosperity had progressed under a lasting peace; some foreign peoples had been subdued, and revolts suppressed, but now Rome possessed the best parts of the lands and seas, and it was sensible to preserve these possessions without attempting to extend her dominion indefinitely over barbarians, out of whom no profit could be made (though they were all actually ready to offer submission and to receive their kings from Rome); already there were parts of the empire which cost more than they brought in, and which were retained only because it was dishonourable to give them up (*pr.* 7). (Britain was the most obvious instance.) Appian is not indeed indifferent to the claims of imperial glory, but in his view it did not need to be increased, since in magnitude and duration the empire surpassed all those recorded in the past (ib. 8–11); its acquisition, over a period of 700 years (the same figure as Florus gives), had been the result of good fortune, and of 'love of honour' (*philotimia*) but also of prudence (*euboulia*), which now acted as a restraint on further acquisitions (11, cf. 7).

In his panegyric on Rome Appian's contemporary Aelius Aristides elaborates a similar comparison between the Roman and earlier empires; that of Alexander had been ephemeral (24–7), and the Persians had failed to win the consent of their subjects (22) or to establish internal peace within their domains (29); Rome had done both. Aristides everywhere writes as if Rome ruled over the whole *oikoumene* or *orbis terrarum* (e.g. 9); if none the less he cannot avoid admitting that not all peoples are their subjects, he minimizes this concession in various ways. The area of the empire is too vast for measurement (28 f.); one may recall Pliny's *'immensa* pacis Romanae maiestas' (*NH* xxvii. 3). Persian rule was bounded by the shores of the Mediterranean, whereas Roman reaches the Atlantic (16); he chose to forget that it did not embrace all the lands beyond the Euphrates which had belonged to the Achaemenids. At least Rome is the emporium for all the products of the world, from India, Arabia, Babylon (11 f.). If the empire has boundaries, that is no reason for censure (28); they have been freely determined by Rome, not imposed by some other power, and they are not fixed, i.e. Rome can advance them, when and if she chooses (10). No doubt Aristides too might have said that if there were peoples beyond Roman dominion, it was only because in Roman estimation they were not worth conquering, and indeed that they were unfortunate in not enjoying the blessings of the Roman peace.

Some imperial writers by using such expressions as 'orbis noster' (or 'Romanus') would implicitly acknowledge that the empire and the world were not coterminous. But even they commonly wrote elsewhere as if they were, probably on the basis that Rome's title to universal dominion was intact. The globe continued to appear on Roman coins as a symbol of this title. Augustus had been termed *moderator, pater, rector, custos* of the *orbis terrarum*; Hadrian would be its *locupletator* or *restitutor*; and amid the disastrous wars of the third century and apparently imminent disintegration of the empire their successors would be similarly honoured; so too Diocletian or Julian would be styled *dominus orbis*. Similarly it could be said of emperors that they were saviours of the human race.[81]

X

Thus the assertion of Rome's right to rule the world was never given up. Only efforts to convert it into reality ceased. Growth in geographical knowledge might well have convinced men that it was futile to pursue a will-o'-the-wisp. But in fact it had proved that Rome lacked the resources, or the resolution, or both, to subdue even peoples immediately contiguous to the frontiers, living in lands whose dimensions were already roughly known. Panegyrists consoled themselves with the reflection that at least Rome ruled over all peoples who were worth ruling and that in extent and solidity the empire far surpassed all its predecessors.

[81] Vogt, (n. 2) 161–8.

It was a commonplace that Rome's success was due to virtue and fortune. In fortune men discerned a divine power. Under the protection of the gods Rome was certain to defeat all enemies. *Victoria* became a cult symbol of the state, connoting the peace and prosperity that Rome maintained. Emperors assumed the title of *invictus*, and in the very period when the most fearful defeats were suffered. Men had come to believe, if not in the indefinite spatial extension of the empire, at least in its eternity, guaranteed by a Providence which could be represented as immanent in its rulers.[82]

Historical experience fortified this belief. It was easy to forget that in Parthia and Germany Roman arms had been repelled for ever. After all, the disasters at Carrhae and in the Teutoburg forest had not imperilled the fabric of the empire. It was still true in 247, when Rome celebrated her millennium, that since Hannibal Rome had not had to fight for survival. The greatest alarm had perhaps been stirred by the irruptions of the Cimbri and Teutones, and of northern peoples in Marcus Aurelius' reign. They had been triumphantly overcome. No territory annexed to the empire for more than a year or two had yet been lost.

In fact for centuries all Rome's neighbours had been individually far inferior to her in might, and incapable of concerting attacks on her from every side. Even by accident they had not assailed her simultaneously, nor, except on rare occasions (Mithridates in 88 BC and the Parthians in 40), had they launched formidable invasions when Roman armies were preoccupied in civil wars. It had therefore been safe for the imperial government progressively to string out its troops thinly on prolonged and distant frontiers, protecting settled and civilized life in the most remote extremities of the empire; if the defences were breached in one sector, it had always been possible, before any grave damage had been inflicted, to repair the breach by transferring forces from some more peaceful quarter. A strategy that worked well for many generations cannot be justly censured. But it depended on luck. Fortune served the Romans better than they could discern, for it was conditions of which they knew little and which they could not control that kept their neighbours relatively weak and little disposed to invade Roman territory. In the third century luck ran out. The *Völkerwanderungen* in the north, set in motion from the far steppes of Asia, and the coincident resurgence of power in Iran, exposed the empire to pressure on every side at the same time, and just when civil wars had become endemic, encouraging hopes of booty or conquest

---

[82] Victoria: *RE* viii A 2518–2521 (Weinstock). *Invictus*, occasionally used of emperors since Commodus, becomes a regular and official title (varied by *invictissimus*) from Gordian III. Providentia: M. P. Charlesworth, *Harv. Th. Rev.* (1936), 107 ff.; *Proc. Br. Ac.* (1937), 15 ff.

from the enfeebled giant. The empire recovered from this crisis but only at the cost of a permanently greater strain on its limited economic resources. Moreover it increasingly depended on the barbarians themselves for its defence; they could infiltrate provinces which initially they could not conquer. The external onslaughts were heaviest in the west (at least until the emergence of Islam), and there Roman rule dissolved; in the east it survived under different forms and with progressively diminishing territory for another millennium. Rome's eternity (save in so far as it was newly embodied in the Church) proved in the end to be another illusion.

The causes of Rome's decline and fall have been and will be endlessly debated. Though it is beyond question that the process was triggered at every stage by external attacks, their success has been attributed to a variety of internal weaknesses. However, in one respect the empire was stronger by the third century than it had been in the days of Caesar and Augustus. The hatred that the Republic inspired among many of the subjects[83] is no longer in evidence. Everywhere the upper classes, who had been admitted to an equal share in such political rights as subsisted under an autocracy, felt themselves to be Romans. There were no 'national' revolts (except in Judaea): the indispensable leadership was lacking. Oppressed peasants, in blind resentment at their sufferings, could at times co-operate with invaders, but it is not evident that *jacqueries* contributed much to the dissolution of Roman power.[84] Moreover in manpower and wealth the empire was stronger on the eve of the great invasions than in the times of its most spectacular conquests. The Severi had a larger army than Augustus, not to speak of the Republic. It was indeed composed almost entirely of provincials, but it was not their loyalty that failed in the crisis of the third century. Then 'Illyrian virtue' did most to restore Rome's fortunes.[85] Moreover, the resources of Egypt and Gaul in particular had immensely augmented revenues since the time when Rome made herself mistress of the Mediterranean shores. It is far from clear that if in the Republic or the early Principate Rome had been under such external pressures as led to the gradual disintegration of her dominion

---

[83] Cicero publicly acknowledged this, *De Imp. Cn. Pomp.* 65, cf. *Verr.* ii. 3. 207 and *Fam.* xv. 1. 3 (to senate). Cf. Mithridates' successes in Asia and Greece in 88–87.

[84] G. E. M. de Ste Croix, *Class Struggle in the Ancient Greek World* (1981), 474–84. The civil wars were of course far more damaging: they sprang from the institutional weakness of the Principate, in which the lack of any established law of succession opened the way to military pronunciamentos.

[85] A. Alföldi, *St. zur Gesch. der Weltreich des 3 Jahrh. nach Christus* (1967), 228 ff. But after the 3rd c. the defence of the empire rested more and more on barbarian troops. By then Gauls, Illyrians, etc. would or could not fight either in regular units of the imperial army or in local self-defence as hard as they had once fought against Roman conquest. Thus there was little true imperial patriotism.

from the third century onwards, she then had greater material strength
with which to have withstood them. The frequency of usurpations and
civil wars, which stemmed from defects in the political structure of the
imperial autocracy, manifestly contributed to disintegration, but this
danger had never been absent in the Principate, and the discords of the
late Republic would no less have exposed the empire to disruption had
any of Rome's neighbours then been capable of launching powerful
attacks.

However, when the need came, the fervent patriotism characteristic
of ancient city states, and of the Roman Republic, or of nation states in
modern times, was wanting in the state that could be called 'communis
nostra patria' (*Dig* xxvii. 1. 6. 11). Men of culture like Aelius Aristides
and Rutilius Namatianus extolled the greatness and beneficence of the
empire, but its defence was left to mercenaries (cf. n. 85). It is doubtful
if the emperors, though represented as gods or as God's viceregents on
earth, inspired the personal devotion, feudal in origin, often felt for
modern kings. Little fidelity was shown to those who were the victims
of conspiracy or rebellion. There were no Jacobites in the empire,
ready to 'throw lands, honours, wealth, away' for their liege lords. Be
this as it may, there are no signs of that martial spirit in the upper
orders that had been manifest down to the time of Augustus.[86] The
dream of world empire had reflected and perhaps fostered that spirit,
and the renunciation of efforts to realize it perhaps betokened its
decay. The illusion of Rome's eternity, in so far as it truly affected
men's minds, might rather have tended to produce complacency and
torpor, and left them unprepared to surmount a crisis which had never
been expected; when it came, it was for the autocrat as the instrument
of divine providence to find the remedy. Naturally any such moral
factors in the process of decline will always elude demonstration.

[86] Cf. my remarks in *Alte Gesch. u. Wissenschaftsgesch.* (ed. P. Kneissl and V. Losemann) (1988),
54–6.

Addenda

CHAPTER I

Addendum to n. 22. The question cannot be resolved by the very fragmentary *SC de agro Pergameno* (Sherk, *Roman Documents from the East* (1969) no. 12), which is probably, but not certainly, dated to 129 rather than to 101. It plainly concerns a dispute over the liability of the city to make payments to publicans on certain land. Now Pergamum was a free city (Magie, *Roman Rule in Asia Minor* (1950), 1045 f., 1258 f., 1270 f.), and freedom may have carried with it immunity from tribute from such time as tribute was imposed on the Asian cities in general. The question may thus have been whether certain land belonged to the city's territory or the old royal domain. The document refers to 'the revenues of Asia' leased to publicans at Rome. But the Greek words presumably render the Latin 'Asiae vectigalia', and as Latin has no definite article, the phrase need not denote *all* Asian revenues including tribute, as distinct from those revenues which were farmed to publicans, and these might be restricted to (*a*) *portoria* and (*b*) dues (*scriptura* and rents, no doubt tithes, on cultivated lands) from the royal domains, which had become *ager publicus* (cf. Cic., *de leg. agr.* ii. 50). If indeed publicans were already collecting tribute as well on the lands of cities which were not immune, then the dispute could have arisen on the delimitation of the territory of Pergamum from other city lands, on the footing that it was immune. But there is no proof in the fragments that this was the case. Still I do not think that we can rely on the accuracy of what Appian implies (*BC* v. 4 ff.), on the immunity of all Asian cities from tribute until Gracchus' measure, as against Velleius ii. 38. 2, who is no less undependable. But we must be content with ignorance.

CHAPTERS 2 AND 3

The changes made in the original text only affect points of detail; some were prompted by the kind private criticisms of K. Wellesley. As to Vindex the view I took seems to be generally accepted. Disputes on the role of Verginius continue, see most recently B. Levick, *Rh. Mus.* (1985), 318 ff., with full bibliography and discussion of rival theories; I see no reason to think that I was in error. Walser's thesis on Civilis was revived with variations by L. Bessone, *La rivolta Batavica e la crisi del 69 d.*

C. (1972), who failed to meet my objections. It is clear that Civilis took up arms as an ostensible partisan of Vespasian, but that from the moment when he persisted in the siege of Vetera, after the Rhine legions had, however reluctantly and insincerely, sworn fealty to Vespasian, and still more when he continued the struggle against Vespasian's own general Cerealis, he was in revolt against Rome. Conceivably Tacitus was mistaken in supposing his initial attachment to the Flavian cause to have been a mere pretence; no Roman writer need have had any information about his true intentions at the time; but what may have been a mere inference from his subsequent conduct could none the less be correct. Bessone is no more persuasive than Walser to those who think with Syme (*Tacitus* (1958) 173) that Tacitus' 'story of the Batavian war commands assent and admiration, in the face of all the stock charges levelled against a writer who insists upon style and colour', charges that derive from 'petulance or pedantry'.

The intensity and perversity of modern scholarly attacks on Tacitus constitute in themselves a historiographic puzzle; some may originate not only in the prejudice to which Syme alludes, but in a more or less unconscious idolatry of imperial Rome and a natural hostility to Tacitus' iconoclasm. Just as R. S. Rogers could not bear to think that the state he admired could have been governed by any emperors as regardless of law and justice as Tacitus (and indeed all our sources) makes out (cf. *Cl. Phil.* (1960), 10 ff.), and devoted misplaced ingenuity in countless writings, too often treated as valuable, to distorting and discrediting his evidence, so others have blamed Tacitus for fixing his attention on the political scene at Rome, and neglecting the beneficence of Roman rule in the provinces and the steady extension of prosperity and civilization, a process hardly touched by the crimes and follies of individual emperors. Whatever truth may be found in this criticism, it must be borne in mind that Tacitus was the prisoner of the canons of ancient historiography. History was a recital and explanation of memorable events, chiefly political and military. It was more proper to a geographer like Strabo (e.g. iii. 2. 15; 3. 8; iv. 1. 2; 1. 5) to describe from observation the civilizing effects of the Roman peace at a given moment. To have traced historically the gradual evolution by which these effects were realized would have required the collection, in a multitude of diverse and often remote communities, of records of the establishment of schools, gymnasia, theatres, aqueducts, market buildings, and the like, the kind of research that no one thought of undertaking before the nineteenth century, and which Tacitus would not have been alone in regarding as beneath the dignity of history, even though in a general way and a cynical tone he could refer to the civilizing process (*Agr.* 21). Nor is it true that he excludes provincial affairs from his purview. But he chooses to record events of the type with which the ancient historian was traditionally concerned and of which evidence was readily accessible in Roman records: chiefly revolts or complaints of misgovernment. He thus illuminates important aspects of Roman rule, oppression and the resistance it evoked, which its modern eulogists prefer to slur over. Nor again were the political transactions at Rome, which form his main subject, so irrelevant to the welfare of the provinces as critics imply. The alienation of the higher orders at Rome from an emperor whom they regarded as tyrannical (never in my judgement without reason) might lead to his downfall; civil wars might then disrupt the peace and stability of the empire. It was good luck for Rome that the crises of 68–9 and 193–7 did not last long (while in 96 civil war was avoided altogether) and that grave and simultaneous attacks from without did not coincide with internal conflicts. When this good fortune ran out in the third century, there was universal distress among Rome's subjects, and the wounds inflicted were perhaps never completely healed.

Note on Hist. *ii. 97 and iv. 13*

Chilver and Wellesley in their edition of the *Histories* (p. 12) adhere to Münzer's view that the apparent incongruity concerning the attitude of Hordeonius to Civilis shows that he was following two discordant sources. They are not satisfied with my explanation in App. 8. I therefore offer another. Tacitus himself evidently did not notice the incongruity, nor does the ordinary reader. Equally it need not have impinged on the earlier writer, probably Pliny, whom he followed. Pliny (or whoever) must have collected his information orally. Let us suppose that Pliny was told by persons cognizant of Vitellius' preparations at Rome that in reply to his demand for reinforcements Hordeonius pleaded the danger from the Batavians as a reason for non-compliance, and that Pliny, when recording transactions at Rome, accepted this without question. Only later, when he turned to events on the Rhine, would he have learned from those whom he took to understand Hordeonius' intentions that the legate was Civilis' accomplice, and he could then have failed to revise what he had already written.

Note on the Druids

Tacitus (*Hist.* iv. 54) mentions a Druid prophecy as one source of unrest in Gaul in 69–70. This unrest was far from resulting in any national insurrection. On p. 24 I maintained that the Druids played no significant part in perpetuating anti-Roman feelings in Gaul. However, the opinion that Roman hostility to the Druids must be explained by the awareness of the imperial government that they constituted 'a subversive element in the empire' continues to reappear in modern scholarship, e.g. in N. K. Chadwick, *The Druids* (1966), where various theories are reviewed; for a succinct statement of the evidence on the Druids see also *RE* v. 1730–8 (Ihm).

It should first be noted that Roman persecution of the Druids was not tantamount to a persecution of Gallic religion, any more than the suppression of the Jesuits by Catholic states in the eighteenth century was an attack on the Catholic faith. Though the Druids had taken part in some, perhaps in all, acts of sacrifice when the Gauls were independent, there is nothing to show that they actually performed them; their presence was probably ancillary, like that of Roman priests in rites conducted by magistrates. At all times the Gauls were free to worship their own gods (whom they might identify with Roman gods), presumably after their own fashion, except that the old practice of human sacrifice was prohibited; so too the British prohibition of suttee was not a proscription of Hinduism.

The imperial government is said to have taken three successive measures against the Druids. Augustus barred 'Druidarum religionem apud Gallos' to Roman citizens (Suet., *Claud.* 25. 5). This may mean that no citizen was permitted to be a Druid, or that none was allowed to participate in rites in which Druids were concerned. Tiberius procured a decree of the senate which 'abolished' ('sustulit') the Gallic Druids and 'hoc genus vatum medicorumque'; in consequence the 'art' crossed to Britain, so Pliny says (*NH* xxx. 13); there it was still practised evidently in his own day, but probably only among peoples not yet subject to Roman rule. We may connect this measure with the decree dated by Tacitus to AD 16 'de mathematicis magisque Italia pellendis', and its wider extension by the decree that Ulpian dates to the next year, 'quo cavetur ut mathematicis Chaldaeis ariolis et ceteris, qui simile inceptum fecerunt, aqua et igni interdicetur omniaque bona eorum publicentur, et *si externarum gentium quis id fecerit, ut in eum animad vertatur*' (*Coll.* xv. 2. 1). This enactment would have proscribed, without mentioning the Druids expressly, the practices in magic and soothsaying which are ascribed to them in various other ancient texts, and to which Pliny alludes in his 'hoc genus vatum medicorumque', but it would not seem to have been aimed especially at them; rather, they were implicated in a ban on practices which Libo's conduct had rendered obnoxious.

However, Pliny himself links it, in its effect on the Druids, with the prohibition on human sacrifice at Rome in 97 BC (ib. 12), and implies that Tiberius ended human sacrifice in Gaul by adding a comment on the great debt mankind owed the Romans for their abolition of 'monstra, in quibus hominem occidere religiosissimum erat, mandi vero etiam saluberrimum', presumably for its magical effects (ib. 13). Now the Gauls are said to have performed human sacrifices by Cicero in his own time (*Font.* 31) and by Dionysius of Halicarnassus in that of Augustus (*Ant. Rom.* i. 38); Diodorus (v. 31. 3 f.; 32. 6), who certainly followed Posidonius, and Caesar (*BG* vi. 16) and Strabo (iv. 4. 5), who may have done so, attest that the participation of the Druids in the rites was essential, and Diodorus associates it with their role as prophets. Strabo indeed claims that by his time the Romans had put an end to such sacrificial rites and divination in Gaul as were contrary to 'our customs'; he could have written this under Tiberius and have taken this to be the effect of Tiberius' measure, or he may simply have held that under Roman rule the Gauls had become more enlightened. That enlightenment might well have progressed at a different pace among different Gallic peoples; or Strabo may have been too optimistic about the efficacy of Tiberius' measure; even bans on magic and soothsaying in Italy did not succeed (cf. Tac., *Hist.* i. 22). On either view we can see why Claudius found it necessary to legislate on the matter once more, if Pliny was right that Tiberius had done so, and did not make the false assumption that a measure adversely affecting some Druidic activities also proscribed human sacrifice; the assumption would have been natural, given his knowledge that it certainly had been proscribed by his own time. At any rate according to Suetonius (loc. cit.), who knows nothing of any relevant legislation by Tiberius, Claudius 'Druidarum religionem apud Gallos dirae immanitatis et tantum civibus sub Augusto interdictam penitus abolevit'; the words 'dirae immanitatis' clearly indicate that this enactment was directed against human sacrifice.

On the whole it is perhaps best to hold that an enactment of Tiberius either proscribed Druids as such or led to their proscription, because they were given to the suspect practices of magic and soothsaying, but that they did not all flee to Britain—some went underground (Chadwick 77 f.)—and that Claudius found it necessary to repeat and reinforce the ban. As the participation of Druids in human sacrifices was apparently indispensable, even Tiberius' measure should have led to the abandonment of the practice in public and official cults, but it may have continued in private. On one view of a perplexing passage of Tertullian (*Apol.* 9. 2) it was also Tiberius who forbade the immolation of infants in Africa to 'Saturn', i.e. to Baal-Hammon; there too it persisted in secret (see T. D. Barnes, *Tertullian* (1971), 13 ff., but the text, its interpretation, and its reliability all remain in some degree uncertain). Augustus' measure surely indicates that he regarded human sacrifice as inappropriate to Roman citizens, even though he must have thought it imprudent to suppress a national custom, and left it to the infiltration of Roman ideas to bring about its discontinuance, with some success, if we believe Strabo. Tiberius and Claudius went further. There is no difficulty in supposing that emperors shared the repugnance to it evinced by Pliny and Suetonius. It is no objection that Romans were blind to the inhumanity of their own gladiatorial shows; it was easy for them to accept what was all too familiar. Pliny indeed says that 'our own age has witnessed' the ritual burial alive of a Greek and a Gallic woman in the Forum Boarium (xxviii. 12), but this may refer to some aberration by Gaius or Nero, and a statement by Plutarch (*Marc.* 3) does not attest the regular continuance of this ritual at Rome (cf. K. Latte, *Röm. Religionsgeschichte* (1960) 256 n. 3). We may compare with the ban on human sacrifice that on circumcision, which was not directed solely against the Jews, and was soon remitted in their case, but must be explained on the basis that it was regarded as barbaric (cf. Schürer, *Hist. of Jewish People in the Age of Jesus Christ*, ed. Vermes-Millar (1973), i. 536–40).

Even Augustus' limited action against the Druids, reflecting an attitude that might well have become widely known long before it was embodied in legislation, must have affected Gallic notables who had obtained the Roman citizenship or hoped to obtain it. Now the Druids had certainly been men of high social status in Caesar's time (or in an earlier time which he describes, following Posidonius, a theory on which I share the scepticism of D. Nash, *Britannia* (1976), 123 ff.). Caesar sharply distinguishes Druids as well as 'Equites' from the plebs, which had no power (vi. 16). By his account they enjoyed immunity from taxation (vi. 14. 1) and exercised the most important civil and criminal jurisdiction (13. 5–7), though he says nothing of their function in arbitrating or mediating between Gallic peoples of which Diodorus (v. 31) and Strabo (iv. 4. 4) tell us (no doubt they did both draw on Posidonius). It seems to me inconceivable that in an aristocratic society these rights would have been conceded to men of humble birth. It may be objected that their prestige and power rested on their reputation for learning. According to Caesar (14, cf. 13. 4) they gave instruction, sometimes over a period of twenty years, to pupils sent to them by their parents and kin, and Mela at least thought that these pupils, who were obviously to be the Druids of the succeeding generation, were 'nobilissimi' (iii. 19). Cicero's acquaintance, the Druid Diviciacus (*Div.* i. 90), certainly belonged to one of the foremost Aeduan families (*BG* i. 3 etc.). However, Augustus' attitude, to say nothing of the later persecution, would have discouraged men of his type from becoming or remaining Druids. We may suspect that Mela's statement was long out of date, even though, writing *c.* 40, he could give contemporary information: he says that human sacrifice had been abandoned. It must of course be assumed that an order of which Augustus disapproved no longer had any part in that jurisdiction which had not been transferred to Roman courts and was still retained by local authorities.

It is not surprising that after Claudius' measure Druids in Britain, on the isle of Mona, were fervent in calling on tribes yet unsubdued to preserve their freedom from the Roman yoke (Tac., *Ann.* xiv. 30); apart from sharing the common desire for independence, they knew from the Gallic experience what they in particular had to expect, if it were lost. By contrast Caesar is absolutely silent on any part the Druids bore in resisting his conquests; though by his account they had a pan-Gallic organization with its centre among the Carnutes, and an arch-Druid (vi. 13), he does not mention that they fomented the pan-Gallic movement led by Vercingetorix, to which a rising among the Carnutes was the prelude (vii. 2 f.). Diviciacus was actually pro-Roman. We may indeed assume that in general Druids were then as zealous for freedom as lay aristocrats, but no more. The anti-Roman prophecy of 69/70 reveals of course that some were now hostile to Rome, and probably all were, but this hostility would have been the natural result of the persecution, and there is nothing at all to show that it was antecedent to persecution and in fact inspired it. Nor is there any other evidence of their stirring up resistance to Rome. We hear nothing of their activity in the risings of Florus and Sacrovir, or of Vindex, or of Mariccus, nothing to show that they were influential in the counsels of the few Gallic *civitates* that rebelled in 70. Given that they were now humble people, this is not surprising; the Gallic *civitates* were oligarchical. If Druids tried to spread sedition among the masses, nothing came of it. They were unable to maintain or revive Gallic nationalism. It had little or no part in the first-century revolts, and thereafter Gaul was tranquil.

CHAPTER 4

A. General Remarks: Standards of Government

In arguing that the prospects for provincials of obtaining retribution or redress for maladministration were not high in the Principate, though higher than in the Republic, when Cicero had said that they should complain of governors, if at all, only 'animo demisso atque humili' (*Font.* 33), and had remarked that the Sicilians 'solent muti esse in iniuriis suis' (*Verr.* ii. 3. 96), and that before 70 they had never brought an indictment of *repetundae* 'publico consilio' (ib. 2. 8, on which see my

Fall of Roman Republic (1988) 529 f.), I missed one consideration that might be adduced for a contrary view. It was the upper class who were most worth pillaging; the individual victims of Verres, for example, were chiefly men of rank and wealth, though by collusion with the farmers of the Sicilian tithe he was able to extend his depredations more widely to the middling sort. But it was precisely men of the former class who were progressively raised to senatorial and equestrian status in the Principate. Their advancement would make them personally less vulnerable to rapacity, and they would also have been better able and more likely to protect and vindicate their own friends and communities; by contrast in the Republic the aristocratic Roman patrons of provincials might do as little for provincial clients as those of the Sicilians did in Verres' time, cf. Brunt, *Chiron* (1980), 273 ff. (We must indeed allow for the fact that families of provincial origin, like that of the emperor Pius, would come to be domiciled in Italy, and might then be divorced in interest and sentiment from their places of origin.) There is indeed no actual evidence that this kind of protection was commonly available to the subjects in those provinces, the most Romanized or Hellenized, from which provincial senators or Equites usually originated, but then our evidence comes almost entirely from the period before the relevant process had reached its full momentum. However it must also not be forgotten that the feuds within and between provincial cities must have meant that a provincial who had attained great influence at Rome would not necessarily have been well disposed to all those of the same province or city.

Some emperors themselves despoiled the subjects in order to meet the needs of empire or of their own personal extravagance. But even they would hardly be ready to connive in the unjust enrichment of officials, except perhaps for a few favourites. But if the moral standards prevalent in the official class were no better than I think, and my views coincide with those of Marcus Aurelius (cf. Brunt, *JRS* (1974), 10 f.), they could only do what Dio (lxxi. 34. 3 f.) says that Marcus did, be content with picking the least imperfect agents. Marcus too had no confidence in his ability to read men's character (Brunt loc. cit). We do not know that other emperors had more penetration. And the choice made by those who were on bad terms with the Roman ruling class would be limited by suspicions, such as Marcus abhorred; they might prefer to advance those whose political submissiveness was least in question, irrespective of their other qualities.

My remarks on the administration of Tiberius and Domitian (p. 87) are thus not intended to suggest that these emperors did not frown on malpractices but only to question whether eulogies on their administration, ancient or modern, can be justified.

Tiberius certainly disapproved of novel exactions (cf. n. 2). Tacitus says that the provinces were not 'novis oneribus pressi'; such impositions could have had the effect, which Pliny insinuates to have resulted under Domitian, that they 'ad vetera tributa deficiunt' (*Paneg.* 29. 4, cf. n. 92). But when Tacitus also asserts (*Ann.* iv. 6) that in Tiberius' reign 'corporum verbera, ademptiones bonorum aberant', he is making a claim which could not have been substantiated by reference merely to imperial prohibitions, the only evidence that he or his sources can have had at their disposal, but only by the investigations of a fact-finding commission. It may also be noted that the contemporary Philo gives a very different picture of conditions under both Augustus and Tiberius (*Flacc.* 105–7); governors were commonly guilty of corruption, plunder, and the punishment of innocent men of rank. He adds that on their return to Rome, when they had to give an account of their conduct, they were tried impartially by the emperors, especially if there were complaints against them by embassies from the communities they had wronged, and this is certainly unreliable: at no time of which we know was there a regular scrutiny of the conduct of ex-governors, and when the provincials preferred charges, it was not the emperors who tried them, at least in Philo's day. But it does not follow that this provincial view of the frequency of misgovernment is to be rejected in favour of Tacitus' encomium.

Domitian too can be credited with good intentions towards the provincials (cf. nn. 120, 132). But the attempts made by H. W. Pleket (*Mnem.* (1961), 296 ff.) and others to show that he took special and effective measures for their welfare rest on uncertain and implausible interpretations of every document invoked to sustain the thesis (cf. B. Levick, *Latomus* (1982), 50 ff.). Moreover, if we credit Frontinus (*de aquis* 9, 64, 72, 74–7, 87 f., 91, 101, 110, 112–18, 130), the administration of the water-supply at Rome by his curators was slack and corrupt; this is the only branch of administration of which we have detailed information from his reign, and we must ask how likely it is that he was more vigilant in remote provinces. Pleket's notion that he was particularly solicitous for his humbler subjects is hardly relevant to the operation of the *repetundae* law, since it was not they who would generally suffer from a governor's extortions, but it also strikes me as quite fanciful. No doubt Domitian adhered to the general principle that they were to be protected from local magnates, but though fear or greed might have induced him, in his dealings with eminent Romans, to violate the accepted standards of justice that guaranteed life and property, there is no sign that he or any other emperor wished in general to subvert the advantages that the law afforded to the *beati possidentes* (cf. Addendum to chapters 6 and 14). Pleket relies heavily on the express testimony of Suetonius as to his rigour in enforcing the *repetundae* law. He fails to answer the question what evidence Suetonius had, or to see its importance. Even if Suetonius collected material for the life of Domitian while he still had access as *ab epistulis* to imperial archives (which the content of the life hardly suggests), I do not find it credible that these ever contained reliable reports on the conduct of officials. Still less can we believe that he made sedulous enquiries of subjects in every part of the empire. If he came from Africa (which is far from certain, cf. A. Wallace-Hadrill, *Suetonius* (1983), 5), he might *more suo* have generalized from a single instance: the experience of the one province about which he knew. I still think it most probable that he made an unjustified inference from the relative frequency of trials and convictions under Domitian and his successors. Pleket discounts as biased rhetoric what Pliny avers in the *Panegyricus*: yet could Pliny have claimed (70. 7) that Domitian allowed 'male consultis impunitatem' if condemnations for misgovernment had been common? (I may add that I would dispute many of Pleket's general assumptions about Domitian: that he was in conflict with the senate alone (cf. *JRS* (1983), 63 ff.), that this conflict did not begin till 89, that persons convicted of conspiracy were necessarily guilty, or that it was only for alleged conspiracy that men were charged with *maiestas*.)

It should not need saying that the records we have of long and distinguished careers in imperial service by themselves prove only that the men concerned were those whom the emperors favoured; in the absence of other evidence we cannot tell if they deserved it. Nor do the honours that provincial communities conferred on many eminent Romans furnish unimpeachable evidence that they were merited. In discussing this on p. 81 f. I failed to cite the statements of Dio Chrysostom that the Rhodians, like many other Greeks, found it necessary to put up statues of 'the rulers' ($\tau\omega\nu$ $\dot{\eta}\gamma o\upsilon\mu\acute{\epsilon}\nu\omega\nu$), i.e. of Romans, including those who merely passed through their city, in the fear that but for such flattery their prized freedom might be in jeopardy (xxxi. 26, 43, 105, 112-14); he distinguishes these honorands from the true benefactors of the city in earlier times. I do not think that he can have in mind only (if at all) emperors and members of the imperial house.

B. Long-Serving Governors under Tiberius and Nero

The very incomplete evidence of provincial *Fasti* suggests that governors and other officials appointed by the emperor held office on average for two to three years (see p. 219 and Brunt, *JRS* (1983), 47, 49). This was not necessarily true under Augustus, for whose reign the data outside Egypt are particularly scanty. There were probably at least seven legates in Syria from 13 BC to AD 14; for the list cf. Syme, *Roman Papers*, iii (1984) 869 ff. We cannot confirm or refute Suetonius' statement that after Varus' disaster in AD 9 Augustus preferred to prolong commands 'ut a peritis et assuetis socii continerentur' (cf. the prorogation of proconsuls in AD 6, Dio lv. 28); his aim, however, if we believe Suetonius (*Aug.* 23), was not to promote the welfare of the subjects, but rather to hold them down. Tiberius may then have been following the practice of Augustus' last years, which was perhaps prompted by his own advice. Dio says that in the latter part of his reign he kept praetorian legates in post for three and consular for six years, because he had put so many to death that there was a shortage of qualified persons (lviii. 23)! Suetonius ascribes his failure to replace even military tribunes and prefects to sheer negligence in old age (*Tib.* 41). But the prosopographical data show that long tenures for governors were characteristic of his administration from the first.

The list of long-serving governors given in the text (p. 76) needs some amendment. M. Iunius Silanus should be deleted (B. E. Thomasson, *Die Statthalter der röm. Provinzen Nordafrikas* (1960), ii. 28 f.). The long tenure of Apronius in Lower Germany is not quite certain. He was there in 28 (*Ann.* iv. 73), though not before 25 (cf. iv. 22), but if *Ann.* vi. 30 does not prove that he remained till 34, which seems to me probable, it shows that he had held his command long enough to win the special affection of his troops. (His previous service on the Rhine seems to have been in Upper Germany, cf. i. 56.) We can add:

L. Volusius Saturninus (EJ² 367, cf. *ILS* 923, 923a, legate in Dalmatia from 29, if not 21, to *c.*40 (J. J. Wilkes, *Dalmatia* (1969), 442 f.);

Cn. Cornelius Lentulus Gaetulicus, Upper Germany, 30–9 (Dio lix. 22. 5);

L. Munatius Plancus, probably 17 years in Pannonia (Syme, *Danubian Papers* (1971), 190).

Nothing is known of the competence or integrity of these three.

Tiberius' policy was a matter for conjectural explanations in antiquity; I favour Tacitus' final surmise that he selected safe mediocrities like Poppaeus Sabinus (i. 80, cf. vi. 39); there would not be many of the right type to choose from. The notion dear to modern scholars that long tenures conduced to the welfare of the subjects is perhaps suggested in *HA Pius* 5. 3, where the practice is ascribed to Pius, but falsely (A. R. Birley, *Corolla memoriae Erich Swoboda dedicata* (1966), 43 ff.).

Curiously enough, it was Nero's practice that was closest to that of Tiberius. Corbulo had the longest continuous command in imperial history after 37; for years the Sulpicii Scribonii were kept on the Rhine,

T. Flavius Sabinus and Plautius Silvanus on the Danube, and Galba in Tarraconensis. Ummidius Quadratus, appointed by Claudius governor of Illyricum and then of Syria, stayed in the latter province at least from 51 to his death in 59 or 60, when he must have been 70 years old or more. In war or diplomacy Corbulo and Plautius (*ILS* 986) may be thought outstanding, but Ummidius, whom Tiberius had not thought fit to advance in his prime, since quaestor in 14, he was still only a praetorian legate in 37 (*ILS* 972, cf. 190), was unable to maintain discipline in the Syrian legions (*Ann.* xiii. 35), which C. Cassius Longinus had recently restored (xii. 12), or to take effective action in re-establishing Roman influence in Armenia (xii. 44 f.), though he did prove capable of obstructing Corbulo (xiii. 9); no evaluation of his interventions in Judaea can be safe in view of the divergencies between Tacitus (xii. 54) and Josephus (*AJ* xx. 137 ff.). Galba is said to have shown energy at first, but to have degenerated into sloth (Suet., *Galba* 9); we may be reminded of the undistinguished or effete legates he himself appointed or retained in command (Vespasian and Mucianus of course excepted). There is no reason to inculpate any of the governors named in the exactions that ultimately earned Nero the hatred of the subjects (ch. 2, s. II); on the other hand, we can hardly form any opinion of the zeal, efficiency, or honesty that even a Corbulo showed in civil adminstration.

C. The Law of Repetundae *and its Development*

Some points in section I merit amplification, or require corrections; these will not affect any of the main conclusions of the chapter, and indeed mainly concern the evolution of the law in the Republic. On this see especially C. Venturini, *Studi sul 'crimen repetundarum' nell' età repubblicana* (1979), with full bibliography, to which add Sherwin-White, *JRS* (1982), 18 ff.

As before I take the *tabula Bembina* (*FIRA* i². 7) to contain fragments of the Gracchan law (cf. Sherwin-White, *JRS* (1972), 83 ff.; Venturini ch. 1); probably it was amended by a *lex Acilia* earlier than Caepio's law. The latter statute, and those which followed, were surely in part tralatician; for example Sulla and Caesar took over a clause from Glaucia's law *totidem verbis* (Cic., *Rab. Post.* 8 f.); the great length of Caesar's law suggests that it was more elaborate than the Gracchan, and probably than any previous enactment. As our narrative sources refer only to changes in the composition of the court, whereas changes in the substance of the law have to be elicited from casual allusions in the speeches of Cicero, and for the Principate in juristic as well as literary writings, we may suppose such changes not to have been politically controversial (cf. my *Fall of Rom. Rep.*, (1988) 218 f.); in principle no one was opposed to devising more and more stringent rules to curb extortion, though political factors, or the mere personal influence of powerful men, might affect the verdicts on individual defendants. Cf. chapter 14, xi.

In the Principate the *lex Iulia* remained the basis of the substantial law for centuries, as the titles in the *Digest* and *Codex Iustinianus* show. However, it was much modified by decrees of the senate and imperial constitutions. Other Republican or Augustan statutes on the criminal law were amended in the same way, perhaps often with retroactive effect on a current prosecution. Thus under Trajan the senate not only resolved that 'in futurum ad eam legem [sc. *repetundarum*] adici' defendants as well as accusers should be entitled to summon witnesses compulsorily, but also applied the new rule to the case in hand (Pliny, *ep.* vi. 5. 1 f.); for the formula cf. the edict of Claudius that 'adiciendum legi Corneliae [de falsis]' that a person convicted of a new kind of offence 'proinde teneatur ac si commiserit in legem Corneliam' (*Dig.* xlviii. 10. 15 *pr.*). A crime could be punished 'vel ex scriptura legis . . . vel ad exemplum legis' (4. 7. 3) or 'ex sententia legis, quamvis verbis non continetur' (5. 15. 34). Thus the criminal law evolved like the civil by the adoption of legal fictions, expressed by Claudius' formula, or by another that we find elsewhere (8. 4. 2, cf. Tac., *Ann.* iii. 50. 4): 'tamquam lege [Cornelia] teneri'; in this way violations of the *lex Cincia*, itself amended, were brought within the scope of the *lex Iulia repetundarum* (*Ann.* xi. 7. 4). Thus new offences could be created or old immunities from prosecution removed. The jurists often say that by decree of the senate persons guilty of such and such an act are liable ('tenentur'), or subject to penalty, under a particular statute (e.g. *Dig.* xlviii. 5. 15. 1; 7. 6; 8. 3. 3 f.; 10. 1. 2); sometimes they make it appear that liability derived from the terms of the statute, when we know that it really sprang from a senatorial or imperial extension of those terms; thus in *Dig.* xlviii. 11 juristic excerpts make out that the *lex Iulia repetundarum* affected all persons vested with any 'officio munere ministeriove' (1 *pr.*, cf. 3. 5; 6. 2; 7 *pr.*; 9), whereas the statute itself had applied to only a limited category of such persons ((F) below). I now feel no confidence that any of the statements in the Pauline *Sententiae* cited in ch. 4 attest the express terms of the *lex Iulia*.

D. *The Nature and Scope of the Offence*

My essay accepted Mommsen's doctrine (*Strafrecht* (1899), 744 ff.) that in principle the *repetundae* laws forbade unauthorized enrichment by officials to the detriment of the subjects rather than extortion or corruption as such. This now seems to me rather dubious. The Gracchan law entitled claimants to compensation for whatever had been 'ablatum captum coactum conciliatum aversumve' (v. 3; the order of the verbs can be varied), and the same formula seems to have been used in Sulla's law (Venturini ch. V). But Venturini's exhaustive investigation of these terms fails to reveal that any had a precise meaning. The *Verrines* suggest that it was necessary to prove force, intimidation, or fraud (Cicero often speaks of Verres' thefts), except in so far as the law expressly prohibited specific modes of enrichment.

Such prohibitions were doubtless introduced to ban those practices which commonly involved violence or threats or fraud, and to meet the difficulty, to which Mommsen drew attention, of proving anything beyond the overt acquisition of money or valuable objects. The *lex Cornelia* evidently forbade the acceptance of gifts, probably (as in later law) with the exception of those received from kinsmen or those below a certain value. This prohibition may be inferred from another specific exception permitting money to be received for statues etc. in the governor's honour, provided that it was spent for the purpose within five years (*Verr.* ii. 2. 142 etc.), and from Verres' efforts to conceal the fact that the ship he built at Messana was a gift from that city; he made out that he had paid for it himself (4. 150; 5. 44 ff.).

This defence clearly implies that there would have been nothing illegal in his building a ship at his own cost (n. 5). Though debarred from lending money at interest and restricted in the purchase of slaves (p. 55), he was not, as there suggested, precluded from all commercial operations. Cicero charges him with looting works of art; he replies that he had bought them, and in some instances produced documentary proof (4. 8, 35–7, 42 f., 53, 135 f.). Cicero cannot take this as an admission that he had broken the law, but has to argue that the prices allegedly paid were so absurdly low that the sales must have been forced (4. 12 ff.), or that the 'vendor' has testified to coercion (15), or that it is highly improbable that the owner would freely have parted with his property (e.g. 3. 91). In cases where Verres could produce no documentation of purchase, Cicero contends that this shows that his acquisitions were the result of illegal gifts or were sheer thefts (4. 36). Similarly he does not claim that it was illegal *per se* for Verres to set up a 'factory' in the province, only that its existence confirms the immensity of the looted material that Verres needed to work up (4. 58 ff.). Since Verres was entitled to build a ship, we may suspect that it was mere rhetoric when Cicero alleges that he had no right to transport anything from places 'in quibus te habere non licet' (5. 45). The passage I cited on p. 55 from *Flacc.* 85 f. does not support my argument there. The prosecution claimed that as governor Flaccus had no right 'suum negotium agere aut mentionem facere hereditatis'. Cicero is not content to reply that other governors had taken up inheritances: he asserts that it must, but cannot, be proved that Flaccus had resorted to intimidation. The prosecution also 'negavit a privato pecuniam in provincia praetorem petere oportere'; but Cicero retorts: 'extorquere, accipere contra leges non oportet, petere non oportere numquam ostendes, nisi docueris non licere', and he could not have used this language if the law had contained any express prohibition. It is thus evident that the *lex Cornelia* comprised no general ban on all commercial transactions on the part of those persons it affected nor any set of specific prohibitions tantamount to such a ban. But many, if not all, of the gaps it had left were probably closed by the *lex Iulia*, which for example forbade owning and operating ships (n. 5). It was after its enactment that Cicero could say that a defendant had to deny virtually every allegation that a prosecutor might make (*de orat.* ii. 105).

According to Modestinus 'principalibus constitutionibus cavetur, ne hi qui provincias regunt *quive circa eos sunt* negotientur mutuamve pecuniam dent faenusve exerceant' (*Dig.* xii. 1. 33). Imperial constitutions often reaffirm legal rules which were being ignored, but the words italicized may indicate that in this case emperors had found it necessary to stop strictly legal evasions of the terms of the *lex* through the use of men of straw. However, with the extension of liability under the *lex* in the Principate to all officials, it became necessary to grant exceptions from the rules in question to 'perpetui officiales', presumably staff permanently resident in provinces with long tenure: they could lend and borrow (xii. 1. 34), and we may suppose enter into other contracts. It is odd that, according to the same legal source, the Pauline *Sententiae*, a governor too was free to borrow at interest, although he could obviously have used his power to obtain, just as to make, loans on unduly favourable terms. This is in manifest contradiction with Modestinus; perhaps the compilers shortened one or both of the fragments in a way that precludes their reconciliation. All these prohibitions would have entitled claimants under the law to get reparation for their infraction, but would not have invalidated the relevant contracts. However Paul (*ad edictum*) says that the law of *repetundae* (not necessarily the statute) denied *usucapio* to donees of illegal gifts, and invalidated acquisitions by 'venditiones locationes . . . pluris minorisve factas' (xlviii. 11. 8), i.e. on terms more favourable to the official than those of the market; this may also have been the criterion on which reparation was assessed.

The *lex Iulia* also proscribed actions of other types likely to entail undue exactions from the subjects. Of one there is more to be said.

'Exire de provincia, educere exercitum, bellum sua sponte gerere, in regnum iniussu populi Romani aut senatus accedere, cum plurimae leges veteres, tum Cornelia maiestatis, Iulia de pecuniis repetundis planissime vetat' (Cic., *Pis.* 50). Caesar presumably inserted this long-standing prohibition in his *repetundae* law on the ground that the outbreak of hostilities in a province would be apt to result in requisitions for supplies and services from the subjects, which could not be justified if the war were unauthorized and undertaken only to enhance the governor's glory and enrich him with booty. A fragment from one of Cicero's 'leges veteres', the 'piracy' law of 101, shows that it was a defence that the governor had acted 'rei publicae causa' (*JRS* (1974), p. 204, col. III 10 ff.). Obviously all sorts of political considerations would affect the court's discretion in accepting this defence. Gabinius' invasion of Egypt without sanction from Rome was evidently a ground of accusation for both *maiestas* and *repetundae*; though the *lex Clodia*, under which he had received his command, had given him, like Piso, some latitude in enlarging the boundaries of his province (Cic., *Pis.* 37, 49, 57), the prosecutors contended that the expedition was illegitimate, and Gabinius replied that he had acted 'rei publicae causa' (*Rab. Post.* 20). Cicero had half encouraged Lentulus Spinther to assist Ptolemy Auletes to recover Egypt (*Fam.* i. 7. 4), and if Lentulus had moved accordingly, he could no doubt have cited Cicero's advice in support of a claim that he had acted 'rei publicae causa'. Arraigned in 23 or 22 for an unauthorized attack on the Odrysae, M. Primus, proconsul of Macedon, claimed that he had followed the *gnome* (*sententia* or *auctoritas*) of Augustus (who denied it), or of his nephew Marcellus (Dio liv. 3); this was surely to sustain the defence that he had acted in the public interest. (Since Marcellus at least had no legal right to sanction Primus' action, we cannot adduce this incident to show that Augustus had such a right.) See also ch. 14 n. 59.

Another clause of the *lex Iulia* in some way prohibited violations of the privileges of free cities (*Pis.* 90). Like that just discussed, it widened the scope of the offence of *repetundae* beyond extortion to cover other acts of misgovernment. We might ask what was the purpose of this kind of extension, especially as making war without authorization was already forbidden under the law of *maiestas*: perhaps simply to facilitate prosecution in the same process of all illegal and oppressive acts. If the *lex Iulia*, as I argue again in (E), permitted the subjects to prosecute for themselves, it enabled them to do so even when they had no quantifiable claim for pecuniary reparation. We should indeed expect the penalty to be other than pecuniary in such cases (see (G)).

Compensation for the victims of extortion always remained one element in the law, but it had already ceased to be the obvious penalty in another type of offence, which had been brought within the scope of the *repetundae* process at latest by the *lex Cornelia*. That statute had authorized prosecution for the taking of bribes, especially in the

exercise of judicial functions. It is patently unlikely that the giver of a
bribe would expose his own iniquity by suing for recovery of the
money. Charges of this kind would not be brought by or at the instance
of the person or persons from whom illegal enrichment had been
obtained. It may be noted that when Gabinius was accused under the
lex Iulia of receiving bribes from Ptolemy Auletes or from the Alexandrians to effect Ptolemy's restoration, both the king and the Alexandrians denied that they had given him any (*Rab. Post.* 30 ff.). We might
suppose that if a defendant was convicted on this charge, the money
recovered from him on this count would have remained in the treasury,
a possibility envisaged in the Gracchan law if there were no claimants
(v. 66). But conceivably anyone who had suffered pecuniary loss
through his corruption may have been entitled to reparation. In any
event this provision in Sulla's law illustrates the fact that, even if it be
right to assimilate the *repetundae* process in its origins to an action for
delict rather than to criminal proceedings, it had developed into one of
criminal law.

E. Who could prosecute?

It now appears to me that under the Gracchan law Roman citizens
could prosecute for wrongs done to them, or 'alieno nomine' to other
Roman citizens; they certainly had this right under the Cornelian law,
and of course under the Julian; in the Principate ever increasing
numbers of provincials were citizens, and they were obviously not
denied a form of redress available to their unenfranchised countrymen.
On the other hand, under the Gracchan law the right to prosecute
'alieno nomine' belonged in my view only to fellow-citizens of the
persons wronged or to those acting on behalf of their own communities
or their kings; Roman citizens could therefore not bring charges on
behalf of *peregrini*, though of course they might act as *patroni* of *peregrini*,
and as such could be loosely styled accusers. For all this see my *Fall of
Rom. Rep.*, 526 ff.

The right of *peregrini* to prosecute for themselves, conceded by the
Gracchan law, had been abrogated when the Cornelian was in force;
only Roman citizens could now take action on their behalf. Hence, if
the *divinatio* between Cicero and Q. Caecilius had been decided in
favour of the latter, the Sicilians would have been unable to prosecute
Verres themselves, although they regarded Caecilius as unfit for the
task and suspected him of collusion with Verres. Their preference for
Cicero was only one of the considerations that the court was called on
to weigh in making its decision. *Divinatio* was indispensable in cases in
which more than one would-be Roman prosecutor came forward,
given that the wishes of the victims were not binding. We find it

already in operation *c.*100 under Glaucia's law (Cic., *Div. in Caec.* 63). This is proof that the law authorized prosecution by Romans in respect of wrongs done to *peregrini.* Venturini supposes (pp. 419 ff.) that *peregrini* had lost their own right to prosecute, perhaps under Caepio's law, which on this matter Glaucia had left untouched. But he has to admit that Latins retained it, and the text that demonstrates this (*Balb.* 53 f.) does not imply that it was a privilege exclusive to Latins. Even if *peregrini* were free to prosecute on their own behalf, *divinatio* would be necessary if Romans too could initiate proceedings in the interest of provincials, and competed for the role of prosecutors. Under the *lex Iulia* it was required to determine who should have the right to prosecute Gabinius for *repetundae* (Cic., *Qu. fr.* iii. 1. 15; 2. 1). Yet under that law the *socii* could act for themselves; why not under Glaucia's?

The rights of the *socii* under the Julian law are clear from the *senatus consultum Calvisianum.* Ostensibly designed to assist them in 'taking proceedings on account of wrongs done to them and to obtain compensation' (v. 92), it prescribed that if any of them, communities or individuals, 'wish to recover what has been exacted from them, provided that they do not wish to bring a capital charge', they are to be brought before the senate, which will then set up a special court; it will also give them a *patronus,* to plead for them, as under the Gracchan law, but though he would doubtless assist them at every stage, it is they, not he, who are entitled to reject *iudices* (v. 122), and there is no sign that he was the principal in the proceedings, any more than under the Gracchan law. So too in Trajan's time, when cases were heard by the senate itself, Pliny and others acted for the complainants merely as *advocati,* ordered by the senate to 'stand by' ('adesse') the *socii* who bring the charges (*ep.* ii. 11. 1; iii. 4. 2 and 6; 9. 7; vi. 29. 8); their own *legati,* who might indeed happen to be Roman citizens, conduct the *inquisitio,* as Cicero had done when himself the prosecutor of Verres, and plead before the senate (iii. 9. 20; v. 20. 4; vii. 6. 6 and 14; 10. 1), arguing points of procedure (v. 20. 2; vi. 13. 2). Pliny can indeed write, 'accusavi Marium Priscum' (vi. 29. 9), and Sherwin-White (ad loc.) suggests that it was he who had 'converted the case into a full-scale indictment for *saevitia*', thinking perhaps that he was now the prosecutor, but 'accusare' does not necessarily mean 'take criminal proceedings', as distinct from 'make an oratorical attack' e.g. as *patronus*; it can indeed also mean 'instigate proceedings' formally taken by others; hence the Sicilians could be said to be Verres' accusers. This ambiguity (for which see my *Fall of Rom. Rep.*, 527) means that the texts from Tacitus cited in n. 19 fail to confirm the right of *socii* to prosecute for themselves, and in fact it was a notorious *delator* who prosecuted Vibius Secundus, despite Tacitus' 'accusantibus Mauris' (*Ann.* xiv. 28. 2; *Hist.*

ii. 10). But the evidence of the *senatus consultum* and of Pliny is enough to prove my case.

F. Who could be prosecuted?

The Gracchan law permitted charges only against holders of specified posts, roughly those who were senators or were embarking on a senatorial career, and in some cases sons of senators (Brunt, *Fall of Rom. Rep.*, ch. 4 nn. 10 and 19). *Legati*, who are not expressly mentioned but were certainly liable under the *lex Cornelia* (*Verr.* ii. 1. 42 ff.), would normally have been senators. Some of those liable under the Gracchan law would have been *equites equo publico*, but Equites holding unlisted posts would have been immune. Their immunity was maintained even under the *lex Iulia* (n. 6, cf. Brunt, *Fall of Rom. Rep.*, 198 f.); they were still exempt then from prosecution for judicial bribery (*Rab. Post.* 16–8). Equites could indeed be among those who could be required to compensate successful plaintiffs under the rubric 'quo ea pecunia pervenerit'. But the applicability of the law to holders of non-senatorial posts did not, as later jurists make out, spring from its terms but from imperial extensions of its scope, cf. C above.

It was of course only reasonable, once Equites could attain posts in the administration comparable with those open to senators, that they should be subjected to the same rules and penalties in cases of extortion. Kunkel has made it plausible that the development had its origin in the senate's action against Cornelius Gallus, prefect of Egypt, in 26 BC (*Kl Schr.* (1974), 277 ff.); it is relevant that a statute had granted the prefect *imperium* like that of a proconsul (*Dig.* i. 17). Ammianus xvii 4. 5 refers to complaints of his extortions, and Dio liii. 23. 5–7 says that the senate decreed that he should be condemned in the *courts*; the plural indicates that the formality of a trial was envisaged on at least two different kinds of indictment, of which *repetundae* was presumably one. No doubt the senate decreed that he should be convicted 'quasi lege Iulia repetundarum teneretur' (cf. (C)).

The few known cases of charges of misgovernment brought against equestrian officials are listed in the Appendix. *Repetundae* is first given expressly as the charge in the case of Vibius Secundus, though Tacitus' vague language makes it a natural assumption that it was also the offence of Vipsanius Laenas and Celer. All these cases belong to the reign of Nero, and it may be that it was not until his accession, and in the period when Burrus and Seneca were in control, that equestrian officials were arraigned for *repetundae* before the senate; Lucilius Celer was probably charged with *vis publica*, and the other equestrian defendants, not necessarily accused of *repetundae*, went before the emperor. Kunkel (*Kl. Schr.* 333 f.) argues that the story in Dio lx. 33. 6 shows that Iunius Cilo was not actually on trial at all, since it does not fit the formalities of a legal process, but it was perhaps not only *intra cubiculum* but in public too that Claudius disregarded proper legal procedure; in any case, if the story is true, but Kunkel is right in his interpretation, we still have an instance in which aggrieved provincials could not get justice, or even a fair hearing. It may be that most emperors preferred to try equestrian officials themselves, and perhaps with little or no publicity, and that this is why senators so greatly preponderate in the records we have, drawn from proceedings in the senate.

Once senatorial status had ceased to be a condition of liability, the law could affect any person, not only Equites, engaged in public administration (*Dig.* xlviii. 11. 1; *h.t.* 6. 2 and 7 *pr.*). In the posthumous proceedings against Classicus even private persons were inculpated as his agents (n. 30). An enactment of 382 was to make the principal culprit liable to fourfold damages for what his agents took (*CJ* ix. 27. 2 under the rubric of the *lex Iulia*). The same title (ib. 3) gives a rule of 383 that makes *cognitores* even in civil suits liable for corruption; they ranked as officials (M. Kaser, *Das röm. Zivilprozessrecht* (1966), 419 f.). The *iudices pedanei*, to whom in the Principate the governor might refer judication either under the formulary system or under *cognitio extra ordinem*, did not have that standing, but the governor might try them for corruption (*Dig.* xlviii. 19. 38. 10). Was this too under the *lex Iulia*? This might be so, if we adopt a conjecture made by Kunkel, (see (G)), that certain trials for *repetundae* could take place within a province. Macer's statement that that law forbade *anyone* to take money 'ob litem aestimandum iudiciumve capitis *pecuniaeve* faciendum' (*Dig.* xlviii. 11. 7 *pr.*) is wide enough to include them. We could suppose that 'perpetui officiales' (cf. D above) could be indicted before the governor, at least if they were not alleged to have been his own agents. Charges might also have been laid in his court against provincials of no official status. Private persons could certainly be brought within the scope of the law, for instance advocates for transgressing the *lex Cincia* (Tac., *Ann.* xi. 7). Venuleius says that the law prohibited taking money 'ob accusandum vel non accusandum', and likewise for giving a corrupt *sententia* 'in senatu consiliove publico' (*Dig.* xlviii. 11. 6. 2). What is meant by 'consilium publicum'? May it include provincial *concilia* and city councils? Cf. n. 32 for at least one case in which the *lex* was applied to them. The *lex Iulia repetundarum*, like the *lex Iulia ambitus* (xlviii. 14), could have been extended from Rome to the municipalities. We might thus understand the rule that it covered illicit gains made by *anyone* responsible for leasing public contracts and approving the work done, and for the distribution and conveyance of public grain, hardly perhaps designed to refer only to Rome (xliii. 11. 7. 2), or by those 'qui munus publice mandatum accepta pecunia ruperunt' (*h.t.* 9). All this would suit Kunkel's conjecture.

I have stated that governors at least could not be prosecuted while in post (p. 71). Evidence that this rule, which appears in a constitution of 390 (*CJ* xi. 27. 5), already held in the Republic and Principate needs to be considered. It is well known of course that Caesar's enemies were unable to prosecute him after his first consulship so long as he retained his proconsular *imperium*. In the particular case of *repetundae* the Gracchan law barred prosecution of any magistrate or holder of *imperium* until he demitted it (vv. 8 f.) The immunity of magistrates, except when indicted before a higher magistrate (Mommsen, *StR* i³. 705 ff.), is indeed irrelevant to provincial administrators in the Principate, since none were magistrates. Nor did all of them possess *imperium*. But all should have been covered by the *lex Memmia*, passed in or before 113 BC, which prohibited reception of criminal charges against persons absent from Rome 'rei publicae causa' (Val. Max. iii. 7. 9; vi. 8. 1).

Now Modestinus says that such absence ran from departure from the city until return, and that the category included proconsuls and their legates, all provincial governors and procurators in the provinces, military tribunes, prefects, and *comites legatorum* registered with the treasury or in imperial *commentarii* (*Dig.* iv. 6. 32); the list as transmitted cannot be exhaustive, as it omits *legati legionum*, *iuridici*, and *comites proconsulum*; Paul adds among others commanders of detachments of troops and recruiting officers, and cites a rescript of Pius extending immunity to persons serving in the army units at Rome (iv. 6. 35). The privilege covered civil as well as criminal proceedings. Papinian, however, says that under the *lex Iulia de adulteriis* it was permitted to serve notice of prosecution ('postulare') on a person 'in honore ministeriove publico' but that, on his giving sureties for appearance, further proceedings were deferred until he vacated office (*Dig.* xlviii. 5. 39. 10); we do not know if this applied to other criminal charges.

A special case arose in AD 31, when Sejanus promoted the indictment, probably for *maiestas*, of an unnamed enemy, who can be identified with L. Arruntius, appointed legate of Tarraconensis ten years earlier but never allowed to go out to his province (*PIR*² A 1130). On Modestinus' doctrine he was not strictly 'rei p. causa *absens*'. Dio lviii. 8. 3, our source, tells that Tiberius frustrated this move by granting immunity to all persons designated for public posts. R. S. Rogers (*CP* xxvi. 40) rightly connected this with a fragment of Venuleius (*Dig.* xlviii. 2. 12); 'hos accusare non licet: legatum imperatoris [id est praesidem provinciae] ex sententia Lentuli dicta Sulla et

Trione consulibus [AD 31]: item legatum proconsulis ['provincialem' codd.], eius dumtaxat criminis quod ante commiserit quam in legationem venerit; item magistratum populi Romani eumve qui rei publicae causa afuerit, dum non detractandae legis causa abest.' It is easy to suppose that Tiberius' ruling was given effect by a senatorial decree (a formality Dio is apt to ignore, cf. Brunt, *CQ* (1984), 423 ff.), which was moved by Lentulus, probably the consul of AD 1 (*PIR*² C 1380). It is not clear from the fragment whether the words from 'item' onwards refer to the substance of the decree rather than to later interpretation or extension. In any case the fragment cannot be verbally correct as the change in tense from 'commiserit' and 'afuerit' to 'abest' shows. It has probably been greatly abbreviated, as comparison with the other lists of persons 'rei p. causa absentes' suggests. More important, it seems unlikely (even if the *lex Memmia* had been repealed or forgotten) that it was a decree of AD 31 that first granted immunity to governors in post and others absent on public business, especially if the decree was occasioned by the circumstances related by Dio, which made it necessary to grant immunity to a man who was not absent at all. All this makes it risky to give any precise significance to the reservations introduced by 'dumtaxat' and 'dum', which may also not have been correctly excerpted by the compilers. If the first reservation is taken seriously, it would mean that a man in post could be prosecuted for alleged offences committed in that post though not for any committed earlier; this is hard to reconcile with the fragment of Papinian on adultery, or to credit. E. Weinrib suggested that Dio too is inaccurate, since Arruntius was legate, not legate designate (*Phoenix* (1968), 32 ff.; (1971), 45 ff. for other views with which I am not in full agreement). But, if the real purport of Tiberius' innovation was to confer immunity on legates and perhaps other officials from the moment of their designation, and not from the moment when they actually left Rome to take their posts up, a fact (if it be such) also not revealed in the juristic fragment, Dio's error would be venial. It must also be noted that a rule to this effect is ignored in the excerpt from Modestinus already cited. Perhaps it only applied to legates, and the special rule for them was overlooked by Modestinus or omitted by the compilers; or perhaps it had passed into oblivion, since cases like that of Arruntius ceased to occur. On the whole it is best to rely on the testimony of Modestinus and Paul.

G. *Penalties*

The Latin law of Bantia, which is surely post-Gracchan, though its precise date is unknown, prescribes that persons convicted of an offence, the nature of which can at best be conjectured, were to be debarred from membership of the senate or of a public court, in which they also might not bear witness, from acting as *iudex, arbiter*, or *recuperator* in civil cases, and from voting in the *comitia* (*FIRA* i². no. 6. 1; cf. Brunt, *Fall of Rom. Rep.*, 139–43). Such political and civil disabilities, which can be summed up as *infamia*, were certainly a consequence of condemnation for *repetundae* in the first century BC, just as in the Table of Heraclea (*FIRA.* i². no. 13 vv. 108 ff.) *infamia* followed condemnation for theft or in civil *bonae fidei* actions. But there is no hint of it in our fragments of the Gracchan law, and C. Cato (*cos.* 114) retained his senatorial rank after condemnation for illegally taking 4,000 HSS, which would have required payment of double that sum in reparation (Cic., *Verr.* ii. 3. 184, cf. *Brut.* 128, Vell. ii. 8). Now the Gracchan law obliged the defendant to furnish sureties for payment due on condemnation to the quaestor, on pain of sequestration of his property; the quaestor was to exact payment from sureties, if the defendant did not pay himself (*FIRA* i², 57—69). No doubt Cato did pay up. It seems probable that if the person condemned failed to do so, he would have automatically suffered *infamia*; under the Table of Heraclea (loc. cit.) a man is ineligible for local magistracies 'pro quo datum depensum est erit', or if his property has been sold up even in proceedings for civil bankruptcy (cf. M. Kaser, *Das röm. Zivilprozessrecht* (1966) 306 ff.). *A fortiori* this should have been the consequence of public sequestration. It may well be that it was an innovation of Glaucia's law, taken over in all later statutes, that *infamia* should follow conviction for *repetundae*, whether or not the defendant made reparation.

Payment of even simple compensation, when the sum was large, might be ruinous to a man without sufficient liquid assets; Lucilius (573 M.) characterized the Calpurnian law as 'saeva'. As early as 173 two ex-governors of Spain, convicted of *repetundae* by an extraordinary court, went into voluntary exile (Livy xliii. 2). It is unlikely that they had been required to make more than simple reparation, as the Calpurnian law was later to prescribe; but defendants who had squandered their illicit gains might find this ruinous, and if sequestration ensued, they probably incurred *infamia* too, ending their public careers. The double reparation demanded by the Gracchan law was still more likely to bankrupt those condemned. It was therefore better for them to remove themselves with any liquid assets beyond Roman jurisdiction. With their remaining wealth, and with the influential connections they might preserve with kinsmen and friends at Rome, they could acquire importance or dominance in their new homes: C. Antonius Hybrida (*cos.* 63) affords another instance (Strabo x. 2. 13), besides those of Verres and Memmius (p. 61). If they chose to accept citizenship in their city of refuge, they automatically forfeited Roman citizenship (Cic., *Balb.* 27–30), and thus lost their *caput*, but in any case its value had been diminished by self-imposed exile. This explains why Cicero, writing of course after Verres' flight, could say that his *caput* was at stake in the *repetundae* trial (e.g. *Verr.* ii. 3. 152), why in 106 L. Crassus could assail the cruelty of equestrian *iudices*, which 'cannot be satiated except with senatorial blood', when advocating that they should be deprived of exclusive judication for *repetundae* (*de orat.* ii. 225), and why M. Antonius in 98 should plead for a defendant on that charge, 'retinendus in civitate' (ib. ii. 194). None of these texts proves that at the relevant time *repetundae* carried a capital penalty. Cicero could actually say that the *caput* of a client was at risk in purely civil proceedings, when he was at most liable to bankruptcy and *infamia* (*Quinct.* 32 f.). There is no justification for Venturini's claim that in 98 at least the loss of *caput* had been prescribed in certain eventualities by Glaucia's law.

He contended that the penalty was capital in appropriate cases under the Cornelian law, and that this being so the innovation would have been due to Glaucia and taken over by Sulla. His argument is not persuasive. In *Cluent.* 116 Cicero maintains that a *litium aestimatio* made by the *repetundae* court after a defendant was condemned did not bind any other court. A man might be convicted for *repetundae*, and assessed for pecuniary reparation, on account of actions which could also give rise to criminal charges for some other offence, such as *maiestas* (cf. *Verr.* ii. 4. 88), but according to Cicero very many had been acquitted of *maiestas*, 'quibus damnatis de pecuniis repetundis lites maiestatis essent aestimatae'. But 'lites' in the sense of penalty is unattested: it means pecuniary compensation, and this was not a consequence of condemnation for *maiestas*, the penalty for which was indeed capital, nor could the *repetundae* court condemn a man for *maiestas*; if that had been possible, it would have been pointless to prosecute him subsequently in the *maiestas* court for an action for which he had already been convicted on that very charge. All that the *repetundae* court could do was to award compensation on account of an action which also laid him open to prosecution for *maiestas*, and 'lites maiestatis' must be short-hand for this. Cicero proceeds to discuss the case of P. Septimius Scaevola. As we know from *Verr.* i. 38, he was condemned for *repetundae*, whereupon 'lis aestimata eo nomine, quod ille ob rem iudicandam pecuniam accepisset'. Now this was also a capital offence under the *lex Cornelia de sicariis*. In *Cluent.* 116 Cicero makes out that that it was really on other counts that Scaevola was convicted for *repetundae*, and that no one took seriously the implication in the *litium aestimatio* that he was also guilty of judicial corruption, although 'omni contentione pugnatum est uti lis haec capitis aestimaretur'; he argues that if the *litium aestimatio* had had the authority of a *res iudicata*, Scaevola would have then been indicted under the *lex de sicariis*. Again we must take 'lis haec capitis' to be shorthand; it cannot mean that the *repetundae* court had itself imposed a capital penalty, in which case there would have been no need to indict him under the *lex de sicariis*, but only that compensation had been awarded on a count for which he would have incurred that penalty, if he had been tried by a different court under another law.

However, given that the same actions could expose a man to prosecution both for *repetundae* and for a capital crime, it was a natural development that the *repetundae* court should in appropriate cases itself be empowered to impose the capital penalty on conviction. I now think that Sherwin-White was right in supposing that the Julian law provided for this. I was hesitant in asserting with confidence what many scholars continued to deny, but further reflection has convinced me that they have been blinded by the authority of Mommsen, who of course never saw the *senatus consultum Calvisianum*; read without *parti pris*, this document is decisive. Kunkel has also reinforced Sherwin-White's case (*Kl. Schr.*, 284 ff.). (1) An argument that no capital condemnation is attested under the Julian law in the Republic would have no cogency, given the paucity of available evidence; in fact most probably Gabinius suffered loss of *caput*. (2) The fragment of the Pauline *Sententiae* discussed in n. 28 need not bear on the Julian law at all. Kunkel himself would read conjecturally 'nemo in p[rovincia accu]satur', explaining that imperial practice allowed the bringing of charges of *repetundae* within a province against local agents of a previous governor, but only if merely pecuniary compensation were sought. Cf. p. 500 for possible types of trials for *repetundae* by governors. It must be urged against this that no theory can be substantiated by conjectural supplementation, but this objection is equally valid against all supplements of this text. (3) The Julian laws on *vis* and *peculatus* also on Kunkel's view prescribed a scale of penalties for the various offences they covered; why not the Julian law on *repetundae*?

No difficulty is presented by a fragment of Macer on the *repetundae* law which reads: 'hodie ex lege repetundarum extra ordinem puniuntur, et plerumque vel exilio vel etiam durius, prout admiserint'; for example taking money to condemn inocent persons deserves deportation, if not execution (*Dig.* xlviii. 11. 7. 3). Macer is contrasting the current practice of imposing penalties *extra ordinem* with that of some earlier period, but not necessarily with the prescriptions of the statute. The classical jurists treated all criminal proceedings for offences defined by Republican or Augustan statutes as arising from the statutes concerned, even though charges were no longer heard by the courts to which the statutes had given the jurisdiction, and though penalties had been varied by decisions of emperor or senate. Thus in *Dig.* xlviii. 8. 3. 5 Marcian contrasts the scale of penalties 'now customary' under the *lex Cornelia de sicariis* with the *poena legis*, viz. deportation to an island and confiscation of property, but though Sulla had certainly made the crime capital, deportation to an island was a form of capital penalty devised in the early Principate. No doubt Macer is contrasting the severity of his own time with the milder treatment accorded to *repetundae* culprits in earlier reigns. In any case the excerpt from his work has certainly been abbreviated; for example the reference in section 1 to 'hoc capite' is obscure as a result.

CHAPTERS 6 AND 14

Both these chapters concern the way in which acquiescence in Roman rule among the subjects developed into a sort of imperial patriotism. I have perhaps not emphasized sufficiently that what we know of this process very largely relates to the higher orders. Though the empire was defended by soldiers who were increasingly recruited from the provincial peasantry, it would be hard to determine how far their loyalty was due simply to material rewards and privileges, to the discipline maintained by officers from the higher orders, and to *esprit de corps*, rather than to the patriotic ardour characteristic of the armies of ancient cities or of modern nation states. For the rest what we know of the readiness of the subjects to accept their lot with gratitude, and eventually to identify themselves with the Romans, derives from literary works composed by, or at least addressed to, members of the élites, or from monuments, often inscribed, most of which were erected by or for such persons or by the communities which they controlled. This is true for instance of the copious evidence that the living emperor, the incarnation of Roman sovereignty, was honoured as a god; the cults were normally authorized by local councils and celebrated by magistrates or priests drawn from their ranks; whatever view we take of the mentality which underlies them, they reveal little or nothing of the sentiments of the masses. No doubt the urban poor relished the festivals, but it is significant that except in a few regions there is little testimony to the extension of the imperial cult in rural areas (cf. S. R. F. Price, *Rituals and Power* (1984), ch. 4).

From the first the local élites must have been best able to discern the futility of isolated revolts and the impossibility of concerting widespread resistance to Roman rule. In the course of time the advantages of submission must have become more and more manifest to them. Not that they are likely to have been conscious of the superior excellence of Roman administration, which may have been neither better nor worse than that which they had previously experienced; in any case honest and efficient government seldom wins the loyalty of subjects, whose distorted recollections may hallow 'the good old days', and who may hold their rulers, sometimes unjustly, to blame for any current evils. But the long and unexampled continuance of the Roman peace was an undeniable blessing. Even the humblest people had far less reason to fear slaughter, enslavement, and pillage from foreign invaders or raiders. Still it was the class in which literacy best preserved the memory of the endemic warfare of the past who could most clearly appreciate the tranquillity of the present. Peace ensured and promoted a higher level of material prosperity, within the limits imposed by technological backwardness, and the diffusion to once uncivilized lands of the delights of Greek or Roman culture. But it was men of property and leisure who had the best opportunities for accumulating wealth, and for enjoying novel amenities in the cities or in their country villas. Few of them had to pay for these benefits in the loss of political liberty, for not many communities had at the time of conquest possessed more than the local self-government that Rome too allowed. And it was in the élites that this self-government was vested. Increasingly they were also given a part in the central administration. They then were, and felt themselves to be, Romans, and Roman rule ceased to appear alien. But all these benefits appertained far less, if at all, to the masses. Town dwellers of every station certainly had a share in the amenities of city life. But these hardly extended to the workers on the land, who must have composed the vast majority of the population. An unknown proportion (in the cities too) consisted of slaves (though the standard of life enjoyed by the free poor was not necessarily higher). It may be doubted if folk memory even enabled men to draw comparisons with the pre-Roman past, and to see that their condition had improved, if it had.

I have said little of the attitudes to Rome of the 'voiceless millions', precisely because they are almost voiceless; even the papyri which tell us much about humbler folk in Egypt hardly illuminate their views about the sovereign power. There and elsewhere a few documents show them seeking, and perhaps getting, relief from oppression by appeals to governors or emperors; their petitions need not betoken that they had much confidence in success, only that they had no other resort. In general such people did not put up inscriptions, or leave literary works to reveal their sentiments. Some Christian writings emanate from the lower classes, but they chiefly reflect the special concerns of their sect.

They may betray, like Revelations, a deep hostility to the state, which was only natural as it was hostile to them. More often Christians complied with scriptural commands to pray for their persecutors and to submit to the higher authorities instituted by God, or sought to persuade them that they deserved tolerance and protection; this was also the course of prudence, or necessity.

According to Aelius Aristides, himself a biased witness from the upper class, Rome held an even balance between rich and poor (*To Rome* 65 f.). The principle had long been an acknowledged mark of just government (Aristotle, *Pol.* 1310^b 40; Cic., *de Offic.* ii. 85). Dio makes Maecenas counsel Augustus to protect the masses from violence and injustice at the hands of the powerful, but not to expose the latter to false accusations (lii. 37). Governors were mandated to prevent the *potentiores* from wronging the *humiliores* with illegal exactions, forced purchases, and the like (*Dig.* i. 18. 6 *pr.*, 2 and 4). The Julian criminal laws or law on violence penalized not only popular 'seditions' but the conduct of magnates who took the law into their own hands, sometimes with the help of armed retainers (xlviii. 6 f. *passim*); the civil law too provided numerous remedies for the use of violence or intimidation. We may recall Tacitus' allusion of provincials who commonly employed their preponderance of influence and riches to injure their inferiors (*Ann.* xv. 20). Governors were also to ensure that in litigation the weaker party was fairly heard and competently represented by advocates (*Dig.* i. 18. 9. 4–6). This would have been primarily of benefit to the middling sort, for the very poor do not litigate. Humbler people, detained in bonds (in contravention of the law on violence), might be given refuge, if they could escape, at a statue of the emperor, and could then procure a hearing, though not if they brought malicious charges (xlviii. 19. 28. 7). Pliny supposed that many governors treated local magnates too harshly and spitefully for fear of seeming to defer overmuch to their influence, but I should guess that this was much rarer than that respect for 'discrimina ordinum dignitatumque' which he enjoins (*ep.* ix. 5). Apart from that social prejudice, they might have personal ties of friendship with provincial notables (*Dig.* i. 16. 4. 3), and of course with their patrons at Rome, and the warning that they should avoid undue intimacy with particular individuals implies a principle that probably had little correspondence with the realities of practice (i. 18. 19. 1). They were also instructed to curb extortions by soldiers and officials, who might rob the poor man of his one means of lighting or few bits of furniture (i. 18. 6. 3. and 5). These vexations were incidental to the system under which government servants in transit could requisition at fixed rates of compensation shelter and transport. Numerous constitutions in the *Theodosian Code* show how vainly emperors in the later period tried to check the abuses of this right; the far scantier records of the Principate suggest that their predecessors had been just as well intentioned, and just as impotent to restrain what Claudius called the 'nequitia hominum' (S. Mitchell, *JRS* (1976), 106 ff.). The few surviving petitions in which peasants seek redress from oppression by appeals to the emperor indicate that they had failed to get protection from governors; in one it is alleged that the procurators were in collusion with the contractors who collected imperial rents and who were exacting more than their due (Abbott and Johnson, *Municipal Administration in the Roman Empire* (1926), no. 111, cf. perhaps 142: see also 113, 132, 139, 141, 143 f.; in some cases the petitioners complain of outrages by municipal officials or police as well as by soldiers and civil officials of the state).

Whatever intermittent protection the government afforded to the lower classes against sheer illegalities, its true sympathies did not lie with them. It sustained an increasingly hierarchical social structure. The civil law was developed in its substance to suit the interests of the *beati possidentes*, and its procedures favoured the strong (J. M. Kelly, *Roman Litigation*, (1966)). The criminal law exempted the *honestiores* (most members of the upper class, but soldiers too) from torture and the savage punishments to which other free men were liable like slaves, and in all courts the testimony of the former carried more weight (P. Garnsey, *Social Status and Legal Privilege in the Roman Empire* (1970), with my review in *JRS* (1972), 166 ff.).

In any cities where democratic institutions had survived until the Roman period, they were eroded (G. E. M. de Ste Croix, *Class Struggle in the Ancient Greek World* (1981), 518 ff.). Everywhere the masses lacked the political rights with which they might legally have defended themselves, though within the cities they had means of applying pressure on their oligarchic rulers (p. 522). If petitions failed, peasants could only resort to banditry or at least to flight from their lands: Egyptian fellahin were apt to disappear 'up-country'. To keep up cultivation and revenues from the land, the government would in the fourth century attach the peasants hereditarily to the soil, a measure that did not necessarily stop them running away. At the same time indeed persons, including even city councillors, were bound, and their children after them, to many other occupations under rules that were doubtless often evaded (A. H. M. Jones, *The Roman Economy* (1974), chs. XIV and XXI). These regulations were inspired by the supposed needs of the state, rather than by the interests of the higher orders; it was an inconvenience to large landowners that they were also forbidden to remove their own slaves from the farms where they were working. And it may be said that most peasants desired nothing more than safe tenure of lands which they and their forefathers had tilled. However, once 'adscripti glebae', they were made legally subject to harsh coercion by their landlords. Oppression by officials also made freeholders place themselves under the greater magnates who could offer them some protection. If slavery, as often supposed, had long been in decline, it was replaced by a serfdom which was in some ways no less grievous.

We must always remember that Roman rule might impinge little on the ordinary man. Very few troops were stationed in provinces not contiguous to the frontiers. Soldiers were hardly to be seen in many areas, except in transit on the great roads. In most communities the direct taxes were collected by city officials and other imposts by tax-farmers, whose agents might be local men. Jurisdiction was divided between the courts of the governors and of the communities. The line of division is imperfectly known, but while only the governor could impose capital sentences, minor crimes must have been repressed by local authority, and local courts would also determine most suits for small sums; this was an advantage to poorer litigants, inasmuch as the assize towns where the governor dispensed justice would often be too distant for them to travel to, leaving their farms or trades for periods that might be unforeseeably protracted. (It may well be that the *potentiores* could get cases transferred to the governor to the prejudice of the weaker party.) Such social benefits as government provided were supplied by the cities and not by Rome (except for occasional imperial benefactions), and they accrued chiefly to town dwellers. In so far as the masses showed discontent by urban riots, banditry, or flight, it must usually have been evoked primarily by their local masters. Rome was indirectly responsible in that it was by her will that they possessed authority, and they might at times be acting under pressure from Rome, especially in response to fiscal demands. But we must be wary of taking such discontent, most evident to us in the defections to barbarians and peasant risings of the late empire (Ste Croix 474 ff.), as proof of specifically anti-Roman feeling, rather than of class discords (cf. ch. 13 and Addenda).

The Christians had inherited from Jewish morality the belief that men had special obligations to widows, orphans, and the poor in general, a belief alien to Greek or Roman mentality, cf. H. Bolkestein, *Wohltätigkeit und Armenpflege im vorchristlichen Altertum* (1939). The charitable practices of the early Church may have helped to win converts (A. von Harnack, *Mission and Expansion of Christianity*, book II, ch. IV). Once Christianity had become the official religion, almshouses, hospitals, and orphanages, previously unknown, were established (A. H. M. Jones, *Later Roman Empire* (1964), 901); of course they can have done no more than mitigate distress here and there. And now we have writings, from the hands of Christian authors such as Shenute (Ste Croix 446), Augustine and John Chrysostom (ib. 226), and Salvian (p. 342), which denounce oppressors of the poor, the landlords and the *curiales* who collected the taxes and shifted their burden on to those less able to bear it, rather than the imperial government as such.

In the late empire barbarian inroads and increased taxation may have aggravated social misery, but we cannot be sure, since we could not expect from Aristides and his like any account of sufferings such as the Christian writers depict. From generation to generation the condition of the masses may have changed little. Ste Croix's discussion of 'the ideology of the victims of the class struggle' (441 ff.) shows, however, that it evoked no doctrinal opposition to their rulers; there were no proto-Marxists in the Roman world. The masses had no memories of a golden past (which had never existed) and no hopes of a future millennium. (As usual, we must except the Jews.) At most they could break out in movements of violent but blind protest against their lot, or even side with invaders in the illusion that a change of masters might be for the better. More commonly their attitude was probably apathetic. No doubt Phaedrus' fable of the donkey who would not flee from the enemy, since no one could lay on him a heavier burden than that which he bore, to which Ste Croix has called attention (444), was often applicable. But the demands of officials and landlords may well have appeared as familiar and inevitable as the alternations of seedtime and harvest, and the exceptional distress in crises brought about by the crimes and follies of the powerful analogous to such natural calamities as floods and droughts, earthquakes and plagues. We may recall T. S. Eliot's Canterbury women:

> 'we know what we must expect and not expect.
> We know of oppression and torture,
> We know of extortion and violence,
> Destitution, disease,
> The old without fire in winter,
> The child without milk in summer,
> Our labour taken away from us . . .
> And meanwhile we have gone on living,
> Living and partly living,
> Picking together the pieces,
> Gathering faggots at nightfall,
> Building a partial shelter,
> For sleeping and eating and drinking and laughter.'

CHAPTER 9

In *Epigraphica*, 42 (1980), 64 ff., Simonetta Segenni published an inscription, which with a plausible supplement gives us an equestrian recruiting officer in Mauretania Caesariensis under Pius, together with a list of such officers, senatorial as well as equestrian. This list includes some whom I had overlooked, two in Italy, if the supplements are accepted; that of *CIL* x. 1259 (Pius or Marcus) is convincing, that in the career inscription of C. Aufidius Victorinus, which ascribes to him the '[adm]inistrati[onem dilectus tironum]' in Transpadana under the *divi fratres* (G. Alföldi, *Fasti hispanieses* (1969), 38 ff.) very hazardous. In *ILS* 1341 we have an equestrian 'delectator' under Hadrian, where is not clear (Pflaum, *Carrières procuratoriennes* (1960), no. 113). A recruiting officer in Thrace is known from *IGR* i. 824. Segenni herself missed the inscription of a Pamphylian recruited by the procurator M. Arruntius Aquila (*PIR* A 1138) for a Syrian legion, probably in 45 (Bean and Mitford, *Denkschr. Akad. Wien. Phil–hist. Kl.*, 102 (1970), p. 21 no. 4). It was not germane to her list to cite the recruiting activity of a Thracian phylarch, a local official (L. Robert, *Bull. ép.* (1960), no. 23a), or the curious case of the *ordinarius* in Thrace deputed to enlist brigands (*Bull. ép.* (1941), no. 92a). The *Historia Augusta* alleges that in the manpower crisis brought about by the great plague Marcus Aurelius made soldiers of brigands in Dalmatia and Dardania, and also *diogmitai*, municipal police in Asia (*Marc.* 21. 7). This is one instance in which the untrustworthy writer was evidently drawing on good information; we also know of a *diogmites* dispatched to his wars from Aezani (*OGIS* 511). Probably brigands were attracted into service by an amnesty. An inscription first published by A. Plassart, *Mél. Glotz* (1932) ii. 731 ff., see now C. P. Jones, *GRBS* (1971), 45 ff., shows that in this crisis recruits were raised at Thespiae. Jones cites *TAM* iii. 1. 106, which shows that Greater Termessus too despatched a contingent to Marcus about the same time. No doubt Thespiae and Termessus were not the only Greek cities to supply soldiers in the emergency. I do not suppose that conscription was regularly employed in such places (n. 21). The Thespian decree refers to the recruits as eager to serve. None the less, Jones argues plausibly that the city was under pressure from the emperor to furnish soldiers, and he calls them 'conscripts'. That description may not be quite correct, since Thespiae conferred various privileges on those who joined up. A mixture of quasi-compulsion and extraordinary incentives (offered by the city, not the emperor) may be conjectured. But the co-operation of local authorities in recruitment would not have been so unusual. If it is not attested epigraphically in the regions from which soldiers were principally drawn, the reason may simply be that there is little epigraphic evidence in those regions for any activity of local authorities. Very probably it was through them that *dilectatores* operated and the Thracian phylarch's role was more typical than we can demonstrate. Cf. the Appendix to chapter 9.

An analogy might be found between those auxiliary regiments of the first century AD which were commanded and perhaps enlisted by tribal chiefs and at first employed not far from their homelands, and the British regiments raised during the eighteenth century in the Scottish Highlands. In his *Mutiny: Highland Regiments in Revolt 1743–1804* (1977) John Prebble writes (429) of the Highlanders' 'intense hatred of compulsory military service'; they were, however, ready to join the colours out of feudal loyalty to their chiefs, and later, when this sentiment had been dissipated by ruthless exploitation, to protect their families from the penalty of eviction by the chiefs from their crofts (e.g. 100 f., 147). The chiefs ingratiated themselves with the government by raising troops, and made substantial profits in the process. Clansmen often enlisted in the false expectation that they would not be required to serve outside their own country, or at least not overseas. They resented being mixed with soldiers or commanded by officers even from other clans, much more Lowland Scots or Englishmen, and being subjected to the common discipline of the British army. (See e.g. 25, 29 f., 37 f., 43, 49 ff., 98, 113–17, 150, 433 ff.). Hence a series of mutinies, inspired by grievances not dissimilar to the causes that Tacitus gives for the Thracian and Batavian revolts, which modern scholars can treat as his inventions. Eventually of course Highlanders were fully incorporated in the British army, as were Thracian and Batavian *auxilia* in the Roman.

The conscription and removal to lands far from their homes of recruits drawn from the most warlike and recalcitrant of Rome's subjects was surely designed in part to reduce the chance of continued resistance among those peoples, cf. pp. 474 f.

It should perhaps be emphasized that it is impossible to determine the proportions of volunteers and conscripts in the Roman army at any time. Arrius Menander implies that conscription was not wholly abandoned even in his day. We may suppose that it had once been more common than it then was. Some possible reasons why it became easier to enlist volunteers are given in the text. G. R. Watson may be right in conjecturing that the innovation introduced about 140, whereby the existing sons of auxiliaries granted citizenship on discharge did not share in the grant, made it more likely that they would join up to gain the higher status, and was designed to produce that effect (*Proc. Afr. Class. Ass.* (1982), 46 ff.).

CHAPTER 10

The text has been altered in places to take account of the revision of the
list of prefects (see Appendix) and of some other prosopographical
data published since 1975.

In *JRS* (1976), 163, A. K. Bowman questioned my conception of the
amateurism of the higher administrators in Egypt on the ground that
'the varied experience of administrators trained them to be at once
flexible and sensitive to local detail'. But only an exceptional quickness
of comprehension could have enabled them to penetrate local complexities until a considerable time had elapsed, during which they
would tend to rely on expert subordinates. In *JRS* (1983), 47–52, I
gave reasons for thinking that there was a general lack of specialized
expertise in the equestrian service, but by a strange oversight neglected
to cite the valuable article of R. P. Saller, *JRS* (1980), 44 ff., which
seems to discredit the common assumption that men were advanced by
seniority in accordance with any norms, or for specialized competence;
rather, appointments were made on the ground that they possessed the
requisite integrity and ability; the 'evidence' for this often consisted in
the commendations of influential patrons, cf. also his *Personal Patronage
under the Early Empire* (1982). No doubt we should also allow that
favourable reports by governors on the way in which an official had
discharged his duties (cf. Pliny, *ep.* x. 21 with *AE* 1972. 575) might have
assisted his future career.

Saller himself argues that little or no financial experience was
demanded for tenure of the highest financial posts (54 f.), and that at
most 'men with military experience were preferred for procuratorships
with military duties, and legal expertise and experience in oratory were
thought useful for certain procuratorships related to the lawcourts'
(57). I would minimize the knowledge of law conveyed by training in
rhetoric or even by advocacy in the courts. Certainly rhetorical
education was as much esteemed as a preparation for public life as a
classical education used to be in this country. F. Millar, *The Emperor in
the Roman World* (1977) 83–109, shows how common it was for
emperors to pick their secretaries among *littérateurs* (though surviving
specimens of imperial letters hardly suggest that flowers of rhetoric
were expected in their drafting). There is actually much less evidence
for the promotion of jurists, though some of the most eminent of course
rose high in senatorial posts, and even commanded armies (ch. 10 n.
80). At a lower level Pliny could commend friends to military
tribunates and the like partly for their literary proficiency or practice
at the bar (*ep.* iii. 2. 2 with Sherwin-White's note). J. B. Campbell also
seems to me to have shown that very few senators who held great

military commands were truly professionals (*JRS* (1975), 11 ff.). Agricola is a good example of the so-called *viri militares*. After a year or two of campaigning in Britain (*c.* 60–1), and holding a levy of recruits in 70, he was made legionary legate in Britain, a post he may have held for three years; thus some five or six years' service was held to fit him for command of one of the largest of Rome's armies. And no doubt he was exceptionally qualified!

CHAPTER 12

No change of substance has been made in this chapter. But a little should be added to what is said on p. 274 and in the last paragraph of ch. 14 on the privileged position of Italy and Rome.

The immunity of Italy from direct taxation is generally held to have been ended by Diocletian, but T. D. Barnes, *Constantine and Eusebius* (1981), 9 and 29, argues that his innovation affected only north Italy and that it was left to Galerius in 306 to extend the burden to Rome and the 'suburbicarian' provinces (cf. Lact., *de mort. pers.* 23. 2, which might, however, in my judgement relate only to the imposition of *capitatio* on the urban plebs, cf. 26. 2). If de Laet is right, which I doubt (chapter 17, Appendix 4) there were also no customs-duties on Italian imports and exports as such. Of course Italians had to pay the *vicesima hereditatium*, but so had provincials, if Roman citizens, and to them its incidence was peculiarly vexatious, at least until the reforms introduced by Nerva and Trajan (Pliny, *Paneg.* 37–40).

Trajan made it obligatory for all candidates for office at Rome, and therefore for all senators, to have one third of their patrimony in Italian lands, a proportion reduced by Marcus to one fourth. According to Pliny (*ep.* vi. 19) he thought it unseemly for them 'Italiam non pro patria sed pro hospitio aut stabulo quasi peregrinantis habere'. In so far as the rule was strictly enforced, it must have compelled provincials pursuing a senatorial career to exchange some provincial for Italian lands, not altogether to their economic disadvantage, even if their provincial no less than their Italian property was tax-exempt (*Dig.* i. 9. 12), since in the first century at least they were expected to reside in or near Rome, and might not leave Italy to visit estates except in Sicily and Narbonensis, unless with the emperor's leave (Dio lv. 26, cf. Tac., *Ann.* xii. 23). Rome still remained the legal domicile of senators in the Severan era (*Dig.* i. 9. 11; l. 1. 22. 6). We know indeed that in the late empire they commonly resided on their estates and seldom visited Rome. When this practice arose we cannot say: perhaps after Rome had ceased to be the seat of the emperor's residence and of the government. See R. J. A. Talbert, *The Senate of Imperial Rome* (1984), 39–42, 139–42.

It was also under Trajan that the alimentary system, restricted to Italy, was developed (see esp. R. Duncan-Jones, *The Economy of the Roman Empire*[2] (1982) ch. 7), and in other ways he sought to foster the prosperity of Italy from imperial funds (cf. e.g. *CAH* xi. 207 f.). Yet he was the first emperor of provincial descent (though the *nomen* Ulpius suggests that he came from an Italian family settled at Italica in Spain). It would not be easy to show that either he or the other 'Spanish' emperors felt any special affection for Spain; the provincial benefactions of Hadrian were bestowed chiefly on Greek cities. So too Pius, whose paternal grandfather came from Narbonensis, is said, admittedly in an unreliable source (*HA Pius* 2. 10, 3. 8), to have remained, while a private citizen, except when proconsul of Asia, on his Italian estates or in Rome, and as emperor he never left Italy. We may recall the Septimius Severus from Lepcis who could be flattered by being called an Italian and who delighted to dwell in his father's house at Veii (Stat., *Silvae* iv. 5. 45–56), yet he was not even a senator. We may suppose that many provincial families elevated to the senate came within a generation or two to feel themselves to be Italians by adoption, a consideration not always taken into account in the lists of attested provincial senators, on which the statistics of M. Hammond (*JRS* (1957), 74 ff.) were based. In any case it is to be remarked that even in the third century, when Italians were a minority of senators whose origins can be detected, they still formed a larger component in the senate than men of any other single region.

Italian cities, like provincial, had indeed to meet their expenses from their own funds. All alike might enjoy occasional grants from the emperor, which modern as well as ancient writers are apt to credit to his beneficence and liberality, without reflecting that its source consisted in taxes, or rents from imperial domains, largely paid by the peasantry; by modern criteria imperial gifts deserve praise only when they were designed to relieve special distress caused by earthquakes and the like, and not when they exhibit the capricious favour of a particular ruler, for example Hadrian's partiality for Athens. We cannot tell if Italian cities had in general a larger share in these benefactions.

Rome itself was in a category of its own. The *urbs* was never clearly distinguished from the state; it was more than the capital of the empire, for the empire was that of Rome. Administered in the Republic by the magistrates of the state and in the Principate by imperial officials, it never had the limited autonomy that every other city possessed, nor any revenues other than those of the state. But these revenues were lavished on the city and its inhabitants, paying for much of their food, for their water, for festivals and games, for protection against fire and crime, and for public buildings, whose construction gave employment to the poor (Brunt, *JRS* (1980), 81 ff.). For the emperors themselves residing at Rome, life was more agreeable and secure if the population were reasonably content. However, by force of tradition, the privileges of the city outlasted the removal of the imperial presence, and even Constantine's creation of a new Rome in the east, which was itself to enjoy like favours. Thus at all times the empire was exploited in some degree by the inhabitants of Rome. Everyone seems to have taken it for granted that this was right and natural. Thus Dio makes Maecenas (who patently expresses the historian's own ideas) urge Augustus to restrict public and private outlay on all other cities, but to spare no expense in enhancing the splendour of Rome and its festivals, for 'it is fitting that we [Romans] with so many subjects should surpass them at all points' (lii. 30). A Greek by culture, who can speak of his Bithynian fatherland (lxxx. 5), Dio was a senator of at least the second generation, and feels himself to be also a Roman of Rome. Similarly, in the fifth century for the Gallic senator and poet Rutilius Namatianus Rome is 'regina tui pulcherrima mundi' (*de reditu suo* 47): it is to the *urbs* that he credits the blessings of Roman rule on mankind (63 ff.), and it is only proper that the subjects should sustain her with their produce and taxes (143 ff.).

CHAPTER 13

It was my aim in this chapter to document the statement in chapter 12 that the Jewish revolt of 66 'was almost as much directed against native landlords and usurers as against the heathen rulers', by collecting the evidence that Josephus gives for social tensions in Judaea both before and during the revolt, and for the adverse or lukewarm attitude of the upper class to the struggle for independence: I did not attempt any complete and balanced analysis of the causes of the insurrection. This has been essayed most recently by M. Goodman in *The Ruling Class of Judaea* (1987), with learning, subtlety, and expository elegance. He too brings out the social discords in the province, and delineates the populist character that the revolt assumed. Yet in the end he fixes the responsibility for it on the ruling class. This seems to me perverse. On the other hand I now think that I somewhat overstated the significance of the animosity of the masses to the élite. It is unlikely to have been confined to Judaea, and some further explanation is required, if we are to understand why the Jews of Palestine, unlike other peoples which had been so long under Roman rule, fought with such fervour to recover their independence.

Independence was sought by all the peoples which at one time or another resisted conquest or tried to throw off the Roman yoke. But most revolts occurred soon after subjugation, sometimes immediately, and were essentially resumptions of the initial struggles against conquest, even when provoked by Roman actions which the rebels regarded as oppressive and of which fresh recollections of freedom made them least patient. Usually they had not lost the practice of fighting in their own ethnic units under native commanders, sometimes in auxiliary regiments of the Roman army. They mostly dwelt on the periphery of the empire, as it was at the time, and might be encouraged by the proximity of free, perhaps kindred, peoples beyond its frontiers from whom they could hope for aid, and by the possibility that Rome would acquiesce in the loss of territory not yet evidently integral to her power.

These revolts cannot be described as national in the modern sense. There was no tradition of political unity even among peoples who like Gauls and Greeks shared a common culture; they were divided between communities each attached to its own identity. This particularism was still alive under Roman rule in the petty rivalries of neighbouring communities of the same speech, religion, and customs (ch. 4 nn. 89 f.). In many regions, like Spain, there cannot have been any sense of a larger unity even in culture.

By contrast the Jews of Palestine, while at least as conscious as Gauls or Greeks of a common cultural heritage, also had memories of an independent ethnic state in their homeland, which corresponded to the traditions of individual Greek cities or Gallic *civitates*, and they were of course far more numerous and to that extent more formidable than Spartans, Aedui, and the like. However, unlike many of Rome's wilder subjects, who were most stubborn in resistance, they were no longer accustomed to fighting, and though Judaea lay on the edge of the empire, no one with any perception of geographical facts could have had rational grounds for supposing that Rome would readily relinquish a province that lay athwart the land route between Egypt and Syria. It is hard to believe that educated Jews of the upper class did not realize this. They must also have been conscious that loyalty to the sovereign power assured their authority in local affairs and their property rights, and that peace and order conduced to their material interests. Such considerations commended submission to them as to their counterparts elsewhere. With the latter they were at a comparative disadvantage in one point: access to posts in the imperial government was denied to Jews, who did not recognize Rome's gods, and would not, like Tiberius Iulius Alexander, forsake the ancestral faith; however, in 66 the advancement of other provincials in the service of the state was only in an early stage, and this difference was less significant than it became later. In fact, despite endemic and increasing local disorders, Judaea had remained submissive for two generations. The outbreak of a movement for independence after such prolonged acquiescence in Roman rule is unique. (By contrast first-century revolts in Gaul were not general and did not have liberation as their aim, cf. chapters 2 and 3.)

In seeking some special explanation for the revolt, we must not assume that all the conditions that probably contributed to it were peculiar to Judaea. Some or most of them could have been present elsewhere, and yet failed to ignite resistance, because there was no such combustible combination as in Judaea, or because there alone some additional element produced combustion. We must never forget that Josephus' works, supplemented by other Jewish and Christian sources, provide a wealth of evidence for conditions and events in Judaea to which there is no parallel. The documentation of customs, social, and economic life in Egypt is more ample, but furnishes no equivalent to Josephus' detailed narratives of events, while the accounts of affairs in other provinces are not only briefer than his, but are not written from the standpoint of the subjects, and less is known of conditions except perhaps in a few cities. But the scattered evidence for other regions allows us to glimpse social and economic relationships not altogether dissimilar to those more clearly revealed for Palestine.

Goodman notes in chapter 1 many factors which complicated and embroiled the relations between Rome and the Jews that also operated in other provinces. In Tacitus' judgement the Jewish revolt was provoked by misgovernment: 'duravit patientia Iudaeis usque ad Gessium Florum procuratorem: sub eo bellum ortum est' (*Hist.* v. 10). The story that Josephus tells illustrates the greed, malice, or ineptitude of many of the governors, and he too says that Florus' oppression 'drove the Jews out of their senses' (*AJ* xviii. 25). Still we cannot be sure that the standard of Roman administration was markedly worse especially under Nero (ch. 2) than in other provinces, for instance in Asia, 'provincia dives ac parata peccantibus' (Tac., *Agr.* 6. 2), for which there are no comparable records, (cf. ch. 4 with addenda). Nor were the Jews alone in resenting the burden of taxation by an alien power; one may think, among other examples, of the Cietae, a tribe which revolted under Tiberius 'quia nostrum in modum deferre census, pati tributa adigebatur' (*Ann.* vi. 41). And the Jews were at least spared conscription, a grievance among some of Rome's subjects (pp. 204 f.). The Jewish quarrels with pagan communities in the province, from which ill-feeling against Rome ensued, have an analogy in the widely attested feuds among contiguous cities. Still, in Judaea they had a unique origin in religious differences. And religion gave a special complexion to all the dealings between the Jews and Rome. Although in principle the imperial government respected the national creed (it was perhaps Sabbatarianism that excused Jews from service in the army), on occasions the emperor himself, or the procurators, flouted Jewish pieties. Even the taking of a census in AD 6 had given trouble, because it could be seen as a violation of divine commands (*AJ* xviii. 3–5, cf. 2 Sam. 24: 1; 1 Chr. 21).

In Judaea, as elsewhere, Rome entrusted local authority to the rich. Goodman supposes that they were less able than magnates in other provinces to win popular acceptance of their role. In his view they lacked the inherited prestige of other oligarchies (ch. 2). Many must have been upstarts who had replaced the leading men of the Hasmonaean court proscribed by Herod; he had probably enriched them with grants of land. Even his nominees to the high priesthood, whose families continued to hold it under Rome, almost all came from Alexandria and Babylon, and had no traditional claims to allegiance. They did not then enjoy the influence that the élites in other provinces derived from patronage (ch. 5), though Goodman thinks that one aristocratic leader in the revolt was supported by his clients (224). They were simply distinguished by wealth. But among the Jews wealth inspired no esteem *per se*; honour was accorded to learning and lineage, but these were attributes that might as well belong to those whose relative poverty excluded them from a share in local authority. Some Jews actually thought that riches conduced to sin (p. 129); this was an attitude that we might expect to have become more prevalent on Goodman's plausible account of the conduct of the upper class at Jerusalem (see also his article in *Journal of Jewish Studies* (1982), 417 ff.). He argues that, having accumulated large profits from the swarms of pilgrims to the Temple and from the great building programme in the city (which was completed only in 66), they invested partly in loans to the surrounding peasantry, and were ultimately able to turn small owners into tenants, or force them to seek an alternative livelihood in the city, where the cessation of the building programme would eventually have superimposed urban unemployment on rural. The distress of the poor was in his view aggravated by the exceptional proclivity of Jews to increase and multiply in obedience to Scripture. He concedes that by bestowing alms the rich will have prevented outright starvation, but suggests that this did not procure them any special gratitude, as they were merely fulfilling an obligation incumbent on all Jews. And while they spent lavishly and ostentatiously on private luxury, they did not practise the civic munificence recorded of magnates in communities of the Greek or Italian type, where in his belief it did much to mitigate social discords.

However, Goodman has surely overdrawn the contrast between the élites in Judaea and elsewhere and overstated the extent of social harmony in other parts of the empire.

In the first place it would be hard to prove that most local oligarchies consisted chiefly of families with high lineage and hereditary claims to patronage. Probably there were analogies everywhere to the rise of new families at Rome itself, where they were always replacing those which had died out or sunk into poverty, and where some were tainted with servile blood (Tac., *Ann.* xiii. 27). Increased economic activity under the Roman peace must have enabled many entrepreneurs to amass fortunes in trade and industry, which would be invested in land, and become in later generations the source of social and political distinction. Numerous *curiales* were probably descended from such rich freedmen as figure in the inscriptions of *Augustales*; the frequency of imperial or excessively aristocratic *nomina* among the city councillors of Canusium in AD 223 (*CIL* ix. 338) is one indication of this process. Marcus Aurelius regretted that descendants of slaves could no longer be excluded from the Athenian Areopagus (J. H. Oliver, *Hesperia*, Suppl. 13 (1970), vv. 57 ff.). Cf. P. Garnsey, *The Ancient Historian and his Materials*, ed. B. Levick (1975), 167 ff. and *ANRW*, *Principat* ii. 241 ff. Patronage of the types familiar in Italy and Gaul is not recorded in many parts of the empire any more than in Judaea, but where it did exist, it had not precluded class conflicts, either in republican Italy, or in the Gaul of Caesar's time (e.g. *BG* vii. 4. 3) or of Tiberius' reign (Tac., *Ann.* iii. 40); in 69 Mariccus 'e plebe Boiorum' raised a peasant revolt which the 'electa iuventus' of the Aedui put down (*Hist.* ii. 61).

The acquisition of land by the rich must often have involved the dispossession of indebted peasants, as for instance in Republican Italy. The ill-feeling between cities and peasants disclosed for Galilee by Josephus' *Vita* probably had its origin in the operations of urban money-lenders, and social conflict at Antioch surely had a similar cause (ch. 13 n. 14). At most the wealthy at Jerusalem had exceptional opportunities for making profits and using them to enlarge their landholdings.

Similarly civic munificence is mainly attested in communities within the Greek or Italian traditions, and its apparent absence in Judaea need not be unique. But where it is found, it did not necessarily resolve class conflicts. Only the theorizing of recent scholars has turned this 'euergetism' into an integral part of the social structure. We do not know that even one of ten of the wealthy practised it. The benefactions which Plutarch likens to 'the flatteries of harlots' (*Praecepta Reipublicae Gerundae* 802 D, 818 C, 821 F, 822 F, all passages in which he has contemporary conditions in mind), public banquets and shows, distributions of food or oil or cash, and even the grandiose buildings, which, as at Rome (Brunt, *JRS* (1980), 81 ff.), must have given employment to free labour, certainly assisted or gratified the city dwellers of every station, but did little for the peasantry, from whom most of the benefactors must have drawn income as tenants or labourers on their estates, just as the cities themselves could also finance much of the expenditure from the rents of municipal domains. Cities might have funds to keep down the cost of grain (*Dig.* l. 8. 2. 3 f.; 12. 2 f.), the imperial government might penalize unfair rises in the price (xlviii. 12. 2), landowners might sell to their cities at less than the market rate (vii. 1. 27. 3, cf. l. 4. 18. 25), sometimes in terror of disorder (xlviii. 12. 3 *pr.*; l. 1. 8; 8. 7 *pr.*); but all this was probably for the benefit mainly of the urban poor, and designed to minimize the risk of riots which there were no ready means of repressing. The peasants who produced the food might in a scarcity be deprived of wholesome subsistence (Galen, quoted by R. MacMullen, *Enemies of the Roman Order* (1967), 243). Experience of other ages suggests that rural brigandage is normally the result of economic distress; it was common in Palestine, as we know from Josephus, but perhaps equally in other regions where the evidence is inevitably sparse; most of it is collected by MacMullen (ch. V and App. B).

Nor did munificence always endear the magnates even to the populace within the city walls. At Prusa Dio Chrysostom, who had once been personally endangered in a food riot (*or.* xlvi), had to assuage the resentment of the *plebs* against those who, he says, were the city's benefactors (xlviii. 9 f.). For all his princely gifts the Athenian millionaire Herodes Atticus was the object of bitter hatred among his own fellow-citizens (*PIR²* C 902 pp. 278 ff.). It would be naïve to read popular sentiments into all the surviving decrees that commemorate the liberality of the rich: they were drafted by the honorands themselves or by their oligarchic partners. Plutarch says that the recipients of honorific statues were often looked on as oppressors of the people (820 B).

The essay cited (*Praecepta Reipublicae Gerundae*) indicates indeed that the urban *plebs* was not so powerless in Greek cities under Roman rule as we might infer from the obsolescence of the formal institutions of democracy (on which see G. E. M. de Ste Croix, *The Class Struggle in the Ancient Greek World* (1981), App. IV). With police forces inadequate or non-existent, and Roman troops distant from the scene, the danger to life and property from riots was omnipresent; Plutarch refers to the perils of mass turbulence (798 E). As we have seen, decurions might be terrorized into selling their grain cheap, and the imperial government itself thought it prudent to penalize unfair devices for keeping up prices (xlviii. 12, cf. A. H. M. Jones, *Greek City* (1940), 217–19). In any case local politicians might naturally prefer popular applause to showers of abuse or stones. Largesses must often have been prompted by these considerations, and Plutarch is idealistic when he urges that the masses should rather be kept content by moderation and justice. He also takes it for granted throughout the essay that the art of persuasion remains important in addresses to the people. *Exempla* he cites from the political life of independent Greek cities or from the Roman Republic evidently seemed relevant to his own day, and could be used by contemporary orators (814 A). Although he more than once observes that Roman sovereignty had transformed the conditions of political life, *stasis* had not altogether ceased; he alludes to some recent cases (815 D). We may recall the Ephesian magnate Claudius Aristion, who in Pliny's judgement was 'munificus et innoxie popularis' (*ep.* vi. 31. 3); in fact he had incurred the enmity of his peers. Trajan at least was intent on stamping out factions in Bithynia, which disturbed public order and to that end banned *collegia* which would be recruited from plebeians (*ep.* x. 34. cf. 93, 96. 7).

In one respect, which Goodman does not bring out, the ruling class had less authority in Judaea than elsewhere. The religious apparatus of pagan communities was wholly under the control of the local magistrates or of priests who belonged to the same class. In my judgement native religions outside Judaea hardly tended to foment anti-Roman feeling, even in Gaul (cf. pp. 481 ff.); one, though not the only, reason might be that the ruling class were able to hinder their exploitation for this purpose. But in Judaea the high priests and Sadducees were plainly in no position to determine the religious sentiments of the people. Their teaching was repudiated by teachers of the other sects which Josephus calls philosophies. The mere existence of such sects, and the emergence of popular prophets, show that every Jew could form his own opinion on religious matters, and thus on the practical and political obligations that the national faith might require. We are not even entitled to assume that every shade of belief among the population is represented by the particular kinds of teaching which we happen to hear of.

However, in all other matters the relationship of the ruling class to the lower orders need not have been more than marginally different from that which obtained in other provinces, cf. pp. 508–11. In some degree the social tensions to which Josephus bears witness were probably found everywhere. And in general the local élites, who best understood the virtually insuperable difficulty of throwing off Roman dominion, were ready to act as its instruments, all the more because it preserved their own privileges and power. It was quite exceptional if a few of their number, like Florus and Sacrovir in Gaul, put themselves at the head of an anti-Roman movement which drew its strength from the lower orders. On Josephus' showing the élite in Judaea, except for some individuals, were just as reluctant to resist Roman rule. Moreover, as Goodman shows, the revolt had the appearance of a populist movement: mass meetings took important decisions and their acclamations gave authority to the leaders, who all represented themselves as democrats (217 f.). It therefore comes as a surprise that he denies that the social cleavage, which he himself has conceded, had any significant part in the outbreak or course of the rebellion, and that (without even a word on the culpability of the Roman administration) he should conclude that the entire ruling class was implicated in and responsible for the revolt (169): it was their 'ambitions and divisions that brought war on to their country' (231). His analysis is not convincing.

He seems to trace the issue to the factional struggles within this class which marked the period of procuratorial administration and formed the prelude to the internecine feuds among the rebel leaders. He shows how its members were before 66 competing for local authority, generally by currying favour with the procurators. This was another phenomenon not peculiar to Judaea. Plutarch censures Greek city politicians who relied on their friendship with governors and Roman patrons to procure their own dominance, inviting unecessary Roman intervention in civic affairs (815 D). Goodman notes that on the eve of revolt some Jewish magnates were wooing the masses, and ingeniously suggests that they hoped that success would make the procurators look to them to curb popular turbulence (150). But we have seen that such demagogy was not unknown in Plutarch's world. In Judaea some such *populares*, notably Eleazar ben Ananias, were to take the further step of inciting revolt. Goodman contends that most of the rebel leaders were men of rank. Though Menahem ben Judas is an admitted exception and, despite his pleas, Simon ben Gioras and John of Gischala may be others, this seems to be true; in particular Eleazar and Ananus ben Ananus, who was for some time at the head of the insurrectionary government, came from high priestly families. But such men need have been no more typical of their class than were the Gracchi of the Roman aristocracy or Mirabeau and Lafayette of the French *noblesse* in 1789. It is more significant that Eleazar's father and other kinsmen perished fighting the rebels and that Ananus and his chief upper-class associates were put to death on suspicions, well founded on Josephus' account (and Goodman allows that he may have been right), of treason to the cause. Executions, massacres, and desertions of the élite went on throughout the struggle.

Goodman's case rests above all on his interpretation of the course of events that issued in general revolt. He will have it that the revolt was precipitated by the refusal of the magnates at Jerusalem to identify and surrender to Florus the young men who had insulted him, and who (so he conjectures) belonged to their own class (*BJ* ii. 295, 302–4). But in Josephus' story this is only one link in the chain of events that led from popular disorders in Caesarea (284–92) to the mass insurrection at Jerusalem. The magnates certainly did not conceive their refusal as tantamount to treason: they continued to work for peace, trying to propitiate Florus, and warning the people not to take up arms (316–25). After the revolutionaries (*stasiastai*) had invested the Roman fortress Antonia, by demolishing the porticoes that connected it with the Temple, they offered to re-establish order, if supported by a Roman cohort (332). At the same time they sought to secure protection from Florus by protesting against his conduct to the legate of Syria (333), invoking the mediation of Agrippa (336), and proposing an appeal to Nero (342); all this shows that they had not in their own estimation thrown off Roman authority. They were ready to rebuild the porticoes and collect arrears of tribute (405). It was against their earnest pleas that the sacrifices for Rome were discontinued (409–17), and when these pleas failed, they actually invited Florus along with Agrippa to repress the rising by force (418), and took up arms themselves with their followers against the insurgents (422); eventually they were massacred in Herod's palace.

Their fate, and the defeat of Cestius Gallus, must have made the rest of the élite look on further resistance to the rebels as not only dangerous but futile. What were they to do? Flee to territory under Roman control with a predominantly pagan population (as Goodman suggests), abandoning their property and hoping to subsist on Roman charity? It was more reasonable to adopt the course attributed to Ananus and his associates, and take charge of the revolt on the chance of negotiating terms later. It must also be borne in mind that hardly any would have disapproved of the aspiration for independence in itself: they would at most have condemned the revolt as an act of folly doomed to failure. Goodman may well be right that the prolonged ineffectiveness of Roman measures to suppress it could have fostered a delusion that after all, contrary to any rational calculations at the outset, it might be successful (p. 180). Moreover, any hope of an accommodation with Rome inevitably depended on putting up a fight which might induce the Roman government to come to terms, just as it apparently did with the Batavians (Tac., *Hist.* v. 24–6, cf. *Germ.* 29).

Goodman seeks to show that in fact the élite took as zealous a part in the revolt as any other class; he surely distorts the testimony of Josephus. The latter tells us that many of the well born in Jerusalem were moved by his own plea during the siege that they should surrender, and that some deserted, though others were restrained by fear (vi. 113-16): Goodman infers from their continued presence within the walls that they were fully involved in the revolt (p. 199)! He thinks it significant that in massacring their opponents the Zealots and Idumaeans spared young men of high birth in the hope of winning their adherence (201); he does not add that they all refused and died by torture (iv. 327 ff.). He argues that the Romans did not view the deserters as loyalists, since they compelled them to live in specified places (232). But the texts cited (iv. 444; vi. 115) show that these were places where they would be safe for the time and would be supported by the local inhabitants, and that they were promised ultimate restitution of their estates. It is true that after the initial phase of the revolt no Jews actually fought against the rebels, and it was easy for the Romans to treat the revolt as universal. Neither in Galilee in 67 (Goodman 182) nor after the fall of Jerusalem were they careful to discriminate between those active in the revolt and those who had merely acquiesced. Yet in fact the fight was kept up only by a resolute minority, in Goodman's view by relatively small bands recruited chiefly by incentives of pay and booty (213-15, 224 ff.), though one leader could perhaps call on personal clients (224). Most people in Jerusalem were unarmed and helpless. We cannot be sure that the majority even among the humbler folk wished to fight on to the death. But there is nothing to rebut Josephus' testimony that with the exception of some individuals this was not the wish of men of rank and property. And, if he is right, their attitude is just what we should expect it to have been.

Goodman thinks that Vespasian's settlement shows that he put no trust in this class, since he did not restore their local authority. Of course with the destruction of Jerusalem and the Temple, the high priests and Sanhedrin disappeared. But there is no evidence for Goodman's hypothesis that Judaea, in its narrow connotation excluding Samaria and Galilee, was largely divided among the 'Greek' cities. Obviously this did not apply to the land around Jerusalem, which was available to constitute the territory of the future Hadrianic city of Aelia Capitolina. Josephus says that Judaea 'is divided into eleven toparchies' which he then specifies (*BJ* iii. 54 f.). Pliny gives a list of ten toparchies (v. 70), with discrepancies from Josephus, which can be explained (Schürer, *History of Jewish People in Age of Jesus Christ*, revised by Vermes and Millar (1973), ii. 191). Josephus uses the present tense, which could perhaps be taken as a historic present, excluding the interpretation that he was describing the position as it was after the revolt, when he was writing. But that can hardly be the correct interpretation of Pliny, who gives the name of Orine to the toparchy of Jerusalem and expressly refers to the fact that that city no longer existed. It may be assumed that the administrators of Orine no longer enjoyed the supremacy over other districts which the Sanhedrin had had (though the extent of that supremacy is not clear). Within the toparchies there had been towns and villages with their local councils, which had apparently existed under and before the rule of Hellenistic kings. The allusions to these local authorities for any period are sparse (Schürer, 184 ff.), and in particular there is no clear evidence about the function of the toparchies. This being so, it is not surprising that there happens to be no testimony to local administration in Judaea after the revolt, since there are no literary sources for this period such as furnish the only evidence for the period before 66. But Rabbinic texts show that in Galilee the same type of administration survived and was in the hands of the propertied class (Goodman, *State and Society in Roman Galilee, AD 132–212* (1983), ch. 8). We should expect this to have been the case in Judaea too, at least before the second revolt under Hadrian. Even if most of the soil had been taken into the royal domain, which is not clear, this would not obviate the necessity for some form of local government, as in Egypt, and it was inevitable that Rome should prefer to entrust it to persons whose property constituted security for performance of their tasks. Presumably it was such village officials to whom orders for arms deliveries were addressed under Hadrian (Dio lxix. 12. 2).

Everything in my view goes to support the thesis that the revolt was essentially a popular movement, whose aristocratic leaders were unrepresentative of their class, and that the majority of that class, after failing to prevent its outbreak, were passive or actually disloyal to it thereafter. It does not, however, follow that it was directed almost as much against them as against their Roman masters. Goodman notes that though most of the rival leaders appealed to debtors and resorted to cash distributions, none of them propounded any programme of social reform, not even a redistribution of land, a measure that would have been hallowed by the precedent of Nehemiah's reform (*Ruling Class*, p. 66). Of course such a programme might well have appeared manifestly impracticable in the course of a life and death struggle against Rome, and likely to stir up more active opposition to the national cause. Still it remains true that the movement was essentially anti-Roman. Moreover, if the social tensions attested in Judaea were present in other provinces, they fail to explain sufficiently why similar rebellions did not occur elsewhere. We must look for another factor, peculiar to Judaea. This is surely to be found in the Jewish religion.

Goodman, who concedes the religious fervour of the insurgents, minimizes the part that it played in bringing the insurrection about (ch. 4). He argues that of the various sects whose beliefs Josephus reviews only the adherents of his 'fourth philosophy' advocated resistance to Rome on religious grounds, and that there is no sign that they had much influence in 66. Some teachers of other persuasions actually commended resignation to the status quo, or the unworldly pursuit of individual salvation. However, Sadducees, Pharisees, and Essenes on one estimate constituted together no more than 7 per cent of the nation (T. W. Manson, *The Servant Messiah*, (1953) ch. 1), and not all of them, still less of Jews in general, need have accepted these counsels of passivity.

Certainly Judaism could foster more militant attitudes. Every Jew could learn from the Scriptures read in the synagogues of the relationship throughout history between Yahweh and his chosen people, whom he would chastise for transgressions, but vindicate when they were faithful to his commands. We may think, for instance, of the belief expressed in Psalm 118, apparently a thanksgiving for victory in battle, sung each year at the major festivals: 'When in my distress I called to the Lord, his answer was to set me free. The Lord is on my side, I have no fear; what can man do to me? The Lord is my refuge and defence, and he has become my deliverer. Hark, shouts of deliverance in the camp of the victors. With his right hand the Lord does mighty deeds, the right hand of the Lord raises me up' (*New Eng. Bible* tr.). Unlike the tutelary gods of pagan peoples, the one true and omnipotent God of the Jews could be restrained neither by the opposition of other gods nor by ineluctable fate. With his favour only two centuries earlier the Maccabees had freed and aggrandized their people against seemingly overwhelming odds, and Jewish memories, unlike those of peoples who knew their past only from an ever fading oral tradition, were kept alive by written records.

Some Jews hoped for the coming of the Messiah, and though not all of these saw him as a political liberator (Goodman p. 90), others certainly did (cf. *Psalms of Solomon* xvii f.). No leader of the first Jewish revolt appeared in the guise of the Messiah, as Bar Kokhba was to do in the second (Schürer i. 543), but many rebels were buoyed up by a prophecy that a world ruler would arise in Judaea (*BJ* vi. 312–14), which Josephus held to have been fulfilled in the person of Vespasian. Moreover belief in divine deliverance was not necessarily connected with the Messianic hope: that is not present in the *Assumption of Moses*, which none the less predicts that 'God will come openly to take vengeance on the Gentiles and destroy all their idols' (ch. x). Josephus makes Agrippa argue on the eve of revolt that the only hope of success rested in the conviction that it would be assisted by God, and that this was based on a mistaken interpretation of his will: he had given the Romans their empire (ii. 390). The speech is a fiction, but doubtless represents much of what was thought and said at the time. To the last the insurgents relied on the invincible aid of God (vi. 100, 286); I find it incredible that this faith did not also stimulate the outbreak of the revolt and foster its progress. Its early success might well have persuaded many Jews for the moment that opposition to it would be opposition to God (cf. Acts 5: 33–9). Once it had been put down, since the divine will could be read in history, not only Josephus but the Rabbis (Schürer i. 527) could see it as sinful, and its failure as a divine punishment.

It may be objected that religion could hardly have contributed decisively to the outbreak of revolt, since the Jews had little reason to complain of the Roman government's treatment of their faith. It was its policy to uphold the right of the Jews to practise the religion of their ancestors, not only in the homeland, where genocide would have been the only alternative, but in the diaspora, where Jewish communities were allowed in some places a measure of self-government and protected against occasional anti-Semitic outbursts among their 'Greek' neighbours; in particular, Jews were not to be hindered from making their annual contributions to the Temple. The Romans, however, like most other pagans, never acquired any understanding of, and still less sympathy with, the beliefs of the Jews, whose religion, unlike that of polytheists, could not be assimilated to their own. No doubt it was the peculiar Jewish way of life, prescribed by the Mosaic law, with its rules for purity, which did most to separate Jews from Gentiles, where they were contiguous: perhaps more important for their relationship with Rome was their exclusive monotheism and repudiation of idolatry. In his brief sketch of the origins of the revolt Tacitus was percipient in signalling Gaius' command that his image should be set up in the Temple (*Hist.* v. 9. 2). It was never carried out; the special providence of his assassination supervened; but it probably undermined Jewish trust in Roman intentions, and both before and after this incident, the oppressiveness of procurators was compounded on occasions by insensitive disregard of Jewish pieties. The first spark for the revolt was ignited by Florus' failure to respond to Jewish complaints of sacrilegious outrages committed by Gentiles at Caesarea (*BJ* ii. 285–92), and he then 'fanned the flames' by laying hands on money in the Temple treasury (293). A little later the masses were afraid that the sacred ornaments of the Temple would be removed and the treasures of the house of God pillaged (321). Josephus makes king Agrippa assume that it would be the one aim of insurrection to keep the national religion inviolate (393). Eleazar's action in rejecting the daily sacrifices offered in the Temple on behalf of the emperor (Philo, *Leg.* 157, 317), on the basis that no gifts should be accepted from aliens, and his suspension of sacrifices offered by the priests for the emperor (409), symbolized an overwhelming feeling that Roman rule had proved incompatible with the preservation of the people's faith. It is irrelevant that this feeling was irrational. And beneath it there surely lay a deep-seated resentment that Jews should be subject to one of 'the lesser breeds without the law'.

Goodman finds that there is more evidence of hostility in the Roman world to Judaism after 66 than previously (ch. 10). If this be so, it would show that it was recognized that religious fanaticism had been a large element in the revolt. But the nature of our evidence is such that we can hardly tell whether the misunderstandings and abuse of Judaism which Josephus would try to discredit were more prevalent when he wrote than in earlier times. The imposition by Vespasian of a poll-tax payable by Jews to the *fiscus Iudaicus*, which was certainly not a penalty for disloyalty, since it fell on Jews of the diaspora as well as of Palestine, need not have been a mark of disapprobation on an abhorrent superstition; more probably, it was merely one of his expedients for replenishing imperial funds, which he might have thought to be no economic burden on persons who were now spared equal contributions to the Temple; naturally to Jews it was an abomination that the payments should be diverted to Jupiter Capitolinus (cf. Jos. *BJ* vii. 218), and their consequential resentment may help to explain the risings in the diaspora under Trajan. Still the state tolerated Judaism, as in the past. But once again it would disregard Jewish religious susceptibilities. Hadrian's prohibition of circumcision, which can hardly have been enforced and which Pius would withdraw, did not affect the Jews alone (p. 486), and was probably inspired by dislike of a practice viewed as barbarous, and he doubtless did not foresee that his plan to found a Roman and idolatrous colony on the holy site where Jerusalem had once stood would be taken as sacrilegious; but together these measures provoked yet another rebellion, the causes of which were primarily religious, even if, as argued by S. Applebaum (*Prolegomena to the Study of the Second Jewish Revolt* (1976)), there was a background of social discontent among an exploited peasantry.

That brings me back to the subject of chapter 13. What significance, if any, is to be assigned to the class cleavage that Josephus reveals? There is no answer of *demonstrable* truth. But it may seem plausible to suppose that the religious teachers who urged acceptance of the existing order in submission to God's will found the readiest response among its material beneficiaries, and that millenary prophecies appealed most to those who suffered under it, and gave them an encouragement to take up arms, unknown to the weak and oppressed in other lands; moreover, their alienation from the élite would make them the more heedless of its warnings against rebellion, whether given on grounds of expediency, such as those which predominate in Agrippa's speech, or on the basis of an interpretation of the divine purpose, which Josephus also imputes to him (ii. 390 f.).

CHAPTER 15

1. I am more convinced on further reflection that much revenue from rents and taxes was exacted in kind. This is of course clear for Egypt. According to Josephus (*BJ* ii. 363) Egypt provided one-third of the grain required by the city of Rome, Africa two-thirds, but he has certainly neglected other sources of supply; it is inconceivable that Sardinia and Sicily in particular, which had ranked with Africa as the 'tria frumentaria subsidia' of the city in the Republic, altogether ceased to perform this role in the Principate. It would have been senseless for the government to exact taxes in money from the producers and then to use it to buy what they produced; it may be noted that peasants on imperial domains in Africa paid their dues in kind. The same applies to regions which supplied the armies.

The local authorities or publicans (as the case might be) responsible for collection of revenue in kind might be required to deliver it at any point within the province concerned that the government designated, e.g. at the barracks of a military unit, or at a place convenient for its transportation to some destination such as Rome beyond the limits of the province. The local authorities might perhaps employ contractors for the purpose; eventually 'res pervehendae vel prosequendae' became a civic *munus* (Arcadius Charisius, *Dig.* l. 4. 18. 3). I suggest on p. 379 that it was one function of the *conductores* of African domains to convey to a central point for shipment the rents they collected from the peasant cultivators, who could not themselves have undertaken this task. It is not clear who bore the costs of the shipment down the Nile to Alexandria of the grain brought by Egyptian cultivators to the state storehouses; here the task was organized by the government through contractors or liturgical officials (A. C. Johnson *ESAR* (ed. T. Frank) ii (1936), 400 ff.). The subjects could be induced to pay bribes to escape directions for delivery at remote and inconvenient places in the province, cf. ch. 4 n. 127 and Jones, *Later Roman Empire* (1964), 458 (Egypt). Some of the texts cited may refer not to the proceeds of taxes paid in kind but to *frumentum emptum*, supplementary supplies compulsorily sold to the state at prices which it fixed (cf. Cic., *Verr.* ii. 3. 163–87), but similar orders could have been issued concerning tax grain.

Beyond the province of origin the conveyance of commodities in state ownership must have been the responsibility of the state. Only in the late empire do we find a sort of public transport service operated by officials for such movements of government goods, which could include that of revenues collected in kind (Jones 429, 459, but cf. A. Móczy, *Germania* (1966), 312 ff.). In earlier times we can conceive that military detachments or fleets, including river flotillas, may have taken delivery in appropriate conditions of supplies destined for the armed forces. More generally the state must have contracted for the transportation. For example it must have taken shipping space in privately owned vessels for grain in its ownership needed for the *frumentationes* at Rome.

However, there is a problem here. The *frumentationes* went to only a minority of the inhabitants of Rome. Most of them had to buy their grain (as well as other foodstuffs) in the market. At times the government had to intervene to keep prices down. These interventions would hardly have been necessary if all the grain furnished by the provinces concerned as tax or rent had remained in public ownership and been released as required from public storehouses. Even in that case the government was ultimately engaged in selling grain to merchants, and it looks as if it was in fact the practice to sell it at some earlier stage, perhaps at points of shipment. I know of no evidence that clarifies this problem. In the same way, if rents or taxes were collected in kind from regions that supplied the armies, there must have been regular or occasional surpluses for the government to dispose of. All this means that it was able to obtain revenue in money by sales to merchants, even when that revenue had been paid in kind. Naturally it must at times have made profits from the transactions.

Columella i. *pr.* 20 says: 'nunc ad hastam locamus, ut nobis ex transmarinis provinciis advehatur frumentum, ne fame laboremus'. So the contracts, whether for the shipment to Italy of grain that remained in public ownership or for its sale as well as for shipment, were made at state auctions. See generally G. Rickman, *Corn-Supply of Ancient Rome* (1980).

2. F. Jacques, *Ktema* (1977), 285 ff. and M. le Glay, *ZPE* 43 (1981), 175 ff., have tried to list the census officials for Gaul/Germany and Thrace respectively in chronological order, sometimes on a conjectural basis, whereas in the Table col. II the epigraphic data are not so ordered. (In revision I have supplied two or three omissions out of their

lists.) It does not seem to me that the evidence they give permits any conclusion about the regularity or frequency of censuses in the regions concerned. The proliferation of testimony to censuses in Gaul is puzzling. Granted that elsewhere governors usually took the census without recording it in career inscriptions, it remains hard to see why in Gaul consular commissioners should so often have been appointed specially for the purpose. Again, while I am not disturbed by the small number of attested equestrian officials assisting in censuses, since such low-ranking officials are relatively unlikely to be documented in inscriptions unless they rose higher (Brunt, *JRS* (1983), 73 f.), it is strange that so many of those who are known operated in Gaul. It looks as if for reasons that elude us the government adopted a special policy for Gallic censuses; alternatively, we might after all conclude that a census was held in Gaul more often than in other regions, where it may have been much less frequent than I argued.

The census obviously required the registration at least of landed property, and census records, e.g. as to delimitation of estates, were accorded great evidentiary weight in court proceedings, but that does not mean that they were up to date, and in one of the relevant texts (*Dig.* x. 1. 11; xxii. 3. 10) Papinian expressly says that at any given time there might have been material changes. The fact that in passing through Anatolia Caracalla ordered a survey of the territory of Pessinus (*AE* 1948. 109) suggests that there at least census records were defective or antiquated. Yet it was not only for purposes of taxation that some assessment of individual wealth was needed: it must also have been the basis for determining both eligibility to local offices, where there was a property qualification, and for liability to civic *munera*, which 'pro modo fortunarum sustinenda sunt' (*CJ* x. 42 (41). 1), but the cities might have made their own assessments wherever registrations ordered by the state were not serviceable (cf. n. 3). Given the disturbance that Quirinius' census provoked in Judaea, we may think it strange that Josephus mentions no later registration, not even to remark on the absence of protests. I now feel less sure that censuses were taken in the Principate as often and as systematically as they should have been for fair and efficient distribution of the tax load.

3. Again I now doubt if all personal estate was registered everywhere. The registration of ships might have been specially required in maritime cities. The difficulty of ascertaining and estimating personal possessions in general was clearly great. Apuleius' novel introduces a rich banker 'qui metu officiorum ac munerum magnis artibus magnam dissimulabat opulentiam'; it was not liability to tax that he feared; could cities have tried to obtain an assessment of a man's total resources which the census did not furnish (*Met.* iv. 9, cf. i. 21)? Where

tributum soli took the form only of levies on produce, and *tributum capitis* was nothing but a flat poll-tax (which incidentally did affect the personal wealth of slaveowners, who would pay on the number of their slaves), only registration of lands and persons was required. Whatever earlier practice may have been, extant census returns from the late empire register only lands and their products, together with persons working on the land and animals (but not the *instrumentum fundi*), and Lactantius (*de Morte Pers.* 23) is consonant with this, though he laments Galerius' innovation in numbering the *plebs urbana* in Pontica, which may have occurred in other regions (Jones, *Roman Economy* (1974) ch. X, cf. XIII; cf. 207 f.); yet it would have served Lactantius well in dilating on the horrors of the census to expatiate on inquisitions into domestic belongings and personal ornaments, had there been any. Admittedly Constantine was to introduce the *collatio lustralis* on the assets of *negotiatores* both in town and country, which had to be entered on a separate *matricula* (Jones, *Later Roman Empire*, 431 f.), and this might have been an attempt to revert to a practice of taxing personal property, which had been followed in the Principate in some regions at least, and which Diocletian had given up. But probably this had never been universal; the data for Syria suggest its adoption there, but the new census return from Arabia (n. 5) seems to show that it did not extend at least to rural parts of that province. It is one possibility that more comprehensive returns of assets were demanded within towns whose riches derived from industry and trade, places like Gades (a Roman *municipium*, where the great number of citizens with equestrian status cannot be explained by their landholdings; see Strabo iii. 5. 3). It may be noted that Dio lii. 28. 6 makes Maecenas advise Augustus to tax all property, individual and communal (i.e., I suppose, municipal lands), from which income was drawn, but we do not know how far this imputed recommendation was implemented at any time, except in Egypt.

4. For appointment of senators to organize collection of *arrears* cf. Dio lx. 10. 4 with the inscription re-edited in *Madr. Mitt.* (1968), 181 ff.

Communal assessments are implied in two documents that I overlooked; in *AE* 1971. 190 there is mention of a successful *legatio censualis* sent to Marcus Aurelius by a Spanish city, and in *AE* 1973. 317 a Spanish magnate is honoured for squaring city accounts with the *fiscus*. In Italy itself the direct property tax on citizens had only been suspended in 167 BC, and it was revived in 43 (Cic., *Fam.* xii. 30. 4; *ad Brut.* i. 18. 5, cf. Dio xlvi. 31. 3 f.), and something like it was raised by the triumvirs (Dio xlvii. 14. 3; App., *BC* iv. 34). I conjecture that it was then levied through the municipalities; it was perhaps with this possibility in mind that a law preserved in the Table of Heraclea had required the local magistrates not only to take declarations from their fellow-citizens on the occasion of a Roman census but to enter them in the municipal records (*FIRA* i². no. 13). Dio lix. 22. 3 may refer to Gallic census records kept centrally in that country, but each *civitas* must have had its own, as in the later empire (Jones, *Later Roman Empire*, 456).

As to the tasks of *assessment on particular properties and collection from individuals*, it is obvious that they involved personal activity, and what Arcadius Charisius writes of his own day must always have been true: 'qui annonam (sc. 'militarem', now the chief form of direct tax on land) suscipit vel exigit vel erogat, et exactores pecuniae pro capitibus, personalis muneris sollicitudinem sustinent', like those 'qui acceptandis sive suscipiendis censualibus professionibus destinantur' (*Dig.* l. 4. 18. 8 and 16). But men under 25 and over 70, the infirm, women of course, and various other categories of privileged persons including veterans were excused the performance of personal *munera*, whereas there was no exemption from patrimonial except poverty (*Dig.* l. 4. 6. 4). If the collection of tribute is none the less defined as a patrimonial *munus*, which could thus fall on even those who were physically incapable of doing the work involved, this can only mean that their property furnished the state with a guarantee that the full sum due was gathered in. No doubt it was in the interest of the rich, who were automatically liable in this way, to assume, when they could, the actual tasks of assessment and collection, which gave them the best chance of protecting themselves and their friends. Hence the *munus* could realistically be described as *mixtum*, since the actual assessors or collectors would normally be found among those who also bore the patrimonial obligation. This fell even on veterans (*Dig.* xlix. 18. 2. 1 and 4 *pr.*), though they retained the right to refuse appointment as collectors (*h.t.* 5. 1). It may be that other classes of persons excused from personal *munera* could also exercise this right, if they chose.

I envisage the theoretical relation between communal and individual liability as follows. The census of any community involved the registration of all persons and property subject to tax, with valuations of the property, except where the tax consisted in quotas or fixed amounts of produce. The liability of the community consisted in the total resulting from these individual assessments. It was the community that received from the government a demand for the appropriate amount in cash or kind each year, a demand that might rise or fall, if rates were increased or reduced, and that might be followed by supplementary demands like the *superindictiones* of the late empire. It then had to apportion this total among the individual taxpayers and collect what was due from each. If there was a shortfall, the government would demand the payment of the arrears from the community, or in response to its pleas grant a remission. If payment in full was insisted on, the community had to put pressure on defaulters; in some circumstances the government might itself send in representatives to enforce payment. The defaulter could be sued by the *fiscus* and not by the community, probably in the Severan period in the procurator's court. If judgement went against him, he had the right of appeal. In granting a remission to Banasa, Caracalla excepts defaulters already condemned in the courts, unless an appeal was pending (*AE* 1948. 109). After judgement the defaulter's property could be sold to the extent necessary to cover his liability. If it was not enough, recourse could be had against those who had a patrimonial obligation to make good the communal deficit, or in the last resort against their sureties. We can imagine *longueurs* in the legal proceedings. The defendant might challenge the assessment on his property or, where quotas of produce were due, the calculation of the actual returns from his land; he might claim that he had paid in full, and that the collector had been guilty of embezzlement; or he might contend that someone else was liable. (It may be noted that there was a double penalty on collectors who took more than was due, *CJ* ii. 11. 2, AD 197.) If the government was in urgent need of revenue, it could perhaps threaten or take immediate action against those on whom lay the patrimonial obligation to cover deficits without awaiting the results of suits against individual defaulters.

This procedure was well enough suited to more or less isolated cases of default, but hardly to a situation in which there were numerous and widespread deficits in communal payments; at any rate it was not pursued with invariable rigour, as is shown by the periodic remissions of accumulated arrears, on which see now R. MacMullen, *Latomus* (1987), 737 ff. Very probably governors and procurators had inadequate staffs for enforcement in such conditions, and in many provinces, including most of the richest, too few troops to protect their agents in effecting extensive sequestrations. Moreover, if estates were sold up on a large scale, who would buy and at what prices? Yet the alternative, that of taking them into public or imperial ownership, might be just as unattractive. Few imperial freedmen capable of managing them might be available, and suitable private contractors to whom they could be leased as hard to find. The process, if ruinous to any considerable number of the local ruling class, would be subversive of the political and social order. The magnates concerned might also have influential protectors at Rome. No doubt the cities could advance all sorts of special pleas in mitigation. Of the embassies they often sent to the emperor many may have sought reductions in fiscal claims. In grave natural calamities emperors could see at once that they had no alternative but to lower or suspend imposts. But there might be many other causes of distress, real or alleged. A decree of Mylasa, which reveals a complicated currency crisis about 210, seems to have stated that it was slowing down tax payments (*OGIS* 515). But communal deficits probably meant almost always that it was the class responsible for assessments and collection who had evaded or postponed their own payments, and they were the chief gainers from remissions, whereby the government renounced its right to make them fulfil their liabilities as guarantors of the revenue; at least this was certainly true in the late empire, as MacMullen has shown once more.

I am not forgetting that some emperors did confiscate large individual estates: what I envisage, in order to account for the accumulation of arrears, is a situation in which there was a widespread and simultaneous failure of cities to pay tribute in full, with the result that the government drew back from the penal remedy of massive sequestrations. In the tradition habitual resort to confiscations is attributed to those emperors marked as tyrannical; they were seen to be the result partly of their fears of disloyal opposition, partly of their need to finance personal extravagance and prodigality. Many scholars tend to discount the budgetary importance of court and household expenditure, lavish building programmes, and liberalities. The evidence long ago collected by Friedländer (*Sittengeschichte Roms* ii[9]. 265 ff.) on the extent to which such expenditure absorbed revenue in the states of early modern Europe should give them pause. The debts that Charles II incurred early in his reign by court extravagance materially affected his relations thereafter with Parliament and foreign powers. In the reigns of some emperors similar practices emptied the treasury, which they then tried to replenish with confiscations. This was a device that such rulers as Trajan, Hadrian, and Marcus wished to avoid, and apparently would not employ to any marked extent even to curb tax defaulting. (It may incidentally be noticed that in halving the direct property tax paid before conquest by Macedonians and Illyrians in 167 BC (Livy xlv. 18. 7; 26. 14) and in reducing that paid by Cappadocians (Tac., *Ann.* ii. 56), the Roman government probably took account of the fact that there was no longer a royal court to support.)

5. *P. Yadin* 16, of which I had notice before publication in a class given by Professor Naphthali Lewis, comprises census declarations of 127 made to the governor of Arabia of four estates of which the location but not the area is specified, producing dates and barley, on which fixed quantities of both products are payable, or in one case, half the barley grown, plus cash payments of *aurum coronarium*.

*　　*　　*

The English 'land tax' of the eighteenth century (for which see W. R. Ward, *English Land Tax in the Eighteenth Century* (1953), developed from earlier experiments in the Commonwealth and Restoration periods (cf. C. D. Chandaman, *English Public Revenues, 1660–88* (1975)), may suggest in some particulars how the Roman system worked.

Like its predecessors this so-called land tax was in principle levied on personal as well as on real estate, but in practice the former yielded a small and decreasing part of the returns, owing to the difficulty of assessing it.

The rate on rentals from landed property was determined from year to year and in wartime was normally 20 per cent. But these rates only represented a maximum beyond which no individual was liable. Each year Parliament set a total sum to be raised, which was apportioned by fixed assessments on counties and boroughs. For historic reasons the apportionment, which had never been based on any census of property, was inequitable from the first; an unfair share in the burden was laid on the south-east as compared with the north and west; and this was never put right. Within each county the sum to be raised was again apportioned between districts by Parliamentary commissioners, who were men of high status, and within each district among individual owners by local persons designated for the purpose; the collectors too were local men. All concerned were often bent on protecting so far as possible their own interests or those of patrons and friends. The money collected passed to receivers, whose appointment was also subject to powerful local influences, and who might make a personal profit by delaying its transmission to the treasury. The machinery for administration became progressively less efficient. With rates of tax at their highest, the Coke family paid at 17.3 per cent on their Norfolk estates in 1708–10, but 13.2 per cent on all their property in the Napoleonic wars (R. A. Parker, *Coke of Norfolk* (1975), 3, 127), a Lincolnshire estate 18 per cent in the 1740s and 9.5 per cent in the late 1770s, and Earl Fitzwilliam on his Yorkshire lands only 3.5 per cent in 1796 (E. Mingay, *English Landed Society in the Eighteenth Century* (1963), 82 ff.; J. Cannon, *Aristocratic Century* (1984) 146). In 1709 a decade's arrears equalled the nominal proceeds for a year at 20 per cent. Collectors or receivers were often holding back moneys in their hands. In London current intakings were set against arrears, which at once grew again (Ward 27, 38 f., 58). It is easy to see that conditions in the Roman empire may have been not dissimilar.

(*a*) The apparent absence of an imperial bureaucracy charged with conducting provincial censuses must have meant that to a considerable extent the communities assessed themselves and that within them assessments on individuals must have been generally decided by those vested with local authority, who (as alleged in the late empire) would tend to shift the burden on to the backs of their inferiors. Governors or census commissioners with their equestrian assistants could at best have checked the most flagrantly suspicious data. Not only were different provinces taxed in different ways but there was no guarantee that within a province with an apparently uniform rate, like the 1 per cent levy on capital in Syria, the apportionment was equitable between either communities or individuals. In so far as censuses were irregular or infrequent, new inequities would develop.

(b) The government was no better equipped to ensure that collection was fair and thorough, or even that the money collected was not partly embezzled by official receivers in the procuratorial offices. Seneca's brother thought that the procuratorial career was the quickest way to get rich (Tac., *Ann.* xvi. 17. 3), and it may be doubted if he counted only on savings from his salary. At a lower level an imperial slave employed in the fiscal administration of Gallia Lugdunensis visited Rome (where he died) with a retinue of his own slaves (*vicarii*); they included two keepers of his silver plate (*ILS* 1514); Pliny tells of one in Tarraconensis with plate weighing 2,500 pounds (*NH* xxxiii. 145), and of another concerned in the pay and supply of Corbulo's army in Armenia who could purchase his freedom for thirteen million sesterces (vii. 129). Accounting procedures might well fail to uncover peculation, when conducted by those who might be involved themselves. In Gaul Augustus' freedman procurator Licinus was detected in having exacted a sixth more in taxes than was due, presumably by making excessive assessments on the *civitates*; he pretended that he had only aimed at enriching the treasury, and Augustus condoned his misconduct (Dio liv. 21), just as Vespasian was alleged to have winked at the rapacity of his procurators, in the belief that he could ultimately squeeze out of them their ill-gotten gains (Suet., *Vesp.* 16. 2). As usual, we hear more of extortions by officials from the more copious testimonies of the late empire, when they sometimes usurped the function of collecting as well as that of enforcing payment of arrears (Jones, *Later Roman Empire*, 457 f.).

(c) The accumulation of arrears (n. 4) not only led to remissions to taxpayers in general or to particular cities, but presumably, when the needs of the treasury were especially pressing, to additional levies; the *superindictiones* of the late empire certainly had earlier precedents (p. 344). There is an analogy in the practice of the British government in doubling the rate of land tax in wartime, which would have been unnecessary if the tax had been fairly distributed and efficiently collected at lower rates.

(*d*) The persistent and often unjustified complaints made by the English gentry of the burden of the land tax suggest that we must be wary of crediting similar complaints made by Rome's subjects. To some of them, especially those recently conquered, regular taxation on their persons and property was detestable *per se* as a form of servitude, to which they had not been accustomed. The true weight of Roman taxation is unknown. We cannot even get a reliable estimate of a normal budget. At best we can put an upper limit on probable expenditure on the army and on the Roman corn-dole, perhaps also on official salaries, but we can hardly guess at the variable outlays on building programmes, the court, and all sorts of liberalities, or at the extra military costs apparently incidental to large-scale campaigns. But even if we could determine what the state had to spend, or did in fact spend, on average, we could still not say what proportion it formed of 'the gross national product'; the total population of the empire is itself a matter of mere speculation (Brunt, *Italian Manpower* (2nd impression, 1986), 718–20), and so is production per caput; models in the air, such as those cited by MacMullen (*Latomus* (1987), n. 30), will not supply the almost entire absence of factual information. MacMullen finds that 'the conventional view of the taxation in the empire, that it became much more severe and heavy after AD 300, seems in summary to be well-founded in the evidence, *for certain places and strata of the population*' (753, his italics). But the evidence in question consists partly of numerous constitutions preserved in the late law codes, partly of Christian indictments of the oppression of the poor. In the Principate we have no comparable series of imperial enactments on administration, while pagan writers were never so solicitous as Christian for the lower classes, and the latter were naturally more prone to expound their moral views on matters of state, when they were the spokesmen of the established Church and not of a small persecuted sect: they now had some hope of influencing persons in authority which in earlier times had been altogether lacking. Thus we cannot expect from the earlier period more than scattered hints of the kind of exactions well attested later, and these hints we do find. None the less, it may well be true that in all periods some complaints of over-taxation, especially with MacMullen's qualification, were justified, and that in the late empire a burden which had not sensibly increased in absolute terms became relatively harder to bear as security and prosperity declined.

Index of Names

Most of the essays in this book are not concerned with discussions of individual persons, peoples or regions, to which there are numerous allusions merely incidental to their themes. Many of these allusions are ignored in the following index, though some are registered as useful indications to the subjects discussed, or because exceptionally something is said of the persons, etc. mentioned which may be thought noteworthy. Information about particular peoples or provinces may be discovered from the entries under Augustus, census, languages, misgovernment, *portoria*, recruitment, revenues; 'north Africa' includes all the Latin speaking provinces there, Asia Minor all the provinces in that region, Narbonensis is subsumed under Gaul, and Illyricum embraces all the Danubian provinces; particular *civitates* are usually not registered. Most persons mentioned, e.g. those accused of *repetundae*, are not listed at all, and some casual references to names which do appear are omitted. Material in notes is registered by the pages on which notes begin.

Index of Subjects

Printed in the United States
104444LV00001B/3/A

9 780198 144762